IN FROM THE COLD

IN FROM THE COLD

National Security and
Parliamentary Democracy

LAURENCE LUSTGARTEN
and
IAN LEIGH

CLARENDON PRESS · OXFORD
1994

Oxford University Press, Walton Street, Oxford OX2 6DP

Oxford New York Toronto
Delhi Bombay Calcutta Madras Karachi
Kuala Lumpur Singapore Hong Kong Tokyo
Nairobi Dar es Salaam Cape Town
Melbourne Auckland Madrid
and associated companies in
Berlin Ibadan

Oxford is a trade mark of Oxford University Press

Published in the United States
by Oxford University Press, New York

British Library Cataloguing in Publication Data
Data available

Library of Congress Cataloging in Publication Data
Lustgarten, Laurence.
In from the cold: national security and parliamentary democracy /
L. Lustgarten and I. Leigh
p. cm.
Includes bibliographical references.
1. Human rights—Great Britain. 2. Intelligence service—Great Britain.
3. National security—Great Britain. 4. Human rights—Australia.
5. Intelligence service—Australia. 6. National security—Australia.
7. Human rights—Canada. 8. Intelligence service—Canada.
9. National security—Canada.
I. Leigh. I. (Ian) II. Title.
JC599.G7L87 1994 351.89—dc20 94–9680
ISBN 0–19–825234–X

1 3 5 7 9 10 8 6 4 2

Set by Hope Services (Abingdon) Ltd.
Printed in Great Britain
on acid-free paper by
Bookcraft Ltd., Midsomer Norton, Avon

To our families

Preface

I

Let us begin with what this book is not. It makes no claim to be as it were a book of revelations, casting light into dark corners and on shadowy figures and organizations engaging in fanciful conspiracies or elaborate deceptions. There are more than enough such books, of variable quality, purporting to reveal 'the truth' about the intelligence agencies, without us adding to them. There also exists a vast literature on spies, 'moles', ancient secrets, and antique treasons, much of which is manifest nonsense and even more of which concerns matters that, at best, are of historical interest. We were able to avoid having to venture into this intellectual quagmire because it was never our purpose to uncover secret information about previously unknown operations. Apart from the names of a few people who spoke to us on condition of anonymity (see below), we make no claim to knowing any more secrets than anyone else. Our aim is quite different.

As academic public lawyers our principal interest has been in exploring the application of the recurring themes of constitutionalism to the realm of security and intelligence. Our starting point is that the maintenance of national security is a function of government like (say) education or transport policy. As such it raises a host of questions familiar to political scientists and public lawyers: how is policy decided upon and implemented? What institutions are involved in these stages? What discretion exists? What democratic input or control is there over the processes and agencies involved? What mechanisms exist for exercising such control and how effective are they? How do decisions taken within this policy field affect individuals, and what avenues of redress exist for persons aggrieved by the outcome?

In exploring these questions in the study of national security as one might in any other field of government policy, two complicating factors add particular interest. The first is the secrecy. We discuss in Chapter 1 the relationship between security and secrecy, but it is unquestionably and necessarily the case that government concern over secrecy affects the processes and institutions involved here. The more difficult questions are how far that concern is justified, and how it is to be reconciled with the state's other commitments to democracy and protection of human rights. The second factor which sets national security apart is the importance of the interests involved, certainly to the state and arguably to its citizens. It is usually claimed in political and legal discourse that these interests are not merely matters of convenience or even desirability, but rather are vital to the very existence of the state. This presents a formidable challenge to a democracy: to preserve itself without losing precisely those attributes which make it worth preserving, especially the rights of individuals to pursue their own concerns alone or with others without official harassment.

As the main government institutions which act in the area of our interest, security and intelligence agencies naturally feature prominently in this study, but they are far from being its sole focus. Security agencies take their *raison d'etre* from the state they are supposed to protect. Since, in Britain, that state embodies a particular vision of democracy, the question of how national security intersects with other values such as privacy, freedom of expression, and freedom of movement becomes critical. Hence our lengthy treatment of those issues in Part II. Moreover, security organizations are merely one component of the machinery of government. It is therefore essential to study how other state institutions, notably the remainder of the executive, Parliament, and the courts, approach decisions involving considerations of national security. Our analysis of their performance will emphasize constitutional questions concerning allocation of power and institutional competence, and equally the perennial problem of accountability, oversight, and review—terms used interchangeably throughout. It will also consider how the treatment of these matters reflects the dominant political culture of the nation, and the strains within it.

Since our topic inevitably goes to the heart of the democratic state we discuss the nature of national security in that context in Chapter 1. This is intended less as a definition than as a conceptual map of the political and normative functions that national security serves. We argue there for a conception of the state unequivocally grounded in democratic values and respect for human rights, which alone is worthy of measures taken to maintain its security. Although the discussion ranges far more widely and on a conceptual plane different from the rest of the book, it would have been dishonest for us not to set out clearly the assumptions underpinning the critique which follows. An examination of national security in a specifically legal context, that of the statutory mandate of the Security Service, appears in Chapter 14.

Another dimension of our approach is that of comparative constitutional analysis. We have taken for this purpose two other Westminster democracies: Canada and Australia. The parliamentary and legal traditions in each country are closely allied to those in the United Kingdom: each has a parliamentary executive, a cabinet system, a politically neutral civil service, and a legal system derived fundamentally from the common law. These similarities are sufficient to enable meaningful comparisons of the development of models of intelligence oversight and accountability. In the field of legal doctrine the differences are more pronounced in view of Australia's federal, written constitution and Canada's patriated constitution with its Charter of Rights. However, even here the systems are united by a common attitude to precedent and to statutory interpretation: the result is that judicial decisions from one state are commonly cited by the courts of the others. We have nevertheless tried to be sensitive to genuine differences and to avoid a simplistic attitude to legal transplants. One state with which we consciously chose not to make extended comparison is the United States. This is not for shortage of available material, nor unfamiliarity with the legal system, but because the differences between the parliamentary and congressional systems and the very different constitutional culture within which American courts operate would have rendered comparisons too distant to be genuinely useful. This point is taken up in greater detail in Chapter 15.

Our emphasis is on the treatment of security within the political and legal systems of three nation states. Where relevant in the case of the United Kingdom we have supplemented this by references to the European Convention on Human Rights and, more occasionally, to European Community law. The relative lack of emphasis on EC law is symptomatic of the current ambit of the underlying constitutional order—as yet there is no notion of Community security, and no common defence policy. Yet it is more than conceivable that the focus of security concerns will soon shift away from the nation state. Should the clear trend of the shift of power to Brussels continue, it may well produce a corresponding reorientation in popular thinking. For the position of the nation state as the focus of its citizens' loyalty owes much to its role as guarantor of security, which may become redundant. This proposition is at present too conjectural to be sketched in detail in the chapters which follow, but it is worth contemplating some of its possible implications.

Following Maastricht, there now exists a notion, legally recognized, of Community citizenship. The import of the loss of sovereignty at Westminster goes well beyond the juridical. In so far as being British has been defined by singularity—separation and differentiation from if not downright opposition to 'the Continent'—this identity is being eroded. If in the future British citizens can no longer look to their MPs for redress of many significant grievances, or to Westminster because Parliament lacks competence to change the relevant law, will they not tend to regard the remaining demands of their government as oppressive? The much-proclaimed principle of subsidiarity is supposed to prevent excessive concentration of decision-making in Brussels but may well rekindle regional or local allegiances if competences devolve to the level that most people will find more accessible and responsive. Finally, and though further on the horizon potentially the most significant development, it seems inescapable that a principal remedy for the so-called 'democratic deficit' from which the Community visibly suffers is a legislature elected directly by all its citizens. A democratically elected Community parliament, making laws over a widening range of subject areas which are supplemented and enforced by the Commission administration, will leave both Westminster and Whitehall with an increasing sense of vestigiality surrounding them. Even where nation states retain formal legal independence, political pressure for combined policies or action in matters like defence and international relations—traditionally the heart of the sovereignty of nations—will not extinguish but will greatly reduce the scope for a distinctive national political role. The national government, seen as at once ineffectual and irritating, will gradually cease to be the cynosure of public allegiance. Thirty years from now the institutional focus of this book (though we would hope not its wider perspective nor its discussion of substantive issues) might be of interest only to historians of political development.

It will already be apparent that a discussion of national security of the kind we intend is not defined by legal categories and will not fall tidily within the boundaries of a legal work. We have made liberal and grateful use of research and concepts developed by historians, political scientists, and international relations specialists. Indeed our work should be seen as a contribution to, and arising from, the growing community of scholarly interest of social scientists and lawyers who since the 1970s have begun to take an interest in security and intelligence as a subject worthy of analysis.[1] With our subject already so vast, it seemed unwise to engage in extensive discussion of matters treated exhaustively by others. This is particularly true of terrorism. Not only have two comprehensive legal studies of the subject been published recently,[2] but consideration of the subject from an almost endless range of other perspectives made any effort on our part otiose.[3] The same applies to the legal and wider security situation in Northern Ireland. And although in Chapter 14 some attention is paid to the changing context of espionage in the aftermath of the Cold War, it seemed unnecessary to traverse ground covered by a recent study of legal aspects of the subject.[4] We have also said nothing about another subject of great interest—the organization and use of intelligence in the processes of policymaking. This is well treated in a growing historical and contemporary political science literature.[5]

II

Like political scientists and others who study contemporary policymaking and implementation, we also faced the difficulty that published material relevant to our subject was either limited and uninformative, or was out of date with respect to current practice. Secrecy obviously accounts for part of this, but the problem of obsolescence arises because the area of security generally has been

[1] However, all British legal academics stand metaphorically on the shoulders of Sir David Williams for his earlier seminal work: D. Williams, *Not in the Public Interest* (London, 1965).

[2] C. Walker, *The Prevention of Terrorism in British Law* (2nd edn., Manchester, 1992), and A. Vercher, *Terrorism in Europe: An International Comparative Legal Analysis* (Oxford, 1992).

[3] A. Lakos, *Terrorism 1980–1990—A Bibliography* (Oxford, 1991), contains no substantive discussion but fills well over 400 pages merely listing works on the subject.

[4] R. Thomas, *Espionage and Secrecy* (London, 1991).

[5] In Britain the quarterly journal *Intelligence and National Security* regularly publishes articles on all facets of the subject.

subject to unusually rapid changes in the 1990s. To some extent reliable information may be found in the quality press; journalists are often the only people able to gain access (often on an unattributable basis) to those currently working in positions or institutions from which the public is barred. Such material—unlike purported 'exposés' trailed in sensationalist headlines—is neither more nor less reliable than other reportage of current political developments. The media is also the only channel by which information from insiders may reach the public—the example which appears most frequently in these pages is the disclosure in 1985 by Cathy Massiter, a former MI5 officer, of official activities against political dissidents in Britain. None the less media coverage is slight and spasmodic, and of course not primarily concerned with the deeper constitutional questions which have given our study its distinctive shape. Moreover, in view of the aura of secrecy, rumour, and suspicion surrounding security matters, we thought it necessary to interview those actively involved in the field.

Our quest was not only for accurate information about policies, processes, and procedures, but also to gain a sense of what the people engaged in the work thought was important and—most difficult of all—to try to tease out some of the unspoken assumptions that seemed to guide their actions. This interest was not limited to the actions of officials. For example, we thought it worth interviewing a number of journalists to understand the practical impact that rules restricting disclosure of government information have on their ability to inform the public about security matters. (The findings are set out in Chapter 10.) We also spoke with people in Australia and Canada who were engaged in oversight work, or had been influential in framing legislation, or chaired tribunals.

Possibly because we were quite firm in disclaiming any interest in operational details of particular cases, we were fortunate enough to obtain a very large number of interviews with persons actively involved in security and its oversight in all three nations. A complete list of everyone to whom we spoke appears in the List of Interviewees below. In some cases, and particularly in Britain,[6] we have broken new ground in terms of access. It may have helped that we started in Australia and Canada and were able to approach people in Britain with names of their counterparts. Yet that is not the whole story, for a sort of snowball effect began to operate: in some important instances, interviewees suggested others who might be useful to talk to. Although Britain has a very long way to go in this respect, our experience in gaining access suggests that a discernible shift towards greater openness—a move in from the cold—is now under way. There was a certain nervousness, partly where—as was true of the Security Service—no one from the institution had previously spoken on an authorized and attributable basis to any researchers. As with our Security Service source, several present or former officials were willing to be interviewed but insisted

---

[6] Pete Gill, author of *Policing Politics: Security Intelligence and the Liberal Democratic State* (London, 1994), conducted several interviews in Canada as part of his research.

upon anonymity. This condition seemed due less to fear for personal safety (although some did have considerable knowledge of current operational matters), than to compliance with either an imposed policy or their own sense of propriety. However, it was one we could readily accept, since other well-respected works in this field, some of which appear repeatedly in our footnotes, are replete with references to 'personal communication' or 'private information'.[7]

None the less there were some unusual aspects to the interview part of our research that are worth noting. One is that nothing was tape recorded. During one of the first interviews, in Australia, we were warned that people working in security and intelligence were 'allergic' to tape recorders, and that he (the then Inspector-General) and probably everyone else would be far less forthcoming in their presence. One soon develops a heightened ability to scribble notes quickly, or even to dictate a rapid summary into the machine upon leaving an office. Moreover, the risk of inaccuracy is certainly no greater than that experienced by those undertaking participant observation or other field research within criminal subcultures, or among the police or football supporters.[8]

The condition which gave us most pause was that one of our Home Office sources and our Security Service informant both wanted to see those parts of the manuscript in which material identifiably attributed to them appeared. This raised the obvious question of censorship, an intention they firmly disclaimed. Their stated reason was that they wished to ensure absolute accuracy of reportage: more precisely, to avoid mistaken factual statements that could be attributed to them. As for expressions of judgment and opinion, one of them rather neatly turned things round by pointing out that he could not comment critically on any of these, because failure to comment on the others would then imply approval of them. With some trepidation we agreed. In the end, the comments we received were either helpful factual clarifications of matters of detail, or extremely narrow corrections, for example, where we had mistitled the Director-General as 'the Director'. They were in fact archetypical civil servant comments, very similar in tenor to what might be expected to emanate from any Whitehall department. In only one instance was there a subtle hint of an attempt to persuade us that a critical comment in the text was mistaken. This took the form of calling attention to some published material. We read it, remained unconvinced, and left the text unaltered.

The question that must trouble any researcher who gains unprecedented access is, why? This was not an issue in Canada and Australia, much more open societies where state officials are used to interchange with academics, and where in 1989 the Director-General of ASIO listed his private telephone number in

[7] e.g. C. Andrew, *Secret Service* (London, 1986), and B. Simpson, *In the Highest Degree Odious: Detention Without Trial in Wartime Britain* (Oxford, 1992).

[8] e.g. the PSI field research on the Metropolitan Police: D. Smith *et al.*, *Police and People in London*, esp. vol. 4 (London, 1983); and D. Hobbs, *Doing the Business* (Oxford, 1988), which is embellished with some splendid quotes from criminal informants which were certainly the product of memory.

the Canberra directory. Perhaps unfairly, there was the suspicion of co-optation, or an attempt to steer us toward a view of the Security Service that accords with the image that it would like to present to the outside world. Of course the question of who is using whom is present in any research, if not in any human relationship. It may be expected that police and especially intelligence officials, who use information as the primary tool of their trade, are better at its manipulation than most people. Our response was simply to undertake more intensive preparation, and in effect cross-examine the statements made more rigorously, than was the case with any of the other interviews. Readers must judge for themselves whether our critical guns have been spiked.

In the main body of the text we have tried to take account of developments up to the end of July 1993, although we have inserted a few footnotes referring to material which became available during copy-editing. The flexibility of the publishers has enabled us to add a Coda dealing with the government's proposed legislation on the Secret Intelligence Service and GCHQ, along with plans for oversight of the Security Service, which were put forward late in November 1993.

Acknowledgements

It would not have been possible to undertake such an ambitious and geographically wide-ranging study without the financial and other material support from an unusually wide variety of sources. Laurence Lustgarten is more than pleased to acknowledge the assistance received from the following:

1) The Nuffield Foundation's Small Grants Scheme, whose award helped make possible a visit to Australia in March–April of 1989.

2) The Centre of Criminology, University of Toronto, and its Director, Professor John Beattie, for the award of a Research Fellowship for six weeks in August–October 1990 which covered all the costs of travel, subsistence, and research visits. Still more, it provided excellent facilities, a friendly and stimulating intellectual environment, and the opportunity to teach some postgraduate seminars. Particular thanks are owed to Professor Philip Stenning, who organized the visit, established a number of indispensable contacts, and literally provided a home.

3) The Joseph Rowntree Charitable Trust, whose Democracy Project provided the funds to support two terms' unpaid leave to finish the writing. Their generosity made possible the concentration of energy and time which conditions of university life these days are steadily undermining, but which remain indispensable to any major project.

Ian Leigh would like to thank the University of Newcastle upon Tyne for a Small Research Grant which facilitated conducting various interviews and visiting libraries.

During the years in which this book has been in progress we have individually or together benefited by discussing aspects of it with academic colleagues in seminars at Aberystwyth, Adelaide, Durham, Hull, University College London, Manchester, Newcastle, Toronto, and Warwick. Portions were also presented to the Society of Public Teachers of Law Public Law Group, the Seventh Law-Politics Colloquium, and the London Public Law Group. We are grateful to all those who have encouraged, challenged, or stimulated us, often simultaneously.

Some paragraphs of the text first appeared in articles in the *Modern Law Review* and *Public Law*. We are grateful to the editors of these journals for permission to reprint that material.

It is a truism that the burden of research and writing falls also on marriage partners and families. In this instance, Ecclesiastes 12: 12: 'there is no end to the writing of books', proved almost literally true. Ian Leigh thanks Sue for her patience and understanding, and Eleanor, Judith, and Jenny for their healthy sceptical intolerance, as The Book exerted its excessive influence over family life. Each was an encouragement to finish the job. Laurence Lustgarten thanks Gill for her sensitive combination of forceful prodding in times of idleness and gentle support in black moments when the whole enterprise seemed overwhelming, and The Tribe—Anders, Nicholas, Pip, and Sarah—for their co-operation in keeping the music down, interruptions to a minimum, and generally letting the Ancient One get on with it.

Finally, both of us would like to thank Richard Hart, our editor at OUP. His support, enthusiasm, genuine interest in the subject, and commitment to ensuring that the book would be sold at a price which most people could actually afford have made it a real pleasure to work with him.

Contents

Contents

List of Interviewees

Note: The positions indicated are those occupied by the person named at the time of interview. Those listed collectively were interviewed together.

1. UNITED KINGDOM

Anonymous sources

Assistant Director, Security Service
Assistant Secretary, F6 Division, Home Office
Assistant Secretary, F4 Division, Home Office
Former Member, Security Commission
Senior official, GCHQ (retired)
Senior Minister, Home Office, in 1974–9 Labour government

Attributed Sources

S. R. Davie, Cabinet Office
Gerald Warner, Intelligence Co-ordinator
Hugh Taylor, Senior Secretary, Security Commission
Rear-Admiral W. A. Higgins, Secretary of the D Notice Committee
Sir Murray Stuart-Smith, Security Service Commissioner and Lord Justice of Appeal
Sir Anthony Lloyd, Interceptions Commissioner, Chairman of the Advisory Panel on Deportations, and Lord Justice of Appeal
Sir Peter Imbert, Commissioner, Metropolitan Police
John Howley, Deputy Assistant Commissioner (Security), Metropolitan Police
John Stevens, Chief Constable, G. McMurchtrie, Assistant Chief Constable, Detective Chief Superintendent; all Northumbria Constabulary
Rupert Allason MP
Jim Cousins MP
Robin Robison, Executive Officer, Cabinet Office (resigned)
Peter Jones, Secretary to Council of Civil Service Unions
David Leigh, Thames Television
James Adams, *Sunday Times*
Alastair Brett, Company Solicitor, Times Newspapers
Anthony Whitaker, Legal Manager, Times Newspapers
Michael Evans, *The Times*
Stuart Patrick, Legal Adviser, *Daily Telegraph*
Andrew Hutchison, Managing Editor, Nigel Wade, Foreign Editor, *Daily Telegraph*
Brian Raymond, Solicitor, Bindman and Partners
John Wadham, Legal Officer, Liberty

2. CANADA

Richard Thompson QC, Inspector General, Michael de Rosenroll, Assistant Inspector General
Ronald Atkey, former Chairman, Security Intelligence Review Committee (SIRC)
John Bassett, Chairman, SIRC
Jean-Jacques Blais, Member SIRC and formerly Solicitor General of Canada
Maurice Archdeacon, Executive Secretary, SIRC
Maurice Klein, John Smith, Directors of Research, SIRC
Blaine Thacker MP, Chairman, Special Committee to Review the CSIS Act
John Brewin, Member, Special Committee
Derek Lee MP, Member, Special Committee
Stuart Farson, Research Director, Special Committee
Robert Kaplan MP, Solicitor General of Canada, 1981–4
Victor Gooch, James Kitching, Office of the Solicitor General, Police and Security Branch
Senator Michael Pitfield, formerly Clerk to the Privy Council
John Starnes, formerly Head of Security, RCMP
Murray Rankin, Faculty of Law, University of Victoria
Peter Russell, Department of Political Science, University of Toronto
Reg Whitaker, Department of Political Science, York University

3. AUSTRALIA

Justice R. M. Hope, Court of Appeal of New South Wales; former Royal Commissioner on Security
Justice G. J. Samuels, Court of Appeal of New South Wales; Chairman, Security Appeals Tribunal
John Moten, Director-General, Michael Boyle, Assistant, Australian Security Intelligence Organization
Alan Wrigley, former Director-General, ASIO
Neil McInnes, Inspector-General of Security
Ann Hazelton, Secretary, Parliamentary Joint Committee on ASIO
William Pinwill, journalist and author
Brian Toohey, journalist and author
Jack Waterford, *Canberra Times*
Desmond Ball, Strategic and Defence Studies Centre, Australian National University
John McMillan, Faculty of Law, Australian National University
John Nethercote, Department of Government, Australian National University

List of Acronyms

Part I
Conceptual Foundations

1

A Democratic Conception of National Security

Few concepts are more complex, contentious, and of such practical importance for the exercise of political power than 'national security'. It cannot be defined, or even discussed, in the abstract. Where one stands (and, politically speaking, whether one is able to stand) is critical. The unstable arena of world politics, in which co-operation, rivalry, law, and anarchy coexist and overlap, is still above all a world of *states*.[1] Each of these will vary in its character, interests, and vulnerability. Many consequences, to be discussed below, flow from this fact, but the point for the present is that the operative meaning of national security will therefore also vary correspondingly for each state.

Thus at various points it will be necessary to link the conceptual analysis which follows to specific characteristics of the United Kingdom today. And our point of departure is that the UK is a strong, rather than weak state. Current discontents notwithstanding, it is relatively cohesive socially and politically; has a long tradition of political stability; continues to enjoy a sense of popular attachment to most of its institutions despite obvious and grievous faults; in world terms is relatively prosperous; and is able to take vital decisions independent of other states if and when it chooses to do so.[2] Nor is it under attack, covertly or openly, from foreign powers: our approach to the subject would not have been sustainable in Weimar Germany, in Nicaragua or various black African states subject to 'destablization' in the 1980s, or possibly some of the fledgling east European democracies now. Assertions about fragility and vulnerability that would demand serious consideration elsewhere can readily be dismissed here.[3]

---

[1] Our analysis owes a great deal to the work of the international relations scholar Barry Buzan, as set out in *People, States and Fear* (2nd edn., London, 1991, orig. pub. 1983). However, the arguments presented are in no sense an attempt to apply Buzan's commentary directly, nor does he bear any responsibility for any of their flaws.

His long introductory chapter includes a very useful review of other literature emerging from this discipline. Of these works, we have found the following particularly helpful: F. Trager and F. Simonie, 'An Introduction to the Study of National Security', in F. Trager and P. Kronenberg (eds.), *National Security and American Society* (Lawrence, Kan., 1973); A. Wolfers, *Discord and Collaboration* (Baltimore, 1952), ch. 10; and R. Berki, *Security and Society: Reflections on Law, Order, and Politics* (London, 1986). See also the more recent discussion in P. Gill, *Policing Politics: Security Intelligence and the Liberal Democratic State* (London, 1994), 92–7.

[2] Buzan also uses the terms strong and weak states, but in a notably different way (above n. 1), 96–107.

[3] The quarter-century of political violence in Northern Ireland, which might seem to make this premiss questionable, paradoxically supports it. The conflict has largely been localized, and elsewhere both people and state have managed, though at considerable costs which have yet to be fully reckoned, to contain a guerrilla war without overwhelming disruption to normal life most of the time.

For the weaker the state, the more it needs to have recourse to extreme measures to preserve its existence; though by doing so, the more it is likely to act
oppressively and thus alienate its citizens. Strong states by contrast can endure
constant dissent and argument, and even periodic turbulence, with equanimity.

A TWO-PRONGED APPROACH

As Buzan suggests, national security is an 'essentially contested concept'.[4] This
means not only that it contains an ineradicable ideological or moral element
which makes empirical refutation impossible, but equally that the contest for
acceptance of any particular definition is itself a highly political one, in the sense
that a competition for power at an ideological level is involved. Therefore any
analysis must approach the concept in two complementary ways, which are so to
speak *internal* and *external*. The former seeks to unravel the concept analytically,
in the way a political philosopher might discuss 'liberty' or 'equality'. The latter
concentrates upon the functional impact of the concept: how and by whom it is
used in the political and legal arenas, and with what consequences in terms of
decisions taken, policies adopted, and the exercise of power more generally.
Obviously the two are connected, for different philosophical constructs will have
different functional implications; moreover, in reality those who propose a particular meaning for any essentially contested concept almost invariably do so
with an eye fixed firmly on those implications. Political theory may be expressed
in abstract terms, but is very rarely abstracted from the political circumstances in
which the theorist lives.

THE INTERNAL PERSPECTIVE

'National security' is actually a compound of two complex ideas: nation or
state,[5] and security. We shall examine each in turn, though as will be seen, the
two elements of the compound are never entirely separable.

What is to be secured?

Axiomatically it is only human beings who count morally. Therefore the state, as
a cultural institution, can only be worthy of protection or security in a derivative

[4] See n. 1 above, 7, borrowing the term coined by W. B. Gallie nearly forty years ago.
[5] Unlike political sociologists, who often distinguish between the ethnic or other characteristics of
a people (the nation) and governmental institutions (the state), we use the two interchangeably, as is
generally the case in legal terminology. Thus, lawyers talk of international law, but also of treaties
between states; of state sovereignty but also of national authorities. Nor, in using the term 'state', do
we mean to enter the theoretical territory of the debates surrounding 'state' and 'society'; for discussion from quite different angles, see e.g. K. Dyson, *The State Tradition in Western Europe* (Oxford,
1980) and P. Dunleavy and B. O'Leary, *Theories of the State* (2nd edn., London, 1992).

sense; that is, because of its purported necessity for human well-being. Put another way, why is national or state security a valid concern at all?—Why is all inquiry not cast in terms of individual security? The answer is not a moral but a practical one. Far more than race, gender, age, or even physical handicap, the nationality into which one is born or (what is for most people the same thing) the nation in which one is settled, is the single most important determinant of most people's conditions, chances, and expectations of life. One can only enjoy personal security[6] within the framework of life in a nation which can maintain a number of fundamental preconditions such as liberty, safety, a certain standard of living, and other social institutions.[7] Nothing attests to that fact more starkly than the flow of millions of refugees around the world, and the attempted migration of millions more.

Many readers may find this argument discomforting because they will assume that it necessarily leads to a corollary which indeed is often asserted: that actions taken for the maintenance of national security therefore justifiably override such rights of individuals as may be affected. No such conclusion follows. The supposed corollary embodies a basic fallacy:[8] that national security and individual freedoms are inherently conflicting values, in some way locked into a zero-sum contest of values which necessitates that an increase in one precipitates a corresponding loss in the other. On the contrary, a critical element of our position is that political and civil rights are major constituents of national security *itself*. To defend that proposition it is necessary to consider the nature of the state which is the object of protection.

THE 'STATE' OR 'NATION'

Buzan's impressive exposition, developed within the framework of international relations, identifies four indispensable elements of the state: 'physical base of population and territory'; governing institutions; sovereignty, in the sense of self-government; and some idea of the state which confers legitimacy and commands the loyalty of the inhabitants.[9] These are a mixture of the tangible and

---

[6] Which we define in a deliberately minimal sense as physical integrity, safety of home and goods, and the ability to participate voluntarily in public life without intimidation. All have a psychological dimension: absence of reasonably based fear that they cannot be enjoyed or exercised in peace.

[7] Other institutions, such as the family or the market, which exercise other forms of control in more limited spheres, ultimately depend upon institutional and ideological elements of the state for their effectiveness.

[8] It also contains a dangerous assumption that should never be accepted without careful scrutiny: that because an action is taken in the (presumptively genuine) belief that it will further national security, it was in fact necessary to achieve that end. It may be wholly in excess of what was required. This criterion of proportionality is critical to much of the discussion throughout this book. See esp. Ch. 2.

[9] See n. 1 above, 65–7, and more generally 57–109 (ch. 2). An additional prerequisite is size, which serves to distinguish states from tribes, families, or communes, but this attribute is not germane to the present discussion.

the intangible, of fact and value. They also feed back upon one another: a government by its actions may diminish or strengthen the legitimating ideology or ideal.

All states within the international order which are comprised of those basic elements share certain fundamental concerns or values. It has been suggested that the latter include continued existence of the state, maintenance of its territorial integrity, survival of its governing regime, independence from dictation by other states, and physical survival of its citizens.[10] This conception helps to identify one of the foremost genuine elements of security: the state as guardian of its constitutional order from foreign threat. In states where the possibility of invasion is remote, the main concern is over attempts by foreign officials or nationals acting at their behest (sometimes called 'agents of influence') to influence the conduct or outcome of democratic politics *covertly*. The clandestine character of the activity is critical, because open subsidy of a political party or journal by a foreign state, or payment to a politician, would alert citizens to the fact that the recipient was neither independent nor to be trusted to differentiate between the interests of the foreign state and their own. Such attempts at covert influence are a general or public injury, going far beyond that suffered by any individual. They are a menace to the integrity of the political system. They are also more dangerous than an attempt by a domestic political group to infiltrate some institution, because of the infinitely greater resources accessible to any state likely to want to attempt such operations. Moreover, a domestic group[11] is ultimately concerned to reshape the institutions of the state according to its vision of what is good for its fellow-citizens. However bizarre and unwelcome that vision may be to the intended beneficiaries, the group is at least not compromising the independence of the nation. Hence whilst all forms of domestic political activity free of violence should be kept firmly outside the remit of security institutions, foreign-influenced covert activity of any kind ought to be one of its major concerns.[12]

The perspective provided by international relations, though valuable, encompasses only a fraction of the state's activities and relationships. Thus whilst there may be considerable persuasiveness in theories of interactions between states which see them solely in terms of power,[13] the same approach cannot govern

[10] Trager and Simonie (n. 1 above), 44 and *passim*.

[11] i.e. one genuinely independent of foreign direction.

[12] This point is developed further in Ch. 13 below.

[13] Of this so-called Realist school, the most distinguished English exponent was E. H. Carr, whose *The Twenty Years' Crisis, 1919–1939* (London, 1939) is still very much worth reading, particularly for those opposed to its general position. One of the purposes of this chapter is to advance the argument for state respect for democratic values in starkly Realistic terms: to propagate the belief that states which fail to meet this test should be regarded by their own citizens as illegitimate. Realism is usually contrasted with a rather less cohesive school of Idealism. Though historically the latter has emphasized the search for peace, often based on collective security (see Buzan (n. 1 above), 2–12), it has also included a strand emphasizing human rights which has helped advance their recognition at international level.

the relation between states and their citizens. This point may be illuminated by a brief consideration of Thomas Hobbes, whose social contract theory owed its origins to the search for security.

Contemplating the political violence endemic throughout his long life, Hobbes equated legitimacy with physical security from internal violence and external invasion. The normal requirement of absolute obedience to the Sovereign dissolved only when he could no longer provide that security. But the condition Hobbes dreaded and described in a famous phrase—a life 'solitary, poor, nasty, brutish, and short'[14]—is not, certainly in our time, most likely to result from anarchy and hostile armies invading, raping, and pillaging. Even in his elemental sense, 'security' is not provided merely by a government's success in keeping the peace within its borders and repelling physical threats from other states. This is because the means by which order is maintained and foreign forces are kept at bay may themselves be as destructive of personal security as those threats which obsessed Hobbes. For every Bosnia or Somalia there have been ten polities in which the population has been brutalized by internal repression and dictatorship, often justified by some ideology or self-serving slogan like communism, anti-communism, or the supremacy of some ethnic group or religious dogma. Underpinning Hobbes's equation was the assumption, natural enough in the seventeenth century, that the absence of democracy, or the violation of what the twentieth century knows as political and personal rights, would not of themselves be a permanent source of dissatisfaction producing discord, instability, and cycles of revolutionary and counter-revolutionary violence. The ubiquity of those demands in a democratic age invalidates Hobbes's influential view that mere authoritarian order and maintenance of well-patrolled borders is sufficient to command people's obedience.[15]

For *citizens*, security has a very different and more demanding content than for *subjects*. This is at one level a simple empirical observation, a datum that no Realist can safely ignore, borne out above all by the overthrow of communism in eastern Europe.[16] Yet it is more: it is also a moral judgment. That judgment necessitates two amendments or supplements to the elements Buzan identified as comprising the state: that the governing institutions be those of constitutional democracy; and that the basic human rights of citizens be respected. Their addition has profound implications for two of the four constituent elements of the state. 'Institutions' would not merely comprise any machinery capable of exercising control over the population at a particular time; that would permit government by decree and torture chamber to be included. Certain essential conditions

---

[14] T. Hobbes, *Leviathan* [1651] (Harmondsworth, 1981), pt. ii, ch. 19

[15] In certain extreme and tragic circumstances—Somalia, Angola, Bosnia—where there exists literally a 'war of all against all', the Hobbesian Leviathan will appear as the most attractive prospect. Yet such cases are not only extreme but infrequent. And there is always the danger that once in place, Leviathan will wreak its own horrors.

[16] It is not necessary to overstate the case: the worsening failure of over-centralized economies to provide living standards meeting rising expectations was very important as well.

of democracy must be met: not just a system, but so far as is practicable, a just system. Secondly, the idea of the state, which Buzan rightly identifies as one of its essential constituents (in the Realist sense of being necessary for effective governance), ought to include respect for individual and democratic rights. There is no reason in principle why legitimacy—the psychological power of obedience enjoyed by governments over their citizens—should be enjoyed by a government that functions dictatorially and oppressively, any more than by one which cannot command the allegiance of different ethnic groups.[17] At this point the path cut by Realism unexpectedly joins that of one branch of Idealism, and language more resonant of the latter may be used to express a similar conclusion: a state which does not provide effective protection for human rights—judged by the standard of international Conventions[18] and including a real possibility of freely and regularly choosing those who exercise political power—does not fulfil the conditions of moral legitimacy necessary for recognition as a state whose security is worth protecting. More starkly, such a state does not count as one which may legitimately claim the allegiance of its citizens.

If these be accepted as the core values, then danger to them is properly described as a threat to the state. They are 'basically conservative and defensive',[19] and so exclude territorial expansion or ethnic subjugation.[20] National security is bedrock, and therefore limited. Conversely, other interests, goals, or desires—however pleasant they might be to achieve or acquire—cannot claim the same importance. Hence more extravagant declarations about the needs, claims, or rights of a state couched in the language of 'national security' ought to be treated with extreme suspicion. They are likely to prove dangerous in their effect on relations with other states, and to turn out on closer examination to be no more than disguised attempts by a favoured class, ethnic group, or political-military élite to seize some advantage for itself.[21]

Thus the state is the political embodiment of a complex of foundational values. Once it is conceived in these comprehensive terms, it is no longer tenable to assert that the continued functioning of government institutions, whatever their quality and character, is its paramount security requirement.[22]

[17] Buzan's discussion of the 'legitimating idea' necessary for a nation (n. 1 above), 69–82—is cast in terms of ethnicity because as matter of practical politics the problem of minority 'nationalities' is one of the prime causes of instability and bloodshed throughout the world. Our hope is that states which fail to protect human rights will, as a matter of brute political fact, come to be as unstable and effectively illegitimate as those which cannot manage the nationalities question.

[18] For Britain the most relevant is of course the European Convention on Human Rights, but there are analogous Conventions in other regions, such as the African Charter on Human and Peoples' Rights of 1981. All draw upon the United Nations Universal Declaration on Human Rights of 1948.

[19] Trager and Simonie, (n.1 above), 41.

[20] For present purposes we need not discuss the case, often important in international relations, of a state with irredentist claims based on the presence of large numbers of ethnic kinsmen in and under the rule of an adjacent state.

[21] See further below, p. 29.

[22] Potential antagonisms between democratic values and other considerations are by no means the

This understanding has profound implications in a range of settings, many of which will be explored in this study. At this stage it is necessary only to emphasize that the often-assumed polarity between human rights and national security is a false one. To use the metaphor of balance that is so often employed, particularly by legal writers and judges: if an action taken in the name of national security represses human rights, its justification cannot be established merely by 'weighing' the needs of national security against the loss of individual liberty. The loss of liberty must be counted on *both* sides of the scale and thus deducted from any asserted gain in national security, as well as recognized as a loss to the individuals or groups specifically affected. This is to give jurisprudential and concrete application to what is too often left as a rhetorical or moral sentiment: that an attack on the freedoms of some diminishes the freedoms of all.[23]

Scepticism about the overworked metaphor of balance can of course be put to a different use. In the course of a judgment washing all judicial hands of the internment of Iraqis and Palestinians during the Gulf War, Lord Donaldson MR wrote:

although they give rise to tensions at the interface, 'national security' and 'civil liberties' are on the same side. In accepting as we must, that to some extent the needs of national security must displace civil liberties, albeit to the least possible extent, it is not irrelevant to remember that the maintenance of national security underpins and is the foundation of all our civil liberties.[24]

This is almost exactly the inverse of our approach. 'Civil liberties' (a narrower concept than democratic rights) are subsumed within an authoritarian conception of national security which gives overwhelming predominance to maintaining the state machinery.[25] The two are indeed no longer opposed as in the classic 'balance'—but only because 'liberties' are submerged under 'security'. Our conception, which places democracy at the core of national security, seeks to integrate the two, to amalgamate them indissolubly. National security is itself cast in the mould of democracy.

only, or most serious, that may arise. Maintenance of governing institutions and control over existing territory may also conflict. Thus, if a geographically concentrated ethnic minority determines to secede and form its own state, the choice may be between loss of population and territory, and political survival of the regime if it is too weak to sustain a military campaign.

. [23] Perhaps the most telling expression of this truth is found in the famous words of Pastor Martin Niemoeller, the Lutheran minister and former U-boat commander who had initially welcomed the advent of Nazi rule, but whose opposition to their attacks on independent Protestant churches spurred him to a more principled resistance that led to seven years imprisonment in concentration camps. He later reflected: 'In Germany they came first for the Communists, and I did not speak up because I was not a Communist. Then they came for the Jews, and I did not speak up because I was not a Jew. Then they came for the trade unionists, and I did not speak up because I was not a trade unionist. Then they came for the Catholics, and I did not speak up because I was a Protestant. Then they came for me, and by that time no one was left to speak up.'

[24] *R.* v. *Secretary of State, ex p. Cheblak*, [1991] 2 All ER 319, 334.

[25] Proof of this characterization is to be found not only in the *Cheblak* case itself (see Ch. 7), but in Lord Donaldson's astonishing proposal that government ministers be given power to suppress a publication by decree, subject to an appeal to the courts: below, p. 274.

There is another reason for equating democratic principles with the ideological component of the modern state. It is that in the international arena the state acts in a sovereign capacity, as the representive of its citizens in relations with other, legally equivalent, states. That status endows it with a capacity, recognized by other states as a matter of international law and practical politics, to exercise power over those citizens, with which they will interfere only very sparingly. The nurturing of democratic values is left overwhelmingly to domestic politics.[26] Thus it is important that citizens be encouraged to regard their rulers as lacking legitimacy and therefore unfit to command their obedience if the regime does not satisfy the criteria of the democratic state.

Taking Western liberal democratic practice[27] as our touchstone is admittedly a form of moral absolutism, though hardly a controversial one since the political context of our study is that of Britain and closely related parliamentary democracies. None the less, in view of the obvious riposte that this is yet another manifestation of intellectual and cultural imperialism, it may be appropriate to make three brief points. One is that human rights norms have been accepted by numerous states outside Europe and North America.[28] Secondly, though it is easy to argue that Enlightenment individualism—the most influential source of contemporary human rights theory—is entitled to no more respect than (say) Islamic norms or those developed through three thousand years of Chinese political thought, it is striking that movements for democracy are virtually universal, not least in China itself. Although the specific demands may not precisely replicate a western European constitution, democratic values palpably have a global resonance which suggests that they are more than a localized cultural artefact. Finally, it is worth noting the conclusion of a recent magisterial study, which in its appraisal of forty of the world's poorest nations found a marked correlation between successful provision for human welfare, as measured by indicia such as life-expectancy and income per person, and the existence of civil and political freedoms.[29] The idea that liberal democracy is an expensive luxury precluding economic advance for the ordinary person, always morally troubling because of its implications for the idea of human equality, turns out to be empirically dubious.

A final issue concerning the character of the state can only be posed tentatively, and perhaps best as a series of related questions. The converse of the idea of a legitimating ideology is the acceptance of that legitimacy, with varying

---

[26] Though since the 1970s there has been an interesting development: Western nations have begun to impose (albeit highly selectively and only on those states too weak to resist) standards of democratic and human rights practice as a precondition for economic relations or grants of aid.

[27] Which for our purposes includes widely divergent socio-economic systems, ranging from Scandinavian social democracy to Thatcherite free marketry. The magnitude of the differences between them, which looks vast when seen from within Europe, contracts dramatically when comparison is made with China, or with most of Africa or Latin America.

[28] Such as the African Charter (above n. 18), and a Latin American equivalent of 1969.

[29] P. Dasgupta, *An Inquiry into Well-being and Destitution* (Oxford, 1993), 116–28.

degrees of self-consciousness, by the citizens. Yet this factual (as distinct from normative) sense of attachment or affiliation has always been part of a two-way process, an implicit contract between ruler and ruled. In the modern democratic state the notion of dynastic allegiance has been replaced by the idea of citizenship, but the element of reciprocity has remained: the state has both symbolized certain ideals and provided certain material support which at least partly justified demands for loyalty and service. Yet in Britain during the last decade this equilibrium has been profoundly shaken by the attack, as a matter of government policy, on both the idea and the practice of public provision—of state responsibility for social security in its original sense of security against individual misfortune which society would take responsibility for controlling or mitigating. In its place has come exaltation of the private market and the value of competitive individualism. This is not the place to debate the justice of the ideology or to consider the distributional effects of the policies. However, both seem to raise pressing questions about the bases of allegiance and legitimacy.

If a government acts on the belief that 'there is no such thing as society', what is the basis of social obligation? If people are told that market forces determine their chances in life, and that it is illegitimate to interfere with the unregulated workings of the market, what moral claim has any political institution on their compliance, let alone their disinterested service? It is inconceivable that people could feel allegiance to the market as they have to nations. The market's purported virtue is precisely its impersonality, its unconcern with any factor but relative prices. Unquestionably this contributes to productive efficiency, but it has nothing to say about emotion nor, except in the narrowest sense, about morality. In this regime, the function of the state apparatus is increasingly reduced to enforcing market exchange.

Yet there remain awkward questions. What is the impact on the stability of a political order when it is no longer grounded in the Christian or equivalent secular social values which hitherto have supported Western states, but simply on the promise of *more*? If individual choice is the highest value, why should anyone choose to accept a system that produces consistent, or even appreciable, denial of their wishes? Why should a rational person choose to sacrifice any interest or defer any gratification in order to support a state or social order, in a world of free movement of labour and capital, tax havens, and relatively easy acquisition of citizenship?

Through exalting individual choice, the market makes a deep incision in any form of legitimation of the state beyond calculated self-interest. It is very doubtful, however, whether a state which relies on such a contingent alliance of rationality and materialism can continue in the long term to draw from the well of legitimacy that governments have previously been able to exploit as a sort of natural resource; and its character, stability, and relations with its citizens will be altered in consequence. The resultant damage can only be repaired by force: a society no longer held together by tradition, habit, ethical principles, or fellow-feeling must rely increasingly on laws and prisons.[30] Instinctive loyalty has no doubt been fed by docility and indifference. But political passivity, whilst natural and endemic, may also be cultivated by the machinery of the state—including its 'security' institutions. And the large question, which we can only raise and leave for events to answer, is whether the altered relation of the state to its citizens will inevitably place those institutions in a more overtly political role as the social bonding in Britain increasingly comes unglued.

THE STATE AND SECURITY: THE JANUS HEAD

People tend to think (and politicians and commentators invariably talk) of the state in which they live as a source of security, necessary for their protection against actual or reasonably likely threats from other states. There is often sharp disagreement about the genuineness or seriousness of any particular threat, and of the appropriate response to it, but seldom is the role of the state as guarantor of security called into question. However, some more free-thinking scholarship originating in quite distinct concerns and disciplines has done just that. In an imaginative exploratory essay, Charles Tilly, a distinguished historian of early modern Europe, has suggested a sharp alteration of the focus through which the state is generally viewed. He begins his essay, 'War Making and State Making as Organised Crime',[31] by rejecting the traditional perspectives: the state as the product of a social contract; as the emanation of a society with shared norms and expectations; or even as the provider of services in competition with other possible providers. Rather, as his title suggests, war making and state making are inseparably connected, and 'belong on the same continuum' with banditry, piracy, gangland rivalry, and policing.[32] This is not presented as a normative argument, but as an analysis of the historical experience of recent centuries of European history. Tilly contends that 'coercive exploitation played a large part in the creation of the European states', with mercantile capitalism and state-making reinforcing one another. He justifies the arresting analogy of his title as follows:

To the extent that the threats against which a given government protects its citizens are imaginary or are consequences of its own activities, the government has organised a protection racket. Since governments themselves commonly simulate, stimulate, or even fabricate threats of external war and since the repressive and extractive activities of governments often constitute the largest current threats to the livelihoods of their own citizens, many governments operate in essentially the same way as racketeers.[33]

Compelling demonstration of the validity of this thesis would of course require far more empirical analysis than Tilly's single essay could provide. For our pur-

---

[30] A point made pithily by the title of an excellent study of the Thatcher achievement: A. Gamble, *The Free Economy and the Strong State* (Basingstoke, 1988).

[31] In P. Evans *et al.* (eds.), *Bringing the State Back In* (Cambridge, 1985), 169–91.

[32] Ibid., 170.   [33] Ibid., 171.

poses, however, it is richly suggestive. It illuminates a previously darkened corner: at least an element of brigandage and, far more important, a substantial imprint of aggression and menace to the citizenry, has been stamped upon our constitutional inheritance. And, as in so many aspects of political modernization, England led the way: the Tudors achieved the state monopoly of legitimate violence more than a century before the process was even begun in France under Richelieu.[34] Thus the institutions and practices of government in Britain have, with a firmness unparalleled elsewhere, been shaped by these imperatives. If we are to shake this historical weight off our shoulders, we must reject its authoritarian, aggressive, and exploitative elements. It is impossible to imagine a state organized and operated on the bases Tilly describes conducting its affairs along open, democratic lines. This is hardly surprising, since the formation of European states long preceded the advent of modern democracy, institutionally or philosophically. It follows, however, that a people which values democracy must alter the character of the state it has inherited.[35] Moreover, in the century which has experienced both total war and, for more than forty years, the overhanging threat of nuclear war, the 'security' and 'protection' which states can credibly promise their inhabitants is almost unprecedentedly slight, at any rate in English-speaking democracies which have enjoyed the fortuitous advantage of great natural moats. Yet this in turn undermines— truly subverts—what we have seen has been the dominant justification for obedience of the citizen to the state since social contract theory was invented in seventeenth-century England.[36]

From the very different perspective and vocabulary provided by the discipline of international relations, Barry Buzan has made strikingly similar points. The contradiction between security at different levels, or of different entities— individuals as opposed to the state or nation—is central to his effort to rethink the concept of security. He views it as multi-dimensional, embracing not only individuals and states but also the international system; security cannot be achieved at any one level alone, but requires consideration of all three and of the interaction between them.[37] Within this complex structure, Buzan argues

---

[34] Ibid., 173–4.

[35] Consider also the view of the conservative American political scientist Samuel Huntington, who argues that in Europe, unlike the USA, national security bureaucracy, military forces and traditions, foreign offices, and police systems all pre-dated democratic institutions and ideas like equality and individual rights. (S. Huntington, 'American Ideals versus American Institutions' (1982) 97 *Pol. Sci. Q.* 1, 15.) His general thesis, supporting our historical analysis but exactly the reverse of our normative argument, is that this is regrettable and a hindrance to what he views as American security needs.

[36] Above, p. 7. John Locke, less motivated by fear than Hobbes, saw the state as a convenient contrivance to protect property and enforce the natural law. However, his conclusion (notwithstanding that his theory of limited government inevitably produced a much less powerful sovereign) was similar: when the sovereign failed to protect the interest for which it was granted power, the subject is released from the obligation to obey. (*Second Treatise of Government* [1692] (Oxford, J. Gough ed. 1946), ch. 19. Locke would, of course, also subscribe to the legitimacy of revolution where the sovereign exceeded its proper role.

[37] (Above n. 1), 1–9. Since our subject is not the workings of the international system of states,

that the tension between individual and state security is permanent and inescapable. Hence his emphasis on 'the state as a source of threat': domestic law enforcement, direct political action by the state against individuals or groups, struggles for control over state machinery, and the results of the state's external security policies can all produce direct threats to the well-being of individuals subject to it.[38] Whilst Western democracies produce overall a lower level of these sorts of threat to their citizens than, say, Iraq, El Salvador, or Ceauçescu's Romania, it is specious to pretend that such threats are absent, trivial, or could not be significantly reduced.

Tilly's historical and Buzan's theoretical analyses have thus led to the intersection of two profound problems: the character of the political order which governs us, and the search for security in a violent world organized into sovereign states. They do not simply intersect, but intertwine: the ruling conception of security shapes and dominates the political order, whilst the historical development and present character of the state structures the perception of the requirements of security and the means used to achieve it.

Our emphasis on the state or nation as embodying values and institutions with certain moral qualities has important implications. It gives a particular content to the legitimating ideology which forms part of the state: one which includes a paramount respect for human rights. It is, however, neutral with respect to the issues that are the stuff of daily political controversy. A state may support one or more religions or be wholly secular; its economy may function according to any number of possible principles, as may its system of taxation, so long as these and other critical choices are freely and democratically made.

This conception of the state transforms and magnifies the significance of Buzan's insight about 'the state as a source of threat'. Official actions may indeed threaten individual security, but they may equally threaten the security of the state itself, as defined here. There is an inherent antinomy between many of the measures taken to protect governmental institutions and the effect of those measures on the state's democratic legitimacy.

Acknowledging the existence of the contradiction involves accepting certain corollaries. Perhaps the most important is the reversal of the usual axiom which exerts so powerful an ideological hegemony over public debate: that acts done by state institutions purportedly for reasons of security are presumptively valid and necessary, albeit subject to a subsidiary concern for democratic liberties. The onus of persuasion ought to be reversed, above all by accounting violations of rights as a loss to the whole society, not merely to individuals or minorities directly affected.[39] At the same time, the government should be required to present a comprehensive elaboration of the character of the danger, its degree of

we need not ponder conundrums such as whether security can ever be absolute or is about acceptable degrees of risk; and whether it must always be competitive or what game theory calls 'zero-sum', or whether certain acts or policies can produce gains for all states.

[38] Ibid., 43–9.   [39] cf. above, p. 9.

seriousness and immediacy, the interests and range of persons affected, the reasonably anticipated duration of the proposed measure,[40] and a credible explanation of why it is likely to achieve results beyond the capability of existing repressive powers. We are not seeking to preclude curtailment of human rights in the name of state security under any circumstances. As will be seen, there are strong reasons to be instinctively sceptical about any such alleged necessity, but it would be reckless to assume as a fixed principle that a relatively secure democratic state will never experience a crisis that would demand even a temporary sacrifice of this kind.

However, the acceptance of such a possibility is not a conclusion but a midpoint in an extended line of thought. Here a paper by Ronald Atkey, the former chairman of the Security Intelligence Review Committee (SIRC), offers two particularly fruitful ideas.[41] The first is that it is pointless, if not positively unhelpful, to search for what is no more than fool's gold: one all-embracing definition of national security appropriate to all circumstances. Rather, it is essential to 'unpack' the term to identify exactly what is at stake in any particular situation. Precision rather than emotive evocation or unthinking assertion is the hallmark of his approach. Following from this, Atkey proposes a 'sliding scale analysis' drawing heavily on the concept of proportionality, which requires consideration of the kind of questions we have suggested governments should be required to address when taking any security measure affecting human rights.[42] His aim is 'to place practical limits on the powers available to a government when pursuing each type of interest, to set up a process for reviewing the invocation of these powers, and to ensure that the breadth and severity of these powers *is* in fact proportional to the interests being pursued'.[43]

The sliding-scale analysis joins seamlessly with the idea of treating democratic practice as a prime object of security. That fusion gives rise to a further corollary: precisely because in some instances protecting some other national security value requires interference with human rights, not only the extent of that intrusion but also the mechanisms of oversight and review of those undertaking the necessary measures must themselves be appropriate to the seriousness of what is being done. Accountability is not a philosophical abstraction, a public relations exercise, or a bone tossed in the direction of those who make insistent noises

---

[40] Consider the oxymoron of the Prevention of Terrorism (Temporary Provisions) Act 1989, which has been continuously in force, with a number of modifications, since its hurried passage through Parliament after the Birmingham pub bombings in 1974.

[41] R. Atkey, 'Reconciling Freedom of Expression and National Security', (1991) 41 *U. Tor. LJ* 38, esp. 50 ff. Atkey's signal contribution to the oversight process in Canada is discussed below, pp. 458–65.

[42] Above, p. 14. Atkey's article is limited to freedom of expression, whilst in this book we attempt to identify the full range of rights and freedoms that may be affected. One need not agree with his proposed application of his methodology in particular cases to appreciate the sophistication and sensitivity of his approach.

[43] See n. 41 above, 49. The statutory model which Atkey commends, and which has influenced his approach, is the Emergencies Act, discussed p. 19 below.

about human rights. Institutionally and ideologically, it is a keystone of the state which is itself being protected; and in Britain's unique constitutional structure, accountability to Parliament and the public is the heartbeat of that state. Therefore limitation on powers and effective review of their use are inseparable elements in considering whether 'the state' is receiving adequate protection— against its own agents.

Although the sliding-scale analysis has been most fully developed by a Canadian lawyer writing within a constitutional framework incorporating judicial power to annul legislation contrary to the Charter of Rights and Freedoms, it would be a grave error to confine the conceptual approach to judicial review, and not only for the obvious reason that no such power exists in Britain at the moment.[44] Judicial control of administration is reactive, intermittent, and erratic almost to the point of randomness; the main importance of public law principles lies in their absorption into the ethos of good public administration. Nowhere is this more true than in relation to national security, for as we shall see, this is an area which British judges generally take pains to avoid.[45] Thus the principles discussed in this chapter and throughout the work generally would have their primary application and value in administrative practice and public debate.

THE BEGUILEMENT OF 'NECESSITY'

This heading serves as a bridge from what we have termed 'internal' analysis of the nature of national security to consideration of its political role and impact. For at this point the two become unseverably linked. We noted the political power of the argument that if the exigencies of national security—in the unacceptably narrow sense of maintenance of the machinery of government—so demand, democratic freedoms must always give way. Rather than leave this proposition hanging contentiously at the level of abstract principle, it is worth pursuing a brief historical review designed to test it in light of experience—of the circumstances and outcomes when actions have been taken under the justification it provides. With one exception, chosen for its jurisprudential as well as political relevance, we shall limit ourselves to examples drawn from English-speaking democracies.

The circumstances of war would seem to provide the strongest justification for measures paying scant heed to any claims of liberty, and there is no shortage of such examples. In May and June 1940 the British government took measures Churchill himself described as 'in the highest degree odious', and interned thou-

---

[44] At many points in this study, however, we examine the jurisprudence of the European Convention on Human Rights (ECHR), which, in rulings of the Strasbourg court, has had a direct bearing on security-related matters. Moreover, some British judges are beginning to explore ways in which concepts like proportionality may be fitted into a common law mould. See esp. J. Laws, 'Is the High Court the Guardian of Fundamental Constitutional Rights?', [1993] *PL* 59, 71–5.

[45] See further the discussion in Ch. 12 below.

sands of aliens and British citizens whom security sources alleged were Nazi or Fascist sympathizers. It was the time of Dunkirk and the impending fall of France. Britain was fighting alone and enduring the horrors of nightly bombing; and a considerable margin for error on the side of safety must be allowed, particularly because, for a few months at any rate, a German invasion was a real possibility. None the less, any dispassionate and balanced evaluation must conclude that the measures taken were grossly excessive. For one thing, the authorities could not be bothered to distinguish between varieties of people holding German passports, so by a particularly cruel irony Jewish refugees from Hitler who remained technically German citizens ended up in detention camps, which they found themselves sharing with unrepentant Nazis.[46] Four thousand Anglo-Italians were rounded up, soon provoking a caustic (but wholly internal, and quite ineffectual) response from a senior Foreign Office official: 'As the discussions with MI5 proceeded there grew up a strong suspicion that in actual fact they had little or no information, let alone evidence, in regard to more than a fraction of the persons they had led the Home Secretary to describe to the Cabinet as "desperate characters".'[47] For hundreds of them the mistake had tragic consequences: they were put aboard the transport ship *Arandora Star* and dispatched to Canada. The ship was torpedoed in the Atlantic, and more than one thousand people drowned.[48]

Nor was Britain alone in its reaction. The most sweeping and in retrospect clearly unnecessary round-ups occurred in the United States and Canada, where all ethnic Japanese living on the West Coast were deported thousands of miles into the interior, and were held *en masse* far longer than the British detainees. Despite the greater provocation of Pearl Harbor, the American government acknowledged the injustice some forty years later, and agreed to pay compensation in some cases.[49] In neither instance was any attempt made to individualize the alleged dangers or present any credible suspicion, let alone legal proof, that the internees were endangering lives, property, or the war effort. Indeed in the

---

[46] For details, see P. Gillman and L. Gillman, *'Collar the Lot!'—How Britain Interned and Expelled its Wartime Refugees* (London, 1980), *passim.*, and R. Stent, *A Bespattered Page? The Internment of His Majesty's 'Most Loyal Aliens'* (London, 1980).

[47] Quoted in B. Simpson, *In the Highest Degree Odious: Detention Without Trial in Wartime Britain* (Oxford, 1992), 195. Though it oddly omits discussion of the internment of Jews, this otherwise excellent study (whose title is drawn from Churchill's remark quoted in the text) is a valuable detailed account of the whole process of internment, appeal, and release. One of the key points which emerges is that which is encapsulated in the quoted passage: Security Service information was often out of date or inaccurate, but was none the less often used to deprive people of their freedom because other officials or minsters were unwilling to challenge it, having no independent source of intelligence. See esp. chs. 9–19. See also N. Stammers, *Civil Liberties in Britain During the Second World War* (London, 1983), ch. 2.

[48] Stammers, previous note, 46–7. The 'passengers' were a motley, if not random, collection of internees, some genuine fascists, others anti-fascists, others wholly unpolitical who happened to be of Italian origin. Britain was not alone in its treatment of Italians; there were internments in Australia and the USA as well.

[49] The Bill of Rights and 14th Amendment proved of little value, though there was some judicial dissent when the challenge was heard: see *Korematsu* v. *United States*, 323 US 214 (1944).

case of the Japanese, the internment was but the most discreditable chapter in the long history of racism they had encountered in both nations since their emigration in the late nineteenth century.[50]

A second example is particularly apposite because it shows how the inadequacies of security institutions can induce a wild, indeed panicky, response. In October 1970 a small Quebec terrorist group, the *Front de libération du Quebec* (FLQ), made world headlines when it murdered the provincial labour minister and kidnapped the resident British Trade Commissioner. The Canadian government responded by invoking the War Measures Act, effectively putting the province under martial law, with armed soldiers on the streets, press censorship, and the internment of nearly 500 people who were denied access to legal assistance whilst under interrogation. In the end, however, almost all were released without charge, and most of those convicted received minor sentences for membership of a prohibited organization.[51] It is hard to disagree with Stuart Farson's conclusion that: 'While the decision to invoke the Act still remains clouded in secrecy, it is now clear that it was a gross over-reaction on the part of the Trudeau government.'[52] The reason for this over-reaction is strikingly analogous to the failings responsible for similar injustices in Britain thirty years earlier. The Royal Canadian Mounted Police (RCMP), which then functioned as Canada's internal security agency, was an almost entirely Anglophone organization with a Cold War orientation, which knew very little about Quebec politics or personalities. It therefore did what security agencies are universally prone to do: exaggerated the threat, telling the Prime Minister that there was a real possibility of insurrection. This faulty premiss provided the basis for invoking the emergency powers.[53] It is noteworthy that Canada has learned from this episode and has

---

[50] Eventually the authorities permitted some of the younger 'Nisei' (American-born) men to leave the camps in order to fight in the American army in Europe—though their parents remained interned.

[51] The prohibition was, in effect, retrospective. For a critical analysis see N. Lyon, 'Constitutional Validity of Sections 3 and 4 of the Public Order Regulations, 1970', (1972) 18 *McGill LJ* 136, whose arguments, however, had been rejected by the Quebec Court of Appeal in *R. v. Gagnon and Vallieres*, (1971) 14 CR (NS) 321, 327, 350.

[52] S. Farson, 'Restructuring Control in Canada: The McDonald Commission of Inquiry and its Legacy', in G. Hastedt (ed.), *Controlling Intelligence* (London, 1991), 158.

[53] This interpretation, emphasizing 'intelligence failure', was subsequently offered by the Liberal government and its supporters as a justification for the invocation of extraordinary repressive powers. The ethnic, or linguistic, element was highlighted by Jean-Jacques Blais, Solicitor General in a later Trudeau government and subsequently a member of SIRC, in an interview. This dominant version was hotly contested, also in interview, by John Starnes, head of the RCMP security branch at the time of these events. It has subsequently, and rather unexpectedly, received strong support from research conducted by Professor Reg Whitaker based upon archive material obtained by use of the Access to Information Act. His article, 'Apprehended Insurrection?—RCMP Intelligence and the October Crisis' (1993) 100 *Queen's Qu.* 383, only became available to us after the manuscript was completed. In brief, it argues that: 'The Quebec ministers in Ottawa deliberately chose to excalate the political magnitude of the crisis to justify emergency powers as a means of intimidating nationalists and separatists' (p. 404), and that the security service, which had provided an accurate, less alarmist report to the Cabinet, was subsequently made the scapegoat for what came to be seen as an intemperate, even panicky, response.

For our purposes, the accuracy of the competing versions is irrelevant: whether self-interested

sought to impose a far more rigorous discipline upon the Executive's actions in any similar circumstances in future. In 1985 it repealed the War Measures Act and replaced it with the Emergencies Act, which incorporates a finely graded set of provisions setting out a range of emergencies, each of which 'enables the federal government to use a particular set of powers that is specifically fashioned to deal with the emergency in question and that is sensitive to [its] severity'.[54]

The conclusion to be drawn from incidents such as these is that official responses to emergencies which were overwhelmingly viewed at the time as not merely justifiable but compelling, have consistently turned out to be excessive, unnecessary, and often shameful. When the cry of 'the nation in danger' is heard, what is called for above all is an instinctive, hard-headed scepticism. The same conclusion emerges from an (also necessarily abbreviated) examination of the ideas of perhaps the most interesting exponent of the contrary view, the German constitutional lawyer and polemicist Carl Schmitt.[55]

Schmitt was writing in a specific context: the weak, unstable state of Weimar Germany, under threat from those, especially on the Right, who sought to use its liberties and procedures to overthrow its parliamentary institutions. In extended debate with other scholars, notably Hans Kelsen, he sought to justify the use by the President of the emergency powers permitting rule by decree under Article 48 of the Constitution, as necessary to safeguard the existence of constitutional freedoms. In particular, he argued that those powers should be used to suppress movements like the Nazis which did not subscribe to democratic norms—a notion that now receives expression in the concept of 'militant democracy' written into the post-War German constitution.[56]

This specific controversy inspired Schmitt's wider jurisprudential argument: that the legal order depends—as a matter of brute fact, not of normative discourse—on a non-legal exception which defines the norm; and 'sovereign is he who decides on the exception'.[57] This is intended to be much more than an unusual way of saying that, as a matter of political sociology, other factors than the constitution and its norms determine whether a nation will enjoy a stable democratic political order. It is saying that ultimately both stability and democracy depend on some agency within the political order being capable of acting

political calculation or faulty intelligence was the cause of the excesses, on either account the infringement of freedom was clearly unnecessary.

[54] (Above n. 41), 46. See RSC 1985, C. 22 (4th Supp.).

[55] Several of Schmitt's books have been translated into English in the last twenty years. See esp. *Political Theology*, trans. G. Schwab (Cambridge, Mass., 1985), and *The Concept of the Political*, trans. G. Schwab (New Brunswick, NJ, 1976). For accessible accounts of his work, see J. Bendersky, *Carl Schmitt: Theorist for the Reich* (Princeton, NJ, 1983), Pt. 3; J. Finn, *Constitutions in Crisis: Political Violence and the Rule of Law* (Oxford, 1991), ch. 4; P. Hirst, *Representative Democracy and its Limits* (Cambridge, 1990), chs. 7 and 8.

[56] See Finn, previous note, ch. 5. Schmitt's own later fawning acceptance of Nazism served to discredit his views for decades, but the thrust of his arguments until the Nazis came to power was to advocate measures which would have stopped them.

[57] *Political Theology* (n. 55 above), 5.

extra-legally to enforce legality, and that such power must transcend legal constraint.

The appeal of Schmitt's doctrine in the circumstances in which he wrote, or in those of any weak state under siege from within or (especially) without, is very great. Yet its allure should be resisted, for a number of important reasons. The argument fails to recognize any notion of proportionality, and is therefore virtually guaranteed to produce the kind of over-reaction that our historical examples have illustrated. More fundamentally, the allure is so powerful that it is likely to become addictive: like an opiate which, once successful in relieving severe pain, is resorted to more readily at each recurring twinge. Attempting to secure constitutional democratic values by deeply authoritarian means is not a paradox but an essential contradiction: something has to give, and what gives is constitutionalism. The 'exception' becomes the norm. This is precisely what happened with Article 48, which was invoked on literally scores of occasions during Weimar's brief history. And it is more than arguable that the habit of relying on rule by decree both denied Germans the experience of making parliamentary institutions work, and stifled the development of loyalty to them; it certainly minimized the contrast between Hitler's avowed authoritarianism (not then of course including concentration camps and the Holocaust) and the conduct of governments in office after 1930. Schmitt's 'exceptionalism' is an impossibility, a sophisticated attempt to have one's constitutional cake and eat it; and to use a more contemporary figure of speech, it assigns the safekeeping of children in a school playground to a pit-bull terrier.

THE STATE AS THREAT: THE POLITICAL USES OF 'NATIONAL SECURITY'

Far too often, the cry of 'security' functions in the political world as a sort of intellectual curare, inducing instant paralysis of thought. It is such a potent yet indefinite symbol[58] that those in positions of power are able to curb criticism and shut off debate by conjuring it up and claiming to possess vital knowledge—which of course cannot safely be revealed—to support their actions or policies. They have drawn, too, on conjoined traditions of deference and non-partisanship in such matters that has made it unnecessary for governments to provide reasoned justifications where security is purportedly involved. Illustrating the curious but vicious circularity that surrounds the whole area, that deference is in part sustained by ignorance—itself fostered by claims of indispensable secrecy. Thus instead of fully reasoned explanations, the public receives only the barest, most conclusory justifications, which are supposed to be taken on trust.

Thus perhaps the primary political function of security is as a part of the

---

[58] Hence the title of Wolfers's influential essay (above n. 1): 'National Security as an Ambiguous Symbol'.

coinage of power, hoarded and used by ministerial and bureaucratic élites to ignore or short-circuit normal democratic processes. Buzan describes the functional implications of this 'symbolic ambiguity' as follows:

The appeal to national security as a justification for actions and policies which would otherwise have to be explained is a political tool of immense convenience for a large variety of sectional interests in all types of state. Because of the considerable leverage over domestic affairs which can be obtained by invoking it, an undefined notion of national security offers scope for power-maximizing strategies to political and military elites . . . Cultivation of hostile images abroad can justify intensified political surveillance, shift of resources to the military, and other such policies with deep implications for the conduct of domestic political life.[59]

To apply these general observations more concretely, the use of 'national security' in the internal politics of Western parliamentary democracies has, theoretically and as a matter of historical fact, numerous dangers and undesirable consequences.[60] Among the most important are:

1. *Enthronement of a political orthodoxy*, or at least imposition of penalties on those who hold 'extreme' views, that is to say, views unacceptable to those who have power to define the range of the acceptable.

2. *Exercise of new and greater powers*—sometimes secretly and illegally, at other times under lawful authority—over political conduct and expression. These powers may be wielded by police or security agencies over the population as a whole, as in the case of telephone tapping.[61] However, and very much a product of state practices in this century and particularly after the Second World War, they may operate as a form of what has been called 'partial sanctioning'.[62] This refers to the imposition of deterrents or penalties on only a portion or segment of the population which finds itself in certain circumstances or with certain needs or wishes. Examples include vetting of those seeking state employment,[63] or refusal of admission or deportation of an alien for conduct which might not even be a crime if undertaken by a citizen.[64] Not only do such sanctions affect only a limited class of persons; they are 'partial' as well in the sense that those persons remain unaffected in other respects. For example, someone refused state employment on 'security' grounds is not forbidden to work in the private sector. None the less, such losses are significant to those who suffer them, and serve to discourage any conduct which might produce them.

3. *The conduct of government in an arbitrary manner.* Policies or actions are taken, not necessarily irrationally, but without adequate explanation and with the terms

[59] See n. 1 above, 11.

[60] These effects may be even more severe in dictatorships or states committed officially to a particular ideology or faith, and in such states use of 'national security' may have other evil results, notably persecution of ethnic or religious minorities.

[61] Below, Ch. 3.

[62] J. Whyte and A. Macdonald, 'Dissent and National Security and Dissent Some More', in C. Franks (ed.), *Dissent and the State* (Toronto, 1989), 23.

[63] Below, Ch. 6.   [64] Below, Ch. 7.

of debate sharply skewed in favour of those in office. Normally, when challenged on the wisdom or efficacy of any particular policy, governments' defence of their policies present an evaluation of gainers and losers. However, where action is taken in the name of national security, there are allegedly no losers, for everyone is said to benefit when the state is more 'secure'. This places critics at a deep disadvantage, because those opposing a measure which must by definition benefit everyone can easily be branded as unpatriotic or as actuated by hidden motives.

4. *Secrecy, the boon companion of arbitrariness.* The difference is that secrecy may go beyond simple failure to account for what is done, to include concealment of actions taken, or—an inevitable step down the slippery slope—flatly lying about them in order to maintain the subterfuge. Secrecy however, is not limited to actions but extends more widely to information that may be several stages removed from any tangible form of conduct. Its broader embrace makes it all the more dangerous. However, though secrecy as related to national security is only one dimension of secrecy in government generally, we must limit ourselves to this facet of the problem.

5. Finally, *national security is regularly invoked in the perennial tussle of fiscal and social priorities*—between, to use Hermann Goering's well-known phrase, guns and butter. One of the most effective means of disposing of the claims of disadvantaged people, or of other services such as education which are at any particular time used by a relatively small minority, is to raise the spectre of national peril. However, this conflict does not involve the sort of legally recognized human rights or protected interests, or the conduct of democratic politics, that are the focus of our concerns. It involves purely political choices concerning competing social interests, and we have therefore not pursued the issues it raises.[65] In a different politico-legal environment, in which economic and social rights as expounded in certain international documents[66] were part of domestic legislation, we would be writing a substantially different book.

Common to the dangers and abuses of national security we have identified is their impact on political freedom and dissent, and on the constitutional processes of accountability. They share the quality identified by Buzan: that of the state as threat. The threat is not confined to the personal security of its citizens, however, but extends equally to the good order of its political institutions. Since we have argued that there are some values and institutions embodied in the state which genuinely merit being 'secured', we cannot dismiss the problem by contending that 'national security' is simply a sham, a dishonest slogan designed to favour 'sinister interests'[67] and to legitimate various forms of repres-

---

[65] Moreover, in recent years the dominance of the ideology of competitive market individualism has been powerful enough on its own to defeat calls for greater social and compensatory spending.

[66] e.g. the International Covenant on Economic, Social and Cultural Rights, 1966, or the European Social Charter, 1961.

[67] A fine phrase of Jeremy Bentham's, which recurs throughout his writings.

sion. Rather, the state is simultaneously protector and threat to vital personal and political values, and we must all live with the inescapable contradiction as best we can.

Concretely, this means constitutional thinking and institution-building: devising principles, and methods to implement them, that will best confine the dangers whilst retaining the benefits. Thus, throughout this study specific issues and problems are continually related back to structures and principles of public law. Public debate tends, understandably, to focus on what are felt to be abuses and to demand a remedy without realizing that what is likely to be effective will depend critically on its compatibility with political institutions generally. There is a close analogy with transfusions and transplants: matter which is incompatible is rejected by the recipient organism. This is not an over-subtle way of saying that no serious change is possible because anything new must fit within the existing governmental machinery. To the contrary: if the need is great enough, the conclusion is surely that the machinery must be altered as well. But it is idle to offer suggestions which fail to take account of the magnitude of what is entailed; that is the certain way to sabotage any movement for reform. Hence our grounding the analysis in our understanding of the possibilities and limits of the parliamentary form of democracy, and more specifically in what is often called the 'Westminster model'.[68]

Having considered the concept of national security from an internal and external perspective we move now to tease out some of the implications. Our understanding of national security as rooted in protection of democratic values can be used to distinguish between security and several related and rival concepts. In the sections following we discuss the relation between it and, in sequence, defence, economic prosperity, and secrecy. Despite some overlap in all three cases, it is crucial to maintain the distinctions, something modern governments are prone to erase.

WHAT'S IN A NAME?: NATIONAL SECURITY VERSUS DEFENCE OF THE REALM

'National security' is today such a familiar phrase in political and legal usage that it is difficult to imagine its absence. Yet it is a relative newcomer, virtually unknown until the coming of the Cold War. Throughout both World Wars there were a great number of statutes and regulations giving extraordinary powers to the Executive and its officials. These were generically entitled, and explicitly drew their justification, from the need for Defence of the Realm—DORA as she was called.[69] It is not clear precisely when or why, in Britain,[70] national

---

[68] See above p. viii and below pp. 412–15 for the implications of this limitation.

[69] Defence of the Realm Acts 1914–15; the same phrase was used in regulations made under the Emergency Powers (Defence) Acts 1939–40, notably in the notorious Reg. 18B.

[70] The change come somewhat earlier in Australia; see below, p. 327. However, in 1918 the War

security replaced DORA in official usage. Lord Diplock once suggested that the two were synonymous, that use of 'national security' in various United Kingdom statutes reflected the influence of our adhesion to the European Convention on Human Rights.[71] Even if correct, this explanation merely raises the further question of why the term made its appearance in the Convention, which British lawyers had a great influence in drafting.[72] Its presence cannot be explained by difficulties of translation, because the French *défense* has the same meaning as its English equivalent. And a search through the *travaux préparatoires* of the Convention—the discussions of the national representatives who considered its draft provisions and approved its final form—sheds no light whatever, for the matter seems never to have been discussed.

There is another possibility, which is that in this, as in so many militarily related matters in the immediate post-war period, American practice predominated.[73] If so, much more is at stake than a mere label, for American historians have documented a parallel transformation from 'defence' to 'national security' as the guiding concept of US foreign policy at that time. Their work demonstrates that the choice of terminology was deliberate, intended to express a more grandly ambitious conception of that nation's role in world affairs.

Daniel Yergin's excellent *Shattered Peace*[74] traces the post-war emergence of an American 'national security state', supported by an ideological fusion of anti-communism and the new doctrine of national security. He focuses particularly on the influence of James Forrestal, Secretary of Defence and a key figure in the change of policy from seeking accommodation with the Soviet Union to all-out antagonism. Traditionally, American policy had been governed by the notion of territorial defence. Forrestal disparaged what he called the 'somewhat passive concept of self-defense', and even before the Second World War ended began quite deliberately to talk in terms of national security rather than defence, specifically to express a more activist policy calling for permanent 'preparedness' and an assertion of American interests and responsibilities that was without restriction and global in its breadth.[75]

Office drafted and circulated a National Security Bill, designed to replace the Official Secrets Act 1911. Its proposals, though, were modified and what emerged was the Official Secrets Act 1920, amending the 1911 Act. The term then seems to have disappeared from British official usage for over twenty years. See R. Thomas, *Espionage and Secrecy* (London, 1991), 10.

[71] *Council of Civil Service Unions* v. *Minister for the Civil Service* [1985] AC 374, 410. Lord Diplock knew more about the subject than most judges, having been Chairman of the Security Commission and judicial monitor of interception of communications, and having much earlier served on the Swinton Committee directing internment in 1940: Simpson (n. 47 above), 185–7.

[72] On the role of Foreign Office lawyers in this respect, see A. Lester, 'Fundamental Rights: The United Kingdom Isolated?', [1984] *PL* 46, 49–50.

[73] An amusing and less weighty example of US influence was their insistence, much to Churchill's fury as a matter of linguistic purity, on uniform use by the UKUSA states of the classification 'Top Secret' rather than the British 'Most Secret'. J. Richelson and D. Ball, *The Ties That Bind* (London, 1985; 2nd edn., Sydney, 1990), 165.

[74] D. Yergin, *Shattered Peace* (Harmondsworth, 1980).

[75] Ibid. 194, 218, and more generally ch. 8.

Yergin describes the key elements in the new concept of national security which, he argues, continued to dominate American policymaking thirty years later:

It postulates the interrelatedness of so many different political, economic, and military factors that developments halfway around the globe are seen to have automatically a direct impact on America's core interests. Virtually every development in the world is perceived to be potentially crucial. An adverse turn of events anywhere endangers the United States. Problems in foreign relations are viewed as urgent and immediate threats. Thus, desirable foreign policy goals are translated into issues of national survival, and the range of threats becomes limitless. The doctrine is characterized by expansiveness, a tendency to push the subjective boundaries of security outward to more and more areas, to encompass more and more geography and more and more problems.[76]

A later study of American national security thinking in the same period reached a similar view.[77] Indeed its author concluded that by 1948 the Americans had defined their security needs as including: a strategic sphere of influence in the Western Hemisphere and both Atlantic and Pacific Oceans; an extensive system of outlying military bases; control over polar air routes; access to the resources of and markets of most of Eurasia and denial of that access to any prospective enemy; and maintenance of nuclear superiority.[78]

This general line of interpretation is controversial, but it is noteworthy that whilst its critics differ on details of interpretation and, even more, in the degree of sympathy with which they view American actions in this period, they do not contest that a significantly more expansive policy was adopted in this period.[79] Of course this expansion occurred in part because the United States stepped into Britain's shoes as a global power, but the critical national security historians are right to emphasize that much more was involved: an increased assertiveness that manifested itself in what in another context has been described as 'global reach'.[80]

We have undertaken this historical review because it may serve as a cautionary tale in present-day policy debate. The overblown ambition produced by such a conception of 'security' leads both to expenditure of resources and energies better devoted to enterprises more productive in the long term, and to the curbing of freedoms in the name of the measures taken in its pursuit.

Britain suffered these effects, though to a lesser degree. It persisted in trying to maintain its status as a world power long after it lacked the wherewithal to do so. In most accounts, the Suez fiasco is treated as a turning-point, after

---

[76] Ibid. 196.

[77] M. Lefler, 'The American Concept of National Security and the Beginning of the Cold War' (1984) 89 *AHR* 346–81.

[78] Ibid. 379. The list in the text is not exhaustive; there were other matters of lesser importance as well.

[79] See the debate between Lefler, Gaddis, and Kuniholm (1984) 89 *AHR* 381–400, and J. Gaddis, *Strategies of Containment* (New York, 1981), 3–88.

[80] R. Barnet and R. Muller, *Global Reach* (New York, 1974), (a study of multinational enterprises).

which the realities of diminished capability began to be respected.[81] None the less, and despite the subsequent withdrawal of forces east of Suez, Britain continued to commit a substantially higher proportion of GNP to military spending that any other western European state.[82] And those who urged a more defensive orientation towards international politics made little headway, not least because the dominant Cold War cast of mind—cast in the mould of 'national security'—paradoxically insisted upon and propagated the notion of a basic *insecurity* that grew directly out of the expansiveness of its conception of security. Britain, though a strong state, acted in many ways as though it were a weak one.[83]

It was not an accident, but rather an inevitable consequence, that once the United States embarked on its grandiose voyage, McCarthyism followed rapidly in its wake. The more overweening the ambition, the more vulnerable the voyager feels: hence the overwrought and viciously destructive campaigns against domestic dissent (alleged to sap the nation's strength) which claimed thousands of victims. The more modestly—but hard-headedly—a nation defines its interests, the more readily it can protect them and rest content, with itself and with its neighbours. Rather than the octopus or the eagle (a bird of prey), the hedgehog is the most appropriate symbol of a state's role in the world arena; for the hedgehog knows one big thing:[84] that a defensive posture is the best means of safety. Its fate under the wheels of cars shows the dangers of venturing where one need not go and where greater powers hold sway.

Though it is probably too much to hope for at this stage, it would be desirable to return to old ways. We should relearn the language—and still more, the mental outlook—of defence instead of national security, and mean by it a tempered willingness to uphold our fundamental values from serious and specific danger, if necessary by extraordinary means including force; but on the understanding that those values, precisely because they are fundamental, are quite finite. If we cannot escape the terminology of national security, we can insist on confining it to what really matters: defence of democratic practice free of foreign manipulation, along with the ability to defend the nation's independence and territory against military attack.

---

[81] For an account which emphasizes the role of SIS (and draws much of its information from former officers), see A. Verrier, *Through the Looking Glass* (London, 1983), *passim* but esp. ch. 4. More generally, see C. Barnett, *The Collapse of British Power* (London, 1972) and B. Porter, *Britain, Europe and the World 1850–1982: Delusions of Grandeur* (London, 1983).

[82] Taking figures scattered throughout the final chapter of P. Kennedy, *The Rise and Fall of the Great Powers* (London, 1989), in the late 1980s the UK was spending 5.5% of its GNP on defence, compared to France's 4.2% and West Germany's 3.3%. For Japan, the figure was under 1%. Kennedy's major thesis, which he supports with a massive weight of historical evidence, is that '*excessive* arms spending will hurt economic growth' (p. 573, original emphasis).

[83] See above, pp. 3–4. It is not suggested that the American conception was swallowed uncritically by everyone, but it was influential throughout the Cold War and particularly during the 1980s.

[84] According at any rate to the ancient Greek poet whose apophthegm ('the fox knows many things, but the hedgehog knows one big thing') inspired an essay on Tolstoy by Sir Isaiah Berlin: 'The Hedgehog and the Fox', in his *Russian Thinkers*, H. and A. Hardy (eds.) (London, 1978).

NATIONAL SECURITY AND THE GOOD THINGS IN LIFE

Though the title of this subsection has been chosen with tongue firmly in cheek, the underlying point is entirely serious. Governments act for many reasons, notably to maintain the wealth, health, skills, and safety of the persons or property of their citizens, or at any rate of a sufficient number as will maintain them in office. These benefits may be regarded as desires, ambitions, or goals of national policy, and when a state seeks to advance or maximize them in the international political arena, they may be called national interests. Through trade negotiations, tax treaties, extradition agreements, and numerous other instrumentalities and measures, advancement of national interests is the staple of foreign policy and diplomatic activity. What none of this can deservedly be called, however, is protection of national security. That term, as we have been suggesting in various ways throughout this chapter, should be reserved for matters that go to the heart of the character of the state and society. Put another way, in the 'contest' surrounding the concept, it can only validly be claimed by matters that are as near as possible of universal and equivalent benefit to all citizens of the state.

This point demands emphasis because in the post-Cold War era there is increasing pressure to treat economic desires or wishes as matters of national security. This may be part of a wider trend in world politics. A fascinating recent book by two international relations scholars begins with the following premiss:

States are now competing more for the means to create wealth within their country than for power over more territory. Where they used to compete for power as a means to wealth, they now compete for wealth as a means to power—but more for the power to maintain internal order and social cohesion than for the power to conduct foreign conquest or to defend themselves against attack.[85]

Although this passage introduces a study limited to developing countries, it may be prescient about the direction of policies of national governments generally, and perhaps especially to Britain as the economy steadily 'declines' (which really means only that it grows less rapidly than others). As such it alerts one both to grave dangers and to a profound paradox.

The hazards of confusing, or rather conflating, national interests with national security begin at home. Most important is the fact that giving national security so wide-ranging a meaning is potentially extraordinarily oppressive, for it erodes the distinction between the civil and military spheres of social life, or at any rate between a liberal and an authoritarian society. In the latter—fascist or communist regimes, or assorted authoritarian capitalist states in the Third World, of which successful NICs like Singapore or Korea are pre-eminent examples—

[85] J. Stopford and S. Strange, *Rival States, Rival Firms* (Cambridge, 1991), 1.

anything which obstructs productivity and hence 'prosperity' or 'development' is regarded as at best dangerously anti-social, and is often made illegal. Rigorous, often oppressive, measures are taken to control political and economic life so as to ensure uninterrupted production. Hence the co-optation or outlawing of trade unions and strikes. Security institutions become part of the system of internal political repression.[86]

We are not suggesting that it is wrong for governments to regard economic prosperity as an important national interest to be pursued internationally and, if necessary, competitively.[87] But there should be limits as to methods, and more broadly as to the atmosphere or spirit in which such efforts are conducted. The former is particularly critical, in that actions undertaken in pursuit of economic advantage must never be permitted to curtail democratic freedoms. As to the latter, there must be serious concern that treating economic interests in this way will lead to a return of conflicts over spheres of influence, most favoured nation trade agreements, and the like—the nineteenth century without gunboat diplomacy—or a re-creation of Cold War-type blocs, divided along new lines: the European Community versus the United States versus Japan and/or the rest of the Pacific Rim. However, such alliances would have even less internal unity than existed during most of the Cold War, for the internal logic of the situation would dictate that the major EC nations must regard each other as adversaries. The result would be a combination of the worst elements of market competition and autarchic mobilization, creating an enlarged and virtually limitless sphere of rivalry and suspicion: at its extreme a new Cold War, though without nuclear weapons.

This prospect is anything but theoretical, and is perhaps fast approaching. For the world's most powerful nation has shown definite signs of moving in this direction. One of the first straws in the wind was the enactment in 1991 of a statute with the curious title of the National Security Education Act. Under the heading of legislative 'findings' it declared:

(1) The *security* of the United States is and will continue to depend on the ability of the United States to exercise international leadership.

(2) [That ability] will increasingly continue to be based on the political and economic strength of the United States, as well as on United States military strength around the world . . .

(4) *The future national security and economic well-being of the United States* will depend substantially on this ability of its citizens to *communicate and compete* by knowing the language and cultures of other countries. (emphasis added)[88]

---

[86] See further below, pp. 390–93.

[87] There may be rare instances where economic matters do rise to the level of national security, as, for example, where a state is the target of what amounts to economic warfare by a foreign state, as has arguably been the case with Cuba at the hands of the USA. Another is where a state is wholly dependent on politically vulnerable imports of a vital commodity, as in the case of Japan which imports 100% of its oil. Fortunately these are not problems the UK is ever likely to encounter.

[88] PL 102–183, s. 801 (b) (1)–(4).

The practical conclusion of this syllogism was the creation of a $150 million fund to assist universities to improve teaching of previously neglected foreign languages and area studies.

Subsequently, President Clinton's appointee as Director of the CIA stated during his confirmation hearings that the way in which the CIA should treat foreign commercial espionage was second only to nuclear proliferation as 'the hottest topic' he faced. More recent press reports from Washington have chronicled claims by the Agency that it had caught agents of the French intelligence services attempting to steal aeronautical and other civilian commercial secrets of American firms.[89]

We discuss this issue further, specifically in relation to the work of the Security Service in protecting the 'economic well-being' of the United Kingdom in Chapter 14, in which for reasons already foreshadowed we argue strongly that it should not be involved in this area. However, the controversy is also important to the work of the organizations that gather intelligence either overseas or predominantly about foreign entities: SIS and GCHQ. The government has promised that it will introduce a statutory charter for both, at some near but unspecified time, and it makes most sense to discuss the matter in that context.[90]

In addition to the dangers we have highlighted, we noted that the assimilation of economic goals to national security involved a paradox. It is that this development involves the increasing 'nationalization' of economic competition at precisely the same time as several counter-trends appear. National economies are becoming less regulated for reasons of public interest; they are welcoming foreign investment and ownership of companies previously held domestically; public assets are being sold to private owners; and public support for the meeting of individual needs of the relatively poor and of social needs generally is sharply diminishing. These policies are directly contrary to a view of the world which equates economic prosperity with benefits that are both purely national and shared throughout the society. Yet that view is the only credible justification for using government agencies granted extraordinary powers and employing secret and sometimes dubious methods to promote the interests of particular sectors of the economy, let alone those of individual companies. The development we have criticized is a classic instance of trying to have things both ways—and also of powerful élites attempting to wrap themselves in the flag for their own advantage. Sectional or class interests are proclaimed as something greater. It is worth recalling that Boswell, seeking to clarify Dr Johnson's famous scathing remark about patriotism, explained 'that he did not mean a real and generous love of our country, but that pretended patriotism which so many, in all ages and countries, have made a cloak for self-interest'.[91]

---

[89] See the reports in the *Guardian*, 4 Feb. 1993 ('Uncloaking Clinton's Spies') and 8 May 1993 ('Now, the Spy Who Looks at the Books').

[90] See below, in Coda.   [91] *Boswell's Life of Johnson*, Globe edn. (London, 1922), 302.

There is also a practical problem. In the 1990s, what is a British company? In the age of multinational enterprises (MNE) and free movement of labour and capital, the answer is no longer self-evident. To use a prominent example, is Nissan UK, with its large investment and substantial contribution to employment in various depressed areas, a British company, or does its remission of profits and ultimate subordination in decisionmaking to its Tokyo parent make it foreign? How does one characterize a company whose head office or major plants are located elsewhere in Europe, but which is part of a joint venture or is partly owned by a British company and hence earns profits that find their way to this country? One need not multiply such conunudrums, for the point will be clear: even if there were no reservations about the principle of using security and intelligence agencies to assist companies, in many cases it will be unclear whether a particular company qualifies on the criterion of national advantage. What Marx misguidedly proclaimed of the worker is actually true of the multinational enterprise: it has no country, and a government which acts on the assumption that its interests and those of a locally based MNE coincide is apt to find that its sovereign powers have been used to the advantage of others, perhaps rivals, far away.

NATIONAL SECURITY AND SECRECY

In the minds of many people, and particularly in discussions in the media, national security and secrecy are so entangled that they seem to be identical. This is a mistaken equation and an unfortunate confusion, for although there is some overlap, they are for the most part unconnected. Justifiable secrecy has other and, in quantitative terms, more important grounds than national security, which could conceivably cover only a small proportion of the matter involved.[92] Conversely, national security as we have expounded it in this chapter encompasses matters whose gravity demands that they be at the forefront of public knowledge and discussion. The question—whose answer must be reasoned through, not merely assumed—is whether it may also require maintenance of the secrecy of some material.

Our first proposition is that decisions as to secrecy should be based on the nature of the material, not on the official position held or formerly held by any person. This might seem, indeed should be, reasonably obvious—except that it is directly contrary to one of the most important provisions of the recently enacted official secrets legislation.[93] Officials of a security agency may possess

---

[92] The most compelling argument for secrecy in our view is protection of personal privacy, which is far removed from most of the arguments put forward to defend secrecy about government policy and activities. Since this book is not about secrecy as such, we cannot explore the issues involved in any depth. For one good legal study, see P. Birkinshaw, *Freedom of Information: The Law, The Practice and the Ideal* (London, 1988), and more generally, S. Bok, *Secrets* (Oxford, 1984).

[93] See Ch. 9.

information which it is vital to put before the public to prevent a government from deceiving Parliament and the electorate. They may also possess other information whose disclosure could place lives in jeopardy. The test of secrecy is the interests served by concealment or revelation, not the source of the information.

Secondly, the decision that a particular class or category of information should be kept secret says nothing at all about the means of doing so, and in particular about penalties for disclosure. This again is discussed at length in Chapter 9; all that need be stated at this point is that safeguarding secrecy does not necessarily require criminal sanctions.

Legitimate secrecy in our conception involves a paradox: much of the most sensitive information is either of no relevance whatever to policy and democratic debate, or is completely incomprehensible to any but a handful of technical experts—or both. Moreover, the vast bulk of it concerns activities undertaken either overseas or with respect to the actions of foreign governments, and thus has little impact on democracy in Britain. This is best seen by considering examples, real and hypothetical.

A paradigm case is that of the identity of active officers, agents, or sources, particularly those working overseas in circumstances where exposure could mean physical harm. A good example, especially because it has been established as true beyond doubt, is the fact that Matrix Churchill executive Paul Henderson acted as an agent for SIS during the 1980s.[94] Had that fact been published during one of his visits to Iraq, he might well have been killed after a summary 'trial'.[95] Had disclosure occurred while he was safely in Britain, obviously his ability to acquire information would have been destroyed, as would his business prospects in Iraq. In the absence of any countervailing public interest to set against these great risks or forms of damage, it was right to maintain the wall of secrecy about his activities.[96] The same reasoning would apply to the identity of anyone who operates secretly on behalf of an agency of the British government, not only because of the risks involved, but because the ability of the agency to protect his or her identity is an absolute precondition in persuading people to take on the risks.[97]

What is vital to emphasize however, is that absolute protection of the identity of serving officers and those with whom they work does not entail secrecy about the policies their efforts are directed to achieving. Quite the reverse: whether the British government should permit sale of machine tools (let alone

---

[94] See below, Ch. 11, on the Matrix Churchill trial.

[95] As happened to the journalist Farzad Barzoft.

[96] The overwhelming public interest in not convicting people known to be innocent (not to mention safeguarding Mr Henderson's own freedom) shifted the scales radically when he was charged with deceiving the government in relation to export licence applications, and his relations with SIS were rightly revealed.

[97] Which leaves one wondering what effect the Matrix Churchill trial will have on the capabilities of future SIS recruitment efforts round the world.

military equipment) to Iraq or anywhere else should occupy the centre stage of politics, and no information about what the government is doing in this respect should be withheld from the public. Mr Henderson's personal endeavours were of no public importance; the government's attitude to his commercial activities was. The same analysis would apply to virtually any other secret agent, unless his activities are morally repugnant and exposure of his identity the only way to stop them.[98] What ought to be revealed are dishonesty, false or misleading statements, unacknowledged policies, and deniable operations authorized or engaged in by policymakers at the highest level in the safety of Whitehall, not the identities of their minions in the field.

A second category consists of activities or operations which depend upon secrecy for their success because they are susceptible to counter-measures. It may be known in a general sense, for instance, that Britain is engaged in trying to intercept telephone and other communications of various governments and multinational companies. The rightness, efficacy, and efficiency of such endeavours should receive a great deal more discussion than they have. But once the political debate is properly held and the course determined, public identification of particular targets, or the methods used against any of them, serves no valid purpose and merely impairs the undertaking. This is particularly so when the specific target, such as an underwater cable lying in a certain location, may not be suspected by the nation using it.

One question raised by both these examples, involving agents and operations, is how long the secrecy needs to be maintained once the activity is concluded. The length of time governments claim is essential is often ludicrous,[99] but they are able to have their way because it is impossible to set out hard and fast universal rules. The decision calls for judgment informed by a full knowledge of the circumstances of each case; since this is restricted to the agency involved, challenging the exercise of that judgment becomes almost hopeless in any particular case. However, some general guidelines may be suggested. One is that operations undertaken within the United Kingdom should be revealed within a very short time (perhaps five years) of their taking place, unless a very strong case can be mounted that those involved face a genuine risk of physical harm. This short period is necessary so that the public may become aware of activities that might, even indirectly and inadvertently, have affected the conduct of domestic politics. Secondly, what has become known to an enemy (or at any rate, those in relation to whom secrecy was sought) ought to be known by the public. To use

---

[98] e.g. if his or her work leads to the deaths of innocent people, or involves destablizing a democratically elected government on behalf of the UK. This justification might support the naming of some, though hardly all, of the CIA agents exposed by Philip Agee in the 1970s.

[99] For instance, an Australian parliamentary committee recently recommended that names of agents be concealed from material released to the public for a period extending thirty years after the agent's death (which may itself have been decades after he or she ceased working). For a discussion of this report and the work of this committee more generally, see pp. 455–58 below. On UK practice in this respect, see Ch. 5.

a Cold War example only for ease of reference, what is known to the KGB should not be concealed from readers of the *Sun*. The only purpose served by continued deception is to cover up the incompetence that enabled the information to be inadvertently 'shared'.[100] And finally, when political relations with a former enemy have permanently altered, material should not be kept secret beyond a relatively short period—perhaps a decade. Due caution should be observed before the conclusion of permanent alteration is reached, but Britain ought to be as open as its former adversaries—though it hardly need emulate the KGB practice of offering files for sale.

Very much the largest body of secret information consists of technical details about the components and capabilities of weaponry, targeting, order of battle, and other military matters. With respect to nuclear weapons and technology, we argue at length in Chapter 13 that preventing the spread of information and *materiel* should be one of the most important priorities of British military and security policy. The obvious corollary is that preserving their secrecy is essential and an equally high priority.

Most of the information in this category would be valueless to a politically interested person seeking to reach an informed judgment about defence policy. Its main, and overwhelming, value would be to technical experts working for another nation or company which lacks the same degree of technological advance. Its release therefore serves no public interest, and indeed is likely to cause harm.[101]

It does not at all follow from this reasoning, however, that a decision to acquire or develop weapons or other equipment which has major financial or foreign policy implications ought to be taken in secret and hidden from the public. From the atomic bomb to Chevaline,[102] British governments have a hallowed tradition of taking such decisions with the public totally excluded. Some have had momentous implications—the 1947 determination to become a nuclear power cemented the growing hostility in relations with the Soviet Union, seriously hobbled further advance of the Welfare State for fiscal reasons, and was indispensable in maintaining an inflated role for Britain in world politics that over many years proved economically and morally unsustainable. Whatever advantage

---

[100] In rare instances this principle may not apply. Information may have been received under circumstances which make its reliability doubtful. It may then be important not to confirm its veracity, and indeed to attempt to make it appear false. In this example—unlike one where no such doubts exist—the opponent cannot really be said to 'know' the truth.

[101] The nuclear proliferation example is the most obvious one, but even cancellation of a potential military advantage enjoyed through technical superiority due to an adversary's ignorance must be accounted a harm. Once a nation decides to equip itself with a particular weapons system, it is reasonable to seek to achieve all possible advantage from that decision.

[102] Chevaline, a secret programme of modernization of the Polaris missile, received over £1,000 m in 1967–80, an expenditure hidden from Parliament, not to mention the public. It was subject to massive cost overruns, which continued during times such as 1976–7 when announced public expenditure was slashed due to IMF requirements. See M. McIntosh, *Managing Britain's Defence* (Basingstoke, 1990), 102–8.

may be gained by surprise is far outweighed by these other policy implications, but even more by the damage inflicted on the working of democracy. Secrecy in such matters also sustains actions undertaken for the most grotesque reasons: the clinching argument for the British atomic bomb was that the Foreign Secretary, Ernest Bevin, had felt himself humiliated in talks with his American counterpart and concluded: 'We've got to have a bloody Union Jack on top of it.'[103] Such decisions should only be made with fully informed public participation, including the best available global cost estimates; but the technical developments which follow from it may be withheld from the public.

A final category of acceptable secrecy concerns information about the secrets of others—what we know about what they do not wish us to know, and how we know it. This is largely a matter of international relations and the ability of the United Kingdom, as one state in a world of states which follow certain norms of secrecy, to avoid significant disadvantage. It may well be that a great deal of what is learned by various forms of spying is either not worth knowing or can be ascertained through open sources supplemented by sharper analysis. However, both to protect sources and because disclosure would most likely just lead to a new cycle of different mechanisms of secrecy and corresponding attempts to penetrate them, and in the absence of any strong public interest in making the information known, government knowledge of the secrets of foreign governments and major companies need not become public knowledge.

CONCLUSION

Underpinning and guiding our analysis has been a strategy of limitation. Once something is categorized as an issue of national security, it immediately assumes an overwhelming importance in the minds of politicians, officials, media, and public. Other important interests are thrust aside, and specialized institutions hidden from public view and enjoying vast and unique powers are given authority to deal with the matter. The potential for abuse of power in such circumstances should be obvious, indeed axiomatic; we have provided some examples in this chapter and will refer to others in later chapters dealing specifically with security agencies. Although in some instances these violations may have been motivated by ideology, partisan ambition, or ill will, these factors are in general of minor importance in understanding the dynamics of political oppression. In the vast majority of instances, officials were acting in the genuine belief that they were protecting their countries from serious threat.

One possible approach is to treat all claims of national security as at best mistaken and at worst bogus, and to rule out any possibility of special powers, actions, or agencies to protect it. Though attractive in moments of weariness

---

[103] Quoted in ibid. 8; and see also K. Morgan, *Labour in Power 1945–51* (Oxford, 1985), 281–4.

when one contemplates the domestic casualties of security operations, we believe this would be yet another form of the over-reaction that seems endemic in this sphere. At the initial conceptual level,[104] what is required instead is to strip the concept down to its irreducible minimum, a core of validity which can then be accepted as requiring extraordinary measures. We would call this a *democratic conception of national security*. For certain activities—notably political violence and covert attempts to influence a nation's political processes—*are* incompatible with both the institutions and ideals of a democratic state and cannot be tolerated. All states are entitled to protect their territory from invasion or attempts to detach portions of it by insurrection. In addition, efforts to gain access to certain narrow and specific categories of information ought to be prevented to protect any nation's immediate or longer-term defence needs. Therefore these matters deserve to be regarded as ones whose 'security', in the sense of safeguarding, requires protection.[105] Beyond them all further encroachment of the claims of national security must be regarded as highly suspect in a strong democratic state.

[104] Oversight and accountability of institutions created to act in this area are of course vital as well, and are the subject of Chs. 14–15.

[105] Apart from the maintenance of territorial integrity, which we take as unproblematic, the specifics of each are discussed in Ch. 13 in relation to the mandate of the Security Service.

Part II
National Security and Human Rights

2

Surveillance and Privacy: Values and Principles

INTRODUCTION

If the separation between the public and the private spheres of life is one of the central marks of liberal democracies, nowhere do the claims of the public sphere loom larger than in the case of national security. Britain lacks formal constitutional protection in law for a general right of privacy, whereas an individual's home, correspondence, and family life are to be respected under the European Convention of Human Rights (Art. 8), and the Canadian Charter of Rights (section 8) confers protection from unreasonable search and seizure. However, the form of legal protection is not the only difficulty. The problems of defining what should be recognized as the domain of privacy in the law are legendary.

'Privacy' is a term that encompasses many human interests, values, and needs. From the substantial volume of writing on the subject, three emerge as particularly salient: confidentiality, property, and reputation.[1] In a study of national security, it might seem sufficient merely to identify these interests and proceed to concentrate attention on the practices that threaten them. After all, few would dispute that telephone tapping, bugging, visual surveillance, and compilation of personal security files (whether held on computer or manually) involve *some* form of invasion of privacy, and frequently infringe upon more than one of the interests identified.

None the less, 'confidentiality', 'property', and 'reputation' fail to capture the full measure of the importance of privacy for what fully deserves to be called the human essence. Privacy is at the core of the deepest aspects of individual character, and equally of the nature of the society in which individuals live and attempt to flourish. Since those three stark words are inadequate to express the gravity of what is involved, it is necessary to examine in greater depth why it is imperative to create a legal regime and a moral climate in which the powers of agents of the state to intrude upon its citizens' privacy are rigorously restricted.

One of the defining characteristics of a free person is the ability to control information about oneself. This may be important at an instrumental level: if I cannot conceal my peculiar sexual tastes, I may become unpopular, find doors to employment closed to me, or suffer some other disadvantage. More fundamental, however, is the sense of mental and emotional security that this control

---

[1] See Raymond Wacks, *Personal Information: Privacy and the Law* (Oxford, 1989) and *The Protection of Privacy* (London, 1980), both including bibliographical references to the (voluminous) literature; D. Siepp, 'Judicial Recognition of the Right to Privacy' (1980) 5 *Ox. JLS* 325.

entails. Imagine being unable to draw the curtain in your bedroom, so that others can see you naked at any time of their choosing. The fear and revulsion this image evokes has little to do with the beauty or otherwise of one's body, but everything to do with one's sense of *self*. If I have no control over what is known about me, I am seriously diminished as a person both in my own eyes and in those which are capable of intruding upon me. This dual aspect of respect and self-respect is a vital dimension to privacy, which is why in institutions that seek to control or alter personalities—prisons, the military, monasteries, and boarding schools—denial of privacy is a key element of the regime. The promise that 'Big Brother is Watching You' derives its horror from the instinctive realization that it means that one is someone else's subject, that in a figurative but still meaningful sense, one is someone else's property.

As with the eye, so with the ear. 'Big Brother is Listening to You' is no less horrific. Clandestine interception or eavesdropping infringes upon a fundamental choice: with *whom* one chooses to speak. The only defences against it are silence and withdrawal. And here we reach the first point at which the individual character (or micro impact, as some no doubt would call it) connects with the character of a society. Turning inward is not merely bad for the individual personality, it is destructive of a great collective value: sociability. An atmosphere in which people practice self-censorship, avoid sharing thoughts and feelings, and prefer secretiveness for reasons of safety is stultifying and fearful. The knowledge, or even widespread belief, that one's words will be heard by someone other than those to whom one wishes to speak creates a society of timid, furtive creatures.

This point requires particular emphasis because there seems to be a belief in some official circles that we should simply accustom ourselves to the fact that our conversations may be monitored by agents of the state. In the course of his judgment rejecting a challenge to telephone tapping as then practiced,[2] Sir Robert Megarry VC said flatly that people who use telephones are not entitled to assume that the confidence of what they say will be protected.[3]

It is precisely this attitude of mind that must be rejected outright. Citizens should be able to assume without need for hesitation that, unless there are overwhelming reasons to the contrary, their thoughts and feelings will be communicated only to those to whom they choose to utter them.

It is bad enough when the intrusion is electronic and undertaken by unknown agents of the state. Much worse is when a person treated as a friend—one to whom *trust* has been extended—passes on a report of one's speech or actions to the authorities. Friendship, one of the greatest of human goods, is dependent upon trust, and a government whose actions destroy the basis of trust, by creat-

---

[2] *Malone* v. *MPC*, [1979] Ch. 344; see below, pp. 42 ff.

[3] [1979] Ch. at 376. Contrast the ruling of the Supreme Court of Canada in *Duarte* v. *The Queen* 65 DLR (4th) 240 that the surreptitious recording of a conversation (even with one party's consent) constituted an unreasonable search and seizure (see n. 19 below).

ing a pervasive fear that words meant to go no further will instead take flight and land in its files, creates a national psychology that deserves to be called *existential insecurity*. No more odious a society can be imagined than one in which no one dares to speak his or her true thoughts, even in private, for fear that state officials will learn of them.

We realize, of course, that in the legal systems we are discussing there is no Orwellian conspiracy. Rather, most of those practices inimical to privacy are introduced in a sincerely meant attempt to uphold a system of democratic values which includes privacy. However, in attempting to protect democracy from threats such as terrorism, there is the ever-present risk that the cost becomes too great and that which was to be preserved has been lost—like attempting to preserve fresh air by bottling it. W. H. Auden's poem 'The Unknown Citizen' makes the point graphically:

> Was he free? Was he happy? The question is absurd:
> Had anything been wrong, we should certainly have heard.[4]

It is trite to say that what is needed is an optimum level of attainable privacy without loss of other democratic values. In discussing specific threats to privacy authorized under the law, we are more concerned here with the practicalities of how such a balance can be achieved. First we examine the shortcomings of the traditional approach.

THE COMMON LAW APPROACH

Privacy is a need or interest inherent in a person's humanity. It is a matter of what may be called the integrity of the person, entirely independent of social situation or material possessions. As such it was unknown, or at least unrecognized, by the common law. If occasionally, and to the credit of the common law, the judicial rhetoric about protecting the rights of the individual rang true, these were not privacy rights.

The common law is pre-eminently a law of property. In so far as human rights such as political participation, freedom of expression, or privacy received any protection at all, it was as an adjunct to property interests. Maitland, at the close of his great series of lectures, remarked of the Middle Ages that 'indeed our whole constitutional law seems at times to be but an appendix to the law of real property.'[5]

---

[4] W. H. Auden, *Collected Shorter Poems 1927–1957* (London, 1966), 146–7.

[5] F. W. Maitland, *The Constitutional History of England*, ed. H. A. L. Fisher (Cambridge, 1908), 538. The classic instance is *Ashby* v. *White* (1701) 2 Ld. Rayd. 938, the celebrated Aylesbury Voters case, which protected not the right to vote, then enjoyed by few men and no women, but the right to the use of a form of property—the franchise—by the fortunate few who possessed it: see W. Holdsworth, *History of English Law* (London, 1924), x. 540–4 for fuller discussion.

Entick v. *Carrington*[6] has been described as the case to take to a desert island, for its ringing endorsement of the right of the individual to be protected from official encroachments couched in vague terms such as 'state necessity'. The court expressly refuted the idea that a minister had the authority to issue general warrants to search for papers relating to seditious writing. Neither the argument of state necessity nor the alleged long practice behind the issue of such warrants could make up for the absence of an express statutory power of search. However, whatever its merits for those in oceanic isolation, the decision is critically dependent upon the fact of trespass to land. It did not protect privacy as such, but property rights. The seizure of material critical of the King and his favourites occurred in the plaintiff's house, enabling him to invoke the tort of trespass.

Other, equally invasive, forms of intrusion therefore remained outside the common law. Lord Camden himself, in the course of his historic judgment, stated that 'the eye cannot by the laws of England be guilty of a trespass'.[7] The way was thus left clear for visual surveillance and undercover infiltration to be employed without restriction by the emergent police forces of the nineteenth century. But the full implications, for both legal doctrine and the powers of police and security organizations, were never fully expounded until the issue of telephone tapping came, extraordinarily late in the day, before the English courts.[8]

Mr Malone, who had discovered during the course of his trial on a charge of receiving stolen property that his telephone had been tapped by the police, sued for damages in tort. His claim was rejected by Megarry V-C, who in a long and interesting judgment held that it raised no cause of action known to the law. One aspect of this conclusion turned on the absence of need for specific legal authority,[9] but even more important was the question of protected interests, or more precisely, lack of them. For ultimately it is a matter of ownership:

The subscriber speaks into his telephone, and the process of tapping appears to be carried out by Post Office officials making recordings, with Post Office apparatus on Post Office premises, of the electrical impulses on Post Office wires provided by Post Office electricity. There is no question of there being any trespass on the plaintiff's premises for the purpose of either attaching anything to the premises themselves or to anything on them: all that is done is done within the Post Office's own domain.[10]

The Post Office is thus free to do as it wishes with its own property, which includes 'inviting' various government agents to listen in on people's conversa-

---

[6] (1765) 19 How St. Tr. 1030.   [7] ibid. 1066.

[8] *Malone* v. *Metropolitan Police Commissioner* [1979] Ch. 344.

[9] This issue is discussed in Ch. 3 below.

[10] [1979] Ch. 344, 369. Lest anyone imagine that privatization has inadvertently increased our liberties, it should be said that his Lordship's statement stands unaltered, with 'British Telecom' now merely substituting for 'Post Office'.

tions.[11] Moreover, immediately following this passage, Megarry V-C quoted Lord Camden's dictum about the innocent eye, and applied it as well to the ear. The result is that 'bugging' and other forms of surreptitious invasion of the privacy of speech which for various reasons may not amount to a trespass may also be undertaken without restriction by the common law.[12]

It is important to emphasize that it is the intellectual structure and unarticulated moral premises of the common law which have dictated these outcomes, not a 'peculiarity of the English' or their judiciary. This can be seen with illuminating clarity through a brief review of a curious chapter of American constitutional law.

In 1928 the US Supreme Court narrowly held that the Fourth Amendment's prohibition of 'unreasonable searches and seizures' did not encompass telephone tapping. The basis of the majority view was the trespass doctrine.[13] The dead hand of the common law principle continued to strangle development of constitutional protections, whose applicability remained dependent upon the niceties of the law of real property.[14] The first major widening of this tunnel vision came in the 'spike mike' case, which held that the Amendment did apply when a microphone driven through a party-wall made contact with a heating duct, thus turning the entire central heating system in the walls of the house into a sound conductor.[15] The Court's patience with basing constitutional rights on arcane distinctions was plainly wearing thin, and a few years later it proclaimed the principle that 'the Fourth Amendment protects people, not places', and held that the protection extended to any circumstances in which there existed a reasonable expectation that privacy would be respected.[16]

The implication of this history is that adequate legal protection of important freedoms threatened by official surveillance requires recognition of a general principle of privacy inherent in the personhood of all citizens. As will be seen, this is recognized to a limited extent in the European Convention on Human Rights. The crucial point is to identify the interests and moral principles involved, as well as the circumstances in which they should apply. The much less satisfactory alternative is to leave the law's development to the adventitious application of rules and precedents developed in other contexts and designed

---

[11] The artificiality of this approach is now even more striking since the Secretary of State's warrant *requires* the operator to carry out the interception (Interception of Communcations Act 1985, s.2(1)), thereby exonerating what would otherwise be an offence (ibid. s. 1 and Telecommunications Act 1984, s. 45).

[12] Such reasons might include consent of one party to a conversation (below, p. 82) or placing the recording device in a way that does not constitute physical trespass (below, pp.74 ff.). It may well be that the learned Judge did not appreciate the full implications of his remark.

[13] *Olmstead* v. *US*, 277 US 438 (1928).   [14] *Goldman* v. *US*, 316 US 129 (1942).

[15] *Silverman* v. *US*, 365 US 505 (1961).

[16] *Katz* v. *US*, 389 US 347, 351-3 (1967). For extracts of these cases and a more detailed historical account, see Y. Kamisar *et al.*, *Modern Criminal Procedure*, 7th edn. (St. Paul, Minn., 1990). Note that 'privacy' here is conceived in terms of personal integrity and/or confidentiality, and not of reputation, which in *Paul* v. *Davis*, 424 US 693 (1976), was held not to enjoy constitutional status.

for other purposes, or to *ad hoc* balancing exercises by judges whose record of respect for principles of human rights is poor, to say the least.[17]

SOME GUIDING PRINCIPLES

From this point of departure there follow certain principles or axioms whose implications will be explored in this section. First, and of prime importance, is the principle that it is the reality of intrusion, not its form, that matters. *Any* form of intrusion requires a justification sufficient to satisfy the principle of legality or rule of law.[18]

The precise form—telephone tapping, electronic bugging, visual surveillance, or informers (so-called 'human sources')—is relevant, but at a secondary level. It may, purely as a matter of practicality, dictate the most effective and appropriate mechanism of authorization and oversight. The extent or degree of intrusion—which is a matter both of form and length of time—is also relevant to the structure of control, in that the more serious intrusion demands the more rigorous scrutiny. But no form of surveillance should be undertaken entirely at the discretion of officials.

It should also be appreciated that there is a dynamic to the protection of human rights in the area of surveillance. Once one form is subject to legal regulation, failure to control other forms not only becomes morally indefensible, but also in practice undermines the protection granted. This arises from the simple behavioural prediction that, assuming equal effectiveness, measures that can be undertaken free of oversight will be much more attractive to people doing the work than those which are subject to restriction or review.[19] In this respect Britain is a laggard compared with Australia and Canada, with all sorts of odd and indefensible anomalies and gaps currently to be found in the structure of

---

[17] It must be acknowledged, however, that Parliament's record in this respect is also sadly deficient: relatively few statutes protect privacy interests, and where they do the Executive has provided wide exemptions for its own operations, e.g. the Data Protection Act 1984 (see pp. 109–10 below). However, in July 1993 the Lord Chancellor issued a discussion paper (*Infringement of Privacy*, London, 1993) proposing the introduction of a new general statutory tort of infringement of privacy. The essential ingredient would be that the complainant had suffered substantial distress, provided that such distress would also have been suffered by a person of ordinary sensibilities in the same circumstances. For these purposes privacy would include matters relating to health, personal communications, family and personal relationships, and a right to be free from molestation and harassment. Defences would be available of consent, lawful authority, absolute and qualified privilege, and public interest; of these, 'lawful authority' and 'public interest' have obvious possible application to official surveillance.

[18] See nn. 20 ff.

[19] This factor heavily influenced the Supreme Court of Canada when it held use of informants' recorded conversations to be subject to the same Charter of Human Rights standards as other forms of electronic surveillance regulated by legislation conforming to the Charter. It greatly feared that a contrary holding would encourage obtaining information and evidence by this means to avoid the need to meet Charter standards. This important case, *Duarte* v. *The Queen* (1990) 65 DLR (4th) 240, 1 SCR 30, is discussed below, p. 82.

oversight. Ultimately the choice is between no legal regulation—the position Britain was forced to abandon in the 1980s by its adherence to the European Convention on Human Rights —and a comprehensive but sensitively designed and graded regime of controls. Attempts have been made to devise general principles for the protection of privacy from intrusive surveillance, particularly in those countries where clearly documented abuses have been acknowledged. Especially significant for our study are the recommendations of the MacDonald Commission, which found evidence of widespread abuses and intrusions into the privacy of Canadians by the Royal Canadian Mounted Police (the predecessor in the security realm of CSIS). The Commission proposed several principles which should govern the use of intrusive surveillance techniques for security purposes:

(1) that the rule of law should be strictly observed;

(2) investigative techniques should be proportionate to the security threat under investigation and weighed against the possible damage to civil liberties and democratic structures;

(3) less intrusive alternatives should be used wherever possible; and

(4) control of discretion should be layered so that the greater the invasion of privacy, the higher the level of necessary authorisation.[20]

Each of these principles stands in need of more precise explanation, and in the discussion which follows we also suggest some additional criteria which, in our view, are appropriate. Nevertheless, the principles are a useful starting point against which to measure the practices discussed in Chapters 3–5.

The legality or rule of law principle raises more complex issues than may at first appear. At a basic level it requires that intelligence agencies should not use practices which are in any way unlawful (that is, involving either a criminal offence or a civil wrong). However, as we have explained, the paucity of privacy law in Britain especially would allow very considerable scope for intrusion if this was the only criterion. Nor would this latitude necessarily be diminished by the proposed enactment of a general statutory tort of infringement of privacy if, as the Lord Chancellor has suggested, it is accompanied by general defences including 'lawful authority' and 'public interest'.[21]

The classical approach, manifest in *Entick* v. *Carrington*,[22] of treating officials as though they were ordinary citizens is a two-edged sword. Failure to provide adequate legal protection against infringements of rights by private individuals leaves the citizen even more vulnerable when the threat comes from the state. Zellick has pointed to the dangers of treating the private individual and the state alike here:[23] the resources available to the state to engage in interference make it

---

[20] *Commission of Enquiry into Certain Actions of the RCMP, Freedom and Security under the Law* (Ottawa, 1980), i. 513 ff.; for a similar discussion of covert policing techniques, see G. T. Marx, *Undercover: Police Surveillance in America* (Berkeley, Calif., 1988), ch. 5.

[21] See n. 17 above.   [22] See n. 6 above.

[23] G. Zellick, 'Government Beyond Law' [1985] *PL* 283, 294.

an unequal adversary. However, unlike the eighteenth century, there is now no shortage of statutory powers of intrusion in this and in other fields, as the BBC found when it was raided by Special Branch officers during the Zircon affair[24]. So the state wins both ways: by permissive general principles *and* a welter of specific powers.[25]

The legality principle also raises questions about the *quality* of authorization of intrusive practices (whether in law or in administrative or bureaucratic guidelines). Laws authorizing intrusive practices should be framed with precision to announce clearly to the agency and to the public which practices are authorized, for what purposes, and within what limits. For this reason, if the guidelines are found in quasi-legal documents—for instance, circulars to the police or the agency concerned—they should be regarded as suspect: in this field such guidelines tend to be concealed from the public for as long as possible and couched in wide terms. They also lack the democratic legitimacy of legislation and are open to change at ministerial whim.[26] There is no magic, however, in the statutory form and Acts of Parliament may be, and have been, passed which suffer from the same defect of open-endedness.[27] However, it is also necessary that the legal powers of an agency be adequate for the mandate democratically entrusted to it, or the temptation to resort to non- or extra-legal practices will be ever-present. This may involve clothing the agency with powers that are not only exceptional in terms of their intrusiveness, but also authorize actions which would be criminal if performed by ordinary citizens—for instance, covert entry to property—provided the use of such powers is governed by precise and rigorous criteria, and is subject to careful and effective scrutiny after the event.

Consideration of *proportionality*, which requires a balancing of the seriousness of the security threat against the damage to human rights, involves delicate judgments about which reasonable people may disagree. Moreover, whilst a given criterion might in general command acceptance, it seems almost inevitable that in some extreme circumstances it will have to be overridden. For example, combatting an impending act of terrorism is recognisably a more urgent concern than countering an act of espionage in peacetime. The corollary is that less intense and intrusive surveillance should be permitted in the latter case.

However, what if the espionage relates to an advanced device of mass destruction which the state obtaining it, or knowledge of how to produce it, is likely to use?. Nuclear technology is the obvious example. Perhaps almost too obvious: the material or information sought is not likely to be a complete device

---

[24] See p. 254 below.

[25] B. Harris, 'The "Third Source" of Authority for Government Action', (1992) 108 *LQR* 626 argues (following the reasoning in *Malone*, n. 8 above) that the government is also able to do anything physically possible which is not otherwise prohibited. Harris argues that the normal range of constitutional controls (and especially the courts) can prevent abuse of this power.

[26] For general discussion see G. Ganz, *Quasi-Legislation* (London, 1986); R. Baldwin and J. Houghton, 'Circular Arguments: the Status and Legitimacy of Administrative Rules', [1986] *PL* 239.

[27] e.g. the Interception of Communications Act 1985, discussed in Ch. 3 below.

(like the 'Q-bomb' in the wonderful Peter Sellers film, *The Mouse That Roared*), but one small part or piece of knowledge to be added to what is already possessed or known, and which may perhaps permit a significant breakthrough. Yet this 'piece of the jigsaw' argument is extremely dangerous because, starting from the unarguable premise that *some* knowledge genuinely needs to remain secret, it would entrap almost every piece of information even tangentially related to that material in a vast web of secrecy. The damage to scientific research, not to mention intelligent public debate, would be immense.[28] Further, in the classic Catch-22 which is almost the hallmark of national security governance, those claiming the necessity of secrecy would further assert that they could not publicly justify the necessity, without undermining the secrecy itself.[29] This evil is so serious, since it is fatally destructive of both effective democracy and rational decision-making, that the McDonald Commission's emphasis on proportionality[30] is vindicated.

A further corollary, however, may be that from the moment solid information is uncovered that a particular person—for example, a foreign 'diplomat' or someone with a documented record of arms dealing—is engaged in activities that on a balanced judgment appear directed at securing genuinely secret information or material, intrusive and, if necessary, lengthy surveillance becomes justified. The *immediacy* of the threat, the *importance* of the material sought, and the *clarity and reliability* of the information establishing the object of the person's activities would seem to be the main criteria in weighing the balance of proportionality.

Proportionality is also intimately related to mandate. The more a purported danger is itself politically contested, the more unacceptable is any invasion of human rights to 'counter' it. The most important example is 'subversion': because the concept inevitably gives free rein to undemocratic political bias of those making judgments about political activities of their fellow citizens,[31] monitoring those citizens' movements or communications to determine whether they are 'really' subversive is unacceptable, even if only mildly intrusive means are employed.

Finally, it should be clear that the assessment of proportionality must take full account on the negative side of what may be called the second order or 'spillover' effects of surveillance. For example, it seems reasonable to think that, from an individual viewpoint, surveillance in public is less damaging than intrusion into private places, especially if it is announced and avoidable. However, whilst this may well be true when considering whether to target a particular

---

[28] For a discussion of secrecy, science, and government, see S. Bok, *Secrets* (Oxford, 1984), chs. 11–13.

[29] Bok puts the point very well: 'The difficulty is made greater still by official claims to military secrecy not only for what is kept secret but often also for the reasons justifying the secrecy. The public is asked to take on faith the need for secrecy on the grounds that an open debate of the reasons for such a need might endanger national security.' Ibid. 202.

[30] See n. 20 above.   [31] See Ch. 14 below.

person, the analysis cannot stop there. It must also take account of the chilling effect such surveillance—even, and perhaps especially, if publicly announced—will have on others. This can be seen most clearly in relation to participation in demonstrations, signing petitions, or any other form of political activity which enables the participant to be identified individually. Knowledge that some official body is keeping lists of those who sign petitions supporting some policy disapproved by government is guaranteed to intimidate potential signatories. It is not even necessary that such a practice be calculated to achieve that result: regardless of motive, the effect is significant. The case for surveillance of any kind in such circumstances must therefore be far more compelling than what would be sufficent to justify its application to a specific person or small group.

Use of *the least obtrusive effective means* connects with the need for differing *layers of control* according to the level of intrusiveness and also of scale. Controls ought to mesh with the processes of democratic accountability over the agency concerned. It has been one of our fundamental premises that these should have a legal basis. However, controls over operations may take effect at different levels, both within and outside an intelligence agency, and a series of questions need to be considered. Should controls be *ex post facto* or take the form of authorisation of the interference before the event? Are there some circumstances in which both should be required? Should controls be external to the agency concerned or internal? Should they be judicial or administrative in nature? How can the interests of those affected be considered without negating the purpose of the intrusion by alerting the suspect to the proposed action?

At the general level (rather than in relation to specific operational techniques), it is only possible to suggest guiding principles that the legal and administrative structure of control ought to reflect. External and prior authorization should be prerequisites for the use of more serious operational techniques—those involving intrusion on private premises or confidential communications. Such techniques should only be used or authorized where a very precise objective will be achieved by the operation in question: acquiring crucial evidence for a prosecution, preventing a serious security threat, or acquiring demonstrably and identifiably important intelligence.

Whether external authorization should take the form of judicial rather than ministerial approval is contentious. A judge enjoys greater independence by virtue of being divorced from policy concerns associated by the applicant agency. Since requests for authorization for seriously intrusive techniques of surveillance should, in our view, only be countenanced in situations where specific grounds for suspicion against the affected individual exist, the task of weighing the evidence (although only presented by one side) is recognizably similar to other judicial tasks. However, we are sceptical in general of claims that the judiciary protects individual rights. Judicial-type procedures can, however, afford a better opportunity for formally articulating the interests of the suspect, and protecting them by burdens and standards of proof, than less-structured decision-making processes. Moreover, judicial and ministerial procedures are not clear-cut alternatives: ministerial procedures can be structured in an adversarial way[32] and judges can be used extra-curially.[33] The involvement at some stage of non-governmental political representatives (for instance, prominent members of the opposition parties) may act as a safeguard against the dangers of political abuse or ministerial complacency.[34]

Nor should controls be limited to the act of intrusion into privacy. Even where covert intrusion is necessary and justifiably authorized at the time, it will in many instances be possible to provide for *ex post facto* grievance mechanisms for those affected. In other cases there will be a continuing need for secrecy and other mechanisms for review will be appropriate, but these are likely to involve long-term general intelligence gathering where the use of highly intrusive techniques would be less easily satisfied according to the criteria just enunciated. Controls after the event should also extend to the use and disclosure of information obtained by intrusive techniques: how and for what reasons it may be stored, for how long, who it may be supplied to, for what purposes, and under what conditions.

With these general considerations in mind we turn, in the next chapter, to a discussion of individual intrusion and surveillance practices.

---

[32] See the discussion of the Canadian TARC in Ch. 3 below.

[33] As with the UK Commissioners (see Ch. 3 below), but these operate as limited checks after the event.

[34] cf. *Klass* v. *FRG* (1979) 2 EHRR 214.

3

Technical Surveillance

INTRODUCTION

Discussion of the legal structure of surveillance in Britain is complicated by the existence of an extraordinary three-level system of regulation. At the apex, relatively the most visible, is telephone tapping, which is regulated by Act of Parliament and supervised by a High Court judge appointed as part-time commissioner.[1] Second is the use of other forms of technical, largely electronic, equipment to gather information surreptitiously. This can include 'bugging'—recording conversations by means other than telephone tapping—tracking devices, which can be attached to a vehicle and thus permit monitoring of a target's movements by following the signals emitted, and binocular, video, or other forms of visual surveillance. In Britain these are subject to no statutory regulation whatever. There do exist detailed Home Office Guidelines on the matter, but these apply solely to the police;[2] the same activities, if conducted by the Security Service, remain outside any published form of control.

The third and most deeply concealed level concerns the use of what intelligence jargon terms 'human sources': you or your neighbour. This takes two main forms. The first, which is treated in the Guidelines indistinguishably from the surreptitious use of electronic devices, is the recording of conversations where one of the parties is carrying a hidden microphone: the 'wired-up informer' or 'human bug'. The second is the use of informers to furnish information, either at their own instigation, by recruitment of persons already involved in a targeted organization or activity, or by deliberate infiltration of an officer or agent[3] into a position from which he or she may furnish information. The problems of human sources of security information are discussed more fully in the next chapter.

In comparative terms, the legal regime governing surveillance in Britain is at once narrow and lax. It is narrow in that only a small proportion of the full range of surveillance practices is regulated at all. It is lax in that, where rules do exist, in most instances they apply only to the police: the security agencies are left to roam free. Moreover, even where supervision exists, it is undertaken pri-

---

[1] See pp. 55–64 below. Note that the Commissioner's remit under the Interception of Communications Act 1985 (ICA) extends to all telephone intercepts, regardless of who undertakes them, and thus covers equally the police and all the various security agencies.

[2] 'Guidelines on the Use of Equipment in Police Surveillance Operations', deposited in the House of Commons Library on 19 Dec. 1984.

[3] The official booklet *MI5: The Security Service* (London, 1993) uses the term 'agent'.

marily by other organs of the state which work closely with the security bodies, rather than by an external and politically independent body. And such limited external review as does exist takes place long after operations are carried out.

Just as it is important to distinguish between types of surveillance activities, it is equally necessary to treat differently the different uses that may be made of the information obtained. If sought to be used as evidence in criminal proceedings, it is subject to a range of statutory rules and judicial principles which govern its admission—and in certain important instances, its exclusion. However, this information is likely to have been gathered by the police, and to relate to criminal offences, most of which are unconnected to national security. Information gathered by the security services may not directly, or even tangentially, be related to criminal activity. For that and other reasons, only very seldom will it be presented in a court of law: it will remain in the hands, or rather in the files, of the agency which has gathered it. Since their work rarely becomes 'visible' in the form of judicial evidence, there arises a critical question: over and above the issues surrounding collection, what controls do or should exist over the various services' use of information?[4]

In Britain, the legal authority for surveillance is divided between two statutes. The Interception of Communications Act 1985 governs telephone tapping and letter opening, whilst the Security Service Act 1989 covers 'interference' with property.[5] However, despite this division of statutory authority, the administrative arrangements for granting both types of warrant are fused within the Home Office.[6] Thus, although this chapter is concerned with technical surveillance, we deal with the powers under the 1989 Act here also[7], both because of this administrative nexus, and because of the practical use of those powers in planting technical surveillance devices. We begin, though, with discussion of the controls governing interception of communications.

THE HISTORY OF INTERCEPTION OF COMMUNICATIONS

Practices such as telephone tapping and mail opening are forms of search which rely entirely for their effectiveness on being covert. They are, however, more intrusive than conventional searches—especially in the case of phone tapping—in several respects. An 'electronic search' usually lasts longer, affects more people, is more indiscriminate, and is more open-ended than a conventional search.[8] If the result is recorded it may provide a permanent record of what the participants intended to be merely ephemeral, perhaps because it was too confidential to commit to paper. As the Supreme Court of Canada has observed:

---

[4] See Ch. 5. [5] ICA, s. 2; Security Service Act 1989 (SSA), s. 3.
[6] See pp. 57 ff. below. [7] See pp. 75 ff. below.
[8] Cf. *R.* v. *Thompson* (1991) 73 DLR (4th) 596, 613, per La Forest J.

'one can scarcely imagine a state activity more dangerous to individual privacy than electronic surveillance'.[9]

From its inception in the sixteenth and seventeenth centuries, the usefulness of intercepting communications in protecting national security was apparent to the authorities. Porter goes so far as to suggest that the Post Office can be regarded as the first standing intelligence agency in British history: 'Here, then, was a genuine espionage agency, with a structure and personnel of its own, recognized by statute, independent (in one sense) of governments, but there for any minister to use when he wanted: a precursor in a way of today's GCHQ.'[10] The historical norm has been for letters (both domestic and foreign) to be opened and read since they might contain details of plots—whether to place a usurper on the throne, to import revolution, or to stir up domestic dissent. If interception is now used also against drug smugglers and organized criminals it is because these categories of crime have taken on many of the characteristics of political conspiracy. An ordinance of 1657 which, for the first time established a regular post office, unashamedly claimed that it was 'the best means to discover and prevent any dangerous and wicked designs against the Commonwealth'.[11]

Hence the creation of a royal monopoly in mail carrying was inextricably linked with the security considerations. An official (known as the 'secret man') was deployed within the Post Office, with the responsibility of identifying and opening suspicious-looking letters. By the beginning of the eighteenth century things were more formal; a warrant signed by one of the principal secretaries of state was required. This requirement first surfaces in an Act of 1711, dealing with the establishment of a chief Post Office for the colonies. As the Committee of Privy Councillors set up to examine a later scandal noted in 1957, this was not a legal foundation for the issue of the warrant, but rather for the execution of it by the Post Office, which was granted immunity from liability.[12] By the early eighteenth century the secret office had been split into two; one part dealing with domestic letters and one part with foreign mail.[13]

The practice of mail opening apparently continued unobtrusively until a furore caused by the revelation in 1844 that the Italian exile Mazzini's mail had been opened at the request of the Austrian emperor: the foreign mail opening branch was disbanded and domestic mail opening was scaled down[14] until the Fenian bomb campaign in the 1880s caused it to be revived. Interception of for-

---

[9] *R.* v. *Duarte* (1990) 65 DLR (4th) 240, 249, per La Forest J.

[10] B. Porter, *Plots and Paranoia* (London, 1989), 17.

[11] *Report of the Committee of Privy Counsellors Appointed to Inquire into the Interception of Communications*, Cmnd. 283 (Oct. 1957) (the Birkett Report), 8. Cf. the 19th-century official who opined: 'It is not the duty of government to facilitate the conveyance of treason from one end of the country to the other. Nor do right-minded people of the present day think it good for the State that the Postmaster-General should propel correspondence of wicked and designing men from Shetland to Scilly for the price of a Penny'. (*The Times*, 16 July 1993).

[12] Birkett Report (n. 11 above), 8.   [13] Porter (n. 10 above), 17.

[14] See generally, B. Porter, *The Refugee Question in Mid-Victorian Politics* (Cambridge, 1979).

eign mail only recommenced on the eve of the First World War.[15] One lesson of this interlude is that, although the practice of interception may lie dormant, ultimately it is too useful a technique for the authorities to discard permanently.

Whereas at one time simple letter opening was enough, as other forms of communication came into use interception was extended to them also. The Telegraph Act 1868 made similar provision for telegrams carried by the Post Office. Telephone tapping was at first even less regulated: since no offence of interference with telephone messages existed before 1985, it was conducted up until 1937 without even the authorization of a warrant. Today interception extends to all means for transferring data, including fax and E mail.[16]

Telephone tapping was officially acknowledged for the first time in a parliamentary answer in 1952. The Birkett Committee was given details of its use and these were updated and supplemented by a White Paper in 1980.[17] Fresh public concern over the practice led to the appointment of first Lord Diplock and then Lord Bridge as judicial (but non-statutory) monitor of the system in the early 1980s.[18] When interception was given statutory force following the ruling of the European Court of Human Rights that the then administrative guidelines lacked the force of law and hence contravened Article 8 of the Convention, protecting correspondence and privacy,[19] the office of monitor became a model for the function of Commissioner.[20] The Interception of Communications Act 1985 establishes both the grounds and review mechanisms for lawful telephone tapping and mail opening under warrant. In discussing these here we are concerned only with those aspects touching national security, and not with the wider use of these techniques for criminal detection.

THE GROUNDS FOR INTERCEPTION

Although it is one of the grounds upon which a warrant may be issued under section 2, 'national security' is not defined in the 1985 Act. However, following the previous practice under the 1980 White Paper, the Commissioner who oversees the process has chosen to interpret it to comprise the troika of terrorism,

[15] C. Andrew, *Secret Service* (London, 1986), 28–9, 262.

[16] *Interception of Communications Act* 1985, Ch. 56; *Report of the Commissioner for 1986*, Cm. 108, para. 5. Electronic searches may also be pro-active, that is, they may involve unauthorized entry into databanks. Although this would constitute an offence if conducted by a private individual, and does not fall within the terms of 'interception' under the 1985 Act, the government apparently takes the view that it can be authorized by warrant under s. 3 of SSA 1989 (see pp. 75 ff. below). See debates on the Computer Misuse Act 1990, *HC Debs.*, Standing Committee C, cols. 19 (14 Mar. 1990) and 72 (28 Mar. 1990).

[17] *The Interception of Communications in Great Britain*, Cmnd. 7873 (1980).

[18] *HC Debs.*, vol. 982, cols. 205, 208 (1 Apr. 1980); *The Interception of Communications in Great Britain*, Cmnd. 8191 (1981); *HC Debs.*, vol. 74, col. 450 (28 Feb. 1985).

[19] *Malone* v. *UK* (1984) 7 EHRR 14.

[20] We are grateful to the first commissioner, Lord Justice Lloyd, for discussing his role in an interview in May 1991. We have not interviewed his successor, Sir Thomas Bingham MR.

espionage, and subversion. Nevertheless, the Commissioner went further and made it clear in his first report that some warrants issued on grounds of national security defied categorization under any of the three headings.[21] He has subsequently instanced warrants issued for the purposes of defence against a potential external aggressor[22] and the countering of nuclear proliferation.[23]

Less helpful, given the Commissioner's role in oversight, was the comment that further definition of national security was unwise or impossible and that 'each case must be judged on its merits'.[24] Australian and Canadian legislation suggests that the concept can be more precisely defined,[25]and it should be an essential part of legislation conferring intrusive powers of this kind to set clear limits to their use.

The definition of subversion applied is the Harris/Rees one which is criticized in Chapter 14. Little thought appears to have been given to the possibility of adopting a narrower definition of subversion (such as Lord Denning's) which would accord greater respect to civil liberties. However, the Commissioner has taken the view that it is only major subversive activity which constitutes a threat to national security.[26] The Commissioner's practice shows some regard for the sensitivity of counter-subversion warrants: Lord Justice Lloyd adopted a practice of checking each warrant issued on this ground and expressed relief that, with the end of the Cold War, the numbers are declining. The report for 1992 states that the no counter-subversion warrants against individuals were then subsisting.[27]

Allegations of the misuse of interception by conducting surveillance on members of pressure groups such as Friends of the Earth and the Campaign for Nuclear Disarmament received some credence from the revelations of the former Security Service officer Cathy Massiter.[28] In an extensive interview screened in 1985 in a documentary entitled 'MI5's Official Secrets'[29] she stated that key members of CND had been under surveillance and that a warrant was granted to tap the telephone of one of them, Mr John Cox. A challenge in the High Court for misfeasance in a public office in issuing this warrant subsequently failed.[30] Despite the government's posture of un-cooperative silence, the judge, Taylor J, found that the warrant had been issued but that there was insufficient

---

[21] See n. 16 above, para. 27.

[22] *Interception of Communications Act 1985 Chapter 56; Report of the Commissioner For 1988*, Cm. 652, para. 10.

[23] *Interception of Communications Act 1985 Chapter 56; Report of the Commisssioner for 1992*, Cm. 2173, para. 3.

[24] See n. 22 above.   [25] See Ch. 14 below.

[26] *Interception of Communications Act 1985 Chapter 56; Report of the Commissioner For 1989*, Cm. 1489, para. 7.

[27] *Report of the Commissioner For 1992* (n. 23 above), para. 10. There do, however, exist a 'very few' warrants against organizations on this ground. This is a consistent trend: *Interception of Communications Act 1985 Chapter 56; Report of the Commissioner For 1991*, Cm. 1942, para. 5.

[28] D. Hooper, *Official Secrets* (London 1987), ch. 14; I. Leigh, [1987] *PL* 12.

[29] First broadcast on Channel 4 on 8 Mar. 1985 (after a long delay ordered by the IBA).

[30] *R. v. Secretary of State for Home Affairs ex p. Ruddock* [1987] 2 All ER 518.

evidence of an abuse of power. Any future allegations of the same kind will never see the light of day in the courts and will be channelled instead to the tribunal established under the Interception of Communications Act.

Closely connected with national security is the availability of interception under warrant to safeguard the economic well-being of the United Kingdom. Under the 1985 Act warrants may only be issued under this ground where necessary to obtain information about the acts or intentions of persons outside the British Isles.[31] According to Fitzgerald and Leopold the gathering of such economic intelligence is a routine part of the operation of GCHQ.[32] This ground has only been acknowledged comparatively recently: there was no mention of it in the Birkett Report or in the 1980 White Paper. During debate on the Bill, Viscount Whitelaw suggested that interception on this ground might relate to the supply of a commodity from abroad on which the economy was dependent.[33] However, the wording is broad enough to catch the actions of multinational companies, currency speculators, and the diplomatic communications of Britain's EC partners. Furthermore, it has been suggested that interception is used as an aid to the enforcement of the COCOM controls[34] on the export of sensitive technology.[35] The Commissioner's reports, although sketchy on published details concerning these warrants, confirm that in these cases the initiative for seeking a warrant lies with the Foreign Office, rather than the Home Office, with slightly more Foreign Office applications being made on grounds of national security and economic well-being than are made on grounds of national security alone. In both cases the objective is to meet the 'government's requirements for intelligence in support of its defence and foreign policies'.[36]

INTERCEPTION PROCEDURE

The system is one of issue of warrants by a government minister, rather than by the judiciary. This may seem anomalous for several reasons: interception is analogous to search, for which warrants are issued by the judiciary (when required in law), and it offends conceptions of the rule of law and separation of powers for a minister of the crown to authorize interception by another part of the executive. It fails to provide an independent check on the power to prevent potential political abuse. While there may be a strong case for implementing the recommendation of the Royal Commission on Criminal Procedure that interception

[31] ICA, s. 2(4).

[32] P. Fitzgerald and M. Leopold, *Stranger on the Line: The Secret History of Telephone Tapping* (London, 1987), 50–1; T. Bunyan, *The Political Police in Britain* (London, 1977), 191; and see pp. 506 ff. below.

[33] *HL Debs.*, vol. 464, col. 879 (6 June 1995).

[34] See pp. 390–96 and 503–4 below.   [35] Fitzgerald and Leopold (n. 32 above), 43–4.

[36] *Report of the Commissioner For 1986* (n. 16 above), paras. 31 and 32.

warrants should be issued by magistrates in criminal investigations,[37] whether those arguments apply with equal force in the domain of security investigations is more doubtful. Certainly it may be said that the nature of the evidence supporting the application will be different in the two types of case. In these circumstances a minister may, because of access to background information, have a fuller picture than a magistrate or a judge of the overall intelligence significance of the proposed surveillance. However, it is submitted that the deciding argument should be that authorisation of interception raises sharply focused questions affecting the rights and privacy of identified individuals. In view of the fact that the process will of necessity exclude the targeted person from making representations prior to interception,[38] it seems essential to require the authorities to satisfy an outsider of the need for it. We would, therefore, favour the introduction of a greater independent element (though not necessarily judicial control)[39] prior to interception occurring.

The introduction of a system of this kind would be more reassuring than the current process of vetting of warrant applications by civil servants within the Home Office, which takes place prior to an application from the Security Service being passed to the Home Secretary. (The Foreign Secretary, the Northern Ireland Secretary, and the Secretary of State for Scotland also issue interception warrants on security grounds,[40] but because virtually nothing is known of the procedures adopted by those departments we concentrate here on the Home Office.) Prior to being passed to the Home Office, a warrant application will have been reviewed and approved within the applying authority at senior level: within the Security Service these cases are considered by a Deputy Director-General. Special Branch operations are approved by the Metropolitan Police Assistant Commissioner (Special Operations).[41]

Although in Britain the legal authority for surveillance is divided between the 1985 Act and the Security Service Act 1989, governing 'interference' with property,[42] the administrative process for the submission and approval of warrants does not track this separation.[43] All warrants requested by the Security Service and Special Branch[44] are handled within F6, the Division of the Home Office

---

[37] *Royal Commission on Criminal Procedure*, Cmnd. 8092 (1981), paras. 38 and 39.

[38] Although the use of 'devil's advocates' can mitigate this, see pp. 83–4 below. This procedure is not in use in the UK.

[39] Statistics from systems requiring judicial authorization do not necessarily support the view that judges are more vigilant of the individual's rights; see n. 60.

[40] *Report of the Commissioner For 1986*, (n. 16 above), para. 7.

[41] Ibid., para. 9; in the Northumbria Constabulary Special Branch the Chief Constable reviews the file before forwarding it personally to the Metropolitan Special Branch. Other police applications relating to 'serious crime' go through the National Crime Intelligence Service: n. 22 above, para. 5.

[42] SSA, s. 3. The statute also establishes a separate Commissioner to review the issuance of warrants under its provisions: s. 4.

[43] In view of the artificiality of separating discussion of warrants issued under the 1989 Act, this section deals with the procedure governing them as well as interception warrants. The substance of the power under s. 3 of the 1989 Act is discussed below.

[44] GCHQ warrants require the approval of the Foreign Secretary as head of the department

which was established in the run-up to the enactment of the 1989 legislation and which is also concerned with day-to-day relations between the Home Office and the Security Service.[45]

Emergency warrants apart, the authorization for all taps, bugs, and break-ins must come from the Home Secretary personally.[46] Since a Cabinet minister can hardly be expected to read the entire file on each of the hundreds of targets subject annually to various forms of surveillance,[47] the process by which the material that comes before him is assembled is the critical element in determining whether the interference will be approved. Formally, it begins with a letter from the Deputy Director-General of the Service[48] to the Home Office Permanent Secretary, who transmits it to F6, where it is handled by a Warrants Unit. If the Division head is satisfied with the result, the letter will return to the Permanent Secretary and then be considered by the Home Secretary as the basis for his decision whether to approve a warrant.

However, this letter does not land unheralded on a desk in Queen Anne's Gate. It is the product of considerable discussion beforehand, which may have resulted in the Warrants Unit passing the informal request back to the Service if it finds the justification wanting. Conversely, the preparatory consultation does not necessarily guarantee rubberstamp approval once the formal letter is received; on occasion letters have been sent back at this stage with requests for further information or with new questions raised.

F6 and MI5 are not, of course, antagonistic to one another. Rather, the purpose of Home Office consideration is to winnow out weakly based warrant requests and to strengthen the presentation of those thought to be valid; the phrase used was 'smoothing the path to approval'.[49] This of course can be interpreted in two sharply different ways: first, as conscientious control over unjustified warrant requests which genuinely ensures that only defensible ones go forward, whilst simultaneously endowing those approved by F6 with enhanced credibility in the eyes of those higher up. Alternatively, it may be seen as a form of collusion between the Security Service and its Whitehall counterpart to gull their political master. Without following the progress of an adequate sampling of warrant applications there is no knowledgeable way to choose between the two

loosely 'responsible' for it. For further discussion of the position of GCHQ see pp. 65 ff. and 506 ff. below.

[45] The account provided in the following paragraphs is based on an extended interview with the head of this Division, which was granted on the strict condition of anonymity. This same person was the source of the interview data used in Ch. 15. There is also a brief account of the warrant procedure in the *Report of the Commissioner for the Security Service for 1990*, Cm. 1480, paras. 3–6.

[46] SSA s. 3(1); emergency warrants, which are governed by s. 3(3) and (4), may be authorized by an official of Grade 3 (Under-secretary) or higher rank and expire automatically after two working days.

[47] A further compelling argument for a requirement of authorization by an independent body.

[48] A closely analogous procedure exists where the request for a warrant comes from Metropolitan Police Special Branch.

[49] This may also involve highlighting matters F6 believe support the request, but do not appear sufficiently in the formal application.

interpretations. The statutory scheme is of course intended to provide an authoritative answer to precisely this question: that the task of monitoring is the primary function of the Commissioners. The second interpretation, if intended to describe normal behaviour, does imply a hardened cynicism among the people involved that cannot be squared with the impression we have formed of those interviewed.[50] Moreover, the two bodies do not approach their respective tasks dominated by the same considerations. F6 is primarily concerned with legality; MI5, though it does not ignore that limitation, with 'operational secrecy', that is, with remaining undetected.

The criteria for approval of warrants are both legal and political. The former are reasonably straightforward and identical: the intrusion must be 'necessary' either 'in the interests of national security',[51] or in order to obtain information 'likely to be of substantial value in assisting the Service to discharge any of its functions [of protecting national security]'.[52] In both cases the test of necessity includes consideration of whether the information could 'reasonably be obtained by other means'.

The political considerations are inevitably less clear-cut. Perhaps the foremost is embarrassment, the avoidance of. The minute of advice from F6 accompanying the letter seeking approval includes comment on matters such as risk, technical difficulties, and other problems: 'warts and all'. Among these 'warts' are human rights considerations which, though not ignored, seem to be decidedly secondary. This of course is hardly surprising when the work of those in the field is heavily orientated towards countering ill-defined 'threats'; all other considerations inevitably take a back seat, just as they would in any specialized bureaucracy.[53] Officials and politicians are, it is said, aware that actions under warrant are very intrusive, and 'unusual' intrusions (that is, bugging and related acts under the 1989 Act) are treated especially seriously. Support for this claim may be found both in the fact that the number of warrants of the latter kind is 'comparatively small',[54] and in the dwindling number of warrants in relation to the 'subversion' mandate.[55]

It is clear that in one respect the system has notably improved since the mid-1980s. Cathy Massiter[56] described in a judicial affidavit the procedures for obtaining a warrant for telephone tapping during her time in the Service. Home Office officials and the Home Secretary would see only what was called 'the short reason'—a two- or three-sentence paragraph summarizing the basis of the proposed interception. It was on this scant information that authorization would

---

[50] However, even if this impression is correct, borderline cases provide ample scope for collaboration to achieve a desired result.

[51] ICA s. 2(2)(*a*).   [52] SSA s. 3(2)(*a*).

[53] This inevitable fact of administrative life is precisely one of the strongest arguments in favour of outside review.

[54] *Second Report of the Security Service Commissioner*, Cm. 1946 (1992), para. 3. The Commissioner has refused to reveal the precise number of such warrants: see further below, p. 86.

[55] See n. 27 above.   [56] pp. 54–5 above.

be given.[57] However, and apparently as a consequence of the creation of F6, not only is the request now subject to more serious scrutiny within the Home Office, but the Home Secretary now sees the whole letter from the Service, supplemented by his officials' advice. How seriously he considers the matter will vary according to whoever occupies the office, but Douglas Hurd, Home Secretary from 1985 to 1989, insisted that he looked at every request personally.[58]

It is very rare indeed, however, for a Home Secretary to reject a warrant request: testimony either to the effective screening that has gone into the process lower down,[59] or to the use of successive ministers as rubber stamps. A judge or some other form of independent scrutiny would be more detached at this point and would certainly not embody the present confusion of executive responsibility, legal and policy advice, and operational approval. Nevertheless, some jurisdictions operating a system of judicial approval of warrants record equally high approval rates.[60]

Warrants issued on grounds of national security or safeguarding the economic well-being of the United Kingdom can run initially for a maximium of two months. However, thereafter, they are renewable at intervals of six months, with no overall maximum period, provided the minister considers that the warrant remains 'necessary'.[61] The renewal period—which contrasts with one of one month in cases involving detection of serious crime—is indicative of the painstaking, laborious, and long-term nature of surveillance for security purposes.[62] A former Home Secretary has admitted that effectively some phone taps are permanent.[63]

Estimating the scale of interception authorized under the Act on national security grounds is beset with difficulties, and there is a wide discrepancy between official accounts of hundreds of warrants and unofficial ones guessing

---

[57] Quoted in R. Norton-Taylor, *In Defence of the Realm?* (London, 1990), 80; Norton-Taylor also asserts that during the early 1980s it was the practice of the Security Service not to produce to British Telecom a copy of the warrant signed by the minister before interception began: ibid. 77–80.

[58] *HC Debs.*, vol. 143, col. 116 (15 Dec. 1988).

[59] This is the explanation advanced by the Commissioner: 'The highest incidence of refusals (within a very modest total) is in relation to foreign affairs . . . since such applications raise more delicate judgmental questions than applications relating (for instance) to domestic terrorism and serious crime.' *Report for 1992* (n. 23 above), para. 6.

[60] For instance in Australia the *Joint Select Committee on Telecommunications Interception* (Parliamentary Paper No. 306/1986), heard evidence in which the Australian Law Reform Commission was unable to point to a single case of a judge rejecting a warrant application (p. 82); and see the Canadian practice discussed at nn. 197–8 below.

[61] ICA, s. 4.

[62] For these reasons the Commissioner recommended that warrants in counter-terrorist operations by Special Branches be treated in the same way as other national security warrants and renewed for six months at a time, rather than the one month normally applied to other police warrants: *Report of the Commissioner For 1986* (n. 16 above), para. 15.

[63] Merlin Rees admitted the existence of long-term blanket taps in 1985: *HC Debs.*, vol. 75, col. 184 (12 Mar. 1985).

at thousands.[64] Some explanation of the divergence is possible. First, the figures give an incomplete picture: the number of warrants issued in Northern Ireland and by the Foreign Office are contained only in confidential appendices to the Commissioner's reports.[65] The published figures for the Home Office and Scottish Office (in 1992 these totalled 756 and eighty-seven warrants respectively)[66] do not break down into the grounds on which the warrants were issued. The reason for concealment is said, in both instances, to be the need to deny to adversaries knowledge of the intelligence capability. It appears from the extra-statutory system of warrant quotas for telephone tapping imposed on the police and Customs and Excise[67] (but not, it should be noted, on the Security Service) that the technical capacity of the requisite equipment imposes limits.

A further explanation for the wide divergences in estimates may lie in differing units of account. The Commissioner has repeatedly made the point that the number of warrants is a misleading guide to the number of lines tapped.[68] Although warrants specify a 'target', the legislation permits this to be either a 'person' or premises, and addresses likely to be used for the purposes of sending or receiving communications to either.[69] In either case several or many lines may be covered by a single warrant. In the case of a single individual working in an open-plan office, equipped with a modern direct-dialling telephone system, it is easy to see how a single warrant aimed at one target could lawfully cover dozens of telephone lines to which they have access in their work environment. Warrants authorizing tapping of public telephones have also been granted under the premises heading.[70] This effect is further multiplied by the definition of a 'person' in section 10 of the Act, which allows an organization or association of individuals to become a target named in a warrant.[71] The scale of the potential intrusion comes into sharper focus still if one thinks of the number of conversations which may be intercepted under a single warrant.

Furthermore, and most significant of all, as we shall see, there is grave doubt over how interception undertaken by GCHQ and associated US installations in Britain fits into the statutory scheme.

---

[64] For criticism of the figures, see Fitzgerald and Leopold (n. 32 above), 14; R. Wacks, *Personal Information: Privacy and the Law* (Oxford, 1989), 270–1; *Guardian*, 16 July 1991.

[65] Foreign Office figures (115 warrants in 1984) were, however, given in the 1985 White Paper (Cmnd. 9438).

[66] *Report of the Commissioner For 1992* (n. 23 above), App. The figures for letters were 118 and 5 respectively. All figures are to numbers issued during the year. The figures demonstrate a growth of 62% in warrants since 1990; the Commissioner attributed this trend to the growing number of counter-terrorism warrants: ibid., para. 9.

[67] *Report of the Commissioner For 1986* (n. 16 above), para. 53.

[68] He has refused, however, to indicate on the number of people affected (rather than the number of warrants).

[69] ICA, s. 3(1); and see *Report of the Commissioner For 1986* (n. 16 above), paras. 20–2.

[70] Ibid., para. 44.

[71] Ibid., para. 22, where the Commissioner approves the practice of modifying a 'person' warrant covering an organization to include, in some cases, the home telephone of an official of the organization.

The legislation is sketchy on what is to happen to information obtained by interception. Section 6 of the 1985 Act requires the Secretary of State to make, on issuing the warrant, arrangements to ensure minimum retention, copying, and disclosure of information obtained. We discuss the administrative arrangements existing in the various agencies in Chapter 5, dealing with files and records.

CONTROLS

Two important points should be made about the statutory controls over the issue of warrants. First, they operate within a climate of secrecy and outside the normal legal process. Secondly, such review as does take place is *post hoc* and is primarily of the minister's decision to issue the warrant on the information available at the time of its issue, rather than of the intelligence agency's operations.

Two interlocking mechanisms are established under the 1985 Act. A Tribunal of senior lawyers (chaired by a High Court judge) hears complaints of improperly authorized interception. Its jurisdiction is carefully prescribed so that alleged unauthorized interception is excluded: this is made, by section 1 of the Act, a criminal offence and, hence, is a matter for the police (who may, of course, be the perpetrators). If the Tribunal establishes that a warrant exists it will then consider whether it was properly issued, having regard to the same principles as would a court in application for judicial review.[72] The actions of the Security Service are not in issue at all—it is the minister's conduct with which the tribunal is concerned. This may be partly explicable by the fact that the Act predates the statutory charter and the similar complaints mechanism existing under the Security Service Act 1989, which are more concerned with the actions of the Service, but still allow it a wide discretion.[73] Nor is the Tribunal concerned with whether the minister's decision was correct, but rather with whether it was within the bounds of discretion granted under the Act and according to the correct procedure. The test is difficult to apply to warrants on grounds of national security for several reasons: opportunities which at common law would be allowed to an individual to make representations before a decision affecting him or her are taken are excluded by the statute, and also by the courts in analogous cases concerning national security;[74] moreover, the concept of review on

---

[72] S. 7(4).

[73] The Security Service Tribunal has jurisdiction to deal with complaints against the Service, and complaints about the improper issue of warrants under s. 3 of the 1989 Act are routed to the Security Service Commissioner (see Ch. 15 below). The two Commissioners liaise to ensure each is applying a similar standard of review. Overlap between the two schemes is a difficult area: the Interceptions Commissioner has pointed out that some forms of interception may be authorized under either scheme: *Report of the Commissioner For 1989* (n. 26 above), para. 4. These were unspecified but he may have had in mind the placing of bugging devices in proximity to telephone receivers.

[74] *Council of Civil Service Unions* v. *Minister for the Civil Service* [1985] AC 374; *R.* v *Secretary of State for Home Affairs ex p. Hosenball* [1977] 1 WLR 776 ; see Ch. 12 .

grounds of irrationality would seem to have limited application in cases involving national security.[75] It is not clear how the tribunal resolves the fundamental contradictions inherent in its job description.

If the Tribunal finds either that no interception warrant exists or that one exists but was justified, it will simply tell the complainant that there has been no breach of the Act; the complainant who suspects interception will then not know whether it is occurring, nor, if so, whether it is unauthorized or properly authorized. The Tribunal is solely concerned with improperly authorized interception. If it finds that a warrant was issued improperly, the Tribunal is able to quash it, order destruction of intercepted material, and to direct the minister to pay compensation.[76] However, to date these powers remain unused: the periodic release of figures in the Commissioner's annual reports show that, of approximately 250 cases considered in the first six years of its operation, the Tribunal has yet to find a single breach of the Act. This reflects more the circumscribed nature of the statutory inquiry than widespread public satisfaction over interception. Even the Commissioner has commented that there may be 'some force' in scepticism about the utility of the Tribunal to complainants.[77]

A mechanism of review not based on complaints is also established in the second source of control, the office of the Commissioner. Like the Tribunal, the Commissioner's function is to review the minister's performance, but on a continuing basis. The Commissioner is to make an Annual Report to the Prime Minister (by whom he or she is appointed) and, after the editing of matters prejudicial to national security or to economic well-being, this is laid before Parliament.[78]

The Commissioner's review of the minister's discretion is a limited one: the current Commissioner operates a 'Wednesbury'[79] test to consider whether a warrant should have been issued. Hence, the question the Commissioner asks is: 'Could a reasonable Secretary of State form the view that a warrant is necessary?' The weak nature of the test is apparent from the fact that no warrant issued since the introduction of the Act has failed it. Nothing in the Act requires the Commissioner to operate to this low threshold, although its adoption would be natural enough on grounds of judicial familiarity. Since it is the test which the Tribunal is required to follow[80] the line between the two organs has become somewhat blurred. However, the Commissioner also checks that the statutory procedure has been scrupulously followed, and here the standard is a stricter one: all the cases of domestic interception adversely commented on in

---

[75] *R. v Director of GCHQ ex p. Hodges, The Times*, Law Report, 26 July 1988; see pp. 328–9 below.
[76] ICA, s. 7(5).
[77] *Interception of Communications Act 1985 Chapter 56; Report of the Commissioner For 1990*, Cm. 1489, para. 19.
[78] S. 8(8).
[79] *Associated Provincial Picture Houses Ltd.* v. *Wednesbury Corporation* [1948] 1 KB 223, 229 per Lord Greene, MR.
[80] ICA, s. 7(4).

the Commissioner's published reports (a handful in all) have involved procedural mistakes at the stage of executing the warrant. The Commissioner sees all the warrants issued by the minister and has statutory power to call for papers and to interview officers, with no exceptions made for intelligence officers.[81]

In practice, the Commissioner devotes two periods a year away from judicial duties to the office.[82] Review follows randomly selected warrant applications by reading individual files and talking to the officers involved. For this purpose he maintains a base in the Home Office, because of ease of access to the papers and personnel involved. The Commissioner also visits establishments (including intelligence and security establishments) and the ministers responsible for issuing warrants. This process involves looking not merely at the minister's decision but also at the accuracy and completeness of the information submitted with the warrant application. Both in his published reports and in interview, the Commissioner stressed that he has always received full co-operation from the authorities. Although the reports frequently receive press coverage—to an extent which 'astonished' Lord Justice Lloyd—to date they have received virtually no Parliamentary scrutiny.

Although the office of Commissioner is a useful check, in practice it is probably the knowledge in Whitehall that the office exists, rather than the weak standard of review applied, which exerts most influence to ensure that the Act is followed carefully. A judge seconded part-time for a few days or weeks each year is not in a position to subject the entire process to in-depth scrutiny. However, there may be other less tangible benefits: the Commissioner stressed that those involved in interception appeared positively to welcome having access to an outsider with whom they could discuss problems.

Nor do the courts proper act as a check over interception. The Act contains two bars on judicial scrutiny: the decisions of the Tribunal are insulated from judicial review,[83] and evidence tending to suggest either that interception has taken place under warrant or unlawfully is prohibited, except in certain official secrets cases and in those for prosecution for illegal interception.[84] Consequently, the issue of whether the courts can or should control investigatory techniques through excluding illegally obtained evidence (here without a warrant) is rendered largely irrelevant, since evidence obtained from interception cannot be led by the authorities nor challenged by the defendant.[85] In any event, controls through the rules of evidence could only operate where prosecution is envisaged as the

---

[81] S. 8(3). [82] See n. 20 above. [83] ICA, s. 7(8).
[84] ICA, s. 9. The exceptions include prosecutions for espionage (Official Secrets Act (OSA) 1911, s. 1) and disclosing information about police and secret investigative methods, including telephone tapping itself (OSA 1989, s. 4).
[85] This is the effect of the Court of Appeal's interpretation of s. 9 in *R.* v. *Preston and others, The Times*, Law Report, 13 May 1992, upheld by the House of Lords, [1993] 4 All ER 638; see further I. Leigh, 'Evidence from Phone Tapping', (1992) 142 *NLJ* 944, 976; the former Commissioner, Lloyd LJ, has argued that telephone tapping evidence should be generally permitted: 'Telephone Tapping and All That', 1992 Mann Memorial Lecture.

outcome of the investigation: much interception for national security purposes is geared to the acquisition of intelligence and is never intended to result in proceedings.[86]

EVASION OF CONTROLS

In view of the narrow focus of the statutory controls on *authorized* interception, it might be thought that they could be easily circumvented by unofficial recourse to unauthorized interception, secure in the knowledge that detection is unlikely. It is appropriate to record the view of the Commissioner at this point, who emphasized to us that he considered it unlikely that impropriety could be hidden from him. However, he also accepts that if interception without authorization under a warrant were taking place, there would be no reason for it to come to his attention,[87] and in such a case the Tribunal's investigation would not proceed beyond the initial stage of identifying that no warrant existed. Unauthorized interception is unlikely to be an institutionalized practice in the Security Service. However, the well-documented presence of former intelligence officers gaining employment in private security work[88] means that the use of such firms in order to evade controls on the Service cannot be ruled out.[89] Unauthorized interception is, by virtue of section 1 of the 1985 Act, a criminal offence, but there are no special powers or procedures for dealing with it.

The biggest single loophole in the Act is probably the restricted definition of interception in section 1, which refers to messages in the course of transmission. The consequence is that a whole gamut of possible techniques involving variants on bugging are unregulated under the 1985 Act;[90] the minimal controls over these are considered below. In addition, it has been alleged that controls have been evaded in the past by direct applications from the police to BT in cases of urgency and not through the Home Office;[91] the legislation now provides explicit procedures for dealing with urgent cases, but their exclusivity will depend on an absence of local co-operative arrangements between the police and BT. It has also been alleged that since BT never sees warrants issued to the Security Service, it would be unable to know whether one had been issued before commencing interception at the request of a Security Service officer;[92]

---

[86] Prior to the recent cases (previous note) the official position was that the product of interception should not be used in evidence: *Birkett Report* (n. 11 above), para. 152; (n. 17 above), para. 16.

[87] *Report of the Commissioner For 1986*, (n. 16 above), para. 3.

[88] M. Hollingsworth and R. Norton-Taylor, *Blacklist: The Inside Story of Political Vetting* (London, 1988), ch. 10.

[89] Fitzgerald and Leopold (n. 32 above), 190.

[90] See *R. v Uxbridge Magistrates Court ex p. Offomah* (unreported decision of QBD, 10 July 1991) and *Preston* (n. 85 above); although some may fall under the 1989 Act.

[91] Fitzgerald and Leopold (n. 32 above), 58; if such a practice persists after the Act it constitutes an offence under s. 1.

[92] Ibid. 16.

this is at variance with the former Commissioner's own account of the procedure.[93]

Some forms of interception which have legitimate telecommunications engi-
neering purposes in testing line quality or billing customers (by recording numbers dialled from a particular phone—so-called 'metering') are capable of being
abused as a form of interception, otherwise than under warrant.[94] While recording of the numbers dialled from a telephone is not as useful in security terms as
overhearing the conversation, nevertheless it has an intelligence use, especially in
analysing patterns of communication between groups of suspect interest. The
legal controls over metering are weaker than those over interception. Although
the disclosure of metering information by a telephone operator is generally an
offence, there is an express exception for information disclosed in the interests
of national security.[95] No statutory warrant procedure governs the disclosure of
such information to the intelligence agencies, nor have any details been released
of any non-statutory controls. However , during the *Malone* litigation before the
European Court of Human Rights, details of a circular on co-operation by the
postal and telephone operators with the police were released. Among other
things, it covered the practice of metering.[96]

FOREIGN INTERCEPTION AND GCHQ

Discussion of interception of international communications is hampered by the
near-total official silence on the topic and the deliberate opaqueness of the
statutory provisions governing it. Statutory authority for interception of international communications dates back to the Official Secrets Act 1920, section 4 of
which provided for the interception of international 'telegrams' under ministerial
warrants, where the Secretary of State considered it expedient in the public
interest.[97] However, the word 'telegram' was used there in full knowledge of
earlier judicial authority that the term encompassed messages transmitted by

[93] Citing cases of refusal to carry out interception because of a defect in the warrant: Mann
Memorial Lecture (n. 85 above).

[94] Fitzgerald and Leopold (n. 32 above), 64, 186–7.

[95] Telecommunications Act 1984, s. 45 (as amended by ICA, s. 11(1) and sched. 2); *Report of the
Commissioner For 1990* (n. 77 above), para.11. Nor does the prohibition on evidence obtained by
interception (ICA s. 9) extend to information obtained by metering; in his Mann Memorial Lecture
Lord Justice Lloyd suggested that the ruling in *R. v. Preston* (n. 85 above) could have been avoided
had the prosecution used this facility. For examples of such evidence being given see: *R. v. Spilby*
(1991) Crim. LR 195 and *R. v. Neville* (1991) Crim. LR 288.

[96] See J. Michael, 'Malone and Police Use of Metering Information' (1984) *NLJ* 646, 669 and
710; it was reported in 1993 that the Scottish Office had recently issued a circular to ensure consistency in treatment among police forces of metering information: (1993) *Statewatch*, vol. 3, no. 1, pp.
5–6.

[97] The 1920 Act provision was passed following disclosure of an arrangement whereby two
transatlantic cable operators passed copies of all cables to the Admiralty: Fitzgerald and Leopold (n.
32 above) 85.

telephone also.[98] This provision has now been superceded by those in the 1985 Act relating to 'external warrants' (that is, relating to communications being sent or received outside the British Isles).[99] In such cases the warrant need not specify a target, and a certificate must be issued by the Secretary of State specifying the descriptions of material which he considers it is necessary to examine.

In view of the open-ended requirements for external warrants, the creation of a procedure for such additional certificates appears at first sight bureaucratic in the extreme. However, it has been suggested that the explanation lies in the practicalities of interception of international communications. GCHQ is allegedly involved in very large-scale interception of communications which are then 'trawled' for specific items of intelligence interest by the use of keywords and other methods such as speech recognition.[100] However, this process may also involve requiring communications operators to intercept all communications over certain routes or for target countries—these will be specified in the warrant. The processing (or 'examination', as the Act describes it) of this material is a distinct second phase. The certificate relates to the second stage in such cases and the warrant to the first; the operator involved will be shown only the warrant and hence will be denied knowledge of what amounts to an intelligence 'shopping list'.

The confidentiality of the process is further guaranteed by the offence of disclosure of 'information relating to to the obtaining of information by reason of . . . interception and any document which has been used or held for use in . . . any such interception'.[101] The wording is clearly wide enough to cover disclosure of both a warrant and a certificate and the contents of either. Even when a major scandal exploded over the reading of transatlantic telegrams and cables in 1967, the resulting inquiry by Privy Councillors[102] focused solely on the use of the D Notice system in failing to prevent publication and not on the propriety of the practice in issue. The Committee did note, however, that the existing practice required the regular collection of telegrams from the Post Office and other cable operators, which were sorted according to instructions to determine which were of security or intelligence interest.[103]

The controls over the use of external warrants are weak. The Act prevents a specific address in Britain from being targeted by the use of a certificate unless the purpose of the interception is for the prevention or detection of terrorism.[104] International postal interception is governed by the normal warrant process and not by section 3(2), which applies only to public telecommunica-

---

[98] *A-G* v. *Edison Telephone Company* (1880) 6 QBD 244. For a fuller explanation of the reasoning, see J. Baxter, *State Security, Privacy and Information* (London, 1990), 186–8.

[99] ICA ss. 3(2) and 10(1).

[100] Fitzgerald and Leopold (n. 32 above), ch. 4 and pp. 148–9; see further p. 508 below.

[101] OSA 1989, ss. 4(1) and 4(3)(*a*).	[102] Cmnd. 3309 (1967); see further p. 269 (n. 91) below.

[103] Ibid., paras. 14–17; the procedure was further described in an unpublished annex to the report.

[104] ICA, s. 3(3).

tions systems. However, there is no doubt that telephone calls and so on to and from UK addresses can be lawfully intercepted under section 3(2), because the authority for the interception is the warrant and not the certificate, which is merely a procedural precondition to the issue of the warrant. On closer examination the protection offered by section 3(3) is that it prevents the specific targeting of *all* external communications to or from a UK address (which will include a phone number) except in cases of suspected terrorism. In practice, though, where the interception of external communications from a target within the United Kingdom is required the authorities apply for a specific 'overlapping' warrant naming that target.[105] These controls do not prevent trawling for all calls to or from the UK in which, say, the Opec oil price is mentioned; they merely prevent in depth surveillance by this means of particular numbers, except where there is a more precise cause for suspicion.

The Secretary of State is required to make arrangements by section 6(1) about the dissemination of intercepted material, and these provisions apply equally to external communications. It is unclear to what extent intercepted material is passed to friendly intelligence agencies.[106] In one respect more stringent criteria apply in such cases: arrangements must be made to ensure that intercepted material not covered by the certificate is 'not read, looked at or listened to by any person'.[107] The wording is consistent with the alleged practice of computerized trawling. The jurisdiction of the Tribunal over external interception is severely circumscribed, since it can only consider whether there has been a contravention of the Act if the certificate specified an address within the British Isles likely to be used for communication to or by the applicant,[108] and as we have seen this will not be a precondition for the interception and examination of the applicant's international communications in most cases. The Commissioner's functions under section 8 are the same as regards purely domestic interception, but his published reports are almost completely unilluminating on the topic of interception of external interception, beyond reciting the statutory provisions. However, even the oblique published references make it clear that on at least one occasion a certificate has been found which breaches the Act.[109]

The diplomatic context in which international interception occurs is more elusive still, and the account which follows cannot, therefore, be verified from official sources.[110] SIGINT (Signals Intelligence) co-operation between Britain and the United States dates from 1940 when a secret treaty was made for the interchange of decoded Japanese and German communications. A more comprehensive agreement between the two countries, signed on 17 May 1943, provided for interchange of personnel, joint procedures on security, and procedures for

---

[105] *Report of the Commissioner For 1986* (n. 16 above), para. 36.
[106] See J. Richelson and D. Ball, *The Ties That Bind* (2nd edn., Sydney, 1990) generally, esp. ch. 7.
[107] ICA s. 6(1)(*b*).   [108] Ss. 7(3) and 7(9)(*b*).
[109] *Report for 1986* (n. 16 above), para. 35.
[110] The description here is drawn from Fitzgerald and Leopold (n. 32 above), 45 ff. and Richelson and Ball (n. 106 above), ch. 1; and see pp. 508–9 below.

processing and disseminating intercepted intelligence. In 1947 a fresh treaty, to which Canada, Australia, and New Zealand were also signatories, continued these arrangements in peacetime against the newly perceived threat from the Soviet Union. The United States National Security Agency is the major partner in these arrangements, with GCHQ and its Canadian and Australian equivalents, respectively the CSE and DSD, as juniors. Co-operation extends not only in pooling SIGINT on areas of common concern, but also through joint training and staff-secondment arrangements, and division of jurisdiction on a world-wide basis to avoid duplication; these arrangements are part of a much larger web of co-operation within the so-called UKUSA intelligence community. In the SIG-INT field this also involves Britain and Australia hosting on their soil major US installations at Menwith Hill and Pine Gap, respectively. The former is said to be integrated at the heart of the British telecommunications system, though for what purpose is unclear.

The importance and scale of these operations collectively are enormous. Billions of pounds have been invested in providing the equipment they require, which comprises some of the most sophisticated technology human ingenuity has conceived and developed. Although the prime motivation for collection of data on this scale is straightforward military intelligence, given the secrecy which surrounds it in all the member states, there are no guarantees against abuse of these interception capabilities. Until recently neither GCHQ, CSE, or DSD have had statutory charters imposing limits upon their work—each was a creation of the royal prerogative. However, now the British government has prepared legislation to give GCHQ a statutory basis for its work.[111] Even where, as in the case of telephone tapping, limits do exist in domestic legislation, there remains the sinister possibility of mutual arrangements being used to circumvent domestic controls.[112]

INTERCEPTION AND THE EUROPEAN CONVENTION ON HUMAN RIGHTS

In view of the unsatisfactory features of the British legislation on interception, it is tempting to think that the European Convention may provide more adequate safeguards. To what extent does UK practice conform to international human rights standards? Interception of communications has been a fertile source of complaints of infringements of privacy under Article 8 of the European Convention on Human Rights. Where, as in Britain, there is no general legal right to privacy, the possibility of international protection assumes special significance.

Article 8 of the Convention requires that respect should be accorded a per-

---

[111] See Coda.   [112] *Guardian*, 16 July 1991; Fitzgerald and Leopold (n. 32 above), 175.

son's private and family life, home, and correspondence. Public authorities are prevented from interfering with this right except 'in accordance with the law and . . . [where] . . . necessary in a democratic society for the interests of national security, public safety or the economic well-being of the country . . . ', and other specified grounds. The exception imposes a rule of law-type requirement, expressly linking democracy and legal form, on practices which are inherently secretive and discretionary. For instance, the European Court held in the *Malone*[113] case, which involved the use of telephone tapping for the detection of crime, that the absence of an express statutory regime for the practice in the United Kingdom meant that it was not 'prescribed by law' and hence Article 8 was contravened. As a result, the UK government passed the Interception of Communications Act 1985.

However, it is not enough that there should be a legal basis for the interception: the Convention requires that domestic law must set clear limits to its use. The French law of interception failed to meet this standard because, although rooted in the Criminal Code and subsequent judicial interpretation, it did not 'indicate with reasonable clarity the scope and manner of the exercise of the relevant discretion conferred on the public authorities':[114] in particular, a number of the controls which the French government claimed governed telephone tapping existed as a matter of administrative practice and were not specified in the Criminal Code.[115]

In other cases under the Convention, the precise scope of the exceptions has fallen to be determined in situations where the domestic law has allowed for interception for security and intelligence purposes. As a result it may be possible to predict the extent to which the substance of the 1985 Act complies with the Convention. In *Klass* v. *Germany*[116] the German G10 law, which permitted telephone tapping and mail opening in protection of the free democratic system and of national security, was held by the Court of Human Rights not to contravene Article 8. To reach this outcome the Court engaged in a careful analysis of the checks and safeguards contained within the legislation.

In *Klass* the questions of whether the restrictions were prescribed by law, or for the purposes of national security, were hardly discussed. Instead, the Court considered in detail whether the German practice could be said to be necessary in a democratic society. It recognized both the need for interception as a counter-espionage, counter-terrorism, and counter-subversion technique, and the

---

[113] *Malone* v. *UK* (1984) 7 EHRR 14.

[114] *Kruslin* v. *France*, (1990) 12 EHRR 547. The French law then applicable failed to define who was liable to have their telephone tapped by judicial order, or for which offences. Also omitted were legal limits on the duration of tapping, on the transcription of recordings, and on their destruction: ibid. 19; and see *Huvig* v. *France*, (1990) 12 EHRR 528 .

[115] The UK legislation may be vulnerable at this point because s. 2 of the ICA does not define or illustrate national security (contrast SSA, s. 1(2)): this is done instead in administrative documents, and in any case the Commissioner has stated that those definitions are not exhaustive (nn. 21–4 above).

[116] *Klass* v. *FRG*, (1979–80) 2 EHRR 214.

danger to democracy posed by such methods, even where their avowed purpose was the protection of the democratic system. In assessing 'necessity' the court adopted the tests of a 'pressing social need' and whether the measures were proportionate. Attention focused in particular on the absence of a requirement in every case to inform the suspect after the event that tapping had occurred and the lack of judicial supervision of the system. The court held that whilst such safeguards would normally be required in the context of secret surveillance measures, where, as here, other forms of oversight filled the gap, they could be dispensed with. The oversight mechanisms provided under the German legislation were that the Minister of the Interior or the Minister of Defence (each of whom could issue warrants in security cases) should report to a Parliamentary Board at not less than six-monthly intervals on the exercise of the power. In addition, a person suspecting himself or herself to be the victim of interception was able to complain to an independent Commission, appointed by the Parliamentary Board.

It cannot be said that prior judicial authorization of interception is a requirement for compliance with Article 8. The G10 legislation involved a ministerial warrant system, as does the UK system; furthermore, the system of vetting of warrant applications by officials prior to placing them before the minister was cited by the Court as one of a number of safeguards. This is a feature of the UK statutory scheme also,[117] although admittedly it rests on administrative practice rather than a requirement in the legislation.

Less clear is what the Convention requires by the way of review after interception. The Court accepted in *Klass* that a requirement to inform a suspect after the event would in many cases frustrate the purpose of security surveillance, and spoke instead of the need for 'equivalent guarantees'.[118] The presence of the G10 Board (which included members of the opposition parties) and Commission, and a system of retrospective notification of the suspect (which did not always apply in security cases), were held to be sufficient. In order to satisfy Article 8, it is necessary that the review mechanisms be demonstrably independent of the executive, but the overall balance or pattern of control is more important than the involvement of Parliamentarians.[119] Nor is it a requirement that unlawfully obtained telephone tapping evidence be excluded at a criminal trial.[120]

The Convention organs have adopted a realistic threshold test for receiving complaints in cases of alleged secret surveillance: recognizing that a complainant

---

[117] See pp. 56–9 above.   [118] See n. 116 above, para. 55.

[119] In a case from Switzerland, a complaint about an interception relating to the closure of a Soviet news agency for fostering subversion and disinformation was declared manifestly ill founded, where the controls involved a mixture of ministerial and judicial approval, a requirement of strong indications that an offence was being committed or planned, and six-monthly reviews: Application 10628/83.

[120] *Schenk* v. *Switzerland* (1993) 15 EHRR 242 (where it was held that there was no breach of Art. 6, guaranteeing a fair trial; the Court of Human Rights based its reasoning on the view that evidential matters were primarily left to national authorities and in any event there was other evidence which supported the defendant's conviction).

is unlikely to have clear evidence, they have admitted complaints where the complainant was within a class to whom measures might be applied under the domestic law.[121] This contrasts with the more rigorous standards applied to allegations concerning security files.[122] However, the privacy rights of 'innocent' victims of security-related surveillance (that is, those not targeted for interception but affected because they communicate with an individual who is) have received scant recognition under the Convention, perhaps because of the wide approach to potentially targeted complainants. In one case of a counter-terrorist operation a solicitor's telephone had been tapped for several months, involving the recording of thousands of conversations with clients, but no infringement of Article 8 was found to have occurred.[123]

As regards grounds for interception, it is not enough that a statutory basis for the practice exists, the quality of the relevant law is also significant. In *Mersch* v. *Luxembourg*[124] the Commission made clear that a statute authorizing interception must specify clearly when the procedure may be used. In the *Mersch* case the Luxembourgish legislation authorizing interception in connection with offences affecting the 'external security' of the state was upheld, but there the power only arose in investigating conduct which would constitute a criminal offence. The Commission noted that: 'the grand Duchy of Luxembourg houses international organisations and a large diplomatic corps in its small territory and that its external security is consequently exposed to increasing dangers, as the recent terrorist attacks demonstrate.'[125] Accordingly, a legislative scheme which provided for interception, when authorized by the President with the consent of a Board including the President of the Higher Court of Justice, but which denied any notification after the event to the person under surveillance, did not contravene Article 8. The Commission noted particularly that the intelligence service was established by statute under the authority of the President, and that legal guarantees protecting the inviolability of the home were binding upon it.[126] The Commission also placed some emphasis on the ability of persons who suspected themselves to be under surveillance to complain to the Council of State (the highest administrative court) to have authorized surveillance terminated, or to bring a civil claim for infringement of privacy.[127]

The United Kingdom legislation does not fit exactly the pattern of that from Germany or Luxembourg considered by the convention organs. Unlike the German legislation, the absence of judicial controls over secret surveillance is not balanced by a parliamentary input. Nor is surveillance limited in the security realm to activities constituting criminal offences or counterbalanced by enforceable privacy rights as in Luxembourg. However, in the UK scheme the

---

[121] *Klass* (n. 116 above), para. 34; *Malone*, (n. 113 above), para. 64; *Mersch* v. *Luxembourg* (1985) 43 D and R 34, 113–14.
[122] Ch. 5 below.   [123] *A, B, C, D* v. *Federal Republic of Germany* (1980) 18 D and R 176.
[124] *Mersch* v. *Luxembourg* (1985) 43 D and R 34.
[125] Ibid. 117.   [126] Ibid. 116.   [127] Ibid. 118.

Commissioner is able in effect to report possible abuses to Parliament, although the style of the reports to date in practice make this eventuality seem unlikely. The notification of a person that he or she has been subject to surveillance is a requirement wholly, rather than merely exceptionally, absent from the UK legislation. Nevertheless, the ability to complain to the Tribunal and the remedies available to the Tribunal may be a substitute for judicial supervision as far as the convention is concerned, whatever the failings of the tribunal system when judged against an idealized version of procedural fairness.[128] In judging the compliance of the UK Act with the Convention it is necessary in the end to make a qualitative judgment about whether the overall package achieves the balance implied by the phrase in Article 8(2), 'necessary in a democratic society'. Individually the defects within the UK Act would certainly be excusable on the basis of the existing Convention jurisprudence on Article 8. Our (somewhat pessimistic and conservative) prediction is that collectively they cannot be said to fail the test.[129] It will be apparent that the conclusion implies neither satisfaction with the state of UK law nor with the interpretation of the Convention adopted by the Court and Commission of Human Rights.

When we turn, however, to the regulation of other forms of technical surveillance, the rules on interception appear superabundant by comparison.

OTHER FORMS OF TECHNICAL SURVEILLANCE

The laxity and breadth of the law on interception pales by comparison with the lack of regulation of other technical surveillance.[130] The use by the police of technical devices for visual and aural surveillance is governed by Home Office Guidelines.[131]

The Guidelines cover both the use of listening devices and of technical aids to visual surveillance, such as video cameras and night glasses. Some recognition is given to expectations of privacy by the distinction drawn between the covert use of surveillance in public and private places; the latter specifically include private homes and hotel bedrooms. Where the surveillance involves a private place

---

[128] In a separate concurring judgment in *Malone* v. *UK*, (n. 113 above), Judge Pettiti argued that to comply with Art. 8 a system of interception had to incorporate judicial or other equivalent guarantees, at least where its purpose was the detection of crime (pp. 52–3).

[129] For an alternative assessment see I. Cameron, 'Telephone Tapping and the Interception of Communications Act 1985' (1986) 37 *NILQ* 126, 146–7. In *Firsoff* v. *UK, App. 20591/92* (1993) 15 EHRR CD 111, the Commission declared inadmissible a complaint brought following an unsuccessful application to the Interception of Communications Tribunal, on the ground that there was insufficient evidence that the complainant was likely to be subject to clandestine interception of his mail. An earlier action against the Post Office had been struck out: *Firsoff* v. *The Post Office* (unreported decision of the Court of Appeal of 23 Oct. 1991).

[130] For general discussion of the issues prior to the publication of the Guidelines discussed here see, *Report of the Committee on Privacy*, Cmnd. 5012 (1972), ch. 19; R. Wacks, *The Protection of Privacy* (1980); C. Walker, 'Police Surveillance by Technical Devices' [1980] *PL* 184.

[131] See n. 2 above; Baxter (n. 98 above), ch. 6.

the personal permission of the Chief Constable is required; visual surveillance in a public place may be authorized by a Chief Superintendant, and, if no recording is to take place, by an Inspector. Where the surveillance involves participant monitoring (for example, the use of a recording device by an undercover police officer or informer) to record a conversation, the permission of an Assistant Chief Constable is required. Before surveillance of a private place may be authorized certain criteria are to be satisfied: the investigation must concern serious crime, normal methods of investigation must either have failed or be unlikely to succeed, there must be good reason to think that arrest and conviction, or prevention of an act of terrorism, will follow. The Guidelines counsel that the authorizing officer must weigh the seriousness of the offence against the degree of intrusion into privacy. Authorization lasts for one month at a time, but renewal is possible if the relevant criteria are still satisfied. Further safeguards require that a central record of the use of listening devices be kept for two years at New Scotland Yard, and local records of authorized uses of visual surveillance for the same period, to be available to HM Inspectors of Constabulary.

Several criticisms may be made of the Guidelines. They will apply to Special Branches, but not to the security or intelligence services[132]—a paradox in view of the overlap of functions at some points. Essentially the Guidelines provide for internal, hierarchical approval from within the police for operational use of these extraordinary means. This control is administrative in nature but is similar to other controls on policing techniques, which seek to exploit the bureaucratic structure of the organization, for instance governing the questioning of suspects under the Police and Criminal Evidence Act 1984, or crowd control under the Public Order Act 1986. The marked contrast between controls over surveillance devices and these last two examples is, however, that the former are non-statutory and have not been the subject of parliamentary approval. Although no challenge has yet arisen, it is not hard to guess that, as in *Malone*, the lack of legal controls over electronic surveillance of communications by bugging is ripe for adverse adjudication by the Court of Human Rights under Article 8 of the Convention. Arguably the coverage is also too narrow: they do not restrict, for instance, covert attendance by Special Branch officers at political meetings or demonstrations, where no technical device is used.

In the case of bugging, a considerable anomaly exists. Bugging is directly comparable as an investigative technique to interception of communications (indeed, in some respects it is more intrusive, since it will catch conversations

---

[132] Visual surveillance by these agencies remains legally unregulated and requires no specific authorization, unless it involves entry on to or interference with property (in which case SSA, s. 3 applies: see below, pp. 75–8). The ECHR has declared admissible a case which alleges that the unauthorized photographing by police of demonstrators contravened Art. 8 of the ECHR: *H* v. *Austria, App. No. 15225/89* (1993) 15 EHRR CD 70. A complaint alleging that the use of a photograph already contained on a police file for the purposes of identification only has been declared manifestly ill-founded: *Q.* v. *Netherlands, App. No. 18395/91,* (1993) 15 EHRR CD 96.

too private to entrust to the telephone), and yet the authorization procedures and safeguards are markedly weaker. An obscure criminal provision, whose purpose is the protection of the airwaves, makes use of an unlicensed transmitting device (which is how 'bugs' operate) an offence,[133] but presumably the authorities could grant themselves licences: nor has this restriction restrained the proliferation of bugging devices in the private sector. There is no requirement to obtain a warrant before a bugging device is used, and the use of devices of this kind is not within the jurisdiction of the tribunal or the Commissioner established under the 1985 Act. The Guidelines do not rule out the use of bugging devices in proximity to telephones, where they may incidentally overhear a conversation. Instead, they state that bugging without warrant is not appropriate where the 'only reasonably foreseeable result' is to overhear phone conversations—for instance, where a device is placed in a phone box. The limitation on the police circumventing the legislation is, therefore, decidedly a narrow one.

Significantly, the Guidelines are silent on the issue of how devices are to be placed if the surveillance is covert and does not have the consent of the occupier of the premises, beyond stating blandly that 'the use of the equipment must be operationally feasible.' If the placing of a surveillance device involves surreptitious or unlawful entry onto private premises or interference with other property (for instance, a motor vehicle), it may, in the case of the Security Service be authorized by a ministerial warrant under section 3 of the Security Service Act 1989. The position of Special Branch officers engaged in entry of this kind appears more legally precarious; general powers existing for entering onto property with a warrant to search for evidence connected with a serious arrestable offence appear inappropriate, both because of the need for specific suspicion before the warrant is granted[134] and requirements of notice in executing the warrant and doubts over the extent of search permitted by a warrant.[135]

The Royal Commission on Criminal Procedure recommended in 1981 that all police surreptitious surveillance should be governed by a statutory regime.[136]

---

[133] Wireless Telegraphy Act 1949, S.1 (use of unlicensed wireless telegraphy equipment). Section 5 makes it an offence to use wireless telegraphy equipment with intent to obtain information relating to a message (however sent) to which the user is not entitled to have access and to disclose that information, except for the purpose of legal proceedings. However, the Secretary of State may authorize equipment users under the section; receiver-only apparatus (including scanners capable of overhearing conversations on cellular telephones) have been exempted: Wireless Telegraphy Apparatus (Receivers) (Exemption) Regulations 1989 SI 1989/123. In *Francome* v. *Mirror Group Newspapers* [1984] 2 All ER 408, 412 the Court of Appeal held that there was an arguable case that s. 5 created private rights and, accordingly, granted an interim injunction in a case where it was alleged to have been breached, to restrain publication by a newspaper of transcripts of telephone conversations.

[134] Police and Criminal Evidence Act 1984, s. 8.   [135] Ibid., s. 16.

[136] Cmnd. 8092 (1981), paras. 3.56 ff. The Younger Committee on Privacy (Cmnd. 5012, 1972) had earlier recommended that covert surveillance by technical means, conducted by a private individual should be a criminal offence: para. 560; it also recommended the creation of a similar tort to cover surveillance, whether overt or covert. However, its terms of reference did not extend to the public sector. Similarly the Calcutt Report, *Review of Press Self-Regulation*, Cm. 2135 (1993), ch. 7, recommended the creation of new offences and associated civil remedies governing the placing of a surveillance device, and taking a photograph or voice recording, where any of these acts were done on

The Commission saw the advantages, that it would bring 'clarity and precision to the rules; they would be open to public scrutiny and to the potential for Parliamentary review'. The Commission would have required each occasion of use of surveillance devices to be authorized by a magistrate's court warrant, issued in an *ex parte* private application. The suspect's rights would be protected at this hearing by representations made on his or her behalf by the Official Solicitor. The issue of the warrant would be subject to specific requirements:

A warrant should only be issued if the court is satisfied that other methods of investigation have been tried and are ineffective; if there are reasonable grounds to believe that the evidence will be of substantial value, and that its use will enable those responsible for a particular crime to be identified or the particulars of the offence thought to have been committed by particular individuals to be determined and if the matter under investigation is a grave offence.

The warrant itself would indicate with precision the suspect, the place where surveillance was to be conducted, and the reason for the intrusion. The person concerned would be told after the event, unless there was specific judicial authorization relaxing this requirement, to enable the police action to be challenged.

Not all of these suggestions (which have not been implemented) would be directly transferable to security-related surveillance, where different issues are at stake to those of conventional criminal investigation. However, the need for outside authorization, based upon specific evidence or suspicion, and for safeguards limiting the use of the devices and providing for conscious consideration of the 'target's' rights, are valuable features which would be transferable, even in such cases.

The authorization of 'interferences with property' by ministerial warrant under section 3 of the Security Service Act 1989 is equally unsatisfactory. The background to the provision lay in the government's need to regularize covert entry by the Security Service in the light of Peter Wright's free admission in his book *Spycatcher* to having bugged and burgled his way across London. It would have been possible to continue to turn a blind eye to such practices and exercise the *nolle prosequi* to block criminal proceedings[137] against any officer hapless enough to be caught, as was canvassed with apparent equanimity by Lord Donaldson in a quite breathtaking passage in the *Spycatcher* litigation.[138] Instead, the alternative was chosen of creating specific statutory powers,[139] modelled on existing

private property without consent to obtain personal information, with a view to publication. The government has accepted this aspect of Calcutt's proposals and is considering the need for wider reform of the Interception of Communications Act 1985: *HC Debs.*, vol. 216, col. 1067 (14 Jan. 1993). It now seems likely that a general tort of infringement of privacy will be created rather than one to mirror the proposed criminal offences. See Lord Chancellor's Dept., *Infringement of Privacy* (London, 1993), para. 5.34.

[137] See J. Andrews, 'Public Interest and Criminal Proceedings' (1988) 104 *LQR* 410.

[138] See *A-G* v. *Guardian* (No. 2) [1988] 2 WLR 805, 879–80.

[139] A wholly new departure. In his Profumo report Lord Denning stressed the absence of special powers enjoyed by the Security Service: 'No special powers of search are given to them . . . They

Canadian and Australian provisions,[140] and conferring statutory immunity on those responsible for enforcing the warrant.

Authenticated evidence of the use of this power appeared for the first time at the trial of three members of the Welsh nationalist group *Meibion Glyndwr* on explosives and conspiracy charges at Caernarfon Crown Court in March 1993.[141] After the trial judge, Mr Justice Pill, had ruled against a public interest immunity certificate issued by the Home Secretary and a request by the Attorney-General that the evidence be heard *in camera*, Security Service officers gave evidence in open court about surveillance operations they had conducted. These included visual surveillance by an estimated thirty-eight MI5 officers of a nationalist protest march in Caernarfon on 9 November 1991, and three break-ins to plant and recover bugging devices at a flat in Llangefni, Anglesey, in November and December of that year. Although the bugging produced nothing of significance, on the last of these occasions the officers discovered bomb-making materials and alerted police, who then conducted an overt raid, leading to the defendants' arrest.

If section 3 passes the letter of the legality test[142] it fails it in spirit, as it does our other yardsticks of proportionality, and layered and independent control. Every aspect of the provision, from the question of who may issue such warrants, to what they may cover and what use may be made of the material obtained[143] as a result, is seriously flawed.[144] The issue of warrants of this kind by ministers is a direct throw-back to the practice of issuing ministerial search warrants on grounds of state necessity, condemned by the common law in *Entick* v *Carrington* in the eighteenth century.[145] Covert entry and search is directly analogous to the myriad of statutory powers of entry, which in the absence of quite specific suspicion of evidence relating to an offence, generally require advance *judicial* approval. The government's arguments against judicial involvement—that it would be wrong in principle to involve judges in authorizing intelligence operations, and that a judge facing an individual warrant application might see it out of its intelligence context or impose 'onerous conditions'[146]—are unsupportable. It is precisely because of the risk of a myopic view of the need for an intelligence operation deeply intrusive of personal privacy that there should be a requirement for independent approval. The onus should be on those seeking the power to satisfy an outsider by explaining the context that justifies its use; if this cannot be done, that is the best possible rea-

---

have managed very well without them. We would rather have it so than have anything in the nature of a "secret police".' (Cmnd. 2152, para. 273). S.3 is to be amended in the Intelligence Services Bill; pp. 509 ff. below.

[140] CSIS Act, ss. 21–8; ASIO Act, s. 25.   [141] See the *Guardian*, 10 Mar. 1993.

[142] pp. 45 ff. above.   [143] We discuss this issue at pp. 106–7 below.

[144] On the dangers of covert entry for the purpose of planting bugs, see Brennan J in *Dalia* v. *US* 441 US 238 (1979), 259–60, where he states that the practice 'breaches physical as well as conversational privacy' and 'is particularly intrusive and susceptible to abuse since it leaves naked in the hands and eyes of government agents items beyond the reach of simple eavesdropping'.

[145] See p. 42 above.   [146] *HC Debs.*, vol. 145, cols. 266 ff. (17 Jan. 1989).

son for refusing to authorize covert entry or interference with property. Ministerial approval and judicial scrutiny should not be seen as alternatives— Canadian law combines the two, with the Solicitor General approving warrant applications before they go to a Federal Court judge.[147] Ministerial approval is directed at ensuring operational necessity, consistent with intelligence and security policy and priorities. Independent scrutiny is necessary to provide a measure of protection for affected individuals and to set limits to what is operationally desirable. A division of labour along these lines need not compromise the position of the judiciary: everything depends on whether the individual judges involved take seriously the need to behave in an independent and critical way.

When it comes to considering what may be authorized, the language of section 3 is curiously coy. It merely states that: 'No entry on or interference with property shall be unlawful if it is authorised by a warrant issued by the Secretary of State under this section.'[148] Unlike the equivalent Canadian provision, the types of 'interference' which may be authorized are left unspecified.[149] Coyness is one thing, open-ended discretion—which is what this lack of definition confers on the Home Secretary—is altogether more sinister. Crucial details, such as what the warrant itself is to specify, are entirely omitted; presumably these would fall into the category of 'onerous conditions', which the government was anxious to avoid.

The pattern of controls operating over warrants issued under the 1989 Act is similar, but not identical to those applicable to the interception of communications. Whereas in general complaints about the actions of the Security Service go to a tribunal, if these allege 'interference with property' they are routed instead to the Security Service Commissioner. The Commissioner's function is to check first of all whether a section 3 warrant was issued and then, if so, whether the warrant was properly issued, applying the principles applicable to an action for judicial review.[150] Since this is the major function conferred by the Act on the Commissioner,[151] the office may be accurately, if colloquially, described as that of a 'bugging commissioner'.[152] In the first three years of operation of the Act, forty complaints of suspected interference with property were referred to the Commissioner: all were rejected.[153] As with interception,

---

[147] CSIS Act, s. 21(1): see discussion below; the Australian equivalent provides only for ministerial approval: ASIO Act, s. 25.

[148] SSA, s. 3(1).

[149] CSIS Act s. 21(3) specifically itemizes: forcible entry, search, copying and removal of papers, installation of bugging and surveillance equipment, and equipment to monitor vehicle movements.

[150] SSA, sched. 1, para. 4; the Commissioner's decisions are themslves immune from judicial scrutiny: SSA, s. 5(3).

[151] Apart from producing an annual report (s. 4(5)), the other role of the Commissioner is to assist the Tribunal (s. 5(3)). Some categories of other case may be referred by the Tribunal to the Commissioner: SSA, sched. 2, para. 7; the Commissioner is also to receive details of complaints upheld by the Tribunal (sched. 1, para. 5 (1)(*b*)).

[152] A description the present Commissioner accepted when put to him. We are grateful to Stuart-Smith LJ, the present Commissioner, for an interview about his role.

[153] *Security Service Act 1989; Report of the Commissioner for 1992*, Cm. 2174 (1993), para. 8.

unauthorized interferences with property are left unregulated, but here there is much less reason to be charitably disposed towards the presumption of official rectitude, since, by implication, such operations were occurring before the coming into force of the legislation.[154] Nevertheless, the Commissioner has felt it necessary to give four reasons for his belief that such operations are not conducted: tight managerial control within the Service; the complexity and expense of such operations; the difficulty of concealing technical aspects from colleagues and superiors within the Service; and the availability of warrants for legitimate operations and the desire to avoid scandal.[155]

Whereas in Britain the approach to technical surveillance is partial and inconsistent, Australian and Canadian legislation on its use in security cases is more comprehensive.

AUSTRALIA

The Australian Security Intelligence Organization was the first body in Australia to have conferred upon it specific authority to tap telephones: the Telephonic Communications (Interception) Act 1960 made it an offence to intercept messages passing over the telephone system except under a warrant issued by the Attorney-General to ASIO.[156] It was not until 1979 that these powers were extended to the federal police,[157] and then, in 1987, to state police forces, subject to adequate state legislation being in force.[158]

Under the Telecommunications (Interception) Act 1979[159] the normal procedure for authorization of telephone tapping is for the Federal Police to apply for a judicial warrant. This system is overseen by an Ombudsman.[160] However, warrants obtained by ASIO remain a considerable departure from this procedure since they are issued by a minister (the Attorney-General) and the oversight procedures are replaced by a system of reporting to the minister. This follows considerable reluctance in Australia by politicians to involve the judiciary in granting security-related warrants.[161] The use by ASIO of intrusive investigatory techniques falls within the remit of the Inspector-General.[162] This layer of scrutiny is in addition to a specific duty on the Director-General of ASIO to report back to the Attorney-General on the extent to which the execution of each warrant

---

[154] Nor (unlike interception) does covert entry require the participation of an outside body, such as British Telecom, which would check possible illegality.

[155] See n. 152 above.

[156] The Act also regulated communication of intercepted material.

[157] Telecommunications (Interception) Act 1979.

[158] Telecommunications (Interception) Amendment Act 1987.

[159] Pt. IV.   [160] Pt. VIII.

[161] P. Hanks, 'Collecting Security Intelligence', (unpublished manuscript) 27–8 cites the shadow Attorney-General L. Bowen: 'Security matters are not capable of the same precise testing as law enforcement matters' (House of Representatives, *Debates*, 18 Sept. 1979, p. 1206).

[162] Inspector-General of Security and Intelligence Act 1986, s. 4, see pp. 418–22 below.

assisted in the carrying out of ASIO's functions.[163] Nevertheless, these procedures are less stringent than those applicable in Canada (see below) since no independent authorization is required before surveillance commences.

However, ASIO's statutory powers of technical surveillance extend beyond mere telephone tapping. The Royal Commission established under Justice Hope found interception and surveillance was one area where ASIO had frequently exceeded its statutory powers.[164] For instance, Hope found that the then statutory regime empowering telephone tapping under ministerial warrant could be circumvented by the use of listening devices near to telephone apparatus, which was unregulated,[165] and ASIO lacked a specific authority to intercept mail. Consequently, Justice Hope recommended a new regime to confer clearly worded intrusive powers where necessary and to impose safeguards. A system of ministerial warrants for telephone tapping, letter opening, the use of listening devices, and entry and search was proposed. This fell short of a complete charter for the use of surveillance techniques because of the deliberate omission of controls on visual surveillance and on the use of human sources.[166]

These amendments were given statutory force by the Australian Security Intelligence Organization Act 1979.[167] The Attorney-General may authorize, in addition to interception of communications, the following: entry into and search of premises and the inspection and removal of anything relevant to the matter referred to in the warrant;[168] the use of a listening device for listening to or recording of images,[169] signals or sounds; the inspection of postal articles; and inspection and copying of telegrams. The warrant application by the Director-General of ASIO will set out the facts of the case, how these relate to the statutory grounds, and the objectives ASIO wishes to achieve by the use of special powers. If issued, the maximum duration of a warrant will depend on what it authorises: seven days in the case of entry and search, ninety days for inspection of postal articles, and six months where listening devices or interception of communications are involved.[170] During the life of a warrant, the information obtained by use of the special powers will be reviewed against the specified objectives for the operation, and at the end of the warrant period the Director-General is required to report in writing to the Attorney-General on the extent to which the warrant assisted in collection of intelligence.

Before issuing a warrant the Attorney-General must be satisfied that the information to be collected will assist ASIO in performing its statutory

---

[163] Telecommunications (Interception) Act 1979, s. 17; ASIO Act 1979, s. 34.

[164] *Royal Commission on Intelligence and Security, Fourth Report* (Canberra, 1977), para. 117 ff.

[165] Ibid., App. 4K; cf. the current position in the UK.   [166] Para. 172.

[167] Division 2 (amended by the Australian Security Intelligence Organization Amendment Act 1986).

[168] ASIO Act, s. 25.

[169] Ibid., s. 26. The wording covers visual surveillance devices and allows a warrant to authorize entry on to private premises for the installation, maintenance, or recovery of the device.

[170] Ss. 25(4), 27(4), and 26(6) respectively. Provision is made for emergency warrants issued by the Director-General of ASIO subject to ministerial confirmation: s. 29.

functions and that an individual who is the target of the warrrant is, at minimum, reasonably suspected of being engaged in or likely to engage in activities prejudicial to security.[171] Narrower powers exist to intercept domestic communications for the purpose of gathering foreign intelligence. In this case the Attorney-General must be 'satisfied, on the basis of advice received from the relevant Minister, that the collection of foreign intelligence relating to that matter is important in relation to the defence of the Commonwealth or to the conduct of the Commonwealth's international affairs'.[172] However, these powers are not to be used for collecting information on Australian citizens or permanent residents .

In practice, the use of special powers by ASIO forms part of a larger 'intelligence cycle' by which it selects targets for investigation where they are of discernible relevance to its mandate, formally identifies (through administrative documents known as Security Operations Programs) ASIO's objectives, strategy, and collection requirements in relation to the subject, collects information by open sources and use of special powers, and then analyses and reviews the result.[173] Before being passed to the minister, a request for a warrant will have been reviewed within ASIO by the Director-General and a committee known as the 'Operational Resources Group', chaired by the Deputy Director-General, which considers its soundness, appropriateness, and necessity.[174] Figures on the use of these special powers are reported to the Attorney-General in the Annual Report, but are excluded from the version published to Parliament.[175] The Inspector-General[176] acts as an auditor for the minister of the use of special powers, because of the function of the office in checking on legality and propriety by ASIO. The Inspector-General has adopted a system of spot-checks reviewing files on the conduct of ASIO operations involving special powers, and has reported favourably on their use.[177]

CANADA

One basic difference in the study of surveillance practice in Canada compared with Britain is the ease of obtaining information from publicly available printed

[171] These are the criteria for warrants authorizing use of listening devices (s. 26(3)) and inspection of postal packets (s. 27(2)). In the case of warrants for entry and search under s. 25(1) the test is whether 'the Minister is satisfied that there are reasonable grounds for believing that there are . . . any records or other things without access to which by the Organization the collection of intelligence by the Organization in accordance with this Act in respect of a matter that is important in relation to security would be seriously impaired'.

[172] ASIO Act, s. 27A and Telecommunications (Interception) Act 1979, s. 11A.

[173] *ASIO Report to Parliament 1987–88* (Canberra 1988), 23–7.

[174] *Joint Select Committee on Telecommunications Interception*, Parliamentary Paper No. 306/1986, p. 9.

[175] See e.g. *Australian Security Intelligence Organization Report to Parliament 1990–91* (Canberra, 1991), 33.

[176] See pp. 418–22 below.

[177] *Inspector-General of Security and Intelligence, Annual Report 1989–90* (Canberra, 1990), 6–7.

sources. Interview material was of minor importance to our study in light of the details found in official reports, some of which draw upon testimony given to the parliamentary Review Committee by the Director of the Canadian Security Intelligence Service (CSIS). This difference in secrecy is every bit as marked as the differences of substance.

One immediately apparent contrast is that CSIS operates under a tighter legal rein than do Britain intelligence bodies. Its collection and retention of information is subject to the requirement that it do no more than is 'strictly necessary' for the carrying out of its statutory functions.[178] As the limiting adverb implies, this standard is stricter than the merely 'necessary', which as we have seen is the test for surveillance approval in the UK.[179] It is always difficult to judge the practical importance of legal formulations, but it is notable that the Director stressed this principle in describing the workings of surveillance approval within CSIS.[180] The stricter standard may also be responsible for the emphasis given to proportionality as the governing precept of CSIS's surveillance activity in the government's discussion of the subject.[181]

The predominant characteristic of the Canadian system is a series of administrative controls, of which the centre-piece is the Target Approval and Review Committee (TARC).[182] CSIS investigations are categorized according to three ascending Levels. Level 1 investigations are of short duration, and are limited to collection of information from open sources—those accessible to anyone—and records held by foreign police or security bodies. They apparently may be initiated by any CSIS official. Level 2 investigations, which involve greater intrusiveness and can include interviews, the use of informers, and 'limited physical surveillance', must be approved by a senior CSIS manager but can only be renewed by TARC. It is not clear how long the initial investigation may proceed without higher-level scrutiny. Level 3 investigations are those which require warrants and can only be initiated with TARC approval. It should be emphasized that this system, which has been elaborated and changed over several years, is governed by (secret) ministerial directions, as well as by operational rules promulgated internally.[183]

---

[178] CSIS Act. s. 12. [179] p. 58 above.

[180] Quoted in *Report of the Special Committee on the Review of the CSIS Act and the Security Offences Act, In Flux But Not in Crisis* (Ottawa, 1990), 112–13.

[181] *On Course: National Security for the 1990s* (the government's response to *In Flux*, above) (Ottawa, 1991), 59, 64.

[182] Our account is essentially a summary of *On Course*, 59–66, an entire chapter entitled 'Investigating Threats'.

[183] The use and importance of ministerial directions in the Canadian system are discussed below, pp. 422–3. Our Security Service informant stated that there exist in Britain 'very tight' internal controls, exercised by higher-ups, over the initiation of operations by Security Service officers, whether or not these require a warrant. Outsiders cannot judge their effectiveness in either preventing abuses of power or in merely avoiding wild-goose chases. One point, however, is very striking: the British reliance on internal management controls, as contrasted with the Canadian use of formal administrative machinery involving participation by officials from other government bodies, epitomizes the general difference of approach in the two nations to executive control of security agency operations.

TARC is chaired by the Director of CSIS, and includes senior officials of the Service, representatives of other relevant ministries, and since 1987, an Independent Counsel furnished by the Department of Justice in any case which requires a judicial warrant. This official's task is to meet with CSIS personnel and attempt to challenge the factual basis of the warrant request, including questions of reliability and whether the presentation of the information in the affidavit puts things in their proper context. His report is placed before a special Warrant Review Committee (WRC), also chaired by the Director, which then considers the application.

According to the government's account, TARC is definitely not a rubber stamp: 'Not all TARC submissions are approved, nor do they all survive the TARC process unscathed. Some are approved at lower or higher levels than requested, or for longer or shorter durations, while others are rejected.'[184] WRC decisions are then, after consultation with the senior civil servant in the office of the Solicitor General,[185] forwarded to the minister, whose approval is required before it may be submitted for judicial scrutiny. No warrant has ever been rejected by any Solicitor General, but one former minister told the Review Committee that: 'on occasion, I have stipulated, as have previous Solicitors General, that further work and analysis be conducted in relation to applications before they were approved for presentation to the Court'.[186]

Thus the system seems well-adapted to protect human rights, particularly because approval by the Solicitor General is specifically required for an investigation involving any techniques going beyond use of open published sources if the purported threat comes under the head of 'subversion'.[187] Moreover, further protection has come from the decision of the Supreme Court of Canada in *Duarte* v. *The Queen*,[188] which held that so-called 'participant surveillance'— hidden recording of a private communication with the consent of one of the parties—is subject to the Charter of Rights prohibition on unreasonable searches and seizures. Protection of fundamental rights in these circumstances, the Court ruled, requires judicial authorization. Human bugs therefore must be approved by TARC and then may only operate under a judicial warrant.

In other respects the approach of the Canadian courts to the use of intrusive surveillance powers in the security realm has been somewhat mixed. In *Atwal* the Federal Court of Appeal held that Charter protection against unreasonable search and seizure extended to interception for security purposes, since it constituted seizure of verbal communications.[189] However, the court found that sec-

---

[184] See n. 181 above, 62.

[185] The Solicitor General is the minister responsible for CSIS. Rather confusingly, what in Britain would be called the Permanent Secretary is in Canada known as the Deputy Minister, who is the official referred to in the text.

[186] See n. 180 above, 115.   [187] See n. 181 above, 60.

[188] (1990) 1 SCR 30, 65 DLR (4th) 240.

[189] *Atwal* v. *Canada* (1989) 79 NR 91, 106 per Mahoney J.

tion 21 of the CSIS Act satisfied the Charter requirement[190] of reasonable and probable grounds that evidence of the offence is to be found at the place of the search, since different considerations applied in determing the reasonableness of security investigations than in criminal cases.[191] A later challenge to the whole gamut of statutory surveillance techniques used by CSIS, on the basis that in permitting limited surveillance on lawful dissent they violated the Charter, also failed.[192]

Scope for improvement to the statutory provisions remains. In particular, the independent oversight body, SIRC,[193] has suggested that a further layer of protection for the target be introduced. It proposed establishing a 'Devil's Advocate', whose function would go well beyond that of the Independent Counsel (whom he or she would replace), not merely checking the accuracy of the information supporting the warrant request, but rather being 'someone who would challenge the need for a warrant at all—someone to make the case that the proposed target (who does not, of course, even know a warrant is being sought) might make'.[194]

This recommendation, accepted by the Review Committee, was rejected by the government.[195] None the less, it has several powerful attractions. Surveillance, to be effective, obviously must remain unknown to the target. However, in addition to the intrusion into one's life, the accompanying secrecy is a gross denial of natural justice in that it deprives the person affected of any opportunity to contest the justification for it. Nor can third parties who happen to have dealings with the target, of whatever nature, be alerted. Their rights too are sacrificed. A system of *ex post facto* review may conclude that a particular intrusion was unjustified. This may improve practice in future, but equally obviously cannot prevent nor undo the damage in that case. All oversight systems suffer from this serious failing, which has tended to be accepted as a regrettable necessity.

SIRC's idea offers a novel way out of the dilemma because it permits presentation of the strongest credible case against the intrusion *before* it occurs. This task would be undertaken by security-cleared lawyers who can be trusted to maintain the necessary secrecy about the application. SIRC already maintains a list of such counsel who are called upon to act on behalf of appellants in reviews of security clearance (that is, vetting) refusals, a practice that has not

[190] Established in *Hunter* v. *Southam* (1984) 11 DLR (4th) 641.
[191] n. 189 above, 108; Huggeson J dissented vigorously arguing that s. 21 conferred powers that were 'vast and intrusive to the highest degree', and that the section did not demonstrate 'a reasonable and proportionate relationship' between the state interest and the proposed intrusion of privacy: ibid. 119.
[192] *Re Canadian Civil Liberties Association and Attorney-General of Canada* (1992) 91 DLR (4th) 38, Ontario Court (General Division). In the non-security realm the Supreme Court has adopted an extremely permissive attitude towards the details required to be specified in a warrant for interception of communications: *R* v. *Thompson* (1988) 73 DLR (4th) 596.
[193] See pp. 458–66 below. [194] SIRC, *Annual Report 1988–89* (Ottawa, 1989), 61.
[195] Which merely stated rather blandly that the proposal 'would not enhance the rigour of the CSIS warrant application process' (n. 181 above), 64.

caused any problems with leaks or other improprieties.[196] The fact that the Devil's Advocate would be entirely independent of government (unlike the Independent Counsel, who despite the title and any individual's best efforts, remains a government employee), would notably enhance the public credibility of the process. There are several compelling reasons to create the Devil's Advocate, and no good reasons against it.

The Devil's Advocate's presence before the court might also affect the approach taken by judges. According to a SIRC official, only one warrant application has ever been rejected by a judge. This is not at all surprising in light of the fact that judges see only an affidavit from a CSIS officer (as checked and approved by the process described above). Without sight of the complete file, which might put the facts presented in the affidavit in a very different light, they are ineluctably led to view the matter through the eyes of the Service. Moreover, although an early SIRC Report stated that 'searching questions have been asked from the bench and conditions designed to protect individual rights have been imposed in the order granting the warrant',[197] concern seems to focus almost exclusively on protection of attorney–client confidentiality.[198] Important as this undoubtedly is as a social interest, it can hardly lay claim to being the paramount human right threatened by surveillance, and there is a strong whiff of legal professional self-interest about the judges' emphasis. Anything that widens the scope of their awareness can only be beneficial. However, the value of the proposal must be seen in proper proportion. It is the efficacy of the internal controls and the integrity of the people operating them which matter most. External checks, and particularly those undertaken by inexpert judges, are at best of secondary importance.

CONCLUSION

The interest of technical surveillance for this study goes beyond its functional significance as a technique at the call of the state for pursuing national security interests. Interception is a secret technique and has become virtually indistinguishable from the security and intelligence apparatus of the state. One of the key intelligence agencies, GCHQ, has as its main purpose the interception of signals. Similarly, interception may be used as an investigative method where

---

[196] These people, who number about two dozen and work at various places throughout the country, are listed every couple of years in SIRC's Annual Reports. Most are full-time practitioners, although there are a few academics as well.

[197] SIRC, *Annual Report 1986–87* (Ottawa, 1987), 9.

[198] The two illustrations offered by SIRC for its assertion both involved attorney–client relations: see ibid., 20. On the basis of an unpublished review by the Solicitor General's Office covering police telephone tapping approvals over more than fifteen years, Professor Jean-Paul Brodeur (see below, p. 102 (n. 91) also concluded that the judges' principal interest is in protecting the attorney–client privilege. He, it may be noted, is a social scientist, not a lawyer.

official information has been leaked without authority. Interception is surrounded by a perimeter of laws designed to preserve its secrecy. The practice of the tribunal discussed above achieves this effect. The Official Secrets Act 1989 makes it an offence to publish certain details about it.[199] Likewise it is one of the key areas of government protected by a D Notice. Interception is a particularly good example of the creeping effect whereby everything, however peripheral to the maintenance of secrecy, may itself become a legally protected secret.

We can now assess how well the British legislation meets the criteria, discussed in the preceding chapter, by which surveillance practices should be judged: legality (including precision and clarity), proportionality, use of the least obtrusive effective means, and the need for layered control of discretion.

In the case of interception of communications, the legislation only partly satisfies the legality test, because of the omission of bugging from the 1985 Act and the doubtful status of signals interception conducted by GCHQ. It is also widely permissive, owing to the breadth of the definitions of national security, especially where it concerns subversion, and economic well-being. This criticism can be expressed slightly differently as an aspect of proportionality. Concepts such as subversion are inherently inchoate: they embrace a vast range of possible activities. However, the Act fails to give a measure of how serious or urgent a subversive threat must be before interception is justified.[200] The Act itself embodies the least obtrusive alternative test: the Secretary of State is required before issuing a warrant to decide whether it is necessary, and as part of this, whether the information could reasonably be obtained by alternative means.[201] The bureaucratic system for dealing with warrant applications provides layers of control, both within the Security Service and the police, in the Home Office, and before the minister. However, it is doubtful if these can properly be regarded as external or independent controls: although the police and the Security Service are operationally distinct from the Home Office, the pattern of interdependence between them as suppliers and consumers of intelligence is clear.

With the other forms of technical surveillance, the UK practice clearly fails the legality test: administrative Guidelines applicable only to the police, and not to the Security Service, fall far short of what is required. Nor are all surveillance practices covered by the controls. Considerations of proportionality appear explicitly in the Guidelines in the requirement to weigh the seriousness of the intrusion against the seriousness of the conduct suspected. The controls are likewise layered roughly according to the seriousness of the intrusion into privacy, but what is plainly lacking is any element of external control, still less judicial authorization.

In contrast, the Australian and Canadian legislation embody not merely independent controls, but also a more comprehensive and consistent framework

---

[199] S. 4; see pp. 243–5 below.   [200] See further pp. 395 ff. below.   [201] ICA, s. 2(3).

governing the whole range of surveillance practices. The importance of a holistic approach to surveillance cannot be over-emphasized, since only when all intrusive practices are governed by a common, structured regime can it be guaranteed that controls will not be evaded by resort to less regulated forms of surveillance. The Canadian system which combines TARC, the Warrant Review Committee, the Solicitor General, and the judiciary in authorizing surveillance, and the Inspector-General, SIRC, and the minister in checking after the event demonstrates clearly that such a regime is feasible.

One final point may be made about surveillance in Canada, which provides an interesting contrast with Britain, not necessarily in what is done, but in what is made known. SIRC, which has right of access to all warrant files, has repeatedly pointed out that bare warrant statistics are inadequate and misleading, because they may involve one or more powers of intrusion, and affect any number of persons. This approach is in sharp contrast to that of the British Security Service Commissioner who, as we have seen, has been willing only to say that 'because of the comparatively small number of warrants issued under the Act and the restricted number of purposes for which they can be issued, it is not in the national interest that these figures should be known to those who are possible targets'.[202] This statement is deeply unsatisfactory. It is unresponsive to concerns about the number of people affected by a given warrant, regardless of how limited its *purposes* may be. It is also insensitive to the anxieties, not of possible targets, but of the wider public about the extent and impact of various surveillance measures. Paradoxically, one of the great advantages of the extensive review provided by the Canadian system is the ability to offer credible reassurance when a rigorous inquiry reveals that the work of a security agency is not impinging upon human rights.[203] It is certainly true that an attempt to provide similar information in Britain would be much more difficult precisely because almost all Republican terrorists are, despite their wishes, British citizens. None the less, by putting Northern Ireland to one side, it should be possible to provide some useful indication of the extent of the impact of surveillance operations on individuals in Britain. Refusal even to attempt to do so is a political choice, not for the maintenance of security, but merely for the maintenance of secrecy.

---

[202] *Security Service Act 1989; Report of the Commissioner for 1991*, Cm. 1946, para. 3. The Interceptions Commissioner has similarly refused to make public the number of national security-based intercepts: see p. 60 above.

[203] After an extensive review of warrant affidavits and court approvals, SIRC concluded that 'many Canadians have a highly exaggerated view of the extent of the intrusive activities of CSIS using Federal Court warrants', and decided to 'make public the fact that Canadians who may be affected by intrusive activity by CSIS [under warrant] number in the hundreds, not in the thousands' (SIRC, *Annual Report 1990–91* (Ottawa, 1991), 12–13).

4

Agents, Informers, and Infiltrators

INTRODUCTION

In 1863 the constitutional historian, Erskine May wrote:

Men may be without restraints upon their liberty: they may pass to and fro at pleasure: but if their steps are tracked by spies and informers, their words noted down for crimination, their associates watched as conspirators—who shall say that they are free? Nothing is more revolting to Englishmen than the espionage which forms part of the administrative system of continental despotisms. It haunts men like an evil genius, chills their gaiety, restrains their wit, casts a shadow over their friendships, and blights their domestic hearth. The freedom of a country may be measured by its immunity from this baleful agency.[1]

Perhaps the longest-standing method of surveillance involves not technical but human intrusion of suspect associations in order to obtain intelligence. Secret history records that it was not nearly so revolting to Englishmen as May would have liked to believe. Porter has shown that in the period before the establishment of a regular police force this method was used by the authorities.[2] Not long after the uniformed police became an established and conspicuous part of British life, an aversion to Continental styles of political policing was overcome: a plainclothes detective branch was introduced in 1842,[3] and by the 1880s a substantial network of informers was in place to counter the threat from Fenianism.[4] The use of informers was a key part of the government's response to the Chartist movement, and the trial of several leaders resulted from the secret attendance at Chartist meetings of government agents, who were in regular contact with the police.[5] The lineage of such surveillance continues up to recent times, through surveillance of the Sufragette movement and of the embryonic Labour Party in the early years of the twentieth century,[6] of the Communist Party and the British Union of Fascists in the inter-war period,[7] to

---

[1] E. May, *Constitutional History of England*, vol. 2 (2nd. edn., London, 1863), 287–8.
[2] B. Porter, *Plots and Paranoia* (London, 1989), chs. 2–4.
[3] Id., *The Origins of the Vigilant State: The London Metropolitan Police Force Before the First World War* (London, 1987), 5.
[4] Ibid. 41, 57.
[5] See *R.* v. *Dowling* (1848) 3 CCC 509; *R.* v. *Mullins* (1848) 3 CCC 509.
[6] Porter (n. 3 above), 164 and 176 respectively.
[7] R. Thurlow, *Fascism in Britain: A History, 1918–1985* (Oxford, 1988) and 'British Fascism and State Surveillance, 1934–45', (1988) 3 *Int. & NS*, 77; C. Andrew, *Secret Service* (London, 1986), 525–30.

the Campaign for Nuclear Disarmament in the post-war period, including the early 1980s.[8]

Probably no aspect of intelligence and security operations is surrounded with greater secrecy than the use of human sources. It may be relatively easy to avoid using a telephone, but all political activity, violent or democratic, open or covert, involves continuous personal contact and, at its most rewarding, the sharing of ideas, confidences, and plans with one's fellows.[9] Therefore those who gain access to the targets of security agencies at this level of intimacy are potentially capable of delivering the most valuable kind of information possible.[10] The linkage between human sources and invasions of privacy was recognized explicitly by Justice Douglas of the United States Supreme Court in 1966:

> We are rapidly entering the age of no privacy, where everyone is open to surveillance at all times; where there are no secrets from government . . . Police are instructed to pander to the weaknesses and craven motives of friends and acquaintances of suspects in order to induce them to inform . . . The undercover agent may enter a suspect's home and make a search on suspicion that a crime will be committed. He is indeed often the instigator of, and active participator in the crime—an agent provocateur . . . But the 'dirty business' does not begin or end with entrapment. Entrapment is merely a facet of a much broader problem. Together with illegal searches and seizures, coerced confessions, wiretapping and bugging, it represents lawless invasions of privacy. It is indicative of a philosophy that the ends justify the means.[11]

The dangers in human undercover operations of this kind are many and varied.[12] Whereas technical surveillance involves merely an intrusion into privacy, the use of undercover operatives involves also deceit and manipulation and betrayal of personal relationships. If the agent is more than a merely passive conduit of information, there is also the danger, amply attested to by historical examples, that he or she become an *agent provocateur*. Any system of rewarding undercover agents in return for incriminating information more or less encourages such abuse by putting a low value on non-incriminating intelligence. Furthermore, if the agent is in a setting where genuine terrorist activity is taking place, the long-term value of the intelligence source may be purchased at the price of complicity in criminal conduct in the shorter term. If criminal proceedings are eventually brought it will be difficult in such cases to unravel evidence of and liability for offences committed from instigation of the same conduct. The dangers are abundantly illustrated by two recent *causes célèbres*.

The infiltration of the Ulster Defence Association by a military intelligence

---

[8] See p. 54 above.

[9] This is true *a fortiori* of close friends and relations, which makes the use of persons enjoying this relationship all the more odious.

[10] It is certainly the police view that 'the best information comes from people.' It is unnecessary for our purposes to enter into the major debate among intelligence officials about the comparative utility of human versus signals or other technological forms of intelligence sources.

[11] *Osborn* v. *US* (1966) 87 S. Ct. 429, 439–41.

[12] See generally G. Marx, *Undercover: Police Surveillance in America* (Berkeley, Calif., 1988).

agent, Brian Nelson, is one of the few officially acknowledged cases of this kind. Nelson was convicted in January 1992 after pleading guilty to twenty terrorist charges, including five of conspiracy to murder; fifteen other charges, including two of murder, were not proceeded with. According to mitigation given on his behalf by a former head of army intelligence, Nelson had been infiltrated into the UDA and had committed the offences to maintain his cover as a long-term source providing information, enabling the army to avert terrorist attacks.[13] It also was stated that no guidelines exist for the running of agents by military intelligence in Northern Ireland, and that such agents were bound to become involved in criminality. In sentencing Nelson to ten years' imprisonment, the judge recognized the public value of his information, but stated that Nelson had crossed the line from maintaining cover into committing offences, for which he enjoyed no immunity. Following the case a review is reported to have been instigated into the procedures for operating agents in Northern Ireland.

The second example is the state of affairs exposed by the collapse in November 1992 of the trial of executives from the machine tools company Matrix Churchill, indicted for deception in export licence applications.[14] Before the trial was aborted by Customs and Excise, evidence was tendered which showed that both MI5 and MI6 had agents in place in the company who, at considerable personal risk, were feeding them intelligence about Iraqi control of the company and attempts to procure armaments-manufacturing machines. It was one of these agents, Paul Henderson, the managing director of Matrix Churchill, who, with others, subsequently faced trial. Indeed, there was evidence not merely that several government departments were aware of the true nature of the machines to be exported, and that a minister at the Department of Trade and Industry had connived at the deceptive obtaining of the licences, but also that MI6 had specifically supported the granting of the licences in question in order not to compromise a valuable source.[15]

Instances such as these prove the truth of Scott's axiom, 'what a tangled web we weave when first we practise to deceive'. Some distinctions in terminology are perhaps necessary to unravel the complexities: the legal literature[16] commonly distinguishes between informers, undercover police officers, and *agents provocateurs*. In this lexicon an informer is a member of the public rather than an employee of the state who volunteers information.[17] However, this is merely a

[13] The *Independent*, 30 Jan. 1992.

[14] See D. Leigh, *Betrayed: The Real Story of the Matrix Churchill Trial* (London, 1993); other aspects of the trial are discussed in Ch. 11 below.

[15] Ibid. 116.

[16] We are indebted for many references cited hereafter to M. Allen, 'The Law and Practice Relating to Agents Provocateurs in the United States, United Kingdom and Commonwealth Jurisdictions' (LL M thesis, Queen's University of Belfast, 1981); see also A. Vercher, *Terrorism in Europe: An International Comparative Legal Analysis* (Oxford, 1992), ch. 4; J. Heydon, 'The Problems of Entrapment' [1973] *Camb. LJ* 268; A. Choo (1990) 'A Defence of Entrapment', 53 *MLR* 453.

[17] Prior to the Common Informers Act 1951, informers were also a category of persons entitled to bring proceedings analogous to criminal proceedings, for which they recovered a penalty from the

model instance of its use because many informers are paid and may be recruited on the initiative of the state rather than vice versa, and if their assistance is purchased with an offer of immunity from other criminal charges or the promise of a reduction in sentence, plainly its voluntariness is questionable.[18] Police or intelligence officers may obtain information by failing to announce their presence (as in the case of the plainclothes police officer or the unmarked police car), or by actively concealing it in an attempt to infiltrate a suspect group. With both informers and covert policing a further danger exists: that the role goes beyond the passive one of observation and passing of information to one of actively encouraging or initiating questionable activity, either to justify to others the infiltration, or to obtain proof not otherwise forthcoming—this is the forbidden territory of the *agent provocateur*.[19] These are categories which exist principally in the treatment of witnesses in the law of evidence. We will suggest later that their use obscures the most important questions about human surveillance. Nevertheless, they are useful for the purpose of grasping the limitations in the legal regime which we wish to criticize.

THE PROBLEM OF THE HUMAN SOURCE

One quickly learns from talking with anyone officially involved with security matters that the subject of human sources is perhaps the most sensitive and most likely to attract an insistence on absolute secrecy. This cannot simply be dismissed as exaggeration or paranoia. Betraying the secrets of intimates or comrades leaves one in permanent fear of exposure and, at best, great shame. At worst, it leaves one in mortal peril, as the IRA's periodic announcements of the fate of informers within their ranks makes horrifically clear.[20] Consequently the sort of person willing to engage in this sort of activity will tend to be psychologically out of the ordinary, to say the least, and certainly mercurial and difficult.

---

defendant, as an inducement to public-spirited law enforcement—an early example of privatization in the criminal justice field.

[18] A recent survey of police informers has shown that 70% are recruited when in custody at a police station. The Home Office issued a fresh circular to deal with such 'resident' informers in Feb. 1992: (1992) *Statewatch*, 2: 5, p. 3. Walker suggests that the extended periods of detention before charge available against suspected terrorists have facilitated the recruitment of informers in Northern Ireland: C. Walker, *The Prevention of Terrorism in British Law*, 2nd edn. (Manchester, 1992), 295.

[19] Marx (n. 12 above), ch. 4, suggests a distinction between Intelligence Operations, Preventive Operations, and Facilitative Operations. The *agent provocateur* would come within the realm of Facilitative Operations, although Marx also acknowledges use (in the preventive field) of the 'counter-provocateur'—the undercover operative planted to argue against criminal action (ibid. 64). Marx further lists no fewer than ten criteria according to which a particular undercover operation may be categorized: grounds for initiation, specificity in target selection, degree of self-selection, correspondence to real world behaviour, natural and artificial criminal environments, intent and autonomy, carrying out an offence or not, who plays the undercover role, deep and light cover, and use of the results.

[20] See examples given by Vercher, (n. 16 above), 115; and for historical parallels Porter, (n. 2 above), 33–4.

The handling of informers is said to be one of the most delicate skills of an intelligence officer, requiring above all that the source trust him implicitly to ensure that his deceit will remain concealed. According to an official account: 'Substantial resources are devoted to providing support both for the agent and the Security Service case officer, particularly to maintain the security of the operation. Close attention is also paid to the welfare of the Service's agents both during and after their agent career.'[21] Administrative controls on the use of informers and *agents provocateurs* are sparse. Those made public[22] relate only to the police and envisage that prosecution will follow, and hence are less relevant to some Special Branch work, for instance gathering information for public order purposes. These guidelines cover, albeit in very general terms, issues such as the participation of the informer in the offence, disclosure of information to the court, to counsel, and the prosecuting authorities, grants of immunity, payment, and supervision. We note their requirements in more detail where appropriate in the discussion which follows.

Although cases of pure transcendent idealism or epiphanic moral conversion are theoretically possible, in reality informers are motivated by factors ranging from the obscure through the base to the bizarre. In the experience of the police, the key influences are not necessarily what one might have expected. The head of the Metropolitan Police Security Branch[23] emphasized that no one single motive predominates, and cited spite, settling old scores, and ideological schisms as particularly prominent. Greed or need, which would seem the more obvious, are apparently less important in the political field than with 'ordinary' crime like armed robbery, although small sums of money are paid, particularly where the informer is unemployed or otherwise short of funds. On the other hand, this description inevitably did not extend to the operations of the Security Service, who have a lot more money available for this purpose, including the lion's share of a fund also accessible to Special Branch. The Home Office circular counsels that police payments to informers from public funds should be supervised by a senior officer.[24]

Immunity from prosecution can effectively be offered to informers by guaranteeing that the power to extinguish proceedings by the *nolle prosequi* will be used on some future occasion if necessary.[25] This power rests with the Attorney-General and the Director of Public Prosecutions, and if the offer is to be binding it therefore requires the approval of one of them.[26] Although it has been

---

[21] *MI5: The Security Service* (London, 1993), 21.

[22] *Report to the Home Secretary from the Commissioner of Police of the Metropolis on the Actions of the Police Officers Concerned with the Case of Kenneth Joseph Lennon,* HC (1973–4) 351 (hereafter 'the Starritt Report'), App. C; and see (1969) 119 *NLJ* 513 for an earlier published summary.

[23] Interview with Sir Peter Imbert, Commissioner, and Mr John Howley, Deputy Assistant Commissioner (in charge of Security Branch), Metropolitan Police.

[24] Starritt Report, App. C.

[25] On the whole subject see A. Smith, 'Immunity From Prosecution' (1983) 42 *Camb. LJ* 299; see also pp. 304–5 below.

[26] It appears that one Attorney-General cannot give a commitment binding a later one, hence the

stated by one Attorney-General that each case is looked at separately, relevant criteria have been enumerated:

(i) whether in the interests of justice it is of more value to have a suspected person as a witness for the Crown than as a possible defendant;

(ii) whether in the interests of public safety or security the obtaining of information about the extent and nature of criminal activities is of greater importance than the possible conviction of an individual;

(iii) whether it is very unlikely that any information could be obtained without an offer of immunity and whether it is also unlikely that any prosecution could be launched against a person to whom the immunity is offered.[27]

The Home Office Circular states: 'The need to protect an informant does not justify granting him immunity from arrest or prosecution for the crime if he fully participates in it with the requisite intent (still less in respect of any other crime he has committed or may in the future commit).'[28] The courts have occasionally bridled when such an offer of immunity has become known, but they are powerless to intervene.[29]

Exceptional cases apart, in practice, the offer of immunity from prosecution in exchange for working as an informer was largely discounted as a motivation for informers by the police.[30] The Home Office has issued secret formal Guidelines on the treatment of 'participatory informants'. To use an example offered, someone involved in a group planning a bank robbery is exculpated from guilt in the conspiracy when he buys a pick and shovel intended for use in tunnelling in. This immunity requires authorization at Deputy Assistant Commissioner level (Deputy Chief Constable outside London). It does not extend to unrelated crime, for example, handling stolen property as an additional source of income. However, if a valuable source lands himself in trouble, it remains open to the police officers actually handling the informer to attempt to negotiate a deferral of charges or a caution with the Crown Prosecution Service. Moroever, the only real check on lower-level officers conferring effective immunity on a 'blind eye' basis is the professionalism and sense of propriety of those working in Special Branch: a factor not to dismissed out of hand, but one which inevitably is less than perfect.

adoption of the immunity extended to Antony Blunt by successive ministers: Smith (previous note), 304.

[27] Sir Michael Havers: *HC Debs.*, vol. 12, col. 12 (9 Nov. 1981); see also ibid., vol. 973, cols. 679 (15 Nov. 1979) and vol. 974, col. 402 (21 Nov. 1979). These criteria apply equally, as the context (the Blunt case) shows, where it is envisaged that no proceedings against another person will result.

[28] Starritt Report (n. 22 above), App. C, para. (*d*).

[29] Smith (n. 25 above), 313–14, citing *R.* v. *Turner* (1975) 61 Cr. App. R 67, CA; (1978) 68 Cr. App. R. 70, HL. However, in *Turner* v. *DPP* (1978) 68 Cr. App. R 70 it was held that a convicted defendant had no civil cause of action against the Director of Public Prosecutions to challenge the DPP's offering of no evidence in that defendant's private prosecution of an accomplice to whom the DPP had formerly given immmunity in exchange for testimony at the defendant's trial: it was impossible to argue that the DPP was acting *ultra vires* having regard to the breadth of discretion conferred on him.

[30] See n. 23.

The role of the Crown Prosecution Service (CPS) is crucial, because since its creation the police no longer have the final decision as to whether a prosecution will be brought.[31] Moreover—an issue that has emerged as one causing great anxiety—recent judgments of the Lord Chief Justice, inspired in part by gross miscarriages of justice,[32] are interpreted by the police as requiring them to reveal to the CPS full background information, including the role of informers, when referring any case. They expressed particular fear that information relating to sources might have to be disclosed to defendants' lawyers,[33] but the need to inform the CPS was also seen as taking away any ability to grant immunity. None of this would affect the Security Service, whose officers are not constables and have no power of prosecution. They may therefore choose not to reveal activities of their informers, whose information may never become known outside the Service. Moreover, nothing we have learned purports to apply to Northern Ireland, which we have not researched and where there is good reason to believe matters are very different.

A related possible motivation should be mentioned: that of assisting the authorities in exchange for a reduced sentence. Known as 'turning Queen's evidence', this applies only to a particular category of informers—those charged with offences who testify against their associates (now their co-defendants). The practice raises similar problems of uncontrolled discretion, but in a different way to grants of immunity. Since sentencing is subject to statutory maximum penalties, in most cases a matter within the discretion of the trial judge, the authorities are unable to give a binding commitment to a reduced sentence at the close of the trial.[34] The judiciary has generally recognized the principle that, as a matter of public policy, credit should be given to such informers otherwise certain types of offences (especially involving gangs) are less likely to be successfully prosecuted.[35] Failure to give due credit may result in reduction of sentence on appeal,[36] but the Court of Appeal has resisted the idea that consistency requires a 'tariff' for reductions in sentence in these cases.

Whatever their initial motivation, once in place the informer is permanently under pressure to justify his standing and rewards. This requires a continuing ability to 'deliver the goods', and in extreme cases may lead to exaggerating or even fabricating material. The stakes involved in striking the right balance are therefore extraordinarily high. The information gained can be of the highest value; the persons providing it may be at serious risk. They may also be acting

---

[31] Prosecution of Offences Act 1985. [32] See p. 313 below.

[33] This would seem to be the broad effect of the statement in the Attorney-General's 'Guidelines on Disclosure of Prosecution Evidence', which state that all unused material should be made available to the defence solicitor: (1982) 74 Cr. App. R. 302; however, there are a number of exceptions which might justify non-disclosure in the case of informers: see the more detailed discussion at pp. 311 ff. below.

[34] This results in the further difficulty of informer discretion: see below, p. 94.

[35] *R.* v. *Lowe* (1978) 66 Cr. App. R. 122, 125 per Roskill LJ.

[36] e.g. *R.* v. *Sinfield* (1981) 3 Cr. App. R. (S) 239.

for the most discreditable of motives, and be only too prone to providing false and malicious information, or to acting as *agents provocateurs*: the recent history of miscarriages of justice, and more ancient history of convictions that now appear highly disreputable, document these tendencies beyond question.[37] These factors leave the legal system at the mercy of 'informer discretion', where it is the informer *choosing* who to implicate and who to absolve. Nor do the problems disappear once this stage is passed. If the informer is giving evidence against co-defendants in the expectation of a lower sentence, the incentive to minimize his or her part in the offences and maximize theirs, creates an irreconcilable conundrum: if the informer-defendant is sentenced in advance of the trial of the remainder it will be on an incomplete picture, derived mainly from his or her own confession, but if sentencing is deferred so that all the defendants are treated together, there is the suspicion that the evidence may be affected.[38]

The informer's method of operation is, of all surveillance techniques, the most destructive of the paramount values of privacy and sociability, and the most corrosive of the sense of freedom and personal security which citizens who give their loyalty to a government are entitled to demand that it provide. It is therefore morally abhorrent, though hardly politically surprising, that in Britain there exist no legal restraints prior to the use of human sources, and few after the event.

An initial choice which requires consideration where human sources are concerned is whether to institute proceedings (where this is possible), and, if so, whether to use the testimony of the informer. Protection of the informer may result either in no proceedings being brought or in their being based on less than the best evidence. Decisions at this level about human sources are largely invisible (and therefore unaccountable) so far as the legal process is concerned.

Evidence from informers is admissible in a criminal trial, but where the informer's involvement is such that he or she could have been charged as co-defendant, it may attract a warning from the trial judge to the jury of the danger of convicting on the uncorroborated evidence of an accomplice. Here the critical factor seems to be the reason why the informer has joined a conspiratorial organization and participated in its activities. This is best illustrated by an extract from the summing up in a case in which Chartists were convicted on informer evidence:

[I]f his object in entering into the confederacy was not to deceive or entrap any one, but to serve his country, he was entitled to praise instead of censure. If he only lent himself to the scheme for the purpose of convicting the guilty, he was a good witness, and his testimony did not require corroboration as that of an accomplice would do . . . for he did not enter the conspiracy with the mind of a co-conspirator . . . At the same time

---

[37] See Porter (n. 3 above), ch. 9, esp. pp. 135–42; on *agent provocateur* activity during the First World War see N. Hiley and J. Putowski, 'A Postscript on PMS2', (1988) 3 *Int. & N.S.* 326.

[38] Although the modern practice is to defer sentence (*R. v. Weekes* (1982) 74 Cr. App. R. 161), previously some judges advocated the alternative course (*R. v. Payne* [1950] 1 All ER 102).

from the facts of his joining the conspiracy for the purpose of betrayal, and that he had used considerable deceit by his own account in carrying out that intent, the jury would do well to receive his evidence with caution . . . [39]

The extensive use of largely uncorroborated informer evidence against alleged terrorists during the so-called 'Supergrass' cases in the early 1980s in Northern Ireland received an almost total rebuff from the Northern Ireland courts when virtually all the convictions were quashed on appeal.[40] This put to an end the unedifying spectacle of a succession of individual terrorists appearing to testify against dozens of their former associates at a time, in return for immunity, monetary recompense, and resettlement with a new identity after the trial.

It is not just that the law allows informer or infiltrator evidence. There is also a considerable body of case law specifically grounded in public policy which seeks to conceal the identity of informers, even at the cost of restricting a criminal defendant's access to certain evidence.[41] Police informers receive protection from disclosure in criminal trials for reasons of public policy[42]—to protect police sources of information and to prevent reprisals. Interestingly, the origin of this rule lies in eighteenth century treason cases: it has been extended in modern times to all police prosecutions, and to analogous proceedings taken by other public bodies.[43] In 1794 in the trial of Thomas Hardy for treason the Special Commission hearing the case prevented Hardy's counsel, Erskine, from questioning a witness who had attended meetings of the London Corresponding Society and passed to the authorities reports of its meetings: Erskine was debarred from establishing the identity of the (politically embarrassing, no doubt) recipient of this intelligence.[44] In another treason trial some twenty years later, Lord Ellenborough incisively explained the justification: 'there will be no safety in communicating the most important intelligence to government, if such matters are not kept secret, and if the channels of communication are to be revealed'.[45] The protection of sources is thus based on practical considerations: 'the courts appreciate the need to protect the identity of informers not only for

---

[39] *R. v. Dowling* (1848) 3 CCC 509, 515–16 per Erle J; cf. *R. v. Mullins* (1848) 3 CCC 526, 531–2 per Maule J.

[40] For full discussion see S. Greer, 'Supergrasses and the Legal System in Britain and Northern Ireland', (1988) 102 *LQR* 189; D. Bonner, 'Combating Terrorism: Supergrass Trials in Northern Ireland', (1988) 51 *MLR* 23; T. Gifford, *Supergrasses: The Use of Accomplice Evidence in Northern Ireland* (London, 1984); Vercher (n. 16 above) 86–105; Walker (n. 18 above), 295–8.

[41] For general discussion see I. Oscapella, 'A Study of Informers in England', [1980] *Crim. LR* 136; I. Eagles, 'Evidentiary Protection for Informers—Policy or Privilege?' (1982) 6 *Crim. LJ* 175.

[42] *Marks* v. *Beyfus* (1890) 25 QBD 494.   [43] *D* v. *NSPCC* [1978] AC 178.

[44] *R. v. Hardy* (1794) 24 St. Tr. 199; in this instance the protection was invoked to prevent identification of the public official to whom information was passed by a named informer who was giving evidence at the trial. Eyre CJ stressed that it is the 'channel of communication' by which disclosure is made which was protected, although later cases have tended to focus on the protection of informers as such: J. Andrews and M. Hirst, *Criminal Evidence* (London, 1987), 301. The resulting popular outcry at the use of evidence obtained by informers in the Hardy case apparently led the government to decide not to lead such evidence directly in the future: Porter (n. 2 above), 33, 37.

[45] *R. v. Watson* (1817) 32 St. Tr. 102.

their own safety but to ensure that the supply of information does not dry up.'[46] The immunity is, however, subject to one overriding exception: the witness may be required to reveal a source where it is necessary in order to prove the defendant's innocence.[47]

Different procedural devices can be used to buttress this protection: *in camera* hearings;[48] allowing a witness to write rather than to publicly state his or her name;[49] allowing anonymous evidence,[50] and evidence from behind a screen in the courtroom;[51] and by orders prohibiting the publication of the witness's name.[52] These devices are as useful for protecting undercover employees of the state as they are for informers. In addition, in the Northern Ireland Supergrass cases measures were taken to protect the informer from pressures to withdraw evidence before trial.[53]

Any protection or control which the courts do provide is dependent on them being aware of the existence of the informer. The Home Office Guidelines state that a court must not be misled and that if the only alternative to deception is to put the informer at risk by revealing his identity, that is a compelling reason not to use the informer in the first place.[54] Where an informer has taken part in a crime for which others are on trial, the prosecuting solicitor, counsel, and if necessary the DPP are to be told, though the informer's identity may be concealed.[55] However, cases have arisen where evidently these rules have not been followed: for instance, the trial judge in the case of a prosecution of members of the IRA for conspiracy to rob was not informed that the police had been tipped off by an informer, Lennon, who had been infiltrated to supply information. It was only when Lennon was found murdered shortly after making a statement to the National Council for Civil Liberties that his part came to light.[56] The courts have taken the view that failure to disclose the existence of

[46] *R.* v. *Hennessey* (1978) 68 Cr. App. R. 419, 425 (per Lawton LJ).

[47] e.g. see *R.* v. *Agar* (1989) 90 Cr. App. R. 318.   [48] OSA 1911, s. 8 (see pp. 306 ff. below).

[49] Approved in *R.* v. *Socialist Workers Printers and Publishers ex p. A-G* [1975] 1 All ER 142 (for witnesses giving evidence at a trial for blackmail).

[50] The 'Colonel B' manœuvre approved in *A-G* v. *Leveller* [1979] AC 440, 451, 467, and 472 (and see pp. 308–11 below).

[51] The practice presumably rests upon a court's ability to regulate its own procedure and to exclude the public in the interests of justice; cf. the Colonel B case (preceding note), where the use of a pseudonym was held to be an acceptable extension of the same powers.

[52] e.g. under the Contempt of Court Act 1981, s. 8.

[53] These included use of the Voluntary Bill of Indictment, avoiding committal proceedings (see Vercher (n. 16 above), 100) and placing the informer's family into protection (in one reported case the 'protective' measures were sufficiently ambiguous to result in a successful habeas corpus application: *Re Quigley* [1983] NI 245).   [54] Starritt Report (n. 22 above), App. C, para. (*c*).

[55] Ibid., para. (*g*); and now the CPS (see text to n. 31).

[56] *R.* v. *Mealey* (1974) 60 Cr. App. R 59; on the Lennon affair see further the Starritt Report and G. Robertson, *Reluctant Judas* (London, 1976). The non-disclosure of Lennon's status was apparently successful in the short term because he was then involved with other IRA members in a conspiracy to help the first defendants escape from prison: on this occasion his status was protected through placing him on trial with the other conspirators and by failing to tell the court of his true role. On this occasion they were convicted but he was acquitted; the convictions were quashed by the Court of Appeal following revelation of Lennon's role: *R.* v. *O'Brien* (1974) 59 Cr. App. R. 222.

an informer will only amount to an irregularity at the trial where it affects some vital feature of the charge.[57]

POLICE COVERT ACTION

Covert policing abounds with dangers, both real and ridiculous. At the fantastic level, witness the Home Office spy who mistook the strange behaviour of the poets Wordsworth and Coleridge on their holidays in Somerset in 1797 for reconnaissance for a possible French invasion or domestic uprising.[58] On the same level was the discovery of two Special Branch officers hiding under the speaker's platform at a meeting of the Communist Party in 1924.[59] It is not hard to see where Chesterton drew material for his comic masterpiece *The Man Who Was Thursday*[60]—the story of how the members of an anarchist cell discover that each of the others is a secret policeman.

The privilege for informer evidence has been extended by analogy to protect other surveillance practices, particularly to prevent the identification of those who allow their premises to be used for secret surveillance by the police.[61] The Court of Appeal has laid down guidelines on the exclusion of evidence obtained by visual surveillance designed to reinforce this objective by requiring the police to ascertain prior to the trial the attitude of the co-operative member of the public to being exposed to identification at the trial.[62] It has been suggested that public policy might also be used as a justification for excluding questions at a trial about unpublicized police techniques, but that each such claim would have to be considered on its merits.[63]

Infiltration by state officials has been treated benignly by the courts. Despite occasional expressions of distaste at the ungentlemanly conduct involved, judges have in effect sanctioned the use of police techniques of covert infiltration. No defence to criminal liability of entrapment exists in English law. For instance, in *R.* v. *Mealey*,[64] an appeal against a conviction for robbery to raise funds for the IRA failed, despite evidence which had come to light of the role of a police informer in encouraging the defendants. The Lord Chief Justice stated:

In these days of terrorism the police must be entitled to use the effective weapon of infiltration. Infiltration by a police officer into a suspected society is a lawful police activity and the intruder may show a certain amount of interest in and enthusiasm for the objects of the society, though they are unlawful. He must not, though, actually cause an offence to be committed which would not otherwise be committed at all.[65]

---

[57] *R.* v. *O'Brien* (previous note), 227.
[58] Porter (n. 2 above), 39–40.
[59] T. Bunyan, *The Political Police in Britain* (London, 1977), 170.
[60] (London, 1937).
[61] *R.* v. *Rankine* [1986] 1 QB 861.
[62] *R.* v. *Johnson* [1988] 1 WLR 1377; and see *R.* v. *Hewitt and Davis* (1992) 95 Cr. App. R. 81, *R.* v. *Brown, Robson and Wilson* [1992] Crim. LR 78.
[63] *R.* v. *Brown* (1987) 87 Cr. App. R 52.
[64] (1974) 60 Cr. App. R 59.
[65] Ibid. 61; and cf. *R.* v. *McEvilly* (1973) 60 Cr. App. R. 150.

This merely updates and applies to terrorism the approach adopted by the courts from the eighteenth century onwards.[66]

Consequently, challenges to such practices have tended to arise as objections to the admissibility of the evidence obtained by such surreptitious means. Where the evidence of the informer or *agent provocateur* is the most substantial evidence against the defendant, the courts have been reluctant to exclude it, since to do so would be tantamount to operating a substantive defence of entrapment. The legal definition of an *agent provocateur* is strictly limited: 'a person who entices another to commit an express breach of the law *which he would not have otherwise committed* and then informs against him'.[67] Thus, in *R. v. Murphy*[68] a conviction at a court martial was upheld, although the only evidence was of two plainclothes police officers who, posing as members of a subversive organization (unnamed in the report), had induced a soldier to give them information about barracks security. The judgment of Lord MacDermott suggests that while deception should be sparingly used, it could be justified in cases where no other method was available, such as security cases. Although the soldier in the case was already under suspicion as a security risk before the police operation, the testing of a predisposition, rather than an intention, to offend in this way is beyond the acceptable limits of police behaviour in our view. [69]

The question of judicial exclusion of *agent provocateur* evidence appeared a closed issue after the House of Lords held in *R. v. Sang*[70] that no such discretion existed, because to recognize it would in effect be to allow a substantive defence of entrapment. However, it has been reopened by the enactment of a general statutory discretion to exclude unfairly obtained evidence in section 78 of the Police and Criminal Evidence Act 1984. In the terrorist case of *R. v. Gill* [71] the Court of Appeal accepted that this provision was capable of allowing the exclusion of evidence obtained by entrapment. However, they held that evidence of undercover police officers, who had posed as IRA assassins to trap Sikh militants into conspiring to murder Rajiv Ghandi, was correctly admitted by the trial judge. The Court laid stress upon the fact that a police informer had acted as an intermediary in establishing the initial link with the defendants, rather than by

[66] See p. 95 above.

[67] *Report of the Royal Commission on Police Powers*, Cmd. 3297 (1929), emphasis added. The definition was cited with approval in *R. v. Mealey* (n. 56 above).

[68] [1965] NI 138.

[69] While security precautions commonly work on the basis of a probability of security risk, to set out actively to test a hypothesis by inducing someone previously presumed loyal to breach security violates the very trust between the state and its employees which is the rationale for the precautions. See Ch. 6.

[70] [1980] AC 402 (not a security-related case).

[71] [1989] Crim. LR 358; and see *R. v. Edwards* [1991] Crim. LR 45; contrast *R. v. Harwood* [1989] Crim. LR 285 9 (*obiter dicta* that s. 78 being a procedural provision could not in effect introduce an entrapment defence); *R. v. Christou and Wright* (1992) 95 Cr. App. R. 264 (conversations between police officers running undercover operation to handle stolen goods and defendant not excluded under s. 78 although obtained contrary to the Code of Practice on questioning, since the conversations took place on an equal footing). See also *R. v. Smuthwaite, R. v. Gill, The Times*, 5 Oct. 1993.

the initiative coming from the police officers themselves. In any event, as Choo has pointed out, even the judicial exclusion of *agent provocateur* evidence fails to address the central concern in such cases, which is the cause of the offence, not the propriety of how the prosecution may prove it.[72]

The European Convention on Human Rights may provide some safeguards against the use of agents, informers, and *agents provocateurs*. The main Convention provisions of relevance here are Article 6(1), which requires a trial to be fair and public, subject to specified exceptions, and Article 8, protecting privacy. In a case involving use by the Swiss authorities of telephone tapping and an under-cover police agent against an alleged drugs ring,[73] the European Court of Human Rights found that there had been no violation of Article 8, since the telephone tapping was judicially authorized for the purpose of detecting crime. Rather less convincing was the suggestion that in undertaking drugs dealing the defendant had accepted the inherent risk of falling foul of undercover policing.[74] The Court did, however, hold that in refusing to allow the defendant to exam-ine the undercover agent, in order to protect his or her anonymity, the proceed-ings had violated the right to a public trial since the defendant was entitled to be present while the witness was heard and to challenge his evidence. The Court laid stress upon the failure of the Swiss court to consider alternatives such as protection in the courtroom, by which protection could be afforded to the police officer without disadvantaging the defendant.[75] This last point suggests that the procedural devices for protecting informers in English law[76] will not fall foul of Article 6. There may be more scope for argument where the informer privilege prevents the informer's identity being revealed and, because the prose-cution choose not to use the evidence, the defence is deprived of hearing or cross-examining the evidence. (This is different from the situation in *Lüdi* where the prosecution were relying on the evidence.) Although even in this situation the ability of a UK court to set aside the privilege where essential in the defen-dant's interests[77] may well do enough to satisfy the right to a fair trial.

---

[72] Choo (n. 16 above), 464.

[73] *Lüdi* v. *Switzerland*, European Court of Human Rights (1993) 15 EHRR 173. In *X* v. *UK* Appl. 7306/75 DR 7, 45 (which was held inadmissible on other grounds) the Commission suggests that disclosure of an immunity deal with a witness may be a requirement of Art. 6. The Commission has suggested that Art. 6(1) may be invoked by *witnesses* whose testimony puts them in danger in the event of the court refusing to conduct an *in camera* hearing (*X* v. *UK* Appl. 8016/77).

[74] (1993) 15 EHRR 173, 199. The Commission had found a breach of Art. 8 because of the undercover policing element, since, in its view, this took the case beyond one of merely passive interception (it found no violation with regard to the interception as such): ibid. 188. The Commission went on to consider whether the undercover policing was 'prescribed by law' under Art. 8(2), holding that the Swiss Federal Misuse of Drugs Act was insufficiently precise and, because of the breadth of the discretion it granted, paid too little regard to the rights of targets to satisfy this requirement: ibid. 191. This is a more satisfactory approach than that adopted by the Court.

[75] Ibid. 200–2; but see *Q.* v. *Netherlands* (1993) 15 EHRR CD 96, where the Commission held that evidence admitted in a criminal case from anonymous informers did not violate Art. 6, because of the full review of the case on appeal and the wealth of additional evidence.

[76] See nn. 48–52 (inclusive) above.   [77] See n. 47 above.

Various proposals have been made for dealing with the problems of human sources within the law enforcement domain. The Law Commission, while rejecting the case for a general defence of entrapment,[78] concluded that purely administrative controls were inadequate by themselves[79] and therefore suggested that cases of abuse could be dealt with by the creation of a new offence of entrapment.[80] The tentative proposal was for an offence of taking the initiative in inciting or persuading another into committing or attempting an offence, even where the purpose was crime detection: such conduct is not at present a secondary or inchoate offence, because there is no intention involved.

Whatever the merits of such an approach (and it has not been implemented), its main focus is on activities surrounding criminal conduct. Similarly reliance on rules of evidence to enhance the rights of suspects and influence officials' behaviour begs two critical questions. First, the empirical question of whether it works: neither the judges nor the authorities see the function of the courts as being to coach police officers and others in good practice. Secondly, even if it did work, much intelligence work would be immune from this influence, because it is not directed or intended to produce outcomes in court.[81] For this reason, in the security realm at least, specific legal or administrative procedures are worthy of further consideration.

What the appropriate legal regulations might be, and when and how they might operate, can only be determined in light of the wide range of circumstances in which informers may gain access to material. A rough categorization might proceed as follows. At the pole of least concern is the case of someone with no prior connection with anyone in authority who happens upon information which he freely volunteers to a security official.[82] The discovery may even occur wholly by accident, as when a stranger overhears a conversation in a pub. Yet even if the informer is a friend of the person whose activities are reported, the betrayal of trust must be counted less important than the fact that the revelation was made wholly as a matter of uncoerced choice. In this instance the informer is at worst like any other gossip, a social irritant we must all bear and do not seek to regulate by law. At best he or she may resolve a difficult moral dilemma and act out of conscience and a sense of public duty, as when the information relates to serious threats or criminal acts.

At the other extreme where privacy and fellowship are most vulnerable, is the

---

[78] Law Com. No. 83, *Criminal Law: Report on Defences of General Application* (1977), paras. 5.34–40.

[79] Ibid., paras. 5.43–45: the Commission were unhappy about making civil liberties effectively dependent on the enforcement of a Home Office circular through police disciplinary proceedings, and pointed out that many abuses were committed by informers who were not police officers and were beyond the reach of bureaucratic controls and sanctions.

[80] Ibid., paras. 5.48–52; this would envisage the prosecution of police officers in appropriate circumstances.

[81] See Ch. 2 above.

[82] 'Security official' in this context may also include a police officer, although the information may not directly implicate anyone in the commission of crime.

purported friend or political associate who has been deliberately placed[83]—planted—to gather information from conversation or other social contact with people who implicitly but mistakenly assume that he or she will honour, as they do, the normal conventions of trust and confidence. This is the classic technique of infiltration.[84] Not radically different is the case of someone who is already in place within an organization or personal relationship and who then becomes a regular informer, not for reasons of public-spiritedness but out of base self-interest. In both instances enormous damage may be done to important social values and often also to the effectiveness of perfectly proper political activity. It is in these circumstances that the greatest need exists for external review of the use of informers.[85]

The main relevant difference between the two cases concerns the moment at which external controls ought to operate. A person infiltrated into a social setting to obtain information functions as an invader of privacy in a similar way to a clandestine electronic listening device,[86] but with the added advantage (to the authorities) of being able to record demeanour, and impressions. His operations should become subject to review from the instant he begins his work. The suborned person presents a more complex problem. It is often not immediately clear when he has actually 'graduated' to the status of a permanent or recurrent source.[87] His handler will be testing him over an extended period for reliability,

[83] As in the case of Brian Nelson (n. 12 above).

[84] It is possible that worries on this score may be exaggerated. Mr Howley (n. 23 above) stated that planting agents is both very difficult and not too productive, and that the police preferred to 'talent spot' and cultivate people already in or on the fringes of a target organization. He also said that journalists are not used as sources because they were unreliable—that is, they cannot be controlled effectively and directed to uncover desired information. However, we must again note that we know nothing in this respect about the work of MI5 or any security agency in Northern Ireland.

[85] One might identify a sort of intermediate case, where a person is acting as an informant, not in relation to a specific group of which he becomes or already is a member, but simply to pass on information as and when he comes upon it (journalists are particularly useful in this context). This does not raise the same issues of betrayal, and thus is morally far less obnoxious. None the less, there remains a substantial invasion of privacy, in the same way that a tapped telephone may record the tendernesses of a target's lover, and there are also dangers of what we describe below as 'perverse incentives'. It therefore seems appropriate that the warrant proposal we offer below should apply equally in this case.

[86] In other words the infiltrator should be treated as a 'human bug' (cf. Marx (n. 12 above),61: 'the agent's goal is to be like an ambulatory wiretap or bug and reflect back rather than shape what occurs'). The only important qualification to this principle might arise in a criminal prosecution where the informer or undercover police officer is called to testify as to conversations with the accused. He would probably be regarded as less credible than a recording of the conversation. In legal systems where constitutional provisions may mandate the exclusion of evidence, treatment of the human bug has been a remarkably contentious issue: note the divergent approaches in Canada (see *Duarte* v. *The Queen* (1990) 1 SCR 30, 65 DLR(4th) 240) and the USA (*Lopez* v. *US*, 373 US 427 (1963), and *US* v. *White* 401 US 745 (1971)). In the security context, however, the information is not used for purposes of criminal proceedings, so we can treat the infiltrator and the wired-up informer identically, as their impact upon privacy demands in any case.

[87] This difficulty should not be over-emphasized: the regular monthly meetings held between Paul Henderson and his intelligence officer handler suggest a greater degree of formality than might have been expected, see Leigh (n. 14 above).

as well as trying to establish a working personal relationship. Some organizations, such as the American FBI, subject potential informants to background checks and required them to serve a probationary period to demonstrate reliability.[88] At this stage the informer may be particularly skittish, and the prospect of being the subject of some form of warrant may be sufficient to put him off. What is perhaps more important, in some circumstances a potentially valuable source may emerge rapidly and unexpectedly, and demand money immediately. Where the need for the information is truly pressing (for example, if it concerns the movements of a member of a terrorist organization), either it will be impractical to obtain a warrant in time,[89] or the matter will be covered by an emergency warrant, which in terms of hard scrutiny is not much better than no warrant at all.[90]

The problem is clearly a complex one, and no solution can pretend to be neat or fully satisfactory. Equally clearly, however, the undoubted difficulties should not be permitted to justify the present position which clearly fails to satisfy our criteria of legality (in the broader sense), proportionality, and layered control according to intrusiveness set out in Chapter 2. It is paradoxical that access may be obtained by use of informers to confidences which elude other intrusive methods which require statutory warrants or administrative approval, and yet the practice is less regulated. The difficulties are sufficiently accounted for if one accepts the proposal of Professor Jean-Paul Brodeur,[91] that after a fixed period of perhaps twelve months all persons who receive money or other benefits, or provide information on a more than occasional basis, be regarded as official sources[92] and become subject to the same warrant requirements as obtain for other forms of surveillance.[93] The twelve-month period is inevitably a rough-and-ready figure, but would be long enough to sift out the casuals, sources under development, those utilized for a particular emergency, and those whom

[88] J. Elliff, *The Reform of FBI Intelligence Operations* (Princeton, NJ, 1979), 122.

[89] If this is true of an administrative warrant, which is sufficient in Britain and Australia for telephone tapping, bugging, and covert entry, it will be all the more true in Canada, where judicial warrants are required.

[90] Provisions now exist for emergency 'interference' warrants under the Security Service Act 1989. However these automatically expire after two working days: SSA, s. 3(3) and (4). Parallel provisions exist in ICA, ss. 4(1) (*b*) and 4(6) (*a*) (ii).

[91] Director of the Centre Internationale de Criminologie Comparée, University of Montreal; Research Director of the Quebec Provincial Commission which investigated abuses by the RCMP security branch; and a witness to the five-year review on the CSIS Act.

[92] This qualification is needed in any attempt at formulating a legal definition of informer, to ensure that any member of the public who gave information the police under normal circumstances (e.g. an eye witness to a street robbery or someone who reported suspicious movements of a stranger) did not thereby fall within the category.

[93] In Britain at the present time this would mean that warrants would be required for the continued use of the source, that these warrants would expire at the end of the same period provided for other warrants, and that they would be subject to review by a commissioner. Whether a tribunal could be established to hear complaints would bear some hard thinking, in view of the evidential difficulties involved in trying to keep identities secret. Brodeur's proposal was, of course, devised in the context of a system of judicial warrants and a powerful Review Committee (SIRC).

the agency itself rejects after trial as untrustworthy or ineffective. It would enable review to focus upon those who have become subject to perverse incentives—notably a vested interest in exaggerating the danger they purport to combat. Such people are also more likely to have moved into a position where their own contribution to criminality or other social threats can be substantial.[94] Coupled with the ever-present infringement of human rights, the increasing danger of counter-productiveness makes critical oversight by someone outside the system imperative. [95]

The need to subject informers to external review is particularly critical in Britain. Professor Brodeur's proposal has not found favour in Canada, where it would operate in the very different context of judicial warrants, which the CSIS Act requires for most other surveillance operations.[96] Even if one accepts for argument's sake that the process of seeking judicial authorization would 'seriously hamper the Service's collection ability',[97] that problem would not arise within the British system of administrative warrants.[98] Moreover, the alternative proposed by SIRC, the Canadian oversight body,[99] was that the matter be governed by ministerial directive, and one in fact was subsequently issued.[100] However, as will be seen in Chapter 15, Britain has firmly rejected the use of ministerial directives in relation to the management of security, so this option is not available either. The alternative to controlling established informers by warrant is therefore simply not controlling them at all.

[94] In a small group or one with rapid turnover of membership, the long-term informer may actually become the mainspring of its continuing activity, criminality, or even of its existence—an even more perverse incentive.

[95] It might well be argued that less rigorous standards, which means primarily a longer qualifying period, should apply where the informer operates only against foreign nationals, particularly those in an official capacity, like diplomats and the well-known 'commercial attaché'. This would be based on the view that the human rights of those who act as agents for foreign governments, in whatever capacity, are not entitled to the same consideration as those of people who have settled under the protection of one's own government. There is much sense in this. However, the other points about perverse incentives apply equally in this context, so the period should not be drastically longer, perhaps eighteen months.

[96] CSIS Act 1984, ss. 21–4; see pp. 80 ff. above.

[97] The view of the then director of CSIS, expressed in a written response to the parliamentary special review committee and quoted in their report, *In Flux But Not in Crisis* (Ottawa, 1990), 127.

[98] The proposal would apply only to operations within Britain, or rather the UK, since Northern Ireland is the critical area in this respect. Overseas operations would be entirely unaffected, on the grounds that spying in foreign countries raises no human rights issues worth weighing against the need for information under UK law. (The distinction does not arise in Canada since it has no overseas intelligence service.) The treatment of UK citizens or residents who, as business people engaged in foreign travel, are recuited as sources may, however, call for specific provisions.

[99] This institution is examined in detail in Ch. 16 below.

[100] See SIRC, *Annual Report 1988–89* (Ottawa, 1989), 74. The principles embodied in the ministerial directive are set out in *In Flux* (above n. 97), 127.

5

The Intelligence Harvest: Files and Records

Having examined the powers of the state to collect security information about individuals in the preceding chapters, we turn now to the storage and use of such information. At the outset, it is worth making several distinctions.

The question of whether a file may be disclosed can be looked at from two directions: from inside the administration and from the perspective of a citizen. In some cases the disclosure will amount to a criminal offence to which an official (or recipient of the information) may be liable.[1] However, even where it is not criminalized, there may be other legal and administrative impediments to disclosure, from the inside looking out: the disclosure of information not covered by the Official Secrets Act may, nevertheless, put an official in jeopardy of employment disciplinary measures.[2] Potential loss of one's career or pension is a powerful disincentive. Furthermore, so far as security information is concerned, these bars operate in Britain within a culture of secrecy, reinforced by the all-pervasive 'need to know' principle. It is little surprise that figures like Clive Ponting or Cathy Massiter are rare indeed.

The citizen's perspective is different. The absence of penalties for disclosure of information does not mean that an individual has any entitlement to have access to the relevant file. A right of this kind only exists at the point where the state loses control of the choice whether or not to make disclosure and is required to do so by some independent authority, whether a court, ombudsman, or commissioner.

We should also distinguish two types of access to government-held information an individual may wish to have: access to personal files and freedom of information. The first is truly an aspect of privacy as we have defined it in Chapter 2, involving control over information about oneself. Commonly the individual wishes to know what personal information is held because he or she objects to the government sharing information of this kind, or wishes to check its veracity or control its disclosure to others. Freedom of information, on the other hand, is disinterested access to information about decisions or policies. The starting point is with a theory of government (some version of democratic accountability), not with the autonomy of the individual. There are some similarities:[3] the claim that my file is in some (non-legal) sense my property is related to the claim that the government does *not* have property in information about itself. The similarity lies in a common view of what it means to be a person—

---

[1] Official secrecy is discussed in Ch. 9 below.   [2] See pp. 232–3 below.
[3] For reasons of convenience we discuss them both in this chapter.

the state is merely an *artificial* person not to be confused with, nor endowed with the same entitlements as, the real thing.[4] In the context of freedom of information, democratic theory often also suggests the opposite: that we have rights to state-held information, because it is *our* government.[5] The arguments which we consider as the strongest justifications for secrecy concerning the indi-vidual—those based on privacy and property notions—are, conversely, the weakest when advanced on behalf of the government.[6]

Whatever their similarities, access to personal files and freedom of informa-tion are most sharply differentiated when they clash. My control of my file implies that you should not have unrestricted access to it; freedom of informa-tion legislation commonly contains privacy exemptions preventing access to other people's personal files.[7]

ADMINISTRATIVE AND LEGAL CONTROLS

In this section we consider first the controls operative in Britain affecting secu-rity files on individuals and then those concerning access to information gener-ally. Unofficial, but credible, accounts suggest the existence of computing and filing systems held by government agencies for security purposes of enormous potential.[8] The Metropolitan Special Branch was expected to have files on 1.5 million individuals by 1986, with some 600,000 of these computerized. The Security Service Joint Computer Bureau was said to hold files on around half a million people in the same year, containing personal details, including suspected political affiliations and association with groups of security interest, much of it based on rumour and inference.

The keeping of files on individuals for purposes related to security raises complex issues requiring consideration of all of the criteria for control of inva-sions of privacy enunciated at the beginning of Chapter 2. The discussion here will focus on the collection, storing, and release of personal information for these purposes, although this cannot be wholly divorced from the means of acquiring private information and the use to which it is put. The pertinent issues are: what legal controls govern when a file may be opened, what may be stored

---

[4] The failure of the law to make the distinction we are urging here is shown most graphically in the extension of breach of confidence to the government as though it were a private individual: *A-G* v. *Jonathan Cape* [1976] QB 752; this was modified in the *Spycatcher* litigation so that the government was only allowed to enforce confidentiality where it was in the public interest: see Ch. 10.

[5] See pp. 221 ff. below.

[6] This appears to leave as possible justifications for state secrecy, either efficiency (Sir Humphrey Appleby on Open Government: 'you can have openness *or* government') or the protection of the community as a whole from some greater threat (commonly a variation on national security).

[7] The same principle is respected in provisions in the UK restricting access to information about other individuals: *Open Government*, Cm. 2290 (1993), paras. 3.23–27.

[8] The material in this paragraph is based on D. Campbell and S. Connors, *On the Record: Surveillance, Computers and Privacy* (London, 1986), chs. 9 and 10.

in it, who has access to it, and when information may be disclosed from it and for what purposes; what steps are taken to ensure accuracy, adequacy, and relevance of information stored; and what rights does an individual have to check or challenge the contents of a file? The answer to nearly all of these questions in the case of security files held in Britain is monosyllabic—none.

If the information is derived from interception under warrant, there are common requirements applicable to all agencies, derived from section 6 of the Interception of Communications Act 1985 (ICA), which govern its retention and use. This requires the Secretary of State to ensure that the extent to which material is disclosed and copied is the minimum necessary, and that copies are destroyed as soon as no longer required for the purposes for which a warrant could be issued. This requirement extends to summaries, reports, and file entries based upon intercepted material.[9] Derived from these common provisions, each agency has its own administrative procedures.

GCHQ has developed criteria which have been incorporated into secret Guidelines for those parts of its work falling under the ICA, agreed with the Interceptions Commissioner.[10] These Guidelines cover how long material obtained under warrant is retained and how it is disposed of, the treatment of non-security material (for instance, evidence of criminal or discreditable activities) obtained through interception of a target, and the treatment of security-related material on non-targeted individuals which comes to light through interception. In the case of Special Branch and MI5, their treatment of material is also affected by other guidelines affecting their work, contained respectively in the Home Office Guidelines on the Work of a Special Branch, and the Security Service Act 1989 (SSA). The Security Service has standing rules which are issued to all interceptors (the officers who analyse intercepted material) to ensure that ancillary material (such as evidence of unrelated criminal activity) is not retained. Whereas with interception carried out by the police transcripts are destroyed at the close of the investigation, because of the long-term nature of gathering security intelligence, the Security Service retains its transcripts indefinitely.[11] Only exceptionally will the Service supply information to other government departments derived from interception.

The Security Service Act 1989 specifically places a duty on the Director-General to make arrangements 'to ensure that no information is obtained or disclosed by the Service, except in so far as is necessary for the proper discharge of its functions'.[12] This provision applies both to information obtained under a

[9] See definition of 'copy': ICA, s. 10.

[10] This material is based on an interview with a former highly placed GCHQ officer, who requested anonymity.

[11] *Interception of Communications Act 1985 Chapter 56; Report of the Commissioner For 1986* Cm. 108, para. 48.

[12] SSA, s. 2(2)(a). Disclosure (but not collection) for the purpose of preventing or detecting serious crime is also authorized. Consequently, information may only be sought or retained if concerned with national security or for safeguarding the economic well-being of the UK, but evidence of criminality which comes to light may be passed on to others but not stored.

warrant (whether under the ICA or the SSA) and to information from human or open sources and visual surveillance. However, the SSA contains no provision equivalent to section 6 of the ICA (requiring minimum copying and disclosure of intercepted material). This is anomalous from a privacy perspective, since in practice bugging under warrant seems more likely to turn up evidence of ancillary criminality, of which the target might be reluctant to speak on the telephone. In practice the Service's interceptors are instructed to overlook minor criminality and only evidence relating to serious offences will be passed on to the police. Procedures exist for sifting material according to relevance under the Service's statutory remit before it reaches a file. Disclosure of information for employment vetting is governed by more precise minsterial guidelines.[13] However, all these arrangements are unpublished and the Act gives inadequate guidance on the treatment of extraneous material. The Act contains no right of access or correction for an individual complainant to personal files held by the Security Service. Instead, file-keeping may fall within the remit of the Commissioner and the Tribunal with all the attendant shortcomings of those mechanisms.[14] The individual has no right to know whether the Security Service has a file on him or her and the Tribunal has no right to order the destruction of a file. This leaves the controls as administrative ones operative within the Service. The Commissioner has no statutory remit to police the file-keeping operations of the Service. Nevertheless, he may become involved where individual cases referred by the Tribunal[15] raise issues of general policy affecting files. The little that is officially known about MI5 files has come to light in this way.[16]

Controls govern the opening of and additions to files. These divide files into several categories. A temporary file may be opened for a period of up to three years where it is unclear whether the criteria for opening a permanent file are satisfied. The criteria relate to the statutory duties of the Service under section 1 of the SSA.[17] When a permanent file exists it is open for additions and active inquiries may be made for relevant material during a fixed period (varying according to the criteria for opening the file)—the so-called 'green' phase. This period may be extended in the light of material uncovered by active inquiries. At the expiry of this active period the file enters a period in purgatory during which material may be added if it comes to the attention of the Service, but no active inquiries are undertaken—the 'amber' phase. Finally, the file is closed (that is, no further material may be added) but is retained for consultation—the 'red' phase. It seems that the Commissioner directly equates this traffic-light

---

[13] SSA, s. 2(3).   [14] See Ch. 15.   [15] SSA, sched. 1, para. 7.

[16] *Security Service Act 1989; Report of the Commissioner for 1991*, Cm. 1946 (1992), paras. 16 ff. We draw here also on interviews held with officials from the Security Service and Division F6 of the Home Office (see List of Interviewees).

[17] The implication is that in the case of some temporary files, the s. 1 criteria will not be fulfilled; since this involves the Security Service in collecting (though at this stage relatively passively) information outside its remit, three years may seem an unnecessarily long period.

cycle and the requirements of the Act.[18] Presumably the references in the Act to the Tribunal establishing whether since the commencement date the Service has undertaken inquiries relating to the complainant (SSA, Sched. 1, para. 2) were intended to relate only to 'amber' and 'green' files. The general policy of the Service is to retain personal files indefinitely, because it claims that it is impossible to predict when they might be needed in future.[19] The Commissioner has also endorsed the principle of retaining files which would previously have been disposed of in case a complaint is made about them: this is, to put it mildly, paradoxical—especially in view of the small number of complaints.

Information on controls over Special Branch files is equally sparse. There are no statutory controls. The Home Office Guidelines will apply and are particularly concerned with the question of file-keeping. These stipulate that the information collected should be confined to that which relates to the legitimate functions of a Special Branch[20] and that information should never be collected on an individual or organization because they espouse an 'unpopular cause' or on the basis of race or creed. They stress that wherever possible information should be authenticated so that material on file does not give a false or misleading impression.[21] The importance of security is also stressed: access should be limited to those with a particular need to know, and there should be in place stringent and appropriate controls against unauthorized disclosure or unauthorized loss of material. Our interviews with representatives of both the Metropolitan Special Branch and a provincial branch confirmed the seriousness with which these matters are treated.[22]

In the Metropolitan Special Branch there are unpublished guidelines on the weeding of files, and files are reviewed 'frequently'. Where information relates to an individual rather than an organization it is more likely to be 'transitory'—the length of retention will be influenced by the staleness of the material, the individual's age, and his likelihood of future involvement in activities within the Branch's remit. From an interview held with officers of one provincial force, it would appear that a variety of administrative controls operate. 'Careful consideration' is given before a file is opened concerning an individual, guidelines issued by the Security Service are followed, access to the files within the police is restricted to Special Branch officers,[23] and then only on a need to know basis,

---

[18] *Security Service Act 1989; Report of the Commissioner for 1992*, Cm. 2174 (1993), para. 9.

[19] See n. 16 above, para. 18. This policy is based on previous experience where espionage investigations had in the past been hampered by the destruction of files. The Commissioner has stated that in his view the general policy is acceptable.

[20] However, in view of the Special Branch's public order function this may give considerable scope for retaining information on pressure groups.

[21] HC 71 (1984–5), para. 17.

[22] Interview with Sir Peter Imbert (Metropolitan Police Commissioner) and Mr John Howley (Deputy Assistant Commissioner, in charge of Special Branch); interview with Chief Constable, Assistant Chief Constable, and Head of Special Branch, Northumbria Constabulary.

[23] The same applies to the Metropolitan Special Branch; consequently not even officers from the Anti-Terrorist branch have access.

the filing system (in this particular force) is subject to internal biannual random checks by an Assistant Chief Constable, and files are inspected by HM Inspectors of Constabulary during the annual efficiency certificate visitation. Although these safeguards may go some way to satisfying the need voiced by the Select Committee on Home Affairs[24] that careful control should be exercised over Special Branch files, it should be noted that the controls are purely administrative, give no entitlements to an affected individual, and, for the most part, are internal only.

Rights of access for an individual to personal files concerning him or her in the United Kingdom are fragmented.[25] There is no general right of access to manual files, but instead there exists a number of incremental pieces of legislation,[26] none of which has any application in the security realm. If the data is held in computer-processable form then there will be an entitlement under the Data Protection Act 1984, subject, however, to the sweeping exemptions which apply in security cases.

The Data Protection Act 1984 is the United Kingdom's half-hearted attempt to impose controls on users of personal data, through a registration scheme, with attendant administrative powers, and rights of access for individuals for data held concerning them; it also establishes a right of action for loss arising from inaccurate data. A number of exemptions exist from this scheme which considerably dilute its effect in practice, but only those in the public sector which are relevant to our purpose will be considered here. The Act contains, in section 27, a general exemption from registration for personal data held for the purpose of safeguarding national security. One effect of the exemption is that the data protection principles—requiring accuracy, relevance to purpose, updating, data security, and so on[27]—do not apply to such databanks.[28] Another is that the 'subject access' provisions in the Act are also excluded. The importance of the exception is such that section 27(6) provides for a certificate, which is purportedly conclusive,[29] as proof of the applicability of the exemption by a cabinet minister or by the Attorney-General or the Lord Advocate. The extreme novelty and sensitivity of this procedure is underlined by the fact that this is one of the very few references to the Cabinet in a British statute. Nor is the section entirely negative in its effect: section 27(4) allows for privileged access for the purposes of national security to other personal databanks—normally, under the non-disclosure provisions in the Act, this would be prohibited. In addition to

[24] See n. 21 above, Home Office Guidelines, paras. 16 ff.
[25] For proposals to extend these rights (which would not affect security files on individuals), see the White Paper on *Open Government* (n. 7 above), ch. 5.
[26] Access to Personal Files Act 1987; Access to Medical Reports Act 1988; Education Reform Act 1988, ss. 218 and 232; Access to Health Records Act 1990.
[27] Data Protection Act 1984, sched. 1.
[28] However, Special Branch informed us that they apply the principles of necessity, relevance, and accuracy to manual and electronic files equally.
[29] S. 27(2).

the general exemption, *ad hoc* exemptions may be made by ministerial order for data which is prohibited from being disclosed under other statutes; since the Interception of Communications Act 1985, Official Secrets Act 1989, and Security Service Act 1989 contain numerous provisions of this kind, there will be little difficulty in exempting all data held on computer by the security and intelligence agencies, and by the police and Home Office for similar purposes.

Whilst one would naturally expect some computer records to be exempt on security grounds, the breadth of these exceptions is disturbing. Before the legislation was passed the Lindop Committee recommended that a senior and vetted member of the Data Protection Registrar's office should act as a consultant to the Home Office and the Security Service to assist them to devise appropriate (non-statutory) safeguards. The Committee also suggested that the Home Secretary should not be able to extend the national security exemption to cover information received from the private sector.[30] If the draft European Community directive on protection of individuals in relation to the processing of personal data is implemented[31] it should introduce a measure of outside control in this field in the case of data held for purposes where the EC has competence:[32] although the draft directive contains exemptions from subject access for defence and national security, even these are to be subject to checks by the 'supervisory authority'[33] (in Britain this would be the Data Protection Registrar).

Behind any discussion of access to government information lies the shadowy question: is it classified? A common feature of the British, Canadian, and Australian administrative culture is the familiar categorization of documents into bands reflecting their secrecy. The administrative advantage of such a scheme is that it provides a way of determining which officials should be granted access to those papers. In the British and Canadian systems it has been closely linked to the employment practices of vetting and security clearance.[34] In a system of interlocking international co-operation a common currency in such classifications is a vital prerequisite to the free flow of information. It was therefore inevitable that the fourfold classification of Top Secret, Secret, Confidential, and Restricted would come to be commonly used in each country. Prior to its internationalization the fourfold classification seems to have originated in a British government attempt to standardize Whitehall procedures following leaks surrounding the abortive Norway expedition in 1940.[35]

---

[30] *Report of the Committee on Data Protection*, Cmnd. 7341 (1978), paras. 23.23 and 23.25 respectively.

[31] COM (90) 314 (OJ C/277, 5. 11. 90).   [32] e.g. immigration.

[33] See n. 31 above, art. 15(2); the purpose would be to check that the principles contained in Art. 16 are complied with. These include that personal data is collected lawfully and fairly, stored for explicit and lawful purposes, is adequate, relevant, and not excessive, and is accurate and up to date.

[34] See Ch. 6 below.

[35] PRO/T273/4 Bridges to Brook, 1 Apr. 1952 (quoted extensively in R. Chapman and M. Hunt (eds.), *Open Government* (Beckenham, 1987), 19–21); the classification went into Anglo-American use after American objections to the British term 'Most Secret' (Churchill's preferred terminology) were

The meaning of these classification categories supposedly reflects the seriousness of the consequences of disclosure. Hence, disclosure of TOP SECRET documents will result in 'exceptionally grave damage to the nation', SECRET documents will cause 'serious injury to the interests of the nation', whereas leaking of CONFIDENTIAL documents would be merely 'prejudicial', and of those which are RESTRICTED, would be 'undesirable' to the interests of the nation.[36] These categories are not tied to criminal liablity. However, they may affect the reasonableness of a defendant's belief that the document was not concerned with security, defence, and so on where that is relevant under the Official Secrets Act 1989.[37] Rather, the classification governs who has access to the document and the steps taken to ensure its physical security.

The dangers of over-classification have often been noticed.[38] There are strong administrative arguments against the practice also on grounds of the unnecessary work and expense of security precautions.[39] Over-classification probably occurs more as a by-product of administrative culture and bureaucratic caution than by conscious design. One institutionalized practice capable of abuse drawn to our attention by an official is 'the whole file principle'—the classification of a file is determined by the status of the most confidential document it contains.

Although the United Kingdom lacks freedom of information legislation conferring a right to see government papers, some documents are, nevertheless, released under the provisions of the Public Records Acts 1958 and 1967.[40] The purpose of these Acts is to ensure that important historical documents are preserved and made available for research. Thus government departments transfer their records to the Public Records Office, which after a given period (now thirty years), may make them available to the public. This system has severe limitations, some general and some of specific application in the security field.

overcome by substitution of 'Top Secret' (a term apparently derived from the top layer of secret material).

[36] *Reform of Section 2 of the Official Secrets Act 1911*, Cm. 408 (1988), paras. 75 and 76. The Franks Committee had earlier recommended that classification and criminal liability should be partially linked, with ministers personally checking that a document was correctly classified before a prosecution was authorized: *Departmental Committee on Section 2 of the Official Secrets Act 1911*, Cmnd. 5014 (1972), vol. 1, paras. 144–69. In addition to the classifications cited in the text other levels of clearance may be designated to delineate circulation of information classified at TOP SECRET level on the 'need to know' basis; for examples, see J. Richelson and D. Ball, *The Ties That Bind* (2nd edn., Sydney, 1990), 164–7. There also exist privacy classifications to denote documents whose disclosure would affect individual or commercial interests, but where no national interest would be jeopardized: Franks Committee, para. 63.   [37] Ch. 9 below.

[38] e.g. Lord Scarman in *Secretary of State for Defence* v. *Guardian Newspapers* [1985] 1AC 339, 365, where he expressed the view that it could be misused to cover information whose disclosure would be politically embarrassing.

[39] These considerations were cited by the Security Commission in recommending a thorough review to reduce the number of highly classified documents: *Statement on the Recommendations of the Security Commission*, Cmnd. 8540 (1982), para. 8.

[40] See M. Roper, 'Access to Public Records', in Chapman and Hunt (n. 35 above); N. Cox, 'The Thirty Year Rule and Freedom of Information', in G. Martin and P. Spurford (eds.), *The Records of the Nation* (Woodbridge, 1990).

Apart from the lengthy statutory embargo, the most general problem with the legislation is that the overwhelming majority of papers (estimated at 95 per cent) are destroyed by departmental 'weeders' before transfer to the PRO: this is a requirement of efficient administration rather than anything more sinister.[41] Exemptions from the legislation operate both at the stage of transferring the documents from departments to the PRO and with respect to the 'closure period' of transferred documents. The Lord Chancellor is able to authorize the retention of files by departments,[42] and does so in cases of records containing highly sensitive information relating to national security. Approvals of this kind have been given for records concerned with security and intelligence matters[43] and for civil and home defence planning in the period 1945–55, and with defence uses of atomic energy. Outside these blanket approvals files on other topics with a high security content may be exempted subject to suitable arrangement for regular review.

The arrangements for closure were reviewed in 1992 and now require it to be shown (*inter alia*) that the release of the file would cause demonstrable damage to national security, international relations, defence, or the economic interests of the United Kingdom;[44] the insistence on actual harm is more stringent than the notion of public interest which formerly applied. The normal period of extended closure is now forty years in such cases.[45] Applications from departments for extended closure are considered by an administrative process involving an Inspecting Officer of the PRO and consideration by an Advisory Council[46] before the draft instrument is passed to the Lord Chancellor. In practice no more than 2 per cent of PRO records are closed in this way.[47]

The operation of the closure provisions mainly affects the secondary product of the intelligence agencies' work recorded in the files of related departments.

[41] Further selection of papers takes place once they are handed over to the PRO; see K. Smith, 'Sampling and Selection: Current Policies', in Martin and Spurford (n. 40 above), for details of the process and the criteria adopted for retention.

[42] Public Records Act 1958, s. 3(4).

[43] Thus the files of MI5, MI6, GCHQ, and the Home Office and Foreign Office files connected with their work will be exempt from transfer to the PRO.

[44] The 1993 White Paper listed as examples of when these criteria might be satisfied documents which: 'refer to possible plans for intervention in a foreign state; concern security or defence of a UK dependent territory, where the release would jeopardise the security of the territory concerned; comment on unresolved border or territorial dispute, not necessarily one directly involving the UK; or comment adversely on leaders of, or the internal affairs of, foreign states.' (n. 7 above, para. 9.14).

[45] Ibid., Annex C. Longer periods of extended closure (up to 100 years) are reserved for highly personal files, thus apparently giving greater weight to privacy interests.

[46] These procedures are now to apply also to applications from departments for retention of records: 1993 White Paper (n. 7 above), para. 9.30. However, the Council does not inspect the records in question (see *32nd Annual Report of the Keeper of the Public Records on the Work of the Public Records Office and 32nd Report of the Advisory Council on Public Records*, (1990–1) HC 561, p. 40); a recommendation that sensitive records should be considered by a confidential committee of the Advisory Council (*Modern Public Records: Selection and Access, Report of a Committee Appointed by the Lord Chancellor*, Cmnd. 8204 (1981), para. 315) has not been implemented.

[47] *32nd Report* (n. 46 above), para. 4.

Files of the intelligence agencies themselves will be covered by the exemptions allowing them to be retained and not passed to the PRO, rather than closed. The need for this policy has recently been reaffirmed on gounds of protecting 'their methods of operations which, despite the passage of time, are still extant' and 'the identitities of people who put themselves at risk in the service of the State'.[48] The cumulative effect of these provisions is to make informed public debate about security and intelligence matters extremely difficult, due to lack of reliable historical data. Occasionally academics have been given privileged access for the purpose of historical study to records to which there was no entitlement,[49] or through sheer persistence and ingenuity have tracked down security-related documents which have escaped weeding on released files of other government departments.[50] Although it is clear that papers relating to the intelligence agencies are retained against the possibility of availability under the Public Records Acts at some future time,[51] the authorities remain firmly in control of the data necessary for a historical, and still more a contemporary, debate of the agencies' effectiveness. It will be apparent that there is no independent control outside government on the operation of these exemptions, and few in practice outside the relevant department.[52]

In the absence of any statutory entitlement to files or information the courts have been powerless to fashion a substantive right from the procedural protections afforded by judicial review. Thus, although plainly affronted by the Ministry of Defence's refusal to release to the bereaved parents of a soldier killed in an accident in the Falklands the report of the board of inquiry on his death, Rose J held that the minister was under no legal duty to do so in the absence of a Freedom of Information Act.[53]

---

[48]   White Paper (n. 7 above), para. 9.27.

[49]   For example limited access to intelligence files was granted for the research on one official history, F. H. Hinsley, *British Intelligence in the Second World War* (London, 1979). The government has also recently invited historians to submit requests for release of retained material: 1993 White Paper (n. 7 above), 9.28.

[50]   See Andrew, *Secret Service*, 15–16; A. Simpson, *In the Highest Degree Odious* (Oxford, 1992), 422–3.

[51]   Wilson Committee Report (n. 46 above), paras. 197–200.

[52]   Where exemption from transfer to the PRO is sought officials from the PRO can do no more than inspect a small sample of the records for which exemption is sought; the Advisory Committee has claimed that it is inconsistent that it should not be consulted in these cases: ibid. 40.

[53]   *R.* v. *Secretary of State for Defence, ex p. Sancto*, (*The Times*, Law Reports, 9 Sept. 1992); there was at the time of accident no right to sue the army over the fatality to which a claim for discovery could be appended. With the repeal of s. 10 of the Crown Proceedings Act 1947 this is no longer the case. However, in the later case of *Barrett* v. *Ministry of Defence* (*The Times*, Law Reports, 24 Jan. 1992) a similar claim failed on the grounds that it was too early in the proceedings; the judge, nevertheless, doubted whether public interest immunity could have lain (see p. 335 below).

THE APPLICATION OF THE EUROPEAN CONVENTION ON HUMAN RIGHTS

It is questionable to what extent the European Convention on Human Rights can be utilized by complainants to make good the lack of firm rights of access to information in UK law.

In general terms the Strasbourg jurisprudence provides that keeping a file relating to an individual by an official body can fall within Article 8 if the file contains personal information, over and above the person's name and address. What counts as personal information for these purposes has not been clearly defined, and the Convention organs do not appear to differentiate that question from the logically subsequent one of whether any interference with privacy was 'necessary in a democratic society'.

In *Gaskin* v. *UK*[54] the Court of Human Rights held that where an individual claims access to a file about him held by a public authority, Article 8(2) may allow access to be denied to protect the confidentiality of the information and its sources, but that proportionality required an independent mechanism in British legislation for weighing the individual's claim against the assertion of confidentiality. The absence of such a mechanism led the Court to hold that a violation had occurred. The creative aspect of this judgment is the finding that Article 8 can encompass a positive right of access to information about one's private life, as well as negative protection from state interference. However, the judgment does not amount to a right in the Convention for access to all files, since it turned on the highly personal nature of the files in question,[55] which made them indistinguishable from the individual's privacy interests;[56] the same reasoning would not apply to other categories of non-personal information. The Commission has held that the mere compilation and retention of a file about an individual does not constitute a breach of Article 8.[57] This seems an unrealistically restrictive approach. The files in *Gaskin* were not related to security, and while the same general approach has been taken to security files, the standards applied have been somewhat diluted. However, the Convention organs have in general adopted a realistic approach in requiring only that a complainant show a reasonable likelihood that a file has been maintained on him or her before accepting a complaint as admissible: anything more would create an unenviable catch-22.[58]

The Court in *Leander*[59] explicitly stated that safeguards would be necessarily diluted in the security realm where the state would enjoy a wide 'margin of

---

[54] (1990) 12 EHRR 36.   [55] Which related to Gaskin's childhood in local authority care.
[56] Cf. pp. 104–5 above.
[57] *Hilton* v. *UK* App. No. 12015/86, p. 20: 'an interference with the right to respect for private life only occurs when security checks are based on information about a person's private affairs.' For discussion of the *Hilton* case see Ch. 6 below.
[58] Ibid.; *N* v. *UK*, App. No. 122327/86.   [59] *Leander* v. *Sweden* (1987) 9 EHRR 433, para. 59.

appreciation' (that is, discretion as to whether interference with privacy was necessary). In other cases affecting the United Kingdom, the Committee of Ministers concluded enigmatically that in the light of the passage of the Security Service Act 1989, no further action was necessary on two complaints relating to files maintained by the Security Service on former officers of the National Council for Civil Liberties.[60] Since then the Commission has declared admissible a complaint from the Netherlands which alleges a breach of Article 8 in the refusal of access to the complainants to files allegedly held by the security and intelligence service.[61] This matter is discussed more fully in Chapter 6, where we argue in the context of employment vetting that the Act is insufficient to satisfy the Convention. It is likely that the *Harman* and *Hewitt* cases will return to the Convention organs now that domestic remedies under the Act have been exhausted fruitlessly.[62] In the case of files held by Special Branches, or by the other intelligence agencies, which are outside statutory control, the absence of a legal mechanism for balancing the state's interests with the individual's would suggest that the United Kingdom is in breach of Article 8 where the information held falls within the field of 'personal' information.

In addition to protecting freedom of expression, Article 10 of the Convention speaks of the right to receive and impart information.[63] Although the Convention organs are now, belatedly, taking seriously the right to receive information,[64] it has still been restricted to situations where the holder of the information wishes to communicate. Hence, in *Gaskin* a claim under Article 10 failed, because the Council did not wish to part with the information. Consequently the main use of Article 10 in this area is likely to be against government restrictions on the free exchange of information between willing parties in the private sector, and not for the obtaining of government information.

In Canada and Australia the question of public or personal access to security-related documents or files has been more directly addressed, because of the creation of wider legislative rights to government information, which Britain lacks.

---

[60] *Harman and Hewitt* v. *UK*, (1992) 14 EHRR 657.

[61] *V and others* v. *Netherlands*, Application No. 14084/88 ((1991) 12 *Human Rights Law Journal* 282.

[62] In *R.* v. *Security Service Tribunal, ex p. Harman and Hewitt* (unreported decision of Kennedy J sitting in the High Court on 14 Feb. 1992, available on LEXIS) judicial review of the Security Service Tribunal's finding that their complaint was unjustified was refused. Two complaints have been declared inadmissible and a third adjourned by the Commission in the cases of three applicants who had offers of jobs withdrawn following negative vetting and who unsuccessfully brought proceedings in the Tribunal: *G, H, and I* v. *UK* App. Nos. 18600/91, 18601/91, and 18602/91 (1993) 15 EHRR CD 41.

[63] Omitted is the right to *seek* information, which is expressly mentioned in Art. 19 of the Universal Declaration of Human Rights and Art. 19 of the International Covenant on Civil and Political Rights: P. Germer, 'Administrative Secrecy under the European Convention on Human Rights', in *Secrecy and Openness: Individuals, Enterprises and Public Administrations, Proceedings of the Seventeenth Colloquy on European Law* (Strasbourg, 1988) 61, p. 62.

[64] *Guardian* v. *UK* (1991) 14 EHRR 153; *Open Door Counselling Ltd., Dublin Well Woman Centre and Others* v. *Ireland*, Judgment of the European Court of Human Rights, 29 Oct. 1992 (64/1991/316/387–88); and see (1992) 14 EHRR 131 for the Commission proceedings. For a review of earlier (less favourable) decisions see Germer, n. 63 above.

It is to how considerations of public access and security are reconciled in those jurisdictions that we now turn.

CANADA

Canada possesses a freedom of information Act (the Access to Information Act 1982) and a sweeping right for Canadians and permanent residents to have access to personal information held about them by government departments (the Privacy Act 1982).[65] However, both pieces of legislation provide for the withholding of information on security grounds.[66]

The exceptions to the Access to Information Act operate both to allow for the exemption of records held by *agencies* with law enforcement or security functions[67] and for *categories* of information. The latter include information whose disclosure could reasonably be expected to be injurious to the conduct of international affairs, the defence of Canada or any state allied or associated with Canada, or the detection, prevention, or suppression of subversive or hostile activities.[68] The burden of proof lies with the government in claiming the benefit of the exception,[69] but the legislation does not require the projected harm to be serious.[70] In addition, papers which have gone to the Cabinet are exempt, giving rise to the fear that some politically sensitive security matters may undergo a process of 'Cabinet laundering' to prevent disclosure.[71]

An applicant aggrieved by a refusal to disclose information has a right of review before the Information Commissioner (an independent officer with access to all documents except Privy Council papers) and, thereafter, to the Federal Court. Where information is sensitive the legislation provides that the review both before the Commissioner and the Court may take place *in camera* and *ex parte* at the request of the government.[72] However, whereas the normal function of the Federal Court under the Act is to consider the entitlement to access on its merits, the security exemptions are one of a number of provisions where the court is limited to considering whether there are reasonable grounds on which the refusal is based.[73]

The practical operation of the Act is described in the Information Commissioner's Annual Reports. In the first five years of operation of the Act there were forty-five refusals of access by CSIS, of which the Information

---

[65]　See J. Wallace, 'The Canadian Access to Information Act 1982', in N. Marsh (ed.), *Public Access to Government-Held Information* (London,1987); P. Birkinshaw, *Freedom of Information: The Law, the Practice and the Ideal* (London, 1988), 48–52; R. Thomas, 'The Experience of Other Countries', in Chapman and Hunt (n. 35 above).

[66]　For a detailed and critical account: M. Rankin, 'National Security: Information, Accountability, and the Canadian Security Intelligence Service' (1986) 36 *University of Toronto LJ* 248.

[67]　S. 16(1)(*a*).　　　　[68]　S. 15.　　　　[69]　S. 48.　　　　[70]　Rankin (n. 66 above), 267.

[71]　Ibid. 269.　　　　[72]　S. 52; and see the duty to prevent disclosure: ss. 47 and 62.

[73]　S. 50.

Commissioner upheld twenty-six and overruled nineteen. In the circumstances a 40 per cent success rate is a minor victory for open government. Among the information whose release the intervention of the Commissioner has secured at least in part are: Privy Council Office records on terrorism in Quebec, material on Soviet intelligence activities in Canada in 1963–5,[74] a CSIS Operational Manual and Technical Aids, Policy, and Procedures Manual, and a CSIS file on a named individual (where most of its contents had been public knowledge since 1945).[75] However, the Commissioner has also upheld a number of refusals of access to security-related information. These include: documents related to the Cuban missile crisis (on the grounds that information was supplied in confidence by a foreign government), a CSIS manual on counter-espionage and counter-subversion, and CSIS counter-intelligence on Soviet espionage activities in Canada in 1963–4.[76]

The need to police the use of exemptions by government agencies is self-evident if the legislation is to be made to work. One critical issue is that reasons for refusal of access should be narrowly restricted to the necessary interests and that their use in practice should be as publicly accountable as possible. The record here is rather disappointing. In *Re Information Commissioner of Canada and Minister of National Defence*,[77] a refusal to supply documents under the Access to Information Act relating to agreements entered into by the Canadian government with the United States concerning nuclear weapons was challenged. The Federal Court upheld a certificate of denial of access which simply recited the broad statutory exclusion of matters reasonably considered injurious to foreign relations, defence, or the detection, prevention, or suppression of subversive or hostile activities[78] without giving precise particulars of which paragraphs were relied on. The court reached this conclusion despite a statutory requirement to identify the 'specific provision'[79] relied on for denial and a detailed list of no fewer than nine possible types of such harm,[80] which were available to be so specified.

More invidious are the cases in which an agency refuses to give any reason at all for the refusal of access on the grounds that even to do so would compromise a statutorily protected interest. The Information Commissioner has upheld such a refusal from the Department of National Defence.[81] Likewise, a department may in certain circumstances be entitled to refuse to confirm whether a file exists.[82] A response (if it can be called such) of this kind is intended to prevent the legislation from being used to defeat genuine security-related surveillance. The Commissioner has upheld a case of this kind involving CSIS where it was admitted that, if the file existed, it would be only partly exempt.[83] Although

---

[74] *Report of the Information Commissioner for 1985–86* (Ottawa, 1986), 37, 54.
[75] *Report of the Information Commissioner for 1986–87* (Ottawa, 1987), 56 and 59.
[76] See n. 74 above, 35, 59, and 60. [77] (1990) 67 DLR (4th) 585.
[78] S. 15(1). [79] S. 10(1). [80] Set out in s. 15(1).
[81] See n. 74 above, 49. [82] S. 16(1); cf. *Re Zanganeh and CSIS* (1988) 50 DLR (4th) 747.
[83] *Report of the Information Commissioner for 1987–88* (Ottawa, 1988), 72–3.

the outcome was reached with understandable regret, the result in practice was to extend the exemptions beyond those authorized under the Act.

The Privacy Act 1982 contains a similar system of exemptions and review of decisions relating to refusal of access to personal information, under a similar commissioner (the Privacy Commissioner[84]) and with review by the Federal Court.[85] Under the scheme personal information banks may be exempted by Order in Council on security grounds.[86] In such cases, an applicant requesting information will not be entitled to know whether or not a file exists, although the Privacy Commissioner has powers both to review exempt information banks to ensure that they comprise only information which is properly exempt,[87] and to apply to the Federal Court in the case of non-compliance with any remedial action ordered.[88]

However, one category of security file receives particular treatment, namely files relating to security clearances:[89] information may be withheld by an agency if it derives from CSIS and could reasonably be expected, if disclosed, to reveal the identity of an individual who was a source. The same issue has arisen in the courts in a case where an applicant challenged the confirmation by SIRC of the denial of enhanced security clearance to him. The court upheld a certificate filed by CSIS objecting to discovery in the judicial proceedings of the relevant documents, which they had made available to SIRC, relating to the applicant's involvement in (named) allegedly subversive organizations. In view of the importance of the effect of denial of security clearance and the relevance of the evidence to the case, the trial judge examined the documents and then upheld CSIS's claim to withholding discovery under the Canada Evidence Act 1970, cE-10, section 36.2. Among the reasons given for upholding the non-disclosure were that the information would identify, or tend to identify, either human sources, individuals, or groups subject (or not) to surveillance, or past or present members of or operational techniques of CSIS. Moreover, the judge feared that disclosure might jeopardize the security of CSIS's telecommunications or cypher systems, and that it would reveal the intensity of any investigation and its degree of success.[90]

In several other decisions the Canadian courts have refused to review denials of information based on these exemptions. Refusal of access to personal information contained in databanks held by CSIS has been upheld.[91] In the same case an argument based on the Charter of Rights also failed, with the court holding that the limitation in section 1 of the Charter enabled the government to refuse to say whether a file existed at all on the applicant. Muldoon J com-

---

[84] Although the office is seperate from the Information Commissioner, there is a common staff.
[85] In camera and *ex parte* hearings may be held in security cases: Privacy Act 1982, s. 51.
[86] Ibid., s. 18.   [87] Ibid., s. 36.   [88] Ibid., s. 43.   [89] Ibid., s. 23.
[90] *Henrie* v. *Canada* (1989) 53 DLR (4th) 568; and see pp. 314–17 below for discussion of the Canada Evidence Act.
[91] *Re Zanganeh and CSIS* (n. 82 above).

mented: 'some Canadians may shudder to realize that the security needs of a free and democratic society are, in a few basic essentials, much the same as those which totalitarian societies arrogate to themselves. Utter secrecy, subject to certain checks, in security intelligence matters is one.' However, he then went on to point to the safeguards provided through the jurisdiction of the Privacy Commissioner in such cases.[92]

Nevertheless, in theory, the jurisdiction of the courts to police the security exemptions to the Privacy Act has been enhanced by judicial interpretation. In an early case arising under the Act the Federal Court held that, despite the scheme giving the Privacy Commissioner access to exempt databanks, it too had jurisdiction to conduct an examination into whether a security file existed in the relevant databank and, if so, whether it contained predominantly information which was within the scope of the exemption.[93] The government's contention that the court had no jurisdiction to consider whether access was properly denied would, in the words of Strayer J, have left the Court with only the 'trivial and inconsequential function' of reading the exemption order and comparing it with the databank designation.[94] The decision is an important blow to the very concept of exempt banks and it is significant that, far from responding with legislation to repair the breach, the Canadian government has accepted the outcome and, under pressure from the Privacy Commissioner, the number of exempt banks has been steadily reduced.[95]

The judge in *Ternette* ordered that the RCMP (the predecessor in this instance of CSIS) provide confidential evidence to the court about whether there was information within the exempt databank on the applicant, to be considered at a later *in camera* hearing.[96] However, when the court had reviewed the file (which in the interim had been inadvertently admitted to exist), it upheld the denial of access, holding that there was no basis for finding that the refusal was not made on reasonable grounds.[97] Nevertheless, the history of the case shows the strengths of the Canadian procedures. The file to which Ternette was seeking access was one related to his allegedly subversive activities. Following repeated reviews of the file both by CSIS and by the Privacy Commissioner, 186 documents from his file were released in full, and a further seventy-eight documents with deletions. The remainder, for which exemption was sought, were reviewed by the court. The proceedings were conducted in part in open court (during which a CSIS witness was cross-examined on general matters), partly *in camera*,

---

[92] Ibid. 756–7.   [93] *Re Ternette and Solicitor-General of Canada* (1984) 10 DLR (4th) 587.
[94] Ibid. 595.

[95] By 1987 there were only five (out of an initial nineteen) exempt banks remaining: three at the Department of National Defence (Military Police Investigation files, on the Communications Security Establishment, and Intelligence Investigation files), at the Privy Council Office (Security and Intelligence files), and the RCMP (Criminal Intelligence Operational Records). The Privacy Commissioner found that a number of banks had been incorrectly exempted without any outside review of the files contents before designation *Privacy Commissioner Annual Report* 1987–88, 21.

[96] See n. 93 above, 598.   [97] *Ternette* v. *Canada* (1992) 86 DLR (4th) 281, 306.

and partly *ex parte* (that is, in the absence of the applicant and his representatives). The Privacy Commissioner was represented at the *ex parte* hearings, although her counsel declined the applicant's suggestion that he should act to represent the applicant's interests in his enforced absence from the proceedings. The court made clear that in the *ex parte* session it had received evidence about both the file keeping processes of CSIS and each individual document.

This procedure goes a long way towards reconciling secrecy with procedural fairness. It could be improved by providing express representation by independent, security-cleared counsel at the *ex parte* hearings. However, in view of the presence of representatives of the Privacy Commissioner to provide a dispassionate viewpoint, that might seem unduly adversarial. A second suggestion, made by the applicant but rejected by the court in *Ternette*, was that the government be ordered to provide a list, describing each document withheld and the specific ground relied on so that the applicant could make some representations about it.[98] Although Strayer J rejected the request that this information be supplied to the applicant, it should be noted that the CSIS affidavit admitted at the *ex parte* hearing did discuss the purported damage the release of each document would cause.[99]

A review of the Canadian legislation by a Parliamentary Committee has suggested a number of reforms.[100] A proposal that the whole concept of exempt databanks be abolished in view of their small number and dwindling significance in the light of the *Ternette* decision[101] has not been implemented. On the question of review by the Federal Court, the Committee argued that the Federal Court should be given the power to substitute its own judgment on whether a document should be released irrespective of the claimed ground for refusal of access.[102] This too was rejected by the government, which argued that executive responsibility for security was better protected through limiting the review to one of the reasonableness of the refusal.[103] There is no automatic correlation between the security classification of a document in Canada and the statutory exemptions.[104] This is perhaps surprising because since 1986 the grounds for security classification of documents have been identical to the language of the exemptions used in the Privacy Act and the Access to Information Act.[105] Information may be security classified if it falls into one of six areas: national

---

[98] A so-called Vaughn index, from the US freedom of information case in which the approach was first adopted: *Vaughn* v. *Rosen* 484 F.2d 820. A Vaughn Index has been used in the USA in security cases: *Roy* v. *Turner* 587 F.2d 1187.

[99] See n. 97 above, 306.

[100] *Open and Shut: Report of the Standing Committee on Justice and the Solicitor General on the Review of the Access to Information Act and the Privacy Act* (Ottawa, 1987).

[101] Ibid. 46–9.   [102] Ibid. 38–9.   [103] See n. 95 above, 22–3.

[104] *Open and Shut* (n. 100 above), 85–6; and see Rankin (n. 66 above), 275–9.

[105] Solicitor General's statement, *House of Commons Debates, 1st Sess. 33rd Parliament*, vol. 10, col. 14615 (18 June 1986); for critical discussion see S. Farson, 'Propriety, Efficiency and Balance: "A Preliminary Appraisal of Canada's "New", "Improved", Administrative Secrecy Program"', in P. Hanks and J. McCamus, *National Security, Surveillance and Accountability* (Cowansville, Que.,1989).

defence, national security (including hostile and subversive activities and threats to the country's security), confidences of Cabinet, federal–provincial affairs, and selected economic interests of Canada. As in Britain, security classification is related to the question of who in government, rather than outside it, is to allowed access—it is the life-blood of the vetting system.[106]

AUSTRALIA[107]

In Australia the freedom of information legislation (Freedom of Information Act 1982)[108] also contains similar exemptions which are relevant. Unlike the Canadian arrangements, key parts of the intelligence community are completely outside the legislation, rather than on a document-by-document or databank basis: ASIO and ASIS are wholly exempt from the Act.[109] The Senate Committee which considered the proposed legislation was divided over this approach. Some argued that if ASIO were subject to the Act it would prejudice its operational capability by deterring informants and opening it to disruption by 'excessive demands orchestrated by extreme groups'.[110] The opposing view was that some access should be allowed 'for the purpose of ensuring a degree of accountability and deterring, to some extent, the use of illegal methods and procedures'. The Act also contains an exemption applying to other agencies on grounds of national security. Documents are exempt where their disclosure would be contrary to the public interest because it could reasonably be expected to cause damage to the security, defence, or international relations of Australia, or where it would divulge information communicated in confidence by a foreign government or by an international organization (for instance, NATO).[111]

The pattern of review of refusal of access to a document follows a model in common use in Australian administrative law: the applicant will first ask the department concerned to reconsider ('internal review'), and if the refusal is confirmed may then apply to the Australian Administrative Tribunal (AAT),[112] which generally has powers under the Act to order disclosure.[113] However, the

---

[106] See Ch. 6 below.

[107] See P. Bayne, *Freedom of Information* (Sydney, 1984); Mark Aronsen and Nicola Franklin, *Review of Administrative Action* (Sydney, 1987), 290–2 and 349–53; Thomas (n. 65 above).

[108] As amended by the Freedom of Information Amendment Act 1983.

[109] Sched. 2, Pt. I. Documents originated by these agencies are also exempt in the hands of other government departments.

[110] *Freedom of Information, Report by the Senate Standing Committee on Constitutional and Legal Affairs on the Freedom of Information Bill 1978 and Aspects of the Archives Bill 1978*, para. 12.22. US experience suggests that intelligence agencies can be subject to relatively heavy and costly demands for access: in 1985 the CIA estimated that it spent '107 man years' in that year on processing FoI requests; in 1989 the FBI spent $14.5 m. on complying with the legislation: P. Birkinshaw, *Freedom of Information: The US Experience* (Hull, 1991), 23–4.

[111] Freedom of Information Act 1982, s. 33(1); other exemptions protect State–Commonwealth confidences (s. 33A(1) and Cabinet papers and records (s. 34).

[112] S. 55.   [113] S. 58.

minister may issue a conclusive certificate where the national security exemption is invoked, restricting review of the decision by the AAT.[114] In these cases the AAT refers to the Tribunal President the question of whether reasonable grounds exist for the claim.[115] Although this will appear unexceptionable to British readers, normally the AAT considers the merits rather than the reasonableness of a decision—the procedure represents, therefore, a dilution of the normal standard of review.[116] The provision of review by the AAT President is an attempt to preserve a more secure environment for sensitive issues to be determined.[117] The Tribunal is given power to inspect the document,[118] but hearings at which documents protected by a certificate are produced or arguments are addressed by the government or agency about the document are to be held in private.[119] The President does not have power to revoke the certificate,[120] but instead executive responsibility is preserved by limiting the power to one of non-binding recommendation to the minister. The minister then has twenty-eight days in which to decide whether to revoke the certificate:[121] if he decides to do so the document is released. Where he decides not to do so a political safeguard exists in a requirement to notify not only the applicant but also both Houses of Parliament.[122]

As in Canada, the exemptions purportedly operate in isolation from the system of security classification of documents, although critics argued that bureaucrats would tend in practice to undermine the spirit of the legislation by automatically claiming conclusive exemption for all classified documents.[123] However, the wording of section 33(1) corresponds to that controlling the designation of documents as 'Classified'.[124]

Mention should also be made of the Australian equivalent to the Public Record Act, the Archives Act 1983, the provisions of which have prompted a continuing debate about historical access to ASIO records. In general the Act provides for the transfer of Commonwealth files to the Archives after twenty-five years and for public access after thirty years.[125] The records of ASIO and all other Australian intelligence agencies are exempt from transfer,[126] with the effect that the agencies retain control of these files. However, under the public access provisions narrower exemptions attach to the individual files, rather than on an agency basis.[127] Records are exempt if they include information the disclosure of which 'could reasonably be expected to cause damage to the security,

---

[114] S. 33(2).   [115] S. 58(4) as amended.

[116] The Senate Committee had wanted the review to take the form of an appeal on the question of whether the document was one which could cause damage if released, but not on the question of whether it should be released in the public interest (n. 110 above), 195.

[117] Originally the legislation provided for these questions to stand referred to a Documents Review Tribunal, s. 58(4), 66, and 67 repealed.

[118] S. 58E.   [119] S. 58C.   [120] S. 58(3) as amended.   [121] S. 58A(1).

[122] S. 58A(3).   [123] See Senate Standing Committee (n. 110 above), 187.

[124] Following the recommendation of the Senate Committee (n. 110 above), 188–9.

[125] Archives Act 1983, ss. 27 and 3(7), respectively.   [126] Ibid., s. 29(8).

[127] Contrast the freedom of information legislation (n. 109 above).

defence or international relations of the Commonwealth'.[128] A pattern of review (and comparable restrictions) similar to those applicable under the Freedom of Information Act operates in such cases. A conclusive ministerial certificate may be issued[129] which has the effect of limiting the basis of an appeal to the AAT against a refusal based upon the exemption to considerations of reasonableness.[130] Parliament must be notified if the minister decides not to follow a recommendation of the AAT that the claim of exemption is unreasonable.[131]

Although it might be thought that these conditions are not unduly onerous ones to apply to files that are thirty years old, ASIO has, nevertheless, maintained a steady barrage of criticism in its annual reports at being subject to the legislation, with the result that the first act of the Australian Parliamentary Joint Committee was an investigation of its operation.[132] The Joint Committee rejected ASIO's arguments for exemption from the legislation or for a fifty-year closure period, but recommended that security concerns could be met by extending the closure period in the case of intelligence files by delaying the running of the thirty years until the death of the relevant operative, agent or source.[133] On the other hand, changes were proposed to bring greater independence into the review process: conclusive certificates should lapse after three years, and the Inspector-General of Intelligence and Security should be involved in the review of refusals of access.[134] Whilst noting the diversion of resources involved in ASIO's compliance with the legislation, the Committee believed that these difficulties should be dealt with by increased government funding and the establishment of a specialist Archives Unit within ASIO rather than by restricting rights of access.[135] These proposals will mainly be of interest to historians and researchers trying to establish the record of ASIO during the crucial post-war period of Australian history.[136] However, one interesting proposal has a more direct contemporary relevance. The Committee also recommended that an individual concerned about potential inaccuracy on a personal file held by ASIO should be able to raise this matter with the Inspector-General, who might in turn bring it to the attention of ASIO, without confirming to the individual the existence of any such file.[137]

---

[128] Archives Act 1983, s. 33(1)(*a*).   [129] Ibid., s. 34.

[130] Ibid., 44(5).   [131] Ibid., s. 45.

[132] Report of the Joint Parliamentary Committee on the Australian Security Intelligence Organization, *ASIO and the Archives Act: The Effect on ASIO of the Operation of the Archives Act* (Canberra, 1992), ch. 1. On the work of the Committee see further below, pp. 455–8.

[133] Ibid. 28. Cf. p. 32 above.   [134] Ibid. 45.   [135] Ibid. 52.

[136] For an evaluation of the report by a historian see: F. Cain, 'The Right to Know: ASIO, Historians and the Australian Parliament'. (1993) 8 *Int. & NS* 87.

[137] See n. 132 above, 55; the proposal is modelled on a practice adopted by the Canadian Privacy Commissioner.

REFORM

This is not the place to canvass general arguments for or against the introduction of legislation giving freedom of information or wider access to personal files in the United Kingdom. The government has recently rejected the former while allowing only a modest approach (predictably not in the security realm) to the latter. Instead, it has proposed a weak substitute: a Code of Practice on Government Information policed by the Parliamentary Commissioner for Administration.[138] It is clear, however, that if *legislation* were introduced it would inevitably contain exemptions covering issues such as national security, defence, foreign policy, telephone tapping, and the detection and prevention of crime. The important questions would be what form the exemptions took and what review or appeal mechanisms were established.[139]

The most generous forms of exemption to the executive are those exempting whole departments or agencies ('agency exemptions'), and those excluding all documents within a designated policy area ('class exemptions'). The narrowest are those which require a specific claim that the individual document would harm a designated interest ('contents exemptions'). The exemption of ASIO and ASIS under the Australian legislation are instances of agency exemptions. The Canadian legislation contains instances both of class exemptions and a variant, lying somewhere between an agency and class exemption, the exempt databank. In Australia the exemptions for matters such as defence are contents exemptions. While the agency- and class-exemptions approaches have on their side administrative convenience and symmetry, particularly in instances where the majority of information is sensitive, the danger is that they effectively pre-empt consideration of whether any information can be released.[140] We prefer the Canadian exempt databanks approach to the wholesale exemption of bodies like MI5 and MI6. However, apart from the intelligence and security agencies, other departments should, in our view, be subject to contents exemptions, although

---

[138] See n. 7 above, Annex 1. The Code would apply to bodies covered by the Ombudsman's jurisdiction (Parliamentary Commissioner Act 1967, sched. 2), hence the intelligence agencies will be exempt. Other departments will be able to claim the benefit of exemptions including those for: information whose disclosure would (or could reasonably be expected to) harm defence, security, and international relations, internal discussion and advice, prosecutions and the administration of justice, and personnel records (including security vetting). For discussion of the proposals see: P. Birkinshaw, "'I only ask for information"—the White Paper on Open Government', [1993] *PL* 557.

[139] We refer below to the provisions of the most recent serious attempt to introduce freedom of information in the UK: the unsuccessful Right to Know Bill 1992–3 (introduced by Mark Fisher, MP, hereafter the Fisher Bill). This Private Member's Bill passed its second reading in the House of Commons on 19 Feb. 1993 (*HC Debs.*, vol. 219, cols. 583 ff.).

[140] Contrast the government's position: 'The Government believes that information should in general be protected only where its release would cause, or be likely to cause, actual harm; but sees no merit introducing access rights in respect of categories of information which are so sensitive as to be largely secret in nature.' (n. 7 above, para. 3.7).

quite exceptionally (for instance in the case of wartime operation planning), there may be a case for class exemptions.[141]

The prerequisites for a system of review of refusal of access to a document are that it should be independent; easy, quick, and cheap to use; secure in its procedures for dealing with sensitive information; procedurally fair both to the government and the citizen; and binding in its determinations. To some extent these are conflicting objectives: for example, while it would be possible to devise a procedure for review of a refusal by a High Court judge, this would elevate independence and procedural fairness so far above accessibility and cheapness that it could be guaranteed to deter all but the most persistent and wealthy of claimants from ever appealing. This is quite apart from the procedural convolutions that would be necessary for allowing fair adversarial argument to a claimant in countering a claim for exemption in part based on secret perceptions of the public interest. The other possibilities are review by an ombudsman-type figure[142] or by a specialist tribunal, or the first followed by an appeal to the second. An ombudsman has the advantage that the procedure can be inquisitorial, specialist, and requires little expertise to use: once an appeal was made the ombudsman would take the case up, investigate it, and issue a determination of whether the exemption was made out. The ombudsman could also have a pro-active role in advising government and individuals about use of the legislation and a duty to keep it under overall review. This would be a brief similar to that of the Canadian Information and Privacy Commissioners. However, such a procedure, in which an impartial individual goes behind the veil of government on the citizen's behalf, is weaker on procedural fairness. For that reason it would be best if an appeal was possible against the finding of the ombudsman to a tribunal. The tribunal would have the advantage of having access to the inquisitorial findings of the ombudsman but allowing representations by the government and the citizen in a more adversarial way than the ombudsman procedure.[143] Although most cases would be resolved at the lower level, the tribunal would build up specialist expertise and procedures for approaching access questions and would be a prime source of interpretation for controversial aspects of the legislation. The practice of the Canadian Federal Court in the *Ternette* litigation[144]

---

[141] The Fisher Bill (n. 139 above) contained exemptions where disclosure was likely to cause '*significant damage*' to defence (cl. 15), to the *lawful activities* of the security and intelligence agencies (cl. 16) or to the interests of the UK in the conduct of international relations (cl. 17). These took the form of contents, rather than agency, exemptions. However, the exemptions were overridden in the public interest if the benefits of disclosure outweighed the probable damage on various grounds (including evidence of significant abuse of authority, injustice to an individual, and unauthorized use of public funds): cl. 30. The Bill also contained protections from employment disciplinary measures for 'whistleblowers' (cl. 66).

[142] We have in mind an independent officer with coercive and binding powers, something far removed from the British Parliamentary Commissioner.

[143] The Fisher Bill (n. 139 above) proposed the creation of a Commissioner, to receive individual complaints and to report on the implementation of the legislation, and a Tribunal, with both an original and an appellate jurisdiction.

[144] See nn. 97 ff. above.

offers a possible model of good practice for the tribunal. If necessary, a limited appeal on a point of law to the High Court could be available or judicial review would extend to the tribunal's procedures.

There is no prospect that proposals like these will be implemented in Britain in the near future. However, simply to state the prerequisites for an independent and fair procedure is to demonstrate the weakness of what currently exists.

6

Employment and Security Vetting

The United Kingdom, in common with other Western states, found it necessary to introduce comprehensive national security controls and exemptions in its employment law in the post-war period to counter a perceived espionage threat arising from infiltration of sensitive positions by foreign intelligence agencies and other groups. The measures taken involve both pre-employment screening of applicants and periodic reassessment of the security clearance of those already employed. These practices are by no means limited to employees working in the defence- and intelligence-related parts of government. Large numbers of state employees working in other departments are affected, particularly if they are of sufficient seniority to have access to classified information. The British obsession with restricting access to information about the working of government inevitably has carried with it broad personnel security measures. The world view which saw Communism as an international conspiracy to gain influence was also capable of justifying similiar controls in what, constitutionally speaking, are non-governmental independent bodies such as the BBC, the Atomic Energy Authority, and British Telecom, on the grounds that their strategic importance made them obvious candidates for infiltration. The private sector has also been significantly affected because of controls extended to it to protect work carried out by defence contractors. In strictly quantitative terms these arrangements directly affect more people than any others discussed in this book; according to Linn, employment vetting on security grounds is applied to at least three-quarters of a million people.[1]

Employment relationships are regulated by the contractual arrangements between the employer and employees, but are subject to fundamental statutory rights which will be read into and override the contractual arrangements on such questions as unfair dismissal and protection from racial and sexual discrimination. Employment law is also concerned with the collective enforcement of rights by trade unions and therefore governs both the freedom to join a trade union and the legitimate limits of collective action. National security appears in an employment context partly as an exception to this statutory floor of rights. Although the relationship between private sector employers and employees is

---

[1] I. Linn, *Application Refused: Employment Vetting by the State* (London, 1990), 19. For other accounts of vetting see M. Hollingsworth and R. Norton-Taylor, *Blacklist: The Inside Story of Political Vetting* (London, 1988), introduction and chs. 1 and 2 ; S. Fredman and G. S. Morris, *The State as Employer* (London, 1989), 232–6. However, all these accounts should be read in light of the 1990 revisions discussed below.

contractual in nature, the dominant economic position of government allows it to insist on the inclusion of its own security requirements in such contracts as a pre-condition of the award of defence-related work. Such requirements are legislative in effect if not in name.

With these general introductory observations in mind this chapter will first consider the context in which employment restrictions operate in the public and private sectors. We then discuss the development of vetting, the procedures involved, and the administrative and legal entitlements to challenge adverse decisions, both domestically and under the European Convention on Human Rights. Finally we compare the position with the analogous, and more satisfactory, Canadian and Australian procedures, and set out proposals for reform.

THE CONTEXT OF SECURITY RESTRICTIONS

In so far as vetting was introduced against a background of political restrictions in the civil service in the name of ensuring political impartiality, it may appear merely as an extension of an established tradition.[2] Traditionally the British civil service has perceived itself to be politically neutral and was, therefore, concerned to preserve appearances by controls on the political activities of civil servants, whilst remaining unconcerned with their personal beliefs. Broad loyalty to the state was presumed from citizenship, hence restrictions were imposed limiting appointments to British citizens.[3] The one notable historical exception to this approach to some extent prefigures political vetting, namely the imposition of religious tests, dating from an age when religious nonconformity was seen to be deeply subversive of the existing order and of the very structure of the state.[4]

However, several differences of emphasis should be noted. The purpose of vetting is to attempt to exclude the disloyal or those considered prone for various reasons to disloyalty, not those who appear to lack the necessary impartial public stance. The archetypal 'mole' or 'sleeper' insinuated into the public service would not be someone whose public activities would give rise to doubts. Whereas the restrictions on political activity are concerned with the manifestation rather than the substance of the political views held by the civil servant, vetting may punish opinions *per se*—on the assumption that those holding certain opinions lack the necessary commitment to the existing constitutional order.

---

[2] A fairly detailed list of restrictions on the political activities of civil servants (who for these purposes are divided according to grade into restricted, intermediate, and unrestricted classes) has been operative since 1953 when the White Paper *The Political Activities of Civil Servants*, Cmd. 8783 (1953) was introduced (partly implementing the recommendations of the Masterman Committee, Cmd. 7718 (1949)). The current restrictions are based on modifications proposed by the Armitage Committee (*Committee on the Political Activities of Civil Servants*), Cmnd. 7057 (1978).

[3] Act of Settlement 1700, s. 3; Aliens Restiction (Amendment) Act 1919 (as amended by Aliens Employment Act 1955, s. 1); Army Act 1955, s. 21; Air Force Act 1955, s. 21.

[4] See further below, pp. 203–5. St John Robilliard, *Religion and the Law* (Manchester, 1984), App. describes the progressive removal of religious disabilities.

The system of vetting of public servants excludes those whose views are inconsistent with parliamentary democracy, rather than requiring a positive demonstration of allegiance. A further distinction should be drawn between restrictions on political activities and vetting. Whereas the former are most concerned with those in contact with ministers and with the public (since it is here that the appearance of impartiality is vital), vetting is driven by the need for secrecy. In cases where ministers are involved with high-level and often confidential policy, the civil servants involved may be the same ones, but this is not always so. The filing clerk at the Ministry of Defence may raise acute problems of secrecy whereas the Permanent Secretary (for instance) at the Ministry of Agriculture may raise none related to security.[5]

In addition to these restrictions on public sector employees many restrictions on employment justified by reason of national security operate in the private sector also. For instance, this applies to arrangements for vetting, to the exclusion of unfair dismissal legislation by ministerial certificate,[6] and to various offences under the Official Secrets Act 1989 which may be committed in relation to government contractors.[7] Where the private sector is concerned the government is not (as it is with the civil service) in the anomalous position of being both employer and defender of national security. However, the peculiar circumstances under which the defence sector (where most of these restrictions apply in practice) operates are of importance in understanding their significance.

There are several aspects of the defence industry which give it importance in security terms. The most obvious is the military secrecy surrounding some of the research, development, and production work undertaken by defence contractors. This is the immediate justification for the extension of employment restrictions into the private sector. However the macro-economic and strategic importance of the defence industries should not be underestimated, because of the size of the defence budget. Governments regularly face a choice between economy and other considerations (such as preventing regional unemployment or preserving the viability of a UK defence contractor) in decisions about defence procurement: the debates in 1993 about the future of Swan Hunter Shipbuilders and the naval dockyards at Plymouth and Rosyth are but the latest examples. The European Community recognizes such considerations by allowing protectionism towards domestic industries for reasons of national security as exceptions to the general rules on competition policy and forbidding state aids.[8]

---

[5] G. Cunningham, 'Vetting Investigation and Interrogations', in A. Gale (ed.), *The Polygraph Test: Truth, Lies and Science* (London, 1988), 42.

[6] Employment Protection (Consolidation) Act 1978, s. 138(4).

[7] e.g. ss. 2–4, and 8; on the scope of these offences see Ch. 9 below. 'Government contractor' is defined in s. 12(2).

[8] Art. 223(1)(*b*) EEC Treaty allows Member States to take measures for the protection of security which are connected with the production of or trade in arms, ammunition, or war materials provided they do not adversely affect competition in non-military products: see R. Whish *Competition Law* (3nr edn., London, 1993), 355.

The formal device by which state controls are imposed on private sector employers is by incorporating appropriate terms in defence contracts.[9] By such means the Ministry of Defence can, for instance, compel the dismissal or veto the employment by private companies of individuals about whom it entertains security doubts.[10] These practices do not cease to have constitutional significance because they are contractual in form. Daintith has argued persuasively that governments as frequently use their control on expenditure to rule as they do formal lawmaking: the former he calls *dominium* in contrast to *imperium*.[11]

Indeed, the defence sector is so highly regulated that to describe it as part of the 'private sector' bargaining with government through contracts is to strain the concepts intolerably: this regulation of the 'private' sector in defence matters even extends to control by committee of the rate of profit under defence procurement contracts.[12] Such arrangements are an almost inevitable outcome of the economic conditions under which defence manufacturing takes place: in particular, the very high research and development costs on defence projects restrict competition and the political and diplomatic interest in the supply (or preventing the supply) of armaments to other possible buyers. In these circumstances there has developed in Britain a defence sector in which a handful of major companies supply one customer. To contrast these arrangements with the 'public' sector is clearly somewhat artificial, whatever the legal form of the network of relationships between government, employer, and employee.

THE ORIGINS AND DEVELOPMENT OF VETTING

The origins of state employment vetting in the international ice age is not merely a matter of chronology: its roots lie there in ideological and diplomatic terms also. The latter is the hardest to document since the contents of the international agreements between Britain, the United States, Australia, Canada, and New Zealand based upon post-war co-operation in nuclear energy and weaponry and signals intelligence remain secret.[13] However it has been reliably asserted

---

[9] See *First Report from the Select Committee on Defence, Session 1982–1983, Positive Vetting Procedures in Her Majesty's Services and the Ministry of Defence* HC (1982–3) 242 and the Radcliffe Report (Cmnd. 1681, 1962), ch. 7.

[10] The *cause célèbre* was the dismissal of ICI's assistant solicitor John Lang in 1956 because the government had refused to place further contracts with the firm unless he was prevented from seeing them: *HL Debs.*, vol. 197, cols. 1226 ff. (21 June 1956); for an instance of refusal of employment in the private sector following vetting see the *Nimmo* case (n. 110 below).

[11] T. Daintith, 'Regulation by Contract: The New Prerogative' [1979] *Current Legal Problems* 41; J. Jowell and D. Oliver, *The Changing Constitution* (Oxford, 1985), ch. 8. This is part of the wider phenomenon of corporatism, which in this context is no less prevalent now than in 1979: P. Birkinshaw, I. Harden, and N. Lewis, *Government by Moonlight* (London, 1990).

[12] C. Turpin, *Government Procurement and Contracts* (Harlow, 1989), 163–6; I. Harden and N. Lewis, *The Noble Lie* (London, 1986), 177–8. G. Kennedy, *The Economics of Defence* (London, 1975), 126–33.

[13] J. T. Richelson and D. Ball, *The Ties That Bind*, 2nd edn. (Sydney, 1990) describes intelligence co-operation in the UKUSA alliance.

that the introduction of the purge procedure in Britain in 1946 was a direct result of American pressure following the exposure as a Soviet agent of the atomic scientist Alan Nunn May.[14] It is easier to trace the ideological pedigree of vetting through the official accounts. The post-war spy scandals demonstrated clearly that the normal assumptions about loyalty from nationality (and more informally) background were quite unequal to the threat posed to Western public and defence agencies by ideologically motivated espionage.

The initial purge was aimed at communists (and, ostensibly, at fascists) in key designated posts, on the avowed ground that their loyalty to the Communist Party might, for some, conflict with loyalty to the public service. Since there was no way of distinguishing potentially disloyal Communists from those who were not, all were to be removed from sensitive posts. Where transfer to other suitable, non-sensitive work proved impracticable, they would be dismissed.[15] Not surprisingly the purge procedure has been regarded as of dwindling importance since Positive Vetting has been applied to new entrants to sensitive posts in the civil service for more than thirty years.

Positive Vetting (PV) was introduced in 1952 initially to protect a small number of posts dealing with highly classified information, supposedly that connected with the atomic energy programme.[16] The purpose was to attempt 'positively' to confirm the reliability of those to whom it was applied. Initially unreliability was to be deduced from membership of the Communist Party or a fascist organisation or from a civil servant's association with such bodies in such a way as to raise legitimate doubts. The Conference of Privy Councillors on Security (established following the disappearance of Burgess and Maclean) confirmed the view that ideological communism was the major security threat, but emphasized that 'character defects' (drunkenness, drug addiction, homosexuality, and 'loose living') could seriously affect an individual's reliability by exposing him or her either to blackmail or to the influence of foreign agents. Accordingly the guidelines introduced following the Report categorized as unreliables not only members of the Communist Party but also anyone who 'in such a way as to raise reasonable doubts about his reliability, is or has been recently sympathetic to Communism, associated with Communists or Communist sympathizers or is susceptible to Communist pressure'.[17]

When the Radcliffe Committee examined security procedures in 1962 follow-

[14] P. Hennessy and G. Brownfield, 'Britain's Cold War Security Purge: the Origins of Positive Vetting', (1982), 25 *Hist. J.* 965–73. However, later research has shown that the antecedents of this programme were put in place in the 1930s: see L. Hannant, 'Inter-war Security Screening in Britain, the United States and Canada' (1991) 6 *Int. & NS* 711, 713–17.

[15] *HC Debs.*, vol. 448, cols. 1703–8 (15 Mar. 1948).

[16] The definitive official accounts are: *Security Procedures in the Public Service*, Cmnd. 1681 (1962) (hereafter 'the Radcliffe Report'); the *Statement on the Recommendations of the Security Commission*, Cmnd. 8540 (1982) and (in relation to the Ministry of Defence and government contractors) *First Report from the Select Committee on Defence* (n. 9 above).

[17] *Statement on the Findings of the Conference of Privy Councillors on Security*, Cmnd. 9715 (1956), paras. 4–10; *HC Debs.*, vol. 563, cols. 151–2 (29 Jan. 1957).

ing the Blake case, it did not recommend any change of substance to these grounds, although it was sceptical of the security value of the evidence obtained (especially with regard to character defects) by Positive Vetting.[18] However, an oblique reference in the Committee's description of the procedure involved made clear that the check made with Security Service files would reveal adverse information not simply about communist association or sympathies but also about 'other forms of subversive activity'.[19] Some twenty years later a further major review was carried out by the Security Commission. It is plain that in the intervening period Communist Party membership or association had come to be regarded as simply one species of a genus 'subversion'. Indeed the statement summarizing the Commission's recommendations justified the shift of emphasis in terms, pointing to the: 'proliferation of new subversive groups of the extreme left and extreme right (mainly the former) whose aim is to overthrow democratic parliamentary government in this country by violent or other unconstitutional means . . .'[20] Somewhat alarmingly, the Commission apparently saw no cause for concern in the implications for civil liberties of the creeping definition of subversion. The trend was confirmed by a 1985 Statement of Procedure issued by the Prime Minister which talked of membership of 'a communist or fascist organisation, or of a subversive group, acknowledged as such by the Minister, whose aims are to undermine or overthrow Parliamentary democracy in the United Kingdom of Great Britain and Northern Ireland by political, industrial or violent means'.[21]

THE NEW VETTING GUIDELINES

Against this background, the revised policy on vetting announced in July 1990[22] would appear to mark a significant change of emphasis in security effort. The new grounds state that:

no one should be employed in connection with work the nature of which is vital to the security of the state who:

(*a*) is, or has been, involved in, or associated with any of the following activities threatening national security:

(i) espionage,

(ii) terrorism,

(iii) sabotage,

(iv) actions intended to overthrow or undermine Parliamentary democracy by political, industrial or violent means; or

---

[18] See n. 16 above, paras. 62–3 and 69.   [19] Ibid., para. 12.

[20] Cmnd. 8540, para. 4.

[21] Referred to at *HC Debs.*, vol. 76, col. 617 (3 Apr. 1985). For the text see: National Council for Civil Liberties, *The Purging of the Civil Service* (London, 1985), app. B and Linn (n. 1 above), app. II.

[22] *HC Debs.*, vol. 177, cols. 159–61w (24 July 1990).

(*b*) is, or has recently been, a member of any organisation which has advocated such activities; or

(*c*) is, or recently has been, associated with any such organisation, or any of its members, in such a way as to raise reasonable doubts about his or her reliability; or

(*d*) is susceptible to pressure from any such organisation or from a foreign intelligence service or hostile power; or

(*e*) suffers from defects of character which may expose him or her to blackmail or other influence by any such organisation or by a foreign intelligence service or which may otherwise indicate unreliability.

The grounds represent a broadening and rationalization of national-security concerns in relation to vetting. Overt mention of communism and fascism has been expunged (although these could still fall within (*a*)(iv)), and instead the activites catalogued in paragraph (*a*) mirror closely the threats to national security to be regarded by the Security Service.[23] The formal inclusion of terrorism, espionage, and sabotage (none of which is defined)[24] in the list is a change of form but scarcely one of content, since there can be little doubt that association with such activities would have been clear evidence of disloyalty or unreliability under the previous criteria. However, when taken with the new levels of vetting (discussed below) it does represent a greater emphasis on physical security of premises and people rather than on the prevention of long-term infiltration of government departments. It should be noted, though, that the grounds are in the main extended rather than curtailed. The core definition of subversion and association with it remains, although sympathy with and association with those sympathetic to subversion (mentioned in the Prime Minister's 1985 Statement) have been deleted. In view of the vagueness of the concepts of subversion and of association in the first place, it would be premature to claim that this represents a significant loosening of attitudes.

The major change announced in the Statement is a new classification of different levels of security vetting for different purposes. Five different bands are enumerated. However, it is plain that there is sufficient flexibility to enable *ad hoc* (designer?) vetting for particular posts—especially so at the lower levels. The critical determinant of the level of vetting is the level of access to information or premises. Hence vetting remains inextricably wedded to the system for the classification of documents, notwithstanding its semi-official status (there is no necessary connection with offences under the Official Secrets Act 1989),[25] and the obvious dangers of idiosyncratic or over-classification. There is, however, a

---

[23] SSA, s. 1(2). Additionally MI5 is charged with investigating threats to the 'economic well-being' of the UK; ibid., s. 1(3). See further Ch. 14 below.

[24] A definition of terrorism may be found in the Prevention of Terrorism (Temporary Provisions) Act 1989, s. 20. Non-statutory definitions of the latter two terms may be found in the Home Office guidelines which govern the work of Special Branches: *Fourth Report from the Home Affairs Select Committee 1984–85*, HC 71 (1984–5); and see Ch. 14 below.

[25] The government argued against any linkage in its White Paper, *Reform of Section 2 of the Official Secrets Act 1911*, Cm. 406 (June 1988), para. 76. See pp. 110–11 above.

break from this approach at the lower level, with the introduction of two new checks (Reliability and Counter-Terrorist Checks), which are to be applied 'irrespective of the degree of access to classified information'.

At the highest level is Enhanced Positive Vetting (EPV), which applies to members of the intelligence and security services and those staff employed on closely associated work in government departments.[26] EPV comprises not merely departmental, criminal, security, and credit-worthiness checks but also in-depth interviews with the applicant and home and work acquaintances. The next level—PV(TS)—is applicable to those with regular and constant access to information classified Top Secret and, on a discretionary basis, to certain others. These include diplomats posted overseas, members of the police service with access to Special Branch information, departmental security officers, and ancillary staff working for the intelligence and security services. The checks carried out are the same as those for EPV, but at a lesser depth. For access to Secret material clearance at level PV(S) is required. PV(S) may also be applied to individuals who do not yet have access to Secret material, but whose promotion would otherwise be jeopardized without such clearance. It involves a check with departmental and criminal records and those of the Security Service and Special Branch. PV(S) may be augmented by further enquiries, including an interview with the applicant as necessary. Although the statement provides no indication of numbers of employees affected, presumably these three levels of vetting encompass the 68,000 positively vetted posts identified by the Security Commission in 1981.[27]

The remaining two levels of clearance (Reliability and Counter-Terrorist checks) are an extension of the officially acknowledged practice and amount to an admission of the existence of 'Normal Vetting'. This process, akin to the Purge, is said to involve a check on the applicant's files (if any) held by Special Branch and MI5 made without informing the applicant and without supporting field enquiries.[28] A recent investigation by the Home Affairs Select Committee confirmed that normal vetting, involving a check on police criminal records, was taking place on a massive scale.[29] The 1990 Statement regularizes these unofficial practices. Although in their basic form Reliability and Counter-Terrorist Checks are less intensive than the varieties of Positive Vetting, they will be applied to a much larger number of people. The Select Committee was surprised to discover that nearly 1 per cent of the population (508,942 checks) was the

[26] The special status of these officers is also recognized in the specific offence governing all disclosure of information by them: Official Secrets Act 1989, s. 1. However, a Home Office official informed us that officers in that department working closely with the Security Service are not at the present time to be subject to EPV.

[27] In 1983 the government informed the Council of Civil Service Unions that there were 41,000 posts subject to PV in the civil service.

[28] For earlier allegations of such a practice see Hollingsworth and Norton-Taylor (n. 1 above), 24–5 and Linn (n.1 above), 18–20.

[29] *Third Report from the Home Affairs Committee 1989/90*, HC 285 (1989–90).

subject of enquiries by government agencies to the National Identification Bureau 'for the protection of national security' in 1989 alone.[30] Reliability checks are applicable to individuals who have unescorted access to premises in which highly classified information is held; this could include cleaners, porters, night security staff, and office equipment servicers and fitters. They are also applicable to individuals with access to categories of confidential information mainly relating to defence and foreign affairs. Reliability checks involve a criminal record check; presumably the major interest will be in recorded offences of dishonesty. The statement is chary about what is involved in Counter-Terrorist checks except to state that 'criminal record information may also be taken into account'. However, since the purpose is to search for any connections with or vulnerability to terrorist organizations in the cases of those with access to public figures or sensitive establishments, presumably it involves a limited check with Special Branch files and, possibly, those of the Security Service. Otherwise it is hard to see how any terrorist connections would be revealed. Whereas in the past Normal Vetting has taken place without the individual concerned being made aware, in future he or she is to be told and asked to complete a security questionnaire, thus providing the necessary personal details.

THE PROCESS OF VETTING[31]

Governments concerned about espionage, sabotage, subversion, and terrorism will naturally try to identify persons predisposed (whether voluntarily or under pressure) to such activities and ban them from access to protected matter and places. How such proclivities can be spotted with any tolerable degree of certainty is anything but obvious, so those conducting vetting have had to fall back on factors of varying reliability. These include, or have included at various times, criminal or discreditable personal conduct (because threat of disclosure might leave a person open to blackmail); large debt or other economic pressure that would make payment for breach of security particularly tempting; family members living in a foreign country deemed hostile to the United Kingdom, or otherwise vulnerable to pressure by a hostile state or organization such as the IRA; alcohol or drug abuse; 'assimilation' (for those of foreign origin); psychological inadequacies of various kinds relating to the inability to work in conditions of tension and secrecy; and most dubiously (under the heading of 'subversion'), political attitudes or peaceful activities that those in authority dislike.

The weighting of any of these factors at a given time is dependent on the

---

[30] Ibid., para. 16. An explanation of the figure is contained in the government's response: Cm. 1163 (July 1990).

[31] This section draws heavily upon an interview with Mr S. R. Davie, Principal Establishment and Finance Officer, Cabinet Office, and Mr Hugh Taylor, Secretary to the Security Commission, conducted on 12 Dec. 1990. All direct quotations are taken from this interview.

current perception of risks and probabilities. For instance, in the early 1980s there were complaints that the vetting process was giving undue and illegitimate emphasis to inquiring into applicants' political views.[32] All indicators suggest now that counter-subversion is no longer a major area of concern likely to prompt detailed scrutiny of political attitudes, although subversive activities remain a bar and it is not unforseeable that it could be extended in future (say) to views such as radical Muslim fundamentalism. At present, however, the factor which weighs most heavily is economic difficulty—a reflection of the lessons drawn from a series of American spy cases of the 1980s, all of which involved financial inducements, and an ironic recognition of the deterioration of pay levels in the civil service during that period. Homosexuality still creates difficulties, despite long-standing legalization and the avowed removal of an absolute bar for vetting purposes: as the unfortunate Mr Hodges learned, honesty can still exact a high price.[33] The increased emphasis on physical security—matters like the whereabouts and movements of ministers and the vulnerability of government buildings to bombs—has led to the extension of vetting to enterprises and people not previously covered, notably building contractors. The problem has an inescapable ethnic dimension, for the building trade, particularly in London, is notoriously heavily Irish. Although the officials interviewed were at pains to emphasize that being Irish or of Irish descent is not of itself a suspect characteristic, it seems that more people of that background will be caught up in the process than ever before.

Several distinct sources of information converge in the making of vetting decisions. Depending on the level of vetting, information will be available from: personnel records, a questionnaire completed by the person concerned, interviews with family, friends, and referees, MI5 and Special Branch files, and financial and medical data. Decisions about individuals' clearance are made by each ministry on the basis of the information supplied. It has been a strong feature of the British approach to security to encourage each department to take responsibility to counter the danger that would otherwise be left to specialists.[34]

The security questionnaire enjoys a prominent and perhaps symbolic place in the information-gathering process. It provides basic information which may then be followed up in other checks and in some instances by interview. Under the new vetting arrangements the questionnaires in use progress in length and intru-

---

[32] For criticism see Ch. 14 below. See also Linn (n. 1 above), 29–31 and Hollingsworth and Norton-Taylor (n. 1 above), ch. 2. For an official account of the propriety of some questions about political attitudes (but disavowing those referring to herself) see Mrs Thatcher's answer at *HC Debs.*, vol. 72, cols. 386–7w (4 February 1985).

[33] See n. 65 below. The Security Commission recommended that openly acknowledged homosexuality should not generally act as a bar to security clearance (except in the Diplomatic Service and in the armed forces): (n. 16 above), para. 5. In July 1991 the government lifted the ban in respect of most diplomats serving overseas: *The Times*, 24 July 1991.

[34] See the Radcliffe Report (n. 16 above), para. 13.

siveness the higher the level of vetting. Those for the Reliability and Counter-Terrorism checks merely request details of nationality, residence, marital status, overseas employment or residence, convictions, and brief details of partners and parents. The questionnaires for vetting to the levels of Secret, Top Secret, and Enhanced Positive Vetting ask for fuller details of education and employment and (perhaps optimistically) ask the applicant to give details of involvement or association with terrorism, sabotage, or subversion and other circumstances or characteristics which might affect suitablity for secret work. The questionnaires for PV(TS) and EPV ask for details of visits to and relatives who have lived in communist or former communist countries, for character referees (four in the case of EPV), and for medical history and access to the applicant's doctor (coupled with a warning that refusal may lead to refusal or withdrawal of security clearance).[35] The EPV questionnaire also manifests an interest in other relatives (partner's parents, brothers and sisters, children), those living at the same address, contacts with nationals of communist or former communist countries, and all visits abroad since the age of 14. Questionnaires to be completed on reviews of vetting are less intensive, merely asking for information where changes have occurred. Each questionnaire contains on its face a clear summary of vetting policy and of the other checks which will be made, but no indication of the procedures for review of an adverse decision.

Following completion of the questionnaire an interview will be held with the applicant in the case of posts requiring PV(TS) and EPV and may be held with those for PV(S) posts. The interviews are, in the case of most departments, conducted by field investigators from the Personnel Security Investigation Unit (PSIU) housed in the Ministry of Defence. However, the Security Service, GCHQ, and MI6 carry out their own field investigation. Concern has been expressed about these interviews in the past, partly on account of the restricted background of the interviewing officers (who are predominantly male retired police or service personnel) and partly because of the pattern of questioning of political beliefs (including previous voting habits) and sexuality.[36] Clearly, in a system so dependent on subjective assessments of character, attitude, and risk, the field investigator will enjoy a critical place and the unrepresentative character of the people involved is cause for concern.[37]

The one attempt in recent years to replace the human factor in this process with technology—by introducing the polygraph (or lie-detector)—foundered amid considerable controversy. A ministerial written answer, in response to an

[35] See Linn (n. 1 above), 15.   [36] See n. 32 above.

[37] cf. McDonald Commission (Commission of Inquiry Concerning Certain Activities of the Royal Canadian Mounted Police), *Freedom and Security under the Law* (Ottawa, 1981), Pt. VII, p. 799: 'Those who serve as security staffing officers should be mature individuals well versed in the variety of political ideologies relevant to Canadian society, sympathetic to the democratic principles which the security screening process is designed to protect, knowledgeable about and interested in human behaviour and the various methods used by foreign intelligence agencies to compromise people, and above all competent at interviewing a wide variety of people.'

obviously planted Parliamentary Question, quietly interred the idea in 1988, after review of a pilot project in GCHQ and MI5.[38] This closed a chapter unsatisfactory from any point of view and which, as a far from minor side-effect, brought confrontation with the unions and the resulting ban at GCHQ. American influence—though not, our informants stressed, American arm-twisting—was an important element. In the wake of the Prime case[39] the Security Commission recommended the introduction of the polygraph, having been impressed with the arguments of American officials, who extolled the virtues of the device as a means of checking the truth of applicants' statements. In the background also is the existence of the 'fairly rigid' vetting standards in NATO which, not surprisingly, bear a strong US imprint. Although use of the polygraph was described as 'not quite British', greater sensitivity to personal liberty cannot be described as the dominant factor in its rejection. Rather, the Security Commission had bought a pup, or had at any rate failed to understand the very different context which supports polygraph testing in the United States. For one thing, its use is far more widespread than would be conceivable in Britain (especially in the private sector)—its ready acceptance in the security area is part of a wider cultural practice that is quite alien to this country. Moreover, American security agencies accept polygraph 'evidence'[40] as sufficient of itself to deny someone a clearance, which the British authorities were always unwilling to do. Though this restraint shows a laudable scepticism about the reliability of gadgetry, it does seriously undermine the arguments for using the polygraph at all. Finally, there are the labour market realities—the Americans have always had a surplus of applicants for security-related jobs, whereas in the 1980s Britain faced a shortage. It was thought inadvisable to erect yet another deterrent to good candidates.

The Security Service remains in the background during the vetting process—it supplies any information it may have on its files to the PSIU investigator, but otherwise takes no active part. More generally, however, it supplies the Cabinet Office with its 'expert assessment' of what constitutes a threat to national security—a sensitive and contentious judgment about a range of activities and organizations which few in government service would have the inclination or the stature to dispute.

However, in individual vetting cases the final judgment rests with the department concerned—often the PSIU report will not even make a formal recommendation, merely set out alternatives. The level at which a decision is taken will vary among departments, and depends upon how a given Permanent Secretary

---

[38] *HC Debs.*, vol. 143, cols. 268–9w (8 Dec. 1988).

[39] Cmnd. 8876 (1983). In 1982 Geoffrey Prime, an employee of GCHQ, was sentenced to thirty-five years imprisonment after an *in camera* trial for espionage offences described by Lord Lane LCJ, the trial judge, as causing 'incalculable harm to the interests of security of this country'.

[40] The main issue is precisely whether polygraph readings are in any sense 'evidence' on which one can ground reliable conclusions about a person's truthfulness. See D. Lykken, *A Tremor in the Blood* (New York, 1981); *House of Commons Select Committee on Employment, Third Report for 1984–85*, HC (1984–5) 98; and Gale (n. 5 above).

chooses to delegate a decision. However, any decision to refuse clearance is in general taken at a high level. Consistent with the Permanent Head of department's responsibilities as chief establishment officer, procedures exist at this level (described below) for review of refusals based on character defects. By convention ministers are not involved in departmental personnel matters,[41] although paradoxically the procedures governing review of 'security' cases refer repeatedly to the participation of 'the minister'. If this is more than a piece of civil service reticence to admit who in reality would review the case, it is open to grave objection. The relationship between vetting and conventional personnel management is a close one: past and previous supervisors may be interviewed as a part of review of the applicant's PV and it is part of a supervisor's continuing responsibility to report between reviews any signs (such as sudden changes in behaviour or evidence of stress) which might be early indicators of a possible security-related problem.[42] At times there may be a conflict between personnel practices which are in part paternalistic, individual loyalty to colleagues, the protection of security, and the strict procedural entitlements of the employee concerned. This is the context within which the procedural protections over vetting must be considered.

PROCEDURES FOR CHALLENGING VETTING DECISIONS

Separate and long-standing procedures exist for challenging adverse decisions about reliability according to whether a 'character defect' or a doubt on security grounds is in issue. 'Character defect' cases are subject to internal appeal to the Permanent Secretary of the department. In the case of doubts arising on security grounds, because of an individual's involvement in or association with a subversive organization, a hearing before the 'Three Advisers' is available.[43] The panel comprises a retired Permanent Secretary, a retired Deputy-General Secretary of a civil service union, and a High Court judge.[44] Although this procedure has been justifiably the subject of criticism, this should be tempered by the realization that, according to official accounts, it has not been invoked since 1969.

The explanation lies partly in the fact that the procedure only applies to existing 'public servants' (a term widely defined in this context to include many who are not civil servants). Hence, applicants refused employment in either the

---

[41] Fredman and Morris (n. 1 above), 209.

[42] See e.g. the criticism of the Security Service management for failing to do so in the Security Commission report on the Bettaney case: Cmnd. 9514 (1985).

[43] Although the 1990 *Statement* envisages necessary amendments to the *Statement of Procedure*, no procedural changes to the existing arrangements or to the terms of reference of the Three Advisers are made by it. At present these remain as described in this section, although officials have stated they are to be revised.

[44] Implementing a recommendation of the Security Commission (n. 16 above), Annex, para. (*m*).

public or the private sector for security reasons cannot invoke the procedure. This will be the case with the majority of those subject to Reliability and Counter-Terrorist checks under the new arrangements. Common law offers no remedy for an arbitrary refusal to enter a contract of employment, and *a fortiori* none which could be invoked in these cases.[45] Indeed the common law rule that civil servants are dismissable at will has been attributed to the need not to fetter future executive action in the interests of the community should it be thought desirable to dispense with the services of an employee.[46] Thus, in the New Zealand case of *Deyzner* v. *Campbell*[47] a civil servant failed in his attempt to challenge his transfer to less-sensitive work because of his refusal to say whether he was a communist; the court relied partly on the common law rule and partly on an unrestricted statutory power of transfer.

Other reasons for the paucity of instances in which the procedure has been invoked have been offered. The Security Commission has stated that the majority of cases which arise involve alleged 'character defects' rather than doubts on security grounds.[48] However, it has also been asserted that the lack of appeals on security grounds is attributable to a widespread policy of not informing civil servants whose PV clearance comes into doubt.[49] If the clearance is allowed to lapse (clearances are reviewed every five years) rather than being revoked, the individual may be transferred in the interim to a post not requiring clearance (or clearance at a lower level) without ever being informed of the true reason. Only in cases such as the Foreign Office and Diplomatic Service, where all posts require clearance, will it become apparent to the affected officer what has occurred. Purportedly this practice (which is the 'normal' response to security doubts over existing employees) does not adversely affect a civil servant's career, since it is possible to rise quite high in the civil service without having need to have access to material classified Top Secret. Indeed, moves away from secret work are apparently often welcomed by those involved because of the resulting decrease in stress. Furthermore, it is unlikely that if the individual is transferred out of a security or intelligence department, any adverse material in his or her personnel file will follow. Although the practice may be generally benevolent, it gives no formal protections to the individual concerned and is at variance with the text of the Statement of Procedure, which gives no hint that it will operate only if the department chooses to inform the civil servant or to revoke the PV clearance.[50]

---

[45] *Dunn* v. *The Queen* [1896] QB 116.

[46] Per Rowlatt J in *Rederiaktiebolaget Amphritrite* v. *R.* [1921] 3 KB 500, 503–4.

[47] [1950] NZLR 790. See now New Zealand's Public Service Act 1962, s. 38.

[48] Cmnd. 8540, para. 19.

[49] Linn (n. 1 above), 32–4, citing in particular evidence given by a Ministry of Defence official to the Defence Select Committee.

[50] The *Statement of Procedure* states that 'the Minister will have before him information on which to decide whether the reliability of a public servant is prima facie to be regarded as in doubt on security grounds.' (para. 2.). Presumably the procedure is circumvented by simply exercising a discretion not to refer the case to the minister.

Where the procedure doubting reliability on security grounds is invoked, the prima facie determination that the 'public servant's' reliability is in doubt may be contested before the Three Advisers. Their function is to advise ministers whether the ruling has been substantiated or, in cases of uncertainty, to present their own assessment of the available evidence.[51] The limited nature of the Advisers' function is made clear by a paragraph which excludes from review all questions about whether the post in question has any bearing on security and therefore needs to be vetted.[52] The procedure provides for the public servant to be given an indication of the nature of the allegations against him and then an opportunity to make representations in person or with the help of a friend.[53] However, the Three Advisers are enjoined not to disclose either evidence as such nor sensitive sources to the appellant.[54] It follows that there is no right to hear the evidence on which the allegation is based, still less to challenge it by cross-examination. The report of the Three Advisers to the minister is not available to the appellant, nor is the minister bound to follow the findings. However, where the minister is minded to confirm a prima facie ruling of unreliability the procedure provides a final opportunity for representations by the appellant to the minister.[55] Where a finding is upheld the result would usually be a transfer to less sensitive work or as a last resort, if that were impossible, dismissal.[56] Dismissals on grounds of national security are exempt from the unfair dismissal legislation where the minister issues a certificate stating that this was the reason.[57]

REVIEW BY DOMESTIC COURTS OF SECURITY CLEARANCE DECISIONS

Although it is apparent from the foregoing account that the procedures by which a decision to revoke public servants' security clearance may be challenged

---

[51] *Terms of Reference of the Three Advisers* (1985), para. 2. The Terms of Reference also extend to cases where a minister issues a notice of refusal to negotiate with a trade union official on similar grounds, to withdrawal of clearance due to overseas connections which may strain a civil servant's loyalties, and to security decisions about British citizens employed and seconded to an International Defence Organization (ibid., para. 8).

[52] Ibid., para. 7.

[53] *Statement of Procedure*, para. 8.

[54] Ibid., and *Terms of Reference* (n. 51 above), para. 5.

[55] *Statement of Procedure*, para. 9.

[56] Ibid., para. 10.

[57] Employment Protection Consolidation Act 1978, s. 138(4). For similar exemptions in anti-discrimination legislation see: Sex Discrimination Act 1975, s. 52 (a procedure for conclusive ministerial certificates under s. 53 of the Act was repealed by the Sex Discrimination (Amendment) Order 1988, SI 1988/249 following *Johnstone* v. *Chief Constable of the RUC* [1986] 3 All ER 135); and Race Relations Act 1976, ss. 41 and 69(2) and (3). In *R.* v. *Secretary of State for the Foreign and Commonwealth Office ex p. Vidler* (an unreported decision of the Queen's Bench Division of January 22, 1993) Popplewell J refused to quash a certificate signed under these provisions in an unfair dismissal action brought by an employee of the diplomatic service (described as working in 'the security services') whose positive vetting had been withdrawn following an incident which had occurred during his posting to Russia.

tilt the balance of fairness in favour of the state,[58] the courts will do little to redress the balance. Where national security is involved judicial review is normally restricted to at most an examination of whether some evidence exists that the executive's assertion is in good faith.[59] Clearly this restricts to vanishing-point any possible review of the substance of a vetting decision and, as the cases following show, procedural standards may also be displaced as a result.

The fairness of a procedure which followed very closely that of the Three Advisers was in issue in the *Hosenball*[60] case, which arose under the analogous procedure for review of orders of deportation for reasons of national security before the panel of advisers appointed by the Secretary of State.[61] Hosenball, who had availed himself of this procedure, sought to challenge the Home Secretary's decision to confirm the deportation. His argument that the procedure was contrary to natural justice since he had been given inadequate details of the allegations against him by the Home Secretary failed in the Court of Appeal. The Court held that it would not interfere with the Secretary of State's assessment that national security required that the sources of information against Hosenball should be protected and that this outweighed any unfairness to him resulting from the failure to specify the allegations. As Lord Denning MR put it: 'when national security is at stake even the rules of natural justice may have to be modified to meet the position.'[62] Although the judgments concentrated on the refusal of the Home Secretary to give fuller details, it is also apparent that their Lordships considered that any apparent unfairness in the procedure before the advisory panel (where Hosenball was simply invited to make representations but given no further details of the allegations or evidence against him) was outweighed by considerations of national security.[63] Lord Denning MR did, however, suggest that had the advisers refused to hear representations from Hosenball the court would have interfered.[64]

Review of the withdrawal of a civil servant's positive vetting clearance was the central issue before the Divisional Court in *R.* v. *Director of GCHQ ex p. Hodges.*[65] The applicant's security clearance had been withdrawn following an interview in which he had revealed to his superiors that he was a sexually active homosexual. Although he had volunteered full details of his homosexual activities, after consideration of the frequency and nature of his homosexual relationships management at GCHQ considered that he was nevertheless 'vulnerable to pressure or blackmail from a hostile intelligence service'.[66] His appeal to the

---

[58] Official accounts admit as much: *Statement on the Findings of the Conference of Privy Councillors on Security*, Cmnd. 9715 (Mar. 1956), para. 15.

[59] *Secretary of State for Defence* v. *Guardian Newspapers* [1985] 1 AC 339; *CCSU* v. *Minister for the Civil Service* [1985] AC 374; see further Ch. 12 below.

[60] [1977] 3 All ER 452. See also *R.* v. *Secretary of State for Home Affairs, ex p. Cheblak* [1991] 2 All ER 319.

[61] See pp. 185 ff. below.			[62] See n. 60 above, 457.

[63] Lord Denning MR, ibid., at 456h–i and Geoffrey Lane LJ at 461j, 462a.

[64] Ibid. 459h.			[65] *The Times*, Law Report, 26 July 1988 (available on LEXIS).

[66] The facts in *Hodges* bear a striking resemblance to those in the American decision of *Webster* v.

Director of GCHQ against the decision also failed. He then applied for judicial review, seeking an order of *certiorari* to quash the withdrawal of the PV clearance, *mandamus* requiring it to be restored, and a declaration that he was a fit and proper person to be employed. Notwithstanding that the Divisional Court rejected the applicant's contentions that the decision had been both unreasonable and unfairly arrived at, the judgments do exhibit at least a minimal preparedness to review security clearance decisions. The court rejected the argument advanced by the Crown that a claim of national security deprived the courts totally of jurisdiction. Rather, Glidewell LJ relied on the speeches in the *GCHQ* case for the view that, while an inquiry into the reasonableness of a decision based on national security was prohibited, this did not prevent consideration of the fairness of the procedure adopted for reaching the decision, unless it was further claimed that the procedure had itself been followed for reasons of national security.[67] Hence, the court could not inquire into the applicant's claim that the decision to withdraw clearance was irrational (although for good measure Glidewell LJ found that it was not). However, the argument that the failure to give the applicant notes of his initial interviews was unfair could be considered, although it too failed on the facts. The implication of the judgment is that those parts of the security clearance procedure which are not required to be kept confidential will be subject to judicial review and that national security will not be allowed to cloak the entire process. This is to be welcomed, although it may turn largely upon the openness which Hodges' case had been dealt with (since it was based on information volunteered by him), which stands in stark contrast to the treatment meted out to Hosenball (where the relevant information was derived from other sources).

Considering the combined effect of the decisions, what emerges is a picture of the courts' extreme deference to the executive, only slightly tempered by their reluctance to relinquish entirely supervision of minimal standards of fairness in security cases. Since substantive justice will almost invariably depend on the civil servant's ability to answer and challenge in detail the case against him (*Hodges* was exceptional this respect), the courts' preparedness to allow these matters to be kept absolutely confidential is disquieting. Clearly, gross cases apart, domestic courts will do little to assist civil servants wishing to challenge either the Three Adviser's reference procedure (as in *Hosenball*) or a departmental review in a 'character defects' case (as in *Hodges*).

Doe (1988) 486 US 592 in which the Supreme Court refused to quash the dismissal of a CIA employee following his announcement that he was a homosexual.

[67] Citing Lord Fraser of Tulleybelton at [1985] AC at 402C, Lord Diplock ibid. 412F and Lord Roskill at 420D.

EMPLOYMENT VETTING AND THE EUROPEAN CONVENTION ON HUMAN RIGHTS

It might have been expected that the application of the ECHR would afford an opportunity to invoke substantive as well as procedural rights against employment vetting, and that international judicial bodies would be more sceptical of claims of national security than domestic ones.[68] In fact neither is the case: the way in which the Court and the Commission of Human Rights have interpreted the Convention in employment vetting cases to date is extremely restrictive.

The major difficulty for public sector employees or prospective employees challenging vetting decisions arises from the omission from the Convention of a unequivocal positive right of free access to employment in the public service. In this respect the Convention contrasts with the Universal Declaration of Human Rights (Art. 21, para. 2) and the International Covenant on Civil and Political Rights (Art. 25), both of which confer such a right. Accordingly, to bring themselves within the terms of the Convention complainants have tried to allege either that restrictions imposed on civil servants amount to an infringement of freedom of expression or that the process of vetting involves an interference with the individual's private and family life. These rights are guaranteed respectively by Articles 10 and 8 of the ECHR, but in each case the state is allowed to impose restrictions if they are 'prescribed by law' and 'necessary in a democratic society' for the protection of, *inter alia*, national security. If either of these substantive rights is successfully invoked there also arises the possibility of claiming denial of an effective remedy to enforce them in domestic law contrary to Article 13, or, since political opinion and sexual orientation are often deemed relevant to employment vetting, unlawful discrimination contrary to Article 14. Another possible impediment lies in Article 17, which denies protection to actions 'aimed at the destruction of any of the rights and freedoms set forth herein or at their limitation to a greater extent than is provided for in the Convention'. Although if applied widely Article 17 could give considerable scope for denying rights to those judged 'subversive', in fact it has rarely been invoked.[69]

The first major attempt to challenge employment vetting under the Convention came in two cases involving the so-called *berufsverbot* in the Federal Republic of Germany.[70] The *berufsverbot* is in effect a test of loyalty to the

---

[68] For a more general assessment of the performance of the Convention organs, see pp. 344–7 below.

[69] It was so used by the Commission in the German Communist Party case (*Application No. 250/57*), but this is an isolated example see: P. van Dijk and G. van Hoof, *Theory and Practice of the European Convention on Human Rights* (2nd edn., Deventer, 1990), 562–7.

[70] For a discussion of the *berufsverbot* see: G. Braunthal, *Political Loyalty and the Public Service in West Germany* (Boston, 1990) and G. Brinkman, 'Militant Democracy and Radicals in the West German Civil Service' (1983) 46 *MLR* 584.

Constitution which requires public servants to declare allegiance to and a preparedness to protect the 'free democratic system'. Political extremists or those who have advocated support for such causes therefore stand to be debarred from public office. In the cases of *Glasenapp*[71] and *Kosiek*[72] the applicants who were, respectively, a probationary grammar school teacher and a technical college lecturer, challenged their dismissals for activities allegedly showing a lack of allegiance to the Constitution, as interfering with their right to freedom of expression under Article 10.

The Commission considered that the imposition of a loyalty test and the requirement made of the applicants to dissociate themselves from a particular political party, prima facie, amounted to a restriction of freedom of expression and, therefore, it fell to be examined whether the restriction was justifiable.[73] In the Commission's view the *berufsverbot* could be said to be 'prescribed by law', not only in the sense of having a legal basis but also because it fulfilled the requisite standard[74] of being sufficiently accessible, foreseeable, and certain.[75] The Commission also held that the loyalty test was capable of furthering the justifiable aim under Article 10(2) of protecting national security since, although not directly concerned with security considerations (for example, espionage), it was intended to institutionalize the democratic structure and hence render impossible any return to totalitarianism.[76] However, when it came to consider whether the restriction was 'necessary in a democratic society' the Commission distinguished between the two cases. Applying the test laid down in the *Sunday Times* case, necessity required that there should be 'a pressing social need' and that the steps taken were proportionate. The Commission found that the measures taken against Glasenapp were disproportionate because of the indiscriminate nature of the loyalty test (which applies to many teachers), the tenuous link between the applicant and the KPD (the German Communist Party) and the fact that the opinions punished were wholly unrelated to her work.[77] In *Kosiek* the Commission found that factual differences in the applicant's circumstances compared to Glasenapp's made the dismissal justified.[78] Kosiek had been an extremely active member of the NPD, an extreme right wing party, which frequently attacked the 'rotten' and 'corrupt' system of parliamentary democracy in the Federal Republic of Germany.

When the European Court of Human Rights came to consider these two cases it took a radically different approach to the Commission.[79] In both instances it found, by a majority of sixteen to one, that there had been no

---

[71] *Glasenapp* v. *FRG* (Commission) (1984) 6 EHRR 499; (Court) (1987) 9 EHRR 25.
[72] *Kosiek* v. *FRG* (Commission) (1984) 6 EHRR 519; (Court) (1987) 9 EHRR 328.
[73] (1984) 6 EHRR, paras. 67–77.
[74] From *Sunday Times* v. *UK* (1979) 2 EHRR 245, para. 49.
[75] (1984) 6 EHRR, paras. 79–84.   [76] Ibid., para. 87.
[77] Ibid., paras. 100–28.   [78] (1984) 6 EHRR 519, paras. 109–16.
[79] See nn. 71 and 72 above. Cf. *Application No. 10942/82* v. *Germany* (1989) 11 EHRR 46 (declared inadmissible on the same grounds).

violation of Article 10 because it considered the real issue at the heart of the case to be that of access to the civil service, which was not protected by the Convention. It held that the applicants' opinions had been taken into account simply in order to assess their suitability as civil servants. Application of this approach made it unnecessary for the majority to consider whether the restriction was justified under Article 10(2), since no question of a restriction of free speech arose. It should be noted that two judges departed from this analysis. Judge Cremona found (because of the artificiality of treating dismissals as decisions about appointment) that the freedom of expression issue was central, but then went on to hold that the restriction was justified under Article 10.[80] Judge Spielman, applying a similar analysis to the one adopted by the Commission in the *Glasenapp* case, found in both instances that the dismissals were in violation of Article 10.[81]

In presenting the issue as one of access to employment the Court in effect abdicated any attempt to control the reasonableness of state decisions in vetting cases. Since in both cases the way in which the applicant's opinions were inferred to assess their suitability was through their published views, freedom of expression was firmly in issue. Even if adopted, however, this approach would not avail the applicant whose unsuitability was inferred solely from membership of a party or organization considered suspect. In fact, subsequent to the Court's decisions in *Glasenapp* and *Kosiek* the Commission has held to be manifestly unfounded a complaint from a UK civil servant relating to disciplinary action against him taken because he gave an unauthorized television interview. The civil servant in question, a senior Ministry of Defence scientist at a radioactive plant, was interviewed in his capacity as a County Councillor about safety at the plant where he was employed. The Commission had no difficulty in finding that such a restriction could be justifiable under Article 10(2) for the protection of national security or for the protection of others, namely his employer.[82] It is apparent that even where the organs of the Convention consider that a freedom of expression issue does arise, Article 10(2) may easily be satisfied in relation to civil servants.

Employment vetting in the public sector has also been challenged as being incompatible with the Convention because of its secrecy and intrusiveness. Both issues were central in the case of *Leander* v *Sweden*,[83] which concerned a refusal to employ a carpenter at the Naval Museum at Karlskrona, because of an unfavourable vetting report (a 'personnel control'). The applicant alleged that the use of information about his private life in a police register in checking his suitability breached Article 8 and that the denial of employment to him, presumably

---

[80] (1987) 9 EHRR, 46–7 and 342–3.   [81] Ibid. 47ff and 343 ff.

[82] *Application No. 10293/83* v. *UK* (1987) 9 EHRR 255. Cf. limitations on freedom of speech justified under Art. 10(2) in the case of military personnel: *Engel* v. *Netherlands* (1979–80) 1 EHRR 647, para. 100 and *Application Nos. 111565/85 and 11568/85 Le Cour Grandmaison and Fritz* v. *France* (1989) 11 EHRR 67.

[83] (Commission) (1985) 7 EHRR 557; (Court) (1987) 9 EHRR 433.

because of his political views, and the refusal of access to his police file amounted to restrictions on his freedom of expression and freedom to receive information contrary to Article 10. He further alleged that the opportunities he was afforded in the domestic arena to challenge the decisions fell short of Articles 6 (the right to a fair hearing by an independent and impartial tribunal) and 13 (the right to an effective domestic remedy). At the heart of the applicant's case was his inability to discover what was recorded on his police record, to establish why it made him a security risk, and to verify or contradict the information recorded.

Although the Commission found that the keeping of a police file which presumably dealt with the applicant's acts, opinions, and associations based on assessment of his behaviour and possibly his personality (the file was not produced for the proceedings) contravened Article 8(1), they found it to be justified under Article 8(2), since such files were prescribed by law and were necessary in a democratic society for the protection of national security. The Commission regarded as self-evident the need, for national security considerations, to maintain files on individuals of radical political views.[84] Likewise it had no doubt that vetting on such grounds was capable of justification. However, the issue was whether the safeguards and controls surrounding the practice in Sweden's case were sufficient to satisfy Article 8(2).[85] Of twelve possible safeguards cited by the Swedish government, the Commission found four in particular to be independent safeguards against abuse: the presence of parliamentarians on the body responsible for supplying information for the personnel control system (the National Police Board); the Parliamentary Ombudsman, (whose jurisdiction extended to personnel control complaints); the independent complaints jurisdiction of the Chancellor of Justice, and a Standing Committee of the Parliament on Justice with power to oversee the procedure.[86] Purely ministerial controls over vetting were brushed aside.

The Court endorsed this reasoning, holding that in order to be 'in accordance with law' the interference with privacy must be foreseeable and authorized in terms accessible to the individual. In the context of security vetting this did not require that the applicant should be able to predict the process entirely (which would make it easy to circumvent), but rather that the authorizing law should be sufficiently clear to give a general indication of the practice.[87] If part of the practice was unpublished, the government was only entitled to rely under Article 8(2) on the published part.[88] When considering the necessity of the restriction the Court, like the Commission, accepted unquestioningly the legitimacy of security vetting in general and that this justified collecting information and retaining files for assessing the suitability of candidates for posts of importance for national security.[89] Although this affected the applicant's private life in limiting

---

[84] Ibid., para. 68.
[86] (n. 83 above), para. 80.
[88] Ibid., para. 54.

[85] cf. *Klass* v. *Germany* (1978) 2 EHRR 214.
[87] Ibid., para. 51.
[89] Ibid., para. 59.

access to sensitive posts, it did not otherwise constitute an obstacle to him leading a private life of his choosing. In these circumstances the state was to be
allowed a wide margin of appreciation,[90] and, in view of the safeguards, the
Court concluded that the interference with Leander's right of privacy 'cannot
. . . be said to have been disproportionate to the legitimate aim pursued'.[91]

With regard to the claim under Article 10, Leander's inability to demonstrate
the content of the file meant he could not satisfy the Commission that it related
to his freedom to express opinions.[92] Furthermore, the Commission held that
Article 10 could not be extended to include a right to receive information contained in such a file, since absence of notification of the file's contents could be
consistent with Article 8, in view of the safeguards.[93] The Court adopted a more
restrictive approach and, following *Glasenapp* and *Kosiek*, held that the real issue
was access to the civil service rather than freedom of speech. Since the information was stored and used solely for assessing job qualifications accordingly it did
not infringe Article 10.[94]

For the majority of the Commission the aggregate of remedies and safeguards
satisfied Article 13;[95] however, a minority dissenting found that since none of
the remedies could actually deliver details of the file to Leander, collectively they
could not be said to be 'effective'.[96] The Court upheld the majority, holding
that: 'for the purpose of the present proceedings, an "effective remedy" under
Article 13 must mean a remedy that is as effective as can be, having regard to
the restricted scope for recourse inherent in any system of secret checks on candidates for employment in posts of importance from a national security point of
view.'[97]

Some aspects of the *Leander* judgment may be applauded: for instance, the
insistence on looking to published sources of law and the requirement that independent remedies should be provided for alleged breaches of privacy. However,
on other points the Commmission and the Court adopted what may fairly be
called a craven attitude in the face of assertions of national security. Strikingly
absent is any serious attempt to consider whether vetting and the means and
scope of vetting adopted were proportionate to the alleged threat to national
security.[98] Whilst it would be over-ambitious to expect that a supervisory international organ could conduct a serious enquiry into the threat to a country from
subversive activity, a proportionality test would have the merit of requiring from
the state concerned a higher standard of proof of the threat to national security
in cases where the alleged threat was indirect as opposed to direct (for example,
from espionage and terrorism). Of course it is possible, in an extreme version of

---

[90] (Commission) (1985) 7 EHRR 557; (Court) (1987) 9 EHRR 433 para. 59.
[91] (Court), para. 67.   [92] Ibid., para. 84.   [93] para. 86.   [94] Ibid., paras. 71–3.
[95] Ibid., paras. 88–102.   [96] (Commission) 578–9.   [97] (Court), para. 78.
[98] Proportionality was adopted as the major criterion of compatibility with Art. 8 in *Dudgeon* v.
UK (1982) 4 EHRR 149, para. 61. In *Leander* it received no detailed separate treatment, apparently
being subsumed under the questions of foreseeability, accessibility, and legality. It was, however,
invoked by the Commission (but not the Court) in *Glasenapp* and *Kosiek* (nn. 71 and 72 above).

the argument, to allege that any citizen of a country is a potential future candidate for a position sensitive to national security, but this would be a decidedly thin justification for keeping files on the entire population. Yet the Court's approach in *Leander* fails to provide firm ground for striking down such indiscriminate file-keeping, provided its ostensible purpose is related to public employment.

There is an arid formalism in the Court's treatment of Article 10 in these cases that oddly recalls an earlier chapter in American constitutional law. Oliver Wendell Holmes, whilst still a judge of the Supreme Court of Massachusetts at the end of the last century, dismissed the appeal of a policeman, sacked for expressing political opinions when off duty, with the remark, 'the Petitioner may have a constitutional right to talk politics, but he has no constitutional right to be a policeman'.[99] This decision was frequently cited in years following to uphold various restrictions on activities of government employees or access to government benefits, and it took several decades for the fallacies contained beneath the pithiness of Holmes's prose to be appreciated.[100] None the less the dangers of what we have described in Chapter 1 as 'partial sanctioning'[101] should be obvious. If a legal provision protects freedom of expresssion, that protection should not be arbitrarily limited to invalidating criminal penalties or formal censorship. If a person knows that he will lose an important material advantage—employment, citizenship, or a pension—if he exercises that freedom, the threat of loss is likely to be at least as effective in inhibiting the exercise of the protected rights as any formal sanction. From a slightly different perspective, the threatened loss means that an individual's access to some desirable thing is made conditional on forgoing exercise of the protected right. The concept of 'chilling effect' here conjoins with that of 'unconstitutional conditions', and from the 1950s onwards various restrictions on public employees' rights were invalidated as violating freedom of expression.[102] Persons like Mrs Glasenapp do not claim a 'right to public employment'; their claim is that they should not be penalized for exercising their rights under Article 10 by loss of public employment. This is surely a realistic understanding of what protection of freedom of expression entails.

United Kingdom Cases and the ECHR

Security vetting and file-keeping have also been challenged in several recent complaints from the United Kingdom under the European Convention on

---

[99] *McAuliffe* v. *Mayor of New Bedford* (1892) 155 Mass. 216, 220.

[100] For a review and critique see: W. van Alstyne, 'The Demise of the Right–Privilege Distinction in Constitutional Law' (1968) 81 *Harv. LR* 1439.

[101] p. 21 above.

[102] See, for analysis and details: 'Note: Unconstitutional Conditions' (1960) 73 *Harv. LR* 1595; 'Note: The Chilling Effect in Constitutional Law' (1969) 69 *Col. LR* 802; and K. Sullivan, 'Unconstitutional Conditions' (1989) 102 *Harv. LR* 1413.

Human Rights. Unfortunately none of these has resulted in an authoritative determination from the Court, but the Commission reports give useful guidance on the application of the principles discussed above to the UK practice of vetting. They are also of significance because officials confirmed to us that the realization that 'we were vulnerable on procedural grounds' under the Convention in relation to vetting was the single most important reason for the introduction of the Security Service Act 1989. As a litigation strategy the enactment of the statute proved brilliantly successful, although as we argue below, UK practice remains in breach of the Convention.

The case of Isobel Hilton[103] concerned a variation on Normal Vetting at the BBC which was made public for the first time by the *Observer* in 1985. Hilton was a journalist whose offer of employment by the BBC was withdrawn allegedly following an adverse security report from MI5 under a long-standing informal practice for vetting BBC applicants. The application failed at the admissibility stage and provides a graphic illustration of the difficulties in challenging secretive practices, about which the applicant will have little hard information: Hilton only became aware of the vetting several years after the event, and the time-lag was to count critically against her.

The case was unusual in that, contrary to its frequent stance in security-related litigation, the government was prepared to confirm not only that a check had taken place with MI5, but also to contradict the applicant's account of the chronology and her assertion that the objection to her could only have been based upon a mistake about her involvement in a (benign) Scotland–China cultural organization. It did not, however, explain what the real objection was. Hilton alleged that the collection, retention, and application of personal information by the BBC and the Security Service so as adversely to affect her prospects of appointment without any opportunity for her to comment on the accuracy of the information was a breach of Article 8. She also alleged a breach of Article 10 in two respects: that the decision not to appoint her amounted to a penalty imposed for the expression of her views, and that the Security Service's part in that decision was an infringement of her right as a journalist to impart information and ideas to the public.

In part the Commission rejected the complaint under Article 8 because of the view it took of the evidence: it was not satisfied that adverse security reports had been made before Hilton accepted another job—in which case it could not be said that she had suffered detriment. More importantly, the Commission also rejected the assertion that compilation and retention of a file was in itself an invasion of privacy: 'an interference with the right to respect for private life only occurs when security checks are based on information about a person's private affairs . . .'[104] However, the Commission also went on to hold that 'it is not necessary that the person actually shows that the information has been used to

---

[103] *Application No. 12015/86.*   [104] Ibid.,19.

his detriment'. The claims under Articles 10 and 13 fell with that under Article 8.

The Commission's reasoning has erected a high hurdle for complainants. Hilton failed to clear it because the BBC had written to assure her that it had no remaining papers about her job application and because the Commission considered that she had not shown that the Security Service compiled and maintained a file of personal information about her. The Commission held these facts to be insufficient to establish the continued retention of a personal file by MI5. What is unclear about this reasoning is whether the Commission considered the apparent recording of involvement in a cultural association not to be a personal detail, or whether the decisive factor was the inability of the complainant to show the continued retention of such information. Whatever the rationale, it is unsatisfactory. If involvement in an association of this kind does not count as an aspect of one's private life the protection of Article 8 is considerably narrowed, especially when one considers the failure to extend Article 10 to involvement in such activities.[105] On the other hand, once it was shown that MI5 had been in possession of such information the onus was surely upon the government to satisfy the Commission that it no longer retained it. This particular trap for complainants is one that has been concealed by other vetting cases such as *Leander*, where it was freely conceded at the outset that the file contained personal information. The Commission tempered the severity of the burden on the complainant somewhat by stating 'that it should be possible in certain cases to raise a complaint such as is made by the applicant without the necessity of proving the existence of a file of personal information. To fall into the latter category . . . applicants must be able to show that there is, at least, a reasonable likelihood that the Security Service has compiled and continues to retain personal information about them.'[106]

Whilst the test appears unobjectionable, what is puzzling is why Hilton was held not to have raised such a 'reasonable likelihood'. No evidence was adduced by the government, either about the destruction of Hilton's file nor even of any general system of file-weeding or reviewing. In such circumstances the reasonable (rebuttable) presumption should be 'once on file always on file'. Nevertheless, later complainants have, somewhat paradoxically, found it easier to satisfy the test enunciated by the Commission than did Hilton.

The complaints of surveillance and file-keeping by the Security Service brought by two former officers of the National Council for Civil Liberties, Harriet Harman and Patricia Hewitt,[107] arose from allegations made by the former MI5 officer Cathy Massiter in a television documentary, screened in 1985. Massiter had sworn an affidavit to the effect that Security Service files existed

---

[105] See p. 149 above.   [106] *Application No. 12015/86*, 20.
[107] *Harman and Hewitt* v. *UK* (1992) 14 EHRR 657. Another application arising from Massiter's allegations by the CND was withdrawn after the announcement of the Security Service Bill: *Application Nos. 11745/85 and 13595/88*.

on the complainants which would include personal details. The case was one of extreme sensitivity for the authorities, not least because of the subsequent careers of the complainants: Harman became a Labour MP and is currently an opposition spokeswoman on economic policy, and Hewitt went on to become a personal assistant to the former leader of the Labour Party. Although not citing any specific instance of prejudice through vetting, the complainants alleged that the gathering of information for possible vetting infringed Article 8, had a 'chilling effect' on the expression of opinions contrary to Article 10, and contravened Article 11 (since others would be deterred from associating with them); the complaint also challenged the lack of an 'effective remedy' under Article 13 for these breaches.

The Commission's report (adopted by the Council of Ministers) found breaches of Article 8 and, associated with them, of Article 13. Massiter's evidence was found to be sufficient to satisfy the 'reasonable likelihood' test and it, therefore, had to be considered whether the interference with the complainants' right to respect for their private life was justified. As in the *Malone* case,[108] it was the absence of a specific statutory basis which was held to be fatal to the claim that it was 'in accordance with the law'. The government could only point to the Security Service's administrative charter—the Maxwell-Fyfe Directive of 1952— as authority for the surveillance and file-keeping. However, this did not have the force of law, its contents were not legally binding or enforceable, and it was couched in language which failed to indicate 'with the requisite degree of certainty the scope and the manner of the exercise of discretion by the authorities in the carrying out of secret surveillance activities'.[109] It followed also that there was no effective remedy.

Obstacles also stand in the way of complainants who allege vetting in the private sector, for instance, in connection with defence contracts. The major difficulty is that the Convention only creates enforceable rights against the contracting state and its organs but not against other private bodies and individuals. Thus in so far as the complaint in *N* v. *UK*[110] related solely to the activities of a defence contractor which had withdrawn its offer of employment for a financial analyst's post after vetting, the Commission held it inadmissible as being incompatible with the Convention. However, in so far as vetting was a collaborative exercise with the Security Service, the complaint was admissible and was subsequently upheld. The complainant was unable to catalogue the course of the vetting nor give any details of what his security file might contain, but nevertheless the Commission was prepared to make a 'reasonable inference from the facts' that he had applied for a post in the defence sector, and that he was turned down when security enquiries proved unsatisfactory, that a security check had been carried out with a Security Service file containing reference to his private affairs. Once it had established to its satisfaction the involvement of

---

[108] (1985) 7 EHRR 14; see further p. 69 above.   [109] *Application No. 12175/86*, para. 40.
[110] *Application No. 12327/86*.

the Security Service, the Commission's reasoning followed the same pattern as in the *Harman and Hewitt* case.

These cases leave much unresolved: the issue of whether files for use in vetting are solely within the permitted exceptions under Article 8, or were limited to what is necessary in a democratic society were not reached because of the Commission's other findings. In view of this, it is unfortunate that both cases went to the Council of Ministers rather than to the Court of Human Rights. Accordingly, they were dealt with in secret and in a political forum, each of whose members can be assumed to have some interest in an expansive treatment of issues involving national security. The resolution[111] which emerged at the end of the process adopted the Commission's findings but decided 'that no further action was called for' in view of the subsequent passage of the Security Service Act 1989 and the payment by the government of the applicants' legal expenses. Apart from the obvious point that an Act which came into effect on 18 December 1989 can have no relevance to cases arising on earlier facts, there are substantive grounds also for doubting the adequacy of the remedies provided in it for vetting complaints and their compliance with the Convention. It is to those we now turn.

THE SECURITY SERVICE ACT AND VETTING

Any involvement of the Security Service in the security vetting process is subject to the—admittedly weak—controls contained in the Security Service Act 1989.[112] The statutory aims in section 1 of the Act[113] provide a broad base for the collection, storing, and dissemination of information in employment vetting and for other tasks connected with national security. A limited safeguard to the over-wide collection of personal information exists in section 2(2), which requires the Director-General of MI5 to ensure that there are arrangements limiting the collection of information to that necessary for the proper discharge of the Service's role or for preventing or detecting serious crime. By virtue of section 2(3), these arrangements are to ensure that such information is not disclosed by the Service in connection with employment vetting except in accordance with ministerial provisions. However, the guidelines are not included in the Act. There is no duty to publish them and they have not been published.

Individuals who allege that they have been prejudiced by the actions of the Security Service have the right to complain to the Security Service Tribunal.[114] Where a complaint relates specifically to disclosure of information by the Security Service for employment purposes the Tribunal is required to determine whether the Service did so and if so whether it 'had reasonable grounds for

---

[111] Resolution DH(90) 36 of 13 Dec. 1990.   [112] See more generally Chs. 15 and 16 below.
[113] Ch. 14 below.   [114] S. 5 and scheds. 1 and 2; Ch. 15 below.

believing the information to be true'.[115] Members of the Service are under a duty to disclose documents and information to the Tribunal, but the tribunal in turn must ensure that, except by consent, these remain confidential and are not disclosed to the complainant.[116] If the Tribunal concludes the 'reasonable grounds' test has not been satisfied, it must give notice to the complainant of a determination in his or her favour and report to the Home Secretary and to the Commissioner established under the Act.[117] In the reverse instance, the complainant will simply be informed that no favourable determination has been made.

Where the Tribunal upholds a complaint its powers include ordering that inquiries be ended and that files and records be destroyed. In addition, if the Tribunal finds in an employment case that no reasonable grounds existed for believing the information disclosed to be true, it may order the payment of a specified sum of compensation.[118] The basis on which compensation is to be assessed is left undetermined by the Act.[119] Although it cannot provide a remedy, the Tribunal may also refer two types of issues which may be raised in a vetting case to the Commissioner, the judicial monitor established by section 4 of the Act. The latter may then, entirely at his discretion, undertake an investigation into the matter and present a report to the Home Secretary. The issues which may give rise to such a reference are, first, whether the category of persons regarded as proper objects of inquiry is overly broad, for example, all members of a purportedly subversive organization,[120] and secondly, any other unreasonable conduct by the Service in relation to the complainant or his property.[121]

In Parliament, the Home Secretary was able to claim that the Act gives a remedy to those whose careers are disrupted because of the activities of the Security Service. It is correct that, unlike the vetting review procedures, access to the Tribunal will be open to those affected by pre-entry vetting. However, there are a number of unsatisfactory features about the way in which the Act deals with employment vetting. Since the legislation creates an institutional rather than a functional framework, other actions in the process of vetting are left unregulated. The Act will only prove of any use in vetting cases with regard to the decision to supply information and the accuracy of the information supplied, since these are the only respects in which the Security Service will be involved. Information supplied by Special Branch remains beyond the reach of the Act. It does nothing to provide a remedy for a decision not to employ, to withdraw security clearance, or to terminate employment by a government department or a defence contractor based upon the information supplied. Indeed even the

---

[115] Sched. 1, para. 3.   [116] Sched. 2, para. 4.
[117] Sched. 1, para. 5.   [118] Sched. 1, para. 6.

[119] e.g. whether for defamation or for loss of opportunity of career prospects in cases in which the information supplied results in the complainant not being offered employment.

[120] The Tribunal's function in such cases is limited to review of the reasonableness of regarding the complainant as a member of the suspect category: see sched. 1, para. 2(4)

[121] Sched. 1, para. 7.

decisions to supply information in the first place will be immune in all but the clearest cases of abuse, since the only issue for the Tribunal would be whether the Service had reasonable grounds for complying with the request as touching national security. The Tribunal is unlikely, on such a fragile statutory instruction, to develop its own independent view of which categories of posts should be vetted on security grounds. Since the Act only covers the Security Service's involvement, and then only very sketchily, the basis of public sector vetting remains a pastiche of statutory and administrative guidelines.

A problem area is the interaction of the Act with the Three Advisers' procedure and with the departmental appeal in 'character defects' cases, both of which are left intact notwithstanding the introduction of the Security Service Tribunal. Strictly speaking, the Tribunal's function can be diffentiated from the review mechanisms: it exists to investigate MI5's actions (here in the vetting process) whilst they are challenges to the decisions based on the information obtained (*inter alia*) by those actions. Whereas a finding by the Tribunal in a vetting case in the complainant's favour would surely be material in an attack on the refusal of security clearance, it is possible to envisage other such challenges which ought not to be precluded by a Tribunal decision against the complainant; for instance, the information supplied in vetting may be accurate but the judgment based upon it open to question. Thus whilst a person may indeed have participated in a particular demonstration, or have an uncle living in Poland or West Belfast, the pertinent question is whether these facts justify refusal of the position he has sought. The Tribunal has no jurisdiction to consider that question, which remains a matter for the Three Advisers. Furthermore, it should be remembered that the Tribunal is in the nature of judicial review proceedings, in which the review is a limited one, whereas the other remedies are analogous to appeals.

It will be clear that even in those instances where it is possible to complain under the Act, the controls are minimal. The purpose of mentioning vetting in the Act appears to have been to give it a legal foundation so as to satisfy the European Convention on Human Rights in view of the impending cases against the United Kingdom.[122] However, because the Act is institutional rather than functional in outline, those parts of the vetting process not involving MI5 continue to lack an explicit legal basis. Even in respect of MI5, whether the Act does enough to make its role in the process 'prescribed by law' will depend on the view taken of the balance between the published statutory language, published administrative practice, and unpublished ministerial guidelines about the

---

[122] Inconclusive arguments along the line advanced here were put in *G, H, and I* v. *UK* (1993) 15 EHRR CD 4, three cases each involving the withdrawal of a job offer following vetting. Each applicant had unsuccessfully applied to the Security Service Tribunal. However, the Commission declared two of the cases inadmissible because it accepted the government's argument that no security vetting had taken place, since the long periods the applicants had spent living abroad effectively prevented it. An admissibility decision was adjourned in the third case.

release of information by the Service. Following the reasoning in *Leander*,[123] there are two issues.

The first is whether the Act satisfies the 'quality' of law test: it is not enough that there should be a statute. Clearly the statutory objectives of the Service in section 1 of the Act are capable of providing justification for the collection, storing, and release of information for permitted reasons within Article 8. However, the statute must indicate with reasonable certainty when, to whom, and on what grounds the discretion within this secret process is to be exercised.[124] In applying this test it would certainly be permissible to read the text of the Act. However, the unpublished ministerial directions should be discounted (following the practice in *Leander*). Equally, the published statements regarding vetting policy do not have legal a quality at all. In view of the almost total absence of operational detail in the Act, arguably it fails at this first hurdle.

Even assuming that we are mistaken on this point, does the Act build in sufficient safeguards to satisfy the second test, that the interference be 'necessary in a democratic society'? Unlike in Sweden, there is no input into oversight of the process from parliamentarians[125] nor from the Parliamentary Commissioner.[126] The only independent controls are the Tribunal and the Commissioner. In some respects these are more efficacious than those found sufficient in Sweden because of the powers of the Tribunal to order deletion of files (but not, apparently, their rectification) and the payment of compensation. It is likely, in view of the independent nature of the personnel comprising the Tribunal and the judicial character of the Commissioner, that these remedies will be held sufficient, as regards the narrow issue referred to the Tribunal.

What this discussion shows is that even if (which we regard as unlikely) current UK practices comply with the Convention, the Security Service Act is very far from being a comprehensive or satisfactory treatment of the issue. This becomes clearer still if a comparison is made with the statutory schemes in Canada and Australia.

CANADIAN AND AUSTRALIAN PRACTICE

Canada and Australia inherited from Britain the tradition of a politically neutral civil service serving a parliamentary executive. However, unlike Britain, where regulation of the civil service has remained a matter governed by the prerogative, both countries have long-established statutory regimes for their public offi-

---

[123] n. 83 above.   [124] Ibid., para. 51.   [125] See Ch. 16 below.

[126] The Ombudsman's jurisdiction will be excluded certainly because of the national security exemption (Parliamentary Commissioner for Administration Act 1967, Sched. 3, para. 5) and in relation to the civil service because of the personnel exemption (Sched. 3, para. 10) The personnel exemption also extends to ministerial directions given about employees in the private sector, e.g. those employed by defence contractors (ibid., para. 10(*c*)). In so far as a complaint relates to the activities of MI5, the alternative legal remedy bar (s. 5 of the Act) would also operate.

cials. It is noteworthy that, notwithstanding this administrative climate, security controls were introduced at approximately the same time as in Britain (in Canada in 1946[127] and in Australia 1948[128]) and remained on an administrative basis until they were incorporated into major reforms of their respective intelligence charters. It is probable that the need for conformity within the UKUSA intelligence alliance—at least so far as the minor partners were concerned—overrode domestic constitutional considerations.

The statutory charters of the Canadian and Australian domestic intelligence agencies expressly state that the provision of security assessment is an agency function.[129] In both instances the keeping of records from which such assessment will be made is subject to their overall statutory remit, which places clear limits on the kinds of activity which may attract official attention. Both Canada and Australia have resiled from the broad category of subversive activities[130] used in the UK Statements on vetting and in the Security Service Act 1989, thus providing the rights of public servants significantly better protection. As regards the procedure for appealing against denial, limitation, or revocation of security clearance, the legislation is, by British standards, remarkably detailed. In Australia there is a binding statutory appeal procedure of a specially constituted tribunal, the Security Appeals Tribunal.[131] In the Canadian legislation the task of reviewing security clearance decisions is given to the SIRC as part of its jurisdiction over complaints.[132]

The appeal procedures rest upon the right of the public servant[133] to be informed of an adverse security decision. The CSIS Act provides that an individual is to be informed if the denial of security clearance is the sole reason for

---

[127] See McDonald Commission (n. 37 above), pt. VII, ch. 1; R. Whitaker, 'Origins of the Canadian Government's Internal Security System, 1946–1952' (1984) 65 *Can. Hist. Rev.* 154; P. Hanks and J. D. McCamus (eds.), *National Security: Surveillance and Accountability in a Democratic Society* (Cowansville, Que., 1989), ch. 11. For the historical antecedents, see Hannant, above n. 14. Prior to the passing of the Canadian Security Intelligence Service Act 1984 it had been held, in *Lee* v. *A-G of Canada* 126 DLR (3d), 1982, 1, that the statutory Public Service Commission had no jurisdiction to review a security-clearance decision.

[128] R. Whitaker, 'Fighting the Cold War on the Home Front America, Britain, Australia and Canada' (1984) *Socialist Register*, 47–8. An attempt was made *inter alia*, in the Communist Party Dissolution Act 1950, s. 10 to place a statutory bar on the employment of communists by the Commonwealth or designated key industries of the economy. However, in *Australian Communist Party and Others* v. *The Commonwealth* (1951) 83 CLR 1 the Act was held to *ultra vires* the Australian Parliament; see further, pp. pp. 349 ff. below.

[129] ASIO Act ss. 17(1)(c) and 37(1); CSIS Act s. 13.   [130] See Ch. 14 below.

[131] ASIO Act, ss. 41–83.

[132] CSIS Act, ss. 34–5. The McDonald Commission (n. 37 above), Pt. VII, ch. 1, para. 80) had recommended that security clearance appeals should go to a Security Appeals Tribunal modelled on the Australian one and headed by a Judge of the Federal Court of Canada. For specific criticism of SIRC's procedure in security clearance cases, see M. Rankin, 'The Security Intelligence Review Committee: Reconciling National Security with Procedural Fairness', 3 *Can. J. of Admin. L. & Prac.* 173. A vetting scheme introduced outside this framework in the interests of airport security was declared *ultra vires* in *Swan* v. *Canada (Minister of Transport)* (1990) 67 DLR (4th) 390.

[133] Private contractors and their employees are expressly within the ASIO Act provisions: see s. 35.

a decision to deny employment, demote, dismiss, or refuse promotion or transfer.[134] Although more comprehensive than the UK Statement of Procedure, this still requires positive action to have been taken in relation to the employee before the duty to notify arises. SIRC has recommended that the duty to notify should turn on the security clearance decision and not on an ancillary one about employment; it has also suggested that the requirement that the denial of clearance be the only operative factor should be removed from the legislation.[135] The ASIO Act goes further and requires that the individual be notified (subject to an exception where the Attorney-General certifies that the withholding of notice is essential to the security of the nation) wherever an adverse or qualified security assessment is made on him or her, even if it does not at that time result in any action being taken.[136]

The giving of background information to the person affected is handled differently under each scheme. Under the ASIO Act the onus is on the department or government agency to give the individual a copy of the security assessment when informing him or her of the decision.[137] However, details may be excluded if the Attorney-General certifies that their inclusion would be 'prejudicial to the interests of security'.[138] Where this occurs the official is not even told that material has been excluded and, although the Tribunal will have access to the unedited assessment, it too is under a duty not to divulge the existence of the Attorney-General's certificate or its contents.[139] The Canadian legislation places the onus on the SIRC to give a summary to the complainant to enable him 'to be as fully informed as possible of the circumstances giving rise to the denial of the security clearance'.[140] However, this must be read in the context of the Committee's duty to comply with security requirements.[141] Although in preparing the statement SIRC is obliged to consult the Director of CSIS, the relevant section (section 55) falls short of giving the CSIS a veto on the information disclosed.

Although on paper the Canadian and Australian Acts exhibit a fundamental difference in emphasis, with the former the more investigatory (in keeping with the SIRC's other statutory functions), in practice both follow an adversarial pattern.[142] The Canadian legislation has been substantially supplemented by rules of

---

[134] CSIS Act, s. 42.

[135] Security Intelligence Review Committee, *Amending the CSIS Act: Proposals for the Special Committee of the House of Commons* (Ottawa, 1989), 10–12 . This proposal has been endorsed in *In Report of the Special Committee on the Review of the CSIS Act and the Security Offences Act, In Flux But Not in Crisis* (Ottawa,1990), 168. The government undertook to consider how best to provide a remedy in such cases: Solicitor General of Canada, *On Course: National Security for the 1990s* (Ottawa, 1991), 74.

[136] ASIO Act, s. 39(1) and note esp. the definitions of 'assessment', 'prescribed administrative action' and 'qualified security assessment' in s. 35.

[137] Ibid., s. 38(1).   [138] Ibid., s. 38(2)(*b*).   [139] Ibid., s. 57.

[140] CSIS Act, s. 46.   [141] Ibid., s. 37.

[142] Rankin (n. 132 above) argues that the conduct of SIRC investigations in s. 42 cases is more adversarial than the Act would suggest because of various procedural devices which the Committee has adopted.

procedure adopted by SIRC for hearing security clearance cases; when acting in this capacity SIRC has been described (in a Parliamentary review of the legislation) as an 'administrative tribunal'.[143] Both statutes provide that the hearings are to be in private, with a right for the complainant to make representations, but not to hear the representations made by the intelligence agencies.[144]

However, the ASIO Act expressly states that the 'parties' are the complainant and the ASIO (with the department concerned having a right to be heard).[145] The Director-General of ASIO is, however, under a duty to lay all relevant material (including that favourable to the applicant) before the Tribunal. Section 58 of the Act provides for a discretionary pre-hearing review between the parties and, at the hearing, for first the ASIO and then the applicant to put their cases. The Tribunal is required, after hearing the representations of the Director-General, to consider what further details may be given to the applicant to enable him to make representations. Here the tension at the heart of the use of the adversarial process is exposed, for the Tribunal is required to consider the interests of justice 'consistently with the requirements of security'[146] and, in doing so, it must consult the Director-General as to the requirements of security if it intends to give particulars of his submissions as evidence.[147] Further limitations are placed upon the disclosure of evidence by the Tribunal by section 59, which permits the Attorney-General to certify that disclosure would be contrary to the public interest. If the grounds for the certificate are related to security, defence, international relations, or because disclosure would involve revealing Cabinet secrets, the certificate is conclusive. In other cases the President of the Tribunal may, notwithstanding the Attorney-General's certificate, allow disclosure if the interests of justice require it.[148] Even where no certificate is given the Tribunal is required not to communicate information contrary to the requirements of security.[149] The Tribunal has powers to hear evidence on oath, to subpoena witnesses, and to punish for contempt.[150] There are also powers to grant legal assistance[151] and to award costs from public funds.[152]

The CSIS Act treats investigations into complaints of denial of security clearance under section 42 of the Act as an aspect of SIRC's investigatory brief. As an investigatory body, SIRC is equipped with powers to obtain access to information[153] and to subpoena evidence.[154] All its investigations take place in private[155] and are subject to general requirements to protect security.[156] The

[143] *In Flux* (n. 135 above), 163.

[144] ASIO Act, ss. 58(5)–(7); CSIS Act, ss.48 (1) and (2). In both instances the intelligence agency is also to be excluded when the complainant is giving evidence.   [145] ASIO Act. s. 58 (2).

[146] Ibid., s. 58(9), and likewise when inviting a party to give fresh evidence in response to evidence submitted by the other: s. 58(12).

[147] Ibid., s. 58(13).   [148] Ibid., s. 59(4) and (5).   [149] Ibid., s. 59(10).

[150] Ibid., ss. 70, 74, and 76 respectively.   [151] Ibid., s. 72.

[152] Ibid., s. 72A.   [153] CSIS Act, s. 39(2).   [154] Ibid., s. 50.

[155] Ibid., s. 48(1).

[156] Ibid. s. 37. s. 55 contains a specific duty to consult the Director of CSIS over the material to be included in a report at the conclusion of an investigation.

modifications to this scheme in the cases of section 42 complaints are a specific right for representations to be made by CSIS and the complainant and for them to present evidence (but in each other's absence),[157] and a discretion for the Committee to reveal such of its recommendations and findings as it sees fit to the complainant (in addition to the Solicitor General and to the CSIS).[158] Although full cross-examination of CSIS evidence is not practical for security reasons, SIRC has, nevertheless, developed practices which attempt to ensure fairness to the complainant.[159] These involve, so far as possible, giving the gist of allegations to the complainant to enable him or her to challenge them. Even where access to confidential information must be excluded, SIRC has adopted the practice of using its own security-cleared counsel to vigorously cross-examine the CSIS evidence. These individuals are identified in SIRC's annual reports, and include academics and practitioners, many with a record of commitment to civil liberties. An agreed (but censored) summary is presented on the complainant's return to enable further questions and cross-examination by the complainant.[160]

There are differences between the Australian and the Canadian legislation at the remedial level following the review. Under the ASIO Act the Tribunal may record in its findings about the challenged security assessment, its own view of any opinion, advice, or information contained in the assessment.[161] Since these findings supersede the security assessment where there is a conflict[162] this amounts to a power of rectification—but only where the Tribunal forms the view that information in the assessment is 'incorrect, incorrectly represented or could not reasonably be relevant to the requirements of security'.[163] The Tribunal's findings go to the Director-General of ASIO, the Commonwealth agency to which the assessment was furnished and, subject to a discretion to exclude information not previously given to him or her, to the complainant.[164] The complainant is free, subject to any directions from the Tribunal, to publish the findings.[165] The Tribunal also has power to report more general matters raised by an individual complainant with ASIO and with the minister.[166] This power would be of obvious relevance if a complaint demonstrated an overpreparedness to regard a particular category of individuals or an organization as a security threat[167] or some general deficiency in the assessment process. Under

---

[157] ASIO Act, s. 48(2).   [158] Ibid., s. 52(2).   [159] See Rankin (n. 132 above).

[160] These procedures have been held by the Supreme Court to comply with s. 7 of the Charter of Rights, which protects life, liberty, and security of the person: *Chiarelli* v. *Canada* [1992] SCR 711. Nevertheless, the Special Committee earlier recommended that a procedure be introduced creating a bar of security-cleared counsel who could cross-examine CSIS evidence representing the complainant: *In Flux* (n. 135 above), para. 12.5.2.

[161] ASIO Act, s. 60(1).   [162] Ibid., s. 61.   [163] Ibid., 60(1A).

[164] Ibid., s. 60 (2)(3).   [165] Ibid., s. 60 (4).   [166] Ibid., s. 60A.

[167] Long before the end of the Cold War the Security Appeals Tribunal held that the Australian Communist Party was not a subversive organization on the basis of a very careful and extended analysis of developments since the Second World War and the Party's own publications: *Rix* v. *Director General of Security* (Security Appeals Tribunal, 1 June 1983). We are grateful to Samuels J, President of the Tribunal, for sending us a copy of this decision.

the CSIS Act SIRC reports its findings and any recommendations,[168] but there is nothing on the face of the Act to make these binding.[169]

The position of the courts under the two schemes is different. Although in Australia judicial review of the actions of ASIO itself is in general possible,[170] all decisions relating to security assessments are immune from challenge in the courts[171] and the decisions of the Security Appeals Tribunal are also beyond question or review.[172] In Canada no attempt has been made to restrict access to the courts.

The Canadian and Australian legislation demonstrates the difficulties of reconciling the requirements of justice to the individual public servant with the requirements of national security. Access to information to enable an effective appeal to be made is clearly a problem area. Both schemes recognize that access may have to be restricted. In the CSIS Act it is SIRC which goes behind the veil of secrecy on the complainant's behalf, but it has also developed imaginative practices for protecting the complainant's interests consistent with the requirements of national security. The ASIO Act places greater emphasis on informing the complainant as fully as possible. Either approach is preferable to the weak or non-existent entitlements to information which a civil servant enjoys under British procedures. In both cases the basis of the review procedures is very much wider than under the equivalent processes in the Britain.

CONCLUSION

Vetting is a necessary evil. It is necessary because there needs to be reasonable assurance that those with access to the small proportion of government-held information which genuinely needs to be kept secret can be relied on to maintain that secrecy, and similarly that those with access to government premises do not commit, or assist in committing, politically motivated violence. It is an evil for several divergent reasons. Some of these are inherent in any system of evaluation of individuals, but others result from defects in the system Britain has chosen to adopt.

Vetting decisions are a matter of probability and prediction; they seek to assess the degree of risk and entail judgments of future behaviour. The nearest

---

[168] CSIS Act, s. 52(2).

[169] In *Thompson* v. *Canada* [1992] 1 SCR 385 the Supreme Court held (reversing the Federal Court of Appeal (1988) 3 FC 108) that such recommendations were not binding on the minister. The government has rejected suggestions that SIRC decisions on security clearance complaints should be final: *On Course* (n. 135 above), 75.

[170] See *Church of Scientology* v. *Woodward* [1983] 57 AJLR 42. The allegations in that case concerned general 'targeting' of a body by ASIO (on the facts, not *ultra vires*), which was held not to be excluded from judicial consideration by the existence of the statutory security appeal scheme; see further pp. 000–0 (Ch. 12).

[171] ASIO Act, s. 37(5).   [172] Ibid., s. 62.

analogy is to the 'dangerousness' debate in relation to sentencing offenders;[173] and in both contexts there are profound moral objections to making a person's employment or deprivation of liberty dependent on the fragile rationality of such judgments. The difference is that while alternative bases exist for calculating criminal punishment, there seems to be no way of avoiding decisions of this kind in the context of security. One must insist instead that the criteria used be open, definite, and do not incorporate political bias or irrelevant matter. They must be applied in a reasonably systematic and consistent matter, and anyone adversely affected must have what the European Convention describes as an 'effective remedy'.

By these standards, the British system is highly unsatisfactory—at both the levels of substance and of procedure. In this chapter we have concentrated on reviewing the latter, but the need for reform of the criteria in use should not go unnoticed. Some of the specific criteria are perfectly acceptable. If someone on a yearly salary of £15,000 has debts of £30,000 and is known to frequent gambling casinos, it is reasonable to conclude that he or she will find the prospect of a large and quick financial gain more alluring than the average person. Yet however reasonable any particular rule of thumb used by administrators may be, in terms of the publicly enunciated criteria, this example would fall into the catch-all category of 'defect of character', which leaves too much arbitrary power to government officials to include within it any behaviour of which they happen to disapprove. We have seen what can happen in the case of Mr Hodges; however distasteful his promiscuous homosexuality, it was both legal and unconcealed. The danger of blackmail, and hence to security, was therefore minimal. Elsewhere the criteria are more contentious: for instance, in the light of the events in Eastern Europe since 1989, the case for abandoning vetting on ideological grounds entirely is now stronger than ever.

Even without such radical reform of the criteria there is much scope for improvement. Comprehensive legislation is a requirement for the United Kingdom to be able to take advantage of the national security exceptions to Articles 8 and 10 of the European Convention where the restrictions must be 'prescribed by law'. The administrative practice based upon the prerogative governing the civil service is exactly the quality of rule which was found to be deficient in the *Malone* case. The provisions in the Security Service Act 1989 do not cover the deficiency because they do not purport to provide a legal basis for vetting *per se* and in any event provide only a partial remedy. Where an applicant wishes to challenge the truth of information supplied by the Security Service, rather than the reasonableness of their belief in it, or whether it justified an adverse decision, recourse to the Security Service Tribunal will be to no avail. Futhermore, it is plain from the *Leander* judgment that in order to meet the test that the law be foreseeable and accessible to the individual, the legislation should

---

[173] J. Floud and W. Young, *Dangerousness and Criminal Justice* (London, 1981), *passim*; A. Bottoms and R. Brownsword, 'The Dangerousness Debate After the Floud Report' (1982) 22 *BJ Crim.* 229.

be sufficiently clear and comprehensive so that any implementary administrative practice is firmly rooted in it. Unpublished guidelines will not suffice. Open-ended and administratively manipulable phrases like 'defect of character' lack the necessary precision. It is doubtful whether the reference to the Three Advisers would satisfy the tests because of its procedural deficiencies and non-binding quality; *a fortiori* the review of a case by a departmental head. Still less could these processes individually or collectively be said to constitute an 'effective remedy', although the limited availability of judicial review may mitigate some of the inadequacies.[174]

What is needed is legislation which itself specifies the grounds for vetting, the rights of review or appeal, and the relationship between vetting, security clearances, and the jurisdiction of the Security Service Tribunal.[175] In view of the severe self-imposed limitations under which British courts operate in national security related cases, a separate statutory security clearance review tribunal would be the most appropriate forum to hear appeals in individual cases. By creating the Interception of Communications and Security Service Tribunals, the government has already shown its preparedness to confer similar powers to obtain evidence and to grant remedies (but within an unsatisfactorily narrow jurisdiction) in security cases. These Tribunals are rather nearer the Canadian than the Australian model of a security clearance tribunal, but with coercive powers to grant redress. One possibility would be to expand the jurisdiction and powers of the Security Service Tribunal to deal with all aspects of vetting cases. On the whole this is not to be recommended, because it would distort that body's focus on a single institution. A separate tribunal is required to deal with vetting cases, although this in turn would require clear lines of demarcation between it and the Security Service Tribunal as regards complaints over MI5's involvement in vetting. While such a tribunal needs to be fashioned so that it tones in harmoniously with the existing constitutional decor, the models already in use in Australia and Canada, if suitably adapted, have much to commend them, especially because of the procedural protections they offer the complainant.

Although as the inactivity of the Three Advisers for over twenty years attests, the system has not in the recent past generally operated oppressively against those already employed, it certainly has the potential to do so. It also provides precious few rights for people never employed at all because of adverse security reports. The official expansion of vetting to several hundred thousand more cases each year, confirmed by the 1990 Statement, requires something better than the existing cosy patchwork of administrative and personnel procedures. For the way the state makes decisions over whom it will employ has a symbolic significance far exceeding even the issues of individual justice at stake.

[174] *Soering* v. *UK* (1989) 11 EHRR 439, 481–2.
[175] A Home Office consultation paper was issued in 1993 inviting comment on a proposal to establish a statutory vetting agency to oversee the disclosure of criminal records for (non-security) employment vetting: *Disclosure of Criminal Records for Employment Vetting Purposes*, Cm. 2319 (1993).

7

Detention, Immigration, and Deportation

In an age before the instant spread of ideas by mass communications the control of the entry of persons whose presence was politically undesirable was an
effective means of ensuring state security. An island state like the United
Kingdom had a considerable additional protection against the arrival of those
with threatening ideas. In fact, though, people of heterodox views were often
tolerated in nineteenth century Britain as political refugees. In the twentieth century immigration and immigration policy has been more dominated by economic
and racial factors, especially since the Second World War, but a continuing interest in security remains. The terrain has changed—anarchists and revolutionaries
have given way to refugees (who are no longer so welcome if they are black)
and students; the European Community and the Irish troubles have, in different
ways, left their mark. Nevertheless, in the era of international terrorism the
·physical migration of persons of interest to security officials is as significant as
ever.

Immigration law has never been divorced from either domestic economic or
foreign policy. The broadest conception of national security interests (which we
have criticized in Chapter 1), demands a tight control over both the entrance
and departure of people regarded as either dangerous or especially valuable to
the state. Whilst those whose political or religious views may 'contaminate' the
native population are excluded (the long-established American law and practice),
strategically significant sections of the workforce are prevented from leaving, as
was done by Soviet bloc states during the Cold War. However, more commonly
it is specific persons, rather than the volume of migration, who are seen to pose
a security problem. In addition to possible direct threat to domestic security
interests, questions of diplomacy may also be involved, especially when the presence or activites of a particular individual in the country is an embarrassment
and a threat to the continued good relations with a foreign state.

In addition to describing the history and operation of these controls this
chapter is also concerned with internal measures applied to what the law
quaintly terms 'aliens' (that is, non-British citizens). The legal position of such
people is always precarious, their civil rights substantially fewer than those of
their 'hosts' and, as that description suggests, their invitation to remain ever
likely to be terminated by deportation if their activities displease. In addition, in
times of international tension or outright conflict, 'enemy aliens' may face a
number of other disabilities—not least mass internment or expulsion. Both
major wars saw the introduction of such measures, as, to a much more limited

extent, did the Gulf War. In addressing freedom of movement we are not, however, solely concerned with immigration matters. We deal also with the imposition of non-criminal forms of restraint on liberty on British citizens. Though in much smaller numbers than 'enemy aliens', British citizens were also detained during the Second World War. Uniquely, Northern Ireland has caused a form of internal exile (the exclusion order) to be introduced even against British citizens.

In what follows we first consider the connection between immigration procedures and security. This discussion highlights the theme with which the remainder of the chapter is concerned—the scope of executive discretion. We illustrate the breadth of the discretion by focusing first in outline on a whole range of ministerial powers to control the movement both of foreigners and citizens. We then demonstrate the unsatisfactory nature of the procedures involved by dealing in greater depth with three modern problem areas: detention in wartime, the use of exclusion orders, and deportation on grounds of national security. The procedural defects inherent in these procedures are largely common ones, and it is appropriate to look for solutions to the equivalent processes for reviewing similar immigration and deportation cases in Canada. Control of freedom of movement is not solely a question of national discretion in Britain's case and we, therefore, also briefly examine the extent to which discretion in the security field is constrained under EC law.

IMMIGRATION PROCEDURES AND SECURITY

The administration of immigration control has since its inception been inextricably linked with national security. Special Branch and MI5 have, as domestic intelligence agencies, been preoccupied with the political and other activities of immigrants since their formation. This pattern can be traced back to the mid-Victorian period.

Throughout much of the Victorian period the presence of a significant refugee population in London was a considerable diplomatic embarrassment.[1] State papers show that the government was under constant pressure to curb the conspiratorial activities of French, German, and Austrian *émigrés* in the 1850s. Despite the overt resistance to the idea of political policing some measures were taken: Mazzini's mail was opened (although there followed a public furore when the interception was revealed), and from 1851 forwards some attempts were made to infiltrate the refugee communities to obtain information and to pass it on to foreign governments. Money was used from the Secret Service Fund (and secretly donated by the French government) to resettle some of the more troublesome refugees in America. Some of these efforts bordered on the farcical— for instance, the polite request from the Home Office to Karl Marx for

---

[1] This paragraph is drawn from the comprehensive and entertaining account in B. Porter, *The Refugee Question in Mid-Victorian Politics* (Cambridge, 1979).

information about communist activities in England, to which he responded with full co-operation.[2] They did not, however, prevent French exiles in Britain from hatching a plot to assassinate Emperor Napoleon III with a bomb: the apprehension of Orsini in France caused a major diplomatic incident bordering on war which the acquittal of one of his conspirators in Britain did little to ease. Palmerston's subsequent attempt to strengthen the law to appease the French led to the fall of his government when the Conspiracy to Murder Bill was wrecked by an amendment. However, the tide of domestic opinion turned against the refugees: the law was quietly amended to introduce conspiracy in the Offences Against the Person Act 1861, extradition was extensively introduced through the 1870 Act, although it contained the 'political offence' exception,[3]

---

[2] B. Porter, *The Origins of the Vigilant State: The London Metropolitan Special Branch Before the First World War* (London, 1987), 9–10.

[3] The political offence exception which became enshrined in s. 3 of the Extradition Act 1870 (see now Extradition Act 1989, s. 6(1)(*a*)) is a fascinating sub-plot in this story. It undoubtedly saved many alleged offenders who would, in modern terminology, have been regarded as terrorists by the requesting state. The rationale of the exception may be partly attributable to a non-recognition of other states' national security concerns and partly to an unpreparedness to assist in what may appear as nakedly political persecution (s. 6 (1)(*d*) of the Extradition Act 1989 now forbids extradition *inter alia* where the fugitive will be punished or persecuted for his or her political opinions). In some respects, however, the exception provided a cover for international terrorists to enter a country for the express purpose of offending by committing an assassination or bombing, hijacking or hostage taking, and immediately fleeing to another state, which would lack jurisdiction to try him or her and also be unable to extradite. The modern importance of the rule is limited by several factors.

First, the courts narrowed the scope of the exception by propounding a distinction between acts whose purpose was to bring about the overthrow of the government and others. In *Re Meunier* [1894] 2 QB 415 the defence was denied to an anarchist who had caused explosions at a café and at a military barracks in France. Cave J decided that the facts fell outside the exception because the incident was not part of a struggle between opposing sides for control of the state. Although later cases had cut back somewhat from the limited notion that the exception only applies in the context of a struggle for power over the state (*Schtraks* v. *Government of Israel* [1964] AC 556), nevertheless, in flexibly adapting the concept to new circumstances, the courts have sometimes explicitly referred to the need not to hamper the international fight against terrorism. Thus in *Cheng* v. *Governor of Pentonville Prison* [1973] AC 931, the House of Lords held that the political nature of the offence must be directed at the state seeking extradition. In *R.* v. *Governor of Winson Green Prison, ex p. Littlejohn* [1975] 1 WLR 893, the Divisional Court refused to apply the exception to a convicted IRA bank robber who claimed that the offence was motivated by an attempt to infiltrate that organization on behalf of British Intelligence: it regarded the evidence of the political character of the offence as insufficient. In *R.* v. *Governor of Pentonville Prison, ex p. Rehott* (1978) 75 LSG 43, the Court of Appeal held that the applicant who, in the course of absconding whilst awaiting sentencing on a charge of assault in Israel, had given information to the Moroccan authorities about Israeli military installations, was not entitled to the defence: even if the facts were as alleged, it did not follow that espionage was an offence of a political character.

Secondly, the government and the courts have been prepared to find ways around the rule where an inability to extradite would cause embarrassment in its relations with a friendly state (as in the 'disguised extradition' cases p. 170 below).

Thirdly, modern legislation has deprived terrorists of the benefit of the rule. Terrorist offenders are now precluded by the Suppression of Terrorism Act 1978 (s. 1 and Sched. 1), passed to give domestic effect to the Council of Europe Convention on the Suppression of Terrorism (see Cmnd. 7031 (1977)). At the same time, in furtherance of the principle of 'extradite or try' the UK has assumed extra-territorial jurisdiction over a number of terrorist offences, e.g. in relation to hijacking of ships and aircraft: Tokyo Convention Act 1967, s. 2; Suppression of Terrorism Act 1978, s. 4(7); Taking of Hostages Act 1982, s. 1; Aviation Security Act 1982, s. 1.

and ultimately the open door policy itself was abandoned with the introduction of immigration control in the anti-Semitic Aliens Act 1905.

Although the Metropolitan Police had had sporadic involvement in political surveillance of refugees in mid-Victorian London, it was the Fenian bombing campaign which began in 1881 which led to the creation of the Special Branch.[4] In the same year regular surveillance of the meetings of refugee socialists began, following the conviction for sedition of Alfred Most for writing in the newspaper *Freiheit* in praise of the assassination of the Tsar.[5] A military intelligence department in the War Office was formed at about the same time, but it took the spy fever of the years proceeding the First World War to lead to the establishment of the Secret Service Bureau (the forerunner of MI5 and MI6). From the start its activities were directed at the sizeable immmigrant refugee populations, who were feared to be harbouring an army of spies.[6]

By the Edwardian period the liberal mid-Victorian feelings of superiority and detachment toward imported subversion had evaporated. The Aliens Act 1905 established an Aliens Inspectorate with powers to exclude 'undesirables', although initially the category comprised those with criminal leanings or infectious diseases, rather than contagious ideologies.[7] The Great War was to change attitudes to immigration irrevocably and to carry with it a machinery of immigration control wedded to the infant security apparatus of the state. The Security Service Bureau instigated the creation of a secret police register of aliens in 1910, in which chief constables were asked to report on the espionage or other unusual activities of aliens within their districts.[8] During the war the list was made overt by requiring aliens to register with the police, and the system was maintained for security reasons in the inter-war period[9] and still remains.[10] A system of passport control was introduced as a wartime measure but retained following the Armistice because of its value in countering the new threat from Bolshevism by excluding known Bolshevik agents and otherwise providing intelligence on the movement of Bolsheviks.[11] 'Undesirability' came to be applied to those with communist associations, and immigration officers were issued with a

---

[4] See n. 2 above, 7–10 and esp. ch. 3. As well as the direct impetus given by the bombings, Porter lays considerable stress on the erosion of mid-centrury liberalism as leading to the introduction of political policing.

[5] Ibid. 42–3; A. Dummet and A. Nicol, *Subjects, Citizens, Aliens and Others: Nationality and Immigration Law* (London, 1990), 94.

[6] C. Andrew, *Secret Service* (London, 1986), 103–4.

[7] Dummet and Nicol (n. 5 above), 103. For responses to earlier fears of imported revolution from France following 1798, see R. Plender, *International Migration Law* (2nd edn., Dordrecht, 1988), 64–5.

[8] Andrew, (n. 6 above), 103.   [9] Dummet and Nicol (n. 5 above), 110–11.

[10] Immigration Act 1971, s. 4(3); Immigration (Registration with Police) Regulations 1972, SI 1972/1758 (as amended by SI 1975/999 and SI 1979/196).

[11] Andrew (n. 6 above), 346–9. The system was under the control of the Foreign Office and, in the inter-war years, the presence of Passport Control Officers at embassies abroad became a cover for SIS (later to become MI6) officers.

blacklist of suspects, whom they had authority to turn away at a port of entry.[12] The popular association of communism and Jewishness was to blight the attempts to resettle many refugees from Germany during the 1930s.[13]

Although following 1945 British immigration policy became dominated by quite different concerns, the administrative marriage of immigration and security persists. In a recent official publication the Security Sevice has claimed that its role in advising on the refusal of visas has 'severely hampered hostile intelligence agencies in their efforts to run and recruit agents'.[14] One of the chief tasks of Special Branch officers is assignment on port duty;[15] although this has much to do with the war against drugs and counter-terrorism, the 'Guidelines on the Work of a Special Branch' states that one of the purposes is to 'gather information relating to their other functions and other criminal matters'.[16] These other functions include assisting the Security Service in its tasks.[17] The Branch is also involved in investigating and reporting on requests for citizenship by naturalization: this will include a check on any security threat from the applicant. It is because of the security aspect that the the the Home Office has rejected calls for a system of appeal against refusal of naturalization.[18] The Home Office Guidelines also state that Branch officers assist with other immigration enquiries and deal with the registration of foreign nationals, although in practice much of the routine work is done by the non-Branch officers. What these 'other immigration enquiries' comprise has not been officially acknowledged, but the experience of those arrested pending deportation during the Gulf War suggests that they may involve monitoring the activities of foreign student and political groups.[19] Presumably, formal avenues exist for relaying Special Branch information on foreign nationals to those in the Home Office reponsible for advising on deportation.

EXECUTIVE DISCRETION

In part the association between security and immigration is also strengthened by the nature of immigration law, which assures the state virtually unfettered discre-

---

[12] Dummet and Nicol (n. 5 above), 146–7.   [13] Ibid. 152–8.

[14] *MI5: The Security Service* (London, 1993), 16.

[15] This appears to date from the assignment of officers from the Metropolitan Police to port duty in 1884: see Porter (n. 3 above), 50. Powers under the Prevention of Terrorism (Temporary Provisions) Act 1989, sched. 2, paras. 7 and 8 and sched. 3 of detention and search of suspected terrorists are in practice operated by assigned Special Branch officers. Similar powers under earlier legislation have been held not to contravene the ECHR: *McVeigh, O'Neill and Evans* v. *UK* (1981) 5 EHRR 71.

[16] *Fourth Report from the Select Committee on Home Affairs* HC (1984–5) 71.

[17] Ibid., 'Guidelines on the Work of a Special Branch', para. 6.

[18] Dummett and Nicol (n. 5 above), 189; *Third Report from the Home Affairs Committee for 1982–83, British Nationality Fees*, HC 248, para. 2 and 'Notes of Guidance for Police Officers Concerning Registration Enquiries', para. 3.

[19] See pp. 187 ff. below. Writing some years earlier, Bunyan suggested that Special Branch work included continuous updating of the lists of those to be interned in the event of war: T. Bunyan, *The Political Police in Britain* (London, 1977), 132.

tion at some critical points, thus making decisions based on security considerations effectively immune from challenge.

Several examples can be given. For instance, the sovereign possessed the ability to exclude particular aliens from entry into the country prior to the modern system of immigration control,[20] although there is controversy over whether this practice was properly founded in the prerogative.[21] In any event the power to refuse entry to non-British citizens is now equally broad, if statutory.[22] Although this power, like the statutory power of deportation considered below, gives ample scope for ministerial discretion in security cases,[23] so that there would be little need to resort to ancient prerogative powers, the position is further confused by an intriguing provision (section 33(5) of the 1971 Act) which expressly preserves the prerogative.[24] Acquisition of citizenship by naturalization depends, in addition to other statutory criteria, on the Secretary of State's discretion—'if he thinks fit'.[25] Deprivation of citizenship is also provided for, by order, where the minister is satisfied *inter alia* that a citizen has, by speech or act, been disloyal or disaffected, and continuance of his citizenship would not be conducive to the public good.[26]

The record clearly shows that British judges have given the administration wide latitude in this area, thus reinforcing the discretion, even where it has been credibly alleged that executive powers are being abused to achieve some impermissible objective. One example is the return to his or her country, outside the normal processes of extradition, of a foreigner who has offended that regime.

[20] S. Legomsky, *Immigration and the Judiciary* (Oxford, 1987), 87 ff.

[21] Ibid.; Plender (n. 7 above), 62; W. Craies, 'The Right of Aliens to Enter British Territory' (1890) 6 *LQR* 27, 29; C. Vincenzi, 'Aliens and the Judicial Review of Immigration Law', [1985] *PL* 93, 99 ff.

[22] There is no right of entry in such cases, which are by leave of the Secretary of State; Immigration Act 1971, ss. 1(2) and 3(1). In practice the discretion is exercised with regard to rules made under s. 3(2); see (1989–90) HC 251, para. 86, which provides for refusal of entry if a person's presence in the country would not be conducive to the public good. Citizens of EC countries exercising their right of free movement are exempt from entry control; see Immigration Act 1988, s. 7.

[23] See e.g. C. Aubrey, *Who's Watching You?* (London, 1981), 141–2.

[24] See C. Vincenzi, 'Extra-Statutory Ministerial Discretion in Immigration Law', [1992] *PL* 300.

[25] British Nationality Act 1981, s. 6 and sched. 1. The government resisted attempts to replace the general discretion with a more precise list of criteria for refusal (including a ground that the applicant threatened national security): *HC Debs.*, Standing Committee F, 19 Mar. 1981, cols. 632 ff. The procedures require the taking of an oath of allegiance in some cases: British Nationality Act 1981, ss. 41(1)(d) and 42(1) and (2) and sched. 5. Allegiance to the Crown is a critical element of the offence of treason: see pp. 200–2 below.

[26] British Nationality Act 1981, s. 40 (3) and (5). A procedure exists for review of these cases by a committee of inquiry with a judicial chairman: ibid., s. 40(7). The procedural rules for these hearings allow for legal representation and a right to call witnesses, but do not grant a right of cross-examination (British Citizenship (Deprivation) Rules 1982, SI 1982/988; British Dependent Territories Citizenship (Deprivation) Rules 1982, SI 1982/989). The committee has discretion to hold hearings *in camera* (although it is unclear if the applicant may be excluded), and to censor the reasons it gives for its conclusions on grounds of national security. However, its conclusions are not binding on the minister, and the procedures has only been invoked in a very few cases, although interestingly five of them involved spies (*HC Debs.*, Standing Committee F, 7 May, 1981, cols. 1841 ff.).

Deportation procedures have sometimes been used as a method of achieving such 'disguised extradition'.[27] When, during the First World War, deserters from the French army were deported by agreement with the French government in circumstances where they could not have been extradited, the courts refused to intervene.[28] Most notorious of all was the case in 1962 of Dr Soblen who had been convicted in the United States on charges of espionage (a non-extraditable offence). Soblen had been deported from Israel (whence he had fled), but he successfully interrupted his passage to the United States by slashing his wrists and forcing the aircraft to land at Heathrow to seek medical treatment for him. At American behest, Soblen was served with refusal of permission to land by the British authorities and detained in hospital pending deportation to the United States. Nevertheless, the Court of Appeal both refused Soblen access to documents which might indicate bad faith in the deportation proceedings and refused to intervene in the decision itself.[29] Soblen committed suicide before the deportation order could be enforced. In effect, the Court of Appeal held that the Aliens Order 1953 (which pre-dated the power now contained in the Immigration Act 1971 discusssed above) could be used to circumvent the Extradition Act 1870. All the members of the Court of Appeal held that theoretically the exercise of the power of deportation was reviewable. Lord Denning held that if it could be shown that the real purpose of the deportation was to bring about extradition then it would amount to abuse of the ministerial power. However, despite news reports of a request for Soblen's return made by the United States, his Lordship went on to hold that there was no evidence of abuse; Soblen's attempt to gain access to the diplomatic exchanges between the two countries foundered on a claim of crown privilege and, in any event, there was nothing to show what weight the Home Secretary had attached to any American representations.[30] Donovan LJ was prepared to infer that the reason for the order was to effect the return of Soblen to the United States, but held that this did not amount to an abuse of the power, since it was open to the minister to conclude that the return of a convicted spy to an ally was conducive to the public good.[31]

The same degree of executive discretion with regard to persons whose movements raise concerns on security grounds can be seen in relation to the controls

[27] See P. O'Higgins, 'Disguised Extradition: the Soblen Case' (1964) *MLR* 521; C. Thornberry, 'Dr Soblen and the Alien Law of the United Kingdom' (1963) 12 *ICLQ* 414.

[28] *R.* v. *Secretary of State for Home Affairs ex p. Duke of Chateau Thierry* [1917] 1 KB 922; *R.* v. *Superintendent of Chiswick Police Station, ex p. Sacksteder* [1918] 1 KB 578.

[29] *R.* v. *Governor of Brixton Prison ex p. Soblen* [1962] All ER 641; cf. the Australian decision of *Taxeris* v. *Liveris* (1962) ALJR 63.

[30] [1962] 3 All ER at 662.

[31] Ibid. 665. It is doubtful that this reasoning could succeed on the present law: the clear policy of the Extradition Act 1989 is that 'extradition arrangements' should either be general or 'special' (i.e. pertaining to a particular case with whom there are not general arrangements) in nature. An arrangement to deport to a particular country should, it is argued, be considered to be a failed attempt at 'special arrangements' if, as in *Soblen*, there are general arrangements with the state in question.

on the travel of UK citizens. Before the modern restrictions introduced to prevent warring football supporters roaming continental Europe, the ability of the state to prevent foreign travel was governed by powers of some antiquity and obscurity. Magna Carta provided in 1215 that: 'It shall be lawful for any man to leave and return to our kingdom unharmed and without fear, by land or water, preserving his allegiance to us except in time of war for some short period, for the common benefit of the realm.'[32] Shortly afterwards the writ *ne exeat regno* was introduced for the purpose of restraining citizens from leaving the country[33] in times of national crisis so that they would be available to defend the realm, and to prevent them from travelling to other kingdoms for prejudicial purposes.[34] However, in practice its use shifted mysteriously from the prevention of medieval draft dodging to restraining the movement of property out of the jurisdiction during litigation. It would not, however, be available against non-citizens; hence when the American wife of the spy Donald Maclean left the country to join him, ultimately in Moscow, the authorities (even had they wished to) could not have prevented her.[35] Although not formally abolished, the political use of the writ is now defunct: in modern times restrictions have been imposed during war by legislation under emergency powers rather than through the use of the prerogative.[36]

However, the prerogative governing the issue of passports is in healthy use, even if practice is somewhat modified due to membership of the European Community. Travel can effectively be prevented through denial or revocation of a passport[37] and, not surprisingly, security considerations feature (although not expressly) among the reasons why in practice these wide discretions are exercised. According to a statement of ministerial practice, passports may be denied to: 'persons whose activities are so notoriously undesirable or dangerous that Parliament would be expected to support the action of the Foreign Secretary in refusing them a passport or withdrawing a passport already issued to prevent their leaving the United Kingdom.'[38] The most extensive modern use of this power was during the Rhodesian crisis, when an advisory committee was established to review cases of those whose passports had been withdrawn because of

---

[32] Art. 42 (HMSO trans., 1965).

[33] J. Bridge, 'The Case of the Rugby Football Team and the High Prerogative Writ' (1972) 88 *LQR* 83; 'Justice', *Going Abroad: A Report on Passports* (London, 1974), 8; *Parsons* v. *Burk and Others* [1971] NZLR 244; L. Anderson, 'Antiquity in Action—Ne Exeat Regno Revived' (1987) 103 *LQR* 246.

[34] Bridge (n. 33), 84 and 88.

[35] *Report Concerning the Disappearance of Two Former Foreign Office Officials*, Cmd. 9577 (1955), para. 22.

[36] Bridge (n. 33 above), 86.

[37] The passport is a practical if not a legal necessity for modern travel: it is acceptable as proof of British citizenship on entry (Immigration Act 1971, s. 3(9)) and in practice British citizens may experience difficulties on re-entry unless carrying one: *R.* v. *Secretary of State for Home Affairs ex p. Minta*, the *Independent*, 21 Aug., 1991.

[38] *HL Debs.*, vol. 209, col. 860 (16 June 1958). See also: *HC Debs.*, vol. 764, col. 1107 (14 May 1968).

their association with the Smith regime.[39] The arm of the Ombudsman reaches the Passport Office, but ministerial decisions to refuse or withdraw passports are excluded.[40] Although the power is a prerogative one, the Court of Appeal has asserted its jurisdiction to review a refusal to issue a passport.[41] However, the case in question was a routine one of restricting freedom to travel because of the issue of an unexecuted criminal warrant for the applicant's arrest; it is probable that the courts would be more deferential in a case in which national security was asserted as the reason for the refusal.[42]

To these ancient rules there must also be added a modern gloss: freedom to travel has repeatedly received recognition as a fundamental human right in international law. However, the major human rights treaties recognize executive discretion by allowing for curtailment of the right on grounds of national security.[43] Exercise of rights of freedom of movement by EC citizens also imply legally enforceable rights to travel; thus, a British citizen will have an enforceable right to a passport to leave the country to travel to work in other EC countries.[44] However, unsurprisingly, the relevant Directive allows restrictions in the interests of public security.

Enough has been said in this general section to establish the broad trend of executive discretion. We turn now to the detailed study of three procedures attempting to provide a measure of administrative justice for the individual, whether a foreigner or British citizen, caught up in executive decisions in this field. These are wartime powers of internment, exclusion orders, and deportation on grounds of national security.

WARTIME INTERNMENT

Wartime internment is an example of one of the most drastic powers of the state exercised in the name of security. Both world wars saw the introduction of a sweeping array of executive powers over all aspects of life, of which the introduction of internment was the most severe. With hindsight and access to official

[39] *HC Debs.*, vol. 766, cols. 723–7 (17 June 1968).
[40] Parliamentary Commissioner Act 1967, s. 4 and, sched. 2; Secretary of State for Foreign and Commonwealth Affairs Order, 1968, SI No. 1657, Art. 4.
[41] *R.* v. *Secretary of State for Foreign and Commonwealth Affairs ex p. Everett* [1989] QB 811.
[42] *Council of Civil Service Unions* v. *Minister for the Civil Service* [1985] AC 374 (see Ch. 12 below). In the USA, the Supreme Court has refused to intervene in a case of interference with the right to travel on these grounds: *Haig* v. *Agee* 101 S. Ct. 2766 (1981).
[43] The International Covenant on Civil and Political Rights (1966), Arts. 12(2) and (3) provide that 'everyone is free to leave any country including his own' but allows for restrictions to be imposed by law where necessary to protect *inter alia* national security or public order. The Fourth Protocol to the European Convention on Human Rights contains a similar provision (Art. 2, paras. (2) and (3)).
[44] Council Directive 68/360/EEC of 15 Oct. 1968, OJ Sp. Edn. 1968, 485, Art. 2(2). Art. 48 EC, contains a similar public-policy exception, see *Rutili* v. *Minister for the Interior* [1975] ECR 1219; *Minister of the Interior* v. *Cohn-Bendit* [1980] CMLR 543; *Van Duyn* v. *Home Office* [1974] ECR 1337.

documents from the time it is possible to state that the holding of thousands of 'enemy aliens' (although many were long-term fully assimilated residents and refugees from persecution) in prison camps was not justified by a realistic threat to national security but was more a device either to assuage public opinion, or to bring home to the civilian population the reality of war.[45] Nor indeed were these measures solely confined to aliens—in both wars certain categories of British citizens fell foul of the Churchillian command to 'Collar the Lot'. Whereas British citizens and neutrals were interned under delegated legislation, aliens were held under prerogative powers; in both cases, though for different reasons, the courts declined to intervene.

At the dawn of the First World War, the Defence of the Realm Act 1914 had empowered the government to make regulations 'for securing the public safety and the defence of the realm'. Regulation 14B made under this scheme allowed for the detention of persons of 'hostile origins or association'. Although the decision was delegated to the Home Secretary, the power was not exercisable except on the recommendation of the military authorities or an Advisory Committee. Legal challenges in the courts proved fruitless. In the famous decision of *R. v. Halliday, ex p. Zadig*[46] the House of Lords upheld the internment of a naturalized British citizen of German birth and found that Regulation 14B was *intra vires* the Defence of the Realm (Consolidation) Act 1914 (which had replaced the earlier Act). It was left to Lord Shaw to deliver a powerful dissenting speech in which he pointed to the absence of an express parentage for the internment scheme in the 1914 Act and refused to assist the executive in filling the gap in such an important issue affecting the liberty of the subject.

At the beginning of the war the Aliens Restriction Act 1914 introduced a duty for aliens to register with the authorities and imposed conditions upon them; these included a power of deportation. From May 1915 internment was introduced for male aliens: ultimately at least 30,000 were interned, with another 20,000 men (those who were not potential combatants), women, and children being repatriated. The legal basis for their internment was the prerogative, and the courts duly held that an order of internment made against an enemy alien for the security of the realm was not reviewable in habeas corpus proceedings.[47]

---

[45] See also Ch. 1 above. For accounts see N. Stammers, *Civil Liberties in Britain During the Second World War* (London, 1983); P. Gillman and L. Gillman, *'Collar the Lot!': How Britain Interned and Expelled its Wartime Refugees* (London, 1980); F. Lafitte, *The Internment of Aliens* (London, 1940); Andrew, *Secret Service* (n. 6 above), 269–70 and 666–71; C. Allen, *Law and Orders* (3rd edn., London, 1965); A. Simpson, *In the Highest Degree Odious: Detention Without Trial in Wartime Britain* (Oxford, 1993).

[46] [1917] AC 260; see also *Ex p. Weber* [1916] 1 AC 421 where the House of Lords held that a German who had resided in Britain for fifteen years and had lost his German nationality as a consequence was, nevertheless, validly interned.

[47] *R. v. Superintendant of Vine St Police Station, ex p. Liebmann* (1916) 1 KB 268. In *R. v. Commandant of Knockdale Camp ex p. Forman* (1917) 117 LT 627 it was held that an alien who had been dealt with until 1917 by restrictions imposed under the Aliens Restrictions Act 1914 was unable to challenge the subsequent cancellation of his exemption from internment. It was held that internment was a prerogative act unaffected by the legislation since s. 1 of the 1914 Act had expressly preserved the prerogative.

The restrictions under the 1914 Act were held not to constrain the use of the prerogative powers since these were in addition to them. In a decision which gave extravagant vent to popular spy fever the Divisional Court took 'judicial notice' of the dangers of clandestine rumour-mongering, signalling with lights, and of passing intelligence by carrier pigeons which could arise from the presence of German citizens at large.[48] It was left to a more moderate Court of Appeal in *Shaffenius* v. *Goldberg*[49] to explain that internment was no smear on the character of the individual alien but was simply due to a policy which the executive had introduced of mass detention as the safest way in its assessment to deal with the risks. The Court of Appeal also explained that the unreviewability of the decision was not due to incapacity to take legal proceedings brought about upon internment, but to its prerogative nature.[50]

In the Second World War the Emergency Powers (Defence) Act 1939 expressly authorized the making of regulations bringing in internment, and separate schemes were introduced for British citizens and for aliens (neutrals were detained under delegated powers and enemy aliens once again under the prerogative). Internment affected comparatively few people in the 'phoney war' period, and it is clear that in these early months the Home Office and MI5 argued against its extension. Several events which occurred within a short space of time changed the policy: Churchill came to power with the conviction that a mass round-up was necessary; the German blitzkrieg swept through much of Europe in April and May 1940, significantly heightening fears of a 'fifth column' operating in Britain; and the veteran head of the Security Service, Vernon Kell, who had argued that internment of aliens was unnecessary, was replaced.[51] In May and June 1940 some 22,000 Germans and Austrians and 4,000 Italians were interned, although most were later released. At the same time the Cabinet took the decision to act against domestic dissidents: around 1,300 British citizens were interned: the power was used mainly against fascists (who accounted for about 750 of this number), although a smaller number of Irish republicans were also detained (communists were markedly absent from this group).

Measures had been taken against enemy aliens from the outset of the war: they were required first to register with police and then to appear before a tribunal in order to be categorized.[52] The purpose of categorization was to determine both which aliens presented a threat to security and also which were

[48] *Ex p. Liebmann* (n. 47 above), Bailhache J at 275 and Low J at 27.

[49] [1916] KB 284 per Young J at 295.

[50] It is likely that even under the 'new' understanding of the prerogative following *CCSU* v. *Minister for the Civil Service* [1985] AC 374 the power would still be held to be unreviewable for reasons of national security: see Ch. 12 below.

[51] Andrew (n. 6 above), 666–71 and R. Thurlow, *Fascism in Britain: a History, 1918–1985* (Oxford, 1986), ch. 9.

[52] The account in this paragraph is based on Gillman and Gillman (n. 45 above), *passim* and Stammers (n. 45 above), ch. 2. On the system of classification see Stammers, 35–6: Category 'A' were those to be interned, Category 'B' were those who were to be left free but subject to restrictions, and category 'C' were to be left unregulated.

refugees. Both decisions were intended to be relevant to the possible introduction of internment at some future date.[53] However, ultimately the government acceded to pressure to intern many aliens who were not recognized as constituting any kind of security threat, and in the rush and confusion of mass internment little regard was paid to the question of whether those affected were refugees from the very regimes against whom the war was being prosecuted. When in May 1940 government policy swung towards mass internments the system was overwhelmed, with the result that many aliens were held for weeks in makeshift camps with little bedding, sanitation, cooking facilities, or food.[54] Contingency planning for internment had been hampered by years of vacillation between the War Office and Home Office over what measures should be taken over aliens in the event of war.[55] Growing public and official concern in the summer and autumn of 1940 led to the establishment of an Advisory Council and Committee on Alien Internees to deal with recommendations about the release of those interned. The adoption of increasingly generous criteria for the release of those interned meant that most had been freed by the end of 1942. However, conflict between MI5 and the Advisory Committee over who was to be released had first to be settled, with MI5's policy of mass internment being thrown over as the release policy became increasingly generous from January 1941 onwards.[56] The intervening period had exposed many inadequacies and mistakes in MI5's preliminary assessment of which aliens were dangerous, but even without these many aliens had been interned for no better reason than because of their German or Italian nationality.

The story of internment of the British fascists during the same conflict sheds considerable light on how such decisions are taken within the intelligence community, and has been explored in some depth by historians.[57] Prior to the war fascist groups in Britain had been successfully penetrated by a number of MI5 agents, enabling the Security Service to reach the conclusion that they posed little real threat—a conclusion confirmed by the open and apparently sincere patriotism expressed by many of their leaders during the early months of the war. Nevertheless, individuals such as Mosley had had high-level contact with and some funding from foreign fascists and this, coupled with rumours of plans for a right-wing *coup d'état*, and evidence of fascist involvement in the

---

[53] Of some 73,000 cases the overwhelming majority (64,000) were placed in Category 'C', with 6,800 in Category 'B' and merely 569 in Category 'A': Stammers (n. 45 above), 36.

[54] Gillman and Gillman (n. 45 above), ch. 20 and Stammers (n. 45 above), 41 ff.

[55] The pre-war policy of encouraging aliens to leave voluntarily changed shortly before the war when, in the light of the influx of refugees, it was realized that few were likely to do so. There followed considerable interdepartmental disputes over who was to be responsible for internment camps: see Gillman and Gillman, (n. 45 above), ch. 3.

[56] The complex changes in release policy and practice may be followed in Stammers (n. 45 above), 51 ff.

[57] Simpson (n. 45 above) is a comprehensive account based on official files; see also Thurlow (n. 51 above), ch. 9.

recruitment of a spy at the American embassy in London (Tyler Kent)[58] led to a Cabinet decision in May 1940 to intern fascist leaders. It is clear from the Cabinet discussions prior to that decision being taken that internment was resorted to precisely because of the improbability of obtaining successful convictions against fascists for recognized criminal offences.[59] Another significant motive was the desire to be able to interrogate the fascists about their contacts with Germany and Italy: some evidence has surfaced of mistreatment of early fascist detainees in an attempt to elicit intelligence from them.[60] Later, in June 1940, an order was made for the internment of 350 local British Union of Fascists officials: criticism that these instructions were based on poor and inaccurate information and that many of those brought in had only tenuous links with the Party appeared to be well-founded, to judge from subsequent events in the review process and in the courts.

The procedure under Regulation 18B was very similar to that employed at the present time in cases of deportations conducive to the public good.[61] Since a fairly full historical record of how it operated is now available from released official documents, it is worth studying in some detail. The grounds for detention were that the minister had reasonable cause to believe that the person was of hostile origins or associations, or had recently been involved in acts prejudicial to the public safety or the defence of the realm, and that as a result it was necessary to exercise control over him. Although the 'reasonable cause' test had been inserted against parliamentary pressure in substitution for the initial regulation which merely required that the minister be 'satisfied',[62] the courts later refused to question the exercise of the minister's discretion.[63] To enable the detention of fascists without proof of 'hostile associations' or 'acts prejudicial' (of which there was none in most cases), Regulation 18B was further amended following the Cabinet's decision to intern them; the new ground permitted internment of members of organizations which were subject to foreign influence or control, or whose leaders had or had had associations with leaders of enemy governments, or who sympathized with the system of government of enemy powers.[64]

The impetus for making an individual detention order in these cases usually originated with the Security Service, or more rarely with the police. After prior consideration by civil servants in his department, the order would be signed by the Home Secretary personally. However, when in the summer of 1940 the policy of mass internment was put into effect these arrangements were effectively

---

[58] Tyler Kent had obtained copies of the secret correspondence between Churchill and Roosevelt demonstrating American connivance in the war despite its professed neutrality (see generally Simpson (n. 45 above), ch. 8). However, at the *in camera* trial one fascist, Mrs Nicholson (the wife of an admiral) was acquitted—she was nevertheless subsequently interned: Thurlow (n. 51 above), 194–7; Simpson, 154 and 214.

[59] Thurlow (n. 51 above), 197.   [60] Ibid. 209.

[61] See pp. 183 ff. below.

[62] See R. Heuston, 'Liversedge v. Anderson in Retrospect' (1970) 86 *LQR* 33, and 87 *LQR* 161; and G. Lewis, *Lord Atkin* (London. 1983) 147–52 for a full account.

[63] *Liversedge* v. *Anderson* [1942] AC 206.   [64] Thurlow (n. 51 above), 197–8.

swamped: personal ministerial consideration of cases was replaced with omnibus orders with up to several hundred names listed in a schedule to an order signed by the minister. The making of the order provided the trigger for the arrest by the police of the detainee. Home Office officials did not normally test in any depth the case put forward by MI5, and this was left to the Advisory Committee established under the procedures if the detainee wished to have the case reviewed. As Simpson has noted, the policy was to detain first and review the evidence later.[65]

Following arrest the detainee's case was subject to review before an Advisory Committee.[66] The Advisory Committe was established in September 1939 and operated under the chairmanship of Norman Birkett, KC. If the case was to go to the Advisory Committee lawyers employed by MI5 would at this stage draft a notice of 'Reasons for the Order' (to be given to the detainee), comprising a recitation of the ground from the regulation which was relied on, after consideration of the Service's files on the detainee, but omitting mention of the evidence which supported the reason. The Committee (but not the detainee) also received a 'Statement of the Case' prepared by the Service which summarized the events relied on and was used by the Committee in questioning the detainee. The Advisory Committee was master of its own procedure but decided at a meeting early in its history to examine detainees in person without granting them the benefit of legal representation at the hearing. Birkett explained in a memorandum that the Committee regarded the lack of legal representation for the detainee as offset by its view that its duty was to assist him or her. However, when it came to making recommendations to the minister any doubts were in practice resolved 'in favour of the country and against the individual'.[67]

After reviewing the case the Committee's report went to the Home Secretary. However, it was confidential and its recommendations were not legally binding. A strong incentive for the minister to follow them where possible lay in the periodic duty to inform Parliament of the numbers of cases in which they had been followed. It is clear that the Committee's advice was followed in the majority of cases; for instance, of 455 recommendations for release that it made up to 6 February 1941, 400 were accepted by the Home Secretary. These figures mask a hidden power struggle over whether MI5's view of the degree of threat posed by the detainees was to be accepted, which was only resolved when the principle was agreed by the Security Executive (subject to MI5's recorded dissent) that the Minister would be recommended routinely to confirm the Advisory Committee's view unless there were exceptional reasons ·not to do

[65] See n. 45 above, 322.
[66] Ibid. 83 ff.. The Committee for Imperial Defence had earlier (in 1937) approved in draft a scheme in which detention would be reviewed by an advisory committee chaired by a High Court Judge, sitting with two MPs; legal representation was to be allowed. An unsuccessful amendment to this effect was moved to the Emergency Powers (Defence) Bill 1939: ibid. 44–5.
[67] Ibid. 86.
[68] Ibid. 292–4; although in some later cases the Advisory Committee protested at further MI5

so.[68] The cases in which the Advisory Committee recommended release have been analysed as falling into four categories: those where decision to intern was based on inaccurate information; where fresh information had surfaced since the decision was taken; where there was convincing evidence of a change in the views of the detainee since Hitler's invasion of the Low Countries; and where the initial internment may have had sufficient deterrent effect in its own right.

Although, as the figures for its performance demonstrate, the Advisory Committee considerably tempered some of the excesses of the internment programme, its own record is not without blemish.[69] The Committee worked from the evidence of MI5 officers, which formed the basis of the questions put to the internee at the hearing. However, detailed knowledge of the allegations was not given to the internee and the Committee itself chose not to examine directly intelligence informants but instead to rely upon the intelligence officers' briefings prepared from their reports; in order to protect sources the Committee was not even given the names of the informants. Naturally this gave rise to criticism that the Advisory Committee was making its recommendations on the basis of second-hand information from unknown informants which had not been tested by cross-examination. In the most important case it had to deal with—that of Mosley himself—it was given an advance briefing by MI5 (apparently derived from surveillance in prison) of the form Mosley's defence would take at the hearings which it was due to conduct—a state of affairs hardly conducive to a judicial, or even moderately fair, hearing.[70]

The major cases reaching the courts where these internments were contested were those brought by alleged fascists in habeas corpus proceedings.[71] The courts consistently refused to intervene.[72] At first they did so on an evidential basis, holding that the minister was not bound to disclose the reasons, thus making legal challenge fraught with difficulty.[73] Then in the infamous decision in *Liversedge* v. *Anderson*[74] the House of Lords held, over Lord Atkin's dissent, that the reasonableness of the Home Secretary's belief was anyway unreviewable in the absence of bad faith. Likewise a blanket order by the Home Secretary covering no fewer than 344 individuals was held to be immune from challenge.[75] Lord Atkin claimed 'even amid the clash of arms the laws are not silent',[76] but the muffling of the ancient safeguard of habeas corpus was to render them

representations being considered by the Home Secretary after the Committee had delivered its recommendation: ibid. 295.

[69] Simpson (n. 45 above), ch. 13.   [70] Thurlow (n. 51 above), 267.

[71] See generally, Simpson (n. 45 above), chs. 14, 15, and 17. No doubt the paucity of cases brought by (the much more numerous) interned aliens was due to the then-prevailing legal view of the unreviewability of actions based on the prerogative.

[72] The solitary exception was *Ex p. Budd* (*No. 1*), *The Times*, 28 May 1941, where the internee was released only to be reinterned (see Simpson, n. 45 above), 318–30: a challenge to the second internment failed: *R.* v. *Home Secretary ex p. Budd* (*No. 2*) [1941] 2 All ER 749.

[73] *R.* v. *Home Secretary, ex p. Lees* [1941] KB 72.

[74] See n. 63 above; and see *Greene* v. *Secretary of State for Home Affairs* [1942] AC 284.

[75] *Stuart* v. *Anderson* [1941] KB 642.   [76] See *Liversedge* v. *Anderson* (n. 63 above), 244.

inaudible. Under the cloak of unreviewability instances of official carelessness in the making of detention orders went unchecked, as is apparent even from the cases reported in the law reports: persons were detained on the basis of evidence later admitted to be unreliable,[77] detained notwithstanding the failure of criminal cases brought in reliance of the same allegations,[78] given the wrong ground for detention,[79] or re-detained on a second ground following the collapse of the case against them on the first.[80]

The function of the courts in this situation was seen to be to assist the government to maintain the state through the crisis, so that in more normal times civil liberties could be restored and guaranteed long term. Judges who drew a line under the powers of self preservation of the state in the name of the rule of law were apt to appear disloyal—Lord Atkin suffered remarkable ostracism at the hands of his judicial brethren following his dissent in *Liversedge* v. *Anderson*, although this may have been partly because of the tone of his speech.[81] However, the danger that the handing of such unchecked powers to the executive is an invitation to abuse is amply demonstrated by the reluctance with which governments relinquished their exceptional powers when the storm was passed. Even after the war the courts proved equally reluctant to gainsay the government's claim of the continuing need for internment.[82]

Overall it is not hard to conclude that human rights were significantly and unnecessarily trampled on as a result of these internments. Despite frequent internal debates and misgivings about the policies pursued and their effects on individuals, the traditional and visible organs of the constitution, Parliament and the courts, did virtually nothing to check the excesses of the Security Service. In Simpson's detailed account of the process it is only the Home Office, and to a lesser extent the Advisory Committee, which emerge with a degree of credit in making slightly more acceptable what was an admittedly inhumane system.[83] In the light of all that has subsequently come to light it is regrettable that in a booklet published in July 1993 MI5 maintained that the internments had successfully deprived Germany of its agents at the outset of the war,[84] without a shred of an apology to the tens of thousands of others who were needlessly interned.

From a power exercised in wartime, we turn now to an exceptional measure available in peace to contain domestic terrorism: the exclusion order. Like internment it involves a severe restriction on the liberty of an individual without the normal preconditions of criminal trial and proof by the authorities beyond reasonable doubt.

---

[77] *Greene* v. *Home Secretary* (n. 74 above); Simpson (n. 45 above), 366–7; Thurlow (n. 51 above), 204; R. Heuston, 'Liversedge v. Anderson: Two Footnotes', 87 *LQR* 162, 163–6.
[78] As in the case of Mrs Nicholson: Allen (n. 45 above), 376–7.
[79] *Greene* v. *Home Secretary* (n. 74 above).   [80] *Ex p. Budd* (*No. 2*) (n. 72 above).
[81] See Heuston (n. 62 above), 44.
[82] *R.* v. *Bottrill ex p. Keuchenmeister* [1947] KB 41—alien enemy internee unable to question Foreign Secretary's certificate that a state of war existed, despite cessation of hostilities on German surrender.
[83] See n. 45 above, 414–16.   [84] *MI5: The Security Service* (London, 1993), 27.

EXCLUSION ORDERS[85]

The origins of the exclusion order lie in powers first taken on the eve of the Second World War when, following a series of bombings, the Prevention of Violence (Temporary Provisions) Act 1939 allowed for the exclusion of suspected Republican sympathizers.[86] With the revival of anti-terrorist legislation in the wake of the 1974 pub bombings, the power was resurrected; it is currently contained in section 5 of the optimistically entitled Prevention of Terrorism (Temporary Provisions) Act 1989.[87] The orders amount to a form of domestic curtailment of movement by preventing named UK and Irish citizens from entering mainland Britain or Northern Ireland (or, in the case of Irish citizens, both).

The prerequisite for the making of an exclusion order is that the Secretary of State is satisfied that the person concerned has been involved in the commission, preparation, or instigation of acts of terrorism[88] connected with Northern Ireland, or is attempting to enter Great Britain with a view to doing so.[89] The effect of an exclusion order is that by section 8 of the Act it becomes a criminal offence to be in or attempt to enter Great Britain; orders last for three years (if not previously revoked) but are renewable. The power can only be exercised against those citizens with less than three years' residence in the relevant part of the United Kingdom. Exclusion orders may also be made against non-British citizens, irrespective of their length of residence. In view of the historical exception of Irish citizens from UK immigration control and powers, the latter provision is a useful substitute for refusal of entry or deportation on public good grounds.

Decisions are made personally by the Home Secretary,[90] after review of evidence by senior police officers and civil servants. The minister will see the

---

[85] This section is heavily based on two sources: interviews held in 1992 with the head of Division F4 (the Police Division) of the Home Office, and with the then Metropolitan Police Commissioner, Sir Peter Imbert and Deputy Assistant Commissioner John Howley, head of Special Branch; a fuller treatment of exclusion orders may be found in C. Walker, *The Prevention of Terrorism in British Law* (2nd edn., Manchester, 1992), ch. 6.

[86] See O. Lomas, 'The Executive and the Anti-Terrorist Legislation of 1939'. [1980] *PL* 16.

[87] See Prevention of Terrorism (Temporary Provisions) Act 1989, ss. 4–8 and sched. 2; on the 1989 Act provisions see Walker (n. 85 above) and D. Bonner, 'Combatting Terrorism in the 1990s: The Role of the Prevention of Terrorism (Temporary Provisions) Act 1989', [1989] *PL* 440, 452 ff.; A. Vercher, *Terrorism in Europe: An International Comparative Legal Analysis* (Oxford, 1992), ch. 2. For accounts of exclusion orders (based on earlier legislation): D. Bonner, *Emergency Powers in Peacetime* (London, 1986), 160–1 and 191–209; G. Hogan and C. Walker, *Political Violence and the Law in Ireland* (Manchester, 1989), 96.

[88] Defined in s. 20(1) as: 'the use of violence for political ends and includes the use of violence for the purpose of putting the public or any section of the public in fear'; see pp. 381–6 below.

[89] S. 6 of the Act gives a corresponding power to the Northern Ireland Secretary over entry into Northern Ireland.

[90] In the rare case of an order excluding an individual from Northern Ireland, by the Northern Ireland minister.

original police reports containing intelligence from informers and police officers, any past convictions, a report of the interrogation of the person detained, and any forensic evidence.[91] Before an order is made the Northern Ireland police will be consulted, because of sensitivity over returning suspected terrorists to the province at large. Our Home Office source stressed that the four Home Secretaries he had worked under had each given personal attention to the making of exclusion orders (and to deportation orders on grounds of national security), and that as a consequence civil servants were conscious of having to justify each case at a high level. This may result in applications being referrred back to the police for 'further and better particulars'. Home Office figures suggesting a refusal rate of 14 per cent in 1974–90,[92] confirm that the process involves a real screening of applications and not a rubber stamping exercise. These powers have been fairly widely used in practice: several hundred exclusion orders were made[93] during the 1970s and early 1980s; however, since that time few fresh orders have been made, although the power has been retained within the statutory armoury.[94]

The most controversial aspect of its use is in situations where no offence is provable: convicted terrorists ought to feel little surprise at finding themselves subject to exclusion on completion of their sentences. However, the use of orders against those acquitted of terrorist offences, released from internment without trial, or associated with 'extremist' (but not 'proscribed') political organizations raises fundamental objections.[95] These concerns can be readily illustrated by the case of John Matthews, who was served with an exclusion order in July 1993 after terrorist charges brought against him were dropped.[96] After detaining him for ten weeks on charges in connection with an explosion in North London, the Crown admitted that the evidence against him did not offer a realistic prospect of conviction. Nevertheless, on his release from the magistrates' court he was re-arrested pending signing of the order by the Home Secretary and later returned to Northern Ireland.

In practice, exclusion orders are used as an alternative to prosecution because of insufficiency of evidence against the suspect. Sometimes this will be because the 'evidence' on which the orders are made is of a kind (for instance, hearsay),

---

[91] The powers are frequently used in practice in conjunction with detention and search powers at ports of entry: see Walker (n. 85 above), 83; Bonner (n. 87 above), 171 ff.

[92] Walker (n. 85 above), 83–4.

[93] For figures see *Review of the Operation of the Prevention of Terrorism (Temporary Provisions) Act 1984 by the Viscount Colville of Culross, Q.C.*, Cm. 264 (1987), para. 11.2.3.

[94] Hogan and Walker (n. 87 above) 96. And may be wheeled out whenever the authorities think fit, as with the service of an exclusion order on the Sinn Fein leader Gerry Adams in order to prevent him attending a meeting at Westminster: the *Independent*, 3 Nov. 1993.

[95] Walker (n. 85 above), 69–72; Bonner (n. 87 above), 191–209, discussing the compatibility of the practice with the ECHR and recommending reform.

[96] *The Times*, 8 July 1993; cf. the similar facts in the deportation case of *In Re Amanulla Khan* [1986] Imm. AR 485 where court upheld the service of a notice of deportation on the applicant immediately following his acquittal on explosives charges.

which would be inadmissible in legal proceedings. However, additional reasons were cited by our sources. Protection of informers was one; proceedings may be difficult to bring where either witnesses are reluctant to come to court, or it is difficult to guarantee their anonymity or safety.[97] The police also cited resource constraints in maintaining long-term surveillance for the purpose of gathering legally credible evidence: exclusion was both pre-emptive and cheaper than prosecution. It is, however, less effective than conviction and imprisonment as a means of curtailing terrorism, and that no doubt accounted for the police preference for prosecution where possible. Exclusion was in the police view a useful second best where good information (but not evidence) of a person's activities was available.

Those who take human rights seriously can only find restrictions of this kind unacceptable. The process of internal exile at ministerial dictat for unspecified activities without the benefit of trial and conviction, and on evidence which has never been tested by cross-examination, has an uncomfortable affinity to powers now abandoned by the regimes of Eastern Europe. However, it is worth recording that concern over civil liberties was expressed by our respondents. The police cited it as a reason for the reduction in the number of exclusion orders in recent years, although there are credible alternative explanations.[98] The Home Office official volunteered 'proportionality', that is, a balance of loss of liberty as against other benefits and costs, as a consideration in the use of exclusion orders.

There is no formal appeal against the making of an exclusion order. Instead, the person affected may object in writing to the order and may also ask for a personal interview with an adviser appointed by the minister.[99] The current advisers (who work singly) are two Queen's Counsel and an industrialist. The case will then be reviewed by the adviser, who will report to the Home Secretary. There is no entitlement for the applicant to hear the evidence on which the order is made or to call witnesses (although the adviser will review the case against the complainant), no statutory right to legal representation, no reasons are given for decisions, and the adviser's opinion is not binding on the minister. The procedure is, if anything, even less satisfactory than the similar one operating in deportation cases,[100] since it embodies fewer formal opportunites for the individual affected to make representations. Nevertheless, in practice it seems its influence has been beneficial: of eighty-nine cases referred to the

---

[97] See Ch. 4 above.

[98] The head of F4 claimed 'we're probably a lot better at it now', by which he meant more precise at targeting the relevant individuals. Greater numbers of exclusion orders in earlier years are also explicable by historical factors: many orders were made initially against long-standing suspects, and a change in the law in 1984 prevented orders being made thereafter to exclude someone from a part of the UK where they had been resident for three years (formerly twenty years residence had been required for exemption).

[99] Sched. 2, para. 3.

[100] See pp. 183 ff. below.

advisers up 1990, thirty resulted in a recommendation to revoke the order, which was followed in all but one case by the minister.[101]

Although challenge in the courts of the making of an exclusion order is not formally precluded, the Act gives no right of appeal as such and the widely drawn terms of the minister's discretion make successful challenge by judicial review a Herculean feat. Thus, in *R. v. Secretary of State for the Home Office, ex p. Stitt*[102] the Divisional Court held that the Home Secretary was not obliged to give reasons when exercising this power: the Divisional Court was impressed by the need, for reasons of national security, not to compromise informers by giving further details of the basis of the case against the excluded person, and by the fact that Parliament had specifically omitted such a right from the legislation despite review of it on two occasions. The effect of the decision is to limit the practical scope of judicial review to clear cases of *ultra vires*, such as the making of an order against a person exempted by the residence rule, since without access to the reason the person excluded will find it impossible to challenge the substance of the decision, even for unreasonableness.

Proposals for reform of the process have produced only unconvincing rebuffs from the government, which has consistently argued that the nature of the information means that any form of binding judicial process would be unsuitable for the review of exclusion orders.[103] However, critics have argued[104] that *in camera* review procedures of an inquisitorial kind could be devised to give greater protection to the individual without necessarily compromising security or detracting from ministerial responsibility. The problem is identical to that concerning deportation cases, and so we return to it below after discussion of that topic.

DEPORTATION PROCEDURES

Until the early twentieth century deportation was governed by the prerogative, emphasizing both its political sensitivity and importance, and its highly discretionary nature. In practice the discretion has vested in the Home Secretary and has been triggered by a variety of anti-social behaviour, some of which, for instance straightforward criminality, is outside our concern here. The discretion was codified, but hardly clarified or constrained, by its inclusion in successive pieces of delegated legislation: the Aliens Orders 1919, 1920, 1953, each of which referred to the deportation when the Secretary of State deemed it to be 'conducive to the public good'.[105] When this ground was included in section

---

[101] Walker (n. 85 above), 77 and 84.   [102] *The Times*, 3 Feb. 1987 (available on LEXIS).
[103] e.g. rejecting an amendment to establish a system of binding inquisitorial review: *HC Debs.*, Standing Committee B, cols. 95–116 (15 Dec. 1988).
[104] Bonner (n. 87 above), 205–207; Walker (n. 85 above), 94–6.
[105] On the history of deportation on this ground, see *Report of the Committee on Immigration Appeals*, Cmnd. 3387 (Aug. 1967); Legomsky (n. 20 above), 87–105.

3(5) of the Immmigration Act 1971, it was elucidated, although somewhat obliquely, by listing the categories of cases not subject to the right of appeal introduced by the Act: namely, 'in the interests of national security or of the relations between the United Kingdom and any other country or for other reasons of a political nature'.[106]

Whatever the legal parentage of the power, the courts have been equally deferential to its use in practice. Thus, during the First World War the courts refused to intervene with a deportation order despite its use to return a French aristocrat who had fled to avoid military service.[107] In this period the courts also took a relaxed view of procedural safeguards: in *R. v. Inspector of Leman Street Police Station ex p. Venicoff* [108] it was held that the Home Secretary was under no duty to grant a deportee a hearing before exercising the power to deport in 'public good' cases, notwithstanding the allegation that the deportation was based on untested and false informer evidence. Although the decision pre-dates the modern revival of the rules of natural justice, and a non-statutory hearing would now be granted, in practical terms the position is little changed today.

When an appeal was introduced against deportation decisions in 1971, a special procedure was provided for reviewing cases involving security considerations. The *Dutschke* case, involving the deportation of a radical student activist, was the first and only case to be heard under this procedure for dealing with security cases in the Immigration Appeal Tribunal.[109] The proceedings took place, mainly in public, before a specially constituted tribunal, but evidence was received from the Security Service *in camera* and in the absence of the applicant. Public dissatisfaction over the form of the proceedings was met perversely by the removal altogether of the right of appeal in security cases.[110] However, the government did provide for a non-statutory hearing before an advisory panel to review the evidence and make recommendations to the Home Secretary,[111] modelled consciously on that applicable to civil servants whose loyalty is in

---

[106] Immigration Act 1971, s. 15(3).   [107] See n. 28 above.

[108] [1920] 3 KB 72.

[109] Immigration Appeals Act 1969, s. 9 and Aliens (Appeals) Order 1970 (SI 1970 No. 151), art. 8; see B. Hepple, 'Aliens and Administrative Justice: The Dutschke Case' (1971) 34 *MLR* 501. The procedure was unusual in that it allowed the Home Secretary to direct that the case be heard by the Tribunal (rather than an immigration adjudicator), chosen from a special panel of members compiled by the Home Secretary and the Lord Chancellor. In security cases the Tribunal exercised an advisory function only. However, unlike proceedings before the advisory panel, legal representation was allowed. *The Report of the Committee on Immigration Appeals* (Cmnd. 3387, 1967) had earlier concluded that security cases could be dealt with by the new appeals mechanism which it recommended for deportation orders, provided that the Tribunal members had been security cleared to hear classified information and the proceedings were *in camera* (but in the appellant's presence): para. 144.

[110] See n. 106 above.

[111] *HC Debs.*, vol. 819, cols. 375 ff. (15 June 1971). After outlining how the advisory procedure would work, the Home Secretary stated: 'I am not sure that it is wise to put this in statutory form. In effect it means importing once again into this matter a justiciable issue, whereas the whole basis of my philosophy is that these are decisions of a political and executive character which should be subject to Parliament and not subject to the courts, arbitrators and so on.' (ibid., col. 377).

doubt.[112] The advisory panel currently comprises Lord Lloyd (although Bingham LJ replaced him on some of the Gulf War deportees' hearings), Mr David Neve (former President of the Immigration Appeal Tribunal), and Sir Robert Andrew (a former Deputy Under Secretary at the Home Office and former Permanent Under Secretary at the Northern Ireland Office).

The procedure followed is that the Home Secretary personally considers decisions to deport on security grounds,[113] and once a prima facie decision is reached the person concerned is told the basis of the allegations (so far as this can be done without disclosing sources) and advised of the right to make representations to the panel. At the hearing (if one is requested) there is an opportunity to make representations, to call witnesses, and to be assisted by a friend. There is no right to be present to hear evidence adduced by the authorities (for instance Security Service officers), to be told of it, or to cross-examine. However, the advisers are enjoined to remember that the evidence will not have been subject to cross-examination. Legal representation is excluded. The unsatisfactory nature of proceedings before this panel ('the Three Wise Men') has given rise to challenges in the courts on two occasions.

In 1976 orders of deportation were made against the American journalist Mark Hosenball and former CIA officer, Phillip Agee. Although they were not told exactly what they had done to make their continued presence no longer conducive to the public good for reasons of national security, the cause was almost certainly Hosenball's investigative interest in telephone tapping and in the activities of GCHQ, and Agee's campaign to expose CIA covert activities.[114] Despite a solemn hearing lasting almost a week before the advisory panel in which they put their case, Hosenball and Agee were given no clearer official indication than the initial statements served on them. In Hosenball's case this recited that he had: 'in consort with others sought to obtain and has obtained for publication information harmful to the security of the United Kingdom and that this information has included information prejudicial to the safety of servants of the Crown'.[115] Agee was told that he had 'been involved in disseminating information', had 'aided and counselled others in obtaining information for publication', and had 'maintained regular contact with foreign intelligence officers'.[116]

---

[112] See Ch. 6 above. However, quite separately, a non-statutory Aliens Deportation Advisory Committee had been in operation in the period 1932–6 until it fell into disuse. The remit was not limited to security cases and it pre-dated any right of appeal generally against deportation cases. See *Report of the Committee on Immigration Appeals*, Cmnd. 3378 (1967), app. III.

[113] It has been held that the Secretary of State may delegate aspects of decision-making in deportation cases: *R. v. Secretary of State for the Home Department ex p. Oladehinde* [1990] 3 WLR 797. In *In Re Amanulla Khan* [1986] Imm. AR 485 it was held that the issuing of a deportation notice on grounds of national security and an order of detention pending deportation immediately after the applicant's acquittal on explosives offences charges could lawfully be delegated in advance to an official without the need for for the case to be referred to the Home Secretary.

[114] For an account written by a close associate see Aubrey (n. 23 above), 94–109.

[115] [1977] 1 WLR 766, 770–1.   [116] Aubrey (n. 23 above), 99.

Some credence was given to Agee's allegation that the decision was taken at the behest of his former employers, the CIA, by his subsequent deportations from France and Holland[117] and by attempts by the American authorities to impede his freedom to travel by revoking his passport.[118] Requests for additional details by both men were refused, and the decision was duly confirmed by Merlin Rees, the Labour Home Secretary.[119]

When Hosenball challenged the decision in the Court of Appeal, alleging that the lack of detailed allegations offended the rules of natural justice by preventing him mounting an effective defence, he fared no better. The Court of Appeal held that the rules of natural justice were flexible according to the circumstances and, as Lord Denning put it, where security was at stake, they would be 'modified to meet the position'.[120] The court noted that the Home Secretary had personally considered both the decision to deport and the refusal to give further details of the allegations, and held that it could not go behind the Secretary of State's assertion that the reason for both was national security. The need to protect sensitive intelligence sources justified the non-disclosure in their Lordships' view.[121]

Agee complained against his order of deportation under the European Convention on Human Rights, alleging that it amounted to a determination of his civil rights without an opportunity for judicial redress contrary to Article 6 and that, as it arose from his exercise of a right to freedom of expression, it violated Article 10. Both contentions were dismissed by the Commission, which found the complaint to be inadmissible.[122] The Commission found that Article 6 does not apply to a decision to deport an alien, underlining once again the fragile position of those in a foreign country. Although the decision does not rest on any discrimination in the Convention between nationals and aliens (Article 6 applies equally to both),[123] but on the absence of positive rights in national law with which to trigger Article 6, this is an unsatisfactory and artificial distinction, since the practical result is clearly to enable states to treat aliens in a way which severely disadvantages them. Hosenball's attempt to circumvent the Commission's interpretation of Article 6 by alleging that the decisions to deport effectively terminated other entitlements which should be regarded as civil obligations (such as his employment in the United Kingdom as a journalist) also failed, since the Commission regarded the interference as contingent rather than direct.[124]

The power to deport carries with it a power of arrest and detention pending

---

[117] Aubrey (n. 23 above), 108.   [118] See *Haig* v. *Agee* (n. 42 above).

[119] See the statement at *HC Debs.*, vol. 926, cols. 495 ff. (16 Feb. 1977).

[120] See n. 115 above, 779.

[121] Per Lord Denning MR, ibid. 782; Geoffrey Lane LJ, 784; Cumming-Bruce LJ 787.

[122] *Agee* v. *UK* 7729/767 DR 164.

[123] Plender, *International Migration Law* (n. 7 above), 230.

[124] *Application No. 7902/77, X* v. *United Kingdom* 9 DR 224; (see also *Caprino* v. *UK* below).

deportation[125] and review of the decision. However, attacks on the legality of the detention have also proved fruitless in 'public good' cases.[126] The later case of *Cheblak*[127] involved the Home Secretary's decision to detain pending deportation the applicant (together with a number of Iraqis and other Palestinians) at the commencement of the Gulf War.

Cheblak was a Palestinian writer of Lebanese citizenship who had been resident in Britain since 1975 as a journalist, student, and research officer. Although he had travelled to Iraq for the purposes of study, he had campaigned for an Iraqi withdrawal from Kuwait and stated himself to be opposed to terrorism. The day after commencement of hostilities in the Gulf he was detained pending deportation and invited to apply for review of his case by the procedure described. Unlike Hosenball he did not await confirmation of the decision to deport before coming to the courts. Instead, he struck a pre-emptive blow by applying for habeas corpus to contest the legality of his detention and judicial review of the Home Secretary's initial decision to serve the deportation notice. Both actions failed in the High Court[128] and also in the Court of Appeal. Notwithstanding that, Cheblak was later released following the Home Secretary's decision not to confirm the deportation order, after review of the case by the advisory panel.[129]

The legality of the detention within the statutory scheme turned upon whether the applicant had been properly served with a notice of intention to deport, complying with regulations made under section 18 of the 1971 Act. The

---

[125] Immigration Act 1971, s. 5(5), sched. 2, paras. 17 and 18 and sched. 3, para. 2.

[126] In *Caprino* v. *UK* 6871/ 75 (adopted by the Council of Ministers (DH (81) 7, 30 Apr. 1981) the Commission held that the provisions authorizing detention pending deportation in a case where the Secretary of State considered it to be conducive to the public good were in compliance with Art. 5(4) of the Convention, requiring an opportunity to be provided to challenge the detention before a court. The availability of habeas corpus was held to be sufficient, in view of the earlier holdings that the Convention did not require that a decision to deport should itself be challengeable before a court. However, habeas corpus proceedings would be bound to fail except in the case of outright non-compliance with the 1971 Act. More realistically, in a dissenting opinion, Mr M. Melchiou argued that in view of the width of discretion granted under the 1971 Act to the Secretary of State, habeas corpus was an ineffective remedy; he also questioned the very wide protection given to sources in such cases, claiming that it made it impossible for a reviewing body to know whether or not the initial decision was an arbitrary one. See C. Newdick, 'Deportation and the European Convention' (1982) 2 *Ox. JLS* 151.

[127] *R.* v. *Secretary of State for Home Affairs ex p. Cheblak* [1991] 2 All ER 319. See also *R.* v. *Secretary of State for Home Affairs ex p. B and B*, the *Independent*, 29 Jan. 1991, and *R.* v. *Secretary of State for the Home Department ex p. Chahal*, *The Times*, 27 Oct. 1993. Although the round-up of deportees and the keeping of them in prisons and army camps, and the speedy release of those still held at the cessation of hostilities, gave rise to allegations of disguised internment these were not canvassed in the proceedings: see generally F. Hampson, 'The Geneva Conventions and the Detention of Civilians and Alleged Prisoners of War', [1991] *PL* 507.

[128] Unreported judgment of 23 Jan. 1991 (available on LEXIS).

[129] Many of those detained during the Gulf crisis were not so fortunate. Deportation notices were served on 167 Iraqi, Jordanian, Lebanese, and Yemeni nationals in total. Of these eighty-one left voluntarily without exercising the right of review. Of the thirty-three cases which went to the advisory panel by 1 Mar. 1991, nineteen detainees had been released. The remainder were released at the conclusion of the war.

relevant regulations provided that a notice of deportation had to include a statement of the 'reason for the decision'.[130] The Court of Appeal held that the service on Cheblak of a notice stating that his departure from the United Kingdom
'would be conducive to the public good for reasons of national security' was
sufficient. Lord Donaldson argued that the court could not, in the absence of
bad faith, go behind an affidavit adduced by the Home Office that to give further details might itself threaten national security.[131] The proceedings did, however, elicit a fuller statement of the reasons. According to a letter read out in
court, Cheblak was informed: 'The Iraqi government has openly threatened to
take terrorist action against unspecified western targets if hostilities break out in
the Gulf. In the light of this, your known links with an organisation which we
believe could take such action in support of the Iraqi regime make your presence in the United Kingdom an unacceptable security risk.' It was argued that in
basing the decision to deport upon this reason the Home Secretary had either
failed to take account of all relevant circumstances or had acted irrationally,
because Cheblak had no terrorist connections and was opposed to terrorism.
These arguments were met squarely at first instance and in the Court of Appeal
with judicial protestations of non-justiciability because of national security.[132]
Lord Donaldson suggested that the 'Home Secretary is fully accountable to
Parliament for his decisions whether or not to deport and . . . for any failure to
heed the advice of the non-statutory panel'.[133] However, 'full accountability' is
likely to amount to little more than the minister's preparedness to suffer the
temporary embarrassment of refusing to answer questions on grounds of
national security.[134] Accountability for failure to follow the panel's advice is simply fictitious—since the panel's recommendations are confidential, there is no
way of knowing whether or not they were followed in a particular case.

The judge pointed to what he claimed was the more satisfactory nature of the
advisory panel's proceedings for dealing with the issues which the applicant
wished to raise:

The approach adopted by the Home Secretary's advisory panel is, perhaps, best described
as an 'independent quasi-judicial scrutiny'. The members all have the necessary security
clearance to enable them to take an active role in questioning and evaluating the weight
of the evidence and information which formed the basis of the Home Secretary's initial
decision. Similarly they seek to discover any countervailing evidence, information or representations which the detainee may wish to put forward and evaluate its weight. Whilst
that part of their task which involves the protection of the rights of the individual would

---

[130] Immigration Appeals (Notices) Regulations, 1984 (SI 2040 of 1984).

[131] Nolan and Beldam LJJ both asserted the court's independent power of inquiry, under the
Habeas Corpus Act 1816, s. 3, into the sufficiency of the reasons, even in cases to which s. 15(3) of
the 1971 Act applied. However, they too found that national security prevented further inquiry in
this case. Beldam LJ laid particular emphasis upon the wording of s. 3(5) of the 1971 Act where it is
the Home Secretary who 'deems' the person's deportation to be conducive to the public good:
[1991] 2 All ER at 338.   [132] See Ch. 12 below.

[133] See n. 127 above, 330.   [134] See pp. 441–2 below.

be easier of performance if they could reveal to the detainee all that has become known to them, it is by no means impossible to perform it effectively where they cannot do so. Sufficient may be already be revealed by the Home Secretary himself to steer the detainee in the right direction and it is always possible for members of the panel to ask questions in a form which is itself not informative, but leads the detainee on to giving as full an account as he wishes of his contacts and activities in the areas which are relevant to the Home Secretary's decision.[135]

The experience of those who underwent these procedures during the Gulf War was less reassuring.[136] In part the difference may be explicable because the Home Office was dealing with and the panel was hearing many more cases and in a shorter time than on previous occasions. Since a large number of deportees were being held in custody, the determination of their cases became a matter of urgency. Whereas Hosenball and Agee had several days in which to make representations and answer questions, the average length of the individual hearings in the Gulf War cases was from forty-five minutes to an hour. The information given to the deportees was no more than the statutory notice and the explanatory two sentences given to Mr Cheblak, which were in fact a standard form explanation used with only minor variations according to nationality in all cases. Any requests for additional information prior to the hearing (such as the terrorist organization with which links were alleged) were met by outright refusal because of the ostensible need to protect sources. Preparation for the hearings had to take place in custody, often in a different part of the country from where the detainee's family, friends, and advisers were. Some detainees were given no more than four or five days' notice of the hearing, although some adjournments were granted. Legal representation was not allowed, but written representations prepared by legal advisers were received: in view of the absence of detailed allegations, summaries were prepared giving individuals' life stories and dealing in depth with their work, social activities, and acquaintances while living in Britain, and their political views. In the hearing the applicant was entitled to be assisted by a friend (an invaluable facility, in view of the fact that English was not the first language of most those involved), and to call character referees.

Before the deportees' hearings the panel had earlier received written reports from the Security Service on each case, and dealt with matters arising from the reports in oral questions to officers of the Service.[137] The deportees were excluded from this part of the process and were not informed that it had occurred. At the hearings the panel asked detailed questions apparently arising

[135] See n. 127 above, 332.

[136] We are grateful for information to Richard Nobles and Cath Sylvester, who were involved with assisting several of the detainees whose cases were reviewed under these procedures. See also Stephanie Grant, 'A Just Treatment for Enemy Aliens', *NLJ*, 8 Mar. 1991. For the questions asked of one applicant see the *Guardian*, 18 Mar. 1991.

[137] We are grateful to Lord Justice Lloyd for confirming the involvement of the Security Service and for discussing with us his perception of the panel's role. We alone, however, are responsible for the interpretation and views expressed here.

from security reports (visibly in use during the hearings), especially about political activities and views of the applicant and of named individuals—in some cases these included questions about specified meetings or social occasions, which were presumably based on information obtained by surveillance or from informers. In a few instances the panel re-interviewed officers from the Security Service in the light of the deportee's answers at the hearing.

These practices were no doubt benevolently intended and it must be remembered that a high proportion of the Gulf War deportees were subsequently released—presumably on the panel's advice.[138] The panel apparently regarded the function of the hearing granted to deportees as being for the purpose of putting their case without revealing sources to the individual affected, and recording his or her views for the Secretary of State, and not as an ordinary appellate procedure requiring legal representation. However, these conclusions should be set against the broader policy considerations, which suggest that the detentions and deportations were unnecessary or certainly excessive. It was the Britain alone of all the Gulf coalition partners which felt it necessary to take these steps, and it was noticeable that in the remainder of the western world there was a total absence of successful pro-Iraqi acts of terrorism. Although it is possible that this was due to brilliant intelligence work of which the British detentions were part, it is altogether more plausible that, just as they had fifty years earlier, the authorities wholly over-reacted.[139]

These procedures represent a confusing *mélange* of ultimately incompatible objectives: confronting the deportee with the case against him or her, reviewing the evidence, and giving non-binding advice to the Minister. They clearly lack the safeguards normally associated with processes whose possible outcome for the individual is so serious: specific notice of allegations, legal representation, and cross-examination. As the judgments in *Cheblak* and *Hosenball* show, two quite distinct defences have been mounted to charges of procedural unfairness in the advisory panel format. The first is based on the non-justiciability of decisions involving national security.[140] Here the argument rests on an assumption that a claim of security necessarily blankets virtually the whole process with non-justiciablity. However, this does not justify the refusal to allow intelligence information in individual cases to be tested by cross-examination. Issues of accuracy, potential bias or self-interest of informers, and alternative interpretations of the facts, could all be dealt with without calling into question the policy underlying the decision contested. The real issue here is the second argument—confidentiality. The challenge is to devise legal procedures which preserve executive responsibility and protect confidentiality but also allow rigorous testing of the case on the appellant's behalf. It is here that an examination of possible

---

[138] See n. 129 above.
[139] Nevertheless it seems an official (but, naturally, unpublished) inquiry by Sir Philip Woodfield acquitted the Security Service of incompetence: the *Independent*, 10 Dec. 1991.
[140] See further Ch. 12 below.

alternative procedures is pertinent. For this we turn to Canadian deportation and immigration procedures.

CANADIAN PROCEDURES[141]

Interestingly, Canada abandoned procedures similar to the Advisory Panel format long ago, in favour of better procedural protections for the deportee. Under the Canadian Immigration Act 1976 permanent residents had a right to have their deportation on security grounds reviewed by a Special Advisory Board.[142] Under this procedure the deportee had a right to a summary of the allegations against him or her, so far as consistent with national security, and to appear in person, to have legal representation, and to call evidence. The Board's reports went in the form of advice to the Cabinet, with whom the final decision rested.[143] Following the McDonald Commission Report these procedures were strengthened by giving a similar role to SIRC, with increased powers to obtain information from intelligence sources. SIRC's jurisdiction in these appeals is similar to that in security clearance cases described in Chapter 6.[144]

SIRC's involvement in these cases follows from its oversight of CSIS, which will be involved with the supply of the information on which the action is based. Investigation and review of decisions to deport and of refusal of entry is expressly within the purview of SIRC under the CSIS Act 1984, section 38 and the Immigration Act 1976, section 39.[145] The 1976 Act lays down some procedural rules which are supplemented by rules for such hearings which the committee itself has promulgated. Within the statutory scheme the committee's

---

[141] A full survey (prior to the Supreme Court decision in *Chiarelli* at n. 153 below) is provided in B. Gorlick, 'The Exclusion of "Security Risks" as a Form of Immigration Control; Law and Process in Canada' (1991) 5 *Immigration and Nationality Law and Practice* 76–82 and 109–15. For a historical treatment of Canadian immigration procedures on this ground see R. Whitaker, *Double Standard: The Secret History of Canadian Immigration* (Toronto, 1987).

[142] S. 41 of the 1976 Act, now amended. Aliens other than permanent residents were in a more precarious position, since a conclusive ministerial certificate could be served, effectively depriving them of the right to challenge before an immigration adjudicator the designation as a security threat: ibid., ss. 39(1) and 119 (unamended version); the courts upheld the inviolablity of similar certificates in *Prata* v. *MMI* (1975) 52 DLR (3d) 383 and *The Queen* v. *Douglas* (1976) 67 DLR (3d) 373 under earlier legislation.

[143] See C. Wydrznski, *Canadian Immigration Law and Practice* (Toronto, 1983), 341–4.

[144] Brief mention might also be made of the equivalent Australian procedures. Deportation cases on security grounds were formerly without provision for appeal, but now there is a right of appeal to the Security Appeals Tribunal (Migration Act 1958, s. 56) rather than the more normal forum for immigration cases, the immigration Review Tribunal. Other categories of immigration cases may receive the same treatment by ministerial certificate (ibid., s. 120 (2) (*a*)). However, this procedure suffers from the defect that it is possible for the minister to serve a conclusive public interest immunity certicate witholding security evidence (ibid., ss. 146 and 147). Appeal lies from the Security Appeals Tribunal to the Federal Court on a point of law (ibid., s. 138).

[145] See M. Rankin, 'The Security Intelligence Review Committee: Reconciling National Security with Procedural Fairness', 3 *Can. J Admin. L. & Prac.* 173 for a detailed assessment of the committee's procedures.

function is to advise the Governor-in-Council on whether the deportation should be confirmed, following an initial report from the Minister of Employment and Immigration. The committee is responsible for sending to the individual a statement summarizing the available information as far as possible to enable him or her to prepare for an investigatory hearing. At the hearing the applicant has the right to be represented and to call evidence. Confidentiality of security information is maintained by requiring evidence to be given in the absence of the applicant or his or her representative. However, there are two safeguards over such evidence: first, the committee uses its own security-cleared counsel in these closed sessions to cross-examine as though representing the applicant,[146] and secondly, a summary (subject to deletions) of the evidence given in this way is released to the applicant.

The attitude of the Canadian courts to these procedures has on the whole been non-interventionist. In pre-Charter cases the Canadian courts also gave a wide berth to ministerial discretions exercised on grounds of national security in immigration cases, upholding decisions to refuse entry to or to deport alleged members of the Black Panthers,[147] of the Australian National Socialist Party,[148] and a former member of the United States Communist Party.[149] However, where a minister exercised discretion to refuse citizenship to a landed immigrant of some thirty-five years standing, because of an adverse intelligence report, he was at least required by the rules of natural justice to grant a hearing first.[150] There has been little difference in outcome in post-Charter cases. The courts have cited with approval the *Hosenball* judgment[151] in holding that the security exemption in the Citizenship Act did not violate the Charter since citizenship was a privilege the state was entitled to withhold, and not a right.[152] The Supreme Court has refused a claim that the procedures adopted by SIRC for determining these cases breaches section 7 of the Charter (protecting life, liberty, and security), holding that there was no constitutional right to an appeal in such cases but that in any event SIRC's procedures strike a reasonable balance between individual and state interests.[153] In doing so the Court reversed an earlier ruling of the Federal Court of Appeal in which the statutory procedures had been criticized as a disproportionate restriction and as 'obliterating' the individual's rights.[154]

A variation on these procedures, involving not SIRC but determination of the

[146] The Special Committee of the Canadian House of Commons suggested that s. 48(2) of the CSIS Act be reformed to allow the complainant's counsel to be security cleared and to cross-examine CSIS evidence: *Report of the Special Committee on the Review of the CSIS Act and the Security Offences Act, In Flux But Not In Crisis* (Ottawa, 1990), para. 12.5.2.

[147] *Jolly* v. *MMI* (1975) 54 DLR (3d) 277.   [148] *Wernberg* v. *MMI* (1968) 4 IAC 292.
[149] *Cronan* v. *MMI* (1972) 3 IAC 42.
[150] *Lazarov* v. *Secretary of State of Canada* (1973) 39 DLR (3d) 738.   [151] See n. 115 above.
[152] *Reyes* v. *Canada* (1983) 149 DLR (3rd) 748.
[153] *Chiarelli* v. *Canada (MEI)* [1992] SCR 711.
[154] [1990] 2 FC 299, esp. Stone JA at 326; see also *Brar* v. *Canada* (1990) 30 FTR 284; *Regalado-Brito* v. *MEI* [1987] 1 FC 80.

issues by the courts, applies in refugee cases. In such cases section 40. 1 of the Immigration Act 1976 (as amended)[155] provides for a form of judicial review of a ministerial certificate in security cases. The certificate has the effect of suspending the application for refugee status. The Federal Court must determine whether the certificate is 'reasonable on the basis of the evidence'. The judge is required to examine the intelligence evidence *in camera* and may do so *ex parte* but must provide the applicant with a summary enabling him to be reasonably informed of the circumstances giving rise to the circumstances leading to the service of the certificate.

It was in a case involving this procedure during the Gulf War that the Federal Court struck a significant blow by quashing as unreasonable a ministerial certificate stating that the applicants (who were Iraqi citizens, claiming refugee status) were a security threat because of alleged subversive and terrorist activities.[156] The decision was all the more remarkable because the applicants had entered Canada on forged papers and in possession of literature from a militant Shiite Muslim organization which had engaged in terrorist activities against the Iraqi government, and of a weapons price list. Nevertheless, after reviewing security intelligence reports and hearing evidence from a CSIS officer *in camera*, the court held that there was insufficient evidence relating to the danger posed by applicants. Cullen J stressed the need for the authorities to satisfy a high standard of proof in cases involving liberty of the person.

At the very least these processes demonstrate that it is possible to devise procedures offering greater protection and information to the deportee, internee, or immigrant faced with security objections without compromising justifiable secrecy. It is striking, however, that the introduction of these advantages in Canadian law was due more to the commitment of the legislature to introduce reforms respecting human rights than to the actions of the courts. The Charter of Rights has had relatively little impact on immigration cases involving national security, as the cases discussed show.[157]

CONCLUSION

It is plain that in the instances of the wartime detentions, of exclusion orders, and of deportation on grounds of national security the courts have done relatively little to protect human rights. Although in these fields the consequences of such decisions are among the most serious a person may face, the executive's

---

[155] The amendment (introduced by the Immigration Act 1988) followed a recommendation that the person claiming refugee status should have the opportunity present his or her case: *Refugee Determination in Canada: A Report to the Hon. Flora MacDonald, Minister of Employment and Immigration by W. Gunther Plaut* (Ottawa, 1985), 86–7.

[156] *Smith* v. *Canada* [1991] 3 FC 3.

[157] This accords with our conclusions about Bills of Rights generally in this field; see further below, Ch. 12, pp. 341–8.

discretion has been left virtually untrammelled. This comment is as true for Canada as for Britain.

However it does not follow that the British procedures are incapable of improvement, or that because of the absence of judicial safeguards the only alternative is the unsatisfactory inquisitorial procedures involving bodies like the Three Wise Men. It is clear that the alternative starkly posed by the Court of Appeal in *Cheblak* between either full adversarial proceedings or inquisitorial proceedings which, however well intentioned, leave the complainant uninformed, is a false one. The procedural innovations adopted in Canada suggest that protections can be introduced for the affected individual without destroying the necessary safeguards for the government. What is needed are binding, statutory procedures which are capable of receiving intelligence evidence in a secure environment, but allow it to be challenged on behalf of the individual. The use of the 'Devil's Advocate' in some form of inquisitorial tribunal (such as SIRC hearings) has much to recommend it in this respect. So also does the introduction of special safeguards for review in court (as in the Canadian refugee provisions).

Nevertheless, it is plain that because of the repeated failure of the courts in Britain to propel reform or the introduction of safeguards and because of their effective endorsement of the *status quo*, it is futile to look in that direction for improvement. As with employment vetting, it is now to Parliament that we should look for the introduction of fair, not to say civilized, procedures in these cases.

Part III
Criticism, Dissent, and National Security

8

Criminal Repression of Freedom of Expression

From the earliest stages of the political history of England after the Conquest, criminal prohibitions and punishments have been central to the strategies of rulers to maintain themselves in power. The oldest criminal statute on our law books is the Statute of Treasons or Treason Act 1351, which, somewhat unbelievably, 'is still the basis of the present law of treason'.[1] The practices of impeachment, attainder, forfeiture of estates, and other forms of persecution of political opponents by legal means have long vanished, though they have left odd imprints on other legal systems.[2] With only slight exaggeration, it can be said that for several centuries criminal law and taxation were virtually the only forms of public law, given the rudimentary structure and limited responsibilities of the national government. Indeed the Statute of Treasons is itself somewhat unusual, in that most criminal law was common law, judicially created and enunciated in response to particular prosecutions. That part of criminal law relating to offences against the state was distinctive in one important procedural respect: though the overwhelming number of prosecutions before the mid-nineteenth century were undertaken privately, generally state security cases were initiated by the Crown or its ministers, and in major cases conducted by a Law Officer. We have a record of unparalleled detail of these cases, including the testimony and cross-examination of witnesses, thanks to the industry of several sets of editors who produced various editions of *State Trials*. Most notable was the work of the great Radical writer and publisher William Cobbett and his partner Thomas Howell, who launched a revived series in 1809. Devoted (unlike those published in the eighteenth century) entirely to political trials, they produced no less than thirty-three volumes in the ensuing seventeen years, concluding with the so-called Cato Street Conspiracy of 1820.[3] The sheer quantity of available material is weighty evidence of the value of criminal law to those in power, though

---

[1] M. Supperstone, *Brownlie's Law of Public Order and National Security* (2nd edn., London, 1981), 230.

[2] The US Constitution, Art. 1, s. 9, forbids 'bills of attainder'. This clause was given an unusual application to strike down a statute making it a crime for a Communist to be a trade union official in *United States* v. *Brown*, 381 US 435 (1965). The constitutional abhorrence of attainder lies not merely in denial of fair process, but in legislative encroachment on what should be a judicial matter—punishment based on a determination of guilt by fair process. These remain live issues, though in different form, see below pp. 349–50.

[3] Cobbett was himself the victim of political persecution, and received a two year sentence for seditious libel for criticism of savage punishment meted out to army protestors. Penniless upon release he sold his interest in the series to Howell who, with his son, was responsible for most of the volumes which bear the family name. See the Introduction by Donald Thomas to his edition of *State Trials* (London, 1972), i. 1–20.

whether their use of it is best described as necessary concern for the safety of the state or tyrannical suppression of opposition depends largely on whether one views the process from the initiating or the receiving end.

The main weapons in the official armoury were, at varying periods, the common law offences of blasphemy, sedition, and conspiracy, supported by an occasional statute, especially the Treason Acts. The law concerning these offences will be discussed in this chapter, though not in the same terms of doctrinal exposition as the textbooks.[4] Instead a historical-political interpretation, which seeks to understand their specific provisions in a wider context, will be presented.

Any such interpretation must seek to explain why, with a partial exception for conspiracy, prosecution for these offences in the context of state security are nowadays very rare. The answer is that they have been replaced. There has been a shift from common law offences—invented or developed by judges to suit what they believed was the need to protect the state and its supporting institutions from criticism—to statutory offences.

The major statutes concerned are the various Official Secrets Acts, which for more than eighty years have restricted disclosure of government-held information.[5] Though it may seem odd to portray them as the successors to sedition, there are two fundamental similarities. The narrow one is that both entail the use of criminal punishment to protect the state and its supposed interests, whereas the great bulk of criminal law is devoted to protecting the lives, personal security, and property of individuals. There is therefore a common aspect of political controversy involved in both instances.

The broader continuity between laws punishing criticism and those punishing the obtaining or publishing of concealed information is that both reflect the major vulnerability of the ruling political élite at various periods. In the eighteenth and even mid-nineteenth centuries, when virtually no one had the right to vote,[6] the majority of people were illiterate, and police forces rudimentary, the great fear was of 'the rabble' inflamed by soap-box orators or broadsheets lampooning ministers and their policies. Hence public orators, authors, printers, and booksellers were the main targets, and it was the substance even more than the manner of their criticism that formed the basis of prosecutions.

---

[4] This can best be obtained from Supperstone (n. 1 above), ch. 11 and J. Smith and B. Hogan, *Criminal Law* (7th edn., London 1992), ch. 11 and pp. 723–5, 749–51.

[5] See Ch. 9 below. There has been some use of the Incitement to Disaffection Act 1934 (pp. 209–10 below), but no noteworthy questions of construction have arisen.

[6] Before the great Reform Act of 1832 the electorate totalled under 370,000—11% of the male population. That legislation did not quite double the electorate (which grew to about 650,000); thus less than 10% of the population was eligible to vote. In 1866, just before Disraeli's vast expansion of the franchise (and well after the use of sedition had declined), the electorate had only risen to about 20% of adult males, and Disraeli's masterpiece of opportunism did not quite double that figure. Political democracy came remarkably late in this country. The figures are taken from E. Evans, *The Great Reform Act of 1832* (London, 1983), 50 and J. Walton, *The Second Reform Act* (London, 1987), 21.

The modern state has far greater legitimacy in the eyes of its subjects. It provides both elaborate trappings and sufficient substance of democracy to create enough identification between the ruled and their rulers to ensure loyalty and obedience. It is therefore quite capable of withstanding the traditional form of generalized and highly emotive criticism, which in any case seems to have lost its audience in an audio-visual culture of mass consumerism. Widened access to secondary and (very restrictedly) higher education has been coupled with (and has perhaps helped to produce) a much reduced deference to those occupying high office. Over nearly forty years a succession of scandals interspersed with several unrelated episodes revealing shocking incompetence—beginning with Suez and stretching from Profumo through Black Wednesday and the Royal *Annus Horribilis*—has caused widespread disillusionment. Concretely this has meant the virtual disappearance of that instinctive willingness to trust our leaders to act for the best and generally tell the truth—a valuable asset enjoyed by politicians even thirty years ago.[7] The result is that the battleground of liberty has shifted. Government is no more secretive now than in the Macmillan era, indeed very much the reverse; but a public and Press no longer content with the official version demand to know very much more. One of the virtues of secrecy from the perspective of officialdom is the ability to deflect or dismiss criticism by pretending to possess more complete and more accurate information. If critics can be portrayed as ill informed, they can more readily be dismissed.[8] Moreover, although concocting and spreading deliberately false information (disinformation) or giving misleading or downright inaccurate accounts to Parliament are certainly nothing new,[9] the government's public relations machinery has expanded enormously in recent times, and as the Westland Affair pointedly illustrated, conventional restraints on leaking confidential material and using civil servants for partisan purposes have lost much of their effective force.[10]

Thus a more aggressive and partisan government, no longer encumbered by the limitations of convention, confronts a more inquiring, less credulous public and Press. No longer can it be expected that significant areas of government decision-making will be regarded as apolitical matters in which the national interest is obvious. Therefore conflicts over the release or partial concealment of

---

[7] For a very perceptive account of this lost world, which now seems as remote as the Jurassic Age, see E. Shils, *The Torment of Secrecy* (London, 1956), 47–57.

[8] A variation is selective leaking of previously secret information that is favourable to the government position, whilst continuing to withhold matter that would give the critics further ammunition.

[9] For two historical examples which are well documented see: B. Weinberger, 'Police Perceptions of Labour in the Inter-War Period: The Case of the Unemployed and the Miners' Strike', in F. Snyder and D. Hay (eds.), *Labour, Law and Crime* (London, 1987) (disinformation campaign against organization of the unemployed in the 1920s) and D. Hooper, *Official Secrets—The Use and Abuse of the Act* (London, 1987) (misleading Parliament and attempted intimidation of critics).

[10] See Defence Committee, Fourth Report, *Westland plc: The Government's Decision-making*, HC 519 (1985–6); R. Austin and D. Oliver, 'The Westland Affair' (1987) 40 *Parl. Aff.* 20. For an account that most fully captures the political flavour, D. Leigh and M. Linklater *Not With Honour* (London, 1986).

all available information have moved to centre stage. This applies to government across the board, but above all to 'security' and foreign affairs. However, the actors are very different than in the past. Journalists and civil servants are far less easy prey than poor and obscure orators. They are much more capable of mounting campaigns of support, generating financial assistance, and gaining vital media coverage. So in considering prosecution the government must tread warily, and political considerations may loom large in the mind of the Attorney-General, whose consent is required before a prosecution may proceed and whose discretion in the matter is absolute.[11] Hence there arises one of the greatest, and inevitable, evils of using criminal law in politically contentious circumstances: selective prosecution. These grave issues will occupy much of the present chapter. First, however, we must examine particular offences.

TREASON

The relevance of an offence which developed under a feudal monarchy striving to keep control of power in the face of periodic rebellion may not appear immediately obvious in a stable modern democracy with very different national security concerns. After all, since the Statute of Treason codified the common law in 1351 only the fine detail of the offence has been filled in. The absence of peacetime prosecutions in the modern era (William Joyce was the last, in 1946) has led the Law Commission seriously to question whether the offence needs to be retained on the criminal calendar.[12] Nevertheless a brief consideration will demonstrate some aspects of the offence which, with due allowance, are not at all unfamiliar in the modern state. Moreover, it has a lineal connection with other offences: as will be demonstrated more fully below,[13] forensic and procedural limitations on the use of treason spurred the development of sedition as a partial replacement.

The essence of treason is a betrayal of trust. Hence in the Treason Act of 1351 'treason' was a generic term which included 'petit treason', committed against a master by a servant or against a husband by a wife. In the case of 'high treason' the basis of this relationship of trust was at the pinnacle of feudal society: the personal allegiance owed by the subject, however great or powerful, to the sovereign. To trace the transformation of the offence until it rests in its modern form on an allegiance owed to the state is quite simply to watch the chrysalis-like unfolding of the constitution. The formal ingredients of the offence bear the mark of its concern with the personal safety of the monarch; the transformation of the offence is due to the extended meaning given to these

---

[11] OSA 1911, s. 8; OSA 1989, s. 9. See further Ch. 11 below.
[12] Law Commission, Working Paper No. 72, *Treason, Sedition and Allied Offences*. For discussion, see L. Leigh, 'Law Reform and the Law of Treason and Sedition' [1977] *PL* 128.
[13] p. 206 below.

concepts, especially by judicial interpretation.[14] According to Maitland, it is a crime 'which has a vague circumference and more than one centre'.[15]

Some elements of the offence, such as the violation of certain royal ladies, are anachronistic on any count and could safely be discarded since the ordinary criminal law protects royal personages no less than the remainder of the citizenry. The same could be said for 'compassing or imagining the King's death', which in its plain meaning would clearly fall as murder or conspiracy to murder. However it should be noted that at times this has been extended to include imagining the King's 'political death'.[16] Two elements of the offence—levying war against the King in his realm and adhering to the King's enemies—are scarcely less relevant to state security in the twentieth century than they were in the fourteenth. It is on these aspects that the account here will focus.

The historical development of the offence rests upon a changing understanding of the importance of protecting the sovereign. This is not simply a matter of the prevailing constitutional doctrine at any moment but also depends on the political conditions of the time. Although Holdsworth was able to trace to the Act of 1351 the idea that the King is 'coming to represent the state',[17] there was no full separation at that time between the King's public and private capacities. Indeed as late as the Reformation period there were extensive temporary statutory extensions of the offence to prevent the personal political embarrassment of the serial monogamist Henry VIII, by criminalizing in turn public criticism of each successive marriage.[18] In so far as Henry's relentless search for an heir did affect the future security of the state, the line between legitimate and illegitimate invocation of state interest is every bit as difficult to draw as with the modern control of official information. The repressive use by Elizabeth I of charges of treason against her enemies, which incidentally involved the use of a sixteenth century precursor to the Security Service, exhibits the same tension, since the plots were Roman Catholic inspired and the future of the English Reformation was inextricably linked to her personal safety.[19]

'Levying war in the realm' had an obvious application to the Lancastrian wars and to any organized attempt at military insurrection. However by extended judicial interpretation it was also applied to agricultural unrest and in 1597 was successfully invoked against a peasants' uprising in opposition to the enclosure of land.[20] Nearly two centuries later it was this same rationale which led Lord Mansfield to state in his summing-up to the jury in a treason charge arising from a riot against legislation emancipating Roman Catholic disabilities:

there are two kinds of levying war—one against the person of the King; to imprison, to dethrone, or to kill him: or to make him change measures or to remove councillors—the

---

[14] Law Commission (n. 12 above), 7–24 and W. Holdsworth, *A History of English Law* (London, 1924), iii. 287–93, iv. 492–500, and viii. 307–22.

[15] F. Pollock and F. Maitland, *The History of English Law* 2nd edn. (Cambridge, 1968), ii. 503.

[16] *R. v. Sheanes* (1798) 27 St. Tr. 255, 387.   [17] Holdsworth (n. 14 above), ii. 289.

[18] Ibid. iv. 493–5.   [19] Ibid. viii. 310.

[20] *R. v. Bradshaw and Others*, Coke, Third Inst. 9, 10.

other of which is said to be levied against the majesty of the king, or, in other words, against him in his regal capacity; as when a multitude rise and assemble to attain by force and violence any object of a general public nature; that is levying war against the majesty of the king; and most reasonably so held because it tends to destroy all the bonds of society, to destroy property, and to overturn government; and by force of arms to restrain the king from reigning according to law.[21]

A similar process of extension occurred in the case of 'compassing the king's death' which, according to Lord Carleton CJ speaking in 1798, included:

forming conspiracies to usurp by force and in defiance of the authority of Parliament, the government of the kingdom, to destroy its constitution and in so doing to destroy the monarchy . . . holding consultations or entering into agreement, or advising, soliciting or persuading others for any such purpose.[22]

The explanation for the prosecution of the members of a society for constitutional reform on this charge in 1794[23] was, no doubt, that very similar demands had shortly before directly led to the death of the French sovereign. It is perhaps not surprising that in this and several other contemporaneous cases juries balked at the use of the most serious offence in the law to stifle dissent. Thereafter political public disorder tended to be treated as sedition or as riot. 'Adhering to the king's enemies' is the charge that accounts for the modern use of treason, especially in wartime. Even prior to the 1351 Act betraying secrets to the king's enemies had been regarded as treason,[24] and it continued to be so regarded. In this respect the offence took the place of the modern espionage laws. Hence in the eighteenth century case of *R.* v. *De La Motte*, Buller J stated: 'The sending or collecting of intelligence for the purpose of sending it to an enemy to enable them to annoy us or to defend themselves, though it never be delivered to the enemy, or the hiring a person for that purpose, is an overt act [of adhering to the enemy].'[25] This aspect of treason has kept up with modern military science since it has been interpreted so as to have extraterritorial effect: Roger Casement was tried and found guilty for recruiting an expeditionary force among Irish prisoners of war held in Germany during the First World War.[26] Likewise at the end of the Second World War the German propagandist, William Joyce, whose broadcasts had all been made from outside the realm, was tried and executed on the charge.[27] 'Adhering' has also been held to apply to seemingly minor acts such as becoming a naturalized subject in an enemy state in time of war;[28] or acting as a cook for a belligerent army.[29]

---

[21] *R.* v. *Lord George Gordon* 21 St. Tr. 485, 644.   [22] See n. 16 above.
[23] *R.* v. *Hardy* 24 St. Tr. 199; *R.* v. *Tooke* 25 St. Tr. 1.
[24] Pollock and Maitland (n. 15 above), 507.   [25] *R.* v. *De La Motte* 21 St. Tr., 808.
[26] *R.* v. *Casement* [1917] 1 KB 98. For discussion of this and Joyce's case see Wharam (1978) 41 *MLR* 681.
[27] *Joyce* v. *DPP* [1946] AC 347.   [28] *R.* v. *Lynch* [1946] AC 347.
[29] Law Commission (n. 12 above), para. 23, citing Kenny's *Outlines of Criminal Law* (19th ed., 1966).

BLASPHEMY

The inclusion of blasphemy in the catalogue of political offences may seem odd, but historically it has played an important role in this sphere. The conception of religion and private morality as separate from the sphere of politics and government is only partly accepted in the twentieth century; in the seventeenth it was anathema. European wars and dynastic rivalries were fatally entangled with religion: Roman Catholic monarchs were supposed to act as 'defenders of the faith' (as the Pope had honoured Henry VIII), whilst Protestant nations created state churches of which the King was supreme head. Monarchs of all Christian denominations claimed divine sanction for their rule; to attack the truth and authority of Christian doctrine was therefore to hack away at one of the main pillars of the legitimacy of the secular powers.

In Restoration England the purely spiritual censures of the ecclesiastical courts, which had for centuries enforced norms of morality and religious observance, had lost their sting. The Court of Star Chamber had been abolished in 1641. The common law courts quickly stepped into the breach. They proclaimed themselves *custos morum* of all the King's subjects,[30] and not long afterwards enlarged their jurisdiction to control religious controversy. This annexation of power had vast long-term consequences throughout the criminal law, for it enlisted the coercive might of the civil state to underpin conventional morality. More narrowly in relation to the law of blasphemy, the first major case remained, in the words of the leading judgment in the House of Lords, nearly two and a half centuries later, 'the foundation stone of this branch of the law'.[31]

The defendant was called John Taylor, normally described in textbooks as a madman, though what sociologists have taught us about the use of emotive labelling ought to caution us against ready acceptance of the term. He had publicly reviled Jesus Christ as a bastard[32] and a whore-master, and called organized religion a cheat. To the plea that the common law courts had no power over such matters, Hale CJ responded that 'wicked blasphemous words were not only an offence to God and religion but a crime against laws, State and Government, and therefore punishable in this court'. Moreover, 'to say, Religion is a Cheat, is to dissolve all those Obligations whereby the Civil societies are preserved, and that Christianity is a parcel of the Laws of England; and therefore to reproach the Christian religion is to speak in subversion of the law'.[33] The defendant's

---

[30] *R.* v. *Sidley* (1663) 1 Sid. 168.

[31] *Bowman* v. *Secular Society* [1917] AC 406, 457, per Lord Sumner, describing *Taylor's Case* (below n. 33). It is, however, arguable that the common law courts were punishing behaviour that they would later formally stigmatize as blasphemy considerably before that decision. See I. Leigh, 'Not To Judge But To Save?' (1977) 8 *Camb. LR* 56, 58–61.

[32] Even granted the Virgin Birth, this presents a difficult conundrum as a matter of family law. The court did not pause to consider whether the defendant's learned opinion was correct.

[33] *R.* v. *Taylor* (1676) 1 Vent. 293, 86 ER 189.

punishment was tailored to his offence: he was made to sit in the pillory, orna-
mented with a placard which read: 'For blasphemous words tending to the subversion of all Government.'[34]

Thus, although *Taylor's Case* is generally cited for the legal proposition that it
is blasphemous to deny the truth of the Christian religion,[35] it is important to
grasp the underlying justification: that in the absence of respect for the Christian
religion and its truths, the bonds of 'obligation' might be thrown off. In other
words, deference and obedience to the ruling powers might be threatened. In
Robertson's words, 'strange gods might subvert familiar government'.[36]

This connection became clearer as the use of the law increased. As the Law
Commission's historical account describes,[37] in the eighteenth century there were
many prosecutions aimed at those who had attacked the Bible or the idea of a
Deity. There was, however, an overlap with the even more obviously political
crime of sedition; defendants who had attacked the Established Church were
prosecuted for seditious libel, whilst those who had confined their scorn to
beliefs rather than a political institution were treated as blasphemers.[38]

The lack of any clear dividing line reflected the fact that the state's primary interest was
its own security. Consequently the state intervened by using the criminal law to punish
those whose attacks on Christianity or the Deity were regarded as a menace to the foun-
dations of established religion and thus to society in general.[39]

Blasphemy prosecutions became ever more important in response to the
French Revolution, which had fiercely attacked the intertwined institutions of
Church and State. The Revolution initially inspired a good deal of sympathy in
England, manifested in numerous constitutional and political societies, whose
leading spokesman was Tom Paine. Paine followed *The Rights of Man* with *The
Age of Reason*, first published in 1795, a work well described by E. P. Thompson
as 'an assault on the ethics of the Old Testament, and the veracity of the New,
a pell-mell essay in biblical criticism'.[40] It was censored, cut, and subsequently
banned, with a number of printers and booksellers gaoled for blasphemy. The
official campaign against the book was unremitting: the last major prosecution
occurred over a quarter of a century after publication, in 1821.[41]

Nor was Paine the sole target. Between 1821 and April 1834 there were seventy-

---

[34] G. Robertson, *Freedom, the Individual and the Law* (Harmondsworth, 1989), 210.

[35] e.g. Supperstone (n. 1 above), 200; Smith and Hogan (n. 4 above), 723.

[36] (See n. 34 above, 210.

[37] Law Commission Working Paper No. 79, *Offences Against Religion and Public Worship* (1981),
chap. xi. A more detailed account may be found in Leigh (n. 31 above).

[38] Technically both offences were described as libel—seditious libel, blasphemous libel—in the
18th-cent. usage of the term meaning a small writing. When erotic literature was censored it was
done by means of prosecutions for 'obscene libel'.

[39] See n. 37 above, para. 2.3.

[40] E. P. Thompson, *The Making of the English Working Class* (Harmondsworth, 1968), 106. Part I of
this classic work presents a detailed description of these societies, their activities, and the persecution
of their leaders.

[41] St John Robilliard, *Religion and the Law* (Manchester, 1984), 26.

three convictions on this charge.[42] Many of the defendants were early socialists who had vigorously attacked the Established Church, but after the failure of the Chartist movement blasphemy prosecutions ceased to be employed by the national authorities to suppress political opposition.[43] The law began then to evolve, with the judges redefining and narrowing the offence to reach only manner rather than matter; that is to say, scurrility and abusive derision of Christian doctrine would be punishable, but reasoned criticism, however strong, would not.[44] Economic and political doctrines had replaced religion as the main ideological prop of the political order; and the subsequent history of blasphemy—its decline and putative demise; its resurrection accompanied by prayer meetings in the halls of the Old Bailey; its proposed abolition by the Law Commission; and its emergence as an important symbol to many Muslims in the wake of the publication of Salmon Rushdie's *Satanic Verses*—must be left for consideration by others.

SEDITION

As noted earlier,[45] sedition was companion in arms to blasphemy, serving much the same purposes but with an explicitly secular and political orientation. It proved a fearsome weapon. Its heyday was perhaps the early decades of the reign of George III, when a clumsy, disaster-prone, but authoritarian government encountered a boisterous opposition enlivened by men with a gift for invective seldom equalled in the history of political rivalry. It was the age of the political broadsheet, John Wilkes, and the *Letters of Junius*. When in 1770 Junius's printers and publishers were acquitted of sedition by a jury acting in disregard of a virtual direction to convict from Lord Mansfield, thousands cheered in the streets.[46] Nonetheless it took staunch jurymen, determined to resist partisan misuse of criminal law, to acquit a defendant, for theirs was a very limited role. Juries were asked to decide only two questions of fact: did the accused publish the alleged libel, and did the publication carry the meaning claimed in the indictment? The question of whether it was seditious was left to the judge—one reason why judges of that era, and Lord Mansfield, the Lord Chief Justice, in particular, were subject to criticisms of a bite and severity that

---

[42] This is reported in Roskill LJ's historical account of blasphemy in *R.* v. *Lemon* [1979] QB 10, 19.

[43] See n. 40 above, 27–8.

[44] For fuller accounts of the historical development of blasphemy, see Law Commission (n. 37 above); Robilliard, (n. 41 above); and Kenny, 'The Evolution of the Law of Blasphemy, (1922) 1 *Camb. LJ* 127. The key cases, in which public order emerges as the primary basis of the offence, are *R.* v. *Ramsay and Foote* (1883) 15 Cox CC 231, and *Bowman* v. *Secular Society* (n. 31 above).

[45] Above, p. 204.

[46] A. Mockler, *Lions Under the Throne* (London, 1983), 165–9. For a general account of Wilkes's career—which wrote a chapter in the history of English law virtually by itself—see G. Rudé, *Wilkes and Liberty* (Oxford, 1962).

subsequent, more reverential, generations have never equalled. Opponents of the Crown argued that judges, regarded as government place-men (indeed, Mansfield was a Cabinet Minister), be stripped of the power to determine the crucial issue in the case. In 1792, just before the killing of Louis XVI turned English sentiment against the French Revolution and inaugurated an intense repression of its sympathizers, Charles James Fox carried his Libel Act through Parliament. Henceforth jurors would decide the question of sedition for themselves.[47]

This parliamentary reform marked the reversal of nearly a century of judicial expansion of seditious libel. Recent historical scholarship[48] has shown that the offence was developed by the eighteenth-century judiciary to effectuate the aims of the Crown in silencing and suppressing printed criticism. This followed earlier attempts by both Crown and Protectorate first to widen the definition of treason by statute and then to use the law against pamphleteers. This was tragically successful in the prosecution of one William Anderton, who in 1695 was tried and executed for publishing a Jacobite tract. Alarmed, Parliament responded with the enactment of the Treason Trials Act 1696, which blocked this promising avenue by granting defendants a number of procedural rights (including, uniquely, the right to counsel). As a result,

Although members of the Parliamentary opposition passed the Treason Trials Act with their own safety in mind, they restrained the government in a way they did not directly intend. Politically-motivated prosecutions of politicians for constructive treason were cut, and convictions for treason based on printed criticism became almost impossible.[49]

Having lost one political weapon, the Crown cast round for another, and seditious libel came into its own. Previously a subcategory of the law of written defamation, the judges developed it as a distinct branch of criminal law with its own precedents. They enlarged the range of prohibited conduct, and circumscribed the jury's role in deciding the relevant issues. Hence the resemblance to treason grew increasingly stronger, as exemplified in the charge to the jury in one of the last cases to reflect the trend:

Sedition is a crime against society, nearly allied to that of treason, and it frequently precedes treason by a short interval . . . The objects of seditions generally are to induce discontent and insurrection, and stir up opposition to the Government . . . the very tendency of sedition is to incite people to insurrection and rebellion. Sedition has been described as disloyalty in action.[50]

However, Fox's Libel Act did not put an end to the government's use of sedition, which featured prominently in the attack on Radicalism. As a Law

---

[47] W. Holdsworth, *A History of English Law*, vol. 10 (London, 1938), 673–92. As Viscount Dilhorne pointed out in *R. v. Lemon* [1979] AC 617, 640–41, the 1792 Act applied to all aspects of libel (see n. 38 above), such as blasphemy.

[48] P. Hamburger, 'The Development of the Law of Seditious Libel and the Control of the Press' (1985) 37 *Stan. LR* 661, from which the following paragraphs are taken.

[49] Ibid., 722–3.   [50] *R. v. Sullivan* (1868) 11 Cox CC 44, 45 per Fitzgerald J.

Commission Working Paper rather demurely put it, before the nineteenth century 'one also finds that prosecutions were usually brought with overtly political motives'.[51] Unfortunately the turn of the century brought no respite. Cobbett's imprisonment was not at all unusual; in one year alone (1817), in the middle of the great political agitations that followed the victory over Napoleon, no less than eighteen seditious libel prosecutions were begun.[52] The use of the offence was not solely at the behest of the Government; Stephen reports the existence in the 1820s of a Constitutional Association, which initiated prosecutions with the aim of compelling left-wing writers to give up their books, pay the expenses of the proceedings, and cease publication.[53] Writing in 1883, he surveyed the previous sixty years and concluded that seditious libel prosecutions had become 'so rare that they may be said practically to have ceased'.[54] This was owing partly to the emergence of seditious conspiracy, considered below, and also, it has been suggested, by the judicial development of the offence of unlawful assembly.[55] But it may also be seen as a result of the growing confidence in the political stability and justice of liberal institutions that led to the growth of tolerance of dissent in early and mid-Victorian Britain. This same attitude, at once liberal and xenophobic, led Britain to become a haven for refugees from Continental 'despotisms'.[56] However, sedition continued to be used in the turbulence of Ireland, and in 1886 was revived with the prosecution of John Burns, labour leader and future Liberal Cabinet Minister; his oratory was alleged to have caused the violence that grew out of the great demonstrations of the London unemployed in 1886.[57] In our own century prosecutions have been rare, but a catalogue of defendants reads like a biographical history of the radical Left: McLean, Maxton, and Gallacher during the First World War; the entire executive committee of the Communist Party in 1925; Tom Mann and Harry Pollitt in 1934.[58] Some of these cases concerned seditious conspiracy, thus compounding the vagueness of the offence and maximizing the procedural advantages enjoyed by the Crown.

Breadth and vagueness were indeed the defining characteristics of sedition. As one commentator notes,

The sources of the decisions on sedition in the first half of the nineteenth century include broad notions. They cover the illegality of conspiracies, unlawful societies, 'combinations against the government', incitement as a misdemeanour, and cases regarded as

[51] See n. 12 above, para. 41.   [52] Thomas (n. 3 above), 12–15.
[53] J. Stephen, *History of the Criminal Law of England*, vol. 2 (London, 1883), 371.
[54] Ibid. 373.
[55] See M. Lobban, 'From Seditious Libel to Unlawful Assembly: Peterloo and the Changing Face of Political Crime *c.*1770–1820' (1990) 10 *Ox. JLS* 319, who also suggests (349–52) that in the mid-19th cent., unlawful assembly began to comprise the central element in conspiracy prosecutions.
[56] B. Porter, *The Refugee Question in Mid-Victorian Politics* (Cambridge, 1979), *passim*.
[57] *R. v. Burns* (1886) 16 Cox CC 355, discussed below.
[58] Supperstone (n. 1 above), 239, n. 9.

examples of unlawful assembly by reasons of a seditious intent. This last group was seen in general political terms rather than the likelihood of breaches of the peace.[59]

The offence was somewhat narrowed in *Burns*, where Cave J, following Stephen's *Digest of the Criminal Law*, instructed the jurors (who acquitted the defendant) that the offence requires

an intention to bring into hatred or contempt or incite disaffection against the person of Her Majesty . . . or to excite Her Majesty's subjects to attempt, otherwise than by lawful means, the alteration of any matter in Church or State by law established, or to raise discontent or disaffection amongst Her Majesty's subjects, or to promote feelings of ill-will and hostility between different classes of such subjects.[60]

The charge was most readily employed against speakers and writers, and hence the modern history of sedition through the common law world is tightly intertwined with freedom of speech and the ability to criticize governments. This is particularly true of the United States, and not only because of the existence of the First Amendment's guarantee of freedom of speech. Less than a decade after the nation's founding, the embattled administration of President John Adams passed the Alien and Sedition Acts of 1798. The ensuing prosecutions of political opponents proved so unpopular that Adams was defeated for re-election and his party, the Federalists, were set firmly on the road to extinction.[61] More unhappily, twentieth century state and federal legislation, aimed at anarchists and Communists, was often sustained by the Supreme Court; dissents by Justices Holmes and Brandeis inaugurated the development of the modern First Amendment, but not until the virulence of McCarthyism had lost much of its political potency did the Supreme Court adopt a tougher reading of the Constitution and significantly curtail the impact of those laws.[62]

Moreover, sedition was important in combatting independence movements throughout the Empire. Highly critical speeches to illiterate audiences who, denied the right to vote, had no democratic means of redress were not surprisingly regarded by the colonial authorities as inflammatory and dangerous.[63] In their eyes, such speeches would appear as archetypical attempts 'to lead ignorant persons to endeavour to subvert the Government and the laws of the Empire':[64] a neat example of adapting a mechanism designed for the control of the masses

---

[59] Supperstone (n. 1 above), 235–6, omitting several footnotes.

[60] (1886) 16 Cox CC 355, 360.

[61] T. Emerson, *The System of Freedom of Expression* (New York, 1970), 99–100.

[62] Ibid., ch. 5, discussing the cases in great detail, and more accessibly E. Barendt, *Freedom of Speech* (Oxford, 1985), 154–7. Indeed J. Boasberg, 'Seditious Libel and Incitement to Mutiny' (1990) 10 *Ox. JLS* 106, argues that even the contributions of Holmes and Judge Learned Hand (whose lower court judgment in a contemporaneous case is often also cited as an admirably progressive interpretation of the First Amendment) were actually less protective of freedom of speech than the slightly earlier analogous English cases of *R. v. Aldred* (1909) 22 Cox CC 1 and *R. v. Bowman* (1912) 22 Cox CC 729.

[63] Cases and statutes are collected in Supperstone (n. 1 above), 235, n. 10.

[64] *R. v. Sullivan* (1868) 11 Cox CC 44, 45.

at home to the subject peoples overseas. Sedition charges were also used against left-wing, particularly Communist, leaders in the white Dominions.[65]

However, in 1951 the Supreme Court of Canada had occasion to consider the offence, and interpreted it still more narrowly than it had been left in *Burns*. In *Boucher* v. *R.*[66] it held that seditious intention must consist of 'an intention to incite violence or create public disturbance or disorder against the institutions of government . . . there must be violence or defiance for the purpose of disturbing constituted authority'.[67] This case has in turn shaped the interpretation of the law in England: it was the basis of the Divisional Court's rejection of the attempt by a Muslim cleric to institute proceedings against Salman Rushdie on this charge.[68]

In Britain sedition has fallen into disuse. There have been no prosecutions for more than twenty years, and only two of any significance since the First World War. The two cases both involved anti-Semitic propaganda, and both ended in acquittals.[69] This aspect of sedition—concerning what Cave J called 'promot[ing] feelings of ill-will and hostility between different classes of . . . subjects'—is now covered by the racial incitement provisions of the Public Order Act 1986; there is similar legislation elsewhere in the Commonwealth.[70] Although in the later case Birkett J emphasized the importance of freedom of the Press,[71] one may doubt whether the authorities' greater sensitivity to civil liberties is the complete explanation. Two others may be explored.

The first is that in one narrow but important aspect, it had been superceded by statute even earlier. The National Government enacted the Incitement to Disaffection Act 1934, after near-universal condemnation of its original proposals forced a radical pruning.[72] What remained, and remains, are the offences of intentionally 'endeavour(ing) to seduce any member of His Majesty's forces from his duty or allegiance to His Majesty', and of possessing documents which would have that effect if disseminated, with the intent to commit or in any way assist in the commission of the main offence.[73] Despite the furore, or perhaps

---

[65] e.g. *Burns* v. *Ransley* (1949) 79 CLR 101, *R.* v. *Sharkey* (1949) 79 CLR 121 (Australia); for Canada see M. Friedland, *National Security—The Legal Dimensions* (Ottawa, 1980), 18–19.

[66] (1951) 2 DLR 369.　　　　　　　　　　[67] Quoted in Law Commission (above n. 11), para. 71.

[68] *R.* v. *Chief London Stipendiary Magistrate, ex. p. Choudhury* [1991] 1 QB 429, 452–3.

[69] *R.* v. *Leese, The Times* 22 Sept. 1936 (the defendants were however convicted of a public mischief); *R.* v. *Caunt*, unreported (1947). The latter defendant, a newspaper editor, published an account of the case, *An Editor on Trial*, in the same year.

[70] Public Order Act 1986, ss. 17–27, and see particularly the 'hate propaganda' statute enacted in Canada in 1970, and upheld in *R.* v. *Keegstra* (1990) 3 SCR 697. For a general view of the problem, which is still valuable for its historical account of English law, see A. Lester and G. Bindman, *Race and Law* (Harmondsworth, 1972), ch. 10.

[71] In what may be unique in the annals of English legal writing, the learned judge wrote a note of his own case: (1947) 64 *LQR* 203.

[72] For an account of this episode, see H. Street, *Freedom, The Individual and the Law*, 4th edn. (Harmondsworth, 1977), 215–20. One strong impulse behind the legislation was a long campaign by the Security Service. See C. Andrew, *Secret Service* (London, 1986) 380–1.

[73] Incitement to Disaffection Act 1934, ss. 1 and 2(1).

because of it, there were very few prosecutions in the years after its passage. Only in the 1970s, as opposition mobilized against the commitment of British forces to Northern Ireland, did it enjoy a brief prominence. Pat Arrowsmith, the veteran pacifist and political activist, was convicted for distributing leaflets at an Army base advocating that soldiers refuse to accept postings to Northern Ireland and giving information about other nations which might accept deserters. It is hard to imagine material that fits within the Act more precisely, and her appeal was rejected.[74] The European Commission of Human Rights rather peremptorily declared inadmissible her claim that the statute violated freedom of expression as guaranteed by Article 10 of the Convention, apparently on the ground that its provisions were necessary to maintain national security.[75]

The Arrowsmith prosecution was only one of several initiated in respect of leaflets and campaigns of the Troops Out Movement. The most spectacular was also the last. The conspiracy cannon was again wheeled out; fourteen defendants were charged with conspiracy to violate the 1934 Act. However, the leaflets they distributed had a very different emphasis, concentrating primarily on explaining how to apply for a discharge from the Forces, or for conscientious objector status. After a fifty-one-day trial the defendants were all acquitted; and the Attorney-General expressed regret that the prosecution had ever been brought.[76] The Act then seems to have been put in cold storage, as has a parallel provision in the Police Act 1964, which penalizes efforts to induce constables to withhold their services or breach their discipline.[77] This provision carries over an offence enacted after the police strike of 1919, and appears never to have been used, at any rate in its present form.

CONSPIRACY

The second explanation for the decline of seditious libel prosecutions is that conspiracy charges in considerable measure took over their political function. This was Stephen's view: after noting the decline of the latter, he traced the emergence of the former. The first case occurred in 1795, 'at a time when associations for the purpose of obtaining political objects first became a marked feature of English political life'.[78] In other words, the rise of radical and working-men's associations was met, in a profoundly undemocratic political order, with a new form of political prosecution. Once again, the list of cases contains virtually every celebrated dissident political leader of the nineteenth century: Orator Hunt, the Charter leaders of 1839, O'Connell and Parnell in Ireland.[79] The conspiracy device proved particularly useful to the prosecution,

---

[74] *R.* v. *Arrowsmith* [1975] QB 678.
[75] 7075/75, *Arrowsmith* v. *UK*, 19 D & R 5., discussed briefly by Barendt (n. 62 above), 158.
[76] *R.* v. *Williams and Others*, *The Times*, 11 Dec. 1975; Robertson (n. 34 above), 176.
[77] Police Act 1964, s. 53.   [78] Stephen (n. 53 above), 377.
[79] Ibid. 378.

because speeches, meetings, or even the establishment of an organization could be considered unlawful acts in furtherance of the conspiracy, once the Crown could establish that the purpose of these activities was in some way 'inconsistent with peace and good government of the country'.[80] It is hard to imagine a more blatantly political offence, or a clearer example of persecution of dissidents through the means of law. However, in one respect the judges narrowed the offence: in the early days the truth of criticisms of the government was no defence, because the truer it was, the more tumult it might cause. As more liberal notions of political freedom grew in influence, the position was altered to exempt from liability criticism in good faith for the purpose of securing improvement in governmental institutions.[81]

Few aspects of criminal law have been as heavily criticized as conspiracy, and the literature on the subject is large.[82] In view of its intellectual interest and historical importance, we must be wary of temptation and limit discussion to those aspects touching upon national security or closely related matters.

Three of the most telling criticisms have in any case prevailed. Conspiracy is no longer a common law offence.[83] This has two consequences. First, judges can no longer make up new crimes,[84] although presumably they can still expand liability by claiming that they were merely applying existing offences to new forms of conduct.[85] Secondly, it means that acts which are not criminal if done by one person can no longer become so because done by two or more.[86]

The third point relates to punishment, which used to be 'at large', so that even if the completed offence was subject to a statutory maximum, that limit could be ignored; indeed there was no requirement that the accused be charged with the substantive offence. This produced the outrageous result in the case of the Shrewsbury Three that a man was gaoled for three years for conspiracy to commit an offence for which the statutory maximum was three months.[87] The

---

[80] Ibid. 379.   [81] Ibid. 380–1.

[82] Most useful are F. Sayer, 'Criminal Conspiracy' (1922) 35 *Harv. LR* 393; Smith and Hogan (n. 4 above). ch. 10; I. Brownlie and D. Williams, 'Judicial Legislation in Criminal Law' (1964) 42 *Can. Bar Rev.* 561; R. Hazell, *Conspiracy and Civil Liberties* (London, 1973); G. Robertson, *Whose Conspiracy?* (London, 1974); Law Commission Report No. 76, *Conspiracy and Criminal Law Reform* (London, 1976); see also L. Lustgarten, 'Common Law Crimes and Trade Union Activities' (1976) 27 *NILQ* 216, Pt. I. R. Spicer, *Conspiracy: Law, Class and Society* (London, 1981) is not entirely reliable in its legal analysis, but can be very useful as an account of particular cases.

[83] Criminal Law Act 1977, s. 5(1). Note, however, the explicit retention as common law offences of conspiracy to corrupt public morals and to outrage public decency in s. 5(3).

[84] The rather extravagant claims made by some of the Law Lords, notably Viscount Simonds, in *Shaw* v. *DPP*, [1962] AC 220, 268, that there exists a residual judicial power 'to superintend those offences which are prejudicial to the public welfare' met with severe criticism and were not followed by great judicial activism.

[85] One of the vices of the still-existing offences (see n. 83 above), is that they are so open-ended that they enable police and judges to apply them to almost any activity they detest whilst avoiding condemnation for having retrospectively imposed criminal liability.

[86] Criminal Law Act 1977, s. 1, overturning *Kamara* v. *DPP* [1974] AC 104.

[87] R. v. *Jones* [1974] ICR 310; Lustgarten (n. 82 above), 227–31, for further analysis.

statutory rule now limits punishment for conspiracy to the statutory maximum for the completed offence.[88]

In the history of conspiracy, certain groups or activities were targeted at particular times. One was trade unions. Although someone committed to the view that the state apparatus is merely, or pre-eminently, the servant of the capitalist class would not agree, the prosecution of trade unionists, though odious for many reasons, cannot be regarded as based upon considerations of state security. This is shown first by the fact that an entirely separate branch of the law of conspiracy was developed by the judges to stifle trade unions; they did not employ seditious conspiracy. Nor did Parliament when it chose to attack trade unions: the Combination Acts outlawed only agreements for advancing wages or regulating hours of work. Secondly, after repeated judicial invention of new heads of liability, Parliament intervened in 1875 in terms that kept criminal conspiracy law out of industrial relations for nearly 100 years.[89] This enactment by a Conservative administration at the height of *laissez-faire* capitalism does not easily fit with the 'capitalist agent' view. Finally, it is noteworthy that during the miners' strike of 1984–5—perhaps the most politically charged industrial dispute since the General Strike—not one conspiracy charge was entered, of a total exceeding 11,000.[90]

A second cluster of conspiracy prosecutions were the public morality cases of the 1960s and early 1970s. Doctrinally, the most notorious is *Shaw* v. *DPP*,[91] in which the House of Lords held that the offence of conspiracy to corrupt public morals exists in English law. That charge was mostly used to prosecute private showings of 'blue' films because the Obscene Publications Act only covered public performances.[92] However, along with the similar offence of conspiracy to outrage public decency it was invoked against the so-called 'underground' press, most notably the magazines *OZ*[93] and *International Times*.[94] There were also numerous raids on 'alternative' bookshops which stocked radical and sexually explicit material and were staffed by people regarded as 'hippies'—disreputable in appearance and disrespectful of authority. There can be little doubt that personal and ideological antipathy on the part of some police officers influenced both the choice of targets and the treatment of those arrested.[95] Nevertheless it is extravagant to claim, as was done at the time, that the defendants were challenging the cultural legitimacy of the state. The ease with which members of the so-called 'counter-culture' made the journey to highly paid employment or suc-

---

[88] Criminal Law Act 1977, s. 3(1), reversing *Verrier* v. *DPP* [1967] 2 AC 195
[89] On the 19th-cent. history, see K. Wedderburn, *The Worker and the Law* (3rd. edn., Harmondsworth, 1986), 513–21.
[90] The figure for total charges is found in ibid. 549.   [91] [1962] AC 220.
[92] Hazell (above n. 82), 32 quoting a statement by the Lord Chancellor in parliament.
[93] *R.* v. *Anderson* [1971] 3 All ER 1152.
[94] *Knuller Ltd.* v. *DPP* [1973] AC 435, in which the existence of conspiracy to outrage public decency was affirmed 3–2 by the House of Lords.
[95] G. Robertson, *Obscenity* (London, 1979), 292–3. And not only the police, as a reading of the judge's direction to the jury in the *OZ* trial clearly shows. See n. 93 above.

cess as entrepreneurial capitalists in the media industry within a few years weakens the claim considerably; so too does the fact that ideas, pictures, and language very similar to what appeared in various 'underground' publications found their way into the mainstream media in a relatively short time afterwards. We therefore need not discuss these examples any further.

The third group of cases, much the most relevant to our subject, concern Irish Nationalists and Republicans. Many of these were nineteenth-century cases, while others have been a by-product of the Troubles of post-1969 Northern Ireland. Unlike the seditious conspiracy cases, these prosecutions usually involve conspiracies to commit substantive offences related to violence or possession of explosives or firearms.[96] Whilst it is perfectly reasonable to believe that the British presence anywhere in the island of Ireland is an act of political oppression, and the existence of six counties outside the Republic of Ireland illegitimate, it is equally reasonable to expect the political authorities in Belfast and London to take the opposite view and defend their powers by both legal and military means. Therefore one cannot object to prosecutions charging people with, for example, violations of the laws prohibiting making bombs or possessing firearms.[97] Further, if persons are engaging in acts leading up to planting bombs or physically attacking someone, it is ludicrous to suggest that the police should wait until the violence occurs and then arrest them for the completed offence, or even wait until the very last moment before completion and then charge them with attempt. It does not, however, follow that the present law of conspiracy is satisfactory even in such contexts.

There are several unacceptable features. The first is that it is possible to charge someone both with committing a particular offence and conspiracy to commit the same offence. This practice, known as a 'roll-up' charge, has been criticized by generations of judges, but prosecutors have continued to use it because of its forensic advantages.[98] Foremost among them is that a jury which remains unconvinced that one or two individual defendants committed any substantive offence may nevertheless convict them of conspiracy. This can happen where there are several defendants and a mass of evidence that applies at times to some, then to others, but never to all. The jury may be persuaded that with so much evidence flying around in their general direction, all those individuals must have done *something*. In some prosecutions 'peripheral' defendants are charged only with conspiracy whilst their co-defendants are subject to roll-up charges, although juries seem to have come to resent such practices and have

---

[96] Spicer (above n. 82), ch. 3, presents a useful descriptive account of several cases.

[97] One cannot imagine any political system accepting that attempts to change any aspect of it by means of violence would be morally or legally tolerable. And even those who see IRA violence as a form of warfare conducted by a national liberation movement cannot ignore the fact that most of the people they have killed have been unarmed civilians, not British soldiers.

[98] Hazell (n. 82 above), 73–8, discusses this issue very fully.

acquitted them.[99] Prosecutors have apparently been slow to realize that jurors are neither docile nor credulous.[100]

The second is that a conspiracy may exist even where the individuals do not know and have never met each other: the 'agreement' to pursue a criminal course of conduct required for the offence is purely notional. It may be inferred from evidence of acts that seem to have a common purpose.[101] Since, however, it is precisely this element of common endeavour to commit crime that constitutes the actual illegality, the defendant may fall into a very nasty catch-22. It is clear why this rule exists: an organization may be constructed like a chain or in parallel cells or units, whose members are kept unaware of each others' identities and know only those immediately above or below them with whom they have specific dealings. However, in an age of large and highly organized police forces, it is hard to see why the mere fact of collective action should be the basis of additional criminal liability, though in some circumstances it may be an aggravating factor in sentencing.[102]

Each of these features may also be seen as particular examples of the more general problem of joint trials. The chances of injustice rise exponentially as the number of defendants increases, for a range of reasons falling well beyond the scope of this study. The late Tom Sargant, the foremost expert and campaigner against miscarriages of justice in England, emphasized this feature as a contributory element in the cases he dealt with;[103] one may simply add an *a fortiori* where an alleged conspiracy of any size is involved.

Thirdly, and because it is permissible to infer the existence of the conspiracy from circumstantial evidence, the prosecution often introduces evidence of the political beliefs and 'deviant life-style' of the defendants. Thus in cases where the accused are supposed to have been part of IRA violence, Republican leaflets found in their homes are introduced as evidence. This is grossly prejudicial and must make any resulting conviction suspect. People may sympathize with Republican aims or ideals and, particularly if they are Irish, regularly read or receive Republican literature, without approving or being willing to participate in violence. That distinction may be clear in their minds, but not in those of English jurors. And the portrayal of someone as a Republican sympathizer is virtually an invitation to the jurors to let anti-Irish prejudices run amok, a particularly dangerous possibility where serious violence has been committed. These points are equally applicable to trials of political radicals, in which evidence of

---

[99] This was noteworthy in the two Angry Brigade trials; see ibid. 76 and Spicer (n. 82 above), 67–77.

[100] The most recent example is the verdict given in the Covenanters' case, discussed at pp. 382–4 below. Whilst one defendant was convicted by a bare majority of a substantive offence after a 2 month trial, the other two were acquitted of conspiracy offences, apparently the sole charges brought against them.

[101] Hazell (n. 82 above), 78.   [102] We return to this point below, p. 219.

[103] T. Sargant and P. Hill, *Criminal Trials: The Search for Truth*, Fabian Research Series 348 (London, 1986), 2, 8–9.

actual possession of weapons may be promiscuously mixed with evidence of their political beliefs and activities, allegedly probative of their participation in conspiracy. The clearest example of this were the two Angry Brigade cases of the early 1970s, though a sceptical jury acquitted many of the 'conspiracy-only' defendants and only convicted any of the defendants by a bare vote of ten to two.[104]

A related matter is that use of evidence about the defendants' lawful political activities, speeches and so on is itself an infringement upon political freedom. There is a real chance in such circumstances that defendants may be convicted for their politics rather than for the commission of any injurious act. Moreover, there is more than a faint possibility that those with unpopular views may be deterred from expressing them if there is a reasonable chance that they may find such views used as evidence against them in a conspiracy prosecution: another instance of the 'chilling effect' on the exercise of rights. Both these points have raised constitutional issues in the United States under the First Amendment.[105] In Britain they have remained in the realm of policy or philosophical argument rather than law, due to the absence of a formally recognized right to freedom of speech. In our conclusion to this chapter we shall suggest that, even taking that underlying legal framework as given, it is possible to initiate some reform which would be responsive to these human rights considerations.

The final disquieting aspect of conspiracy prosecutions in the national security sphere is that they may raise the problem of entrapment and *agents provocateurs*. This is not a new phenomenon. In his painstaking history of the early Special Branch, Bernard Porter investigated a number of cases in which conspiracies were allegedly foiled, Anarchists and Fenians sentenced to long terms of imprisonment, and great kudos earned by the Branch and its parent, Scotland Yard.[106] Allegations were made at the time that in some of these cases police agents had participated in the conspiracy, even to the extent, in one instance, of initiating it.[107] Porter's judicious evaluation is that these claims cannot be conclusively proved or disproved, although in several cases there are suspicious circumstances, such as the failure to charge individuals who had clearly taken a prominent part in the activities. But there can be no doubt whatever that, in the words of the memorandum written by the head of Scotland Yard's CID in 1898, the police had been doing 'utterly unlawful things' in their campaigns

---

[104] Spicer (n. 82 above). The case reached the Court of Appeal on some narrow technical points which were rejected: *R. v. Greenfield* [1973] 1 WLR 1151. Indeed were it not for the abolition of the requirement of unanimous jury verdicts brought in by s. 13 of the Criminal Justice Act 1967, virtually no convictions would have been obtained in any of the politically controversial cases of the last quarter century. The Caernarfon prosecution (above n. 100) fits squarely within the pattern: the only conviction was by a vote of 10–2.

[105] See Note, 'Conspiracy and the First Amendment', 79 *Yale LJ* 872 (1970).

[106] B. Porter, *The Origins of the Vigilant State: The London Metropolitan Special Branch Before the First World War* (London, 1987), 68–79, 88–9, 130–42.

[107] Ibid. 88–9.

against anarchists throughout that decade.[108] As our discussion of informers in Chapter 4 indicates, this problem is still very much with us.

COMMON LAW CRIMES AND NATIONAL SECURITY—AN EVALUATION

The offences we have considered so far have all been directed toward shoring up the political order. Historically they were used to stifle criticism of policies or personalities of leaders, or to check the propagation of new and radical ideas about how and by whom state power should be exercised. Viewed from a contemporary perspective, this use of criminal law looks merely like persecution through the legal process. But it must be emphasized that, at any rate before the diffusion of democratic ideas in the late eighteenth century, such prosecutions were grounded in a genuine belief that public criticism, not only of government but of its religious and secular ideological supports, struck at the stability of the state—what we today call national security. Prosecution for these offences become most markedly repressive in the Europe-wide turmoil begun by the French Revolution as the political oligarchy fought, with remarkable success, to maintain its powers against proponents of democracy. This struggle left a permanent imprint of legalistic authoritarianism upon English political culture which the belated coming of the democratic franchise has only partly blurred—a legacy whose influence we shall see at work at various critical points throughout this study.

The Victorians saw themselves as the bearers of progress and enlightenment, and it is certainly true that—in mainland Britain—their greater respect for liberty of thought and conscience was reflected in legal changes in this sphere. The judges remoulded blasphemy to limit it to extreme attacks on believers' sensibilities, not to heated controversies about matters of truth; sedition was also narrowed, but remained in the background as a threat, particularly in the context of conspiracy. One suspects that the infrequency of its use reflected prosecutors' fears that juries would balk at the charge and refuse to convict, at least as much as judicial solicitude for freedom of expression. None the less the judges have played a liberalizing role, particularly the Supreme Court of Canada in the *Boucher* decision.[109]

In terms of the future, we may consider what role, if any, the various offences we have discussed should continue to play in this sphere.

---

[108] B. Porter, *The Origins of the Vigilant State: The London Metropolitan Special Branch Before the First World War* (London, 1987), 136.

[109] See n. 66 above.

Treason

A fully fledged critique of treason would require consideration of whether, in the age of supranational political organization and a concept of European citizenship implanted in UK law, the degree of loyalty to the sovereign state embodied in the offence is sustainable any longer. Such reflections are, however, more for the future than the present, and in any case there are serious practical objections to retention of the offence in its present form. These arise from its wide scope and the consequent discretion as to whether to charge which inevitably arises. Many terrorist offences would fall squarely within the ambit of treason, but in practice are charged as offences of violence or as explosives offences.[110] The same may be true of espionage. The difficulty is compounded by the continued, and unique, availability of the death penalty for treason. It is hard to envisage prosecutorial discretion carrying more serious consequences.

In practice use of the offence has been restricted to wartime, and our view is that the only proper use for treason is against specific acts of serious disloyalty in war. We would restrict the actions covered to steps which would ordinarily constitute an offence—the treason charge would then be a way of marking the aggravated nature of the conduct, not of catching (with the most serious consequences imaginable) conduct not otherwise criminal. Admittedly this would leave the theoretical possibility that non-violent preparation of a *coup d'état* in peacetime might go unpunished, but the democratic process in the United Kingdom is surely secure enough to bear the risk.

Blasphemy

As a result of the Salman Rushdie affair the question of blasphemy has achieved a new and controversial salience which could not have been predicted even after the revival of the offence in the *Gay News* prosecution[111] reopened a door many had thought had been shut for good. Perhaps fortunately, we need not consider the more difficult questions here.[112] For our purposes the matter is much simpler: nowadays blasphemy has no national security implications whatever, there seems no chance of any regression in that direction, and it is a case of letting sleeping dogs lie.

---

[110] At various times Lords Hailsham, Denning, and Havers have commented on the possible charging of terrorist bombers with treason. See R. Thomas, *Espionage and Secrecy* (London, 1991), 2 for citations.

[111] *R.* v. *Lemon*, (n. 42 above).

[112] A useful starting point is the Discussion Papers, *Law, Blasphemy and the Multi-Faith Society*, and *Free Speech*, each containing several papers presented at two seminars sponsored by the Commission for Racial Equality and published by them (London, 1989).

Sedition

In so far as the existence of sedition (or seditious conspiracy) reflects the idea that any form of expression can *of itself* be a threat to the security of the nation, it cannot be squared with even the most crabbed interpretation of what liberty or democracy entail. This is no less true where speech or writing involves advocacy of violent revolution or overthrow of an elected government, or of acts of economic sabotage designed to achieve the same end. Greater difficulties of principle arise where some form of expression begins to merge in time and place with prohibited, especially violent, action. However, this then becomes a matter of public order, protection of the safety of individuals, or both. The Law Commission in effect recognized this by noting that, under the *Boucher* test, any seditious speech would also amount to incitement or conspiracy to commit a fairly serious substantive offence, such as an offence against the person or criminal damage. It therefore considered sedition otiose, and recommended its abolition.[113] We would agree; and certainly there are no considerations of national security—its original sphere of operation—that would stand in the way of this conclusion.

Conspiracy

Any discussion of conspiracy must take account of the multifarious contexts in which the charge may be brought. It would be difficult to suggest reforms which would apply to cases only purportedly involving national security, not least because the offences are not expressed in those terms but rather in relation to explosive substances or other offences of violence.[114] Indeed the abuses have arisen in several contexts, not merely that of offences relating to national security. Some useful reforms have been enacted but there remain the defects identified earlier:[115] the practice of 'roll-up' charges, impairment of the exercise of freedom of political belief and expression, the inevitable prejudice to individual defendants when tried collectively, and the possibility of entrapment and failure to control *agents provocateurs*.

To these are allied a doctrinal question: whether conspiracy as a separate offence should be maintained in any form. The fundamental analytical difficulty is that there are two quite distinct, indeed wholly unrelated, justifications for the existence of the offence.[116] Historically, the more practically powerful justification has been the heightened menace of collectivity. As one judge expressed it:

---

[113] Law Commission, Working Paper No. 72, (n. 12 above), para. 77.

[114] The key statute is the Explosive Substances Act 1883, as amended, s. 3 of which includes a conspiracy offence.

[115] Above pp. 213–14.

[116] For a fuller discussion see I. Dennis, 'The Rationale of Criminal Conspiracy' (1977) 93 *LQR* 39.

It is useless to try and conceal the fact that an organised body of men working together can produce results very different from those which can be produced by an individual without assistance. Laws adapted to individuals require modification if they are to be applied with effect to large bodies of persons acting in concert.[117]

This fear of a turbulent 'ungovernable people'[118] lies at the heart of conspiracy law, explaining many of its technical aspects. It is not often enough emphasized, however, that conspiracy law was developed by judges in the years before the creation of an organized police force. With only the local Dogberry to keep watch—provided he remained sober—it is understandable that groups of men whose organization, co-ordination, and ability to provide alibis for each other made them appear far more efficient than the constabulary, seemed a powerful menace to society in the eyes of the judges, who were the real administrators of criminal justice until Victorian times. This is not to deny the political utility of the offence to the ruling élite in the contexts we have examined; but it is to say that in other spheres the public interest was genuinely served. In this sense, conspiracy may be seen as the rather inadequate substitute provided by English criminal justice for an organized police force. This institution came to Britain later than anywhere else in Europe, and most forces made do without a specialist detective branch until well into the present century.

Today policing without detective squads which cultivate networks of informers and maintain ongoing awareness of and information about criminal activity would be inconceivable. We also live in the age of the Police National Computer, ACPO, Regional Crime Squads, and most directly on point, the National Criminal Intelligence Service. The idea that the police cannot come to terms with the co-ordinated activities of criminals is simply not convincing. They have themselves become 'an organised body of men working together', backed by expensive technical resources. The justification of conspiracy as a sort of redress of the balance of power between law enforcement and criminality no longer exists.

The second justification for conspiracy is inchoacy: the need to punish people who take steps to commit an offence but are foiled from carrying their intention into practice. This is obviously desirable, and there are interesting philosophical and doctrinal questions as to whether punishment of attempts alone, or creation of some novel concept, would adequately protect the social interests involved. For instance, one commentator did propose that conspiracy be scrapped entirely, to be replaced by criminalization of 'acts preparatory' to serious

---

[117] Lord Lindley in *South Wales Miners Federation* v. *Glamorgan Coal Co.* [1905] AC 239, 252. This was a tort action, and the law of tort and crime was haphazardly mixed in the early development of conspiracy law. We have not considered the implications of our analysis of the criminal offence for civil actions.

[118] A description applied specifically to the colliers of Kingswood Forest in the 18th cent., but taken by the editors of an excellent collection of historical essays on crime, law, and social control in that period as symbolic of the governing class perception of the masses in that era: J. Brewer and J. Styles (eds.), *An Ungovernable People* (London, 1980).

substantive offences.[119] The Law Commission rejected the idea on what may be called technical grounds: they believed it would cause as many problems of application and interpretation as it would solve.[120] However, this riposte did not really meet the point that there is little reason why the decision of two or more persons to commit an offence should by itself, be deserving of punishment.

However, we are much less concerned here with the precise moment when behaviour should become criminal, than with elimination of the abuses that have emerged in conspiracy trials. These either create prejudice against defendants in the course of trial, or penalize dissenting political activity. The former require no legislative intervention: they can be rectified by judges in the course of their control of proceedings, by dismissing 'roll-up' charges and more readily granting motions for separate trials of individual defendants. Parliament, however, would have to act to overturn established jurisprudence,[121] and recognize a defence of entrapment where a government agent takes an initiating role in the criminal activity in which the defendant participated. And it should also create an exclusionary rule of evidence that would forbid introduction of any testimony relating to the accuseds' political beliefs or their non-violent expression. If defendants are not permitted to offer evidence about the political or moral basis of their refusal to pay the poll tax or that part of their income tax devoted to nuclear weapons,[122] or why they have demonstrated at sites where nuclear missiles are stationed—as has almost invariably been the case when magistrates and judges are faced with pleas of civil disobedience[123]—then an equivalent prohibition should in fairness be enforced on the prosecution.

---

[119] G. Robertson, (n. 82 above), 46
[120] Law Commission (n. 82 above), para. 3, citing its Working Paper No. 50 (London, 1973).
[121] Notably *R.* v. *Sang* [1980] AC 402.   [122] *Cheney* v. *Conn*, [1968] 1 WLR 242.
[123] Best illustrated by *Chandler* v. *DPP*, [1964] AC 763.

9

Criminal Law and the Concealment of Public Information

At the heart of the debate over 'freedom of information' are the terms on which government information is held. In a state with democratic institutions but an élitist political culture, officials and the majority of politicians regard the conduct of government as falling within their province, subject to two constraints: the requirements of offering occasional explanations of a highly general kind, and periodic elections. Information about the government's activities and the basis of its decisions is thought to be, literally and metaphorically, the property of government itself, to be distributed to the wider public as and when it thinks proper or necessary. Criticism is viewed as often carping and politically motivated; it is thought to be a compelling argument against making information more readily available that thereby criticism will be stimulated.[1]

A democratic political culture considers material held by the government to be *public*, not *official* information. The state has gathered or generated this material on behalf of the citizenry, and stands as trustee of it for them. The information is presumptively theirs, and officialdom must justify any withholding; and in doing so must carry a weighty, through not crippling, burden of proof.[2]

The constructs of élitist and democratic political cultures are meant as Weberian ideal types, useful as conceptual models. They are designed to assist comparisons of different states, which will diverge from one or other of the polarities in varying degrees. And when considering any state's practices, regardless of where on the spectrum it lies, one must always remember Weber's own analysis of 'the Power Position of Bureaucracy' in such matters:

Every bureaucracy seeks to increase the superiority of the professionally informed by keeping their knowledge and intentions secret. Bureaucratic administration always tends to be an administration of 'secret sessions' . . . The pure interest of the bureaucracy in power, however, is efficacious far beyond those areas where purely functional interests make for secrecy. The concept of the 'official secret' is the specific invention of bureaucracy, and nothing is so fanatically defended by the bureaucracy as this attitude . . .[3]

---

[1] The clearest and most unembarrassed expression of this outlook may be found in the judgment of Lord Reid in *Conway* v. *Rimmer* [1968] AC 910, 952. Note also the similar sentiment expressed by Lord Wilberforce in *British Steel Corpn.* v. *Granada Television* [1981] AC 1096, 1168. Professor John Griffith, who also found in these passages particularly illuminating examples of the world-view we have identified, has chosen a particularly apt word for it: 'patrician'. See his 'The Official Secrets Act 1989' (1989) 16 *JLS* 273, 289.

[2] For a more fully elaborated statement of a view close to that taken here, see A. Mathews, *The Darker Reaches of Government* (Berkeley, Calif., 1978), chs. 1–3.

[3] M. Weber, 'The Power Position of Bureaucracy', in H. Gerth and C. W. Mills (eds.), *From Max Weber: Essays in Sociology* (New York, 1958), 233.

In the 1970s a sophisticated comparative analysis emphasized that factors such as the number of political parties and their degree of internal discipline, inherited institutional and intellectual influences, and legal structures all conditioned the approaches to secrecy found in democratic states.[4] At that time, whilst 'the British influence' was cited as one of the factors contributing to maintenance of secrecy in some of the non-European countries studied,[5] Britain was not seen as notably more secretive than France or the Federal Republic of Germany. However, the ensuing decade and a half saw a major wave of change, with freedom of information legislation enacted in numerous nations round the world, including Canada, Australia, and France.[6] Moreover, there emerged major radical parties, movements, and pressure groups in countries like the former FRG and the Netherlands which challenged the practices of secrecy in key policy areas like defence, nuclear power, and the environment.

These forces have been far less influential in Britain. Single party domination, the result of an electoral system—unique in Europe—capable of producing a minority party with outright control of legislature and executive, has managed to resist and contain them. It has been the arena of law in which the most sustained and intense struggles concerning state secrecy have taken place. Despite a series of campaigns, the Conservative government has flatly refused to enact Freedom of Information legislation.[7] Whilst denying increased public access, it has taken successive measures actively to lock the gates more securely with the machinery of criminal law. Its initial venture, characteristically called the Protection of Official Information Bill, had two main features.[8] First, where the 'confidential' information fell into the category of defence policy or international relations, it was an essential element of the offence that harm would result. Proof of this element required a certificate submitted by a minister stating that, at the time of the offence, unauthorized disclosure of the information would cause serious injury to the nation or endanger the safety of a UK citizen. This certificate was to be conclusive: it could not be subject to rebuttal evidence, nor its maker to cross-examination. In effect, executive fiat would carry the prosecution's case a considerable distance on the road to success—that is, conviction of the defendant. The potential for political abuse of such power was and is obvious, as is the danger of allowing a minister to influence the judicial process in such a fashion.

Secondly, the Bill marked a major extension of criminal liability, in that for

---

[4] I. Galnoor, 'What Do We Know About Government Secrecy?' in Galnoor (ed.), _Government Secrecy in Democracies_ (New York, 1977). For conceptual clarity it should be emphasized that criminal legislation protecting official secrets and freedom of information laws are not opposite sides of the same coin. Absence or repeal of the former does not lead directly to the latter, which require enactment of specific rules and procedures enabling citizens to get effective access to state-held information as a matter of right.

[5] Ibid. 283, specifically in relation to Canada and Israel.   [6] See Ch. 5 above.

[7] Whatever the merits of the Citizens' Charter alternative, effective access to information held by government has not proved to be among them.

[8] Details may be found in D. Leigh, _The Frontiers of Secrecy_ (London, 1980), 259–62.

the first time, publication of *any* information relating to security or intelligence, or that had been obtained by authorized telephone tapping or mail opening or related to those forms of information gathering would have been unlawful. This Bill was introduced in October 1979. Almost simultaneously the storm broke over the public identification of Sir (as he was soon no longer to be) Anthony Blunt as the 'Fourth Man' of the celebrated group of spies whose activities in the 1930s and 1940s seem to arouse a continuing fascination inversely proportional to their present importance. When it was pointed out that the material leading to Blunt's unmasking[9] could not have legally been published had the Bill been in force, it was withdrawn by an embarrassed Government.

In place of new legislation, the Government relied on increasing use of prosecutions under section 2 of the Official Secrets Act 1911 (OSA) which—to oversimplify considerably—prohibited unauthorized disclosure or retention of any government information or documents except in the interest of the State. Although the then Attorney-General, Sir Michael Havers, insisted that he authorized such prosecutions 'sparingly and only when absolutely necessary', more prosecutions were brought under his regime than under any other Attorney in the history of the Act. Civil servants were particularly at risk, although in most cases there was no claim that national security was involved.[10] That policy came to a crashing halt with the acquittal of Clive Ponting in February 1985, as a result of a jury verdict in the teeth of the trial judge's summing up that was widely interpreted as rendering section 2 virtually unusable.[11] The Government then turned almost immediately to civil suits and injunctions,[12] and indeed announced in October 1986 that it had no plans for repeal of the section.[13] This statement was either disingenuous, or the Government felt it had to respond to the pressure for reform which developed round the Private Member's Bill introduced by Richard Shepherd, a Conservative MP who had long been involved in the campaign for greater freedom of information. In June 1988 it issued a White Paper announcing its proposals for repeal and reform,[14]

[9] A. Boyle, *The Climate of Treason* (London, 1978) drew heavily upon material the author was able to obtain in the USA under its Freedom of Information Act, an irony not lost on the Bill's critics.

[10] For Sir Michael's comment, see 58 *HC Debs.* (9 Apr. 1984), cols. 13–15. His standing at the top of the prosecutorial league table, and the absence of alleged injury to national security, is documented by D. Hooper, *Official Secrets—The Use and Abuse of the Act* (London, 1987), 3 and a forty-page Appendix (345–85) briefly summarizing more than seventy non-espionage official secrets prosecutions from 1915 to 1989. See also K. Ewing and C. Gearty, *Freedom Under Thatcher: Civil Liberties in Modern Britain* (Oxford, 1990), 138–9.

[11] *R.* v. *Ponting* [1985] *Crim. LR* 318. See Hooper (previous n.) ch. 12, and Ponting's own account of his trial in C. Ponting, *The Right to Know* (London, 1985), chs. 6 and 7. It is worth emphasizing that at no time did the prosecution allege that Ponting's disclosures had jeopardized national security.

[12] The use of injunctions is considered below, pp. 279–85. For an earlier analysis of the government's legal strategy, see L. Lustgarten, 'Learning From Peter Wright: A Response to D. C. Watt' (1989) 60 *Pol. Q.*, 222, 230–3.

[13] *HL Debs.*, vol. 480, col. 119 (7 Oct. 1986).

[14] *Reform of the Official Secrets Act 1911*, Cm. 408 (HMSO, 1988). For details of the Shepherd Bill, see P. Birkinshaw, *Freedom of Information: The Law, the Practice and the Ideal* (London, 1988), 84–6.

which were enacted with little change after the guillotining of Parliamentary debate as the Official Secrets Act 1989.[15] Analysis and critique of this legislation as it relates to national security and matters closely related will form the main part of this chapter. However, such criticism can only carry conviction if it emerges from a framework of principle—in this case, of the proper role for criminal sanctions in controlling and punishing disclosure of public information.

CRIMINAL SANCTIONS AND DISCLOSURE

A preliminary point requiring strong emphasis is that the present discussion will not attempt to address all the circumstances in which the issues can arise. Thus whether disclosure of intimate personal details taken from an individual's medical or criminal records, or of technical data that is of great economic advantage to the recipient (as when a public official reveals confidential information about one manufacturer's product to a competitor) should be governed by criminal law involves a range of considerations and arguments quite different from those relevant to this study. We shall discuss only the area of security and intelligence.

Perhaps the most important distinction to consider is that between public disclosure and espionage. The latter is a concealed transfer of information whose value is multiplied exponentially if the information holder ('holding state') is kept unaware of the transfer. Unlike official secrets legislation, almost entirely a peculiarity of the British and their Empire, espionage statutes are universal and impose far greater penalties for their infraction. The differences between the two activities—which in Britain purportedly justifies the difference between a maximum sentence of fourteen years as opposed to two[16]—are both moral and practical. Espionage entails revealing information to an agent of a hostile or potentially hostile foreign state[17] which seeks to gain an advantage over the holding state. The agent who covertly obtains and releases the information,

[15] For general evaluation of the legislation, see Griffith (n. 1 above); S. Palmer, 'Tightening Secrecy Law: The Official Secrets Act 1989' [1990] *PL* 243; Ewing and Gearty (n. 10 above), 189–208; P. Birkinshaw, *Reforming the Secret State* (Milton Keynes, 1990), 16–30; and G. Robertson, *Freedom, the Individual and the Law* (London, 1989), ch. 4.

[16] OSA 1911, s. 11; OSA 1989, s. 10(1).

[17] S.1(*b*) and (*c*) of the Act of 1911 talk of information, documents, etc. that might be 'useful to an enemy'. In the first case decided at the appellate level under that Act, 'enemy' was held to include 'potential enemy': *R* v. *Parrott* (1913) 8 Cr. App. R. 186. This ruling ensured that s. 1 could be used in peacetime as well as during war.

It also raised an interesting point of construction: who determines which state is an enemy? Apart from an obvious case like Iraq, the demise of the Cold War may make this problematic. If, for example, someone clandestinely passes secret information relating to military technology to an agent of the government of Pakistan, does he come within s. 1? And—as would certainly happen—if the matter is disputed at trial, is it decided on the basis of (*a*) an unchallengeable ministerial certificate; (*b*) evidence of some high official called by the prosecution, at least some of which cannot be challenged in cross-examination (see discussion of *Chandler* v. *DPP* [1964] AC 763, see TAN 86 below); or (*c*) whatever evidence either side chooses to call in order to persuade the jury? See also below pp. 000–0, discussing a parallel issue in relation to the mandate of the Security Service.

whatever his or her personal motives, is favouring the interests of the recipient state over that of the holding state. In a world where all states seek to keep most military and intelligence matters secret, and pursue policies based on self-interest, any contention that the spy's activities were of benefit to mankind is, in all but the rarest cases, wholly specious. His act has simply altered the balance of advantage as between equally amoral competitors. If—as is true of most, and certainly the most effective, spies—he is a citizen or permanent resident of the holding state, he has betrayed the obligation of loyalty that may legitimately be demanded of him. If a foreign 'controller', he may have induced that betrayal by someone else. Thus not only does espionage lack the moral justification that might support public disclosure in some circumstances, it is (apart from certain extreme cases) positively immoral.[18] It may also, in some, but by no means all, instances, endanger genuine national security interests or the safety of individuals. These are important social interests.

Public disclosure of information the government wishes to keep secret is a very different matter. We have had more than our fair share of examples in Britain in recent years, as the names Clive Ponting, Cathy Massiter, Miranda Ingram, Sarah Tisdall, Duncan Campbell, and Peter Wright attest. There are three significant contrasts with espionage: those of motive, social value, and method.

The first two are usually tightly intertwined. The discloser (D), particularly if he or she is a public official, is generally moved to make information public because it reveals immoral or criminal conduct, corruption, political chicanery, or actions that may be described as unconstitutional in the traditional Diceyan sense of violating accepted norms of political behaviour. Recent examples have included Ministers lying to or concealing information from Parliament,[19] misuse of the Security Service and Ministry of Defence officials against political opponents of the Government,[20] and alleged cover-ups of incompetence and treason.[21] D's motive is to make the political or legal process work as it is supposed to in our constitutional theory, and prevent it from being perverted by those in power. The social value of this activity is obvious, and even where D's views on examination seem to be irrational, there may well be accompanying information revealed in passing which enriches public debate and understanding of how government has behaved, and which makes the disclosure worthwhile.[22] The fact that D may reap financial reward may be relevant when judging his or

---

[18] Such an extreme case might arise where espionage is committed against a state planning aggressive war, genocide, or developing nuclear or chemical weapons capacity.

[19] Which led to the Sarah Tisdall and Clive Ponting sending documents exposing the deception to, respectively, a newspaper and an MP, and to their subsequent prosecutions.

[20] Below, pp. 363–64.

[21] See Boyle (above n. 9), C. Pincher (below n. 55), and of course P. Wright, *Spycatcher* (New York, 1987).

[22] The clearest example of this *Spycatcher* itself. For an analysis of the book from this perspective, see Lustgarten (n. 12 above), 222–8.

her credibility, but it is likely to be mixed with other motives and in any case is wholly irrelevant to the social value of the material revealed.[23]

Equally important, D's method is publicity, not furtive funnelling of information to an interested party. The public as a whole receives the information; much of the advantage gained by a hostile or potentially hostile state is cancelled by the government's inevitable awareness that its secrecy has been destroyed. The question then becomes whether the damage, if any, done by the revelation is such as to outweigh the public benefit.

This cannot be judged in isolation from the constitutional context. One of the key elements of British political practice is selective leaking by Ministers, usually through favoured individual journalists or newspapers. It is not an aberration; rather as Lord Gordon Walker, a former Foreign Secretary, has argued, it is a linchpin of the system of Cabinet government. It makes the principle of collective ministerial responsibility tolerable to office-holders who have many political reasons to make their personal views known.[24] Moreover, Ministers—and especially Prime Ministers—regularly use the Lobby system of unattributable briefings to an inner circle of journalists to release information in a manner calculated primarily to maximize political advantage, and certainly not to inform the public or contribute to intelligent policy debate.[25]

Thus the real constitution—the norms of accepted political practice—tolerates and facilitates misleading (because partisan and selective) release of information by self-interested political actors and subordinates under their direction.[26] In these circumstances, unauthorized disclosure and publication of materials that exposes misconduct or corrects half-truths and falsehoods does not deserve criminal sanction.[27] Indeed there is an argument, considered below,[28] that it should be assisted, and the Pontings, Massiters, *et al.* should be encouraged to speak out and be protected from retaliation by their superiors.

The constitutional context is of great importance, but there is another, equally important consideration in analysing the proper role of criminal sanctions in this area. Although there is a large and interesting literature on the justifications for punishment,[29] much less attention has been devoted to the question, which logi-

---

[23] This factor can be exaggerated, and deliberately was during the government's campaign against Peter Wright. The publicity engendered by the world-wide attempt at judicial suppression gained him an infinitely greater financial reward than his rather clumsily written text could have earned had it been studiously ignored.

[24] P. Gordon Walker, *The Cabinet* (rev. edn., London, 1972), 33–9.

[25] M. Cockerell *et al.*, *Sources Close to the Prime Minister* (London, 1984); J. Tunstall, *The Westminster Lobby Correspondents* (London, 1970).

[26] Perhaps the most blatant example of all in this respect was the Westland Affair, from which the Prime Minister emerged unscathed.

[27] This is to assume for purposes of argument only that there may be circumstances in which criminal penalties for unauthorized disclosures would be justified. See further below.

[28] pp. 257–59.

[29] Notably in recent years, A. Ashworth, *Sentencing and Criminal Justice* (London, 1992); A. von Hirsch and A. Ashworth (eds.), *Principled Sentencing* (Edinburgh, 1993); N. Lacey, *State Punishment* (London, 1988). A conversation with Professor Ashworth was of great help in clarifying the issues involved.

cally and morally requires prior determination, of when criminalization of particular conduct is justified.[30] Although this is not the place to attempt a lengthy and systematic analysis of the issues involved, we must offer an introductory discussion if our conclusions on the particular issue we are addressing are to carry conviction. And whilst the punishment literature as such provides little guidance, some of the concepts found in it are of great help.

The criminalization decision is an amalgam of two issues: deciding that certain activity is harmful, and that criminal sanctions are the most appropriate means of preventing it and sanctioning those for whom prevention fails. As in any amalgam the two become commingled, but the issues are best approached in that order.

As our discussion has indicated, the harm caused by espionage is real, and can in some circumstances be grave indeed.[31] There is also a strong element of breach of trust, a factor to which the courts purportedly give great weight.[32] Disclosure of public information without proper authorization by superiors involves more complex questions. Two harms may be said to result. One is the damage to some public interest when the matter becomes public knowledge. The second is the threat to civil service discipline, in the sense of its faithfully executing the wishes and policies of ministers. Historically this has been an important part of the convention of ministerial responsibility and arguably it would be weakened by unpunished disclosures, to the extent of breakdown if the practice became commonplace. (There are echoes here too of the notion of breach of trust.) It may be noted that in so far as the second point has validity, it is limited to officials, and would not extend to those who disseminate the material, such as journalists.

Criminal stigmatization and punishment are evils which should be avoided if equally effective methods, less destructive of liberty, peace of mind, and reputation, can be employed. The alternative is civil sanctions in various forms. These generally involve restitution or compensation; where that is insufficient or inappropriate, other or additional sanctions may include loss of some economic advantage, such as present employment, promotion, or a pension.

Justification for criminal sanctions can either be based on considerations specific to the individual wrongdoer, or be more broadly concerned with the social order. The former relate either to the individual's moral blameworthiness or to negating the advantage he or she has gained from the activity. The latter may include an intended *in terrorem* effect—a calculation that only threat of criminal punishment would be sufficiently powerful to deter others in or potentially in the same position as the wrongdoer from behaving in the same way. There may

---

[30] There is of course the well-known Hart–Devlin debate about the enforcement of morals, but that is largely concerned with issues of privacy and the notion of purely personal harm, which are far removed from those under discussion here.

[31] Above, pp. 224–25.

[32] See Ashworth (n. 29 above), 107–09, 134–5, who notes, however, that actual sentencing practice frequently fails to reflect this principle.

also be a more morally grounded reason: that only criminal sanctions are strong enough to proclaim society's disapproval of the conduct involved, even though civil penalties might deprive the wrongdoer of any benefit and satisfy the victim, if there is one.[33]

Applied to espionage, understood in the terms described earlier, both individual and societal considerations support criminalization. Mere financial penalties, however great the amount, are insufficient to punish the betrayal of trust involved; and if lives were truly put at risk this consideration is greatly strengthened. It is also important, and justifiable, for a democratic society to send a clear message that favouring a foreign state over one's own is not acceptable under any circumstances. Where foreign citizens acting on behalf of their country are involved, their minds ought to be concentrated in advance on the threat of lengthy imprisonment. Few crimes are more carefully calculated, and therefore punishment as deterrence is far more appropriate here than is usually the case.

The problem of unauthorized disclosures is much more controversial, and involves a multitude of practical considerations. Having outlined the constitutional and penological principles that will guide our analysis, we shall defer presenting any conclusions until we have examined the current legislation in depth.

THE OFFICIAL SECRETS ACT 1989

The Government's approach to 'reforming' section 2 of the Official Secrets Act 1911 was very astutely gauged and presented. Although the jury's acquittal in the Ponting trial delivered the death blow, the section had already been tottering under a heavy and increasing barrage of criticism from a vast range of political, legal, and journalistic commentators.[34] Much of this criticism emphasised the excessive breadth of the section. *Any* official information, obtained by a person in contravention of the Act or as a result of his present or former position as a holder of an office under the Crown or as a government contractor, fell within

---

[33] As Durkheim argued in his classic work, this outlook has only emerged relatively recently; for most of human history justice was a private or family matter, and compensation to the victim or his or her family was the norm, even for serious violent crimes. E. Durkheim, *The Division of Labour in Society* ([1893] (New York, 1933).

[34] In addition to the works cited in n. 10 above, see esp. the first major study, D. Williams, *Not in the Public Interest* (London, 1965), *passim*, and the same author's 'Official Secrecy and the Courts', in P. Glazebrook (ed.), *Reshaping the Criminal Law* (London, 1978), 154–73. Judicial exasperation received influential expression in Mr Justice Caulfield's direction to the jury in *R.* v. *Aitken* (1971, unreported), the prosecution of the editor of the *Sunday Telegraph* and a journalist for publishing a confidential assessment of the Nigerian political situation during the Biafran war. (Twenty years later, Mr Aitken became a Minister of State in the Department of Defence.) The jury acquitted, apparently influenced by His Lordship's suggestion that s. 2 be 'pensioned off'. In response, the government set up a Departmental Committee chaired by Lord Franks whose Report, *S. 2 of the Official Secrets Act 1911*, Cmnd. 5104 (1972) described s. 2 as 'a mess' and recommended its replacement by narrower and more specific offences. For one of the few defences of the section in general principle, if not in every detail, see K. Robertson, *Public Secrets* (Basingstoke, 1982).

its reach. Critics had great fun with the potential absurdities, such as the fact that revealing the number of cups of tea consumed in government departments could render one liable to prosecution. From the point of view of human rights and democratic government, there was much to be said for the presence on the statute books of a law whose excessive scope made it virtually unusable. Unsurprisingly the Home Office did not take this view, and leaner, meaner, and considerably more complex provisions were introduced in its stead. This exposed the true issue, which is that the primary objection to legislation of this type is not its potential application in situations where fear of looking silly ensures that it will never be invoked, but rather its repressive effects in circumstances where it may well be.

In addition to targeting the prohibited areas more precisely, the new legislation had to make provision for two other elements in the old section 2. The first, which exempts communication of information if a person is 'authorized' to do so, has simply been carried over. It is of critical importance, yet the 1989 Act does not define official duty and purports to define 'authorization' in a convoluted series of subsections which leave unanswered who precisely has the power to authorize.[35] As Birkinshaw suggests, the result is probably to leave the matter as described by the Franks Committee, which accepted that Ministers and senior civil servants were self-authorizing, and by implication the only valid sources of authorization for subordinates.[36] Hence senior people remain effectively outside the 1989 Act, whose target is really lower-ranking officials whose crises of conscience or constitutional scruples are given short shrift.

The second element proved technically rather more difficult. The 1911 Act also excluded information communicated to 'a person to whom it is *in the interest of the State* his [the defendant's] duty to communicate it'.[37] In the Ponting trial, the Defence's major contention was that the information—communicated to an MP, not to a journalist—revealed that Cabinet Ministers were, to put it no higher, 'misleading' the House of Commons and the public in their account of the sinking of the Argentine ship *General Belgrano* during the Falklands War. Therefore, it argued, it was in the very highest interest of the State, in the sense of our constitutional order, that the deception be revealed. Otherwise, ministerial responsibility to Parliament—the fundamental convention of the British Constitution—would become a sham. The trial judge rejected this view, and equated 'interest of the state' with the policies of the Government then in

---

[35] OSA 1989, s. 7(1)–(6). In the only case in which the issue has been relevant, the Court of Appeal made no attempt to elucidate the concept. In *R.* v. *Galvin* [1987] QB 862, it was content to quash a conviction under the old s. 2 on the grounds that the defendants' claim that the person who gave them sight of a weapons manual had been 'authorized' to do so had not properly been put to the jury.

[36] See n. 14 above, 17—18.

[37] OSA 1911, s. 2(1) (emphasis added). An interesting discussion of the origins of this phrase is found in R. Chapman, *Ethics in Public Service* (Edinburgh, 1992), ch. 8.

office. Apparently the authoritarian implications of this position were too much for the jury to swallow.[38]

This issue cannot arise under the 1989 Act. The 'interests of the state' formula no longer appears. It has been replaced in most instances by the requirement that disclosure be 'damaging', which is then defined in broadly similar ways in various specific contexts.[39] Although we will offer criticisms of the definition as it applies to security, the basic approach is to be welcomed, for at least in principle it is a move in the direction of greater precision and specificity, qualities not often found in legislation or case law in the areas covered by this study. Regrettably the same cannot be said about the most controversial innovation incorporated in the new legislation.

Section 1 of the 1989 reads in relevant part as follows:

(1) A person who is or has been—

(*a*) a member of the security and intelligence services; or

(*b*) a person notified that he is subject to the provisions of this subsection,

is guilty of an offence if without lawful authority he discloses any information, document or other article relating to security or intelligence which is or has been in his possession by virtue of his position as a member of any of those services or in the course of his work while the notification is or was in force.

One preliminary point concerns the notification provision (subsection 1(1)(*b*)). This is designed to ensure that all persons with access to security and intelligence material are covered by the prohibition, whether they are employed by the security services, or in other positions which allow them similar access. Thus officials in particular branches of government departments like the Home Office and Foreign Office, and members of the armed forces, who may work alongside or liaise with MI5, MI6, or GCHQ or receive their intelligence product in some form, will be subject to notification. So too are senior members of the police who occupy a similar position: all Metropolitian Police Special Branch officers of the rank of Inspector or above—more than 100 people—have received notification.[40] Constitutionally it is a little odd that the decision of a Minister[41] may determine whether a given person will fall within the scope of a penal statute, but this provision is not in any real sense oppressive. It provides fair notice, and actually allows a more precise, individualized delineation of those affected than

---

[38] For the best discussion of the deeper issues involved, see N. MacCormick, 'The Interests of the State and the Rule of Law', in P. Wallington and R. Merkin (eds.), *Essays in Memory of Professor F. H. Lawson* (London, 1986), 169–87. See also R. Thomas, 'The British Official Secrets Acts 1911–39 and the Ponting Case' [1986] *Crim. LR* 491, 496–500.

[39] Below, pp. 237–40. See also ss. 2(2), 3(2), concerning respectively defence and international relations.

[40] Interview with Deputy Assistant Commissioner John Howley, 22 Sept. 1992.

[41] The notification must be served in writing by a Minister (s.1(6)), but almost certainly the administrative reality will be that the latter merely rubber stamps a list drawn up by the most senior officials of the particular department.

would be possible in a statute, which would inevitably be drafted in terms of rather cumbersome generalized categories.[42] There of course remains the possibility—there has been no known complaint from anyone—that notification will be made not because of a genuine connection with the security or intelligence services, but because a person may be in a position to reveal matters politically embarrasssing to the government. In theory the notification could be challenged by judicial review, but as opponents of the Bill pointed out, in the absence of a requirement that the Minister justify his decisions with detailed reasons, this route would be effectively foreclosed.[43] However, the real problem is not deliberate misuse of the power, nor the number of people covered, but what they are prohibited from doing.

The striking characteristic of section 1 is its absolutism. As has been seen, all other sections of the Act require proof of 'damage'. Section 1 is unconcerned with effect. It lays down a total prohibition on dissemination of any information, for whatever reason or however trivial, by any person within its scope. The *only* defence is perhaps best described as the idiot's gambit. If D did not know and had no reasonable cause to believe that the material at issue related to security or intelligence, he or she cannot be convicted.[44] Since only persons with long and intimate knowledge of this field can be prosecuted, it is a moot point whether anyone successfully pleading this defence would be mentally competent to stand trial. More seriously, it is hard to see how someone in this position could possibly put forward the defence with any credibility.

Section 1 is best understood as an offence of strict liability, requiring no *mens rea*—intention, recklessness, or negligence—for its commission. Given that the maximum punishment is two years imprisonment, this is quite remarkable. Strict liability usually, though by no means always, is confined to regulatory offences which are 'not criminal in any real sense', for which punishment is generally no more severe than a fine.[45] Although in some recent instances the House of Lords has supported a strict liability interpretation of certain criminal statutes,[46] it surely requires extraordinary justification to imprison someone without allowing the jury to consider the moral quality of their actions, or the social harm— or possibly benefit—they have created. What must be examined is whether that justification is present here.

The Government's position, set out in the White Paper preceding the Bill[47]

---

[42] Although the notification lasts for five years and may be renewed indefinitely, it may also be revoked at any time, and the statute instructs the Minister to do so when he or she determines that the person concerned is no longer doing work justifying the designation: OSA 1989, s. 1(7) and (8).

[43] See Griffiths (n. 1 above), 281–2, summarizing the extended debate on this point on 25 Jan. 1989: *HC Debs.*, vol. 145, cols. 1113–39.

[44] OSA 1989, s. 1(5).

[45] For a good recent discussion, see A. Ashworth, *Principles of Criminal Law* (Oxford, 1991), 135–45.

[46] Notably in *Pharmaceutical Society of Great Britain* v. *Storkwain Ltd.* (1986) 83 Cr. App. R. 359 and, in a Privy Council appeal, *Gammon* v. *A-G for Hong Kong* [1985] AC1.

[47] See n. 14 above, esp. paras. 38–43.

and repeated by the Home Secretary in the House of Commons,[48] was that everyone connected with the security services should be subject to a lifelong duty of confidentiality in respect of all information or documents to which they had access in the course of their work. Such a duty was held to exist, or more accurately was created, by the House of Lords in the last round of the *Spycatcher* litigation, but only as a matter of civil law, enforceable by injunction proceedings against those who sought to make public disclosure.[49] Even here there remains an important unresolved question. Scott J declared forcefully that where 'the public interest required disclosure', the duty of confidence would no longer be binding, even on an 'insider' and even where the matter related to national security. He also held that in such instances the Press were appropriate recipients of the information.[50] The House of Lords judgments are both less robust and less clear, and not all address the point of principle. Some of them, however, do leave room for the possibility that public interest may override the duty in some circumstances.[51] With such ambiguity surrounding even civil law, it seems quite wrong that the absolutist position should be imposed where the graver sanctions of criminal law may be imposed.

The most concise defence of the government's position appeared in the White Paper. *All* disclosures by members or former members of the security and intelligence services, it argued,

are harmful and ought to be criminal. They are harmful because they carry a credibility which the disclosure of the same information by any other person does not, and because they reduce public confidence in the services' ability and willingness to carry out their essentially secret duties effectively and loyally. They ought to be criminal because those who become members of the services know that membership carries with it a special and inescapable duty of secrecy about their work. Unauthorised disclosures betray that duty and the trust placed in the members concerned, both by the State and by people who give information to the services.[52]

The reasoning in this paragraph is thin, and heavily reliant on sheer assertion. The idea of 'a special and inescapable duty of secrecy' means no more than: 'We think it right to impose absolute silence, and calculate that backing up that rule with serious criminal penalties is required to deter people in this position from speaking out.' Yet the Civil Service Management Code already contains extensive provisions concerning confidentiality and other duties and responsibilities to Ministers. These are enforced by the normal range of employer sanctions, ranging from warning or reprimand through to dismissal.[53] Since the lesser penalties

---

[48] On the parliamentary history of the Act, see esp. Griffith (n. 1 above), 280–7.

[49] *A-G* v. *Guardian Newspapers Ltd.* (*No. 2*) [1988] 3 All ER 545, 642, 646 (Lord Keith), and at 658 (Lord Griffith) (hereafter *Spycatcher II*). This position was reaffirmed in *Lord Advocate* v. *The Scotsman Publications Ltd.* [1989] 3 WLR 358.

[50] [1988] 3 All ER 545, 585–90.

[51] Lord Griffiths [1988] 3 All ER at 650, and Lord Goff at 660–1.

[52] See n. 14 above, para. 41.

[53] This Code has replaced the former Pay and Conditions of Service Code. S. 4 contains the rules

would also blight promotion prospects, and dismissal under such circumstances would worsen the normal difficulties of finding employment elsewhere, these sanctions already stand as a severe disincentive to disclosure in violation of civil servants' duties. There is little ground to doubt their deterrent effect: the long-retired Peter Wright, obsessed with 'moles', is hardly a typical case. Nor are criminal sanctions needed to deprive the defendant of the fruits of wrongdoing. The House of Lords took great care to announce that Mr Wright and anyone else in his position did not have an enforceable copyright in his book and could not enforce any contract for royalties or other profits earned as a result of their disclosures.[54]

Thus the case for criminalization on either societal or individual grounds seems quite doubtful. Scepticism is further strengthened when one finally comes to the paramount issue: the harm done by such disclosures, a harm allegedly so grave that evaluation of it cannot be left to juries but must in effect be conclusively presumed by incorporation in the Act itself. The first reason offered—enhanced credibility due to the position the officer has held—is by no means convincing in all circumstances and in others undercuts the conclusion. The fact that Peter Wright, a former MI5 official, could draw upon the personal experience of failing to convince his superiors of his conviction that Sir Roger Hollis was a Soviet 'mole' hardly makes his case any more compelling than when it was presented by a journalist, Chapman Pincher, with whom Wright collaborated anonymously.[55] And one circumstance in which the enhanced credibility argument is persuasive is unfortunately precisely where the law can have no effect. A defector who (no doubt selectively) reveals information about individuals and operations does indeed carry great credibility, but is also out of reach.[56]

The most telling circumstance, however, is precisely when the authority of the insider is most valuable to democracy. This is when he or she draws upon personal knowledge to reveal wrongdoing, which it is in the self-interest of the government to conceal. For this reason alone it is essential to preserve the possibility of access to the public, whilst accepting the resulting risk that an individual may behave irresponsibly. A combination of upright official behaviour and careful personnel selection should keep that risk to a minimum.

The only remaining argument for strict liability is the purported reduction of public confidence, which is said to apply both to 'effectiveness' and to

---

of conduct and discipline. There are no provisions specifying particular penalties for particular violations of the Code; this is left to the department or agency in each case, with appeal provided to the Civil Service Appeal Board.

[54] *Spycatcher II* [1988] 3 All ER at 668, per Lord Jauncey, whose view was shared unanimously. Admittedly the White Paper and the Bill preceded the delivery of the Lords' judgment, but the Government had ample time for amendment.

[55] C. Pincher, *Their Trade is Treachery* (London, 1981). It was the Government's failure to try to injunct this book or to prosecute Pincher that was to figure so prominently in the Sydney trial involving *Spycatcher*; see n. 66 below.

[56] e.g. K. Philby, *My Silent War* (London, 1968), written in Moscow.

'loyalty'.[57] Though this is the sort of statement which trips lightly off the official tongue, it is actually rather odd. Unless 'public confidence' is a euphemism for the opinion of ministers of the government in office, it must refer to a question of fact: the actual state of public opinion on the matter. Since the Government did not undertake a survey of a representative sample of citzens to determine their views, it simply tried to hide the ball by treating the matter as self-evident.

In the absence of such evidence, agnosticism is the only safe position, but there are strong reasons even for empirical doubt. Let it be assumed that most people in fact believe that secrecy must surround everything security and intelligence officers do in furtherance of national security, as defined by statute.[58] It hardly follows that they would also believe that secrecy is equally necessary where the information relates to illegal conduct by officials, or to ministerial or other political pressure upon them to act unlawfully. It seems clear from the change in public attitudes towards the police that has followed the avalanche of acknowledged miscarriages of justice since the release of the Guildford Four, that where there is silence, evasion, and suppression of information, there will be widespread suspicion among the public of cover-up and continued abuse.

Ultimately, however, the issue is one of principle, not fact: does the absolute ban advance or retard the working of democracy? It may be accepted that preventing an action which genuinely imperils national security, with no or a lesser anti-democratic effect, would satisfy this test. But the only way to determine that is in particular circumstances, which requires judging the impact of the disclosure on both national security and considerations such as exposure of illegality, human rights violations, or attempts to evade rules of accountability. The matter is ultimately one of proportion.[59] But that is exactly what section 1(1) negates, by in effect deeming all disclosures so damaging to national security that no countervailing considerations could ever prevail, and hence deserving of punishment. This position simply lacks credibility.

Section 1 was viewed by some of its opponents as an act of spite, one which,

[57] Curiously, the claim is not that the *true* effectiveness and loyalty of intelligence officials would be lessened, only that confidence in these qualities would diminish—an argument more modest, but also considerably more feeble.

[58] In the very broad mandate of the Security Service. See SSA 1989, s. 1., discussed extensively in Ch. 14 below. (We would not agree that this degree of secrecy is necessary, but accept the assumption for present purposes, as it strengthens the position we are contending against.)

[59] Consider a somewhat exaggerated example. Officer X of MI6 is convinced that his superior has made false claims and pocketed expenses purportedly used to run agents presently in Iraq. X's complaints with his service are disbelieved. Convinced there has been a cover-up, he reveals his information to a journalist, including the names of the agents involved. Even assuming X is correct about the fraud, on no defensible scale of values could his disclosure be justified. Human life is more important than money, and the agents involved would in these circumstances have clearly put their lives at risk and trusted the organization to conceal their identities. Nor have they committed any killings that might support the sort of argument offered by Philip Agee when he revealed the names of CIA agents operating actively in several countries, that disclosure might save innocent lives. Thus it is certainly possible that a given disclosure would be unjustified, but this conclusion can only be reached by careful consideration of the facts and the values at stake, not by *a priori* assertion.

in the words of former Home Secretary Lord Jenkins of Hillhead, owed 'too much to obsessive resentment at the outcome of the *Spycatcher* and *Ponting* cases'.[60] However its longer term effect, and possibly even its main purpose, look to the future. Its design is *in terrorem*, its riposte to *Spycatcher*: 'Never again!'[61] This has had some unwelcome side-effects. Mr Julian Amery, Conservative MP and son of a long-serving Minister and distinguished memoirist,[62] had initially been assured by the Home Secretary that the new law would have no effect on previous practice whereby former security and intelligence officers were able to publish their memoirs subject to clearance. That turned out to have been misleading: one month later the Minister stated that such authorizations would be 'rare' and would require 'exceptional circumstances'.[63] Mr Amery, in a letter to the *Daily Telegraph*, protested that '[t]he abandonment of the old convention in favour of the new "Trappist" vow was thus not a response to Mr Wright [whose counsel had assured Mr Amery that he had offered to submit the manuscript to the authorities] but a change of policy'.[64]

This 'change of policy' seems to have been an attempt to seal the hole through which the civil action against Wright sunk in the Australian courts. Essentially the government's case was destroyed by evidence that it had permitted publication of material based on disclosures of MI5 officers similar to that appearing in Wright's book, but written by authors more favourable to the official position on the issues involved.[65] To a lesser extent the same factor influenced Scott J's judgment on the merits in the English injunction proceedings.[66]

If section 1(1) operates effectively to deter would-be disclosers, no one will be able to run such a defence in future. Perhaps even more important, it seems designed to ensure that the only information that will reach the public domain is that which fits the official version. This is a problem of historical truth and distortion as well as of contemporary debate. Section 1(1) is unlimited in time, and covers matters concerning Second World War espionage and code-breaking every bit as much as yesterday's IRA surveillance operation. Since the only

---

[60] Quoted in Ewing and Gearty (n. 10 above), at 207.

[61] It cannot of course reach someone like Peter Wright who chooses to leave the jurisdiction, but emigration of people in this position is likely to be exceptional.

[62] L. S. Amery, *My Political Life*, 3 vols. (London, 1951–5).

[63] *HC Debs.*, vol. 145, col. 1104.

[64] *Daily Telegraph*, 28 Feb. 1989. The only solace offered would-be memoirists was the announcement that they could contact the Staff Counsellor (below, p. 430) who would not provide independent review, but might arrange a meeting with the relevant Minister. Ewing and Gearty (above n. 10), 172–3.

[65] See the judgment of Powell J in *A-G (UK)* v. *Heinemann Publishers Australia Pty. Ltd.* (1987) NSWLR 341. The crucial role of this aspect of Wright's defence is emphasized in the entertaining, if inevitably one-sided, account of the trial by his counsel: M. Turnbull, *The Spycatcher Trial* (Richmond, Vic., 1988). (This book contains extensive verbatim quotations from witness testimony at the trial, and is an extremely useful primary source.) A similar view emerges from the account of an Australian journalist who covered the trial: R. Hall, *A Spy's Revenge* (Harmondsworth, 1987), pt. 2.

[66] *Spycatcher II* [1988] 3 All ER at 559–64, in which Scott J reviews evidence of all other books whose publication by former agents had been approved by the government, thus undermining its claims as to confidentiality of the case before him.

lawful disclosures are those which are 'authorized' or in accordance with 'official duty', politicians and civil servants can give permission selectively to those whose views they approve. Given that matters such as the fall of Singapore, British foreknowledge of the Japanese attack on Pearl Harbor, and military and political aspects of the Anglo-Soviet alliance against Germany remain matters of heated dispute with contemporary political implications even now, fear of censorship relating to events long past is by no means fantasy.

However there are difficulties in trying to restrict publications by former officials in this way. The new section has not been written on a clean slate. In the Wright case, the defence entered no less than twenty-six books in evidence relating to espionage, many of them written by British insiders.[67] They included classic studies of scientific intelligence like R. V. Jones's *Most Secret War*, accounts of code-breaking at Bletchley Park and the famous Enigma machine, and Sir John Masterman's account of the Twenty Committee, *The Doublecross System*.[68] Thus to call a halt to future publications now will in many instances not preserve secrecy, but merely freeze public knowledge in the state it happened to reach when the Act and concurrent policy change took effect. Moreover, since few of Britain's secret activities overseas have been undertaken alone, it is entirely possible that Americans in particular will freely produce accounts containing large amounts of information about named individuals and institutions in this country. At first this will merely leave British readers more poorly informed about their own government's actions than Americans, but that state of affairs would quickly be remedied by publication of the work in this country, with the American author (and British publisher) wholly free of criminal, and probably civil, liability. The result may well be to leave us with a skewed, and certainly incomplete, version of events, since the British participants would be prevented from offering their account or even correcting serious inaccuracies.

Much more than historical knowledge is at stake. Many of the most discreditable and immoral activities (which also are often illegal) carried out by agents of the state are carefully concealed and known only to insiders. The result is that a false picture of rectitude and legitimacy surrounds government policy. The best contemporary example is, of course, Northern Ireland. Books like John Stalker's account of his attempt to counter unlawful killing and perversion of justice by members of the Royal Ulster Constabulary[69] have been essential in educating the British public about the true nature of the war in Northern

---

[67] Hall (n. 65 above), 125.

[68] The latter, which described how British intelligence had surreptitiously controlled all the German spies infiltrated into the country during the Second World War was only published in Britain after Masterman, nearing the end of his life and by his own description ruthlessly determined, had made arrangements for publication to occur first in the USA—an uncanny prefiguring of the *Spycatcher* episode. For a useful description of insider publications and their difficulties with the authorities, see N. West, *Molehunt* (London, 1987), 126–33. Masterman's own account in *On the Chariot Wheel* (Oxford, 1975), 348–61 is well worth reading.

[69] J. Stalker, *Stalker* (London, 1988).

Ireland and the institutions enjoying the support of British troops and money. Less popular books, like Fred Holroyd's *War Without Honour*,[70] written by a former army officer who claims to expose horrific and illegal activities undertaken especially by the intelligence services and police there, also contribute to public awareness and debate. Had the 1989 Act been in force, both men would almost certainly have been subject to notification. Suppression of their accounts would have been particularly unfair, since a central element in the case each presents is that public officers have attempted to discredit them by lies, smears, and, in Holroyd's case, abuse of the power of psychiatry to commit him forcibly to hospital.[71] Whatever the truth in either instance—which we are no better placed to decide than any of our readers[72]—both are matters of great public concern which citizens should be allowed to judge for themselves.

Section 1(1), as we have emphasized, applies only to present or former security and intelligence officials. What is the position of those who receive information from such persons, and make it public as journalists or authors? In civil law, the *Spycatcher* litigation distinguished between the two cases, imposing a lifelong and effectively absolute obligation of confidence on the officials, but restraining publication by third parties only if required by the public interest.[73] The Official Secrets Act takes an analogous approach, in that third parties, Crown servants, and government contractors who make disclosures relating to security or intelligence are only punishable if the disclosure is 'damaging'.[74] This is defined as causing

(*a*) damage to the work of, or of any part of, the security and intelligence services; or

(*b*) it is information or a document or other article which is such that its unauthorised disclosure would be likely to cause such damage or which *falls within a class or description* of information, documents or articles the authorised disclosure of which would be likely to have that effect.[75] [emphasis added]

This differentiation produces the obvious anomaly that Officer X who reveals information to Journalist Y will be subject to different standards of liability for the same publication—a problem that would be greatly exacerbated if, as concern for efficient court management might well dictate, they were in the dock together.

Although damage is defined by statute, it remains a question of fact for the

---

[70] F. Holroyd and N. Burbridge, *War Without Honour* (Hull, 1989).

[71] The same point applies to Colin Wallace (see P. Foot, *Who Framed Colin Wallace?* (London, 1989)) who alleges that he was wrongfully imprisoned at the behest of the authorities. That his 'disclosures' appeared in a book authored by another person would have made no difference to liability under s. 1.

[72] For an attempt at evaluation, which credits some of the claims made in these books but rejects others, see M. Urban, *Big Boys' Rules: The Secret Struggle Against the IRA* (London, 1992), *passim*.

[73] *Spycatcher II* [1988] 3 All ER 545, 654 (Lord Griffiths) and 659–60 (Lord Goff). It is worth emphasizing the fact that because there are no jury trials in actions for breach of confidence, the decision as to public interest will be taken by judges alone.

[74] OSA 1989, ss. 1(3) and 5(3).   [75] Ibid., s. 1(4).

jury.[76] However the rather indigestible subsection (*b*) quoted above is a manifest effort to make proof of damage easy for the prosecution. Proof of damage as required under subsection (*a*) would often involve revealing and discussing information the government regards as equally secret. There would seem to be an obvious response. Since 1920 the courts have enjoyed statutory power to order exclusion of the public from hearings on 'grounds of national safety'. This power explicitly applies to prosecutions under the 1989 Act.[77] Formerly a matter of unreviewable judicial discretion, it is now, as a result of the threat of an adverse decision in the European Court of Human Rights, subject to review by the Court of Appeal at the behest of any aggrieved person, which would include a journalist.[78] None the less it ought to be exercised very sparingly indeed, for the decision must have some prejudicial impact on the defendant by supporting the notion that his or her actions had particularly grave consequences.[79] Yet if the trial judge takes the requirement of national safety with proper seriousness, the result may be fairer than feather-lightening the burden of proof, as the italicized phrase 'falls within a class or description of information' was designed to do.

However, there is an inescapable dilemma involved. Elimination of subsection (*b*) would inevitably lead to more requests for *in camera* proceedings, at least for part of the trial. Granting them would not only offend the principle of public justice, it would also increase the necessity for jury vetting, a practice with drawbacks of its own.[80] On the other hand, failure to grant the Prosecution's motion would create what in the United States is called 'graymail', which has led to dropping of charges against defendants like Colonel Oliver North who have been able to escape punishment precisely because of the seriousness of their actions: Catch-22.[81]

This latter point was clearly in the government's mind; the subsection was included to 'allow the arguments before the court to be less specific'.[82] One critic has argued that the result amounts to a sort of conviction by ministerial fiat, accomplishing by sleight of hand what the much-trumpeted rejection of ministerial certificates was proudly proclaimed to have prevented.[83] This is perhaps unduly alarmist. What may be expected is that the jury will be told in

---

[76] Jurors' hands have been tied rather tightly by the Act. If they find damage, they are neither required nor allowed to weigh up the degree or impact of that damage against any public good the disclosure may have done. This was an explicit choice by the government, which rejected proposed defences of exposure of iniquity or a more generalized 'public interest'. On the relation between damage and prior publication, see below, p. 239.

[77] OSA 1989, s. 11(4), incorporating OSA 1920, s. 8(4).

[78] Criminal Justice Act 1988, s. 159, introduced as a part of 'friendly settlement' between the UK government and several Strasburg litigants. See R. Thomas, *Espionage and Secrecy* (London, 1991), 67–8.

[79] pp. 306–8 below.   [80] pp. 295–301 below.   [81] p. 292.

[82] White Paper (n. 14 above), paras. 39–40. Unless the government was worried about jurors leaking, the real point was to prevent supporting arguments about damage becoming public knowledge.

[83] Birkinshaw (n. 15 above), 9–11.

rather general terms, but in person by some senior official rather than by a piece of paper bearing a ministerial signature, that the disclosure is of a type of material which is 'likely'[84] to damage the work of the services. Two things may then happen.

One is that the defence will be able to cross-examine the witness and, perhaps much more important, introduce rebuttal evidence. If, for example, a newspaper has published information about signals intercept technology and the prosecution claims that all such information must be kept secret to protect security, the defence may produce copies of technical journals or foreign periodicals in which identical or even merely similar information has appeared. The jury will then be left to determine (*a*) whether that earlier publication had caused the alleged damage, and further (*b*) even if it had not, whether the fact that the information was already available negatived damage in the present case. Thus a defence of prior publication will be available by the backdoor, despite the government's rejection of amendments designed to incorporate it.[85] Of course it was to block off precisely such arguments in the case of intelligence officers that the strict liability offence was created.

The position is thus quite different from the treatment of 'the interest of the state' under the old section 2 and the still-extant espionage statute, section 1 of the 1911 Act. In the most politically-charged prosecution in the history of the latter provision, the House of Lords upheld the trial judge's refusal to permit counsel either to cross-examine the Air Commodore produced by the prosecution, or to call evidence to show that the defendants' purpose was not in fact prejudicial to the safety or interests of the state. Such matters, it was held unanimously, were purely for determination by the government.[86] Under the 1989 Act's damage test, the contest is less unequal.

The second safeguard is that the jury will still be able to use its common sense. When the government first sought an interdict (injunction) against the *Scotsman* after it published extracts of a book written by a former MI6 official, it presented the judge at first instance with a catalogue of 'classes' of material allegedly damaging to the work of security bodies. Included were anything which might reveal intelligence gathering techniques; lower morale within the organization; or lead to

---

[84] This phrase spares the prosecution the trouble of demonstrating that damage has actually occurred. It is a recurrent feature of the Act, applying to several matters other than security, e.g. ss. 2(2)(*c*) (defence) and 3(2)(*b*) (international relations). Its main purpose seems to be an attempt to load the dice against defendants by inviting the jury to consider all sort of hypothetical horrors. Yet where the dreaded disclosure has in fact occurred, if nothing earth-shaking is shown to have happened the jury may well react with scepticism.

[85] The White Paper (n. 14, above), para. 63, had suggested that the 'damage' test would operate in this way. Even if this interpretation is correct, it is unclear whether the statute will meet the standards of Art. 10 ECHR. The jurisprudence of the Court seems clearly to require a prior publication defence. Both in the *Spycatcher* case itself (*Sunday Times* v. *UK* (*No. 2*) (1991) 14 EHRR 229), and in a criminal contempt case (*Weber* v. *Switzerland* (1990) 12 EHRR 508), it held that prior publication destroys the state's case for proscription on freedom of expression under Art. 10(2).

[86] *Chandler* v. *Director of Public Prosecutions* [1964] AC 763.

foreign agencies seeing their UK counterparts as 'leaky'.[87] A jury would be able to decide that the claim that all such material could cause damage is too hypothetical, attenuated, or downright incredible. A great deal—too much, some may argue—has been laid on the shoulders of the jury. Issues of jury vetting and related attempts by the government to increase the chances of conviction in controversial cases are therefore of overwhelming importance. We have encountered one such on p. 238; others are considered in Chapter 11.

One odd technical point should be noted. Journalists and others who publish information they have received from those with special access are liable where their source is a Crown servant or government contractor, but not where *former* officials—retired, resigned, or dismissed—are involved.[88] This would seem to undermine at least a good part of what the Act purported to achieve: a journalist whose identifiable sources are not serving officials could not be prosecuted, however 'damaging' his or her disclosure. One obvious corollary is that journalists now have an even greater interest than formerly in concealing the identity of their sources. In these circumstances, notes of their conversations would be the most probative evidence, indeed possibly the only evidence, capable of convicting them (and the source). And since, very unusually, journalistic material may be sought under search warrant in official secrets cases,[89] the obvious consequence is to encourage destruction of records and notes after the article or book is written and before a warrant application can be made. This form of self-defence—not a major contribution to accuracy or integrity—is already part of journalistic life, and will be discussed in Chapter 10.

Commentators have described this lax treatment of material from former officials as a 'drafting cock-up'.[90] It is certainly strange, in view of the fact that the omission was pointed out during the debate on the Bill in Parliament. The great irony of course is that anyone publishing information derived from Peter Wright, who retired twenty years ago, would enjoy the exemption. However, there remains the possibility that the judges 'will supply the omission of the legislature', regrettably in a spirit quite different from that expressed by the originator of that phrase.[91] The long history of judicial interpretation of the Official Secrets Acts is indelibly marked by a tendency to define the offences as widely as possibly, without much concern for the ordinary meaning of language. Almost without exception, where there have been two possible readings of the Act, they have favoured the one which extends liability.[92] Not all those cases

---

[87] *Lord Advocate* v. *Scotsman Publications Ltd.* (1988) SLT 490, 496 (Outer House). On this case, ultimately decided on other grounds in the House of Lords, [1989] 3 WLR 358, see N. Walker, 'Spycatcher's Scottish Sequel' [1990] *PL* 354.

[88] OSA 1989, s. 5(1)(*a*)(1).

[89] OSA s. 11(3), overriding the PACE exemptions, discussed on p. 254.

[90] Ewing and Gearty (n. 10 above), 201.

[91] Byles J in *Cooper* v. *Wandsworth Board of Works* (1863) 14 CB (NS) 180, in a judgment requiring observance of a fundamental principle of natural justice.

[92] Thus in the critical case of *R.* v. *Crisp and Homewood* (1919) 83 JP121, it was held that s. 2 extended to information in the public domain. In *Adler* v. *George* [1964] 2 QB 7, the court stretched

produced substantive injustice, but they do point to a worrying possibility: that the judges will simply interpret 'Crown servant' to include 'former Crown servant'.[93] There is unfortunately no safeguard against judicial legislation.[94]

Readers will have noted that most of our analysis is couched in the conditional tense. The reason is simple: as we write there have been no prosecutions under the 1989 Act, let alone any relating to security, so most statements can only be predictive. It is of course possible that the quiescence indicates that the Act has been wholly effective as a deterrent. We doubt this. Precisely because of its sweeping nature and application to matters of great sensitivity and political controversy,[95] the Act could be applied to so many disclosures that there are two connected dangers: over-use, or a public perception, reflected in jury acquittals, of oppressive use. As with nuclear armaments, the sheer magnitude of a legal weapon can produce a sort of paralysis because so few transgressions are seen to be of the same magnitude. In this sense the 1989 Act may share the same fate of effective immobilization as the discredited law it replaced.

Excessive ambition in criminal legislation inevitably results in selective prosecution, which rightly or wrongly can be readily depicted as animated by political bias. Such suspicions are supposed to be allayed by the requirement that the Attorney-General must approve any prosecution.[96] However, after the fiasco of the *Spycatcher* litigation, in which the British government first falsely claimed that the Attorney, Sir Michael Havers—had approved publication of an earlier book and was then, when he made his outrage at the deception known, forced to admit that he had not been consulted at all—it will be difficult to persuade the public that the decision has been fair. The burden will be all the greater since a subsequent Attorney chose not to prosecute, on grounds of 'public interest', Northern Ireland policemen who had obstructed the Stalker Inquiry.[97] The decision to select any particular defendant for prosecution will be greeted with considerable cynicism, and counsel will surely remind the jury of those who have been allowed to get off scot- (or rather ulster-) free.

Moreover, the government which sponsored and guillotined the Bill through the House of Commons has also, by its inaction in a particular instance, opened

the wording of s. 3 of the OSA 1920, which proscribed activity occurring 'in the vicinity of a prohibited place', to include conduct 'in' as well as 'in the vicinity'. And where statute sought to punish 'acts preparatory', the court was prepared to replace the plain word 'and' with 'or' to catch the defendant: *R. v. Oakes* [1959] 2 QB 350. And see also *Stevenson v. Fulton* [1936] 1 KB 320, in the same vein.

[93] This was precisely how the term, used in s. 9(4) of the Evidence (Proceedings in Other Jurisdictions) Act 1975, was construed, so as to prevent a former government forensic scientist from giving evidence in US proceedings arising out of the Lockerbie bombing: *In Re Pan American World Airlines Application* [1992] 1 QB 854.

[94] See esp. A. Smith, 'Judicial Lawmaking in the Criminal Law,' (1984) 100 *LQR* 46.

[95] The Act also covers matters of defence (s. 2), international relations (s. 3), and law enforcement (s. 4), which we do not discuss. For two other security-related provisions, see below, pp. 243–45.

[96] OSA 1989, s. 9(1).   [97] Sir Patrick Mayhew, *HC Debs.* vol. 126, col. 21 (25 Jan. 1988).

all future decisions to prosecute to allegations of partiality or manipulation. George Blake, an MI6 officer, was one of the most notorious, and effective, Russian spies operating against Britain during the Cold War. Sentenced to forty-two years imprisonment, he escaped with the help of fellow prisoners[98] and found his way to Moscow, where he took Soviet nationality and continues to live. In 1990 his memoirs, *No Other Choice*, containing a great deal of information derived from his position in MI6, were published in Britain. He had received an advance of £50,000, though the government moved quickly and successfully to freeze the remainder of the monies owed him under the publication agreement, which he has never received.[99] Because of the position he held, Blake falls squarely within section 1(1), and whilst his absence from the jurisdiction makes prosecution impossible, the same cannot be said of his London publisher, Jonathan Cape. On fairly straightforward principles of criminal law, someone who pays another a large sum of money as a reward for committing a criminal act is guilty of the same crime as a party complicit, and is also a co-conspirator in the commission of the offence. However. no steps were taken to prosecute Cape or any of its directors, no doubt because the presence of eminent publishers in the dock at the Old Bailey would have created a scandal of international proportions. Yet if the Act is not invoked in circumstances involving reward for a man for whom few jurors would be expected to feel any sympathy, when will it be? And when it is, one may expect counsel to underline the contrast between their client and Blake at every opportunity, notwithstanding the absence of any defence in law.

Two other provisions of the 1989 Act deserve at least brief mention. The White Paper identified what is called a 'gap in the law': there was no criminal provision governing publication of 'sensitive' information shared in confidence with other states or an international organization.[100] The result is section 6, which covers any 'damaging disclosure' of such information relating to security or intelligence, if it has been leaked to the discloser without authorization from the recipient state or organization.[101]

---

[98] Michael Randle and Pat Pottle, whose book, *The Blake Escape* (London, 1989) led to a prosecution a quarter-century after the event. They defended themselves and were acquitted in July 1991. See p. 305 below.

[99] The government's action is based on its asserted ownership of copyright in the book, and claims for an account of profits from its publication, and for damages for breach of fiduciary duty. An attempt to unfreeze part of the money to enable Blake to meet the costs of defending the action failed on unrelated jurisdictional grounds before a Deputy Judge in Chancery: *A-G* v. *Blake*, 18 Feb. 1993 (unreported). We should like to thank Mr Blake's solicitor, Mr B. Birnberg, for providing a transcript of this decision and explaining the background.

[100] (Above n. 14), para. 26.

[101] S. 6 also includes defence and international relations, and therefore is broad enough to cover a confidential report submitted to an agency of the UN on the oil price and production policies likely to be adopted by the OPEC states. However, as the White Paper stated, the animating concern behind it is information relating to terrorism which might be shared either with police forces in other states or with international bodies like Interpol or the Trevi Group.

The application of this section spills over the borderline of the ridiculous. It means that confidential information supplied by the British government to the Germans or the Americans, leaked and published in the Press in those countries, cannot be published by the British press without risk of prosecution. These are precisely the circumstances—when confidence has been broken, however wrongly, by the initial recipient—in which the House of Lords unanimously rejected the government's argument that an obligation of confidence could be imposed on third parties as a matter of civil law.[102] To turn it into a criminal offence is therefore particularly objectionable. Since the initial leak would have almost certainly been the act of a foreign national on foreign soil, section 6 seems a particularly cack-handed attempt at admonishing other states which refuse to share the British government's attitude to secrecy: neither the United States nor Germany has enacted Official Secrets legislation, so no prosecution of the person actually responsible for the leak could take place.[103] Moreover, it would seem that a prosecution under section 6 would be mounted only under very unusual circumstances. It seems rather unlikely that a foreign official would leak information specifically to a British journalist rather than to a compatriot. And whilst the fact of previous appearance in a foreign newspaper is not a defence, the allegation that 'damage' had resulted would be seriously undermined.[104] And if the information were of any international significance, even if section 6 deterred the British media from revealing it, the European press and (more importantly because of language) American magazines, newspapers, and satellite television would quickly make it available to any interested person here. This provision seems thoroughly misconceived.

Finally, there are two more strict liability offences relating to security matters, or more precisely to methods of intelligence gathering. Revelation of 'any information relating to the obtaining of information' pursuant to either a telephone tap or mail opening warrant, or a property interference warrant is unlawful.[105] It is noteworthy that this does not extend to revelation of taps, bugging, and so on *not* authorized by warrant, so this provision will not deter and cannot be used to punish exposure of unlawful conduct. Its main purpose is to ensure that all information about these intrusive investigative techniques remains secret. It is not limited to the police or security officials involved, but would extend also to engineers or other technicians. More sinisterly, it could be used against journalists or researchers who reveal information about the organization or techniques of these surveillance activities, for its literal language is not limited to information about a specific tapping or property interference operation under a particular warrant.

---

[102] The main issue in the *Spycatcher* case (n. 49 above).

[103] An even more extraordinary example of the same attitude is s. 15(1) which, in the case of any British citizen or Crown servant, extends the territorial reach of the main offences to the entire world. Thus disclosure by any such person—e.g. a British journalist writing in an American newspaper (or in Australia or Botswana come to that)—is now a criminal offence in Britain. This section would have caught Peter Wright even if his book had been permanently suppressed in Britain.

[104] See above, pp. 237–38.   [105] OSA 1989, s. 4(3)(*a*) and (*b*).

However, it is doubtful whether this was an intended application, or is a likely one.[106]

This provision may be called the 'Massiter clause', after the MI5 officer who revealed that senior officers of CND and other organizations opposed to Conservative Government policies had been stigmatized as 'subversive' and had had their telephones tapped.[107] Her disclosures had an enormously beneficial effect on public awareness of the need to curb abuses of power by security and intelligence organizations; moreover, her action has been acknowledged by an MI5 spokesman to have been a useful learning experience.[108] The justification for putting any future 'whistleblower' in peril of a prison sentence is that the subsequent reforms in the oversight of the security services and establishment of a complaints procedure make public disclosure unnecessary, so there is no benefit to counterbalance the damage such revelations are purported to cause. This 'trade-off' argument is valid only if these mechanisms can reasonably be expected to protect human rights and democratic processes: if one regards them as inadequate or faulty, the justification for silencing those best placed to inform the public of abuses and hence trigger effective remedy disappears. Since the burden of the lengthy critique of the accountability mechanisms presented below[109] is that they fall well short of what is necessary, all we need say at this point is that under present circumstances it is wrong to deprive the public of the benefit of disclosures of abuses.

The other absolute offence forbids disclosure of any information obtained under operations authorized by warrant.[110] This is a privacy protection measure, not something designed to protect governmental secrecy. As such it serves an important purpose, for information gathered by extraordinarily intrusive methods which enjoy legal justification only for rather narrowly defined reasons, often concerns matters of the most intensely private character. It may also be deeply discreditable to the person concerned, and hence a powerful weapon for political blackmail in the hands of those with access to it. This is why the handling of what we have called 'ancillary' material obtained under warrant is such a vital issue.[111] There needs to be an absolute ban on release of such material to anyone except those specifically authorized to make use of it, and solely for the precise purpose for which the intrusion was approved. Improper release of such information can cause grave damage of two distinct kinds: to the person

---

[106] The White Paper (above n. 14, para. 30) sheds only dim light on the intended meaning. It merely states in passing that 'the means by which interception is practised . . . need to be protected'. In view of the amount which has appeared in print or on television about telephone tapping and GCHQ in general, wider use of this provision seems unlikely.

[107] Below, pp. 363–64.   [108] Below, p.403.

[109] These are discussed extensively in Chs. 15 and 16.

[110] It is also found in s. 4(3)(*a*) and (*b*). Strictly speaking it is not an absolute offence, for s. 4(5) provides a defence where the person neither knew nor had reasonable cause to believe that the information had been obtained under a warrant. This is perhaps slightly more plausible than the 'idiot's gambit' discussed above, p. 231.

[111] pp. 106–7.

affected, and to the integrity of the security or policing body. When added to the fact that neither form of injury can be adequately redressed by civil remedies, use of criminal sanctions is justified.

CONCLUSION

There are two contexts within which one might evaluate the Official Secrets Act 1989. One is that of an ideal democratic state, the other, that of Britain of the 1990s. In the former, officials who discovered improper conduct of others, or who felt they were being asked to behave improperly themselves, could appeal to a high ranking superior, or to an independent body ultimately responsible to Parliament. They could do so in the confidence that their concerns would be investigated seriously, that misconduct would be corrected and those responsible exposed and disciplined, and that their own position and career prospects would be protected, if not indeed advanced. Under such circumstances there would be scope for a credible argument in favour of criminal penalties for disclosure of certain tightly defined categories of necessarily secret information held on behalf of the public,[112] since it would not be necessary for the official to make the information public in order to ensure that the source of his or her anxieties is properly investigated.

Merely to state the ideal is to highlight the distance between it and present reality. This observation is not limited to the deficiencies of both the internal and citizen complaints mechanisms which currently apply to the Security Service, significant though they are.[113] More important is the fact that in the political culture of contemporary Britain it is sadly inconceivable that politicians would not try to manipulate any such system. Put with a necessary, if unscholarly, bluntness: the people who ensured that the issues raised by Cathy Massiter remained largely uninvestigated; who prosecuted the Tisdalls and the Pontings for revealing chicanery whilst leaving those guilty of it untouched; who granted effective immunity to organized law-breaking and violence in the Royal Ulster Constabulary; and who deceived Parliament and would have countenanced, and indeed actively assisted in, the imprisonment of the Matrix Churchill defendants, cannot be trusted to allow a full and independent investigation of such grievances. Conversely, it has only been when such matters have come into the public domain, mostly due to the willingness of insiders to break official silence and of newspapers and television to disseminate their disclosures and sometimes investigate the matter further, that those in power have been compelled to make any response. Therefore under present and reasonably foreseeable circumstances,

---

[112] By which we emphatically do not mean the six categories covered under the 1989 Act; the range of protected information would be much narrower. It would go well beyond our present concerns to present a detailed proposal, however.

[113] See Ch. 14 below.

we would conclude that official secrets legislation should be rejected completely.[114] Any social loss incurred as a result, though likely to be marginal,[115] must be regarded as yet another cost of the betrayal of public trust which actions of that kind represent.

However, in light of the inescapable reality that no political party has favoured complete abolition of criminal sanctions in this area, it is perhaps worth sketching a more acceptable form of such legislation as it would relate to national security.

The initial point is that the nature of the harm should be made far more clear than has ever previously been done. Not only is this demanded by a fundamental element of the rule of law, which is that individuals should receive clear advance guidance as to what behaviour they must avoid, it is equally a measure to force government to explain to its citizens just what it believes is at stake, rather than hiding behind generalities. This is both good democratic practice and necessary if those citizens, when they serve as jurors, are to accept the legitimacy of the law. The 1989 Act, perhaps too cleverly for its own good, tries to finesse the issue. Even in cases where damage must be proven, it does not talk of damage to national security, but rather to the work of the security and intelligence services.[116] This is rather like equating the rule of law with the very peculiar practices of the Inns of Court. We arrive, not for the first time, at the necessity for identifying genuine national security interests.

A government daunted by that task might try one other approach: to align the information protected with the administrative system of levels of security classification. This was proposed by the Franks Committee, but within a very different procedural framework and for a very different purpose than we are suggesting. Their proposal would have permitted a prosecution only when the information disclosed was of a particular level of classification. This was to be established by a certificate signed by a Minister which would have served as conclusive evidence.[117] There are fundamental objections to any such practice, which were well expressed in the White Paper[118] and by the Home Secretary during the debate, who congratulated himself on its omission from the Bill.

However the classification system could be used in another way. There are four levels, of which the highest is TOP SECRET, defined as causing 'exceptionally grave damage to the nation'. In light of the legendary endemic over-classification

---

[114] This would of course not affect disciplinary sanctions against civil servants where appropriate. We would advocate retention of the provision penalizing improper disclosure of information gathered under warrant (above, p. 244), but as part of legislation devoted specifically to protecting privacy.

[115] e.g. where someone with no social justification and out of what may be described as malicious motives—perhaps a grievance as a result of dismissal or denial of promotion, or as an act of spite roughly analogous to criminal damage—reveals information whose disclosure does cause harm. Though a conceivable possibility, it is unlikely to occur frequently.

[116] OSA 1989, s. 1(4) (above p. 237).   [117] Above, p. 222.

[118] See n. 14 above), paras. 15–18.

of public information—a fact acknowledged by the Security Commission[119]—it is reasonable to conclude that preserving the secrecy of any material classified *below* this level is not sufficiently momentous to warrant the protection of criminal law. Therefore no prosecution in respect of such information would be permitted. This proposal draws upon one aspect of the Franks Committee recommendations, but we have set the level of information that would be covered one notch higher. This is both to take account of over-classification and, concomitantly, to gather only the most incontestably secret material within the net of criminalization.[120] Moreover, that would only be the beginning, not the end. Certain defences would be available, whose purpose is to introduce precisely that element of balance we have found so wanting in the current law.[121]

Having repeatedly advocated specificity as a vital principle in constructing criminal law, we must maintain our devotion to it and reject the idea of any sort of generalized, open-ended, public interest defence. Though this has had many adherents, it seems not only wrong in principle but unnecessary. It is wrong because it leaves judge and jury roaming free. Given that a conflict of values will inevitably be presented, the constitutional responsibility for determining which are to predominate rests with Parliament, which should give its answer when framing the statute. It is unnecessary because those interests which we believe should outweigh the maintenance of even normally acceptable secrecy can readily be articulated.

The first and much the most important is where democratic and constitutional values are enhanced rather than diminished by the disclosure. The most obvious example is where illegal conduct is exposed, but there are others which are equally important. We would incorporate abuse of power, danger to individual or public health and safety, obstruction of constitutional accountability processes (which would include correction of deliberately misleading statements by Ministers), and violations of human rights.[122] It is right to leave to the jury, the most representative element in the system of criminal justice, the decision as to where the balance of advantage to the constitutional order lies in each particular instance.

The other defence which should be provided is one of public domain or prior publication. It is not sufficient that this be a factor that may serve to negate the prosecution's case that harm has been caused. No one's freedom

---

[119] Cmnd. 8450 (1982), para. 8. On the Security Commission generally, see Ch. 17 below.

[120] We advance this suggestion with some hesitancy, for a possible response is that even more material now classified SECRET ('serious injury' to the nation's interests) would be upgraded to TOP SECRET in order to preserve the threat of criminal prosecution. If that were judged a likely consequence, we would drop the proposal forthwith.

[121] p. 234 above. Of course if the idea of using the classification system as a limiting principle were not adopted it would be even more essential to provide these defences.

[122] Which for present purposes may be equated with the substantive provisions of the ECHR; such conduct would not be illegal in the strictest sense since the Convention is not part of our domestic law. Similar defences were provided in the most recent freedom of information proposal debated in Parliament, Mark Fisher MP's 'Right to Know' Bill (1992–3), cl. 30.

should depend on the fine measurement of intangibles and hypotheticals. Moreover, if the government's security machinery has (by definition) previously failed, prosecuting someone for merely making the information more widely available is no more than scapegoating, perhaps compounded by a wish to distract attention from incompetence. And to argue, as did the White Paper, that a second, more authoritative disclosure can do greater harm than an initial press report, is simply bizarre. Such confirmation, if unauthorized would never be made openly, so the problem would never arise.[123] The real question is whether, once information has entered the public domain by whatever route, it should be accessible to all citizens as equally as possible. To that question there can be only one answer.

Finally, any such criminal provision should exclude journalists, authors, or others who broadcast the disclosure. Not only is the breach of trust issue inapplicable in their case; more important is the principle that those engaged in informing the public be protected from official deterrents and retaliation. Nor is restriction on criminalization sufficient. In our view the media, when dealing seriously with public issues, should be recognized as an important element in constitutional government and assisted rather than discouraged from playing its part. We develop this argument more fully in the following chapter.

---

[123] See n. 14 above, para. 62. Sensibly, the White Paper did not offer the argument sometimes made, that report in a popular newspaper does more damage than previous appearance in an obscure technical periodical. Of course it is to the latter source than any reasonably skilled foreign intelligence officer would look first; hence the first publication would do whatever damage failure to maintain total secrecy would cause.

10

The Role of the Press

In an account of national security rooted in an understanding of the state giving priority to human rights it might be expected that justification would be offered for the value placed on freedom of expression. However, the purpose of this chapter is not to engage in an abstract defence of free speech—a task which has been lucidly undertaken by several recent writers[1]—but rather to examine the specific implications of that primacy in the context of national security for the role of the media. Our exposition originates in a constitutional perspective on the position of the media. It examines the extent to which the law buttresses or hinders that role, specifically through controls over sources of information, bars to publication (prior restraints), and legal penalties for publication. It also draws upon, without further citation, the discussion of disclosure of information in the two preceding chapters.

Despite our opening disclaimer it is worth briefly grounding our constitutional perspective in first principles. Of the three justifications commonly advanced for favouring free expression, two—discovery of truth in the market-place of ideas and artistic self-expression—have little relevance to prohibitions on publication in the name of security. It is the third, which sees freedom of expression as intimately connected with democratic practice, which is important here. Without the right to express ideas and receive information the franchise—the basic democratic entitlement—becomes meaningless: what is one to vote for? Apart from its use in articulating political philosophy and ideals, at a lower but still vital level speech is the method by which the sucesses and failures of governments can be clearly laid before the electorate for their verdict. The vote is a vehicle of expression in its own right, and the Press, like the opposition, is a participant in a great debate. Moreover, in exercising its rights of expression through the ballot box the public is entitled to access to reliable information—which it is the function of the press to provide. Our task in this chapter is to consider the extent to which these axioms hold when the information concerns security. Should these principles apply when the cause of debate is the continuing conduct of a war, or the development of a new weapons system, or revelations of action taken by an intelligence agency?

---

[1] C. Baker, *Human Liberty and Freedom of Speech* (New York, 1989); E. Barendt, *Freedom of Speech* (Oxford, 1987); F. Schauer, *Free Speech: a Philosophical Enquiry* (Cambridge, 1982).

THE CONSTITUTIONAL ROLE OF THE PRESS

The role of the Press may be manifest in two ways. Though distinct they are not incompatible, but they have different histories, lead to different legal conflicts, and require different regimes of legal protection.

The first may be called the 'broadsheet' function. Seventeenth- and eighteenth-century struggles over freedom of expression concerned the ability of critics of government or other established institutions to express their views freely.[2] The common threat connecting publications as disparate as the *Letters of Junius* and Paine's *The Age of Reason* is that they were expressions of opinion, based on ideas formulated by the author. Their purpose was either to persuade readers to adopt a particular point of view, or to discredit those in power by ridicule.

Threatening expressions of opinion were met with straightforward suppression. The ruling élite of England, unlike most of the rest of Europe, did not rely primarily on brute force. Instead, critics faced a barrage of common law and statutory rules, supplemented by institutional controls. Hence the traditional battleground of freedom of expression has been in the arena of censorship. Some of these battles have largely been won: the Licensing Acts and the Lord Chamberlain are no more, and critics of the judiciary no longer fear the arbitrary power of contempt for scandalizing the court. However, the wider war is far from over, and certainly has not yet been won. The most potent force for repression remains the law of defamation, but others are ranged alongside it: obscenity, other forms of contempt, and a recent fearsome recruit, breach of confidence. The latter two are tightly interwoven with the concerns of this study, and the legal conflicts are discussed later in this chapter where they have arisen in a security context. Though they are distinguished by the central role of the judiciary as agents of suppression, they take the same form—'prior restraint'—as identified by Blackstone more than two centuries ago.

The Press retains its 'broadsheet' function, but as its character and readership were transformed into daily publications with mass circulation, it has acquired another of equal importance: provision of information.[3] At their best, journalists uncover information by their own efforts, where necessary surmounting obstacles set up to keep it secret.[4] We have emphasized the significance of this conflict over control of information in relation to criminal offences,[5] but that is not

---

[2] See the discussion of blasphemy and sedition in Ch. 8 above.

[3] This is even more true of television, the medium which reaches by far the greatest number of people, but is subject to a range of restrictions on the expression of opinion by broadcasters. In this section, the term 'Press' includes all media.

[4] The areas covered in this study comprise only a small fraction of those in which these exertions are necessary. Not only are there many other kinds of information governments try to keep secret, there is also a strong public interest in much information tightly guarded by business enterprises and wealthy individuals.

[5] Above, pp. 198–200.

its sole dimension. Other legal provisions which fetter journalists' ability to inform the public are equally grave.

It is necessary to clarify exactly what is at stake in this less traditional arena of conflict. Unlike the classic struggles over censorship, it is not a simple matter of ensuring that dissenting voices are heard. Here the role of the Press is to further accountability of government to the public; it is an essential cog in the mechanism of responsible government. Within its much narrower sphere it has an importance equal to that of Parliament itself: it is no exaggeration to call it a constitutional function.[6]

It is not that journalists or editors are more public-spirited or high-minded than anyone else. Much of what they publish is trivial, sensationalized, salacious, and sometimes all three; and in any case too much even of what purports to be serious coverage of public issues consists of recycling official or corporate press releases. However, in certain circumstances the self-interest of individual newspapers in selling their product by revealing material their competitors could not reach happens to serve the public interest, which is to ensure that incompetence, self-interested manipulation, and deceit are exposed. Surgeons, it is said, bury their mistakes. Politicians seek to do so; and lacking political institutions to do the job effectively, we are left with the Press to conduct the inquest. Parliament was once exalted as the 'Grand Inquest of the Nation', but executive dominance has long made that role an anachronistic, if beguiling, myth.[7] The absence of a legislature securely independent of the executive, or of an ombudsman with a wide jurisdiction, powers of compulsion, and the ability to act on his own initiative (as in several Scandinavian states) heightens the importance of a vigorous, probing, and critical Press—and indeed endows it with a status one may fairly dignify as 'constitutional'.

Four characteristics of the Press make if far more capable of fulfilling this function on behalf of the public than other political actors, such as pressure groups, or opposition parties or politicians. First, it devotes unequalled financial resources and skilled people specifically to obtaining information. Secondly, it enjoys an access to the public, including an international audience, that individuals or small groups can never hope to match. Thirdly, it has the political and economic power to face down legal threats and to fight actions resolutely if they do occur. Individuals faced with loss of a job, payment of legal costs, and possibly a substantial fine may quail at the consequences of a struggle that a newspaper, often backed by insurers, can take in its stride. Nor can the political danger to a government of making enemies among the Press, and of being seen to threaten its liberty, be discounted even in a narrow calculation of advantage.

---

[6] In *Secretary of State for Defence* v. *Guardian Newspapers* [1985] AC 339, in which the MOD demanded return of papers that had been sent anonymously to the newspaper, the latter's counsel sought to place this issue at centre stage by describing the case in precisely these terms. For the majority, Lord Diplock was curtly dismissive: [1985] AC at 345, and even the two dissenters, sceptical though they were of the government's case, did not speak in these terms.

[7] See further Ch. 16 below.

Finally, the Press is not hobbled by a difficulty likely to loom large in the thinking of politicians: that what we say now in opposition may haunt us when in office, and we shall have to deal with the heads of whatever department or agency we are now criticizing.

In the discussion which follows we examine first the critical question of how law affects the access of journalists to information, through the protection or otherwise of those who pass information to the media. The discussion then moves to the treatment of information so received. In discussing the journalistic decision whether or not to publish, we are not concerned primarily with sanctions imposed in judicial proceedings, but rather with the effect those sanctions existence has on journalists perceptions and behaviour, and with other forms of self-censorship. These practices form the context of which legal regulation is but an occasional and sporadically visible part.

DISCLOSURE OF JOURNALISTS' SOURCES

Serious problems surround protection of a vital precondition for effective investigative journalism: the secrecy of documents, notes, and above all, the identity of human sources. The graver the matter—particularly where official misconduct is in issue—the more essential it is to safeguard these forms of information. For precisely the reasons that security agencies take such pains with their human sources,[8] maintaining the anonymity of persons who provide journalists with information is the greatest necessity. Fear of retaliation is certain to still the mouths of those vulnerable to retaliatory prosecutions, dismissal, or physical violence. Journalists therefore need to be able to give an guarantee firm enough to overcome these entirely realistic fears on the part of potential providers of information. The main effect of the present law, which as we shall see provides only a very limited security, is not to force disclosure of the identity of such people; it is to deter them from revealing information which they alone may be in a position to know, and of which the public will not otherwise learn.

Attempts to force journalists to reveal their sources may take three forms.[9] Two are branches of the law of contempt. One arises when a journalist is called before a special tribunal of inquiry which demands to know the origin of information which has appeared in material he or she has written. This was a promi-

---

[8] See Ch. 5 above.

[9] A fourth is a matter of historical interest only: the OSA 1920, s. 6, made it an offence to fail to give information relating to an offence under that or the 1911 Act. Despite earlier assurances from the Attorney-General (Sir Gordon Hewart) that it was not intended to be used against journalists, the journalist Ernest Lewis was later prosecuted for refusing to reveal the source of a leaked police document and the conviction was upheld by Hewart LCJ (as he had by then become) in *Lewis* v. *Cattle* [1938] 2 KB 454. A parliamentary row over an attempt to use the same provision against an MP, Duncan Sandys, led to its curtailment to information about espionage offences only by the OSA 1939, s. 1. See generally D. Hooper, *Official Secrets—The Use and Abuse of the Act* (London, 1987), 46–9 and 54–7.

nent feature of the spy scandals of the early 1960s, when two journalists held firm and served six months in prison for contempt of the Vassall Tribunal.[10] The second is one of the main applications of the law of contempt, under which courts may compel production of information, including journalists' sources, for the reasons enumerated in section 10 of the Contempt of Court Act 1981. These include the extremely vague 'interests of justice', prevention of disorder or crime—and national security.[11]

The latter exception was applied when the House of Lords affirmed a decision to require the *Guardian* to hand back a Ministry of Defence memorandum which had been sent to it anonymously, but which was known to contain markings from which the leaker would be identifiable.[12] The document was a communication between ministers about the arrangements for announcing the arrival of Cruise missiles at Greenham Common. The majority upheld the decision to order its return on the grounds that it was necessary to identify the source because someone with access to information at this level could pose a potential security threat, although the leak itself did not endanger national security.

The third form which attempted extraction of source material may take is a police investigation. This was the subject of extensive debate during the enactment of the Police and Criminal Evidence Act 1984; the government accepted the views of critics and introduced provisions limiting the scope of police powers of search for 'journalistic material' by requiring that any matter of that description be sought only under warrant issued by a circuit judge.[13] The Act lays down a considerable number of 'access conditions', the relevant one being that of 'public interest'. This involves considering the benefit to the investigation if the material is produced and 'the circumstances under which the person in possession of the material holds it'.[14] Thus the court is enabled to take account of a journalist's promise to a source to maintain confidentiality, but the weight given to that factor remains entirely at the discretion of the judge, whose decision is not subject to appeal. The law of contempt then resurfaces, since its punishments await those who fail to comply with an order for production.[15]

---

[10] *A-G* v. *Mulholland*, [1963] 2 QB 477. See also *A-G* v. *Clough*, [1963] 1 QB 773.

[11] For a broader critique of s. 10 than is within our remit, see S. Palmer, 'Protecting Journalists' Sources—Section 10, Contempt of Court Act 1981' [1992] *PL* 61; G. Robertson, *Freedom, the Individual and the Law* (Harmondsworth, 1989), 284–93, and the wealth of material (with reference to specialist treatises) in S. Bailey *et al.*, *Civil Liberties: Cases and Materials* (3rd edn., London, 1990), ch. 6.

[12] See n. 6 above; see further p. 264 below.

[13] Police and Criminal Evidence Act, 1984 (PACE), s. 9 and sched. 1.

[14] Ibid., sched. I, para. 2(*c*). (There is another set of access conditions provided, but they are little used.)

[15] Ibid., paras. 4 and 15, which are to be interpreted in light of *DPP* v. *Channel 4 Television Co. Ltd.* (Div. Ct., 31 July 1992). This case, considered below, involved the virtually identical provisions of the Prevention of Terrorism (Temporary Provisions) Act 1989 (PTA). The judgment of Woolf LJ (Transcript, pp. 8–9), confirms the absence of a right of appeal, though the defendant may apply for discharge or variation of the order, or for judicial review.

Despite its more ominous connotations, the provisions of the anti-terrorist legislation are in this respect virtually identical.[16]

In the case of alleged offences under the Official Secrets Acts 1911 and 1989 wider powers of search are available.[17] In their application to journalists there is a departure from the rules described earlier: the preconditions for search are less stringent,[18] and the opportunity to oppose the issue of the order before the circuit judge may be displaced and a warrant issued after an *ex parte* application if the service of a notice to produce the material 'may seriously prejudice the investigation'.[19] It will not be too difficult to satisfy a judge that that this requirement is fulfilled where there is risk of a journalist destroying a document in order to protect the source of a security-related story. The Zircon satellite affair of January 1987 demonstrated the practical utility of these powers to the authorities.[20] There the police successfully obtained a warrant to search for and seize material relating to the making of a programme in the *Secret Society* series commissioned for the BBC, from the homes of the investigative journalist Duncan Campbell and of the producer of the series. No opportunity to oppose the warrants was given, because the *ex parte* procedure was used. Furthermore in Scotland, where different legislative provisions apply, similar raids were conducted by Special Branch officers on the Glasgow offices of the BBC on the authority of a warrant issued by a sheriff. In all the searches quantities of notes and film unrelated to the Zircon film were seized only to be returned many months later. No prosecutions of any kind followed, and after a delay all the films in the series were eventually screened.[21]

Equally troubling is another, more recent, police investigation into a television documentary. The production order provisions had already been successfully invoked in earlier cases to force journalists to hand over photographs taken during public disorder, which the police sought to help them identify offenders. The ease with which applications succeeded was worrying enough.[22] However, it

---

[16] Compare sched. 1 of PACE with sched. 7 of the PTA. The only difference of note is that orders are granted *ex parte* under the PTA, whilst in applications under PACE the defendant is heard.

[17] OSA 1911, s. 9(1); OSA 1989, s. 11(3). In general searches under this heading are broader than the normal powers to conduct searches of premises during criminal investigations allow in several respects: there is no need to specify the material which is being searched for at the time of applying for a magistrate's warrant; the search may relate to an offence which it is suspected will be committed, rather than merely one which has already taken place; and, exceptionally, such a search may be authorized by a police superintendant if it appears to him or her that 'the case is one of great emergency and in the interests of the State immediate action is necessary': OSA 1911, s. 9(2).

[18] Because a specific power of search exists: PACE, sched. 1, para. 3.

[19] Ibid., sched. 1, para. 14.

[20] See G. Zellick (1987) 137 *NLJ* 160; K. Ewing and C. Gearty, *Freedom Under Thatcher: Civil Liberties in Modern Britain* (Oxford, 1990), 147–52; P. Gill, ''Allo, 'Allo, 'Allo, Who's in Charge Here Then?' (1987) 9 *Liverpool LR* 189. On other aspects of the affair see Ch. 16 below.

[21] The Zircon film was suppressed by the BBC but was later shown by Channel 4 as part of a season on censorship.

[22] *R. v. Bristol Crown Court, ex p. Bristol Press and Picture Agency* (1986) 85 Cr. App. R. 190; note also Professor Zander's summary of the judgment of Glidewell LJ in *R. v. Central Criminal Court, ex p. Carr*, 5 Mar., 1987, which seems to suggest that whenever there is relevant evidence on the

is doubtful whether those who drafted the legislation ever imagined that the power would be wielded when the police themselves were accused of involvement in serious criminal wrongdoing. Yet that is precisely what happened in the autumn of 1991.

As part of its *Despatches* series, Channel 4 had screened a programme presenting credible allegations of the existence of murder squads in Northern Ireland which had links with members of the Royal Ulster Constabulary. The evidence of one person, a member of the group including RUC officers, 'loyalist' terrorists, and business men known as 'the Committee', was vital to the programme's credibility. Known as 'Source A', he agreed to participate (in a heavily disguised silhouette) only on the strictest assurance that his identity would remain confidential, for reasons unfortunately only too obvious. Following transmission the RUC, as part of what purported to be an investigation into the charges,[23] sought to obtain a wide range of documents relating to the programme from the production company, Box Productions, and Channel 4. The defendants complied in the main, but drew the line at disclosing anything that might lead to exposure of Source A, or to subject Box's researcher to the risk of violence. The ensuing contempt motion was heard in Middlesex Crown Court before Judge Clarkson QC, who found the issues so troubling that only 'after straining his conscience'[24] did he order production of the information. On appeal the Divisional Court held that the journalists' and broadcasters' highest duty was to comply with the order of the court and therefore ultimately to co-operate with the investigation. An unconditional assurance could not properly have been given to Source A, said Lord Justice Woolf; any promise should have been subject to a qualification that his name might have to be revealed to a court.

No surer formula for torpedoing the whole enterprise could have been invented. Woolf LJ in the end recognized this, and though his judgment is marred by a strange and rather disingenuous suggestion that Channel 4 should have 'sought advice at the highest level of government' as to the 'propriety' of the undertaking they had given,[25] it ultimately is grounded in what he describes as a issue of 'constitutional significance':[26] the role of the courts as ultimate arbiters of the public interest under the statute. However much one may dislike the result on grounds of policy and wish the Judge's conscience had been strained that bit less, it is impossible to fault the constitutional principle:

premises likely to be of substantial value to an investigation, the 'public interest' test would be satisfied: M. Zander, *The Police and Criminal Evidence Act 1984* (2nd edn., London, 1990), 24.

[23] According to the late Brian Raymond, solicitor for the production company and its researcher, the RUC contacted persons identified in the programme as members of 'The Committee', inquired whether the allegations were true, and has been content to accept their denials.

[24] See n. 15 above, judgement of Woolf LJ, transcript 28.

[25] Ibid., 21. This can hardly be taken seriously in view of the government's public announcment that it would refuse to prosecute those who had admittedly obstructed the Stalker Inquiry, and the complete lack of response to the Sampson Report which carried on after Stalker was dismissed.

[26] Ibid. 22.

Parliament did indeed leave the determination of public interest to judicial discretion. The results, both in this[27] and related cases,[28] and in the highly unsatisfactory decisions under section 10 of the 1981 Act,[29] compel the conclusion that Parliament should itself make the choice and elevate to irremovable precedence the public interest in availability of information. This would require enactment of legislation which positively protects journalists' sources in nearly absolute form. The corollary is that, so far as is humanly and juridically possible, the matter would be removed from the hands of the judges.

We cannot set out proposals in any detail here. It is sufficient to note that at least two legislative treatments of the issue in Europe would bear close attention.[30] One is found in Sweden, where the Freedom of the Press Act, which is considered part of the Constitution, includes provisions protecting providers of information, imposing upon journalists an obligation of confidentiality to their sources regardless of their own wishes, and which may only be overridden in rare instances.[31] Slightly less rigorous is the German approach, which imposes an absolute privilege against disclosure for information received in confidence, though it fails to cover material obtained through the journalist's own efforts.[32]

Common to both statutes is that the only question a judge may be required to decide is whether, as a narrow question of interpretation, a particular person is protected by the obligation or privilege. The judgment as to the value to be given to free flow of information has already been written into the legislation. English judges are peculiarly given to orotund pronouncements about the primacy of the rule of law in cases involving newspapers.[33] Since these are often heard in cases in which the judges appear to be making up the law as they go along, one is left with the strong suspicion that at least part of what is involved

---

[27] The Divisional Court substantially sugared the pill for the defendants by imposing a total fine of £75,000, less than a fifth of what Channel 4 had shortly before paid its Managing Director to remain in post in the face of offers from rival franchises. However, it was made quite clear that in any future case journalists and broadcasters could expect far less sympathetic treatment; Counsel for the DPP had moved for sequestration of Channel 4, which might well have shut it down entirely.

[28] Above n. 22, and see also *R.* v. *Middlesex Guildhall Crown Court, ex p. Salinger*, the *Independent*, 26 Mar., 1992 and LEXIS (order for production of videos of interviews with Lockerbie bomb suspects conducted by an American journalist in Libya).

[29] Above p. 253; and see the cases discussed by Palmer (n. 11 above).

[30] The issue has been much litigated in the USA as well. After the claim for a federal constitutional source protection privilege was rejected (*Branzburg* v. *Hayes*, 408 U.S. 665 (1972)), the majority of states enacted some sort of legislative reform. However, looking at what one expert treats as a typical example, that of Florida, the conditions are very similar to the PACE/PTA provisions in the UK (above n. 16). See W. Korthals Altes, 'Protecting Journalists' Sources—A Dutch Proposal for Legislation', [1992] *PL* 73, 81–2.

[31] Freedom of the Press Act, ch. 3, art. 3. We should like to thank the Swedish Embassy for their extraordinarily prompt response to an inquiry, which produced a full set of the relevant materials in English.

[32] Korthals Altes (n. 30 above), 75–9. Another shortcoming is that for some reason also the privilege extends only to periodicals, not to books or pamphlets. 'Freelances', however, are protected: it is not necessary that one be employed by a newspaper.

[33] Perhaps the most baroque was that offered by Lord Bridge in *X.* v. *Morgan Grampian Ltd.* [1991] 1 AC 1, 48–9.

is a struggle for institutional political supremacy. If that conclusion seems perhaps over-cynical, one cannot ignore both the actual rulings and the tone in which they are often couched. It is beyond question, however, that the British courts emphatically reject the concept of the Press as 'the Fourth Estate', of its having an essential rule in forcing government to be accountable.[34] For this reason alone a shield law is required to give investigative media a protective space.

Of narrow scope but highly dangerous is section 18 of the Prevention of Terrorism Act. This provision makes withholding information about terrorism a criminal offence. Having survived two official recommendations for repeal it has lingered on, little used and restricted by a circular confining its use to 'extreme cases . . . which might lead to death [or] serious injury'.[35] It has never been used against journalists, even though it was quoted in the Channel 4 case as a sort of background context material. If kept at all, it should be amended explicitly to exclude journalists.

PROTECTION OF 'WHISTLEBLOWERS'[36]

A closely related issue is the extent to which the law encourages public officials with knowledge of official misconduct to make it public—or to 'blow the whistle'. Confidentiality of the type just discussed may be an important part of such protection, but equally or more important is protection from legal sanctions for such public-spirited revelations. Without such protection would-be whistleblowers will have a considerable hurdle of self-sacrifice to overcome before making disclosures: in most cases the threat of prosecution or loss of career will be enough to ensure that the public avowal of this kind is rare, and the flow of information through the press to the public will be minimal.

In the United Kingdom the law gives few inducements for such action. In many instances the disclosure will amount to an official secrets' offence, for which there is no public interest defence.[37] However, even if there is no criminal liablity a civil servant may be liable to disciplinary action for unauthorized discosure.[38] There exists no protection for disclosure to Parliament, and instead civil servants operate within a disciplinary framework where they can be forbidden to appear before a select committee, or to answer particular questions.

---

[34] A striking contrast is the article written by a serving US Supreme Court Justice arguing for an interpretation of the First Amendment on precisely this basis: P. Stewart, 'Or of the Press' (1975) 27 *Hast. LJ* 631.

[35] Lord Colville in 1987 and Lord Shackleton in 1978 recommended in their reviews of the PTA that this section should be repealed. The government has refused to follow their recommendations, but has restricted its use by a Circular to all police forces: see Bailey *et al.* (n. 11 above), 292.

[36] See Y. Cripps, 'Disclosure in the Public Interest: The Predicament of the Public Sector Employee', [1983] *PL* 600.   [37] Above, Ch. 9.

[38] Civil Service Pay and Conditions Code, paras. 9911–13; cf. the example of Stephen Thornley, an employee at a defence contractor whose dismissal as a result of writing to the *Guardian* was upheld by the Employment Appeal Tribunal in 1977: Cripps (n. 36 above), 609–13.

Apart from an obscure nineteenth-century statute,[39] the grant of protection to public officials for disclosures lies in the gift of the government itself. Occasionally this is exercised for the benefit of those giving evidence to inquiries: civil servants appearing before the Scott Inquiry (the Arms for Iraq inquiry) were told that their disclosures would be treated as authorized ones for the purpose of the Official Secrets Act 1989, given immunity from prosecution, and informed by the Cabinet Secretary that they would not be disciplined as a consequence of giving evidence.[40]

However this falls a long way short of any protection for disclosure to the press. Indeed the judges in the *Spycatcher* litigation emphasised that whatever public merit there might have been in Peter Wright's disclosures exposing alleged wrongdoing by the Security Service, there was none in his making them by direct appeal to the press and public, rather than to the appropriate authorities.[41] This attitude ignores the ineffectiveness of the alternatives, an important consideration in view of our argument that the press has a constitutional role. The argument would be more credible if there existed some wholly independent figure to whom disclosure might be made, who had then had coercive and effective powers to investigate, deal with, and, where necessary, publish details of impropriety. As it is, civil servants of a Pontingesque disposition are enjoined to contact the Cabinet Secretary, and if they fail to resolve the matter according to their conscience, to resign in silence.[42] Security and intelligence officers are encouraged to use the the Security and Intelligence staff counsellor.[43] These devices are intended as safety-valves to reduce the risk of public disclosure but, in view of their internal and administrative nature, they do not materially increase the possibility that the abuses will be remedied as a result.

In these circumstances it becomes important to provide legal protection for those who leak details of impropriety to the press, as a means of reinforcing the constitutional accountability of the security and intelligence agencies.[44] For instance, procedures allowing complaint to a designated official who reports to the Congress exist in the United States for the benefit of members of the FBI.[45]

---

[39] The Witnesses (Public Inquiries) Protection Act 1892. S. 2 makes it an offence to take reprisals against any person for having given evidence at any inquiry (the definition under s. 1 is broad enough to embrace Select Committees), and s. 4 allows a court to award compensation to any person against whom such reprisals are taken following a conviction under s. 2: see Cripps (n. 36 above), 607. The Act only applies after the event and does not punish attempts to deter testimony.

[40] 'Inquiry into Exports of Defence and Dual Use Goods to Iraq', Press Release, 31 March, 1993.

[41] e.g. Lord Donaldson in *A-G* v. *Guardian Newspapers* (*No. 2*) [1990] 1 AC 109, 183.

[42] 'Note of Guidance on the Duties and Responsibilities of Civil Servants in Relation to Ministers', in *The Duties and Responsibilities of Civil Servants and Ministers*, HC 92 (1985–6), vol. ii, 7–9. A former permanent secretary of the Home Office has suggested that part of the safeguard in this procedure lies in the possibility that the Cabinet Secretary could consult the Prime Minister and, *in extremis*, resign: B. Cubbon, 'The Duty of the Professional', in R. Chapman (ed.), *Ethics in Public Service* (Edinburgh, 1993), 10; apart from the fantastic nature of the scenario, this seems a wholly disproportionate and unnecessary response to a problem which could be resolved at a lower level.

[43] See ch. 15, p. 430.   [44] See further Chs. 15–16.

[45] P. Birkinshaw, *Reforming the Secret State* (Milton Keynes, 1990), 33.

Even more useful as a model is a proposal put forward by the Ontario Law Reform Commission for public employees generally, which drew on the American provision.[46] The core of the idea is the creation of a special counsel, appointed by the legislature and reporting to it, who would stand in a solicitor–client relation to whoever disclosed information to him or her, and would thus be sheltered by legal privilege from identifying the informant. The proposal would combine independence of the executive, anonymity for the whistleblower, access to Parliament, and at least initially, preservation of secrecy until the special counsel and/or the legislative controller decided that publicity was desirable. It thus would be fully responsive to all the values at stake, and be a vast improvement on the present British system, which is designed more to keep matters wholly within the executive than to redress abuses. Only if some such office existed and had demonstrated its independence would disclosure to the Press become wholly unnecessary.

Unfortunately, even where the need for the Press to be free to make disclosures derived from leaks of this kind has been recognized, the force of the argument has not extended to the related issue of protecting the channel of communication by giving immunity to the leaker. Thus, the European Court of Human Rights recognized the valuable role of the press as a 'public watchdog' in its *Spycatcher* judgment,[47] but other pronouncements within the Convention jurisprudence have upheld limitations on the freedom of expression of public employees who speak out.[48]

Having considered the interest (or lack of it) of the law in protecting those with whom journalists deal, we turn now to its effect on them directly. Because of its role in the service of accountable government, any measures that interfere with the ability of the investigative media to gather and retain information are as dangerous to democracy as traditional censorship. This conclusion entails two corollaries: that some current legal provisions ought to be repealed, and that, contrary to the way English law has recently developed, other measures are needed to strengthen the legal protection of the media's constitutional role.

The prime candidate for repeal is found in the Official Secrets Act 1989, for reasons we have explored in the preceding chapter. Even those who believe that legislation of this kind has a legitimate place on the statute book would perhaps recognize that the countervailing values are much stronger where the Press is threatened than where a civil servant or other official (in reality its main targets) is prosecuted. Although our interviews have suggested that the Act has little

---

[46] OLRC, *Report on Political Activity, Public Comment and Disclosure by Crown Employees* (Toronto, 1986). For summary and commentary, see K. Swan, 'Whistleblowing and National Security', in P. Hanks and J. McCamus (eds.), *National Security: Surveillance and Accountability in a Democratic Society* (Cowansville, Que., 1989), ch. 13.

[47] *Sunday Times* v. *UK(No. 2)* (1991) 14 EHRR 229; *The Guardian and The Observer* v. *UK* (1991) 14 EHRR 53, para. 39.

[48] e.g. in relation to disciplinary proceedings against a civil servant working at a radioactive plant: *Application 1029/83* v. *UK* (1987) 9 EHRR 255.

direct impact on some of the newspaper journalists most actively engaged in this field, that state of affairs is not guaranteed, and could readily be upset by the successful prosecution of a shrewdly selected target. And there is good reason to believe that, for economic reasons, the deterrent effect of the Act on television investigative work is far more potent.[49]

RESTRICTIONS IN CONTEXT: MEDIA SELF-CENSORSHIP

The Official Secrets Act 1989 has made very little difference to how journalists do their jobs. What emerged from our interviews, however, was more complex and interesting: a picture of what does motivate and constrain at least some of the journalists most actively concerned with issues of defence and security, as well as lawyers who may be called upon to advise them or their editors.[50]

Perhaps the most interesting point was the dominant role of self-censorship. This takes two forms, structural and individual. The former was most obvious and open on the *Daily Telegraph*, which does not employ a correspondent specializing in national security matters 'because most of our readers believe this sort of material should not appear in the public domain.' Since the *Telegraph* is by a considerable margin the largest-selling quality daily newspaper, that attitude has a sort of self-reinforcing effect, in that so far as this large proportion of educated readers is concerned, such material does not appear.

The view taken by the *Telegraph* management harks back to the tradition of an earlier era, one which maintains strong but diminishing influence. Its defenders would describe it as 'discretion'; a less polite word would be collusion. It is the attitude which underpins both the Lobby system and the D Notice system discussed below.[51] Within this structure editors and politicians know each other on social terms and frequently meet informally. They share the same social background and outlook, which produces a consensual, implicit understanding and permits substantial voluntary agreement about what is and is not fit to become public knowledge. At the end of the First World War Northcliffe, one of the great Press Lords, said: 'The power of the press is very great, but not so great as the power of suppress.' Anthony Sampson, one of the earliest critics of the system, reports a saying common among the staff of *The Times* many years later, 'that if readers knew how much of their subscription went to keeping information from them, they would demand their money back'.[52]

---

[49] See below (in this chapter), pp. 268–69.

[50] All those interviewed are listed on p. xix. They were not chosen as a representative group, but neither was selection random. All of those to whom we spoke were either people who have been actively involved in the area or, as in the case of the *Telegraph*, because the journal is of particular importance. Several people did not wish to be identified.   [51] See pp. 269–76.

[52] Both quotations are from A. Sampson, 'Secrecy, News Management and the British Press', in T. Franck and E. Weisband (eds.), *Secrecy and Foreign Policy* (New York, 1974), 219.

This portrait would have remained accurate through at least the early 1970s, but is not so today. Whilst only one newspaper, the *Guardian*, employs someone to cover national security matters virtually full-time, nearly all have defence correspondents, many of whom are less willing than their earlier counterparts to accept the limitations on disclosure imposed by the Ministry or the military. The more contentious political environment within which defence and security policies are now formulated has led to greater official leaking, or rather definitely unofficial leaking by officials, as various sides to a dispute seek to influence public opinion. Moreover the advent of mass television ownership and satellite transmission has fed an expectation among public and journalists alike that they are entitled to receive information about military operations almost as they occur—an outlook that led to much controversy both in the Falklands and the Gulf wars.[53] Television has also provided a home for some investigative journalism. Its greater impact on public awareness creates a correspondingly more intense hostility from government when critical programmes appear.[54] Moreover television programmes are subject to a regulatory structure quite unlike anything affecting newspapers, with the result that different, and in some ways more insidious, pressures for self-censorship are at work.[55]

Personal self-censorship results from the interplay of complex and conflicting pressures. Professionally, journalists live and die by and for the scoop—the exclusive story. However most of the time they rely on two kinds of official sources. One is public relations officers[56] who, no implication of dishonesty intended, try to limit carefully the amount and content of what they reveal. The second is individual operational officials with whom the journalist has developed friendly relations. To some extent all such sources are trying to use journalists as conduits for the messages they wish to present; one important element of a journalist's job is to resist this by being able to draw upon other sources. Often these will be other officials speaking entirely without authorization, whom the journalist has cultivated over the years. Since in many cases their careers, and in an extreme case their liberty, will be at risk, willingness to protect their

---

[53] See pp. 276–79 below.

[54] The most remarkable example was the furore surrounding Thames Television's *Death on the Rock*, which challenged the official version of the SAS killing of three IRA members in Gibraltar. It provoked an unofficial inquiry (see Lord Windlesham and Richard Rampton, QC, *Death on the Rock* (London, 1989)) which found that government claims of bias and interference with the Gibraltar inquest were unsubstantiated but, nevertheless, this episode is often cited by media people as the reason Thames lost its franchise when the new allocations were made in 1991.

[55] Discussed below, pp. 266–69.

[56] Particularly in relation to the MOD, which has a large and sophisticated public relations network. One of the main differences between the security services and virtually any other form of officialdom is that they have no public relations specialists and indeed, until very recently, have tried hard to avoid revealing anything to the media in any form. It is too early to tell whether the 'charm offensive' of 16 July 1993 has inaugurated a new approach. This was a major media event to mark publication of a booklet, *The Security Service*, and included a press conference with (unattributably) Director-General Stella Rimington, whose photograph appeared on several front pages the following day.

anonymity is all-important; and failure to do so would fatally mark any journalist as an unreliable confidant for the rest of his or her career. One of Britain's more experienced and effective investigative journalists, David Leigh, has contended that 'a journalist is only as good as his unofficial sources'.[57] If this is so, the stakes are very high indeed.

Thus the journalist is squeezed between two equal and coincident needs: for co-operation from officials and for independence from them and access to alternative sources. The result is that journalists will make their own judgments about how to treat material to which they receive official access, and whether and how to use material gained by other means.[58]

One factor whose importance was universally discounted by the journalists we interviewed was the Official Secrets Act. None of them had been threatened with prosecution, and the view was expressed that the Act was not in any case aimed at them but at civil servants, in order to prevent leaks. Asked what sort of material they would themselves refuse to publish if it came their way, their examples would all have come within the 1989 Act, but that was not the reason for their reticence. Very striking was the fact that they were guided by their own sense of what should be suppressed. This varied among individuals, and their views should also be seen in the context of what was claimed to be the existence of an informal, media-wide agreement not to publish certain material relating to anti-terrorist operations and also to particular events such as a terrorist-related kidnapping. Such an agreement can be effective because there is a *quid pro quo*—journalists may be told of the existence of a surveillance operation on the understanding that nothing is to be written until the suspects are seized. They will then receive a detailed briefing before anyone is charged, thus permitting publication without violating the law of contempt of court.

The type of material most likely to induce self-restraint is anything that might put individuals at risk. One informant, for example, was very unhappy that some newspapers had published a picture of an SAS captive of the Iraqis during the Gulf War: he feared that the man's life had been put at risk of IRA retaliation. It is doubtful whether all journalists would have the same perception of risk in any given case, but there also seemed to be substantial agreement that anything which identified sources of information, and particularly any person who might be endangered, should not be published. This preoccupation strongly matched that of the officials we interviewed,[59] and accords with the attitude of the courts toward the protection of informers' identities in the context of criminal prosecutions.[60] This congruence of outlook should surprise no one except those who have led themselves to believe in a caricature of 'irresponsible' journalism.

[57] D. Leigh, *The Frontiers of Secrecy* (London, 1980), 55.
[58] Some of these are distinctly curious, and on more than one occasion have included receipt of lost or mislaid documents anonymously through the post or from fellow journalists who did not know what they were.
[59] Above, Ch. 4, p. 90.   [60] Below, Ch. 11.

The other notable area of abstention concerns what one person called the 'capabilities of the system', which has both organizational and technical dimensions. One reason given was that the latter particularly is quite boring and would be of little interest to most readers;[61] an example offered was the thickness and alloy composition of armour-plating on tanks. In any case there exist specialist journals like the American *Aviation Weekly* in which a 'staggering' amount of such detail appears—a fact which must cast serious doubt on the 'damage' publication of such information elsewhere would allegedly produce.[62] Finally, current operations undertaken in secret were cited as a major no-go area. One reason candidly admitted is that publication would be resented by those involved and would destroy the chances for co-operation on future stories. But at least as important is that journalists operate with their own concept of 'national security' in mind, and genuinely do not wish to endanger it. There is complete agreement on this point; but not on the boundaries of national security or what would constitute a threat to it in any particular instance.

Another tension to which journalists are subject is the conflict between accuracy and their own operational secrecy. Several stressed the paramount importance of 'getting it right', which requires cross-checking of information received. Thus if a journalist hears rumours or is told or shown something by a well-placed but definitely unofficial source, good practice would warrant checking with the only people able authoritatively to confirm or deny the story: the relevant service or ministry. However, the inquiry would alert officials to the leak and impending publication, allowing them to bring pressure either on the journalist or his editor—pressure which could and has ranged from informal suggestions, to a summons to a meeting with very senior people wanting to know the source, to, in an extreme case, threatened legal action. Such pressures could obviously be avoided by publication without checking, but that would risk both serious inaccuracy, which could harm one's reputation, and in some cases disclosure of material whose publication the journalist would accept was genuinely undesirable. One important protection from pressure is the power of their employer: politics, in the sense of the government's willingness to lock horns with a major newspaper or television company, rather than the technicalities of whether some law has been broken, is seen as the motive force determining how a particular incident is handled.

A journalist on a major newspaper will be able to consult one or more members of the company's legal staff. The experience, attitudes, and strategies of those interviewed were most illuminating. Official secrets legislation was seen as peripheral; of much greater concern was the possibility of civil injunctions, contempt of court, and 'Special Branch rampaging through the office looking for [unrelated] national security material'. Whilst insistent that they would not advise

---

[61] Anyone who has had to wade through the technical details of surveillance operations and equipment as lovingly detailed by Peter Wright in *Spycatcher* will no doubt take the point.

[62] Above, pp. 237–40.

breaking the law, they had exercised the lawyer's traditional craft and devised ingenious ways to bend it, sometimes markedly out of shape.

There is a striking parallel between the paramount concerns of security organizations and news organizations: the shared imperative is protection of sources. The Sarah Tisdall affair has plainly had a major impact. A court order forced the newspaper she had contacted to return the documents to the Ministry of Defence, which from markings on the photocopy was able to identify Miss Tisdall as the person who had leaked them.[63] The *Guardian* was much criticized at the time for not covering the trail, and the lesson has been learned: any document is either destroyed, leaving no record, or photocopies of photocopies are taken so as to make the original untraceable.

However, this does not absolve the journalist from the responsibility of verification, since professional hoaxers exist and a document may have been taken out of context.[64] We have noted the irony that the danger of legal action arises precisely when efforts at verification alert officialdom. A number of different tactics are therefore adopted. One is to treat any encounter between a minister or official and a journalist in which the former willingly reveals any information as carrying what may be called a 'presumption of authorization' for purposes of the Official Secrets Act, even if they are told something on a 'for background, not for quoting' basis. Any information freely and frankly given is treated as fair game, for the Act requires only that a person receiving information should not have 'reasonable cause to believe' it had been imparted without authorization: it does not lay down procedures for positive clearance.[65] This interpretation draws upon a well-worn working understanding of government–media relations long preceding the 1989 Act.

Documents cause much more difficulty. Ever since the *Granada Television* case[66] media lawyers have been alive to the possibility of a breach of confidence action seeking return of documents, and the 1989 Act also makes it an offence to disobey an 'official'—which means executive, not judicial—direction to return documents.[67] One tactic is to try to phrase verification inquiries so as to make it appear that the information has originated from a source other than a leaked

---

[63] See n. 6 above. Sarah Tisdall pleaded guilty and received a six-month prison sentence under s. 2 of the 1911 Act. The *Guardian* was not prosecuted, though it may have been equally liable under the Act as a recipient of the documents.

[64] Establishing the authenticity of a document is also essential to establishing the 'iniquity' defence to an action for breach of confidence (see *Initial Services Ltd* v. *Putterill*, [1968] 1 QB 396). Where the document alleges blameworthy conduct of individuals or business entities, determining authenticity is essential if a nasty defamation action is to be avoided.

[65] OSA 1989, s. 5(2). The test from the point of view of the official or minister is more rigorous, requiring the disclosure to be with 'lawful authority' and within the person's 'official duty': ss. 7(1) and (2).

[66] *British Steel Corpn.* v. *Granada Television Ltd.* [1981] AC 1096.

[67] OSA 1989, s. 8(4), (9). This provision appears to render unnecessary proceedings of the kind brought in the Tisdall case: in future a ministerial direction could be given for return of the document. There is no requirement that a prosecution be initiated afterwards.

document. Another is to try to arrange for return of the document after it has been used as the basis of a story.

Sunday papers are in a particularly vulnerable position in injunction proceedings, because of certain judicial practices. An injunction granted at 5.00 p.m. on a Friday, with a hearing set for Monday, will effectively keep a story out of the paper for nine days. And the judicial habit of granting *ex parte* injunctions, even over the telephone subject only to an undertaking by government lawyers to file a writ and appear subsequently for a full hearing after the defendant has received notice, has led to adoption of various strategies of concealment. One of the most effective, because it deprives the government of its usual time advantage, is to keep the story out of the first edition and run it in subsequent ones. The *Sunday Times* received sharp criticism for this in the House of Lords' final *Spycatcher* judgment,[68] without any acknowledgement of the procedural advantages the courts have allowed the government as plaintiff to enjoy.[69] Indeed the Spycatcher Affair was notable for the emergence of what became known as 'pyjama justice'—injunctions obtained *ex parte* from a High Court judge roused from bed.[70] This was done as part of the government's campaign to restrict publication by those not covered by the original injunctions.[71]

Finally, it is believed that quoting directly from a document is much more likely to bring official wrath on one's head, as the ministry will then press to retrieve it in order to trace the 'mole'. One ploy, therefore, in writing the story is to lay a false trail by avoiding direct quotation and still more to 'shade' it so as to give the appearance that it is based on more than one source. Journalists are also advised not to answer police questions in any leak inquiry, notwithstanding the perils that might arise under the ruling in the Jeremy Warner case.[72] Presumably other newspapers would follow the course of the *Independent* in that case and pay any fine imposed. The final point to emphasize is that a key aim is to avoid becoming subject to a judicial injunction, which the lawyers always advise journalists to obey.

To summarize, the national Press is in a relatively strong position *vis-à-vis* the government, in significant measure due to the political risks involved for any government which creates enemies among its editors.[73] Its large financial resources and legal expertise make it an even more formidable antagonist. Journalists, concerned mainly to obtain exclusives and maintain the secrecy of their sources, see the law as a reef to steer clear of, but it is by no means a

---

[68] [1990] 1 AC 109, 260 ('peculiarly sneaky methods', per Lord Keith).

[69] Sunday paper journalists face an additional dilemma: they have extra time for checking, but correspondingly find it very difficult to hold a scoop if anyone from the dailies is circling over the same territory.

[70] Hooper (n. 9 above), 336.   [71] See pp. 284–85 below.

[72] *Re an Inquiry under the Company Securities (Insider Dealing) Act 1985*, [1988] AC 660.

[73] An interesting and important empirical question, which we are in no position to answer, is whether adverse public reaction to invasions of personal privacy would result in diminished opposition to government attempts to curb press activity in relation to public information, or whether the two situations are seen as entirely distinct.

major preoccupation. Stories genuinely involving national security are relatively infrequent compared (to use the categories of the Official Secrets Act) with defence or international relations, and then journalists are mainly guided by their own sense of what is appropriate to suppress, which for some individuals may be quite a broad range of material.

Some of the tactics used to protect sources do nothing at all for the reliability and integrity of journalism. They are a regrettable adaptation to a political and, even more, legal environment which is always potentially, and intermittently actively, hostile. Yet they are necessary if newspapers are to inform the public accurately and critically, and be able to break the mental stranglehold of 'the official version'. That necessity arises ultimately from the refusal of both common law and Parliament to provide adequate protection for the secrecy and anonymity of journalists' sources and other forms of information.

The position of broadcasting journalists is rather different. Radio and television have always been subject to heavy informal pressure, formal regulation, or both.[74] The much-vaunted 'independence' of the BBC has some basis in reality, but equally its journalists have always been subject to serious restrictions. These have included the agreement with the government arrived at in its infancy, during the General Strike in 1926;[75] cuts or banning of programmes at the behest of their superiors (worried, among many other things, by threats to its financial life-blood, the licence fee); and intervention by the Board of Governors, perhaps at the prompting of ministers. For instance, in 1985 the BBC came under direct pressure from the Home Secretary, to which it temporarily acceded, not to screen a documentary in the '*Real Lives*' series which included interviews with IRA terrorists.[76] Subsequently, in Lord Lawson's candid phrase, the 'government leaned on' the BBC to ban the *Secret Society* series.[77] In extreme cases, as during the Suez crisis, there can be threats of direct control. Moreover, as was highlighted when the government imposed a ban on the broadcasting of direct spoken words uttered by members of various proscribed Northern Irish organizations and their political wings,[78] the BBC's Licence and Agreement[79] contains a provision empowering the Home Secretary to issue a direction forbidding the broadcasting of certain matters, or classes of matter.

Nor should it be assumed that pressure is always required. Broadcasting is also consciously used to advance national interests. At the one extreme this may, as with the BBC World Service, be done by making information about Britain, whether favourable or unfavourable, available on an international level. Hence

---

[74] For a sampling of a large literature, see A. Briggs, *Governing the BBC* (London, 1979), ch. 4; G. Wyndham-Goldie, *Facing the Nation: Television and Politics, 1936–76* (London, 1977); C. Munro, *Television, Censorship and the Law* (London, 1979); and T. Gibbons, *Regulating the Media* (London, 1991).

[75] See *Report of the Committee on the Future of Broadcasting*, Cmnd. 6783 (1977), para. 5.10.

[76] A. Milne, *DG: The Memoirs of a British Broadcaster* (London, 1988), ch. 12.

[77] See p. 254 above; N. Lawson, *The View From No. 11* (London, 1992), 314.

[78] Upheld in *R. v. Sec. of State for the Home Department, ex p. Brind* [1991] 1 AC 696

[79] Cmnd. 8233 (1981), cl. 13 (4).

the World Service's purpose is to 'target audiences overseas in accordance with objectives and requirements agreed between the World Service and the Foreign and Commonwealth Office'.[80] From its inception the purpose of the Service was rooted in propaganda,[81] although it retains full editorial independence over the content of broadcasts. It receives a grant from the Foreign Office, which in 1991/92 amounted to £143 million.[82] At the other extreme overseas broadcasting may be used deliberately to destabilize foreign regimes by stirring up domestic dissent, especially against governments operating repressive internal censorship of the media.[83]

Commercial television has been directly regulated under a statutory scheme since its inception, for most of its history under the Independent Broadcasting Authority (IBA) and now (under the new regime of the Broadcasting Act 1990), the Independent Television Commission (ITC). Thus a body with power to review and censor—that is, to demand alterations or forbid transmission of—programmes has always been in place, and its existence has provided a ready pressure point for ministers wishing both to suppress material and not to be seen to be denying freedom of expression. Within this regulatory scheme there is a degree of formal self-censorship: for instance, the ITC has published a Programme Code[84] which reminds licensees of the Official Secrets Act and the D Notice system and counsels referral to senior management of various matters connected with programmes concerning terrorism in Northern Ireland.[85] And of course the power of ministerial direction, unsuccessfully challenged in the *Brind* case, applies equally to commercial televsion.[86]

Within this framework, the Official Secrets Act looms little. In David Leigh's robust phrase, 'the Act is what the political situation at the moment says it is'. Another reason for the irrelevance of legal restraints from the working journalist's perspective is that key concepts remain open-ended. If 'national security' is left undefined, it should not be surprising that people act according to their own conceptions of reasonableness: the alternative is paralysis.

Mr Leigh had serious concerns about restrictions, but they originated elsewhere. The first was that, whilst the old IBA had at times hampered efforts to

---

[80] *5th Report of the Committee of Public Accounts, Management of the BBC World Service*, HC (1992–3), 108, para. 1.

[81] For a history, written by a former Managing Director of the Service see G. Mansell, *Let Truth be Told* (London, 1982).

[82] See n. 80 above, para. 2.

[83] In the Second World War this became institutionalized with the establishment of more than sixty 'black' radio stations organized under the Political Warfare Executive: A. Briggs, *The War of Words: the History of Broadcasting in the United Kingdom, Volume III* (Oxford, 1970), 417 ff. The Cold War saw broadcasting by supposedly independent Western radio stations to Eastern Europe; for a (mostly favourable) account see K. Short (ed.), *Western Broadcasting Over the Iron Curtain* (London, 1986).

[84] Made under the authority of the Broadcasting Act 1990, ss. 6, 7, and 9. The licence conditions for holding a television franchise require the Programme Code to be observed.

[85] *The ITC Programme Code* (London, 1991), sections 5.2 and 6.3.

[86] See now the Broadcasting Act 1990, s. 10.

inform the public—for example when it delayed transmission of the Massiter disclosures for a fortnight—it had served at other times as a protection against government pressure. 'The IBA was set up as a dog to bite us, but we learned to use it as a shield.' Mixed metaphor aside, this comment raises an important question about the future. In line with general government broadcasting policy the ITC is a light-touch regulator, less directly involved in programme review than was the IBA.[87] This may make it a less effective shield, allowing pressure to be applied directly to managers and owners of the regional company proposing to broadcast the programme. They will no longer be able to reply that the programme has been cleared by the IBA, to whom all representations should please be addressed.

The second problem is the new economics of broadcasting, or what Leigh called 'casualization'. Formerly the BBC and various ITV franchise holders employed most programme-makers directly. Thus they would continue to be paid even if they made a programme which was cut or suppressed by higher-ups for political reasons or as a result of legal advice. This job security was an important protection for those whose inquiries incurred official displeasure. Increasingly however programmes are made by independent production companies. These are much smaller, and in several ways are at a significant disadvantage when treading on controversial ground. First, the people involved are dependent on selling their programmes for their livelihood; moreover they may well need to recoup the capital invested in the finished programme in order to make the next. Tying up a major proportion of their limited capital for a possibly extended period whilst a broadcasting company deferred transmission or even a decision to purchase due to concern about legal action in event of transmission could be crippling. If they are not self-financing they may find potential investors wary for the same reason. The safe course is simply to steer well clear of any danger: institutional self-censorship in a new form.

The law also exerts an influence, though in economic guise. Unlike major companies, small production firms do not have in-house lawyers, and might be burdened with considerable expense for legal advice if they anticipated or encountered problems whilst making the programme. Perhaps most daunting would be the legal costs of defending an action, civil or criminal, brought by the government. The broadcasting organization might be willing to meet these expenses from its much deeper pocket,[88] but there is no certainty of that and certainly no legal duty to do so. Finally, the financial structure of the new broadcasting regime has been widely predicted to increase the economic pressure for mass audience programmes, which tends to exclude current affairs generally. Thus although it is far too early to speak with confidence, television may be less willing in future to take on subjects likely to lead to legal confrontation with

---

[87] See *Broadcasting in the '90's: Competition, Choice and Quality*, Cm. 517 (1988).
[88] As Channel 4 did for the production company in the RUC case, above p. 255.

government. This reluctance may be compounded by the fact that the the BBC is scheduled for licence renewal in 1996.

PRIOR RESTRAINTS

Apart from the forms of self-censorship already discussed, the most effective controls are those which prevent stories ever being published in the first place. These can be informal mechanisms for co-operative censorship—like the D Notice system and the arrangements which have operated in the recent Falklands and Gulf wars—or may take the form of court-centred processes such as injunctions to restrain breach of confidence and the closely related use of contempt. In the discussion which follows we move from the informal to the formal. The two are closely related, partly in the sense that legal processes are like the visible part of an iceberg, but also sequentially: resort to legal restraint represents a failure behind the scenes to suppress publication invisibly. Nor is this a one-way effect. Since there is a continuous pattern of contact between press and government, resort to litigation may detract from informal and voluntary co-operation.

D Notices[89]

A minor but noteworthy part of the apparatus of controls on publication of security-related information is the D (for Defence) Notice system.[90] Created in 1912, it operated behind the scenes under government domination to ensure curbing of publication of 'sensitive' material. It achieved notoriety in the 1960s when, for the first time, it was publicly flouted. That episode, which disabused many editors of the assumption that participation would effectively protect them from trouble with the official secrets legislation, led to the decline of the system.[91] However, it remains in the background of decision-making in this area.

---

[89] Following a revision announced in July 1993 these are officially DA Notices. We are grateful to Admiral Pulvertaft (the present DA Notice Secretary) and his deputy, Commander Ponsonby, for dealing with our requests for details of the review. On grounds of familiarity we have retained the old terminology to describe the Notices and the Secretary in the discussion which follows. See generally *The Defence Advisory Notices: A Review of the D Notice System*, MOD Open Government Document No. 93/06.

[90] The official account of the system (now dated) can be found in: *Security Procedures in the Public Service*, Cmnd. 1681 (1962), ch. 9. For other accounts, see D. Fairley, 'D Notices, Official Secrets and the Law' (1990) 10 *Ox. JLS* 430; G. Robertson (n. 11 above), 158–63; A. Palmer, 'The History of the D Notice Committee', in C. Andrew and D. Dilks, *The Missing Dimension: Governments and Intelligence Communities in the Twentieth Century* (London, 1984); J. Jaconelli, 'The "D" Notice System' [1982] *PL* 37; and the useful notes in Bailey *et al.* (n. 11 above), 430–5.

[91] The so-called 'D Notice Affair' grew out of a report by Chapman Pincher in the *Daily Express* that the government was routinely reading private cables and telegrams. The Prime Minister, Harold Wilson, furiously claimed that two D Notices had been violated, but the Committee of Privy

The key characteristics of the D Notice system are its lack of compulsion and its extra-legal status. To an extent it is a relic of the culture of informality, personal contacts, and shared outlook which dominated Whitehall's relations with the media in an earlier time.[92] Palmer[93] likens the co-option of patriotic newspaper proprietors into the pre-Great War system of voluntary censorship to the prefect system in a public school. If the origins of the D Notice Committee lie in the golden Edwardian period, its modern composition and practice dates from the dawn of the Atomic age. The system of issuing *notices* advising the press of matters to which they should not refer was a First World War creation.[94] Between the wars the Committee had so fallen into disuse (it did not meet after 1923) that two of the three Services had evidently forgotten its existence.[95] When the Committee was reconstituted in 1946 it was a direct continuation of the system of wartime censorship: the first Secretary, Admiral Thomson, had been Chief Press Censor during the war. The Press was by then used to working within a system of legal restraint and this, coupled with the expansiveness of the Official Secrets Act, gave the 'voluntary' arrangement a harder edge, offset only by the liberality with which successive Secretaries from Thomson onwards have interpreted their role.

This ambivalence between fear of legal sanctions and co-operative participation has bedevilled the D Notice system ever since. In 1992 the government announced a review of the system, which has produced largely cosmetic change.[96] The important question for the future is whether the system has outlived its usefulness, or can it in a sense be turned on its head and adapted to fill a role that assists development of democratic practice.

Formally, the system is run by the Defence Press and Broadcasting Advisory Committee (DPBAC), co-chaired in 1993 by the Permanent Under-Secretary in the Ministry of Defence and a senior (retired) journalist. Of the fifteen members, only four are government officials; the others all occupy senior positions in print and television media. What is noteworthy about the membership is that

Councillors' Report (Cmnd. 3309, 1967) disagreed. The revised arrangments (see Cmnd. 3312, 1967) made clear that what had been understood as 'clearance' by the Secretary to the Committee could not confer immunity from prosecution. It is very difficult to understand why the affair raised so much fuss until it is appreciated that the vetting of cable transmissions was undertaken by GCHQ, whose existence was not publicly acknowledged for another fifteen years. The government's obsession with the continued secrecy of this body explains its heated response.

[92] p. 260 above. This system of informal contact is not, however, unique: Australia possesses an equivalent system (M. Armstrong *et al.*, *Media Law in Australia* (2nd. edn., Melbourne, 1988), 197) and Israel has an Editors' Committee which polices a voluntary self-censorship system in parallel to the legal military censor (Z. Segal, 'Security Censorship: Prior Restraint (After the Schnitzer Decision)', in S. Shetreet (ed.), *Free Speech and National Security* (Dordrecht, 1991), 218–20).

[93] See n. 90 above, 227–34.   [94] Ibid. 236.   [95] Ibid. 239–40.

[96] See n. 89 above. The number of notices was reduced from eight to six (with the omission of those dealing with War Precautions and Civil Defence and Photography, etc. of Defence Establishments and Installations). However, the wording has also been rationalized. The main changes of substance appear to be the liberation of discussion on civil defence matters and on non-classified details of conventional weapons.

the distance in outlook between journalists and these media elder statesmen and women may be greater than that between the two sides of the Committee. The Committee meets infrequently—normally only twice a year. Its functions include receiving reports from the Secretary, approving the text of D Notices, and discussing proposals for its own reform. The first is the normal business, the second and third are infrequent. Both sides of the Committee agree the appointment of the key figure, who is the Secretary, the only person who occupies himself with the issues on what he estimated to be a 'three-quarter time' basis. In May 1991 the post was held by Rear-Admiral W. A. Higgins; all of the otherwise unattributed information in this section derives from an interview with him.[97]

Most Secretaries have been naval officers, a tradition which seems have begun during the last war and then solidified when Rear-Admiral Denning, younger brother of the Master of the Rolls, was brought in following the 'D Notice Affair' in the mid-1960s.[98] All have reached the end of their active careers, and in senior positions; and both characteristics are important. Admiral Higgins identified the three requirements for the post as including: (1) knowledge of how Whitehall works; (2) sufficient seniority to ring up and speak on terms of equality with senior editors and civil servants;, and (3) being a retired person and therefore not susceptible to pressure. The appointment lasts for five years and can be extended, and he suggested that, despite lack of any contractual guarantee, the appointee could not be dismissed because of the media outcry that would follow.

The critical factor is the independence of the Secretary, who should act as the servant of the Committee, rather than as a government official, though the government pays his salary. Admiral Higgins saw his role as that of 'honest broker' between the media and government, though that must be somewhat compromised by the fact that the Secretary is responsible for drafting answers to parliamentary questions about D Notices. Nevertheless the Secretary has an important part to play in educating government departments in the legitimacy of press concerns, and this extends to refusing to advance unrealistic or unreasonable requests for the maintenance of secrecy. A sense of fairness and absolute confidentiality between competing organs of the press is also necessary: since a suppressed or lost 'scoop' means lost circulation from the media perspective. The Secretary both responds to requests for advice and operates pro-actively, in the sense of looking out for material that he might think would fall within the subject matter of a Notice. Books take the most time; some are received from cautious publishers (at times without their author's knowledge); others are requested after reading announcements of impending publication.

Following parliamentary criticism,[99] the Notices were rewritten and are no

---

[97] In Nov. 1992, Rear-Adm. Higgins retired and was replaced by Rear-Adm. D. M. Pulvertaft.
[98] See n. 91 above.
[99] *Third Report of the Defence Committee, Sess. 1979–80, 'The D Notice System'*, HC 773 (1980); see also *Fourth Report 1982–83, 'Previous Recommendations of the Committee'*, HC 55 (1983), detailing the DPBAC's response.

longer classified 'confidential'. There are currently six, and they are short—none exceeds one page. Given the admittedly contestable assumption that the country benefits from all components of the military machine it has created, most of the material covered by them is of the sort that requires secrecy for reasons of effectiveness. Examples in various Notices include photography and filming of military establishments;[100] codes and ciphers used by British or NATO forces; technical details about electromagnetic or electro-optical transmissions used by British defence forces; and design details, technical specifications, and similar information about military equipment.

However the Notices go much further, and cover material which, whilst seemingly of a similar charcter, would in some realistically conceivable circumstances become important to public debate. For example, the Non-Nuclear Weapon and Operational Equipment Notice (No. 2) covers performance figures and operational capabilities which may become essential public information if the government chooses to buy a particular weapon which knowledgeable critics claim is technically unreliable, or continues to produce a weapon after experts here or abroad discover design flaws.[101] Similarly No. 3, on Nuclear Weapons and Equipment, whilst covering a number of matters whose suppression is likely to help prevent proliferation, also includes detailed information on transport and movements of weapons and fissile material (presumably to make terrorism or sabotage more difficult). Yet for many years anti-nuclear groups have made credible allegations about the safety hazards to ordinary citizens from the transport of nuclear weapons round the country, and inadequacy of precautions. Such information is therefore of the gravest public interest. Other examples could be offered; and if anything of the System is to be salvaged, the Notices would need to be cut back somewhat.

Lacking any legal powers, the Secretary relies on his 'credibility' with both civil servants and editors,[102] which in his view is dependent upon maintaining his independence, thus ensuring that his advice is respected as honest judgment.[103] An episode which illustrates the simultaneous strengths and weaknesses of the system occurred during the Gulf War. A naval officer, travelling in a official car, was carrying a lap-top computer containing details of plans for impending military operations. Exhibiting a touching faith in the honesty of his fellow citizens, he left the car near a showroom in West London, and went shopping for one of his own. On his return he discovered that the computer had gone.

[100] Approving the flight plans of commercial aerial photographers occupies a sizeable proportion of the Secretary's time.

[101] There are several well-documented examples, going back to the 1950s and early 1960s when the much-hyped Blue Streak and Skybolt missiles were cancelled, along with a number of other projects. See A. Cox and S. Kirby, *Congress, Parliament and Defence* (Basingstoke, 1986), 214–16.

[102] He does not talk directly to journalists, both because the final decision on publication rests with the editor, and because he does not trust them not to quote him!

[103] In terms of formal procedure, the Secretary's role is to advise that certain matters be deleted or suppressed. Therefore when he has no objection, the quaint formulation for an OK is: 'I have no advice to offer'.

No one had any idea who the thief was, and the probability was high that the latter had no idea of what was contained in the computer's memory. Admiral Higgins spent an agitated weekend phoning round, and succeeded in gaining universal agreement among media outlets to suppress any report of the incident, in the hope that the Iraqis would remain unaware that this militarily vital information might be purchasable. In these circumstances self-censorship seems both proper and far more effectively organized through voluntary co-operation based on reasoned explanation and persuasion rather than governmental or judicial fiat. It is also more fragile, as the sequel demonstrated: when an Irish newspaper broke the story, several papers took the view that silence was no longer necessary and moved swiftly to publish details.

In a curious way, the military background of the Secretary may favour freedom of publication. Certainly Admiral Higgins displayed a deeply sceptical attitude to claims that national security required suppression of certain materials. He clearly saw himself as a force for openness, reckoned that only seldom did he come across something genuinely affecting national security, and was extremely caustic about how the government seemed to understand it: 'anything that offends Mrs Thatcher.' A lifetime's familiarity with the pomposities of Whitehall and service bureaucracy, laced with a certain suspicion of politicians' motives, may be as good a background as any for the job. It certainly should produce a more knowledgeable approach to what may be genuinely regarded as a national security issue than a quarter-century at the Bar, and may also give the incumbent the confidence to reject executive assertions about alleged perils. It is this aspect of the Secretary's role that could prove useful, for as Bingham LJ admitted, in a judgment otherwise noteworthy for its liberal approach, the courts are virtually bound to accept the government's assertion that national security requires suppression of a particular document.[104]

At one time the phrase 'to slap a D Notice' on a proposed publication was much used. This is quite misleading.[105] D Notices are not slapped, nor are their recipients if they do not defer to what is no more than advice. Many books have been published in deliberate contravention of D Notices as a matter of principle, with no adverse consequences in either civil or criminal law. And even consultation and an 'I have no advice to offer' response will not necessarily help the recipient in other forums.[106] This became most unpleasantly clear when the government moved to suppress the radio series *My Country Right or Wrong*. Not only was the BBC Controller of Editorial Policy (himself a member of the then DPBAC) told that 'my reassurance is as nearly complete as it can be on the

---

[104] *A-G* v. *Guardian Newspapers Ltd* (*No. 2*), [1988] 3 All ER, 545, 628.

[105] However, the possibility of *ad hoc* DA Notices (agreed with the Committee) is specifically reserved (n. 89 above), 'How the System Works', para. 10.

[106] This formula seems to have been adopted after the Aitken affair in 1971 where a journalist was prosecuted, notwithstanding the previous clearance of the story by the Secretary, Adm. Denning: Palmer (n. 90 above), 243.

non-prejudicial nature of the programme',[107] but Admiral Higgins was scheduled to participate himself. This did not stop the government[108] from seeking an injunction, nor a judge from summarily granting one, without sight of any transcript of what was to be said.[109] Nor did consultation with the Secretary save Scottish newspapers a lengthy trip through the legal labyrinth.[110] The Secretary has not played a role in any proceedings under the Official Secrets Act 1989, but Admiral Higgins was quite prepared to contemplate the possibility of being called as a witness by the defence, especially if he had given—or more accurately, not given—advice.[111]

One possibilty for reform of the system, which can be considered and rejected quite shortly, is that offered judicially in the *Spycatcher* litigation. In Lord Donaldson's view the Home Secretary should have power 'to issue instructions equivalent to a D notice, but having the force of an *ex parte* injunction, the media being entitled to appeal to the courts or to some special tribunal to have it set aside or modified, the proceedings necessarily being held *in camera*.'[112] Quite apart from its breathtakingly naïve trust in ministers, contempt for the role of the Press, and marginalization of the courts, this proposal bears so little resemblance to the existing system that it could only be described as a reform in the same sense that abolition would be. It is far from clear why the press would wish to play any part in a procedure where D Notices substituted for injunctions.

If the D Notice apparatus has no power to suppress, and no power to immunize from civil or criminal proceedings, does it serve any useful purpose? Abolition should be seriously considered. The partial loyalty of the media to the D Notice system is its weakest link: with significant non-participating outlets (especially the international Press), it can never hope to do more than delay the publication of stories in which there is any sustained international interest. Nevertheless, as the 1993 review shows, the government has clung on to it like a child to a 'security blanket'—comfortable and familiar, if slightly embarrassing and outgrown.

Not surprisingly, a survey of editors revealed that whilst most of those responding participated in the system, the overwhelming majority said they

---

[107] Quoted in Fairley (n. 90 above) at 435.

[108] In Adm. Higgins's view, this decision had to have been taken by Ministers, particularly the Attorney-General, and possibly the Treasury Solicitor, since all his discussions about the matter had been with senior officials, none of whom had objected.

[109] *A-G* v. *BBC, The Times*, 5 and 18 Dec. 1987. The result was to force the BBC to let the government vet the tapes, delaying transmission of the programme, apparently without alteration, for six months. See Robertson (above n. 90), 257.

[110] Fairley (n. 90 above), 436, on the litigation arising out of the serialization of Anthony Cavendish's *Inside Intelligence*, which the government lost at several judicial levels culminating in the Lords: *Lord Advocate* v. *Scotsman Publications Ltd.*, [1989] 3 WLR 358.

[111] See n. 103 above; the presence of the Secretary as a defence witness would no doubt impress any jury considering whether a particular disclosure had been damaging: see Ch. 9 above.

[112] *A-G* v. *Guardian Newspapers (No. 2)* [1990] 1 AC 109, 200.

would follow the advice of their lawyers rather than the Secretary.[113] (Unfortunately the survey did not, and probably could not, have discovered whether the lawyers' advice led in the main to greater or lesser timidity.) One possible function is that of offering informed and independent advice to editors and publishers, with the six Notices constituting a sort of code of practice. However if that is all that can be expected of the system it will probably, as Admiral Higgins suggested, 'trickle into the sand—until a crisis comes'.

The other possibility is to make use of the office of the Secretary as a shield for publication. Its attraction is that its occupant should be expert, apolitical, independent, and enjoy the respect of editors and officials—a combination that cannot be claimed for the judiciary, and certainly not by the government. He should remain entirely without power to restrain publication. Nor, whatever the formal legal position may be, should consultation become in any practical sense a requirement or form of self-protection; in particular, failure to seek or accept advice should not be regarded as relevant to civil or criminal liability. However, much as receipt of a certificate from the (non-statutory) British Board of Film Certification[114] serves, as a matter of prosecutorial discretion, to protect film distributors and exhibitors against prosecution under the obscenity legislation, so should receipt of a 'no-advice' comment from the Secretary be treated by the Attorney-General as a *de facto* bar to criminal prosecution under the Official Secrets Act,[115] and by the courts as powerful, though not formally conclusive, evidence *against* any claim that publication of a particular item would damage national security. It is, after all, virtually the only knowledgeable and disinterested opinion a defendant is likely to be able to muster in such cases.

To those opposed as a matter of principle to censorship in any form, a proposal to maintain the D Notice machinery at all might seem objectionable.[116] However, the reality is that editors fearing legal complications will take advice from someone, and counsel are frequently inexpert and not notably bold in these matters. The Secretary should be seen as a force for openness rather than the opposite, an effect the continued absence of power to suppress should reinforce. Indeed one concern comes from a quite different direction: any effort to use the Secretary's office in this way might lead the government to try to secure the appointment of a more 'reliable' person. However, so long as the DPBAC continues to make the appointment and the Press representatives remain in the majority, the problem should not arise.

---

[113] Fairley (n. 90 above), 438.

[114] The Board does have statutory functions in relation to videos under the Video Recordings Act 1984, but that is not the case with its long-standing function of issuing recommendations concerning films.

[115] The Attorney-General's consent is required for virtually all prosecutions under the Act: OSA 1989, s. 9(1).

[116] The Labour minority on the Defence Select Committee (above n. 99) opted for a strange compromise: abolition of the System with responsibility for the Notices placed on government departments. This seems likely to lead to increased attempts at suppression rather than the reverse.

Whereas the D notice system operates through *ad hoc* inquiries to the Secretary in a relatively informal fashion, more structured and detailed arrangements for government–Press relations have been adopted in times of war. These provide in effect a case study of government–media relations over defence and security information.

War Reporting[117]

The reporting of intended or actual military conflict raises acute problems for the independent function of the Press. The mutually opposed considerations are strong ones. Public preoccupation with the news in times of danger is heightened and lives may be at risk from premature disclosure of battle intentions or operations. In essence the problem is one ever-present in journalistic coverage: that reporting may itself become a decisive factor shaping the events that are themselves ostensibly merely 'recorded'. This can happen in two ways. Premature release of information may allow a military adversary to obtain an advantage which would not have otherwise been enjoyed: press coverage giving advance warning of attack, or details of the whereabouts or strength, capabilities or losses of military units may supplement information available from other intelligence sources. Conversely the authorities, in full knowledge of this potential, may attempt to compromise the media by using them as a source of disinformation[118]—to mislead an adversary into taking ineffective or unnecessary action, for instance, to commit defensive forces in the wrong location.

There is another, more fundamental, problem. Conventional analyses of the media stress, as we have earlier, its high-minded functions of information gathering and constitutional responsibility. But in truth any newspaper is a mixture of news and much else besides—in the case of some tabloids much confusion arises from applying the term 'newspaper' to what are (and are intended to be) primarily sources of entertainment.[119] This line between news and entertainment is frequently blurred, and in times of national danger the line between informing the public and making it feel better is apt to come under great stress. Critical reporting is seen as having the potential adversely to affect public and military morale, a commodity of strategic importance in its own right. Conversely, poor

---

[117] See generally D. Mercer *et al.*, *The Fog of War* (London, 1987); P. Knightley, *The First Casualty* (London, 1975).

[118] The Defence Select Committee found that allegations of such conduct during the Falklands campaign were partly well founded: *First Report from the Defence Committee, The Handling of the Press and Public During the Falklands War* (1982–3), HC 17, para. 101. However, the Committee found that the incident (a deliberate attempt by the Permanent Secretary to mislead journalists in advance of the San Carlos landings) was justifiable on military grounds. Overall the report concluded that there could be sound military reasons both for withholding the truth and putting out misinformation: ibid., para. 27.

[119] In television and radio the distinction is fairly clear-cut between the two, because news coverage is part of a wider public service ethos and is anyway heavily regulated to ensure accuracy and independence. 'Quality' newspapers make the distiction by consciously subdividing their output.

military morale may itself be newsworthy. In so far as military action is under democratic control, negative reporting may also shape the political conduct of operations. The most common allegation of this kind concerns the reporting of the Vietnam War, which is said to have decisively influenced American public opinion against the war.[120]

The line between independence and patriotism is particularly hard to walk for a broadcasting corporation like the BBC, financed by taxpayers' money. However the burdens are to some degree eased by the competitive framework of modern broadcasting, and by its growing internationalism. Whereas during the Second World War the BBC had a national role to play in supporting morale and the war effort—indeed it was part of the war effort—its role in conflicts since then has been very different. The difference emerged prominently at the time of the Suez crisis in 1956 when the strains between the government and the BBC became so acute that Eden came close to exercising the government's powers of direction to take over the Corporation. [121] There were several sources of controversy, but each can be traced back to a difference in outlook on the function of the Corporation: the government had expected the Corporation to rally support behind the campaign, whereas the Corporation considered its duty was to maintain impartiality in the light of domestic conflict over the policy. When the Labour leader Hugh Gaitskell was granted a right of reply to a ministerial broadcast on the crisis, and used it among other things to incite disaffected Conservatives to remove Eden, the BBC's newly adopted policy of political impartiality came under criticism. When the Corporation refused to censor this broadcast before transmitting it in Arabic on the External Service, the Foreign Office responded with a proposed cut in grant as punishment and by installing a civil servant in Bush House to vet future Arabic broadcasts. The government maintained that to report political dissent in Britain gave comfort to Egyptian morale. The BBC governors, on the other hand, refused to differentiate between the versions of news broadcast for domestic and foreign consumption.

Similarly during the Falklands War the BBC came under criticism for being insufficiently pro-British in its reporting. Among incidents which particularly drew the fire of parliamentarians (supported in less strident terms by Mrs Thatcher) were a *Panorama* documentary which featured interviews with MPs opposed to the government's policy, and news items from Argentina showing the effect of battle fatalities. One news report was suggested to have contributed to British losses by warning the Argentinians of an imminent attack by the Paratroop Regiment on Goose Green, although the Defence Committee later put the confusion between the Ministry of Defence and the BBC down to 'the fog of war' rather than a clear breach of security.[122] Among the attempts to

---

[120] See L. Thompson, 'The Press and the Pentagon: Old Battles, New Skirmishes' (1992) 3 *The American Enterprise* 14, 16.

[121] Briggs, (n. 74 above), 209–17.　　　　　　　　　　[122] See n. 118 above, para. 73.

bring pressure upon the Corporation was a hostile meeting between BBC executives and 120 back-bench Conservative MPs.[123]

Technological change has made an enormous impact not only on war reporting but also on the form of control of it. The change can be illustrated by comparing the Falklands War with the Gulf War. During the Falklands conflict press access to the battlefield was effectively under military control, because of the distances and the type of conflict involved.[124] Censorship of reports took place both in the field and by the Ministry of Defence,[125] although on occasion substantive disagreement over what could be safely broadcast or printed caused confusion.[126] During the Gulf War on the other hand, although the military authorities could control access to active service units, unimpeded access was enjoyed to other places. Advances in satellite broadcasting allowed for direct transmission of television news from the war zone, sometimes live, as with the coverage by a CNN news team of the bombing of Baghdad. Faced with technology of this kind the allied response was to adopt a system of field censorship, abandoning altogether central dictation. The international nature of the media coverage (especially by American networks) also made it impossible to manage news to the same degree as during the Falklands War.

During the Gulf War[127] reporters were issued with detailed Ground Rules about what could and could not be reported without consultation. A limited number of reporters was allowed to accompany active service units (these were Media Pools or Media Response Teams) on condition that they submitted to field censorship. In addition editors were issued with a document, Guidance to Editors, encouraging consultation with the Ministry of Defence before printing stories on a number of topics (other than where officially released) including operational details, equipment capabilities, military losses, details of military command and control structures and communications, and details about the enemy operations which might supplement its own intelligence. This system effectively supplanted the D Notice system for the duration. The experience of the journalists involved was mixed.[128] There was some hostility to the Pool system of privileged access; many journalists operated as unilaterals outside the pool. Field censorship was felt on the whole not to have been unduly intrusive or cumbersome since it was normally restricted to genuine operational matters. The one exception, however, was the insistence (on instruction from the Foreign Office) that details of chaplains and religious services be omitted to avoid embarrass-

---

[123] For an account by the then Director-General of the BBC, see Milne (n. 76 above), ch. 7.

[124] Some television footage of the war took more than three weeks to be transported via Ascension Island to London for broadcasting.

[125] For an example of censorship to a press dispatch see Defence Committee (n. 118 above), 201 ff.

[126] Ibid. para. 91.

[127] We are grateful to the MOD for supplying us with copies of the Guidance and Ground Rules.

[128] See *Reporting the War: A Collection of Experiences and Reflections on the Gulf*, Discussion Paper published by the British Executive of the International Press Institute (1991).

ment with the Arab coalition partners. There was no censorship of the tone and taste of reports: journalists were permitted to mix with troops and freely report their reactions in their own words. Journalists with field units were given free access to briefings and hence advance details of the campaign plan, notwithstanding that the plan involved a conscious attempt to deceive the Iraqis; this required that discretion be exercised over reports of locations of units, for instance, but not that the media should be used for disinformation purposes. The journalists' main complaint was perhaps the absence of briefing about certain matters—for instance assessments of Iraqi casualties—rather than deliberate censorship.

Overall control of reporting during actual military conflict is significantly more justified than the other forms of restraint and censorship discussed in this chapter. We have no difficulty in ranking protection of the lives of service personnel as a higher goal than speedy public access to news. An approach of this kind would justify restrictions, but within limits. It would support news blackouts pending an imminent offensive, but not using the media to spread disinformation. Nor would it justify continuing suppression of information of political significance about the conduct of a war, although publication of such details might be delayed for military considerations. The line between these concerns is obviously not clear-cut and borderline issues are most likely to arise where there is an extended war, especially if it is seen to be going badly. The recent confrontations in the Falklands and the Gulf were too short to raise serious difficulties and the controls adopted were on the whole justifiable.

Spycatcher, *Breach of Confidence, and Contempt*

The other most recent and prolific use of prior restraints has been through the legal action to suppress alleged breaches of confidence. Here we turn to the use of legal sanctions. It is not our intention to add needlessly to the forest of trees already felled in writing about the remarkable *Spycatcher* litigation which began in 1986 and in 1993 is still not finally concluded.[129] The account here will therefore focus on the significant aspects of the litigation for Press freedom.[130] Other aspects, mainly of interest to students of the psychological disorder of obsessive litigation, and/or to equity lawyers, will be given less prominence.

The litigation in Britain[131] began when the government obtained interim injunctions in July 1986 to prevent the *Guardian* and the *Observer* publishing

---

[129] Aspects relating to actions brought against the *Sunday Times* are the subject of outstanding complaints under the machinery of the European Convention on Human Rights.

[130] For fuller treatments see Ewing and Gearty (n. 20 above), ch. 5; Bailey *et al.* (n. 11 above), 435–51; D. Feldman, *Civil Liberties and Human Rights in England and Wales* (Oxford, 1993), 648–88.

[131] This paragraph is not intended as a comprehensive chronology: see Bailey *et al.* (n. 11 above), 435–7; for an insider's account, see D. Pannick, 'Spycatcher: Two Years of Legal Indignations' in D. Kingsford-Smith and D. Oliver (eds.), *Economical with the Truth: The Law and Media in a Democratic Society* (Oxford, 1990).

allegations derived from the former MI5 officer, Peter Wright, the publication of whose memoirs the government was attempting to suppress through civil proceedings in the Australian courts. As the Australian proceedings attracted increasing Press attention across the world and were discussed in Parliament, the Court of Appeal affirmed these injunctions in a slightly relaxed form. Elements of the British Press began to chafe under the restriction, and sought to republish the allegations, only to be met by the government with proceedings which resulted in a novel extension of the law of contempt.[132] In the meantime the entire book was published in the United States (shortly preceded by a defiant act of publishing the first episode of an intended serialization in the *Sunday Times*)[133] and became freely available, even in Britain. Despite this turn of events, in the summer of 1987 a bitterly divided Judicial Committee of the House of Lords not only affirmed but also extended the injunctions binding the Press.[134] Meanwhile the government had lost its proceedings in the Australian courts. When the British action for a permanent injunction began in autumn of that year it was refused first by Scott J in the High Court, then by a majority of the Court of Appeal, and finally, in summer 1988, by a majority of the House of Lords.[135] At this point the British press finally became free to publish allegations from *Spycatcher*. As a sequel, in 1991 the European Court of Human Rights held that the continuation of the interim injunctions after the publication of the book in the United States until their discharge in 1988 had contravened Article 10 of the Convention.[136]

The government's reliance upon the private law action of breach of confidence to restrain publication grew out of a combination of technical legal advantage and political calculation, which converged neatly in the *Spycatcher* case. It is one of the very few means by which it is possible to impose a prior restraint, a vital pre-condition for protecting a secret.[137] Moreover, the use of civil proceedings had the by no means incidental bonus for the government of enabling it to bring its actions solely before judges: after the Ponting acquittal it avoided any further potential embarrassment that an encounter with a jury might have brought.[138] This reluctance was no doubt reinforced by the fact that although the principal actor, Peter Wright, was beyond the reach of the criminal courts, his publishers and the newspapers which serialized extracts were not.[139] Not

---

[132] See pp. 282–85 below .   [133] See p. 265 above.

[134] *A-G* v. *Guardian Newspapers* [1987] 1 WLR 1248.

[135] *A-G* v. *Guardian Newspapers* (*No. 2*) [1990] 1 AC 109.

[136] *Sunday Times* v. *UK* (*No. 2*) (1991) 14 EHRR 229; *The Guardian and The Observer* v. *UK* (1991) 14 EHRR 53.

[137] Another, which arises under the High Court's traditional wardship jurisdiction and is used to protect the anonymity of children, was cited in the judgment of Balcombe LJ in the third party contempt cases, nn. 148 and 150 below.

[138] Neither Cathy Massiter nor Anthony Cavendish were prosecuted, although the attempt to suppress the latter's book went all the way up to the Lords in *Lord Advocate* v. *Scotsman Publications* (n. 110 above).

[139] Criminal action against these parties might have been possible after the event under the then

even a government headed by Margaret Thatcher was prepared for the political blood-letting such a prosecution would have occasioned.[140]

Breach of confidence was a tactically well-chosen means to raise the arguments for secrecy, because it enabled the government to avoid having to rely on the suspect argument that judicial suppression was necessary to prevent publication in order to protect national security.[141] To bring a successful breach of confidence action it was necessary to make the lesser showing that the information in question was confidential, that those against whom the actions were brought (the newspapers) were under an obligation to keep the confidence, and that there were no overriding reasons favouring disclosure. These questions were approached in a different manner by the courts on the applications for interim and permanent injunctions, and the whole issue was further complicated by the (ultimately decisive) question of the publication of the book in the United States while the proceedings were in progress.

The first link in the chain of confidence was the obligation owed by Peter Wright as a former member of the Security Service, which the courts held was part of a lifelong vow of silence to be imposed on all members of the security and intelligence services.[142] In this the judges slightly anticipated the similar duty imposed under the criminal law in section 1 of the Official Secrets Act 1989. The obligation of confidence was capable of binding persons who derived the information from Wright, but whether they would be restrained from publication was more variable according to the circumstances.

The question of when the courts would act to restrain publication proved fundamental. Here the form of proceedings taken was significant, since an injunction is a legal remedy which is only available on equitable principles, and these are sufficiently flexible to act as a vehicle for debate of the important policy questions raised by the cases. The courts held ultimately that where the government as a litigant requested an injunction to restrain a breach of confidence it was in a different position to that of an analogous private litigant. The government was only entitled to an injunction where this could be shown to be in the public interest,[143] since by definition the government could only be asserting

OSA 1911, s. 2; however, publication could only have been restrained if the courts had been prepared to grant an injunction to restrain an anticipated breach of the criminal law, something which they have been very reluctant to do, especially without a previous pattern of illegality.

[140] Cf. pp. 251–52 above.

[141] In the *Scotsman* case (n. 110), the Lord Advocate originally attempted to run this argument, but explicitly disclaimed it by the time the case reached the House of Lords.

[142] See n. 135 above.

[143] Applying *A-G* v. *Jonathan Cape Ltd.* [1976] QB 752; and see *Commonwealth of Australia* v. *John Fairfax and Sons Ltd.* (1980) 147 CLR 39, 51–2 (per Mason J), contrasting the private law origins of the equitable doctrine with the application of the doctrine in protecting government information: 'It is unacceptable, in our democratic society, that there should be a restraint on the publication of information relating to government when the only vice of that information is that it enables the public to discuss, review and criticize government action. Accordingly, the court will determine the government's claim to confidentiality by reference to the public interest. Unless disclosure is likely to injure the public interest, it will not be protected.'

rights held on behalf of the whole community. The concept of 'public interest' was broad enough to embrace both the need for limiting disclosures about the Security Service and the arguments favouring Press freedom. As Feldman comments, this 'places the public interest in open government in a democracy at the centre of any consideration of any governmental claim to confidentiality'.[144]

The effect of the publication of the book in the United States was to destroy the justification for further restraint of the newspapers on grounds of confidentiality. This was recognized by the British courts somewhat late in the day. Lords Bridge and Oliver took the point forcefully in their dissenting speeches when the application for the interim injunctions reached the House of Lords in 1987,[145] but the majority were plainly dismayed that the capacity of the courts to pronounce upon the issues could be so easily evaded, for the effect would have been to render the proceedings for a permanent injunction meaningless: a secret once released can never be recaptured. When the case for the permanent injunctions was heard the following year they revised their view.

It was the delay in lifting the injunctions that the European Court of Human Rights criticized in finding that Article 10 of the Convention had been breached,[146] since although prescribed by law, they were not necessary in a democratic society for maintaining the authority of the judiciary or protecting national security. The judgment rests primarily on the view that the use of the injunctions, following the publication of the book, was a disproportionate restriction of press freedom. The Court was particularly influenced by a constitutional perspective on the role of the press similar to the one advanced in this chapter: 'Whilst it must not overstep the bounds set, *inter alia*, in the interests of "national security" or for "maintaining the authority of the judiciary", it is nevertheless incumbent on it to impart information and ideas on matters of public interest. Not only does the press have the task of imparting such information and ideas: the public also has a right to receive them. Were it otherwise, the press would be unable to play its vital role of "public watchdog".'[147]

The silencing of the press by use of the contempt laws is not a new phenomenon but it did arise in a novel and dangerous way in the *Spycatcher* litigation. If, as we have argued, the Press serves a constitutional function, contempt involves questions of allocation of power in a constitutional sense—a determination that the forum for discussion of some matters will be the courts rather than the media. There are manifest objections to this treatment of the issue. Since the courts themselves draw this boundary there are dangers that they will be influenced by concerns about the preservation of self-interest and status rather than

---

[144] See n. 130 above, 653.					[145] See n. 134 above.

[146] See n. 136 above; see generally I. Leigh, 'Spycatcher in Strasbourg', [1992] *PL* 200. The majority found that the imposition and continuance of the interim injunctions until the first House of Lords' judgment was justified. A minority found that the initial injunctions breached Art. 10, either because prior restraint was not permitted, or because on the facts there had been no 'pressing social need' for the injunctions.

[147] *Guardian* case (n. 136 above), para. 59.

by a balance of the constitutional values of free speech and due administration of justice. The problem is compounded by several factors which tend to be obscured by treating the issue merely as one of weighing two competing public interests. Protecting legal process from prejudice by the media is indeed an important goal, but one which necessarily tends to relate to the interests of the individual litigants. It is only secondarily a public interest in the generalized sense of the community interest of living within a state which upholds legal forms of justice. It is also very much attenuated where, as in all civil actions, there is no jury: cases are heard by judges whose professional experience and, presumably, the personal qualities which led to their appointment, combined with security of tenure, ought to insulate them from the swirl of public debate. The public interest in knowing the details of allegations aired in the courts is perhaps less pressing than the rights of the litigants, but is none the less very strong since, partly because of the privilege accorded publication of matters aired in court, legal proceedings are often the best or even the only means by which matters otherwise hidden can be exposed to public view. What is manifestly undesirable is the use of litigation by the powerful—whether the government or a wealthy individual—as a way of stifling debate until the law's capacity for delay (and the public's attention span) have been fully exhausted.

The use of the contempt laws by the government during the *Spycatcher* litigation illustrates these difficulties in an extreme form. Two factors about the litigation out of which the contempt proceedings grew are important here: it involved the government as a litigant and it was an action to preserve secrecy (through use of interim injunctions to uphold an alleged duty of confidentiality). Whatever the merits of giving priority to a private litigant through the public interest in the administration of justice, the argument plainly requires reconsideration when the litigation is being promoted by those in authority in the name of the public. In these circumstances it can be argued that the government should not be treated as any other litigant, since although it purports to be acting for the public benefit, it has a strong self-interest as well. There is an obvious danger that the government may sponsor litigation for party political, sectional reasons. The law of contempt may then be used to stifle informed criticism of the initial litigation, which prevents the government being called to account for its legal activities, thereby undercutting responsible government.

The use of contempt as a handmaiden of confidentiality poses a conundrum: if the subject matter of the litigation is a confidence that, once released, can never be recaptured, any repetition of the confidence in media comment about the proceedings will render the proceedings worthless. This is similar to the problem facing a person alleged to have been defamed—that litigation will draw additional attention to the defamatory remark—but with one important additional factor: whereas the successful plaintiff in a defamation action will at least have damages to compensate for the process and additional unwanted publicity, in an action for an injunction on grounds of confidentiality the action itself may become unwinnable, because Press coverage destroys the confidence. Damages for the original breach of confidence may not compensate.

The relentless logic of this last factor led to the courts effectively extending the ambit of the government's *Spycatcher* proceedings to embrace through the contempt laws newspapers which were not formally party to the breach of confidence action.[148] Following the instigation of the proceedings against the *Guardian* and the *Observer*, the *Independent* published a story commenting on the proceedings and printing allegations derived from Peter Wright. The *Sunday Times* similarly commenced serialization of *Spycatcher* immediately after a (short-lived, as it transpired) victory for the *Independent* in the contempt proceedings; it did so behind an elaborate web of deception, designed to deflect any prior restraint, which subsequently recieved particular judicial criticism.[149] The Attorney-General brought proceedings and all the newspapers were held to be in contempt of court, although the fines initially imposed were discharged by the Court of Appeal.[150]

One technical but inescapable side-effect of the 'third party' liability in contempt is to extend liability under an injunction to newspapers which had no opportunity to oppose its grant, because they were not parties to the litigation. It may even extend liability in situations where, had proceedings for an injunction been brought directly against the newspaper allegedly in contempt, they could not have succeeded because for some reason the obligation of confidentiality did not extend to them.[151] This is an unfortunate and anomalous effect.

However, this injustice pales in comparison with the constitutional side-effects of the judgment. The result is no less than to allow for total imposition of secrecy throughout the British media by the bringing of a single action against one of their number. This was the position in Britain following the *Independent* judgment: all newspapers were stifled in their comment on the proceedings for many months until the lifting of the injunctions in the summer of 1988. The decision was directly equivalent to the introduction of a legislative system of newspaper control, only much speedier and more efficacious, and without the untidy distraction of democratic debate.[152] These criticisms are not adequately addressed in the technical distinction to which the House of Lords resorted in affirming the *Sunday Times* contempt ruling, between the applicability of civil and criminal contempt.[153] Whatever the niceties of the distinction (the *Spycatcher* proceedings were held to constitute criminal contempt) it has little relevance where

---

[148] *A-G* v. *Newspaper Publishing plc* [1987] 3 All ER 276.   [149] See p. 265 above.

[150] *A-G* v. *Newspaper Publishing plc and others, The Times*, 28 Feb. 1990; the *Sunday Times* unsuccessfully continued its appeal to the House of Lords: *A-G* v. *Times Newspapers Ltd* [1991] 2 All ER 398.

[151] Feldman (n. 130 above), 751.

[152] Parliament has spent several years considering much more ineffectual controls designed to protect privacy in the face of press intrusion.

[153] *A-G* v. *Times Newspapers Ltd* [1991] 2 All ER 398, Lord Oliver at 415 (and see 420–1), Lord Ackner at 409, and Lord Jauncey at 426–7; see T. Ingman, '"Interfering with the Proper Administration of Justice": Some Recent Developments' (1992) 11 *Civil Justice Quarterly*, 175, 176–180.

the government is party to the proceedings being protected: in these circumstances the difference between the Attorney-General bringing contempt proceedings to protect the government's interests as litigant (as in civil contempt) or in the public interest (as in criminal contempt) is simply trivial. The reality of the restraint on press freedom is the same in both cases and it draws the boundary between the domains of the press and the courts at an unacceptable location. If, as the judges plainly feel is the case, there is an undesirable 'loophole' in this aspect of the law of contempt, it is open to Parliament to amend the Contempt of Court Act 1981. It is even more undesirable for the judges to conjure up new forms of press censorship in circumstances brought about by their own too ready acceptance of government assertions that on later examination have consistently proven to be exaggerated.

From a discussion of prior restraints now we move briefly to consider legal action after publication. The discussion is necessarily brief since criminal penalties for publication of information relating to security and intelligence have already been discussed in our treatment of the Official Secrets Act 1989 in Chapter 9. Accordingly we concentrate here on other legal sanctions.

DEPRIVATION OF PROFITS

One form of remedy which has become prominent in recent years for sanctioning forms of free expression of which the government disapproves on grounds of national security is to attack the property rights derived from the publication. This form of sanction is of less concern than prior restraints to those championing freedom of expression on constitutional grounds: it is unnecessary in defence of free speech as promoting the accountability of government that the individuals involved thereby derive a personal profit. However, fear of loss of profit (and the associated legal costs) may discourage newspaper proprietors and publishers from acting as a conduit for such information, and so these remedies may prove an effective means of closing off outlets. The legal actions depriving individuals of property rights in publication have arisen both in a civil law and a criminal context, and have taken several different forms.

One subsidiary aspect of the *Spycatcher* saga was an action for account of profits brought against the *Sunday Times* by the government in respect of the serialization of the book. The obligation to account in this way follows from establishing a breach of confidence, since the law does not enable a wrongdoer to profit from breaching the confidence, even if, as in the *Spycatcher* case, there are other reasons why an injunction should not be issued. Account for profit is a device which has been used in the United States to deprive former CIA officers of publishing royalties, and there it has been held not to violate the First Amendment.[154] By its nature account for profits will be more difficult to apply

---

[154] *Snepp* v. *United States* 444 US 507 (1980).

to newspapers than to books, since there is an obvious difficulty in establishing the extent to which a particular breach of confidence boosted circulation, especially if, as in the *Sunday Times* case, it was unaccompanied by advance publicity.

Protection of or deprivation of copyright may also be a means of protecting property right in publication. However, unlike an account for profits this may involve prior restraint, as when the High Court of Australia granted an injunction to prevent the publication of a book on the East Timor Crisis containing an number of government documents.[155] Since the court in the same case refused to grant the injunction on grounds of breach of confidence on grounds that it was not established to be in the public interest, to enable the government to assert other private law grounds to achieve the same effect appears anomalous: it might have been more appropriate to refuse the injunction and compensate the government for 'misuse' of its documents by damages. It would have been better still to have ruled private law remedies wholly inappropriate to restrain the use of government information (whether it incidentally involved reproduction of documents or not), and require Parliament to pass legislation if such remedies were necessary and there existed a gap in the criminal law.[156]

In any event, government assertion of copyright in such cases turns (somewhat arbitrarily) on whether documents are reproduced: if they are merely used for background information or the author compiles an account based on recollection of information derived while in government employment there will be no infringement of copyright. However, the courts have suggested that in the case of a work derived from an unlawful breach of confidence the author might be unable to assert copyright to protect his or her work from infringement by others. This view, which was propounded in the *Spycatcher* litigation[157], in some respects accords well with our view that disclosure of information about the conduct of government should be freely available. More extreme and punitive was the view expressed *obiter dicta* in the same case that the copyright might vest equitably in the Crown:[158] the Treasury Solicitor has seized upon this novel doctrine to bring proceedings (as yet unresolved) to demand the royalties from George Blake's autobiography, *No Other Choice.*[159]

An alternative route to the same destination was attempted in the criminal proceedings brought against Randle and Pottle, who helped Blake to escape from Wormwood Scrubs Prison in 1966. When proceedings were instituted against them in 1988 for their part in the escape the prosecution applied to have

---

[155] *Commonwealth of Australia* v. *Fairfax* (n. 143 above).

[156] In the *Fairfax* case Mason J rejected an argument that an injunction could be granted because of threatened breach of the Crimes Act 1914 (Cth), s. 79: ibid. 50.

[157] Lord Jauncey at [1988] 3 ALL ER at 668; see Y. Cripps, 'Breaches of Copyright and Confidence: The Spycatcher Effect' [1989] *PL* 13.

[158] See *A-G* v. *Guardian Newspapers (No. 2)* [1988] 2 WLR 805, 832–3 (per Scott J) and (CA) 899 (Dillon LJ) and [1988] 3 WLR 776, HL, 788 (Lord Keith), 800–1 (Lord Griffiths), and 812 (Lord Goff); but for a more sceptical view see Lord Donaldson, MR (CA), at 884.

[159] We are grateful to Birnberg and Co., Blake's solicitors, for information about the case.

the proceeds from their book, *The Blake Escape*, frozen under provisions in the Criminal Justice Act 1988. These provisions, modelled on similar powers introduced to deal with drug-trafficking, allow the proceeds of alleged criminal offences to be preserved by court order so as to be available for confiscation if the defendant is convicted. The court rejected Randle and Pottle's argument that the royalties were not property obtained 'in connection with the commission' of an alleged offence, holding that if they had not helped Blake to escape they would not have been in a position to write a book about it.[160] In any event the defendants were acquitted,[161] and the money would then have been returned.

CONCLUSION

It will be apparent that only a small part of this chapter has been devoted to the actions of the courts in restraining publication. Although the latter are highly visible, as with the protracted *Spycatcher* litigation, the more normal sources of control of the press are those over sources, the attitudes of journalists and their editors, and patterns of informal censorship. It can be argued that in view of these successive layers producing censorship in effect, legal process is an almost unnecessary adornment—except that it provides the ultimate sanction within which the others operate on a more normal basis. However far from recognizing this superfluity of controls, the attitude of the judiciary has been more or less consistently hostile to Press freedom. Nowhere is this clearer than in the extensions of the laws of confidentiality, contempt, and copyright which have been gratuitously handed to the government in recent years. Not only were these extensions of the law entirely unnecessary in view of the sweep of the criminal law,[162] but they are a rejection of the constitutional position of the Press essential to a healthy democracy. These developments are all the more striking when it is considered that they happened in peacetime and when the international threat to the security of Britain was less than at virtually any time since the nineteenth century. To continue to treat the Press as though it, rather than the over-powerful executive, was the main threat to democracy has an air of unreality symptomatic of the late stages of decline which the British Constitution has now reached.

---

[160] *Re R. and Re Criminal Justice Act* [1991] COD 369; and see A. Freiburg, 'Confiscating the Literary Proceeds of Crime', [1992] *Crim. LR* 96.

[161] See p. 305 below.

[162] Although we have argued in the preceding chapter against use of the criminal law in this area, whilst the legislation is on the books, the constitutionally appropriate course is to use it or enact civil law provisions to supplement it.

Part IV
National Security and the Legal Process

11

Criminal Proceedings and State Security Interests

The focus in this chapter is on the practicalities of handling intelligence and security-related material within the trial process; we deal with the substance of the law in Chapters 8 and 9 in different areas and with the overall approach of the judiciary in Chapter 12. At the procedural level a number of competing objectives can be identified. Broadly stated, the purpose of criminal proceedings is to require the prosecution to prove the defendant's guilt beyond reasonable doubt. The defendant is not called upon to respond unless an arguable prosecution case can be established, and even then may choose not to give evidence and in defence merely to rely upon technical arguments, or to attack the prosecution evidence. The defendant is entitled to know the prosecution's case in advance to know what has to be answered. At a deeper level this procedure is supposed not merely to embody protections for the defendant, but also to satisfy the public interest that justice be seen to be done in public and impartially.[1] The community has an interest in the application of the law that is reflected both in open justice and in limited participation in the criminal justice system through the magistracy and the jury.

Other factors must be set alongside this idealized version of the criminal justice system. Although from some perspectives all law enforcement is political, this is particularly true of *offences against the state*. Hence the decision whether to prosecute in these cases vests in ministerial hands.[2] Secrets trials often have the potential for enormous political embarrassment: they focus public attention on aspects of the state (and of government policy) which can be hidden from the population most of the time, but about which civil libertarians feel a distinct ambivalence. Potentially, this is a weapon in the defendant's armoury. The history of the jury system is littered with examples of citizen judges cavilling at political charges, from William Penn in the seventeenth century to Clive Ponting in the twentieth, whatever the legal niceties.

In the types of cases we are concerned with the state's interest can conflict at various levels with fair procedures; we discuss below rules which are designed to protect this interest, not merely from the public, but which also affect the position of the jury[3] and the defendant. The interrelationship between these

---

[1] For a vigorous critique of this (traditional) perspective see D. McBarnet, *Conviction: Law, the State and the Construction of Justice* (London, 1981).

[2] See pp. 301 ff below.

[3] Because of the seriousness of security-related offences, they will, if contested be heard by a jury; the exception is Northern Ireland: see n. 11 below.

interests is complex and can only be properly understood in terms of the chronology of the choices (both for the prosecution and the defence) arising at different points in a criminal trial. We will briefly trace this chronology here in introduction in order to show how the practices described in this chapter are interrelated.

The initial decision facing the authorities is whether in a security case the prosecution should be brought at all: at this stage it may be judged that the harm to secrecy outweighs the public good that would result from conviction. Flexible criteria, such as regard to 'the public interest', encourage a cost–benefit analysis of this kind. Where a prosecution is instigated attempts may be made to limit disclosure during the proceedings in various ways. Under the greatest control of the prosecution is the choice not to offer evidence which discloses sensitive material. This may lead to the case being brought on less than the best available evidence. However, the ability of the prosecution to control disclosure by simply not using intelligence evidence has been greatly reduced in the United Kingdom, at least, by recent reforms extending the requirement to disclose unused prosecution material. If the prosecution is obliged to disclose the existence of the material in any event to the defence, this may again tilt the balance towards using the evidence in court, although that in turn will involve wider disclosure still. It is possible, however, for the prosecution to object to disclosure of unused material under these rules, by service of public interest immunity certificates. Whether the certificates are upheld may affect whether or not the prosecution wishes to continue: it may prefer to drop the charges than release the documents. In practice this may give the defendant a powerful additional tool to use against the state in secrecy cases. In the United States the term 'graymail' has been coined to describe the pre-trial defence tactic of requesting intelligence-related material connected with the defendant's case so that the prosecution is face with damaging disclosures about security matters if it continues to press the charges. Graymail is particularly invidious because it is likely to be most successfully employed by former officials from the heart of the government machine who subsequently face trial,[4] and it is more likely to succeed in serious cases because of the inevitable congruence of secrecy, damage, and sensitivity. Decisions made at the pre-trial stage about disclosure of documents may also affect the defence—inability to extract and use in evidence material which the defence considers vital to defending the charge, because a public interest immunity certificate is upheld, may lead to the defendant changing his or her plea to guilty at this point.[5]

[4] Lawyers representing Colonel Oliver North and Admiral Poindexter, who faced charges in the USA arising from the Iran–Contra affair, used the tactic with some success; see further n. 108 below.

[5] This is precisely what occurred in the trial in 1992 of executives from Ordtech Ltd. charged with contravening export-licence regulations over exports to Iraq. See the *Independent*, 10 Mar. 1993. In the similar case of defendants in the Matrix Churchill trial the public interest immunity certificates were partially quashed and the trial thereafter took a different course: see below.

An alternative strategy for limiting disclosure is through use of *in camera* hearings. Although refusal of an application for exclusion of the press and public is unlikely to lead to the dropping of the case, it may limit the way in which evidence is subsequently presented. Conversely, if the application is granted the defence will be limited in its ability to exploit the evidence to bring to bear public embarassment, in the hope that the trial will at some point be aborted. An *in camera* hearing will automatically carry with it vetting of the jury, an operative and possibly influential factor in its own right.

Even when a hearing is not *in camera*, various protective measures may be used to protect security interests during a trial, and if these are refused the prosecution may once again be led to drop the case in the public interest or to present it differently.[6]

This chronology can be illustrated in practice by reference to the trial of executives from the machine tools company Matrix Churchill, indicted for deception in export-licence applications.[7] Matrix Churchill had been part of a network of European companies acquired by the Iraqis in an attempt at covert armaments procurement. The prosecution was halted after Alan Clark, the former Minister of State at the Department of Trade and Industry and Defence Procurement Minister, gave evidence when cross-examined confirming the defendant's case that there was no deception, because the government was fully aware of the intended use (in armaments manufacture) of the machine tools which had been the subject of the licence application. The judge had earlier partially quashed public interest immunity certificates served by the prosecution, designed to suppress evidence about intelligence sources, about information held by MI5 and MI6, and high-level interdepartmental and ministerial contact over the licence application.

Before the trial was aborted by Customs and Excise, evidence was tendered which showed that first MI5 and then MI6 had recruited agents in the company who, at considerable personal risk, were feeding them intelligence about Iraqi control of the company and attempts to procure armaments manufacturing machines. It was one of these agents, Paul Henderson, the managing director of Matrix Churchill, who, with others, subsequently faced trial. Indeed there was evidence not merely that several government departments were aware from reports from these agents of the true nature of the machines to be exported, but also that MI6 had specifically supported the granting of the licences in question in order not to compromise a valuable source.[8]

---

[6] For instance, in the *ABC* case committal hearings, when the justices ordered that the name of an intelligence officer ('Colonel A') would have to be written down and shown to the defence, although not read out in public, the prosecution claimed that this was insufficient to guarantee his personal protection and called instead another officer ('Colonel B'). It was said that disclosure of Colonel B's name would constitute a threat to national security, but not put him in personal danger: see *R. v. Leveller* [1979] 1 QB 31 (and nn. 93–8 below).

[7] A detailed account of the case, quoting many of the documents and much of the testimony, can be found in D. Leigh, *Betrayed: The Real Story of the Matrix Churchill Trial* (London, 1993).

[8] Ibid. 116.

The information received from Henderson and another agent, Mark Gutteridge (the export manager of Matrix Churchill), fed MI6 with intelligence about Iraqi intentions. This intelligence informed the stance taken by the Foreign Office in interdepartmental negotiations with the Department of Trade and Industry and the Ministry of Defence about successive export licence applications made by the company. These applications fell to be considered by a ministerial committee responsible for adjudicating on export-licence policy in the light of the published 'Howe guidelines', issued during the Iran–Iraq war. Behind the scenes a significant struggle was taking place between the Foreign Office and the Department of Trade and Industry over whether controls should be abandoned altogether. The documents released at the trial showed a progressive relaxation or reinterpretation of the guidelines following the ceasefire in that war, and a subsequent tilt towards exports to Iraq following the Salman Rushdie affair, continuing up to the eve of the Iraqi invasion of Kuwait. Parliament was not informed of these changes of policy either at the time, or in any detail when the Trade and Industry Select Committee investigated the Supergun affair in 1991.[9] Through the partial quashing of the Public Interest Immunity certificates the defence was given considerable ammunition with which to cross-examine prosecution witnesses about the state of government knowledge in order successfully to advance its contention that there had been no deception. After the collapse of the trial the government announced the setting up of the Scott Inquiry, with terms of reference which cover both the prosecution conduct at the trial, the issuing of the public interest immunity certificates, the Supergun affair, and government actions and policy on exports to Iraq.[10]

Having described the interrelationship of these issues both in terms of their political context and their chronology in the trial process, we will now examine the individual procedures in turn.

DILUTION OF JURY TRIAL[11]

Before discussing jury vetting and the abolition of peremptory challenge of jurors it is necessary to consider the purpose of jury trial. An evaluation of these

---

[9] *Trade and Industry Select Committee, Second Report, Exports to Iraq: Project Babylon and Long Range Guns*, HC 86 (1991–2).

[10] The terms of reference are given at: *HC Debs.*, vol. 214, col. 74(w) (16 Nov. 1992); see further Ch. 17 below.

[11] We omit from this account the suspension of jury trial in certain cases ('scheduled offences') in Northern Ireland in the Diplock Courts: for a recent account and review of the literature see A. Vercher, *Terrorism in Europe: An International Comparative Legal Analysis* (Oxford, 1992), 125–39. Whatever the merits of this experiment, it is peripheral to our concern here, because the wide ambit of the offences dealt with in this way are not necessarily related to national security; the purpose is not to provide for the secure treatment of information but lies in the rationale of anti-terrorist measures—a topic beyond the boundaries of this work (above, p. x).

measures can only proceed against an appreciation of the objectives of involving lay people in the trial process at all.

It would, of course, be simplistic to suggest that an institution such as the jury, with nearly a thousand years of development and adaptation behind it will have a single, over-arching, rationale.[12] One ambiguity, critical for discussion of the developments we are interested in, is over the sense in which the jury is a democratic institution.[13] The ambiguity is reflected at the stratum of jury selection and composition by the conflicting objectives that the jury should be randomly chosen *and* representative.[14] A true representativeness would argue in the direction of conscious attempts to construct a balanced jury containing a cross-section of views; this would justify extensive exploration of potential jurors' attitudes, as is common for instance in the United States—something generally discouraged within the British legal system.

It was Blackstone who claimed that the liberties of England depended on the jury 'remaining sacred and inviolate; not only from all open attacks (which none be so hardy as to make) but also from all secret machinations, which may sap and undermine it'.[15] Writing in the eighteenth century he had in mind the then common practice of jury packing (direct attempts by the authorities to put the people of their choice on the jury), an activity which appears as the direct lineal forbear of jury vetting. Although only officially acknowledged in 1978, jury vetting has a longer unofficial history.[16] It was following revelations at the '*ABC*' official secrets trial[17] that the Attorney-General published Guidelines on vetting,

---

[12] For an accessible, recent introduction to the debates over the jury see P. Darbyshire, 'The Lamp That Shows That Freedom Lives—Is it Worth the Candle?' [1991] *Crim. LR* 740.

[13] cf. P. Devlin, *The Judge* (Oxford, 1979), 271: 'Through the jury the governed have a voice not only in the making of the laws which govern them but in their application.'

[14] The representative element in the process is the use of the electoral register. However, this base of potential jurors is substantially modified by a long list of statutory disqualifications and excusals, which are explicable on grounds of social policy, but have nothing to do with reflecting the composition of society: for details see T. Ingman, *The English Legal Process* (4th edn., London, 1992), 17881. Randomness is supposedly ensured by processes of selection of jury panels by court officials, but is questionable in practice: J. Baldwin and M. McConville, *Jury Verdicts* (Oxford, 1979), 97–8 and 126–7.

[15] 4. *Commentaries* 350.

[16] S. Enright and J. Morton, *Taking Liberties: The Criminal Jury in the 1990s* (London, 1990), ch. 3, esp. pp. 29–32 and 38–42, cite numerous examples both of jury packing and jury vetting. In 1966 the Attorney-General gave a radio interview in which he stated that during a spy trial he had had the jury panel checked for communists, and that one potential juror had been stood-by as a result: Standing Committee H, Criminal Justice Bill, 1 Mar. 1988, col. 399. For general accounts of jury vetting see M. Finlay and P. Duff, 'Jury Vetting—the Jury under Attack' (1983) 3 *Legal Studies* 159; id., 'Jury Vetting—Ideology of the Jury in Transition' (1982) 6 *Crim LJ* 138; R. East, 'Jury Packing: A Thing of the Past?' (1985) 48 *MLR* 518. Jury vetting is not solely a UK phenomenon—on vetting in Australia, see M. Finlay and P. Duff, *The Jury Under Attack* (London, 1988), 116–18.

[17] See A. Nicol, 'Official Secrets and Jury Vetting' [1979] *Crim. LR* 284; for an insider's account, C. Aubrey, *Who's Watching You?* (London, 1981). Judge King-Hamilton, who presided at the trial, attempted to suppress contemporary reporting of the jury vetting on the grounds that it was contempt—this included reprimanding the Attorney-General for making the practice public, and previewing and dictating cuts in a television documentary: E. Thompson, *Writing by Candlelight* (London, 1980), 217 and 222.

which had apparently been first issued four years earlier. The practice was all the more discreditable because it contradicted the spirit if not the letter of the published position, stated in the 1973 Practice Direction, that jurors should not be 'excused' from service on the grounds which included their political beliefs.[18] Subsequent revision of the guidelines has made it clear that even then an incomplete picture was painted, by omitting the role of the Security Service.[19]

The current guidelines state that the stand by for the Crown[20] should be used 'sparingly and in exceptional circumstances', and not merely in order to secure a tactical advantage.[21] The exceptional nature has been re-emphasized following the abolition of the defendant's right of peremptory challenge, with the Attorney-General issuing fresh guidelines to restrict its use to cases falling within the jury vetting guidelines.[22] Although they recite the statutory safeguards surrounding the jury designed to ensure the proper administration of justice, the guidelines state that in cases in which national security is involved and part of the evidence is likely to be heard *in camera*, and in terrorist cases, there is a need for further safeguards against the possibility of bias. The official reasoning should be allowed to speak for itself:

The particular aspects of these cases which make it desirable to seek extra precautions are (*a*) in security cases a danger that a juror, either voluntarily or under pressure, may make an improper use of evidence which, because of its sensitivity, has been given *in camera*, (*b*) in both security and terrorist cases the danger that a juror's political beliefs are so biased as to go beyond normally reflecting the broad spectrum of views and interests in the community to reflect the extreme views of sectarian interests or pressure groups to a degree which might interfere with his fair assessment of the facts of the case or lead him to assert improper pressure on his fellow jurors.

In these circumstances 'limited' investigations of the jury panel may be authorized under the Guidelines. This will involve checking the records of Special Branches. In security (rather than terrorist cases) investigation may also be made by what the Guidelines vaguely call 'the security services'. What these investigations may comprise is unstated, but the guidelines suggest that active information gathering is not involved when they continue: 'No checks other than on these sources and no general inquiries are to be made save to the limited extent

---

[18] [1973] 1 All ER 240.

[19] A matter which might have created a misleading impression 'by inadvertence' as the (Conservative) Attorney-General, Sir Michael Havers, put it in expressing his regret in a belated parliamentary answer, following the Bettaney case: *HC Debs.*, vol. 91, cols. 55–6 (3 Feb. 1986); the original announcement had been made by the (Labour) Attorney-General of the day, the Rt. Hon Sam Silkin.

[20] The process by which the prosecution objects, without explanation, to a particular would-be juror before he or she takes the oath; for a detailed account of its history see J. McEldowney, 'Stand By for the Crown' [1979] *Crim. LR* 272.

[21] Para. 1; the revised guidelines can be found conveniently in app. 2 to Enright and Morton (n. 16 above); and see [1988] 3 All ER 1068 .

[22] *HC Debs.*, vol. 91, col. 55 (3 Feb. 1986); guidelines, para. 3.

they may be needed to confirm the identity of a juror about whom the initial check has raised serious doubts.'

A hierarchy for approval of these measures is established, with the onus being put on the Chief Constable to alert the Director of Public Prosecutions of the desirability of checks being made, and the Director obtaining the personal permission of the Attorney-General. Information obtained as a result is fed back to the Director of Public Prosecutions, who decides what use is to be made of it (in other words, whether to stand by). Decisions to 'stand by' jurors require the approval of the Attorney-General and are only taken where there is 'strong reason for believing that a particular juror might be a security risk, be susceptible to improper approaches or be influenced in arriving at a verdict for the reasons given'.

The Guidelines are only administrative in nature and might be argued to extend the categories of statutory disqualifications on jury service[23] in practice in a way not sanctioned by Parliament. Nevertheless, the courts have upheld them. Despite claims in the Court of Appeal of a distinctly Blackstonian flavour by Lord Denning that jury vetting was unconstitutional, the majority in the same case held that vetting of the jury panel for previous convictions on the order of the judge, following a request from the defence, could not be set aside for procedural reasons.[24] A differently composed Court of Appeal later removed any doubt about the legality of vetting for the purpose of identifying those disqualified by criminal convictions.[25] As more of the practice of vetting was progressively revealed, the judicial position changed incrementally from an insistence on the random composition of jury panels[26] to emphasizing the continuity of vetting with other historical inroads upon that principle.[27]

It is the status of checks on jurors' backgrounds in terrorist and official secrets cases which is of more interest for our purpose here. The legality of the practice was challenged in the case of the so-called Winchester Three, Irish persons who were charged with conspiracy to murder after they were discovered apparently surveying the grounds of the residence of the Secretary of State for Northern Ireland, Tom King. At their trial an application by their counsel to have the jury panel discharged because it had been vetted was rejected. On appeal, their challenge to conviction on the basis that the checks upon jurors and the resulting use of stand by for the Crown was unlawful, was dismissed.[28]

---

[23] Criminal records checks might be a way of enforcing the disqualifications (however, the offences recorded are wider than those debarring a juror). Checks with Special Branch and the Security Service are intended to discover information unrelated to any statutory ground.

[24] *R.* v. *Crown Court at Sheffield (ex p. Brownlow)* [1980] 2 All ER 444.

[25] *R.* v. *Mason* [1980] 3 All ER 777; and see *R.* v. *McCann* (1990) 92 Cr. App. R. 239, 247, where Beldam LJ laid stress on the fact that in *Brownlow* the court was not informed of the historical basis of stand by (as set out in *R.* v. *Chandler (No. 2)* [1964] 2 QB 322, 328–9, and 333–4).

[26] 1973 Practice Direction (above n. 18).   [27] Lawton LJ in *Mason* (n. 25 above), 781 ff.

[28] *R.* v. *McCann and others* (n. 25 above). The appeal succeeded on other grounds which are worthy of note: during the closing speeches Tom King had given a widely reported speeech arguing for the abolition of the right of silence because of its 'abuse' by terrorists. Two of the defendants

Beldam LJ rejected the argument because vetting merely comprised the conjunction of three elements, each of which was lawful—namely the use of stand by, the supply by court officials of names and addresses of those on the panel to the police, and inquiries into the background of potential jurors.[29] He argued that despite being informed of jury vetting, Parliament had not curtailed it by legislation.

Several arguments are commonly advanced against jury vetting; namely, that it is tantamount to the prosecution packing the jury to get a conviction, that it involves unacceptable intrusion into the privacy of the jurors, and that it is not even-handed. We will consider each in turn.

The first objection raises the obvious question of whether jury vetting *works*. The answer probably depends on whether it is perceived as a means of preventing perverse acquittals by excluding those with unrepresentative views, or as a way of assembling a compliant jury panel. The criticism is often made that the real concern of the prosecution is to assemble a conviction-minded jury and that this shows an attempt by the authorities to interfere with the autonomy of the legal process in those cases of most importance to them.[30] Without the facility of conducting a control experiment with an unvetted jury there is no way of knowing the impact of vetting. Vetting is, of course, not conducted out of idle curiosity, but so that the information derived can, if necessary, be used to eject would-be jurors by use of 'stand by for the Crown'.[31] However attempts to influence jury verdicts by influencing jury composition beg several questions. First, the available evidence does not support the view that jury composition affects verdicts: in their major study of juries in Birmingham in the 1970s, Baldwin and McConville were unable to find any link between the more obvious indicia of the make-up of a jury and its performance.[32] However, it is true that their research methodology, unlike that of Special Branch and the Security Service, did not extend to the political views or associations of the jurors. Studies done of the related issue of attempts by defendants to influence jury composition through peremptory challenge failed to demonstrate any significant variation in acquittal rates according to whether the challenge had been exercised or not.[33] The second imponderable is the effect of self-knowledge—defence

had refused to make statements and the prosecution case was that King was their intended victim. The trial judge's refusal to discharge the jury and order a retrial led the Court of Appeal to quash the convictions as unsafe.

[29] *R. v. McCann and others* 246–7. One potential juror had been stood by for the Crown. The judge had refused to move the venue of the trial from Winchester (a city with strong military connections), but had directed (without jurisdiction, as it transpired) that the panel should not be drawn from Winchester or Aldershot: ibid. 243–4.   [30] Enright and Morton (n. 16 above), 48.

[31] See McEldowney (n. 20 above); an alternative course would be to challenge for cause. In 1988 the law was amended to allow for *in camera* argument on challenge for cause with a security-related objection to a juror in mind: Criminal Justice Act 1988, s. 118(2).

[32] Balwin and McConville (n. 14 above), ch. 6.

[33] J. Vennard and D. Riley, 'The Use of Peremptory Challenge and Stand By of Jurors and their Relationship to Trial Outcome' [1988] *Crim. LR* 731; nevertheless, peremptory challenge was

counsel can be expected to waste no time in pointing out to a vetted jury that they have been hand-picked for the task to hand. How the jury will react, whether with hostility or quiet superiority, is one of the unpredictable elements the prosecution lets loose when it decides to vet.

The argument from privacy[34] is substantially the same as the discussion of this issue in Chapters 2–5. However it is worth noting the allegation that official surveillance may be instituted specifically to check on the suitability of a proposed juror, which, if anything, is more objectionable than merely trawling files already in existence for this purpose.[35] The working assumption behind these practices is that it is permissible, indeed commendable, to detect, label, and exclude from participation in the criminal justice process those whose views diverge sufficiently from the norm in the view of those involved to be categorized as 'extreme'. Leaving aside the more obvious arguments about the nature of dissent in a liberal democracy, this line of reasoning once again calls into question the very rationale of the jury. If it is to be representative, the logic of artificially limiting the spectrum of opinion it comprises is questionable.[36] The official justification is the 'one bad apple' argument, that it only takes one person of 'extreme views' to skew a jury towards an unjustified acquittal. The argument tends to undervalue the safeguard of the majority verdict (which was introduced specifically to counter such influences), that is, in reality it needs three 'bad apples', or at least over-emphasizes the corruptability of the rest of the barrel. Moreover, if vetting is needed because of the risk of three out of twelve members of a randomly selected jury turning out to have 'extreme' views, this suggests that 'extremism' is surprisingly common.[37]

The third objection is the lack of even-handedness.[38] Under the post-1988 law it is the prosecution alone which has the ability to challenge a juror, without giving reasons. It is far from coincidental that the demise of the (not strictly)

abolished by the Criminal Justice Act 1988, s. 118(1), following a campaign against its 'abuse' by Toby Jessel, MP after the 'Cyprus Secrets' acquittals (see nn. 48–50 below).

[34] For an argument that vetting may constitute a violation of Art. 8 of the ECHR see T. Gallivan and C. Warbrick, 'Jury Vetting and the European Convention on Human Rights' (1980) 5 *Human Rights Rev.* 176, 186 ff. The authors conclude that Art. 8(2) may be satisfied where a legitimate aim of protecting national security is involved in the case of *in camera* hearings (p. 189); but even here a greater element of independent (judicial) control would be desirable to meet the requirement that the restriction is 'necessary in the interests of a democratic society' (ibid. 189–91). The proposals advanced below (pp. 300–1 below) should satisfy these tests.

[35] The allegation was made by Michael Bettaney (who, as a former Security Service officer, ought to have known) about the preliminaries to his own trial on official secrets' charges: see his letter to Stuart Bell, MP reproduced as app. I in Enright and Morton (n. 16 above), 159–60.

[36] One of the more bizarre arguments in favour of the practice was made by Judge King-Hamilton, who, at the end of an anarchist trial in which the jury panel had been vetted, reportedly said in summing up: 'One has heard criticism of "jury vetting" as amounting to abandonment of the random selection of juries. What nonsense! It widens the random selection instead of being limited to the first twelve.' *The Times,* 7 Dec. 1979.

[37] Cf. Finlay and Duff (1982), nn. 16 above, 155–6.

[38] For discussion of compliance with Art. 6 of the ECHR see Gallivan and Warbrick (n. 34 above), 183 ff.

equivalent right which formerly existed for the defence was brought about following its systematic use in an official secrets case where the defendants were acquitted.[39] Behind this lie other considerations, such as the enormous resources available to the state for vetting of jurors. The Guidelines do not require the defence to be told of the reason for standing a particular juror by, but allow discretion for giving a general indication of the reason, without compromising sources.[40] Lack of even-handedness is apparent in the fact that no attempt is made to identify or debar from service jurors who might have strong reasons to support the prosecution: for instance, relatives of soldiers serving in Northern Ireland in the case of terrorist trials. However, where information of this kind is turned up during the vetting process, the guidelines require that a general indication should be given to the defence.[41] The usefulness of the information is, however, hampered by the fewer rights given to the defence to challenge jurors. Since the abolition of peremptory challenge, the defence would need to 'challenge for cause', a course unlikely to succeed, especially if the allegation against the juror is a generalized one.[42] The alternative would be for the prosecution to stand by a juror likely to be inimical to the defence, but it is unclear if the Guidelines allow for this.

Most of the objections to jury vetting would not apply, or would apply with less force, if it was limited to criminal record checks for disqualifications,[43] and to cases where evidence is to be heard *in camera*. (We would, however, also restrict the use of *in camera* hearings.) Where vetting is directed only to potential trustworthiness with sensitive material, the objection on grounds of lack of even-handedness is not an issue to the same extent as where the purpose is to exclude persons of 'extreme' views. The argument over representativeness should also be less cogent, provided the criteria of trustworthiness are not themselves a reflection of political or other bias.[44] The invasion of privacy would be justifiable if vetting were restricted to the few essential cases. Even so, we would advocate other changes. The authorization of vetting should lie in the hands of the trial judge, following approval of the application by the Attorney-General. This would provide an additional layer of external control, especially if, as we suggest, the defence is given the opportunity to object at a pre-trial hearing when applications for *in camera* hearings or other secure procedures are considered.[45] Argument at this stage would be informed by the knowledge on both

---

[39] See nn. 48–50 below.   [40] Para. 11.   [41] Para. 12.

[42] For the relevant authorities on challenge for cause see Archbold, *Criminal Pleading, Evidence and Practice*, Vol. 1 (London, 1993), paras. 4–227 ff.

[43] Vetting for convictions can be justified on the basis that it does no more than enforce the existing disqualifications on jury service, and since it merely involves searching for information already held in database, the extra invasion of privacy is minimal.

[44] This would argue against the inclusion of 'subversive' views, associations, and sympathies (see Ch. 14 below).

[45] Public Interest Immunity claims should also be considered at this point. A pre-trial hearing of this kind to consider the PII certificates occurred in the Matrix Churchill case: see pp. 293–4 above and Leigh (n. 7 above), ch. 5.

sides, and of the judge, of the evidence the prosecution intends to lead. To provide further safeguards against abuse of this more limited form of vetting is problematic, but one possible guarantee would be for the judge to be given in sealed form brief reasons for the use of stand-by against a particular juror in vetting cases. This would help to ensure that the criteria were being properly applied, without giving allegations against the prospective juror a wider circulation than necessary.[46] These procedures should be embodied in legislation, rather than resting, as at present, on a circular, and all other vetting of jury panels should become an offence, analogous to attempting to pervert the course of justice.[47]

The lack of corresponding opportunities for the defence to influence jury composition has been criticized for inequality of arms. This imbalance was a feature of the law even before the abolition of peremptory challenge in 1988, since peremptory challenges were previously limited to three[48] while the prosecution was allowed to stand by any number of jurors until the jury panel was exhausted. The demise of peremptory challenge came as a result of allegations of abuse, culminating in the Cyprus Secrets trial. Here the seven defendants effectively 'pooled' their peremptory challenges to attempt to influence the jury composition by collective agreement. Defence counsel challenged no fewer than twelve potential jurors, who were middle-aged or elderly, in order to arrive at a jury composed of five women and seven men, all under the age of 40.[49] Presumably it was felt that a younger jury would be less authoritarian its attitude to the defendants, not least because the case involved alleged passing of information following homosexual entrapment. However, that the jury ultimately acquitted the defendants probably had less to do with its composition than with the considerable doubt cast upon the defendant's confessions due to allegations about the oppressive interrogation methods of the military police.[50] Given that the entire jury panel had already been vetted by the prosecution, the defence tactics looked to be no more than a proportionate response.

PROSECUTION DISCRETION

Several features of security cases combine to make political control of the prosecution decision essential from the state's point of view. These include liaison

---

[46] If vetting were restricted as we suggest, the case for any disclosure of information obtained to the defence considerably diminishes. It would be inappropriate to have any form of contested hearing about the individual juror's suitability in these circumstances.

[47] Cf. Enright and Morton (n. 16 above), 52.

[48] Criminal Law Act 1977, s. 43; on the history of peremptory challenge see: J. Gobert, 'The Peremptory Challenge: An Obituary', [1989] *Crim. LR* 528.

[49] See R. Thomas, *Espionage and Secrecy* (London, 1991), 201–2.

[50] This aspect gave rise to a separate inquiry: *Report by David Calcutt, QC on his Inquiry into the Investigations Carried out by the Service Police in Cyprus in February and March 1984*, Cmnd. 9781 (1986); and see A. Bradley, 'The Cyprus Eight and the Rule of Law', [1986] *PL* 363.

over evidence with the Security Service and Special Branch, revelations which may be made public if a trial is held; the protection of secret sources of information (especially informers), and of techniques for obtaining information (such as visual surveillance, interception of communications, or bugging); and possible use of Public Interest Immunity certificates. In addition it may be judged more important, especially in espionage cases, to obtain the co-operation of the suspect in order to establish what information precisely has been passed and to whom, than to obtain a conviction. All these factors require exceptional control over the conduct of the case and explain why the Attorney-General, a minister, is given the discretion under the Official Secrets Acts and the Prevention of Terrorism Act.[51] Such is the importance and sensitivity of these cases that the Attorney-General of the day has often prosecuted them in person.[52]

The need for this level of control was endorsed by the Franks Committee in 1972 in its review.[53] The reasons cited by the Home Office to the Committee included:

to secure consistency of practice or to prevent abuse where an offence is drafted in wide terms; to enable account to be taken of mitigating factors which cannot easily be defined by statute; to provide central control of the criminal law in sensitive areas . . . and finally to ensure that decisions on prosecution take account of important considerations of public policy or of a political or international character.

These factors may lead the Attorney to decide that the bringing of proceedings would be more harmful to the 'public interest' than failure to prosecute, notwithstanding that sufficient evidence exists.[54] The Committee laid stress on the need for the individual responsible to have experience of the kinds of issues involved and to be able to consult directly with the minister concerned, to be fully aware of the government's views on the national interest.[55] Although sensitivity to public interest and political considerations when conducted by a government minister can easily be confused with party-political self-interest, the Franks Committee were persuaded by the safeguard, which exists as a matter of convention, that in criminal matters the Attorney-General acts in a quasi-

---

[51] Prevention of Terrorism (Temporary Provisions) Act 1989, s. 19; OSA 1911, s. 8; OSA 1989, s. 9. In proposing the 1989 legislation the government distinguished between prosecutions for disclosure of information relating to defence, security, international relations, interception or information by other governments (all of which would require the Attorney-General's consent), and those relating to information useful in the commission of offences or escape from lawful custody (which would require the consent of the Director of Public Prosecutions): *Reform of the OSA 1911*, Cm. 408 (1988), para. 69; this is the effect of s. 9 above.

[52] For examples and discussion of the Attorney-General's role in these cases see Thomas (n. 49 above), ch. 4.

[53] *Departmental Committee on Section 2 of the OSA 1911, Volume 1 of the Report*, Cmnd. 5104 (1972), para. 243.

[54] Ibid., para. 245; and see J. Andrews, 'Public Interest and Criminal Proceedings' (1988) 104 *LQR* 410.

[55] See n. 53 above, para. 249.

independent capacity.[56] It was also claimed that the Attorney-General's accountability to Parliament presented 'a real safeguard which would not be available if his present responsibility were transferred to anyone else'.[57]

This confused intermingling of politics and detachment must inevitably cause considerable contradiction and tension for the Law Officers. If anything, the accountability of the Attorney-General to Parliament is likely to politicize the whole process, as is the insistence that the decision be taken by someone with ministerial experience.[58] The argument *against* the Attorney-General's role rests upon the fact that where disclosure of official information is concerned the government itself is the victim, and frequently an embarrassed one—not the best perspective from which a government minister can exercise an independent discretion over prosecution. The Franks Report rejected the possibility of amending the law to confer the discretion on the DPP in view of the political aspect of decisions to prosecute. A suggestion that the Attorney-General be advised on these matters by a panel was also rejected. Although the Franks Committee found that in the official secrets prosecutions realm the Attorney-General's fiat had operated 'satisfactorily and with integrity',[59] in the twenty years since the Report there have been numerous controversies over selective prosecution.[60]

Controversy has surrounded the choice of defendants, decisions to prosecute, and decisions not to do so. There is an apparent inconsistency, for instance, over the decisions to prosecute Jonathan Aitken and Duncan Campbell, both investigative journalists who received secrets from government officials, but not Chapman Pincher or Nigel West, who used identifiable intelligence officers as sources for their writings. There is a suspicion that a degree of ideological bias, or at least considerations of political embarrassment, influenced the decisions.[61]

[56] The classic statement of this position was the carefully prepared speech of Sir Hartley Shawcross in 1951, which asserted that the Attorney-General was not bound to consult with ministerial colleagues before deciding whether or not to institute proceedings, but could do so if he chose for the purpose of informing himself of political considerations affecting the public interest; the decision, however, would remain for the Attorney-General alone: *HC Debs.*, vol. 483, cols. 683–84 (29 Jan. 1951). For full discussion see J. Edwards, *The Attorney-General, Politics and the Public Interest* (London, 1984), 318–24.

[57] See n. 53 above, para. 249.

[58] The 'ministerial experience' argument is, anyway, self-refuting—if the Attorney-General's office is independent as is claimed, service in that post would not provide experience of the kind necessary. Nor is it commonly the case that Attorney-Generals have a wealth of other ministerial experience to draw on: often the office goes to career lawyer-politicians following a spell as Solicitor-General.

[59] See n. 53 above, para. 249.

[60] See Thomas (n. 49 above), 101–22 and 141–53. For detailed consideration of older instances of controversy over the Attorney-General's fiat and withdrawing of procedings see J. Edwards, *The Law Officers of the Crown* (London, 1964), chs. 10 and 11 (dealing *inter alia* with the Cabinet decision to withdraw proceedings against members of the Communist Party in 1924—the Campbell case) and Edwards (n. 56 above), 310–18.

[61] Pincher was a right-wing journalist, defence correspondent of the *Daily Express*; Rupert Allason ('Nigel West') is the Conservative MP for Torbay, whose writings, although critical of the performance of the intelligence agencies, have been largely sympathetic to their ideology. For discussion of the non-prosecution of Pincher and Allason see: Thomas (n. 49 above), 151–2. Aitken is now,

Similarly, the status of the informant may have been relevant in some cases: Berry (the informant and a co-defendant in the ABC case) had been a corporal in the Intelligence Corps, but former officers of MI5 and MI6 who had reached a high level were left unmolested by the criminal law, despite giving their co-operation to a series of authors.[62] Political embarrassment must also surely account for the decisions to prosecute Ponting and Tisdall. On the other hand the decisions to prosecute Tisdall, a filing clerk who leaked a document to a newspaper, but not Massiter, a former MI5 officer who gave a television interview, are hard to reconcile, although the acquittal between the two cases of Ponting may account for the government's reluctance to take proceedings against Massiter. The failure to prosecute the *Guardian* for publishing the memo leaked by Tisdall appears anomalous. The overall impression is that discretion to prosecute may well be influenced by the attitude of the government of the day to the politics of the alleged offender, and on how much political leverage he or she is perceived to be able to summon.

Decisions to grant immunity have proved particularly controversial where they involve the Law Officers. This does not merely concern offences requiring the Attorney-General's consent to prosecute, since immunity is granted in effect by use (or promised use should need arise) of the *nolle prosequi*—the power to stop proceedings in the public interest—and this can arise whatever the offence and whatever the prosecuting authority. Recent controversial instances have included the granting of immunity to Anthony Blunt in exchange for co-operation over his spying for the Soviet Union.[63] Although not formally involving a grant of immunity, the decision of the DPP in Northern Ireland not to prosecute members of the RUC against whom there was evidence of perverting or attempting or conspiring to pervert the course of justice, and of obstructing the police, arose out of the investigations into the alleged 'Shoot to Kill' policy.[64] Proceedings stopped by offering no further evidence have included the prosecution of men on trial in 1987 for conspiring to kidnap members of the African

ironically, a junior defence minister, but was at the time of his prosecution a journalist and a Conservative prospective parliamentary candidate. His revelations about government action in Nigeria were embarrassing to the Labour government of the day. Campbell was then a journalist with an alternative magazine, *Time Out*.

[62] In one recent case (Anthony Cavendish) no prosecution was instituted despite publication, within the jurisdiction of a book of memoirs (unsuccessful civil proceedings were brought: *Lord Advocate* v. *The Scotsman Publications* [1990] AC 812); this appears anomalous in view of the government's professed determination to prosecute Peter Wright should opportunity arise: *The Times*, 2 Aug. 1984. Much controversy in 1986 surrounded the position of Lord Rothschild as a source of intelligence disclosures; for a parliamentary discussion of allegations of selective prosecution see *HC Debs.*, vol. 109, col. 1292 (6 Feb. 1987). Contrast the position in the USA, where it is possible to challenge selective prosecution on constitutional grounds: *US* v. *Falk* 479 F2d 616 (1973); *US* v. *Jarrett* 822 F2d 1438, 1443 (1987).

[63] See A. Smith, 'Immunity from Prosecution' (1983) 42 *Camb. LJ* 299; Edwards (n. 56 above), 467–74.

[64] Andrews (n. 54 above), 411 (*HC Debs.*, vol. 126, cols. 21–35 (25 Jan. 1988)). The announcement was made by Sir Patrick Mayhew, then Attorney-General, and currently Northern Ireland Secretary. See also Ch. 9 above.

National Congress, in circumstances where there were substantial allegations of the intelligence connections of the defendants.[65] The danger in the use of prosecutorial discretion in cases such as these is that it may be a means of suppressing politically uncomfortable facts.

More defensible is the grant of immunity where the purpose is to ensure that those holding relevant information make it public. A promise of immunity may on occasion be a prerequisite for obtaining information necessary for a public inquiry touching the conduct of public officials: an announcement of immunity of this kind was made by the Attorney-General to those assisting the Scott Inquiry into Exports to Iraq.[66]

The courts are relatively powerless to control decisions at this level. The recent prosecution, twenty-three years after the event, of two men who had helped the convicted spy George Blake to escape from prison raised the question of prosecution policy in an unusual form. The defendants failed in their attempts to have the proceedings struck out as an abuse of process because of the delay in bringing proceedings.[67] The prosecution argued that it was not until the publication of two books (one was a full account of their own part by the defendants) that there was sufficient evidence to prosecute. The defendants alleged that a decision had been taken not to prosecute them in 1970 following the publication of an earlier book and that it would be oppressive for it to be reversed. The Court of Appeal set aside Public Interest Immunity certificates served by the Home Office covering relevant papers from the Security Service and Special Branch,[68] and heard evidence behind screens from a retired MI5 officer, Miss A.[69] Nevertheless, it refused to interfere with the judge's order that the procedings should be allowed to continue, and found entirely credible the explanation that no prosecution had been brought earlier because of insufficient evidence. The jury, however, formed their own view and subsequently acquitted the defendants.[70]

In some respects the arguments for a greater degree of independent control over prosecutorial decisions, even within this sensitive area, are strengthened by the Matrix Churchill case. The prosecutions fell within the remit of Customs and Excise as the independent body responsible for enforcement of export controls. Unlike official secrets' cases, there was no requirement for the Attorney-General's consent. However, at considerable constitutional cost, theoretically a

[65] See Andrews (n. 54 above), 410.

[66] It was reported that the Cabinet Secretary had also indicated that no civil servant's career prospects would be injured by such testimony, but that some officials nevertheless remained wary: *The Times*, 4 May 1993; see further Ch. 17 below.

[67] *R.* v. *Central Criminal Court, ex p. Randle and Pottle* [1991] 1 WLR 1087.

[68] Ibid. 1104–5, per Watkins LJ: 'on the grounds that the greater public interest favoured disclosure and for the purpose of ridding the applicants' minds of any lingering feeling that the perfectly proper class claim made by the Home Secretary's certificate or any other kind of privilege was made to avoid discovery of material embarrassing for the Crown and Special Branch but helpful to the applicants.'

[69] Ibid. 1107.

[70] *The Independent*, 27 June 1991.

nolle prosequi might have been entered after the overriding of the Public Interest Immunity certificates by the judge. Customs demonstrated independence by resisting executive pressure from several sources[71] before the prosecutions were brought. Although the end-result may have been that prosecutions were instigated when in the public interest they ought not to have been, and the use of public interest immunity certificates was unsatisfactory, to put it mildly,[72] a cover-up was avoided. We are far from confident that the outcome would have been the same if the offences had been subject to the Attorney-General's consent to prosecution. When the case was dropped it was on the decision of prosecution counsel in the light of the damage done to the Customs case by the evidence of Alan Clark, not at the insistence of ministers (who were, however, kept informed).[73]

From direct political control of the conduct of the proceedings, we turn now to more technical questions about the conduct of security-related trials.

PROTECTIVE MEASURES

The conduct of trials *in camera* conflicts with the fundamental objective of open justice.[74] The interest here is not so much the position of the defendant—though the trial processes may be affected by the exclusion of the press and public[75]—but the interests of the community. Justice is done in the name of the public and therefore should be done in public, unless that would itself make it more difficult to achieve justice.[76] However, other public interests are worthy of consideration, namely the preservation of secrecy of genuinely sensitive material. This might suggest that the state should be put to a bare choice between the public interests in having a public trial and conviction, and preserving sensitive material. A simple election of this kind might be suitable for cases where there is a clear imbalance in the two public interests to be weighed, or where the interests, although finely balanced, are not in either case very weighty. However, it is cases of finely balanced, serious public interests in favour of prosecution and non-disclosure that require an *in camera* procedure, otherwise the 'graymail' possibility will surface.[77] Article 6(1) of the European Convention on Human

---

[71] Especially from the DTI (see Leigh (n. 7 above), 7–10 and MI6 ibid. 143 ff). Two officials also refused to give evidence to the Trade and Industry Select Committee investigation into the Supergun: see HC (1991–2) 86, paras. 125–7.

[72] This was one aspect in which the Attorney-General was heavily involved in advising other ministers: *HC Debs.* vol. 213, cols. 743 ff. (10 Nov. 1992).

[73] 'Ministers were informed of developments at various stages of the case': Sir John Cope, *HC Debs.*, vol. 213, col. 1002 (13 Nov. 1992).

[74] See generally, G. Nettheim, 'Open Justice and State Secrets' (1985–6) 10 *Adelaide LR* 281, to which we are greatly indebted.

[75] The conduct of proceedings *in camera* may itself be argued to have a prejudicial effect on the jury: see p. 238 above.

[76] *Scott* v. *Scott* [1913] AC 417.

[77] It is possible, though surely rare in practice, for an application for an *in camera* hearing to be made by the defence; for an example see Andrews (n. 54 above), 410.

Rights, for instance, recognizes the right both in determination of criminal and civil matters to a public hearing and public pronouncement of judgment, but specifically allows for the exclusion of the press and the public from all or part of a trial in the interests of national security in a democratic society.[78]

Several qualifications should be entered. First, the availability of *in camera* processes should be restricted to categories of cases that are self-evidently serious: the provisions in the Official Secrets Acts[79] are arguably over-broad, since they can be applied not merely to espionage trials but also to all categories of criminal disclosure of official information. We would limit the availability of *in camera* processes in the latter group to trials relating to security and intelligence information under section 1 of the 1989 Act, defence material under section 2, and information relating to interception and other investigatory techniques under section 4.[80] Secondly, the need for protection should itself be a matter for argument in open court,[81] and subject to review. Where the order is one relating to a trial on indictment, an appeal against the order may be brought by an 'aggrieved person' (this will include affected journalists).[82] Thirdly, the principle of the least restrictive alternative should apply: non-disclosure should be limited to those parts of evidence and argument where it is strictly necessary, and where possible lesser orders should be made if these can satisfy the desired objective.

As has been seen, the Official Secrets Acts allow for parts of official secrets and espionage cases to be heard *in camera* on grounds that 'the publication of any evidence to be given or any statement to be made in the course of the proceedings would be prejudicial to the national safety'.[83] In any event the passing of sentence must take place in public. Generally the courts appear to have exercised these powers sensibly. Examples of cases where part of the evidence was heard *in camera* include the consideration of 'the Crown Jewels' (a briefing document prepared on the sinking of the *General Belgrano*) at the trial of Clive

[78] Exclusion is also possible, on other grounds, including 'to the extent strictly necessary in the opinion of the court in special circumstances where publicity would prejudice the interests of justice.'

[79] OSA 1920, s. 8(4) (having its origin in wartime Defence of the Realm regulations, see Thomas (n. 49 above), 64) ; OSA 1989, s. 11(4). On the history and use of these powers see ibid. 63–8. Advance notice is normally required of such applications by the prosecution: Crown Court Rules 1982, r. 24A (added by SI 1989 No. 1103). This rule requires notice to be posted of any application in the court precincts, to enable the press to make use of the power under Criminal Justice Act 1988, s. 159 to appeal against such orders. *In camera* hearings are available in other types of proceedings on similar grounds. On coroners' inquests see SI 1984/ 552, r.17. Industrial tribunals may also sit in private: Employment Protection (Consolidation) Act 1978, sched. 9.

[80] In Ch. 9 we argue for the restriction of offences under the 1989 Act.

[81] There is some authority holding closed applications for *in camera* hearings in British law: *R. v. Osbourne* (1989) 88 Cr. App. R. 28; and see *R. v. Davis* (n. 115 below), but see the rules requiring public notice (above n. 79).

[82] Criminal Justice Act 1988, s. 159 (1)(*b*) and (*c*); and see Ch. 9 above. The High Court has rejected an application made by journalists against the hearing *in camera* of evidence in a recent espionage case: the *Independent*, 9 July 1993.

[83] See Ch. 9 above. The terminology (national safety) suggests that 'national security' had not at that time achieved paramountcy in the legal armoury of parliamentary counsel.

Ponting,[84] and the taped conversation between Aubrey, Berry, and Campbell which formed the basis of the *ABC* prosecution. By contrast, espionage trials are commonly conducted mostly in private: this was so, for instance, with the trial of Michael Bettaney. This procedure was criticized in the case of George Blake, the former MI6 officer convicted of espionage, as leaving insufficient information of the reasoning for the forty-two-year term of imprisonment imposed on him.[85]

In addition to the statutory power to conduct *in camera* hearings in official secrets cases, it seems that the inherent power at common law which a judge has to exclude the public in the interests of justice[86] may apply in security cases. This will be available especially where the object of the offence is to prevent publication, and public proceedings would, therefore, be self-defeating. However it may also be important in other categories of cases where the evidence comes from security sources: in these cases it may be more marginal whether the true reason for conducting the proceedings in closed session relates to the interests of justice as such, rather than a desire to protect security similar to that permitted under the statutory provisions. This inherent power was applied in a First World War case involving the seizure of 'documents calculated to prevent or injure recruiting'.[87] Although the judges argued that this was in the interests of justice having regard to the purpose of the regulations in question, one suspects that the motive had more to do with preserving public morale than in any genuine secrecy concern. In a case of similar vintage the High Court decided that a court martial held following the 1916 Easter Rising had been properly held *in camera* in order to prevent retaliation against witnesses.[88]

When similar concerns have arisen in recent cases witnesses have been protected by screens or anonymity, rather than by closing the proceedings. These methods are to be preferred in accord with our principle of the least restricted alternative: the appellate courts have treated orders allowing a witness anonymity as a less serious incursion on the principle of open justice than *in camera* hearings.[89] It is unclear if common law requires a judge to be satisfied that they would be ineffective before excluding the public, but there the courts have repeatedly stressed that *in camera* hearings are only to be used in the last resort.

---

[84] Precautions included sweeping the courtroom for bugging devices: C. Ponting, *The Right to Know* (London, 1985), 170–1.

[85] M. Randle and P. Pottle, *The Blake Escape* (London, 1989), 250–8, argue that this allowed the government to leak a partisan account of Blake's activities through selected journalists.

[86] *Scott* v. *Scott* (n. 76 above); s. 8(4) of the OSA 1920 expressly preserves this common law jurisdiction.

[87] *Norman* v. *Matthews* (1916) 85 LJ (KB) 857.

[88] *R.* v. *Governor of Lewes Prison, ex p. Doyle* [1917] 2 KB 254; the Attorney-General argued that without such a discretion espionage cases would necessarily be heard in public, since (at that time) there was no statutory authority for *in camera* hearings: 261–2.

[89] *R.* v. *Socialist Worker's Printers and Publishers Limited* [1975] QB 637, 651–2 per Lord Widgery, LCJ.

In several recent cases intelligence officers have been permitted to give evidence anonymously and, if still serving, behind a screen.[90] The fullest consideration of the applicability of these protective powers in relation to security and intelligence officers came in a New Zealand decision where the Court of Appeal held that the defendant's defiance of an order by the trial judge in an official secrets prosecution not to publish the names of such officers constituted contempt of court.[91] The court regarded the power as an inherent common law one which was unaffected by the express provision of a power (similar to that in United Kingdom legislation) in the Official Secrets Act 1951, section 15(3) to exclude the public. In exercising this jurisdiction the judge was seen as correctly supporting the requirements of efficiency of the security service as expressed in its statutory charter, having regard to the function of that agency in official secrets investigations.[92]

Comparable reasoning would seem applicable to judicial orders suppressing the publication of the names of intelligence officers made by United Kingdom courts. However, in a contempt action arising from the *ABC* case the House of Lords deliberately left unresolved the question of whether such an order which purported to restrict the publication of such names *outside* the courtroom would be valid.[93] In the same case they did hold, however, that the making of an order by a magistrates' court that a witness who was an intelligence officer was not to be referred to by name was an acceptable extension of the court's power to control its own proceedings. It followed that the deliberate publication of the witness's name by a newspaper was capable of amounting to contempt of court, because it could interfere with the administration of justice, although on the facts it did nòt do so. Section 11 of the Contempt of Court Act 1981 was intended to resolve doubts about the legality of orders directed to the press restricting publication of names following the *Leveller* case by allowing a court to give directions prohibiting publication of a name in connection with proceedings. However the effect is by no means clear since this power is expressed to turn upon whether the court has the power to make an order withholding the name in the first place, and this may depend on the validity of the reasons for making the order.[94]

Such powers to restrict publication of details are open to abuse. As Nettheim

---

[90] For instance at the Matrix Churchill trial (Leigh (above n. 7), 130–1) and at the trial of members of *Meibion Glyndwr* at Caernarfon Crown Court in March 1993: the *Guardian*, 10 Mar. 1993, and see p. 76 above.

[91] *A-G* v. *Taylor* [1975] 2 NZLR 675.

[92] Ibid. 679–80, per Wild CJ and 684, per Richmond J. However, in the Matrix Churchill case Geoffrey Robertson QC opposed the making of the orders allowing anonymous evidence from intelligence officers on the grounds that they diluted the force of the protection against perjury and were anyway unnecessary for the operational convenience of the agencies since the officers could be redeployed to desk jobs not requiring anonymity: Leigh (n. 7 above), 129–30.

[93] *A-G* v. *Leveller* [1979] AC 440, 451 (Lord Diplock) and 456 (Viscount Dilhorne).

[94] A leading commentator concludes that the uncertainty over the extent of these powers remains: C. Miller, *Contempt of Court* (2nd ed., Oxford, 1989), 315–17.

has pointed out: 'It is not beyond the bounds of possibility that this power . . . might be used to achieve dramatic effect, namely to impress upon a judge or, particularly, a jury, the high sensistivity of the material in question.'[95] Formal evidence of the purported danger to national security is not required before a court can make such an order.[96] The *Leveller* case illustrates the dangers: after the prosecution claimed that the protection of the witness's identity was necessary for reasons of national security, the intelligence officer in question was forced to concede that his name and rank appeared in a publicly available journal—this was enough to persuade their Lordships that there could be no contempt through breach of the order, but what it really demonstrates is that the court was misled into making the order in the first place.

It can also be argued that the use of protective orders to protect security *per se* is unrelated to the administration of justice—the supposed rationale of the inherent jurisdiction. It was on this basis that Woodhouse J dissented in *Attorney-General* v. *Taylor*, distinguishing inconvenience that the New Zealand Security Service might suffer by the publication of officers' names, or the disadvantage to the individuals themselves, from what he regarded as the central question of whether the order was justified by reason of the evidence given at the trial.[97] This reasoning is highly persuasive. Likewise Lord Scarman has argued that there is no general inherent jurisdiction in a court to sit *in camera* for reasons of national security in the absence of express statutory authority. Instead he linked the interests of justice and graymail: 'if the factor of national safety appears to endanger the due administration of justice, e.g. by deterring the Crown from from prosecuting in cases where it should do so, a court may sit in private'.[98] This approach is further supported by recent decisions in which the courts have quashed orders made under section 11 of the Contempt of Court Act 1981 because the reason was not strictly related to protection of the administration of justice.[99]

Where the court's inherent jurisdiction is seen by the executive as unduly restrictive, the temptation is to create specific statutory authority for such orders, extending the scope of those available under the Official Secrets Acts. A remarkable instance of statutory protection of this kind arose in Australia in 1984 when criminal proceedings appeared imminent against members of the Australian Secret Intelligence Service for acts committed during a training exercise at the Melbourne Sheraton Hotel. Both State and Commonwealth legislation

---

[95] Nettheim (n. 74 above), 299.

[96] *A-G* v. *Leveller* (n. 93 above), 471 (Lord Scarman); and see Lord Widgery LCJ in the Court of Appeal: *R.* v. *Leveller* [1979] 1 QB 31, 44–5.

[97] See n. 91 above, 690–1. He argued that although an order of the kind affirmed by the majority might be in the public interest, it could not be based upon the interests of justice, since it would be restricted to naming the officers as witnesses in the proceedings, rather than naming them as intelligence officers as such.

[98] *A-G* v. *Leveller* (n. 93 above), 471.

[99] *R.* v. *Malvern JJ, ex p. Evans; R.* v. *Evesham JJ ex p. McDonagh* [1988] 1 All ER 371 .

was passed to enable a court to make effective orders preventing the publication outside court of the information given in any proceedings that might be taken:[100] the purpose of these powers was specifically to deal with the doubts over the position of the press arising from the *Taylor* and *Leveller* cases. In the event the legislation was not used since no proceedings were brought, but the fact that legislation was introduced to deal with a single, sensitive case graphically illustrates the potential for abuse of criminal procedures by the authorities.

The procedures we have been discussing affect whether all aspects of the trial are held in public but do not affect the position of the defendant.[101] However, those to be examined in the next section concern the withholding of information from the defendant.

DISCLOSURE OF EVIDENCE

In a criminal case it is fundamental that no *evidence* (that is, material which is laid before the court) is withheld from the defendant.[102] This raises doubts about the applicability of Public Interest Immunity to criminal cases.[103] Although in principle the courts have extended Public Interest Immunity to criminal cases,[104] there are two major difficulties. One is that before the defendant can challenge the certificate, it is necessary at the first stage to demonstrate that the evidence is relevant to the case: this requirement may negate the defendant's general right in criminal proceedings to keep his or her defence a surprise.[105] Thus, in the Matrix Churchill case the trial judge's reluctance to override the public interest immunity certificates filed by the prosecution was only overcome after Henderson's counsel, Geoffrey Robertson, effectively gave advance notice of his defence in order to demonstrate the relevance of the documents.[106]

[100] See Criminal Proceedings Act 1984 (Vict.); Judiciary Amendment Act 1984 (Cth.), both discussed in detail in Nettheim (n. 74 above), 312–16. A separate attempt by the ASIS officers concerned to obtain an injunction forbidding the disclosure of their names to the state police failed: *Australia v. Hayden (No. 2)* (1984) 56 ALR 82.

[101] In considering procedures for dealing with the admissibility of sensitive evidence obtained by telephone tapping, the Court of Appeal has condemned the exclusion of the defendant from the argument by resorting to an *in camera* hearing attended only by the prosecution, defence counsel, and the judge: *R. v. Preston, The Times*, 13 May 1992; but cf. *R. v. Davis* (n. 115 below), where the Court of Appeal endorsed the exceptional use of *ex parte* proceedings over immunity from disclosure of sensitive prosecution material.

[102] Some forms of administrative procedure, such as those relating to deportation and employment vetting (see Chs. 6 and 7 above) do involve *evidence* being given *ex parte* in a civil forum.

[103] On public interest immunity certificates and national security outside the criminal law context, see Ch. 12 below.

[104] *R. v. Governor of Brixton Prison ex p. Osman* [1991] 1 WLR 281 per Mann LJ; this was not a criminal *trial* as such but rather an application for habeas corpus to prevent extradition. Equally inconclusive was the application of the doctrine in criminal libel proceedings: *R. v. Lewes JJ ex p. Home Secretary* [1973] AC 388. On reported criminal cases from Australian and Canadian courts, see nn. 119 ff. below.

[105] Cf. A. Smith, 'Public Interest Immunity in Criminal Cases', [1993] *Camb. LJ* 1.

[106] Leigh (n. 7 above), ch. 5 and, above, pp. 293–4.

The second difficulty is in reconciling immunity from disclosure with the duty of openness owed by the prosecution. As long ago as 1956 the difficulties were recognized when Viscount Kilmuir volunteered that the government would not claim immunity in the case of crown documents relevant to the defence in criminal cases.[107] Since, where a document is covered by immunity, it cannot be produced for any purpose (the prosecution is debarred also from tendering it in evidence), the main significance is in relation to evidence available to the prosecution which it is not intending to use.[108] In this area a number of important recent developments have generally liberalized the position, although the use of Public Interest Immunity certificates is in danger of snatching away these hard-won rights for the defence.

Guidelines issued by the Attorney-General to prosecuting authorities provide for disclosure of unused prosecution material to the defence. However, an exception is made for 'sensitive' material, including that dealing with national security, identifying 'a member of the Security Services who would be of no further use to those Services once his identity became known'; disclosing the identity of an informer who or whose family would be put in danger; or disclosing some unusual form of surveillance or method of detecting crime.[109] Where sensitive information is involved the guidelines put the *prosecution* in the strange position of considering whether the effect of disclosure would be merely neutral or whether it would assist the defence and, if the latter, of balancing between the degree of sensitivity and the extent to which it would assist in deciding on disclosure.[110] Prosecuting counsel will be asked to advise where the correct action is uncertain, but in cases of exceptional sensitivity where the document cannot be shown to counsel, the Director of Public Prosecutions may be consulted.[111] The Guidelines counsel partial disclosure even in sensitive cases wher-

---

[107] *HL Debs.*, vol. 197, col. 745 (6 June 1956). He made an exception for statements by police informers. On the background to this statement see J. Jacob, 'From Privileged Crown to Interested Public', [1993] *PL* 121, 142–6.

[108] This contrasts with the USA where *ex parte* procedures have been devised for hearing argument about extremely sensitive evidence: Classified Information Procedures Act 1980, 18 USC app. 1–16 (1982), s. 4; see: R. Salgado, 'Government Secrets, Fair Trials, and the Classified Procedures Act' (1989) 98 *Yale LJ* 427; S. Jordan, 'Classified Information and Conflicts in Independent Counsel Prosecutions: Balancing the Scales of Justice After Iran–Contra' (1991) 91 *Colum. LR* 1651; D. Menkhaus, 'Graymail: Constitutional Immunity from Justice?' (1981) 18 *Harv. J. on Legis.* 389. *Ex parte* affidavits have, exceptionally, been used also in civil cases: *Patterson* v. *FBI* 893 F. 2d 595 (3rd Cir., 1990); *Molerio* v. *FBI* 749 F.2d 815 (DC Cir., 1984). See F. Askin, 'Secret Justice and the Adversary System' (1991) 18 *Hastings Constit. LQ* 745. In these instances the government preserves the secrecy of the evidence and is allowed the benefit of relying on it. Such a practice would, if followed in the UK, contravene Art. 6 of the ECHR: *Ludi* v. *Switzerland* (1993) 15 EHRR 173 (see p. 99 above). *Ex parte* hearings are forbidden in criminal cases: Classified Information Procedures Act 1980, s. 6(*a*).

[109] *Attorney-General's Guidelines on the Disclosure of Information to the Defence in Cases to be Tried on Indictment* (1982) 74 Cr. App. R. 302, para. 6. The exceptions are apparently waivable—they are described as 'discretionary'.

[110] Ibid., para. 8. 'Any doubt as to whether the balance is in favour of, or against, disclosure should always be resolved in favour of disclosure.'

[111] Ibid., para. 10.

ever possible,[112] but if there is an unresolvable conflict between the duty to disclose and the public interest in not doing so, conclude that it 'will probably be necessary to offer no . . . evidence'.[113]

Although these guidelines are advisory only, the Court of Appeal has added a common law duty of disclosure which extends to any material which might assist the defence.[114] The same judgment puts decisions about non-disclosure firmly in the hands of the court, rather than the prosecution, as under the Guidelines. The consequence is that where the prosecuting authorities wish to resist disclosure, they must now do so by by way of public interest immunity certificate. It was in applying these principles that public interest immunity certificates were served in the Matrix Churchill case. The consequence is that the prosecution would be required, in effect, to draw sensitive material to the defence's attention for the purpose of claiming immunity for it. The Court of Appeal's response to this conundrum has been to sanction the exceptional use of applications in the absence of the defence.[115] Although defence counsel will normally be told that the application has occurred, even if successful, so as to have the opportunity to make representations to the judge about it, in a few cases even the fact of the application may be kept secret. The court saw this procedure as the lesser of three evils: the alternatives being either to require the prosecution to choose between prosecution and non-disclosure, or to allow defence counsel to participate in the hearing on condition that they did not reveal details to their clients.

The Matrix Churchill trial was a celebrated (and isolated) instance of such certificates being quashed,[116] after the trial judge inspected the documents. Both internal government papers and intelligence reports were released to the defence after the judge had been convinced that they were essential to the defence argument that the government had not been misled by the export licence application.[117]

The use of public interest immunity certificates to suppress information about the involvement of security and intelligence operatives in criminal cases has arisen more frequently in Canada and Australia.[118]

---

[112] Ibid., para. 13. [113] Ibid., para. 15.

[114] *R.* v. *Ward* [1993] 1 WLR 619. See generally: P. O'Connor, 'Prosecution Disclosure: Principle, Practice and Justice' [1992] *Crim. LR* 464.

[115] *R.* v. *Davis* [1993] 1 WLR 613; cf. the consideration of *ex parte* applications for production orders under sched. 7 of the Prevention of Terrorism (Temporary Provisions) Act 1989 by Stuart-Smith LJ (who also acts as commissioner under the Security Service Act 1989) in *R.* v. *Middlesex Guildhall Crown Court ex p. Sallinger, The Times*, 30 Mar. 1992. The *Royal Commission on Criminal Justice*, Cmnd. 2263 (1993) has claimed that the judgment in *Davis* 'strikes a satisfactory balance' (para. 95), but wanted the whole subject of disclosure of evidence covered by a statutory framework (para. 96).

[116] The Court of Appeal quashed certificates relating to Special Branch and the Security Service in *R.* v. *Randle and Pottle* (n. 67 above), but with the agreement of the Crown.

[117] For full details of the certificates and the argument see Leigh (n. 7 above), ch. 5.

[118] The text below describes the use of Public Interest Immunity in a criminal context. Australia has also created special statutory procedures to deal with public interest immunity claims in judicial review actions before the Administrative Appeals Tribunal. These allow for a certificate to be served

Australian courts have confirmed that the final decision about disclosure of information, even where it is in the hands of an intelligence agency, rests with them. In one case Lockhart J stated that where the public interest against disclosure clashed with the public interest that the ends of justice should not be defeated by withholding relevant evidence, the court would give considerable weight to the opinion of the responsible minister, but was nevertheless entitled to reach its own conclusion.[119] However, in several Public Interest Immunity cases the Australian courts have suppressed information about or derived from ASIO or ASIS.[120] In *Alister* v. *R*[121] the court ordered production to the court of ASIO records in an appeal from conviction for a terrorist bombing, but after inspecting them decided they were not relevant to the case.[122] Accordingly, they were not disclosed to the defence. In one respect the judgment was a mild blow against the government, for it rejected a claim that ASIO should be able to decline to confirm whether or not the documents even existed. Claims to secrecy in the context of a criminal investigation arose in a highly unusual form in *Australia* v. *Hayden*[123] where ASIS officers involved in the abortive Hilton Hotel operation[124] tried independently to assert security considerations to restrain the Commonwealth government from disclosing their identities to the Victoria police. The case failed since it was held that it was for the government to take a view on whether security required withholding of the evidence, and not an affected individual.

In Canada Public Interest Immunity is based on statutory authority.[125] Following *Conway* v. *Rimmer*,[126] the Canadian parliament responded initially by a statutory attempt to restore the law to the previous position in the case of docu-

by the Attorney-General certifying that particular evidence would be contrary to the public interest, among other reasons, because it would prejudice the security, defence, or international relations of Australia: Administrative Appeals Tribunal Act 1975, s. 36 and s. 36A (as substituted by the Administrative Appeals Tribunal Amendment Act 1977, ss. 22 and 23). Whereas other categories of certificate are made subject to appeal to the AAT President, in these fields the certificate is conclusive before the tribunal and can only be set aside by the High Court. Additional provisions allow the AAT to sit *in camera*, or with one party excluded: ss. 35 and 36 of the 1975 Act.

[119] *Haj-Ismail* v. *Minister for Immigration and Ethnic Affairs (No. 2)* [1982] 64 FLR 112 (involving ASIO records relevant to a decision to deport; following inspection of the documents the judge ruled against production since they were not relevant). The reservation of the power to the court was attributed in part to the vesting of the judicial power in the courts under the Australian Constitution: ibid. 120.

[120] See (in addition to cases cited in nn. 119, 121, and 123) *Haj-Ismail and Another* v. *Minister for Immigration and Ethnic Affairs* (1981) 56 FLR 67.

[121] (1984) 58 ALJR 97; (1984) 50 ALR 41.

[122] Murphy J dissented on the ground that the defendant's counsel should first have been given the opportunity to address argument on whether the documents were relevant.

[123] (1984) 156 CLR 532.

[124] Purportedly an ASIS training exercise which resulted in armed intelligence officers terrorizing guests and staff at the hotel.

[125] Currently Canada Evidence Act, RSC 1985 c. C-5, ss. 37 and 38 (although many of the cases cited below were decided under the former provision, Canada Evidence Act 1970, ss. 36.1 and 36.2); see generally, T. Cooper, *Crown Privilege* (Aurora, Ont., 1990), 130–8.

[126] [1968] AC 910.

ments concerned with international relations, national defence, or security: ministerial certificates were made conclusive in these instances.[127] This was later relaxed so as to allow claims of immunity in these fields to be heard and determined by a Federal Court panel comprising the Chief Justice or certain other designated Federal judges.[128] In formal terms the courts have been keen to assert that the statute vests authority in them and not the executive, but in nearly all of the reported cases they have upheld the government's claims to immunity.

In the first case decided under the revised procedure, officers of the Security Service of the RCMP (the predecessor of CSIS) on trial for a break-in and theft from the offices of a political party (the Parti Quebecois) sought access to documents which they claimed would support their defence that their actions were consistent with approved investigatory techniques within the RCMP. The case was of special significance since it was these allegations which had led to the establishment of the MacDonald Commission.[129] The Solicitor General's certificate, which stated that disclosure would be injurious, was upheld by the Federal Court without inspecting the documents, because the defendants had failed to raise a prima facie case in favour of disclosure.[130] The judgment repays detailed study because of the analysis it contains of how the court should approach the issues, later approved on appeal.[131]

Thurlow CJ stated that, although the procedure gave the courts a role, the public interest in national security was 'as great and weighty as it always has been';[132] nevertheless, as the common law from the eighteenth century onwards showed, it could be outweighed, especially by the public interest in a fair trial for the defendant.[133] In a revealing passage the judge made clear the difficulty he faced in dealing with the issue:

there is little if anything in the certificate or the secret affidavit or elsewhere in the material to afford a basis for estimating or assessing the gravity of the danger or the injury that might result from the disclosure of any particular information. What impresses me as much as anything else in the material, as indicating the gravity of the risk to national security and international relations is the large volume and comprehensiveness of the material demanded, the disclosure of which it seems to me, could but lay bare to the world the whole structure of the Security Service with its shortcomings, its methods and

---

[127] S. 41(2) of the Federal Court Act, RSC 1970 (2nd Supp), c. 10 (repealed).

[128] See n. 125 above. These provisions may be subject to further amendment; the government has announced that a working group is reconsidering the whole question of the use of security information in the courts: Solicitor-General, *On Course: National Security for the 1990s* (Ottawa, 1991), 49.

[129] See A. Goldsmith, 'Political Policing in Canada' [1985] *PL* 39.

[130] *Goguen* v. *Gibson* [1983] 1 FC 872.

[131] *Goguen* v. *Gibson* [1983] 2 FC 462. Marceau J, while concurring, did, however, stress the judge's independent role and expertise in assessing the possible damage to the administration of justice from non-disclosure.

[132] (n. 130 above), 881.

[133] Citing dicta from *R.* v. *Hardy* (1794) 24 St. Tr. 199 onwards (see Ch. 4 above).

techniques, its resources, its policies and its targets, and its relationship with friendly foreign security agencies as well.[134]

In a sense all this tended to support the defendants' claim that they were engaged in an institutionalized practice, but the judge used it to opposite effect; the quashing of the certificate where a similar defence was involved in the Matrix Churchill case compares favourably. Also of interest was the judge's statement that where disclosure of national security information was sought, the age of the information favoured disclosure less than in other cases, since 'secrets relating to national security may require to be preserved indefinitely'.[135] Another factor to be borne in mind was the international position:

> If a state of war existed I doubt that anyone would argue that the importance of the public interest in national security was not greater than the public interest in the administration of justice for in a war situation the lives of all citizens may be in jeopardy. That the country is not at war militates somewhat in favour of the applicants but, in the present day state of international affairs, political terrorism and subversion, not much. Eternal vigilance is as necessary as it always has been to maintain the security of the nation.[136]

These aspects of the public interest had to set aside the public interest of the applicants in defending themselves against criminal charges. However, the judge took the view that if convicted the applicants would be unlikely to face severe punishment. The fact that many of the documents sought might only be peripherally relevant and that the applicants could only speculate on what some of them probably contained also counted against disclosure.[137] Since both the weighting of the factors and the preponderance of the evidence were against disclosure, there was no reason to suppose that inspection of the documents would alter this view.[138]

This approach was applied in a later case where the court refused access to CSIS profiles of informers in the trial of alleged Armenian terrorists charged with conspiracy to murder, and refused cross-examination of the affidavit by the Director of CSIS filed in support of the certificate.[139] The same result has been reached in a civil case where an applicant was refused access to CSIS files on him which he required in a civil action arising from his refusal of security clearance.[140]

---

[134] (n. 130 above), 904–5.   [135] Ibid. 905.

[136] Ibid.; cf. Lord Simon in *D* v. *NSPCC* [1977] 1 All ER 589, 607: 'If society is disrupted or overturned by internal or external enemies the administration of justice will itself be one of the casualties. *Silent enim leges inter arma.* So the law says that, important as it is to the administration of justice that all relevant evidence should be addressed to the court, such evidence must be withheld if, on the balance of public interest, the peril of its adduction to national security outweighs its benefit to the forensic process—as to which, as regards national security in its strictest sense, a ministerial certificate will almost always be regarded as conclusive.'

[137] See n. 130 above, 906–7.   [138] Ibid. 907.

[139] *Kevork* v. *the Queen* [1984] 2 FC 753; and see the later application during the trial of the same case: (1986) 27 CCC 523.

[140] *Gold* v. *Canada* (1986) 64 NR 261. The judge's ruling that it was not necessary to inspect the documents to uphold the certificate was upheld by the Federal Court of Appeal. Mahoney J did,

However in another trial for conspiracy to murder in which the use of special investigatory powers under warrant by CSIS was challenged, the Federal Court of Appeal quashed the trial judge's decision that the affidavit by CSIS filed with the original warrant application should not be disclosed.[141] The judgment of Mahoney J rests ultimately on the ground that the judge had invoked the Canada Evidence Act immunity on his own initiative and not at the invitation of the government. However it is also adorned with powerful (and rare) statements in support of open administration of justice, even in the face of alleged threats to national security. For instance:

> What must be sought here is the maximum accountability and accessibility of and to the judicial presence in the intelligence gathering system but not to the extent of impairing the investigation of genuine threats to national security . . . the credibility of the Service has a direct and positive, but by no means exclusive, dependency on the credibility of the judicial presence in the system; since judicial credibility is so dependent on openness, the Service, too, has an interest in the openness of that judicial presence.[142]

The public interest immunity provisions have also been considered from a constitutional perspective. Thus, they were held not to violate section 7 of the Charter of Rights, when applied to allow a RCMP officer to refuse to answer questions on grounds of national security in an immigration hearing, although the hearing consequently might result in the applicant being deported from Canada.[143]

however, stress that the new procedure opened the possibility of *partial* disclosure, and the tone of the judgment is anything but deferential. After referring to the revision of the procedure and the reforms following the MacDonald Commission he stated: 'It is not to be assumed that any of this transpired because the government of the day was spontaneously taken by a selfless desire to share its secrets. The executive had been unable to sustain the credibility of the system of absolute privilege . . . The new system was a politically necessary response to serious public concerns. Effective judicial supervision is an essential element of the new system. Among other aspects of the new system, its credibility is dependent on a public appreciation that the competing public interests are, in fact, being judicially balanced. It will not be well served if it appears that the exercise of judicial discretion is automatically abdicated because national security is accepted as so vital that the fair administration of justice is assumed incapable of outweighing it.' (ibid. p. 265–6); and cf. the same judge's comments in *Atwal* v. *Canada* (1988) 79 NR 91, 111–12.

[141] *Atwal* v. *Canada*, previous note (and see further Ch. 3 above); it seems likely that it was this part of the decision which led to the admission that the original warrant application had been deeply flawed, resulting in the resignation of the director of CSIS and the subsequent quashing of the warrant (see *Atwal* v. *Canada* (1988) 80 NR 4).

[142] See n. 140 above, 112. Mahoney J also argued that the court is required to consider national security and the administration of justice as competing public interests, not as connected aspects of a single notion of public interest: 'To adopt the latter approach is to risk the co-option of the administration of justice by other, perhaps only momentarily pressing, concerns. Assuming that its disclosure would not have a cataclysmic impact on our entire social order, it is not the ends of justice which may be subverted by the disclosure of the affidavit.' (ibid. 114).

[143] *Mohammad* v. *Canada* (1989) 23 FTR 186, Federal Court of Appeal. Some of the questions related to information admitted to have been supplied by Israeli intelligence about the applicant for counter-terrorist purposes. It was also alleged against the applicant that he had been convicted in Greece for bombing an airline, had failed to inform immigration officers of his membership of the Popular Front for the Liberation of Palestine, and had been refused entry to Cyprus on security grounds. The details revealed in the report of the conduct of the immigration hearing show that in

If it be accepted that Public Interest Immunity should apply to criminal cases, the ways in which the current procedure could be improved are relatively minor. The pre-condition is an important one: most genuine secrecy needs can be met by use of procedural protections within the courtroom, such as *in camera* hearings and protective orders; public interest immunity certificates should be reserved for cases where these are inadequate. In our view such cases should be rare. The defendant's interests in having access in a criminal trial to all available official information (whether the prosecution plans to tender it as evidence or not) are so strong that they should only be overriden in wholly exceptional circumstances. Having said that, there may be a very few cases where the public interest requires both that a prosecution be brought *and* that some prosecution details be withheld. For these we would suggest the following reforms.[144]

Judicial inspection of the documents in respect of which immunity is claimed should be mandatory in criminal cases, not discretionary. This would be a more effective guarantee against allegations, such as those raised in the Matrix Churchill case, that ministers had abused the power[145] to issue the certificates to suppress evidence embarrassing to them. In a criminal case the interests at stake are so serious that there should be no possibility of a certificate being taken at face value. Although it would obviously be impossible for the defence to have access to the documents at this stage, we are not in favour of the type of *ex parte* arguments sanctioned by the Court of Appeal in *Davis*,[146] because they exclude the defendant from important discussions relevant to the case. A possible intermediate position would be to allow some other independent person formally to represent the defendant's interests in those (very few) arguments over immunity from which he or she would be justifiably excluded. One possibility would be for the defence interests to be protected by giving to the Official Solicitor the task of advancing arguments to oppose immunity in closed session. The Official Solicitor would be able to be informed of the importance of the documents for the defence case and to convey that interest for those parts of the proceedings from which the defence was excluded. Although the Official Solicitor has no role in criminal proceedings, in principle this function is not very different to the office's current role of representing disadvantaged litigants (such as children or the mentally ill) in civil cases. There should also be a pre-

other respects the applicant was given a remarkable amount of detail about why he was regarded as a security risk.

[144] The ECHR has little relevance here because of the attitude of the Convention organs that rules of evidence are primarily a matter of national jurisdiction: C. Osbourne, 'Hearsay and the European Convention on Human Rights', [1993] *Crim. LR* 255.

[145] Much controversy centred on whether ministers were *obliged* in some sense to claim Public Interest Immunity; for the view that they were not see A. Bradley, 'They Did Not Have to Sign', the *Independent*, 17 Nov. 1992 ; 'Justice, Good Government and Public Interest Immunity', [1992] *PL* 514, 518–20 ; and G. Ganz, 'Matrix Churchill and Public Interest Immunity' (1993) 56 *MLR* 564; the arguments in support of government's position are reviewed in T. Allan [1993] *Crim LR* 660 and A. Tomkins [1993] *PL* 650, 662 ff.

[146] See n. 115 above.

sumption that a document will only be withheld in full where partial non-disclosure is inadequate to protect the public interest.

CONCLUSION

We have seen that there are several types of device available to the state to combat the 'graymail' problem inherent in criminal proceedings in security cases. The procedures we have discussed are all exceptional variations from the normal criminal process to overcome supposed difficulties in dealing with sensitive cases. These range from controls within the political arena such as the use of prosecution discretion, through to attempts to protect or limit disclosure of information within the trial process by jury vetting, the use of *in camera* proceedings, orders to protect disclosure of information such as witnesses' names, and limiting the disclosure of available documents to the defence. Some of these powers are capable of use for other legitimate puposes unrelated to security, and all are capable of abuse for political ends or to cover the embarrassment of the authorities and the intelligence and security agencies.

It would be a mistake to evaluate these practices primarily by the standards of accountability of control we apply elsewhere to the actions of intelligence agencies, because this can only be a subsidiary concern of criminal procedure. The central emphasis must be on the effect of the fairness of the proceedings. At this level, though, greater independent control over the actions of the prosecution can, nevertheless, be valuable. Particularly troublesome is the wide prosecutorial discretion exercised in most security cases, which seems often to have led to inconsistent decisions over who comes to trial. The potential of independent control can be seen most readily by looking at recent developments over the disclosure of information, where the courts have made substantial inroads into excessive claims to secrecy, but it is plain that the government is far from ready to concede control.[147] If the recent trend of intelligence officers giving evidence in trials continues as MI5 takes a more central role in counter-terrorism, the problem is likely to be exacerbated.

---

[147] It was reported in *The Times*, 1 May 1993, that ministers are considering responding to the Matrix Churchill case by reverting to legislation making public interest immunity certificates conclusive.

12

Judicial Approaches

Cases involving national security, directly or merely as an undertone, do not bulk large in the judicial calendar. However, those which do appear frequently raise significant issues of curtailment of human rights by some executive action taken in the name of national security. This conflict puts judges in a particularly awkward position in a legal system which does not, in the positivist sense, know anything of human rights; one dimension to the problem is ascertaining in any particular case what residual liberties of the common law a litigant may rely upon. None the less anyone taking even a tally-sheet approach to judicial decisionmaking must be struck by the consistency of results in the cases to be discussed throughout this chapter: in virtually all of them the executive emerged victorious. Statistical randomness cannot explain so striking a pattern, and it is highly unlikely that all the unsuccessful litigants were asserting fanciful claims or suffered from poor representation.

The results require explanation. This may be pursued at different levels: the doctrinal and the external. The latter would include judges' views of their proper role in cases of this type, and their political and ideological orientation. 'Levels' is a somewhat unsatisfactory metaphor, for the two do not remain separate but rather intertwine and shape the evolving jurisprudence. 'Explanation' in the present case involves critique, for we do not believe it either necessary or desirable that human rights should occupy so subordinate a place.

We shall begin the analysis by identifying the various ways in which 'national security' is presented as a legal question, and then trace the development of the doctrine from its origins in the medieval war prerogative to an all-encompassing judicial exception in the twentieth century. We will compare this approach with that taken to similar questions in other jurisdictions and under the European Convention on Human Rights. The wider constitutional framework from which the judicial decisions emerge will receive particular emphasis. An attempt will be made to discern whether the results can be said to express or reflect any sort of political or constitutional theory: a coherent set of ideas about the role of the judicial branch of government within the state. Our own critique will be interwoven with more descriptive accounts, but at the end of the chapter we shall attempt to tie the threads together, to summarize the criticisms, and to offer some specific proposals for a different judicial approach.

THE JURIDICAL FORMS OF NATIONAL SECURITY

1. National security may be invoked as a *source*, and not merely a *justification*, of power for the executive branch of government. That is to say, the legal authority for a given act may be claimed to be the specific Royal Prerogative of protecting national security. Under other names[1] this has a long history, some of which forms the very marrow of the constitution of this country,[2] concerning the struggle for power between monarch and parliament. On one interpretation (which we discuss below) the well-known *GCHQ* decision is an example.[3] There are, however, parallels elsewhere, notably in British-influenced constitutions which confer competence and grant power to legislate or otherwise act in relation to 'defence'.[4]

2. Secondly, 'national security' may be used to describe a state interest or reason for action, usually one which outweighs some right that would otherwise be honoured in a judicial forum. Perhaps the best example in UK domestic law is section 10 of the Contempt of Court Act 1981, which forbids a court from requiring any person responsible for a publication to disclose any source of information, unless the court is satisfied that disclosure is 'necessary' for any one of a number of specified interests, including national security.[5]

It also occupies a major role in the European Convention on Human Rights, in which most of the substantive rights are qualified by a long catalogue of contrary overriding interests. 'National security' plays a prominent role in this respect.[6] Similar exceptions may arise in European Community law. Here, however, because some EC law is directly applicable in national courts, the effect is more complex. It is possible that a conflict may arise between the scope of national security exemptions in EC and in domestic law, in which case, where directly enforceable Community law rights are at stake, the exception will be limited to that available under EC law and the national exemption will be of no effect or cut down accordingly.[7]

However, national security also arises as a judicially created exemption in litigation. Here no explicit statutory exemption is in issue—these cases are typically ones in which a prerogative power touching on security arises (see (1) above) or where the applicability of the judicially created grounds for judicial review is in

---

[1] For the evolution of this prerogative power, see p. 323 below.

[2] See p. 324 below.

[3] *Council of Civil Service Unions* v. *Minister of the Civil Service* [1985] AC 374

[4] We shall consider particularly the defence power (s. 51(vi)) of the Constitution of Australia; see p. 348 below.

[5] This was the provision in issue in *Guardian Newspapers* v. *Secretary of State for Defence* [1985] AC 339. Note also s. 15(3) of the Immigration Act 1971 (deportation for reasons of national security): see Ch. 7 above.

[6] ECHR, Art. 6 (public trial); Art. 8(2) (privacy and family life); Art. 10(2) (freedom of expression), and Art. 11(2) (freedom of association and assembly).

[7] e.g. *Van Duyn* v. *Home Office* [1974] ECR 1337.

issue. It is striking that in such cases nothing required the judicial creation of a national security exemption,[8] but in effect this is what has occurred in cases like *GCHQ*,[9] *Hodges*,[10] and *Ruddock*.[11] Similarly, some domestic courts in interpreting their constitutions will imply a national security limit on enumerated rights even when one is not to be found in the text.[12]

3. The term may be used in a statute as a reason for exemption from rules that would otherwise apply thereunder. As it has been a habit of British governments to provide generous exemptions for themselves, there are many examples, which may be found in anti-discrimination legislation,[13] employment protection law,[14] and in the Data Protection Act 1984.[15] What distinguishes this category from the previous one is the the absence of a function for the courts: these exemptions are commonly coupled with provisions requiring the court to accept a ministerial certificate that the exemption applies.[16]

4. 'National security' can also be pleaded by the government as a reason for withholding information that would normally be placed before the court or made available to a party in litigation. As such it is a peculiar species of the wider genus of Public Interest Immunity, and is considered below.[17] At this point it need only be said that the immunity may be invoked not only when the government itself is party to the litigation (and hence may derive tangible advantage if the claim is upheld), but also as an intervening third party in litigation between private individuals or enterprises.

5. Although 'national security' as such does not appear in any criminal statutes, some equivalent terms appear in a few criminal offences. The old, loose formulations of sedition and seditious conspiracy were common law counterparts.[18] Today the main provision is the espionage law, which prohibits various activities undertaken 'for any purpose prejudicial to the safety or interests of the State'.[19]

6. The term may also be used to describe the range of permitted activities

---

[8] See p. 328 below.

[9] n. 3 above. Although *GCHQ* also concerned a statutory exemption under s. 138(4) Employment Protection (Consolidation) Act 1978, by the time the case reached the House of Lords the sole ground of appeal related to the applicability of a (non-statutory) obligation of consultation prior to the introduction of changes to the conditions of employment: it was this that their Lordships decided was displaced by reason of national security.

[10] *R.* v. *Director of GCHQ, ex p. Hodges, The Times*, 26 July 1988; and see Ch. 6 above.

[11] *R.* v. *Secretary of State for Home Affairs ex p. Ruddock* [1987] 2 All ER 518; and see Ch. 3 above.

[12] See pp. 342–44 below.

[13] Race Relations Act 1976, s. 42; Sex Discrimination Act 1975, s. 52.

[14] Employment Protection (Consolidation) Act 1978, s. 138 (4), exempting from the general coverage of Crown employment, anyone whose exclusion a minister attests is necessary for purposes of 'safeguarding national security'.

[15] DPA 1984, s. 27.

[16] However exclusions of judicial consideration may not be effective in EC cases, see *Johnston* v. *Chief Constable of the RUC* [1986] 3 All ER 135, pp. 352–53 below.

[17] In Ch. 11.   [18] See Ch. 8.

[19] Official Secrets Act 1911, s. 1. Note also that this phrase appeared in the now-repealed s. 2 of that Act; see Ch. 9.

or mandate of a security or intelligence agency. This is central to the discussion in Chapter 14; however, it may also arise if the powers of those agencies are challenged in the courts.[20]

7. Finally, the term may be a ground for judicial authorization of intrusive powers, where these require judicial sanction: an example would be in Canada in relation to the powers of CSIS.[21]

THE DEVELOPMENT OF NATIONAL SECURITY

Our concern in this section is to trace the development of the undoubted judicial deference to national security. Two questions need to be considered. The first is how the concept of national security emerged from earlier notions of the defence of the realm and war powers. The second is how it came to be treated with such universal deference, whatever the legal context. For although we have distinguished the different ways in which national security can come before a court, it is striking that the end result is inevitably a victory for the government. The answers to both questions have their roots in the judicial attitude to the prerogative.

There is a problem, at once terminological and historical, which complicates any attempt to delineate the bounds of 'national security' as a source of executive power. It was a concept unknown to Blackstone and other classical writers on the Prerogative. Joseph Chitty, the early nineteenth century commentator whose treatise is still cited by judges today, wrote of 'making War and Peace' and 'other Rights incident to the War Prerogative'. The latter included deployment of forces, blockade, embargoes, and making and strengthening fortifications.[22] Early in the seventeenth century the courts held that it also included what would today be called maintaining a domestic armaments capability. The King was permitted to authorize the digging of saltpetre (an essential ingredient of gunpowder) on private land, since it was needed for the defence of the realm and he would otherwise be dependent upon foreign supplies.[23] Of course the Stuart kings claimed much wider prerogative powers, and in the case of Charles I with more support from precedent than subsequent Whig historians have

---

[20] See as an example *Church of Scientology* v. *Woodward* (1982) 43 ALR 587.

[21] CSIS Act, s. 21; see Ch. 3.

[22] J. Chitty, *A Treatise on the Law of the Prerogatives of the Crown* (London, 1820), 42–8. In the early 17th cent. the judges emphasized the priority of these powers over private rights: 'but when enemies come against the realm to the sea coast, it is lawful to come upon my land adjoining to the same coast to make trenches or bulwarks for the defence of the realm, for every subject hath benefit by it': *The Case of the King's Prerogative in Saltpetre* (1606) 12 Co. Rep. 12. In the 20th cent., the same reasoning was adjusted in the light of the then-modern threats of attacks by Zeppelins, to justify the requisitioning of a private airfield for use by the Royal Flying Corps: *A Petition of Right* [1915] 3 KB 649. See H. Lee, *Emergency Powers* (Sydney, 1984), Ch. 3.

[23] *The Case of the King's Prerogative in Saltpetre* (n. 22 above).

allowed.[24] None the less the Revolution Settlement of 1688–9 definitively abrogated two of the most contentious and potentially oppressive of the asserted powers: that of maintaining a standing army in peacetime, and of raising money for use by the Crown, without the consent of Parliament.[25] Thus the result of the prolonged and most bitter and bloody internal political struggle in modern English history was a curtailment of the manifestations of the war prerogative, achieved by Parliament and the political process, not by the judiciary.[26] Indeed some of the rulings in favour of the king, notably that the sovereign is the sole judge of the existence of a danger of invasion or less immediate threat from external enemies, remain good law today.[27]

However, it is notable that by the time Chitty came to write, the 'other Rights incident' (in modern terms, ancillary powers) enjoyed by the Crown as a matter of prerogative were limited to those thought necessary to conduct war—what may be called provision of effective means. They were thus tied tightly to the actual conduct or preparation for armed conflict. The existence of prerogative powers less immediately connected to the clash of arms seems not to have been asserted. As Lord Reid pointed out, there is practically no judicial authority on the point after the Revolution until the First World War, for, in the spirit of 1688, in times of war or crisis governments enacted or relied on statutory emergency powers.[28] For instance, when in 1766 an emergency embargo was imposed during the parliamentary recess on the export of wheat it was felt necessary to pass an indemnity Act on Parliament reassembling;[29] similarly, seventeenth and eighteenth century prohibitions on the exports of armaments and on mercenaries enlisting for foreign armies were imposed under statute, not the prerogative.[30] Thus as the twentieth century began, the war prerogative was not at all a broad and free-ranging source of executive power.

It may also be observed that at no time in modern history was the war prerogative ever invoked to justify action against domestic 'enemies' of the government. This was mostly mostly left to the criminal law.[31] In one celebrated eighteenth-century instance where counsel sought to uphold a trespass and seizure of papers ordered by a minister of the Crown by praying in aid the principle of general law perhaps most closely analogous in effect to prerogative

[24] For a measured account making this point, see D. Keir, *The Constitutional History of Modern Britain Since 1485*, 9th edn. (New York, 1969), 184–222.

[25] Both were the subject of prohibitions in the Bill of Rights 1689, 1 Will. & Mar., sess. 2, c. 2. A prominent use of taxation had been to raise the necessary finance to conduct war, and the incremental growth of this power had provoked controversy: W. Holdsworth, *History of English Law*, vol. 6 (London, 1924), 50–2.

[26] Although arguably the security of tenure achieved by the judiciary in the Bill of Rights had important doctrinal implications, given the Stuart habit of dismissing judges who had rejected the Crown's arguments in important cases.

[27] *Case of Ship Money* (*R.* v. *Hampden*) (1637) 3 St. Tr. 825. See also W. Holdsworth (n. 25 above), 52–4.

[28] *Burmah Oil* v. *Lord Advocate* [1965] AC 75, 99–101.

[29] W. Holdsworth, *History of English Law*, vol. 10 (London, 1938), 365.

[30] Ibid. 400.   [31] See Ch. 8 above.

power—that of necessity—the argument was slapped down forcefully by the great Whig Lord Chief Justice, Lord Camden.[32] No such ambitious claim was ever again put forward, although the doctrine of necessity continues to occupy a very small place in English public law.[33] In human rights terms the most dangerous use of the prerogative was in relation to telephone tapping, examined in Chapter 3.

Nor did use of the prerogative suddenly mushroom in either World War. It seems that this was due in part to lack of confidence on the executive's part over the legal limits of their powers. Rubin's research has illuminated a controversy which raged within government on the eve of the First World War, between the military who wanted a statutory code of emergency powers and the government's legal officers, who argued that it was enough to rely on the prerogative.[34] What is interesting about this dispute (which the military won, with the enactment of the Defence of the Realm Act 1914), is that from the military point of view the form of statute law was felt to be better able to facilitate advance planning and to encourage clear judgment among officers on the ground.

Consequently, in wartime statutes were again enacted, and regulations issued under them. Judicial decisions upholding internment of British citizens, though appalling in their treatment of human rights and executive power, involved construction of legislation, not the prerogative of war.[35] Reflecting the fundamental values of the common law, the judges in the earlier period gave much more intensive scrutiny to executive acts involving taking of property without compensation or otherwise limiting its use, but always on the authority of statute.[36] What made the Second World War cases unusual was the deference accorded the executive when broad statutory powers affected property rights.[37] Prerogative was relied upon only in two sets of circumstances, the first being where property was requisitioned or destroyed for military purposes.[38] The other concerned internment or deportation of an enemy alien, a decision taken under the long-recognized prerogative power over aliens, given added force by the

---

[32] *Entick* v. *Carrington* (1765) 19 St. Tr. 1030, 1073.

[33] S. de Smith and R. Brazier, *Constitutional and Administrative Law*, 6th edn. (London, 1989), 69–70 (esp. n. 23).

[34] G. Rubin, 'The Royal Prerogative or a Statutory Code? The War Office and Contingency Planning, 1885–1914', in R. Eales and D. Sullivan (eds.), *The Political Context of Law* (London, 1987).

[35] See *R.* v. *Halliday, ex p. Zadig* [1917] AC 260, and *R.* v. *Leman St Police Station Inspector, ex p. Venicoff* [1920] 3 KB 72. The Second World War cases which became notorious, notably *Liversidge* v. *Anderson* [1942] AC 206 and *Greene* v. *Home Secretary* [1942] AC 284, simply followed in the same track. On the latter and related cases, see Ch. 7 above.

[36] *De Keyser* (n. 22 above) overruling *Petition of Right* (ibid.); *Chester* v. *Bateson* [1920] 1 KB 829; *A-G* v. *Wilts United Dairies Ltd.* (1921) 37 TLR 884 (CA); *Newcastle Breweries* v. *The King* [1920] 1 KB 854.

[37] e.g. the successively reported cases of *Point of Ayr Collieries Ltd.* v. *Lloyd-George* [1943] 2 All ER 547 and *Carltona Ltd.* v. *Commissioners of Works* [1943] 2 All ER 560.

[38] e.g. *The Broadmayne* [1916] P. 64, and the famous *Burmah Oil* case (n. 28 above).

Crown's exclusive power to determine whether a state of war existed with an alien's homeland.[39]

Though it was to be influential in later House of Lords decisions, the real juridical oddity of the two wars was *The Zamora*,[40] a decision of the Privy Council sitting in Prize and applying international law, in which the government's requisitioning of a neutral ship's cargo of copper was ruled unlawful. The court found that international law permitted such requisitioning where the vessel or goods were urgently required for use in connection with the defence of the realm, the prosecution of the war, or other matters involving national security.[41] The court would be required to treat a statement on oath by a proper officer of the Crown as conclusive since, in Lord Parker's much-quoted words: 'Those who are responsible for the national security must be the sole judge of what national security requires. It would obviously be undesirable that such matters be made the subject of evidence in a court of law or otherwise discussed in public.'[42] However in this case the evidence was merely that the Crown *desired* to requisition the copper, without stipulating the reason or the urgency, and that was insufficient.[43] The decision stands out not merely because it was given at the height of the First World War, but also because many later judges would undoubtedly have treated the omission in the evidence as a mere technicality and have made the assumption in the government's favour that the copper was required for the war effort.[44]

Without any apparently intended change of meaning, 'war' gave way to 'defence of the realm' as a description of the particular prerogative power. (Since Britain only entered both wars in response to German invasions of other states, 'defence' was perhaps seen as having a less aggressive and more morally appealing connotation.) The latter was used in emergency legislation enacted during both world wars, and in the Maxwell-Fyfe Directive concerning the Security Service.[45]

The provenance of 'national security' is much more obscure. It seems to have appeared first in the passage quoted above from *The Zamora*,[46] in which it is treated as something distinct, and apparently wider, than defence. Both terms were used without further explication, and it is impossible to deduce what the distinction was intended to convey. The term may have begun to appear in government discourse at this time, and found its way via counsel's argument into the judgment. It was undoubtedly in use immediately after the First World War:

[39] *R.* v. *Vine St Police Station Supt., ex p. Liebmann* [1916] 1 KB 268 and *R.* v. *Bottrill, ex p.Kuechenmeister* [1947] 1 KB 41; see Ch. 7 above.
[40] [1916] 2 AC 77.   [41] Ibid. 106.   [42] Ibid. 107.   [43] Ibid. 108.
[44] See examples at p. 331 below.
[45] Defence of the Realm Acts 1914–15. The first statutory use appears to be in the Defence Acts 1842–73 in the context of requisitioning lands during peacetime: see Rubin (n. 34 above), 147. The phrase is also used in regulations made under the Emergency Powers (Defence) Acts 1939–40, notably in the notorious Reg. 18B. See also pp. 375–78 below on the Maxwell-Fyfe Directive.
[46] n. 42 above.

the government were considering in detail legislation to replace the wartime emergency regulations under the title of a proposed National Security Bill.[47] But the title of the Bill was changed before it was introduced in Parliament (it became the Official Secrets Act 1920), and the legislative debut of the term seems to have come instead when, with the outbreak of the Second World War, Australia enacted the National Security Act 1939.[48] Regulations under that Act were used to govern virtually the whole of the economy during wartime, so it appears that there at least the terminology was intended to express a more all-encompassing view of both the immediate crisis and the legitimate role of the state.[49]

Lord Diplock was probably correct in suggesting that the contemporary prevalence of the term is owing to its appearance in the European Convention on Human Rights.[50] However, implicit in his remark is the suggestion that the change was purely one of labelling, involving no alteration of substance. This, we would contend, is quite incorrect, and the testing case is the *GCHQ* decision itself.

As Forsyth pointed out, the House of Lords in that decision invented 'the national security trump'[51] by extending without authority a rule about the limits of inquiry into a source of power into an apparently open-ended exception capable of being invoked in any situation, regardless of statutory or other authority. To the non-legal reader familiar with the *GCHQ* case simply as one in which the courts affirmed the validity of the government's 1983 ban on trade union membership at an intelligence establishment, this may require some explanation. The point is to do with the source of power to institute the ban: although the government relied upon the prerogative, the majority of the judgments do not found it on the defence of the realm prerogative which, as we have seen, was historically more limited to acts undertaken during armed conflict, or closely (in time and in character) related to military preparedness. Instead the majority of the judges saw the source of the government's power as lying in the prerogative power to regulate the civil service.[52]

---

[47] R. Thomas, *Espionage and Secrecy* (London, 1991), 10. It is noteworthy also that National Savings, National Insurance, and National Service all date from the period 1911–16. A similar trend may be discerned in Britain during the 1939–45 war where foodstuffs made to official specification became known as national butter, national flour, etc.: *The Oxford English Dictionary* (2nd. edn., Oxford, 1989), x. 232.

[48] Adopted more or less simultaneously as the UK emergency legislation. The National Security (Subversive Association) Regulations 1940 issued under it banned a wide range of organizations including the Jehovah's Witnesses, who preached pacifism. The ban was struck down by the High Court as *ultra vires: Adelaide Co. of Jehovah's Witnesses* v. *Commonwealth* (1943) 67 CLR 116.

[49] For examples of uses of the regulations which withstood judicial challenge, see B. Galligan, *Politics of the High Court* (Queensland, 1987), 127–8.

[50] See n. 3 above, [1985] AC at 410.

[51] C. Forsyth, 'Judicial Review, the Royal Prerogative and National Security' (1985) 36 *NILQ* 25, 29 ff.

[52] e.g Lord Fraser (n. 3 above), 397; Lord Roskill, ibid. 416–18. For the argument that this is not a true prerogative since it is not unique to the Crown, see H. Wade, 'Procedure and Prerogative in Public Law' (1985) 101 *LQR* 180, 191–2.

The only divergent approach was that of Lord Diplock, who at points in his judgment seemed to treat the case as one about the defence of the realm prerogative.[53] Treated in that way it would have been possible to approach the case from the traditional viewpoint, stressing the non-justiciability of the power, although it would still have required a breathtaking extension to apply it to what was a essentially a problem of industrial relations: abolition of a long-recognized right to membership of an independent trade union. Since, twenty years earlier, Lord Diplock himself had declared, 'It is 350 years and a civil war too late for the Queen's courts to broaden the prerogative',[54] we confront not merely a serious case of historical amnesia but also of constitutional usurpation.

However, the majority approach was to argue that the exercise of the employment prerogative was inherently reviewable, and to find that the past pattern of consulting with the unions at GCHQ had created a legitimate expectation of future consultation, which would, apart from the presence of national security, have been a reason for holding the order banning trade union membership to be unlawful. National security was therefore used as a judge-made exception of general application to the principles of judicial review which would have applied otherwise. Forsyth argues, correctly in our view, that the parentage of the exception is dubious since *The Zamora* was authority only for the rule in prize law, and other cases have been confined to their particular statutory contexts.[55]

A test of non-justiciability which had previously only applied to the defence of the realm prerogative, to certain statutory exceptions for national security, and in prize law has come to be given general application. The creation of a general judicial exception for national security is all the more curious because it occurs in a case which is otherwise regarded as a landmark in confirming the reviewability of the exercise of prerogative powers. However, the time to reverse this process has now probably passed, since later courts have applied this exception to judicial review without demur.[56]

Lord Scarman was alone in emphasizing a less all-embracing approach when, in *Guardian Newspapers* v. *Secretary of State for Defence*, he interpreted a statute as requiring the court to be satisfied of a factual precondition that the reason was national security, rather than the *Zamora* test.[57] Again in the *GCHQ* case he reserved the possibility that a ministerial decision could be set aside for irra-

---

[53] See n. 3 above, 410. [54] As Diplock LJ, in *BBC* v. *Johns* [1965] Ch. 32, 79.

[55] See n. 51 above, 30–1. However, in the same paragraph in his speech in *The Zamora* Lord Parker makes clear that the principle he is stating is by analogy with that operating in municipal law in the case of requisition of property on grounds of national security under the prerogative (citing *In re a Petition of Right* [1915] 3 KB 649). Warrington LJ stated in the latter case: 'the act in question must be necessary for the public safety and defence of the realm, and on this matter the opinion of the competent authorities who alone have sufficient knowledge of the facts, provided they act reasonably and in good faith, should be accepted as conclusive.' (ibid. 666). If this is the correct rule as regards the defence of the realm prerogative, it still does not justify the creation of a more general exception.

[56] e.g. *Hodges* (n. 10 above); *Ruddock* (n. 11 above). [57] See n. 5 above, 366.

tionality even in this field;[58] the other judges in *GCHQ* did not go so far, and in later cases it is the majority view which has been applied.[59] However, it is plain that the duty to act fairly in reaching a decision in the security realm will only be displaced if there are additional reasons relating to national security why it could not be fulfilled, and not by the mere subject matter of the decision: this was the reasoning in the *GCHQ* case itself. The effect is that, whereas the merits of a national security decision are wholly unreviewable, there may be some marginal review of the procedure by which it was reached.[60]

The *GCHQ* judgments comprise a jurisprudence of the Cold War. They arise from the fear-ridden atmosphere of the days when the Cold War divisions calcified into rival military blocs, and reflect unspoken political assumptions so long dominant and hence lying so deep that the Law Lords may not have been aware of how powerfully those assumptions had shaped their approach to the legal issues. The inflated notion of national security they endorse serves to legitimate unilateral executive action over a range of matters which could never have been encompassed under the older understanding of the war/defence prerogative.

We have reached a point where the development of the courts' attitude to national security can be summarized in Lord Diplock's well known words:

National security is the responsibility of the executive government; what action is needed to protect its interests is[,] . . . common sense itself dictates, a matter upon which those upon whom the responsibility rests, and not courts of justice, must have the last word. It is par excellence a non-justiciable question. The judicial process is totally inept to deal with the type of problems which it involves.[61]

Those words, together with those of Lord Parker quoted earlier,[62] reveal the two related and recurring sources of judicial disquiet about consideration of security questions: the first *constitutional* (that is, the courts are not the proper forum), the second *practical* (that is, judicial scrutiny is inconsistent with maintaining secrecy). The constitutional objection is partly a question of constitutional responsibility, to do with the allocation of functions, and partly to do with the policy-orientated nature of the decisions involved. The practical difficulties are likewise twofold: lack of information to determine the case, and the need to protect security information and sources within an adversarial system of justice.[63] These distinctions are not watertight, either analytically or when employed

---

[58] See n. 3 above, 406.   [59] See the judgment of Glidewell LJ in *Hodges* (n. 10 above).

[60] Glidewell LJ (ibid.) gives this interpretation to *GCHQ*: 'I apprehend . . . that the majority of their Lordships were of the view that once it is established by evidence that a decision had been made on behalf of Government in the interests of national security the whole ambit of that decision was one into which the courts can neither enquire nor intervene . . . I do not think that the same principles apply to the question of fairness.' Since a procedure had been established for reviewing positive vetting cases and there was no further claim (on the facts) that it was tainted by national security, his Lordship went on to consider its fairness. McCullough LJ, sitting in the same case, asserted that parts of the decision were justiciable by severing (somewhat artificially) the parts which solely related to an assessment of the applicant's character.

[61] See n. 3 above, 412.   [62] See n. 42 above.

[63] We discuss the second of these issues in greater detail in Chs. 4 and 11.

in practice by the courts, but we will use them as a useful expository device. We will discuss the constitutional objection later, but it is convenient to begin with the practical objection and with a comparison of what judges say and what they do.

GAMES JUDGES PLAY

Modern judges are understandably reluctant openly to admit to abdication of the judicial role to the executive. Consequently the judiciary engage in a series of elegant manœuvres which enable them to suppress the apparent contradiction between the rule of law and the executive's predominance in this field.[64]

It is no longer the case, if it ever was,[65] that counsel for the government has merely to intone the phrase 'national security' to be assured of success. In both *Ruddock* and *Hodges* the court refused the invitation offered that it should simply decline jurisdiction because the cases involved national security questions. In *Ruddock* the government argued that for the court to decide the issue would be to provide an oblique mean for establishing the existence of a telephone tapping warrant. Taylor J rejected what would have been an open denial of the rule of law: 'Totally to oust the court's supervisory jurisdiction in a field where *ex hypothesi* the citizen can have no right to be consulted is a dangerous and draconian step indeed. Evidence to justify the court's declining to decide a case (if such a course is ever justified) would need to be very strong and specific.'[66] Instead the courts have adopted the stance that they must be satisfied that some evidence exists for the executive's claim. All the speeches in the *GCHQ* case make this point; for instance, Lord Roskill:

> The courts have long shown themselves sensitive to the assertion by the executive that considerations of national security must preclude judicial investigation of a particular individual grievance. But even in that field the courts will not act on a mere assertion that questions of national security were involved. Evidence is required that the decision under challenge was in fact founded on those facts.[67]

But the standard is a low one, made lower still by the inevitable difficulty of the other party in contradicting it.[68] In practice the courts have been satisfied of the

---

[64] These represent approaches to evidence; approaches to law tend to be subsumed under the constitutional objection (see below).

[65] Lord Parker stated: 'the judge ought, *as a rule*, to treat the statement on oath of a proper officer of the Crown . . . as conclusive' (n. 40 above), 106–7 (emphasis added). Warrington LJ made provisos to the principle of conclusiveness he expressed in *Re a Petition of Right* (see n. 22) for challenges to good faith and reasonableness.

[66] See n. 11 above, 527.

[67] See n. 3 above, 420; and see Lord Fraser of Tullybelton at 402, and Lord Scarman at 406.

[68] Cf. Lord Fraser of Tullybelton in *GCHQ*: 'The decision of whether the requirements of national security outweigh the duty of fairness in any particular case is for the government and not for the courts; the government alone has access to the necessary information, and in any event the judicial process is unsuitable for reaching decisions on national security' (n. 3 above), 402.

evidential point provided the government produces an affidavit (a sworn statement) by a senior civil servant that the operative factor was national security and giving a possible reason for reaching that view. In the *GCHQ* case the Cabinet Secretary swore that the reason for non-consultation of the trade unions was that to do so might jeopardize national security by itself precipitating industrial action;[69] the House of Lords would not go behind the assertion. Likewise in *Cheblak*, Lord Donaldson held that in the absence of bad faith the Court of Appeal could not look behind the affidavit asserting that the reason both for the paucity of the reasons and for the decision of deportation was national security.[70]

Control of information is a powerful tool—if the government claims that the information necessary to resolve the case cannot be disclosed without compromising national security, the court is faced with a direct choice between accepting the executive's assertion, ordering disclosure of the information (which amounts to saying that it knows better), or trying to determine the substance of the case on inadequate information. The last option will, in the nature of things, usually result in the benefit of the doubt being given to the government. In order to avoid transparently favouring the government, one judicial strategy appears to be to 'make up' facts. There are examples in the case law of the courts filling in absent facts like the missing pieces of a jigsaw puzzle by judicial inference to resolve the case. In the First World War internment case of *R. v. Superintendant of Vine St Police Station, ex p. Liebmann*[71] the court took judicial notice of the dangers of clandestine rumour mongering, signalling with lights, and passing intelligence by carrier pigeons posed by German citizens left at liberty. With hindsight these 'dangers' existed mainly in the popular imagination, as the government of the day well recognized[72]—indeed it had not put them before the court to justify the internment. Similarly, and more recently, the courts in the *Tisdall* case assumed that the official who had leaked the Ministry of Defence memo to the *Guardian* newspaper was a highly placed security threat whose detection required the return of the memo concerned: she turned out to be a filing clerk.[73] Inference does not seem to work for the individual's benefit in reverse: in the *Ruddock* case evidence from an intelligence officer could have been used to infer the reason for the granting of the interception warrant, but instead the judge chose to highlight the lack of evidence about the minister's motives in issuing the warrant (a matter on which the government's case was itself silent).[74]

This last decision shows also the impossible burden which may be laid upon

[69] The fact that the affidavit appeared only after the government had lost the point in the High Court gave rise to a widespread suspicion at the time that it was an exercise in *ex post facto* rationalization.

[70] *R. v. Secretary of State for Home Affairs, ex p. Cheblak* [1991] 2 All ER 319, 333.

[71] [1916] 1 KB 268. [72] C. Andrew, *Secret Service* (London, 1986), 264–70.

[73] See n. 5 above; as an example see the judgment of Lord Diplock at 354–5.

[74] See n. 11, 534.

a litigant against the government in a security case. The practical effect of requiring a person challenging a security decision to produce evidence which is virtually impossible to obtain is to nullify the judiciary's assertion that the rule of law nevertheless applies.

The European Court and Commission of Human Rights have adopted a more benevolent approach to the difficulty faced by an individual litigant in challenging alleged secret action by the state. In Chapter 3 we saw that it has been held that it is not necessary for the applicant to show specific harm when alleging a breach of Article 8 due to alleged secret surveillance; it is enough that the complainant lives within a society where such surveillance is plausible to initiate an examination of their conformity of such practice with the Convention.[75] This approach allows for the disadvantages facing the individual more even-handedly than does the normal application of adversarial principles.

The British courts have a record of faithful trust in government motives. Occasionally this is formally expressed, as in the First World War internment case which gave rise to what Simpson designates 'the Reading Presumption of Executive Innocence', so called for Lord Reading's comment: 'It is of course always to be assumed that the executive will act honestly and that its powers will be reasonably exercised.'[76]

This is partly a prevailing attitude in public law cases: it is always for the person challenging a decision to impugn it. However, on occasion it strains credibility. The *GCHQ* case is a good example, because the argument that ultimately prevailed in the House of Lords, that the unions could not be consulted over the change in conditions of employment for reasons of national security (especially because of the need to avoid disruptive industrial action), was added to the government's battery of arguments only after it had lost in the High Court over the failure to consult. At that stage the Cabinet Secretary swore a further affidavit. Not surprisingly counsel for the applicants described this document as an 'afterthought'; their Lordships, on the other hand, were troubled by no such doubts and relied upon it as disclosing the true reason for the government's method of proceeding.[77] The inherent improbability of an attitude of mind which considered that the best way to prevent disruption and ensure industrial harmony was through acting unilaterally seems not to have occurred to the House of Lords.

In the nature of things it is impossible to say how often judicial gullibility has been exploited in these cases. However, Simpson's research into the official files behind the Second World War detention cases does show some attempts consciously to pull the wool over the eyes of the courts. For instance, in the case of

---

[75] However, the approach in relation to security files, where the difficulties are fundamentally the same, has been less generous; see Chs. 5 and 6 above.

[76] *R.* v. *Governor of Wormwood Scrubs Prison* [1920] 2 KB 305; A. Simpson, *In the Highest Degree Odious* (Oxford 1992), 29.

[77] The treatment of this affidavit contrasts markedly with that of the Massiter affidavit in the *Ruddock* case (n. 74 above).

the detention of Lees, where it was obvious to the authorities that a mistake had been made in the making of a detention order, that information was carefully shielded from those responsible for (successfully) defending Lees's habeas corpus application, so that no professional responsibility to inform the bench would arise.[78] Likewise, in the case of Ben Greene, the way in which a mistake had been made was dishonestly concealed from the court, because to admit it would have exposed a much more serious procedural flaw in the entire detention process, which the authorities were anxious to conceal.[79]

A further judicial strategy is the preparedness of the courts to accept imprecise official justifications of decisions whose legality is challenged. The zenith was once again in the wartime internment cases. At first the courts held the reasons for a detention order were subject to review, but that they could not go behind the Home Secretary's affidavit describing the reasons for the order (which itself did little more than recite the regulation and the ground given in the detention order): the practical effect of the limitation was to render the supervisory role almost wholly nugatory.[80] This studied judicial unconcern with the factual basis of the cases went at times to extreme lengths—the rule was applied in the second application of Captain Budd, who had been released earlier after a mistake had been admitted to before the courts.[81] Later the House of Lords held that the decision itself was effectively unreviewable,[82] thus resolving entirely the evidential question.

Nor is this judicial willingness to succumb to executive imprecision merely historical. In the Gulf War case of *Cheblak*, the Court of Appeal had some barely concealed misgivings about the grounds for the Home Secretary's decision to deport a long-term British resident who had a background of public opposition to terrorism. Nevertheless, the court interpreted a statutory duty to give reasons for deportation so narrowly that it upheld a statement of reasons which was almost totally uninformative to the applicant.[83] An honourable exception was the ruling of Gibson J in a Northern Ireland case in which the internment procedure was challenged, that the applicant was entitled to a written summary of the case against him, but the minister was entitled to exclude material the disclosure of which would be contrary to public safety because it revealed sources or the extent of official intellligence.[84] UK courts are not alone

---

[78] Simpson (n. 76 above), 301.

[79] Ibid. 358–9. This flaw was that MI5 not the Home Office was drafting the Statement of Reasons for detention, and then only after detention had been authorized by the Home Secretary. In a subsequent false imprisonment action brought by Greene after the mistake had come to light Public Interest Immunity was claimed to suppress this information and other details: ibid. 371–4.

[80] See Ch. 7 above; in *R. v. Home Secretary ex p. Lees* [1941] KB 72 it was held that the minister was not obliged to give reasons for such an order.

[81] See Simpson (n. 76 above), 329–31. Simpson concludes: 'it is not clear that the courts had to wash themselves of responsibility as thoroughly as they did. They could have carved out for themselves a larger role . . . By accepting the laconic Home Office affidavits . . . they hamstrung themselves' (ibid. 421–2).

[82] *Liversidge* v. *Anderson* (n. 35 above).   [83] See n. 70 above.

[84] *Re Mackey* (1972) 32 NILQ 113; and see the note by S. de Smith, ibid. 331.

in this failing—as a Canadian decision upholding uninformative reasons for denial of access under Freedom of Legislation shows.[85] As with evidential inferences, the approach may work in reverse to the detriment of an individual. For instance, in the Canadian decision of *Air Flight 182 Disaster Claimants* v. *Air India et al.*,[86] a civil action against the government for loss arising from the intelligence failure in detecting and averting a terrorist attack, the case against the Director of CSIS was struck out for lack of particularity.

When national security comes before the courts the presence or absence of a security consideration would, theoretically, be a question of fact to be determined by evidence to the satisfaction of the court before the benefit of the exemption or enhanced power would be claimed. However, matters rarely get this far. One reason[87] is that statutory exemptions also commonly prescribe the method of proof of the security claim—a common format is for the issue of a ministerial certificate which is evidentially conclusive. Even where the legislation does not so provide, the common law allows for the suppresssion of evidence through the use of Public Interest Immunity.

PUBLIC INTEREST IMMUNITY AND NATIONAL SECURITY[88]

This may arise in litigation concerned with national security decisions or in other litigation, whether or not the government is a party. Although the protection in the law of evidence goes very much wider than anything possibly related to security, we are only concerned in this account with applying the principles in that field.

The high point of the doctrine, whose early origins we have traced in looking at the position of informers,[89] is in the wartime decision of *Duncan* v. *Cammel Laird*.[90] There it was held, in litigation arising from the loss in sea trials of a submarine, brought by the dependants of perished submariners against the shipbuilders, that an affidavit from the First Lord of the Admiralty that disclosure of

---

[85] *Re Information Commissioner of Canada and Minister of National Defence* (1990) 67 DLR (4th) 585 (see Ch. 5 above).

[86] (1988) 62 OR (2d) 130.

[87] Other reasons are that if the case involves judicial review, evidental matters are rarely canvassed. The evidential difficulties for the individual are also formidable, see below.

[88] See generally M. Howard *et al.*, *Phipson on Evidence* (14th edn., London, 1990), ch. 19; A. Zuckerman, 'Privilege and Public Interest', in C. Tapper (ed.), *Crime, Proof and Punishment: Essays in Memory of Sir Rupert Cross* (London, 1981), and (1983) 99 *LQR* 14; J. Jacob 'From Crown Privilege to Interested Public' [1993] *PL* 121. We discuss the application of Public Interest Immunity to criminal cases in ch. 11; our concern here is only with the general approach taken by the courts.

[89] Ch. 4 above. For other early instances see *R.* v. *Watson* (1817) 2 Stark. 116, 148 (upholding refusal to answer questions about the layout of the Tower of London); *Home* v. *Bentinck* (1820) 2 Brod and B 130; *Dawkins* v. *Rokeby* (1873–5) LR 8 QB 255, 268 (both concerned with the disclosure of reports by a military court on the conduct of an officer).

[90] [1942] AC 624.

evidence of the design and from the salvage report would be contrary to the public interest could not be questioned. The breadth of the decision lay not so much in the outcome[91] but in its (much-criticized) statement that the courts had to defer to the minister's opinion, rather than form their own independent view of the public interest. Among those who suffered as a consequence of this interpretation was the alleged spy Dr Soblen, whose allegations of the abuse of power of deportation were dismissed when the courts upheld a certificate signed by the Foreign Secretary objecting to the production of communications passing between London and Washington, on the grounds that to do so 'would be injurious to good diplomatic relations':[92] Soblen argued that the documents would support his allegation that he was the victim of disguised extradition.[93] It took until 1968 for British courts to reverse this aspect of the judgment.[94] The current position is that a court is both able to form an independent view on a public interest immunity certificate (as such claims are now called) and is able to inspect the documents in question to decide whether they should be released. Despite these changes the courts remain deferential in this area.

Documents which the executive have in recent years maintained that the public interest requires to be suppressed include: a diary kept by a seaman during the Falklands War on board the ship which sunk the Argentine cruiser the *General Belgrano* (in a libel action between private litigants);[95] reports on the private life of a senior police officer compiled for the purpose of positive vetting and disciplinary purposes (in sex discrimination proceedings);[96] the report of a naval board of inquiry into the death after excessive consumption of alcohol of a serviceman (in a personal injuries action by his widow against the Ministry of Defence);[97] and forensic reports compiled as part of the investigation into the Lockerbie bombing (when an English court was requested to take evidence for the purpose of a civil action in the United States).[98]

[91] The resulting civil action was lost by the plaintiffs (*Woods* v. *Duncan* [1946] AC 401) but commentators are divided on the extent to which this was due to the suppression of the evidence (cf. H. Wade, *Administrative Law* (5th edn., Oxford, 1980), 722 and M. Aronsen and N. Franklin, *Review of Administrative Action* (Sydney, 1987), 369).

[92] *R.* v. *Governor of Brixton Prison, ex p. Soblen* [1962] 3 All ER 641, 649 and 652–3.

[93] See Ch 7 above.   [94] *Conway* v. *Rimmer* [1968] AC 910.

[95] See *Sethia* v. *Stern and Others, The Times,* 5 Nov. 1987 (The certificate itself was not challenged but the court held that it did not operate to debar the plaintiff from denying its contents.)

[96] *Halford* v. *Sharples,* EAT, *The Times,* 9 Oct. 1991; CA [1992] 3 All ER 624. The approach of the Court of Appeal is instructive because in upholding the immunity claimed they held that it would operate equally against both parties, i.e. the Police Authority would be barred also from relying on the files in its defence.

[97] *Barrett* v. *Ministry of Defence, The Times,* 24 Jan. 1990. The High Court held that the plaintiff was not entitled to the report at the outset of the proceedings (in order to settle pleadings) since it was unnecessary; the certificate was later withdrawn (see *R.* v. *Secretary of State for Defence, ex p. Sancto, The Times,* 9 Sept. 1992—discussed also in Ch. 5) and a County Court judge awarded damages in excess of £160,000 (*The Times,* 13 May 1993).

[98] See *In re Pan American World Airlines Application* [1992] 1 QB 854. The decision turned upon the inability of the court to order that evidence be taken from a former Crown servant under s. 9(4) of the Evidence (Proceedings in Other Jurisdictions) Act 1975 (Ch. 9 above). However, the Crown had also served several public interest immunity certificates and these would have operated under s. 3(1)

A spectacular and troubling example of the difficulties raised by the use of public interest immunity certificates on grounds of national security arose in a libel action brought by a former member of the Stalker Inquiry team (sent to investigate the alleged 'shoot to kill' policy in Northern Ireland) against the former Chief Constable of the RUC, Sir John Hermon.[99] The action arose from comments made by Sir John, in reply to a television documentary, in which he claimed that the plaintiff had approached the inquiry with a closed mind and had been responsible for it exceeding its terms of reference; although, like Sir John Hermon, the plaintiff was a retired policeman, plainly his reputation was at stake. The government intervened to serve public interest immunity certificates objecting to disclosure of parts of official documents (including correspondence between the RUC and the Northern Ireland Law Officers and the working papers of the Stalker Inquiry) that the plaintiff wished to adduce to support his case. It was claimed that the public interest in the criminal investigation process and national security would be undermined by disclosure. It was argued that the information revealed about the personnel, working methods, and informers of the security forces would compromise their efficiency (thus hindering the fight against terrorism) and could put individuals at risk. In upholding the certificates, Otton J appeared to hold that where a certificate claimed national security as the reason for non-disclosure, the court had no option but to accept the ministerial certificate: there was no question of weighing competing interests.[100] More disturbingly still, he went on to strike out parts of the pleadings (the statement of the case to be advanced at trial) on the same grounds, with the effect that the plaintiff's arguments were so artificially limited that the case could not proceed with any prospect of success. The decision graphically illustrates the complicity of the courts in the subordination of private rights to state interests—a process by which parts of the court records are expunged after the event to leave no trace of how one party tried to clear his name is accurately described as Kafkaesque.

Decisions since this judgement appear to leave more room for an independent assessment by the judge,[101] in line with the generally accepted understanding of *Conway* v. *Rimmer* above. Thus the Employment Appeal Tribunal held, in an immunity case arising from a claim for unfair dismissal bought by a former intelligence officer against the Foreign Office, that it would be inappropriate for

---

of the Act to bear the evidence quite independently. The Act also contains a further exception (in s. 3(3)) for national security, where a ministerial certificate is deemed to be conclusive; contrary to the position in domestic proceedings (n. 94 above).

[99] *Thorburn* v. *Hermon*, *The Times*, 14 May 1992 (QBD).

[100] The judge also rejected the argument that the case for secrecy had been destroyed by extensive publicity already given to aspects of the central allegations, through, amongst other things, the publication of two books.

[101] We discuss the Matrix Churchill case, where public interest immunity certificates were partially quashed, in Ch. 11.

an industrial tribunal to go behind a certificate claiming national security.[102] However, this was not a matter of legal disability; rather, that the tribunal was not competent to assess the dangers involved in the disclosure of documents. The scales were therefore weighted against disclosure, rather than there being no balancing exercise to perform. It was still necessary for the tribunal to be satisfied that there was evidence linking the document to the reason claimed in the certificate. Although it asserts that no class of document is automatically immune from disclosure, the judgment does little to encourage the view that the quashing of a certificate is more than a theoretical possibility and is unlikely ever to arise in practice: the tone may, perhaps, be due to unwillingness to encourage Industrial Tribunals, whose composition includes two lay members out of a panel of three, to run amok with the nation's secrets.[103] The government response to what was no more than an extremely moderate restatement of the accepted position is instructive: amendments were introduced in the Trade Union Reform and Employment Rights Act 1993 to provide for ministerially directed *in camera* hearings with the lay members of the tribunal excluded in such cases.[104]

Public Interest Immunity is pivotal to many cases involving national security, since if the government can prevent sensitive evidence being adduced in the first place there may be no basis on which a plaintiff can establish liability. Furthermore suppression of the evidence effectively prevents the court from forming an independent view of a government claim that the reason for action was national security, even without the self-imposed restraints on questioning such assertions discussed earlier in this chapter. Indeed to claim that the rule of law applied to security decisions, while effectively preventing their challenge by suppression of the evidence would be particularly cynical. Although the judges in the Australian decision of *Church of Scientology* v. *Woodward* acknowledged this argument they, nevertheless, clung to the residual ability to order disclosure exceptionally as a reason for asserting the justiciability of ASIO's actions.[105] It is true that the ability of a judge to inspect a document in order to form an independent view on the claim to immunity allows for a more thorough probing than is common in other security-related cases. But in many cases the judge will

---

[102] *Balfour* v. *Foreign and Commonwealth Office, The Times,* 9 Feb. 1993. The Employment Appeal Tribunal treated the judgment in *Thorburn* v. *Hermon* (n. 99 above) as amounting to a statement by the judge that he was satisfied by the substance of public interest immunity certificates.

[103] This reluctance is, however, difficult to reconcile with the decision in *Johnstone* v. *Chief Constable of the RUC* (n. 16 above) that in the realm of sex discrimination the Industrial Tribunal must be free to decide whether a case falls within a statutory exception for national security, rather than the question being precluded by ministerial certificate: this will presumably restrain the use of public interest immunity certificates in instances where directly enforceable Community law rights arise.

[104] Ss. 36(6) and 37(4).

[105] (1982) 57 ALJR 42. Mason J used the availability of a privilege as a reason for asserting that other ASIO decisions would be justiciable: ibid. 50–1; Brennan J stressed that it would be 'most exceptional' for discovery to be ordered against ASIO:. ibid. 57.

treat the government's argument at face value and not inspect, and we have seen that there is in any event a very strong presumption against disclosure. In these circumstances we view the emphasis in *Church of Scientology* v. *Woodward* insisting on the justiciability of security decisions as simply unrealistic: in the majority of cases either no evidence will be available to challenge the government's claim of national security, or if it is available it will be suppressed. This must be seen to affect any claim that actions based on security considerations are subject to the legal process.

If the scope of Public Interest Immunity was cut down, the reasoning would however carry greater conviction. As it stands, the real practical difficulties in handling security-related material do not justify either the broad scope of Public Interest Immunity or the routine deference to the executive demonstrated in the cases.

CONSTITUTIONAL CONSIDERATIONS

The *constitutional* objection has several aspects. A closely associated difficulty, often unstated, is the feeling that national security is primarily a matter of political judgment: on occasion this is related to the character of the decision at stake,[106] whereas at other times it appears as an argument about which institution a class of decision should be allocated to under the constitution.

It is possible to read statements of judicial deference to the executive in the security realm as an affirmation of a type of intuitive separation of powers. This becomes still more plausible in countries like Australia[107] and the United States,[108] where the defence or war powers function is formally allocated by the constitution to the Commonwealth (rather than the states) or to the President. Britain lacks a formal division of power of this kind. British judges have, therefore, on occasion tempered their unwillingness to intervene by stating that ministers are properly accountable for the use and misuse of security powers in parliament,[109] not in the courts. The institutional allocation argument is hard to understand either in theory (since ministerial responsibility does not generally

---

[106] Cf. Lord Reid in *Chandler* v. *DPP* [1964] AC 763, 791: 'Here the question whether it is beneficial to use the armed forces in a particular way or prejudicial to interfere with that use would be a political question . . . Our criminal system is not devised to deal with issues of that kind. The question therefore is whether this Act can reasonably be read in such a way as to avoid the raising of such issues.' Cf. Lord Devlin: 'they had got together the sort of material that an intelligent voter would want to consider if he were taking part in a plebiscite on unilateral disarmament. The judge's ruling forbade all such evidence' (ibid. 802). But contrast Viscount Radcliffe (at 798–9) who expressly denies that the limitation arises because the subject matter is political and attributes it instead to the diffuseness of the question.

[107] On which see pp. 348–52 below.

[108] See C. May, *In the Name of War: Judicial Review and the War Powers Since 1918* (Cambridge, Mass., 1989).

[109] e.g. Lord Donaldson MR in *Cheblak* (n. 70 above), 330.

preclude judicial review in other areas but is additional to it), or in practice (since, as our account of parliamentary practice makes clear,[110] such responsibility is fictitious). If protection of the individual were the governing criterion, the whole argument could be reversed: the absence of parliamentary controls if anything strengthens the case for judicial intervention.

In Britain judges have not usually been involved in directly sanctioning executive action by warrant in the security realm.[111] Instead ministerial or other non-judicial approaches have been adopted, and this if anything reinforces the argument that such matters are non-justiciable. There is evidence that this arrangement is to the liking both of the executive and the judiciary. After the *Brogan* case,[112] it was claimed that the government was constrained from introducing a sytem of judicial review of investigative detention under the anti-terrorist legislation by the reluctance of the judiciary (presumably expressed through informal consultations) to involve itself in intelligence matters. Lord Donaldson in the *Cheblak* case expressly stated that non-judicial procedures were a preferable alternative to judicial review.[113]

One of the few attempts at a different approach was that of Lord Devlin in *Chandler* v. *DPP* where, in what was admittedly a criminal case, he dismissed the notion that national security decisions were constitutionally unusual and argued that: 'There is no rule of common law that whenever questions of national security are being considered by a court for any purposes, it is what the Crown thinks to be necessary or expedient that counts, and not what is necessary or expedient in fact.'[114] However the difference turned out to be cosmetic only:[115] His Lordship argued that the prerogative and statutory powers were invariably broad enough to make their exercise a matter of discretion,[116] and anyway the question of fact in such cases boiled down to proof of the genuineness of the government's *belief*.[117] He expressly repudiated the idea that the trial judge in *Chandler* should have allowed evidence on the merits or otherwise of the government's policy.

Another difficulty is the diffuseness of national security decisions. Whereas judicial decisions are reached upon the basis of proof beyond reasonable doubt or according to the balance of probabilities, security decisions tend to be taken according to a standard less even than the requirement of reasonable suspicion to which the police habitually work.[118] This itself ought not to make them

---

[110] See Ch. 16 below.
[111] Search warrants under the OSAs 1911 and 1989 and production orders would be isolated exceptions, understandable on the basis that the type of power covers non-security cases but is simply more easily exercised in such cases; see Ch. 10 above.
[112] *Brogan* v. *UK* (1988) 11 EHRR 117.   [113] Discussed in Ch. 7.
[114] See n. 106 above, 811.
[115] Cf. D. Thompson, 'The Committee of 100 and the Official Secrets Act 1911' [1963] *PL* 201, 225–6.
[116] See n. 106 above, 809–10.   [117] Ibid. 811.
[118] Cf. Lord Pearce (ibid. 813): 'Questions of defence policy are vast, complicated, confidential and wholly unsuited for ventilation before a jury. In such a context the interests of the State must in

inherently non-justiciable since legislation in the administrative law domain frequently grants powers where the minister is 'satisfied' and the courts, nevertheless, make sense of these provisions and hold their exercise to be reviewable.[119] However, the difference is that, whereas in other policy fields legislation invariably contains indications which the courts can use to construct the criteria according to which even an apparently unfettered discretion is to be exercised, in the realm of national security the powers are expressed so broadly that there are no such limits. The judiciary has notably refrained from ever offering a definition of what national security is; in view of this it is hard to see how such a power could ever be found to have been abused in law.

Diffuseness is also present in the way in which security decisions may rest upon calculation of complex and largely speculative criteria, uncertain future events, and judgements about the reactions of other states. A good instance is the debate over the value of nuclear deterrence. It is no surprise, then, that the majority of the Canadian Supreme Court in *Operation Dismantle* v. *The Queen*[120] struck out an action claiming that the government's decision to allow the testing of cruise missiles on Canadian soil violated the appellants' rights to life, liberty, and security under section 7 of the Charter of Rights. The applicants had claimed that the testing undermined arms control, made nuclear attack more likely, and escalated the arms race. The majority[121] found that although governmental decisions at this level (the decision here had been taken by the Cabinet) fell within the Charter, the effect of the government's decisions was too hypothetical to give rise to a violation of constitutional rights.

As Peter Hanks has pointed out[122] the constitutional approach of the courts to this issue leads to two paradoxes: national security is held simultaneously to be 'non-justiciable' and 'conclusive' when pleaded against individual rights, and in upholding the elasticity of the term the judiciary is in effect adding its imprimatur to a more authoritarian vision of state interests than that contained in legislative definitions of security. Hanks attributes the courts' difficulty in part to the difference between defining national security for the purposes of a statutory mandate for an intelligence agency, and doing so in a range of other circumstances in which an individual's interests may clash with the state's—the courts have been concerned primarily with the latter. However, as he hints in his conclusion, the danger is that the judiciary may as a result appear committed to maintaining not only the ruling institutions of the state (for instance parliamentary democracy), but also its current dominant ideology. This accords ill with conceptions of the role of the judiciary which emphasize its place as neutral arbiter between citizen and government (such as Dicey's)[123] or upholding rights

my judgment mean the interests of the State according to the policies of the State as they are, not as they ought, in the opinion of the jury, to be.'

[119] *Padfield* v. *MAFF* [1968] AC 997.   [120] (1985) 18 DLR (4th) 481.
[121] For the different reasoning of Wilson J, see n. 139 below.
[122] P. Hanks, 'National Security—A Political Concept' (1988) 14 *Monash LR* 114, 132–3.
[123] A. Dicey, *The Law of the Constitution* (10th edn., London, 1959).

(such as Dworkin's).[124] Rather, the courts appear as supreme upholders of state interests, and national security becomes a tautologous device by which the government may instruct the courts of the supreme importance to it of upholding a particular decision. It is tautologous because it is conclusive and it remains undefined. Therefore national security is not *weighed* against individual liberty, it 'trumps'[125] it. There is nothing for the court to consider except the assertion posited by the government that a given (unspecified) interest is so important that it must be accorded priority: it is a form of 'table thumping'.

We argue in the conclusion that the constitutional objection does have a core of good sense worth recognizing, though one much smaller than the courts have claimed: it focuses upon the limited but valuable role that judges fulfil in the constitutional order. However, first we must consider an alternative argument which is often put forward as a panacea.

The Relevance of a Bill of Rights

It is sometimes argued that the dismal performance of British judges in national security cases demonstrates the need for a Bill of Rights, by which individual rights such as free speech, privacy, and association can be protected from official encroachment.[126] The preceding discussion might suggest that there are strong theoretical reasons to suppose that a more rights-based treatment by the judiciary would not eradicate the national security problem in the law. A review of the performance of judges in legal systems purportedly guaranteeing constitutional rights to individuals confirms this. However, before examining the record of judges in other countries, it is worth making the point that even a Bill of Rights would have to accommodate fundamental state interests in some form. This could be done, as in the European Convention on Human Rights, by explicit exemptions for actions prescribed by law and necessary in a democratic society in the interests of national security.[127] Or it could be achieved, as in Canada, by inference from the fundamental purposes of the Charter of Rights, even in the absence of express exceptions. In either case the task of the court is then to balance national security and some other designated rights. This is a theoretical advance on the British position in that the individual's right is made as explicit in the law as the state's interests, although whether this would make any difference is questionable—British judges are not so myopic that they fail to see that the cases are about individuals' interests as well as the state's.

Various stratagems were suggested in the documentary rush of proposals for

---

[124] See nn. 159 ff. below.

[125] Forsyth (n. 51 above), 29. The terminology neatly reverses Dworkin's famous assertion that rights are trumps: see nn. 159 ff. below.

[126] e.g. Lord Bridge of Harwich in *A-G* v. *Guardian Newspapers* [1987] 1 WLR 1248, 1286. For a recent assessment of the position of the political parties on this issue, see R. Brazier, *Constitutional Reform* (Oxford, 1991), Ch. 7.

[127] Arts. 8–11.

constitutional reform in the late 1980s and early 1990s. The draft constitution proposed by the Institute for Public Policy Research[128] contained express exceptions for national security from the rights of privacy, freedom of expression, freedom of assembly and association, and freedom of movement. However, such exceptions were to be confined to what was strictly necessary in the circumstances[129] and national security was given a detailed definition.[130] Liberty's draft People's Charter contained exceptions on grounds of public safety (a narrower conception than national security) to the right to a public trial, privacy, and freedom of information.[131]

Whatever the formula proposed, there is little encouragement from other countries' constitutional practice for the view that the judiciary can be transformed into protectors of individual rights against national security interests.

Perhaps the most striking example of the judicial tendency to treat constitutional rights as subject to countervailing public or governmental interests is to be found in the United States. The First Amendment to the Constitution is expressed in stark terms: 'Congress shall make no law . . . abridging the freedom of speech, or of the press.' This would seem to admit of no ifs, ands, or buts. Yet the idea that the First Amendment provides unqualified protection for speech—that it is 'an absolute'—has been regarded as an extreme position which only one Supreme Court Justice consistently expounded.[132] Indeed, one of the key questions of First Amendment jurisprudence, which had its origin in criminal prosecutions of anti-war critics and Socialist 'agitators' during the First World War, has been formulating the standard which legal or administrative restrictions on speech must meet to be constitutionally valid. Once the famous 'clear and present danger' test was fully elaborated by Justices Holmes and Brandeis, it failed to command the support of a majority of their colleagues, who thought it too liberal.[133] It took another half century before a consensus was reached that seems to have stood the tests of time and radically changing Court membership.[134]

Thus virtually all American judges over nearly eighty years have treated the

---

[128] Institute of Public Policy Research, *The Constitution of the United Kingdom* (London, 1991).

[129] Ibid., Art. 21.   [130] Ibid., Art. 126.

[131] Liberty, *A People's Charter* (London, 1991), 19.

[132] This was Justice Hugo Black, a member of the Court from 1937 to 1971. His views are set forth concisely in a lecture, 'The Bill of Rights' (1960) 35 *NYU LR* 865, 874–81. The only other Justice who came close to sharing his view was William O. Douglas, who frequently joined his dissenting opinions.

[133] After *Schenck* v. *US*, 249 US 47 (1919), in which Holmes wrote for a unanimous court, subsequent formulations and applications either appeared in dissents by Holmes, as in *Abrams* v. *US*, 250 US 616 (1919) and *Gitlow* v. *New York*, 268 US 652 (1925), or in a concurrence by Brandeis in *Whitney* v. *California*, 274 US 357 (1926).

[134] This was enunciated in *Brandenburg* v. *Ohio*, 395 US 444 (1969). See G. Marshall, 'Press Freedom and Free Speech Theory' [1992] *PL* 40, 46 quoting the presently used test and pointing out that it is largely limited to those areas in which 'speech causes potential problems of public order or induces criminal activity'. Other contexts such as obscenity or defamation in which speech has been restrained seem not to have yielded any articulated standard of restriction.

constitutional guarantee of free speech as *inherently* subject to restriction. Despite the absence of textual authority, they have created a legal standard to justify limitations, whilst often debating vigorously amongst themselves about what it should be. It would seem that the notion of an unqualified right, even one so important as speech, is not one that judges—even in the intensely 'rights conscious' American legal tradition—are willing to countenance. Almost certainly this is because of what they perceive as the importance of the countervailing interests the restrictions are supposedly protecting.

One sees this outlook at work even in the celebrated *Pentagon Papers* case.[135] Though constitutionally vital for the protection it provides for a critical Press, it is in no sense an affirmation of the theory of absolute First Amendment rights. Apart from Mr Justice Black, all the Justices comprising the majority accepted that even these rights would have to give way in certain extraordinary circumstances. To be sure, the rule against 'prior restraint' derived from the Amendment meant that the government had a steep hill to climb, but it could have prevailed had it been able to prove credibly (not merely allege) that publication would cause 'direct, immediate, irreparable damage to our nation or its people'.[136] And in subsequent cases, where less important rights have been in issue, the government has won easily.[137]

Canadian judges have, likewise, strongly resisted arguments designed in different ways to deprive the courts of a role and have regularly been concerned with the limits of CSIS's powers. For instance, the Federal Court of Appeal in *Atwal*[138] rejected the government's argument that since the power to issue warrants under the CSIS Act had been reserved to designated Federal Court judges their decisions ought not to be open to review. Similarly, in the *Operation Dismantle* case the Supreme Court was careful to assert (somewhat unconvincingly) that decisions over allowing the testing of Cruise missiles on Canadian soil were not non-justiciable as such, even though they had beeen taken at Cabinet level under the prerogative. However, the majority went on to strike out the applicant's claim against the testing on the grounds that the claim was too diffuse and hypothetical to found an action.[139]

---

[135] *New York Times Co.* v. *US*, 403 US 713 (1971).

[136] 403 US 713, 730 (per Stewart J); see also Brennan J in very similar terms at 726–7.

[137] These cases have either involved lesser rights such as the right to travel abroad (*Haig* v. *Agee*, 453 US 280 (1981)) or did not involve constitutional rights at all (*Snepp* v. *US*, 444 US 507 (1980)). See also *Kleindeinst* v. *Mandel*, 408 US 753 (1972), in which the existence of First Amendment rights was denied and the matter treated as one of Congressional power to regulate the entry of aliens.

[138] *Atwal* v. *Canada* (1989) 79 NR 91.

[139] See n. 120 above. Wilson J dismissed the action on different grounds of substance rather than procedure: by giving the right to life, liberty, and security a restricted interpretation, so that it only applied where a segment of society was threatened and not in the case of a threat (like nuclear annihilation) to the whole community. This position was founded upon a philosophical consideration of the nature of rights, which would be unthinkable from a British judge: citing Rawls, Dworkin, and Pound, she argued that 'rights' as used in the Charter were rights to live within a political community and therefore some measures necessary to protect that community were implicit in the notion of a right. Nevertheless, as Walker notes (C. Walker, 'Review of the Prerogative: The Remaining Issues'

Nevertheless, despite this formal insistence on judicial review, it is striking that the record of the Canadian courts after the introduction of the Charter of Rights does not differ markedly from the historical trend in upholding security claims.[140] With one exception, the Canadian government has yet to suffer a permanent reversal on a matter of substance at the hands of the courts in a security case. Thus in *Atwal*[141] the intrusive powers of CSIS available under section 21 of the CSIS Act[142] were held not to violate section 8 of the Charter, prohibiting unreasonable search and seizure. Other decisions on the scope of the legislation where it had been held that the government had acted unlawfully, notably *Chiarelli*[143] and *Thompson*,[144] were both reversed in the Supreme Court. Decisions on Public Interest Immunity and exemptions to freedom of information legislation have favoured the government.[145] The exception to this trend was a single instance in which a trial judge quashed as unreasonable a ministerial certificate alleging that a husband and wife who had entered Canada on forged papers and applied for refugee status were ineligible on security grounds.[146]

Any discussion of the approach of the European Commission and Court of Human Rights towards national security must first of all note the anomalous position in which those bodies stand as regards national laws. We are not concerned here with the failure to incorporate the Convention into domestic law, although that marginalizes its usefulness in United Kingdom courts. Rather, the structure of the Convention and the Court's view of its function have diluted potential impact of the Treaty as an international legal standard. The Convention organs do not see themselves as exercising a domestic constitutional function. A complaint under the Convention never takes the form of an appeal; it is a review of the discretion of the member state concerned. This is especially so with the interpretation given to the restrictions which may be imposed under Articles 8–11 for, among other reasons, national security. The concern is to see that the member state has acted within its 'margin of appreciation' and only where it is beyond the bounds of this discretion, or where the restriction lacks a legal basis at all, will it be found to be in breach of the Convention. This is a

[1987] *PL* 62, 68), the paradoxical conclusion if the threat is one to the whole community rather than simply a segment of it is that it becomes non-justiciable by reason of its greater importance.

[140] Certainly the historical record—judged on the upholding of emergency powers legislation in wartime—is as dismal as in the UK: R. Sharpe, *The Law of Habeas Corpus* (2nd edn., Oxford, 1989), 106.

[141] See n.138 above, and see *Re Canadian Civil Liberties Association and Attorney-General of Canada* (1992) 91 DLR (4th) 38.

[142] See Ch. 3 above.

[143] See Ch. 7 above; in *Chiarelli* v. *Canada* [1992] 1 S.C.R. 711 the Supreme Court held that the *in camera* procedure adopted by SIRC in considering a deportation on security grounds case did not violate s. 7 of the Charter.

[144] See Ch. 6 above; the Supreme Court held in *Thomson* v. *Canada* [1992] 1 SCR 385, that a recommendation of SIRC concerning a security clearance under s. 58 of the CSIS Act 1984 was not binding on the minister since the Act did not detract from the prerogative power to decide upon security clearance.

[145] See Chs. 11 and 5, respectively.   [146] *Joseph Smith and Sarah Smith* v. *Canada* [1991] 3 FC 3.

direct international counterpart to the judicial reluctance to interfere with subjective exercises of executive discretion at the national level. Not surprisingly, in view of the fundamental state interests at stake, the national security margin of appreciation has been liberally construed. Thus vetting, surveillance, and deportation practices have been held not to violate the Convention. Where the United Kingdom *has* been found to violate the Convention, it is because of the absence of a legal basis for the purported power and not the substance of its use—the obvious implication is that the defect may be simply remedied by wide discretionary legislation. Controls at this procedural level are not altogether worthless, but they fail to address the central issue.

Furthermore the Convention organs have neglected the opportunity to require from member states effective judicial scrutiny of security decisions at the domestic level. Article 6 of the Convention, which entitles an individual in determination of his civil rights and obligations to a fair and public hearing[147] by an independent and impartial tribunal, has been given a restricted interpretation in this field. Thus in the *Klass*[148] case, the Court held that Article 6 could not apply to a decision to place an individual under surveillance which, to be effective, could not be disclosed to the person concerned. In the same way, Article 13 requiring access to an effective domestic remedy for a violation of rights under the Convention has been diluted in the face of national security.[149]

The Convention organs have failed to supply a definition of what national security comprises, against which national interpretations may be compared. However, by their practice they have readily accepted counter-subversive and counter-terrorist measures as well as those more directly connected with espionage or military questions. It is striking that no attempt has been made to confine state measures to a proportionate response to these threats.[150]

One honourable exception to this trend was the finding of the Court of Human Rights that the continuation of the *Spycatcher* injunctions by the United Kingdom courts after the publication of the book in the United States could not be justified on grounds of national security.[151] However, this was the first and, to date, the only occasion on which a state's invocation of national security has been rejected outright, and on any reading it was a fanciful claim.

In addition to the restrictions available under the various articles on grounds of national security, the Convention allows for the emergency suspension of the rights in the treaty (although not the rights to life or not to be tortured or treated or punished in an inhuman or degrading way).[152] Such derogations from the treaty must meet a number of requirements—some formal, others of

---

[147] Art. 6 allows parts of a trial to be held *in camera inter alia* for reasons of national security.

[148] *Klass* v. *Federal Republic of Germany* (1978) 1 EHRR (see Ch. 2 above).

[149] *Leander* v. *Sweden* (1987) 9 EHRR 433, para. 75; see further Ch. 6 above.

[150] Proportionality has been employed by the Convention organs in other contexts when considering state claims to exemption: *Dudgeon* v. *UK* (1982) 4 EHRR 149, para. 61.

[151] *Sunday Times* v. *UK* (*No. 2*), *Guardian* v. *UK* (1991) 14 EHRR 229.

[152] Arts. 2 and 3 respectively.

substance—in order to be effective. Article 15 of the Convention allows derogation in times of war or 'other public emergency affecting the life of the nation'; any suspension of human rights must be properly proclaimed and registered with the Convention organs. Any measures taken must be limited to what are strictly required by the exigencies of the situation and must last no longer than is necessary. The approach of the Court and Commission of Human Rights to this provision has been to allow states considerable discretion in forming their own assessment of when an emergency exists, whilst maintaining that the ultimate judgment rests at the international level.[153] This is partly a matter of practical realism, since the state is in the best position to make the assessment and is more likely to have the necessary information, but it is also symptomatic of the ultimate weakness of international juristic endeavour when confronted with fundamental state interests.

These points can be well illustrated from recent experience involving powers of detention without charge under British legislation.[154] In the *Brogan* case in 1988 the European Court of Human Rights held that the extended powers of detention before charge (up to seven days on the authority of the Secretary of State) were in contravention of the obligation under Article 5(3) of the convention to bring detained persons promptly before a judicial authority.[155] The government had resisted involving the judiciary in the process of authorizing the detention, because the information on which such detentions were authorized was normally counter-terrorist intelligence rather than anything approaching evidence. It was claimed that to involve judges would compromise their independence and also make them possible terrorist targets. When faced with the Court's judgment, instead of reversing the policy and amending the legislation to provide for a judicial element, the government entered a derogation from Article 5(3). On the face of it this appeared as a blatant disregard of international law, not least because the government had earlier explained to the Court during the course of the case that it had not felt that a derogation was necessary.[156] In these circumstances one might have expected the Court to find that the derogation was of no effect, since the timing indicated bad faith and an attempt to avoid compliance with the *Brogan* judgment, rather than a necessary response to an emergency.[157] Remarkably, faced with an identical case in 1993, the European

---

[153] *Lawless* v. *Ireland* (1961) 1 EHRR 15; *The First Greek Case* (1969) 12 YBECHR; *Ireland* v. *UK* (1978) 2 EHRR 25; for discussion, see D. Bonner, *Emergency Powers in Peacetime* (London, 1986), 83–90 and 152–61.

[154] Prevention of Terrorism (Temporary Provisions) Act 1989.   [155] See n. 112 above.

[156] An earlier derogation, applicable to Northern Ireland, but not in any event covering the issue of detention without charge, had been withdrawn by the government in 1984 as no longer necessary (see Bonner (n. 153 above), 88). The present derogation applies only to Northern Ireland: however, while the government has not sought to derogate from the Convention for the mainland (i.e. Great Britain), it has not amended the legislation either and remains in breach of the Convention.

[157] Cf. P. van Dijk and G. van Hoof, *Theory and Practice of the European Convention on Human Rights* (2nd edn., Deventer, 1990), 557–8, writing about the derogation, but before the case cited in the next note.

Court of Human Rights held the derogation to be effective, the majority limply holding that there was no reason to doubt its genuineness.[158] It was held that the government had not, in the prevailing circumstances, exceeded its margin of appreciation in deciding against judicial control. Nothing could indicate more clearly the lack of commitment to effective judicial scrutiny both on the Court's part and in the way that it has allowed the requirement of domestic judicial supervision to be by-passed.

The judicial record under legal systems which give predominance to rights therefore does little to suggest that the adoption of a Bill of Rights in Britain would produce markedly different results in security cases. There are theoretical reasons also to doubt whether the judicial espousal of rights make a significant difference. Here we turn to the work of the foremost liberal theorist of adjudication, Ronald Dworkin, who has given an account of the judicial function based upon the priority of rights.[159]

Dworkin claims that judges should be solely concerned with rights, that is claims to entitlements by individuals and groups, in deciding hard cases. The legislature may be exercised with policies (goals for the community), but not the judges. On this division between rights and goals one might reasonably expect that national security would be a paradigm goal, since it is by definition a claim affecting the nation as a whole.

At a descriptive level support can be found for treating national security as a community goal, but the evidence tends to show the *judiciary* upholding it, contrary to Dworkin's thesis. Following Dworkin's theory of adjudication, the judiciary would be free to uphold national security restrictions when clearly required to do so by legislation. However, the theory would militate against judicially created national security exceptions tacked on to statutory ones as in the *GCHQ* case. We may note in passing that this is no guarantee of greater freedom since it merely invites the legislature to do what the judiciary will not, but Dworkin also believes in constitutional review, and in his later writing he argues that the legislature should behave consistently in respecting rights.

However, there are also indications in Dworkin's work that national security would not necessarily be forbidden to the judges, since it might not be regarded as a goal at all. Dworkin has attempted to deal with cases of courts apparently upholding community goals in preference to rights through the concept of 'substitutability of rights',[160] which treats such apparent counter-examples as really

---

[158] *Brannigan and McBride v. United Kingdom*, Case No 5/1992/350/423–424, *The Times*, 28 May 1993.

[159] R. Dworkin, *Law's Empire* (London, 1986) and *Taking Rights Seriously* (London, 1977).

[160] *Taking Rights Seriously*, 98–100. The nearest Dworkin comes to applying this strategy to national security is a discussion of the meaning of 'public interest' in Public Interest Immunity (see R. Dworkin, 'Principle, Policy, Procedure', in C. Tapper (ed.), *Crime, Proof and Punishment: Essays in Memory of Sir Rupert Cross* (London, 1981), 215 ff., esp. 217), but it is there obscured by the procedural questions involved. It is unclear to what extent Dworkin would still employ the notion of substitutability in view of the fuller development of his integrity thesis in *Law's Empire*.

instances of upholding rights in disguise. Applied to national security, this would come very close to an argument used by Lord Donaldson that national security is the foundation of civil liberties, and therefore beneath the superficial level the two are not in conflict.[161] Whereas this might be relatively convincing in relation to public safety and public policy, it reduces the difference between rights and goals to one of degree, according to the numbers of individuals involved. In this case the national security is undoubtedly at the far end of the scale because it affects the maximum number of individuals. This may explain why judges uphold it—on a utilitarian basis (which, of course, Dworkin rejects), such claims may weigh heavier. However, such claims are necessarily very diffuse, in the sense that the claimed harm to the nation may be difficult to quantify (certainly in contrast to the pressing harm to the individual) and spread among a very large number of individuals. What is by no means obvious is that a judge should favour a diffuse claim of damage to a large number of people to demonstrable, precise, and concentrated damage to a single individual.

It is clear that national Bills of Rights and their international equivalents are no guarantee, whether in theory or practice, of more favourable treatment for the individual faced with state claims of national security. The only judicial exceptions to this familiar pattern do not in fact proceed from the protection of rights, but rather are founded on the constitutional position of the judiciary. We consider these in the next section.

A DIFFERENT APPROACH

These pessimistic comments should, however, be qualified in the case of the interpretation given by the High Court of Australia to the 'defence power' of the Australian Constitution.[162] The similarity of language, of constitutional function (that is, as a head of power), and the Australian inheritance of British public law make this provision a close equivalent to defence of the realm in Britain. The particularly powerful influence of the British legal tradition in Australia due to the role of the Privy Council as the final forum of appeal,[163] and to the fact

---

[161] See p. 9 above. One commentator has suggested stipulating an exception, designed specifically to deal with emergency situations: 'Principles are subservient to policies whose aim is to preserve or regain a political state of affairs *in which principled decisions would not otherwise be a possibility.* This category of case is obviously justified only by emergencies or catastrophes where rights have to be suspended because that is the only way rights will in future be reinstated.' (S. Guest, *Ronald Dworkin* (Edinburgh, 1992), 62). The similarity here of the two lines of thought is even more striking.

[162] Constitution of Australia, s. 51(vi), which empowers Parliament to make laws with respect to 'the naval and military defence of the Commonwealth and of the several States, and the control of the forces to execute and maintain the laws of the Commonwealth'. We are not concerned in the discussion which follows with the question of the division of power within Australia's federal constitution, which for our purposes is irrelevant. See generally W. Wynes, *Legislative, Executive and Judicial Powers in Australia* (5th ed., Sydney, 1976), 199–230, and H. Lee (n. 22 above), Ch. 2.

[163] Not abolished until the passage of the Australia Act 1986.

that many judges have received part of their legal education in Britain, makes the comparison even more apposite. The obvious difference, that it is not a common law prerogative power but a provison in a federal constitution important in allocating competence between the states and the Commonwealth, may be ignored for present purposes. On the determination of the scope and nature of the power, rather than who exercises it, the issues are precisely the same. So too is the role of the court in delineating boundaries.

The High Court has interpreted the defence power variably according to circumstances: war, transition from war to peace, peacetime, and war preparation.[164] Wide latitude was given to exercise of executive power in wartime.[165] In a leading case from the First World War upholding regulations fixing the maximum price for bread,[166] the High Court held that the relevant test was whether the purported exercise of the power was *capable* of advancing defence. It was not for the judges to consider whether it did so in fact, although if the connection appeared be too remote the exercise of the power would be invalid.[167] In the same case it was accepted that the types of legislation which may be justifiably related to the defence power depend upon the factual situation at any given time: for instance legislation governing commercial matters may appear more closely related to defence in a total war economy than at other times. The practical effect has been that the Australian courts have been prepared to uphold a wider range of legislation under the defence power in wartime than in peace and that the continuation of some wartime measures after the cessation of hostilities has been treated as invalid in some instances.[168]

Towering above these, and demanding detailed examination, is the *Communist Party Case*,[169] on any reckoning one of the most courageous decisions of constitutional jurisprudence in modern times.[170] That courage can only be appreciated by recalling the atmosphere of the time. The Cold War was at its darkest hour. The Berlin airlift, the coup in Czechoslovakia, and similar events were in the forefront of policymakers' minds.[171] The Menzies government, voted into office after a long period of opposition, had sent to troops to Korea. It faced strong

---

[164] B. Gage and M. Jones, *Law, Liberty and Australian Democracy* (Sydney, 1990), 209–25, a useful source for cases and commentary, on this point quoting at 212, C. Howard, *Australian Federal Constitutional Law* (3rd edn., Sydney, 1985) 477.

[165] With unhappy results for human rights: *Ferrando v. Pearce* (1918) 25 CLR 241; *Lloyd v. Wallach* (1942) ALR 359.

[166] *Farey v. Burvett* (1916) 21 CLR 433.

[167] Ibid., per Griffith CJ, 21 CLR.141

[168] For examples see Wynes (n. 162 above), 205–13. Even in wartime the court was unable to see the connection between legislative restrictions on university entrance and the war effort: *R. v. University of Sydney, ex p. Drummond* (1943) 67 CLR 95; likewise restrictions relating to the manufacture of fly sprays: *Wertheim v. The Commonwealth* (1945) 69 CLR 601.

[169] *Australian Communist Party v. Commonwealth* (1950–1) 83 CLR 1.

[170] For a detailed treatment placing the case in context, see G. Winterton, 'The Significance of the Communist Party Case' (1992) 18 *Mel. ULR* 630.

[171] And also of the judges: see the comments of Dixon J (soon to become Chief Justice), 83 CLR at 196–7, which makes his judgment striking down the Act the more remarkable.

resistance from the Communist Party, a powerful force within the well-organized trade union movement. Its response was to enact the Communist Party Dissolution Act, which began with a preamble—a sort of legislative explanation of the necessity for the law—stating that the Party was a revolutionary organization using violence, fraud, and sabotage for the purpose of overthrowing the government. The Act proceeded to dissolve the Party, forfeit its property, and gave a minister power to dissolve other associations and ban members from holding jobs in government or trade unions which he designated as vital to the defence of Australia.[172] Thus to the constitutional weight of Parliament's declaration that a particular state of affairs existed was added a statutory allocation of power to the executive to make a factual determination of certain people as threats to defence. The combined constitutional competence and policy judgment of both branches of government would seem to support the legitimacy of action under the defence power.

The High Court, with only one dissent, would have none of it. The absence of a state of war meant a much-narrowed scope for action under the defence power. Whilst wartime cases had permitted the opinion of a designated person to forge the link between an executive act and a constitutional power,[173] that would not be permitted under less perilous conditions. The Court drew on a long-established doctrine known as 'the stream cannot rise above its source',[174] under which no law can give any person apart from a court the power to determine conclusively any issue on which the constitutional validity of the law would rest. The judges objected both to Parliament taking, and to the executive being given, power to determine their own power.

The judgment of Williams J epitomized their approach.[175] He emphasized that the wartime cases relied on judicial notice of 'notorious facts' to support the expanded defence power, but that other facts proven in the normal way would be necessary to uphold exercise of the power in peacetime. Mere assertion, even if approved by Parliament, would not do. Preparation for war could certainly be undertaken in peacetime, and conduct reasonably regarded as being prejudicial to war preparation could be regulated under section 51(vi). However, the legislature must define the nature of the conduct and the means adopted to combat it, to enable the court to judge whether in the circumstances the interests of 'defence' reasonably supported the legislation enacted. The judgment repeatedly emphasizes reasonableness, considered a 'matter of degree'.

Although the judgments in the *Communist Party Case* do not speak in these terms, they are fundamentally about upholding the values of constitutionalism: in particular, separation of powers and the integrity of the judicial function therein.

---

[172] The latter power in particular was not dissimilar from the decision to ban trade union membership at a defence facility in the *GCHQ* case (n. 3 above).

[173] For references see L. Zines, *The High Court and the Constitution* (2nd edn., Sydney, 1986), 202, and for more general discussion of the defence power, 196–204.

[174] Per Griffith CJ in *Heiner* v. *Scott* (1914) 19 CLR 381, 393.

[175] See n. 169 above at 224–7.

This is accomplished by an insistence upon adequate evidence, to be reviewed under a concept of reasonableness that is genuine rather than nominal.

Contrast this with the House of Lords' treatment of the factual issue in the *GCHQ* litigation.[176] The government's affidavit placed great emphasis on past selective strikes in government installations. Their true incidence remains a matter of dispute, but the suggestion implicit in the government's position was that any but the most trivial interruption of intelligence gathering and analysis constitutes a serious international danger to the state. One may indeed accept that broad policy decisions in this field are exclusively for the executive branch, and allow a generous 'margin of appreciation' in matters of implementation. None the less can the contention put forward be regarded as even remotely plausible? It is one thing to say, as the House of Lords did in the *Chandler* case,[177] that if the government in its conduct of defence and foreign relations establishes a military airfield, it is not open to those attempting to interfere with its normal operation to argue that their acts were not 'prejudicial to the safety or interests of the state'.[178] It is quite another to accept, as a matter of *fact*, that a limited number of intermittent interruptions embellished with some rhetorical rodomontade from union officials constituted a danger to the United Kingdom in early 1984 so great as peremptorily to override important interests that the courts otherwise would have upheld. Had the judges in *GCHQ* seriously examined that assumption, they would have been compelled to acknowledge that they had treated life in post-War Britain as a state of permanent war preparation. They would also have had openly to accept another, even more disturbing implication: that permanent and continuous gathering of information had become an accepted, and acceptable, feature of modern government.[179] It is the sheer taken-for-grantedness of this Cold War outlook that emerges as the determinant influence on the judgments.

The approach of the High Court of Australia did not involve usurping executive powers; rather it kept the executive within the proper channels of its powers. The judgments in the *Communist Party Case* did not venture into evaluation of the wisdom of the policy which led to enactment of the law, but scrutinized the antecedent conditions necessary to sustain it. They were not based upon an extravagant notion of judicial review alien to British public law, and indeed to

---

[176] pp. 327–29 above. [177] See n.106 above.

[178] The term used in s. 1 of the OSA 1911. Argument over this point should not have been allowed to deflect attention from the fundamental issue in *Chandler*, which was that s. 1, entitled 'Penalties for spying', should never have been used against people engaging in public civil disobedience. See generally D. Thompson, (n. 115 above). Also disquieting was the fact that, since the airfield was never in fact immobilized, the defendants were charged with conspiracy, not with an offence under s. 1. Moreover, the sentence of eighteen months imprisonment imposed on the most 'serious' offender seems clearly excessive.

[179] GCHQ is the most advanced technological and bureaucratic mechanism in Britain for what deserves to be called *universal surveillance*. Its activities are not targeted at enemies or even potential enemies, but reach literally everyone: any state, whether ally, friend, or snarling adversary; private companies; and individuals: see Ch. 3 above and Coda.

good democratic principle. However, they did insist as a matter of principle that the legislature not be permitted to erect upon the purported constitutional foundation a structure it could not reasonably bear. Their hallmark is a measured approach to the source of power; and this is what so distinguishes them from the speeches in the House of Lords in the *GCHQ* case.

A more modern example of the robust judicial approach was, perhaps surprisingly, provided by the European Court of Justice, with its insistence in the *Johnston* case upon maintaining the role of the courts in assessing governmental claims to national security.[180] In that case the Court held that a UK provision purporting not merely to provide an exemption from sex discrimination legislation, but also to remove the matter from the jurisdiction of an industrial tribunal, was incompatible with judicial supervision of rights arising under the EC Equal Treatment Directive, EC Directive 76/207, which imposes on member states an obligation to provide a remedy for other aspects of discrimination in working conditions.

Following a decision not to arm women police constables, the Chief Constable of the Royal Ulster Constabulary failed to renew the contract of the complainant, since he took the view that suitable duties could no longer be found for unarmed officers. The complainant's subsequent industrial tribunal proceedings for sex discrimination resulted in the government pleading the defence of national security under Article 53 of the Sex Discrimination Order, and producing a ministerial certificate stating that this was the reason for the decision not to renew the contract. Under the Article such certificates were to be treated as conclusive. However, the complainant contended that this could not prevent the tribunal from implementing Directive 76/207. When the case was referred to the European Court of Justice for a preliminary ruling, it distinguished between the exception for national security and the ministerial certificate provisions of the Article. The Court held that the latter was incompatible with the Community rights created in the Directive and, hence, was to be disregarded by the tribunal. (It has since been repealed.) The substance of the Chief Constable's defence was therefore referred back for the industrial tribunal to consider. The Directive itself contained no exception for acts done for reasons of national security. However the Court held that an exception in Article 2(2) of the Directive allowing a court to consider the 'context' of an exception for occupations reserved solely for men was capable of applying to the situation in Northern Ireland. The 'context' could include the background of civil unrest. The Court refused to allow general exceptions under Articles 223 or 224 of the EC Treaty for security and for serious public disturbances to be read so as to broaden the specific exemptions in the Directive. Subsequently the complainant succeeded in the industrial tribunal proceedings.

The case is noteworthy for its strong insistence on judicial scrutiny at every

---

[180] See n. 16 above. For discussion see P. Morris [1987] *PL* 334.

level. The Court applied the principle that enforcement of Community law requires effective judicial control:[181] to have upheld the provision allowing for a conclusive certificate would have been to have passed control to the executive. The United Kingdom government had argued that a general exception for security was implicit in Community law, because of a number of explicit exceptions for that interest elsewhere in the Treaty. This argument is in a sense the direct counterpart of that which succeeded at national level in the *GCHQ* case. The Court of Justice rejected it:

If every provision of Community law were held to be subject to a general provision, regardless of the specific requirements laid down by the provisions of the Treaty, this might impair the binding nature of Community law and impair its uniform application.[182]

Nor was it permissible to use Article 224 of the Treaty of Rome, which allowed for derogations by member states in times of serious civil disturbance, to uphold the deprivation of judicial review through the ministerial certificate. It followed that the police's action had to be construed by the national courts within the provisions of the Directive. At this level too the Court insisted on strict adherence to the Directive, with the requirement that the exceptions be narrowly construed. In particular, the national court had to be satisfied that the action was proportionate, and that the objective could not have been met in some other, non-discriminatory, manner.[183]

This approach is the antithesis of that of the British courts, which have not merely treated legislative national security exemptions with excessive respect, but have also overlaid them with their own self-imposed limitations on judicial review. Instead the Court of Justice based itself squarely upon the constitutional function of the judiciary in preserving judicial scrutiny of executive claims: to have allowed the ministerial exemption conclusive effect would have been to abdicate the judicial function of protecting and enforcing Community rights. Although the Community law context makes the case unusual, the approach is nevertheless transferable to the position of domestic courts—indeed it was the jurisdiction of domestic courts, whose task it remained to evaluate the merits of the government's assertion—that the Court of Justice was acting firmly to safeguard through its judgment.

CONCLUSION: NATIONAL SECURITY, THE JUDICIARY, AND THE CONSTITUTION

Our analysis has documented a striking pattern of judicial self-abnegation in cases involving issues of national security. We have identified two factors—the

---

[181] See n. 16 above, 156.
[182] Ibid. 157; and see the opinion of the Advocate-General (M. Darmon) at 148–9.
[183] Ibid. 159.

'practical' and the 'constitutional'—which have led to this posture. It is misleading to subsume these quite distinct concerns under an all-embracing notion of 'public interest', as the courts have tended to do. It is true that, though analytically separable, they often in practice appear side by side. However, since the response to each is entirely different, both theoretically and practically, it is necessary to identify in each instance the precise consideration which purportedly requires the judiciary to stay its hand. For the practical objections can be met with practical solutions, and the level of argument about their acceptability is very different from a debate about the constitutional allocation of power.

In so far as courts have felt themselves precluded from involvement because of the danger that material which should remain secret would become public knowledge, it must be said that whilst in at least some circumstances the problem is a real one, their reaction has been excessive. Moreover, as we have discussed at length in Chapters 6 and 7, there are alternative procedures—*in camera* hearings, non-adversarial practices involving more active judicial participation in certain specific circumstances, and representation by security-cleared independent counsel—which would permit courts and tribunals to do their job with proper integrity, without needlessly sacrificing either individual rights or necessary secrecy.

Whilst conceptually severable, the practical objection at certain points merges into the constitutional one. Judges have both a professional competence and a constitutional role which, like lines on a cardiograph, continually touch and overlap. Institutionally, the judicial process is particularly adept at finding facts as a result of disinterested assessment of the accounts put forward by opposing parties—which can only properly occur when each side has equal access to all relevant information. Pre-eminently a judicial function in terms of competence, it is also an important constitutional function. This is because a refusal to ensure that all relevant information is before the court has the practical effect of virtually ensuring that a disputed decision of the executive branch will be upheld, because its presentation of the facts, tailored to support the decision, will be accepted as true.

Another point of intersection of the practical and the constitutional concerns fair procedure. Whether described as the duty to act fairly or more technically as natural justice, the requirement that government act in a fair and unbiased way is perhaps the most fundamental principle of judicially created public law. Both maxims of the traditional notion of natural justice—*audi alteram partem* ('hear the other side'), and *nemo judex in re sua* ('no man a judge in his own cause')— express principles of morality, which also have important constitutional implications similar to those just discussed. Indeed it is the failure to heed these maxims that may produce the one-sided and inaccurate factual record which propels the courts towards a flawed decision. Accepting a certificate of public interest immunity where there is a factual dispute or where the government alone has in its possession information favourable to the plaintiff's case has the result that the court fails to hear the plaintiff's side of the story properly, and goes a considerable way towards making the executive the judge in its own case by placing its decision effectively beyond reconsideration. Once again, the constitutional result is that the power of the executive is reinforced or enlarged, not merely as against the individual who has tried to assail its decision, but as against Parliament and the wider public which is deprived of the information that might enable them to call the government properly to account.[184] Thus, though there may be some limited circumstances justifying modification of normal judicial practices, we contend that both with respect to the finding of fact and to the insistence upon fair procedures, the courts have no less a role to play in cases involving security than in any other.

'Court' should be understood as shorthand for a body which satisfies three criteria: it must be wholly independent of the executive; observe the principles of fair adversarial procedure; and issue authoritative decisions. It may be that for reasons including greater expertise and competence, speed of decision, and cost, Parliament may choose to create an alternate adjudicatory framework. So long as those three principles are satisfied[185] it does not matter whether the body is called a court and staffed by judges. What is important is its ability to exercise its best judgment free of pressure, on the basis of all pertinent information. What is never acceptable is a conclusion that, *even though the subject-matter is appropriate for the adjudicating body to consider*,[186] it cannot do so for practical reasons. The result—executive action without constraint—is constitutionally repugnant.

Though we have emphasized their wider implications as well, the considerations discussed so far relate primarily to securing justice between the parties as is generally understood in common law adjudication. Yet there are others which cut even deeper, to constitutional matters in the most important structural sense: how the judiciary functions in relation to the other branches of government, and how that relationship assists or hinders effective accountability to the public.

---

[184] Anyone who doubts this should consider the critical role that criminal trials particularly have had in uncovering political scandals in the security field that would otherwise have remained hidden. Some of these have been of monumental significance. The impeachment of Richard Nixon, the intensive investigations of the CIA and assumption by the American Congress of a far more active role in the oversight of intelligence agencies, and significant reform of rules governing FBI activities were all set in motion by the trial of the Watergate burglars.

Almost incredible is the fact that the whole process of reform in Canada would never have occurred but for the spontaneous outburst in a Quebec courtroom of Robert Sanson, a former police officer on trial for activities undertaken while moonlighting for criminal gangs, that he had done far worse while working for the RCMP security branch. This forensic indiscretion led directly to the setting up of a provincial commission of inquiry, which forced the federal government to establish the McDonald Commission, and led to the enactment of the CSIS Act.

Although one should not expect such dramatic results, had it not been for the overruling of the Public Interest Immunity claim in the Matrix Churchill case, the Scott Inquiry would never have been established and the whole question of ministerial deception would have quickly faded away.

[185] As, for example, proceedings before the 'Three Wise Men' emphatically do not: Ch. 7 above, pp. 185 ff.

[186] This important qualification, which relates to justiciability, has been noted above (p. 329) and is discussed further below (pp. 357–59).

Considered as a form of communication, judicial decisions have concentric audiences. Most obviously they are addressed to the litigants before the court, but they may also be said to send messages (via legal advisers) to a wider circle, including others who find themselves similarly situated. This is particularly true of government departments, 'repeat players' in litigation,[187] who are both exposed to frequent legal challenge and organizationally structured to be able quickly to inform themselves about and respond to specific decisions and emerging broader legal principles.[188] Therefore a judgment in a particular case may be even more important for what it communicates to administrators than for the specific result: even when an adjudicating body concludes that it must accord great deference to a ministerial decision, how that decision is expressed may have important future resonance. Thus, in describing different approaches to Public Interest Immunity claims, we contrasted one decision holding that a ministerial certificate must be accepted without any judicial attempt to weigh competing interests, with another which held that the tribunal's sense of its own lack of competence required it to give great weight to the government's view, whilst retaining the ultimate power to take the decision itself.[189] Whilst from the point of view of a prospective litigant the difference may be trifling—he or she will find it equally impossible to win under either approach—from the perspective of officials the techniques may have very different impact. The former says in effect: 'Do as you like, and no court will inquire why.' The latter says: 'You must set out reasons, to which we shall accord great respect, but you will be required to work through the process of reasoned, public (though not very precise) justification.' Officials and ministers operating under the latter regime must surely behave more carefully and rationally than when given the *carte blanche* of the former. And since legal challenge is statistically a rarity, a judicial approach which instils in officialdom a permanently heightened awareness of legal values and procedures may go a long way towards curbing arbitrary government, notwithstanding the absence of victorious plaintiffs, or even of reported cases.

Equally important is the role of the judiciary in stimulating and invigorating responsible government. Regrettably its performance has mostly had the reverse effect. When judges say, as they sometimes do,[190] that although they have stayed their hand the matter can be pursued in Parliament, it is hard to take such protestations seriously. For by refusing to force the executive out from behind the curtain of national security, they disable the Opposition, independent-minded backbenchers, and the Press from offering informed criticism. The issue

---

[187] The term coined by Marc Galanter in his well-known article, 'Why the Haves Come Out Ahead' (1974) 9 *Law & Soc. Rev.* 115, to describe institutions which frequently participate in litigation and therefore develop practices and structures which maximize their chances of avoiding defeat.

[188] One example of such adaptation is the drafting by the Treasury Solicitor's Department and Cabinet Office and dissemination to senior civil servants of a pamphlet entitled *The Judge Over Your Shoulder—Judicial Review of Administrative Decisions*; see A. Bradley, 'The Judge Over Your Shoulder' [1987] *PL* 485.

[189] Above, pp. 336–37.   [190] See p. 338 above.

for the courts is not the substance of the decision, but whether it can be supported by rational argument based upon a defensible assessment of the relevant facts. There is a great deal of room for divergence of judgment about both the cogency of the argument and the quality of the factual evaluation; and the views of the executive, as the organ of government charged with taking the decision, should not readily be faulted. The court's role should be to enhance accountability, in the literal sense that the government is made to give an adequate account of its action, not only to the opposing litigant but to the political nation.

To take a specific and controversial instance: in the *GCHQ* case, the Law Lords should have rejected the affidavit of the Cabinet Secretary, which was introduced in a blatant attempt to avoid defeat after its initial arguments—in which this ostensibly overwhelmingly important reason was never mentioned—sank in the Divisional Court. This would not have prevented the government from persisting in its policy, but would have forced it to act in accordance with constitutional principle. Two means were readily available. The most obvious was to honour legitimate expectation, engage in proper consultation with the union, and then to implement the ban if its commitment to the policy remained unswayed. The second would have been to seek formal parliamentary sanction.[191] Either way the result would have been a fuller public debate in which all the influences on the government's action would have been adequately probed,[192] and in which opponents—not least within the Conservative Party—would have had an adequate opportunity to state their position and rally support. In the end the government managed to avoid a vote, but if by ramraiding its policy through it intended to pre-empt resistance and keep the matter out of the public eye, the mass demonstrations and extended litigation falsified that hope spectacularly. And the judges failed as well, fumbling the opportunity to insist upon a quality of decisionmaking appropriate to a democratic state.

Of course, as we were at pains to point out earlier, the case for a more active judicial role exists only when the subject matter at issue is appropriate for judicial determination. Lord Diplock's observations on justiciability—the institutional and constitutional limits to what courts can handle and should decide—make good sense.[193] So too do the parallel comments of Lord Roskill, speaking more generally of certain decisions taken under the prerogative, who

---

[191] Either by means of statute or approval of an Order in Council; the technical differences need not detain us here.

[192] e.g. N. West (R. Allason MP), *GCHQ: The Secret Wireless War 1900–86* (London, 1986), 354, accepts the government's view of the seriousness of earlier trade union disruption at GCHQ. However, he goes on to suggest that, in light of the espionage conviction of Geoffrey Prime, a GCHQ employee, in the preceding year, a critical factor behind the union ban was 'not least to restore the NSA's [the American National Security Agency] confidence in its partner'—an influence the government was wholly unwilling to admit. Acknowledgement of this kind of reason, and of the political dependency implied, is precisely what the public has a right to know and should have an opportunity to debate.

[193] See n. 61 above. This notion, expressed in similar terms, is found in many legal systems: Walker (above n. 139), at 64–71.

described them as not 'susceptible to judicial review because their nature and subject matter is such as not to be amenable to the judicial process'.[194]

One can evaluate this viewpoint most effectively by asking why the decisions to build the atomic bomb, join NATO, or commit troops to the Gulf War ought not to be reviewable in the courts. A rather formalistic answer is that in our constitutional system such decisions are not regulated by statute or (obviously) by constitutional provision, so no question of *ultra vires* can arise.[195] This does not, however, address the question of whether such matters, seen as reviewable executive decisions under the prerogative, should be reviewed for 'irrationality' in the specialized sense commonly used by adminstrative lawyers.

The answer turns on the character of such decisions. Though accurate assessment of fact may be critical to sound decisionmaking, they are not essentially questions of fact. They are based on judgments of national interest, a concept which is an untidy *mélange* of political, economic, and ideological factors involving calaculations of advantage (short-term and longer-term) that in the end can often be no more than intuitive. Yet justiciability does not turn on competence. For all anyone knows, in some hypothetical market testing judges might show greater wisdom in such matters than politicians or civil servants. None the less it would be wholly wrong for the courts to take jurisdiction over them. To borrow a well-known distinction, national interest is the archetype of a matter of policy, not of principle, and decisionmaking according to principle is what should distinguish the act of judging.[196]

There will undoubtedly be borderline cases in which application of the justiciability concept may not point clearly in any one direction. This is a problem common to all abstract legal standards, particularly perhaps in public law, where notions like 'reasonableness' and 'public interest' are notably elastic. However, most of the cases in which unnecessary judicial abstention has occurred have not involved great matters of state policy, but claims of individual rights that are grist to the mills of courts and tribunals. The list includes unfair dismissal,[197] defamation,[198] sex discrimination,[199] consultation with a trade union,[200] and negligence.[201] The objections in such cases—some of which should have been dis-

---

[194] [1985] AC 374, 418. See also the analysis of Taylor LJ (now LCJ) in *R.* v. *Home Sec., ex p. Everett* [1989] 2 All ER 224, 231.

[195] There is no intrinsic reason why legislation could not govern such matters. Post-Vietnam War legislation in the USA attempted to restrict the President's power to commit troops overseas, for example: see War Powers Resolution of 1973, 87 Stat. 555, PL 93–148. For a brilliant evaluation of this and related Congressional efforts, see H. Koh, 'Why the President (Almost) Always Wins in Foreign Affairs', 97 *Yale LJ* 1255 (1988). (The workability of such legislation in a parliamentary system must remain a matter for serious debate.) And several provisions of the German Basic Law regulate the purposes and circumstances in which the nation's forces may be deployed; their interpretation is ultimately a matter for the Constitutional Court.

[196] This distinction, made famous by Ronald Dworkin, seems to originate in his 'The Model of Rules I', in *Taking Rights Seriously* (n. 159 above), 22.

[197] *Balfour* (n. 102 above).   [198] *Thorburn* v. *Hermon* (n. 99 above).
[199] *Johnston* v. *CCRUC* (n. 16 above).   [200] *GCHQ* (n. 3 above).
[201] *Duncan* v. *Cammell Laird* (n. 90 above).

missed as mere knee-jerk arguments for secrecy based on habit, or figments of governmental imagination—have not been to subject matter, but about the need to maintain the secrecy of certain material.[202] Therefore it is the 'practical objections' to judicial involvement which in practical terms are of greatest persuasiveness, and we have offered some specific suggestions to meet them.

For the rest, judicial bodies should operate a strong presumption in favour of justiciability. This has several implications. National security exemptions should apply only to the extent required by clearly expressed legislation—courts should not impose further limitations of their own. We see no case for excluding judicially created norms of fair procedure for reasons of national security. Adopting this approach would put the onus on the executive to claim from Parliament any procedural safeguards it believes are required for its security interests. The use of exemptions should be more strictly policed at the evidential level as well. The *Australian Communist Party* decision and the approach of the European Court of Justice both show how a sceptical attitude to the claimed necessity of security powers is both possible and desirable.

---

[202] Arguably—though no more—this factor was genuinely present in the *Thorburn* case (above n. 99). So too with deportation cases like *Hosenball* [1977] 1 WLR 766 (see Ch. 7 above), where nothing about the nature of decision should foreclose challenge, but matters such as the identification of sources might properly be withheld from an appellant.

Part V
Controlling National Security Institutions

13

The Rationale and Dangers of Security Agencies

Security and intelligence services are given extraordinary powers in order to protect the freedoms enjoyed by citizens in a democratic polity. Yet precisely because of those powers, they are more capable than any other civilian agency of destroying those freedoms, and even democracy itself. This conclusion is platitudinous when stated as a generality: it is necessary to identify more precisely the ways in which security institutions can become dangerous both to freedom and security. Combining the deductive and the inductive—generalizations from specific instances with the logical implications of a priori possibilities—enables one to identify a range of dangers. Yet though grouped together, they do not all emanate from common sources: in particular, it is necessary always to bear in mind the distinction between misuse of powers by a security agency, and misuse of the agency by its political superiors. To the victim, the distinction may appear academic and inconsequential, but in designing mechanisms of control and oversight, failure to address each aspect distinctly will defeat the purpose of the enterprise.

Perhaps the most obvious peril is use of an organization as a political tool by the government in power against its opponents, whether they be opposition political parties, specific campaigns or movements, or ethnic or other minority groups. The names of almost every vicious dictatorship of recent times are associated with an acronym of terror—a 'secret police' known by initials—BOSS, BSS, KGB, SAVAK. In this extreme form such organizations and activities are unknown in Western democracies. However, in these states the targeting of particular political organizations or campaigns because their activities aroused opposition to government policies—opposition being treated as a threat to state security because those policies were arrogantly asserted to be the sole means of maintaining security—has been endemic.

Britain is no exception. The best-known recent example is the targeting of activists in the Campaign for Nuclear Disarmament (CND) for telephone tapping and surveillance, in the service of an electoral and propaganda campaign in support of the Conservative government's nuclear weapons policy. This effort was co-ordinated by a special body established within the Ministry of Defence and known as DS 19, whose purpose was to advance the case for the most controversial manifestations of that policy: the acquisition of Trident and the stationing of Cruise missiles in Britain. This was an overtly partisan use of public money and government machinery, for the latter deployment of Cruise in particular was opposed not only by CND but also by the Labour Opposition, and was an issue in the 1983 election. The inability to respect dissent, and to distinguish it from malfeasance, was expressed with unusual candour by one of the officials involved: 'The case of DS 19 to counter CND is the same as the information unit set up by the government to counter AIDS.'[1]

It was pressure upon MI5 from the Ministry of Defence and its Secretary of State, Michael Heseltine, for information that might discredit CND politically which led to action against its members, notwithstanding misgivings within the Service.[2] Although the officer in charge of the operation, Cathy Massiter, later rebelled against what she described as 'breaking our own rules' and revealed what had occurred on a television programme,[3] the role of Mr Heseltine and other ministers in using the Service for partisan purposes has never adequately been investigated or debated.[4] Other forms of targeting, particularly of trade union leaders whose members were engaged in industrial disputes with various governments which employed them or imposed limitations on their wages, also fall into this category.[5] It is not always clear in such cases whether security officials are acting at the behest of the government, or on the basis of their own decisions. In some instances there may well be a confluence of outlook such that no direction or pressure is required; it is likely that an inquiry into the role of the Security Service during the miners' strike of 1984–5—which thus far has escaped public scrutiny—would conclude that, as with the police, it was 'a case of getting messages they wanted to hear'.[6]

A quite different form of abuse, and one whose potential has long been recognized, is the use by politicians of discreditable information about particular individuals, gained by intelligence agencies under their control. This can have no policy or ideological dimension whatever—the victim may as readily be a rival for office from within the same party as a principled opponent—but the evil effect on the political process is clear enough. Awareness of this problem is clearly manifest in the rather cryptic reference in the Maxwell-Fyfe Directive of 1952 to 'the well-established convention whereby Ministers do not concern

[1] Quoted in M. McIntosh, _Managing Britain's Defence_ (Basingstoke, 1990), 180. The quotation is unattributed, but Dr McIntosh informed us that the person involved was central to the activities of the unit.

[2] Jonathan Aitken, a Conservative MP with good contacts among Security Service officers, reported that there was 'considerable soul-searching' within MI5 before it embarked on investigations of CND, having been explicitly instructed to do so: _HC Debs._, vol. 145, col. 188 (17 Jan. 1989). This is corroborated by Rupert Allason MP, who added that until a known communist was identified as a CND official, the organization limited itself to supplying open source material: P. Gill, _Policing Politics: Security Intelligence and the Liberal Democratic State_ (London, 1994), 225.

[3] 'M.I.5's Official Secrets', broadcast on 8 Mar. 1985.

[4] The Bridge Report (below, pp. 489–90) made no attempt to do so, and the legal action brought by CND officers signally failed to pierce the secrecy: _R._ v. _Sec. of State for Home Dept., ex p. Ruddock_, [1987] 2 All ER 518, discussed on pp.54 and 330 above.

[5] The primary basis for these and other oppressive interventions into domestic politics has been the effort to counter 'subversion'. This demands detailed discussion on its own, which is presented on pp. 395–405 below, where further examples are mentioned.

[6] The comment of an Assistant to the Chief Inspector of Constabulary shortly after the end of the strike: see L. Lustgarten, _The Governance of Police_ (London, 1986), 111.

themselves with the detailed information which may be obtained by the Security Service in particular cases'.[7]

The second danger is that a security agency may become an independent power centre, uncontrolled by ministers or other elected representatives, and determine its own targets, priorities, and mandate. This may occur when ministers fail to inquire into the work of the agency, which they may do for two quite different reasons. One is a belief that it is wrong—unconstitutional in the sense of being improper—for an actor engaged in partisan politics to inquire too deeply into matters which may generate information that is politically sensitive, in that it could be used to discredit others on the political stage.[8] The other is that, so long as they are confident that the agency is choosing the 'right' targets, ministers want to retain the option of 'deniability' if a public scandal erupts. Ignorance can be a convenient shield to hide behind, allowing ministers to absolve themselves from responsibility and foist the blame on over-zealous officials. However, whilst the first reason may be regarded as an excess of scruple and morally more admirable than the second, they can equally produce the undesirable result that a security agency is left to run rampant through the political system, in effect taking sides in political competition by harassing those whose views they dislike and perverting the course of politics in their own ideological interest.[9] This result is not inevitable—a service may be held in check by its own leaders' integrity—but it requires a wildly optimistic view of human nature to believe that such self-denial can be taken for granted. Moreover, it remains possible that elements within an organization would hide such activities from their own superiors.[10] But whereas the first danger is the product of political manipulation, the second arises from the lack of appropriate supervision. The need to navigate between two rocks of manipulation and neglect—or conversely, to ensure necessary independence whilst preventing it from degenerating into irresponsibility—is perhaps the major imperative in establishing proper democratic control over security institutions.[11]

---

[7] Below, pp. 375–77, for full text, see App I

[8] This may reflect a minister's appreciation of the evil discussed in the preceding paragraph. Robert Kaplan, who as Solicitor General in the last four years of the government of Pierre Trudeau was intimately involved in the passage of the CSIS Act, stated that Trudeau had expressed this feeling very strongly. This reticence may have been responsible for widespread misconduct by RCMP security officials who were left unsupervised by ministers. It should be noted, however, that this view of Trudeau is highly controversial; others insist that he was fully aware of RCMP illegalities. See above, n. 53, Ch. 1.

[9] Ideology is far more likely than preference for a particular political party to be the influential factor. See also below, pp. 378, 401.

[10] In so far as there is evidence to support the existence of MI5 attempts to discredit and destabilize the Labour government of the 1970s, it suggests that the efforts took place at a low level within the organization. See further D. Leigh, *The Wilson Plot* (London, 1988), *passim* and more briefly and less reliably, P. Wright, *Spycatcher* (New York, 1987), 368–72.

[11] Cf. the comment of Reg Whitaker of York University, one of the leading Canadian scholars in this field, who speaks of 'the delicate balance which must therefore be struck which is neither too "hands-on" nor too "arm's length".' 'The Politics of Security Intelligence Policy-Making in Canada: I', (1991) 6 *Int. & NS* 649, 651.

The third danger is somewhat more subtle and may arise when ministers and civil servants leave too much to the discretion of the agency. It is a problem of means rather than ends. For example, those politically responsible might identify a particular problem—Irish terrorism, an embargo on military technology to Iraq—quite properly and uncontroversially. However, they might inadvertently or deliberately impose no effective limits on the means the service uses to obtain information or directly counter the threat. Agents may employ violent, illegal, or simply oppressive means to accomplish their task, and be given the impression (whether accurate or not) that no one cares very much about how things are done so long as the threat is countered, or information furnished quickly.[12] This impression may be accurate, a correct interpretation of nods and winks received from political superiors. Or it may be quite mistaken: failure to set out explicit limits might result from inattention due to other pressing problems, a reluctance to become involved in 'operational' matters, or a misguided belief that security officials will give human rights considerations the same weight as would the minister or permanent secretary. Although in such instances the public might feel little sympathy with those affected, and might indeed applaud their targeting, it is in precisely those circumstances that human rights require the most vigilant protection, and the need to rein in those exercising state power is greatest. Even legitimate quarry can be treated oppressively, and controlling methods of operation is at least as important as controlling the range of activities and the criteria for selection of persons to be investigated. The words of a former Canadian Solicitor General, then minister responsible for CSIS, bear remembering: 'Certainly the European experience casts in sharp relief the threat terrorism poses to democracy, not only in the act but in the response.'[13]

Two related ways in which security agencies can inflict severe harm on individuals have been discussed earlier in relation to employment and freedom of movement, and need only be summarized here.[14] Security agencies everywhere are involved in the vetting or clearance of public employees and those employed

---

[12] This observation is particularly applicable to Northern Ireland. It is unlikely that the truth about the conduct of MI5 and MI6 there will ever be publicly established, but there is at least a case to answer involving blackmail, political disinformation, complicity in cover-ups of unlawful violence committed by the RUC and the Army, and possible involvement in political assassinations. See F. Holroyd and N. Burbridge, *War Without Honour* (Hull, 1989) and P. Foot, *Who Framed Colin Wallace?* (London, 1989), and on one aspect of one horrible incident, J. Stalker, *Stalker* (London, 1988), 65–90. Another example of the same phenomenon from Canada: after Pierre Trudeau discovered that he had been persuaded in October 1970 to invoke emergency law on the basis of wholly inadequate information about the FLQ (see TAN 51–3, Ch. 1 above), he insisted that a special effort be made. The result was the establishment of a Francophone unit left to operate on its own which produced far more good information but also engaged in an orgy of illegal activities. See also Whitaker (n. 11 above), 655–6.

[13] J. Kelleher, 'The Counter-Terrorism Program of the Government of Canada: Recent Developments', in P. Hanks and J. McCamus (eds.), *National Security: Surveillance and Accountability in a Democratic Society* (Cowansville, Que., 1989), 251.

[14] Above, Chs. 6 and 7.

by private companies whose work gives them access to secret information. Their precise role varies in particular countries, but everywhere they will at least evaluate a mass of personal data about an individual, retain it, and in some instances offer an assessment of his or her suitability for a particular level of clearance. They thus have great power over the livelihood of hundreds of thousands of people, and release of the information in their possession could seriously damage the reputation, employment prospects, or private relations of those persons.

Agencies have a similar role in relation to immigration controls, and particularly with respect to deportation. Whilst the grounds for expulsion in United Kingdom legislation are extraordinarily open-ended and discretionary—if the Home Secretary deems the deportation to be 'conducive to the public good'[15]—all states have at least partly analogous provisions. The information on which such decisions are based derives primarily from security services; the vulnerability of the persons affected is obvious.

These circumstances create two distinct concerns. The first lies in the recommendations made by the agency. They can be defective for a number of reasons, and based upon false, obsolete, or inaccurate information which has not been adequately checked. Someone may be described as participating in the activities of a terrorist organization on the word of an informant which has been accepted without verification, whereas the informant could be working off a grudge against the person he has named. Secondly, even if the information about the person's own activities is accurate, the agency's evaluation may be warped by political bias. Thus a person would receive an adverse recommendation because of activity in an organization whose views on public policy are disliked by those writing the report.[16]

The second lies in the handling of personal information properly gathered and retained by the agency. Such material should be strictly guarded, and released only to those for whose decision it was compiled, and under specified conditions which adequately protect the privacy of those affected. Its distribution to employers' organizations, private security companies, or other bodies with a private interest is one form of abuse of the power of information control. Another, more overtly political, is the leaking of discreditable information about a person to a journalist. The publication of such information damages its subject's reputation and career; a more insidious variant is to threaten the leak in order to influence his or her actions in politics.[17]

[15] Immigration Act 1971, s. 3(5). 'National security' is one of the most prominent, but not the only, reasons given for deportation under this provision.

[16] This seems to have been at the root of Isobel Hilton's difficulties with the BBC; above, p. 15.

[17] A special dilemma arises with respect to ministers and would-be ministers, and perhaps others who are not formally vetted but equally may be considered for positions involving access to secret information. Assuming that to some degree the secrecy is necessary, important privacy questions concerning the gathering of information about private peccadilloes are raised none the less. Who is the blackmailer: the private individual who threatens to reveal information about Minister X's adultery, sexual peculiarities, etc. to the Press, or the security official who reports the information to the Cabinet Secretary in order to block an individual's chances for ministerial appointment for political

One other matter, which has not received the attention it deserves, is co-operation with other nations' security services by furnishing information. The result may be to assist a vicious regime which does not hesitate to threaten or kill opponents, and could endanger either those who have fled from such a regime or their families or associates who remain within its territory. The problem is of growing importance because of the increasing formal co-operation between nations against what is defined as terrorism, a label which many states too readily apply to the activities of their opponents, when in some cases it applies more appropriately to them. It has arisen in Canada in acute form with respect to some of brutal Central American regimes like those in Guatemala and El Salvador, which have tried to track their dissidents and refugees when they flee northwards. CSIS has had to cope with such requests, and in one case completely ended co-operation with a foreign state for human rights reasons, but SIRC none the less was unhappy about whether effective policies and advisory mechanisms existed to prevent dissemination of information to suspect regimes.[18]

The totality of the dangers we have enumerated, and the achievement of post-War Western democratic states in keeping their armed forces under civilian control, means that security institutions operating internally are now, much more than the police, the greatest potential threat to democratic life that these states have created. In that case, it may be wondered, why have them at all? Why not leave all such matters to the police?

This question is in many ways a peculiarly British one. In Australia and Canada the movement has been sharply in the opposite direction. After scandals involving serious political abuses, South Australia, Victoria, and most recently Queensland have abolished their Special Branches entirely, and New South Wales has sharply reined in its Branch. In Canada, one of the main thrusts of the McDonald Commission proposals, which received virtually unanimous support, was to establish a specialist security agency entirely divorced from the RCMP. There particularly it was felt that the formation of a separate national body, subject to specially rigorous forms of accountability would be the best way to prevent recurrence of misconduct. The impulse behind the opposite tack is distrust of the accountability machinery in Britain, coupled with a view that such matters are better provided for in relation to the police.

In one sense this is simply reasoning backwards: if the problem is the system of accountability, the remedy is to insist on improving that system, not to seek abolition of the organization if it is otherwise well-suited to performing necessary functions. We argue in Chapter 16 for a radically strengthened and widened

---

reasons? And even if there is no bad motive (i.e. if the information is reported solely because of the fear that X may be vulnerable to pressure), what is the legitimate purpose of collecting such information about a considerable number of individuals over many years, if they are prepared to own up to their conduct?

[18] SIRC, *Annual Report 1989–1990* (Ottawa, 1990), 35–7.

system and, closely relatedly, in Chapter 14 for a much-altered definition of what the Security Service should be permitted to do. There is no reason at all to believe that the necessity for such reforms would be obviated by simply transferring functions to the police.

Moreover, implicit in the suggestion is a view of police accountability that seems highly questionable. Although over the last few years some police forces have been responsive to calls for greater openness towards the public, and have taken a range of measures to meet criticisms concerning oppressive conduct and inadequate service from, among others, ethnic minorities, women, and crime victims generally, this has come about largely as a matter of managerial policy. Indeed the one legally required element of accountability—statutory liaison committees[19]—has played very little part in these developments, certainly in urban areas. The moving forces behind the new attitude have been the need to recapture and maintain public support and co-operation, and the unfamiliar circumstances of financial stringency. However in situations where direct public involvement is not required, and where the question of aims may be politically controversial, the police—and in particular, the chief constable—retain a virtually untrammelled discretion in law to act as they think fit in matters of policy, and to be as secretive as they choose in operational matters. In other words, the actual mechanisms of police accountability are no more satisfactory from a constitutional point of view than they were when the subject had a higher political salience in the 1980s.[20] Indeed, in an important respect they are worse. In July 1993 the government announced proposals to extend what has been called 'the new magistracy' to police authorities: the number of elected councillors is to be reduced, and in their place will come central government appointees, mostly with backgrounds in business.[21]

Moreover, the creation of a police authority for London was again rejected, which not only undercuts the argument about a more democratic accountability structure, but in particular raises questions about the value of heightening the police role in security matters. For the Metropolitan Police Special Branch, some 500 strong, is by far the largest complement of police in this area, comprising more than half of those in all British forces; and for them the police authority is the Home Secretary—the minister responsible for the Security Service. Moreover, if London ever gains its own police authority, the question would soon arise why it alone should undertake and pay for what are essentially national functions now performed by the Metropolitan Police.[22] A likely response, particularly if the London authority were to take an active interest in

---

[19] Set up under s. 106 of the Police and Criminal Evidence Act 1984.

[20] For critiques offered then, see T. Jefferson and R. Grimshaw, *Controlling the Constable* (London, 1984); S. Spencer, *Called to Account* (London, 1986); and L. Lustgarten, above n. 6. For an updated view, see R. Reiner and S. Spencer (eds.), *Accountable Policing—Effectiveness, Empowerment and Equity* (London, 1993).

[21] White Paper, *Police Reform: A Police Service for the Twenty-First Century*, Cm. 2281 (1993).

[22] Security and personal protection are perhaps the two most prominent, but there are others.

these matters, would be to remove them from any local accountability structure and place them, along with the small branches found in many other forces, directly under Home Office control. There would be considerable logic to such a move, since protection of the central state can hardly be regarded as requiring a particular local input and accountability.

If it be accepted that no democratic accountability gains would be achieved through any such proposal, most of its appeal vanishes. However, exploration of the issue is worthwhile because it serves to focus attention on the divergent rationales of the two types of organization. As one very useful analysis concludes with respect to intelligence, the difference depends on the ultimate objective pursued.[23] If the aim is to arrest and prosecute lawbreakers, a completely different approach is required than if it is to discover and neutralize a 'threat'. The former involves liaison between police and the Crown Prosecution Service, compliance with requirements that most (though not all) relevant material be disclosed to the defence,[24] and the officers involved giving testimony in court subject to cross-examination. Or as the head of the Met. Special Branch put it, 'today's intelligence may become tomorrow's evidence'.[25]

The latter, on the other hand, might involve identification and expulsion of a suspected person without presentation of evidence or any right of appeal.[26] Alternatively, it might lead to an attempt to 'turn' the agent, and use him as an informer or conduit of false information to those who sent him. Legal considerations here are secondary to prevention of damage.

What blurs distinctions and muddies waters is when criminal activity becomes a threat to national security and is both continuous and conducted by one's own citizens or permanent residents. This, of course, is the problem posed by terrorism, or far preferably (because much less emotively), ongoing politically motivated violence (PMV).[27] People can be convicted of explosives offences or murder, but it is better to prevent acts of death or destruction than to punish their perpetrators. The most effective technique is advance knowledge of the group's plans; hence the overwhelming importance of informers. Although it is possible that the information they provide may be used in court proceedings, far

---

[23] S. Farson, 'Security Intelligence versus Police Intelligence' (1991) 2 *Pol. & Soc.* 65.

[24] Above pp. 311–13.

[25] Before the trial of the Covenanters in 1993 (below, pp. 382–84), Security Service officers had never openly given testimony in a British courtroom. Whether this case is wholly exceptional or marks an important departure remains to be seen.

[26] The classic example, regarded as a great triumph by the intelligence agencies, was the expulsion of over 100 Soviet 'diplomats' from Britain in 1971. As aliens with diplomatic status, no question either of prosecution for espionage or appeal on grounds of wrongful identification or misunderstanding of the activities of any individual arose. This is not a human rights issue because people in that status are not regarded as enjoying any of the liberties of the host society, or having any claims of participation in its system of values. Our critique of internment, deportation, and exclusion orders (Ch. 7) is implicitly based on the assumption that persons who do not occupy that special status are entitled to full respect for their rights.

[27] See further below, pp. 406–7. We continue to use the word 'terrorism' at many places in the text because that is the statutory terminology: below, pp. 381–86.

more likely is that any prosecution will occur much later, and on the basis of material subsequently developed on its foundation. At this critical point 'policing' and 'security' become operationally indistinguishable, and it is this fact which lay beneath the much-heralded turf war between the Metropolitan Police Special Branch and the Security Service which ended in the announcement by the Home Secretary that the latter had assumed the 'lead role' in combating Irish terrorism.[28] The details of who recruits, approves, and handles agents in the field, sets priorities, and has the main responsibility for analysing the information generated, need not concern us, though they caused much grief to those involved. For present purposes the important point is that however those tasks are allocated, they need to be done; and it is difficult to see why, constitutionally, it matters whether they are done by a specialist security agency or a separate arm of the police.

Indeed a strong case can be made for minimizing the police role in respect of terrorism, or more precisely for reorientating it as much as is practicable towards prosecution. Extensive reliance upon informers always entails, however reluctantly, an element of corruption: the use of inducements and rewards; toleration of participation in the activities under surveillance and usually of unrelated criminality; the ever-present temptation to *agent provocateur* activity; and the real possibility of injustice as information is withheld from the judicial process or prosecutions are abandoned in order to maintain cover. The organization participating is inevitably drawn down into the slime. One cannot read John Stalker's account of his investigation into the RUC,[29] or reports from a diverse range of sources about other aspects of the involvement of its specialist squads with Republican and Loyalist terrorists, without concluding that the integrity and legitimacy of the force as a whole has been ineradicably defiled. In a slightly lower key, similar problems have emerged in England as certain officers or even squads within the Metropolitan Police have been discredited by their relations with professional criminals who acted as informers. Active and large-scale police activity of this kind is unhealthy in a democracy and, if unavoidable, better left to a special service further removed from contact with the public and under very tight control.

It would also be inappropriate to assign responsibility for counter-espionage, another key function of a security service, to the police. Although criminal offences are committed, the resemblance to most police matters ends there. The people involved, either as spies or controllers, are often non-citizens who have some direct connection to a foreign state. The methods employed and the counter-measures required, the technicality and secrecy of the information, and the unusual time frame (which may extend over years), further place the area far away from the police realm. This is equally true of other matters in which political considerations play a determining role, and which require unusual methods

---

[28] *HC Debs.*, vol. 207, cols. 297–306 (8 May 1992).   [29] Stalker, (n. 12 above), esp. chs. 1–3.

far removed from the central police mandates of law enforcement and order maintenance. Some of these, such as identifying covert attempts to influence domestic politics, and assisting in the enforcement of embargoes on certain kinds of weaponry and technology, are discussed at length in the following chapter. Along with PMV and espionage, they are among those matters which deserve the name of national security. A specialist agency is required to address them; the corollary is that establishing an effective system of oversight becomes crucial, and the stakes are very high indeed.

CONCLUSION

From our schematic overview of the risks to a democratic state caused by the creation of security agencies there emerge a number of critical points. The first is that controls are required both over the services and their masters. Elected representatives—politicians—or those acting on their behalf must be able to superintend all aspects of agency activity, but the agencies themselves must be protected from partisan or self-interested direction by politicians. This is only an apparent paradox; in fact it is a reflection of the multiple and divergent character of the hazards.

The second point is that the mechanisms of control and supervision must vary with the context. A deportation order served on an individual should be checked by a rigorous and wholly independent appeal process in which the person affected is given full notice of the case against him or her and adequate opportunity to refute its accuracy.[30] Decisions about whether to target a particular organization or its leaders, and the measures to be taken against them, are not matters for review by a court or comparable body. Some aspects of those actions may need to be judged against statutory standards,[31] but the main issues are not those of law but of policy: the definition of the threat, judgment about its likelihood and gravity, the impact on human rights weighed against the need for the information. These determinations will in the first instance be made by the organization itself, but supervision and correction can only be undertaken within the political, not the judicial, process. So, too, with the controls on politicians abusing their positions; protection for the agencies must be sought outside the courtroom. And even when the appropriate sphere of supervision is identical the mechanisms may be different: for example, the political process may be called upon to provide different safeguards for different dangers.

The final point is that controls are not solely a matter of external oversight or even internal organizational checks. A key element is the task set for a security and intelligence agency—its mandate. A clear instruction as to the bounds of its legitimate purpose serves equally to fence off certain types of conduct as forbid-

---

[30] Recall our criticisms of present procedures in Ch. 7.
[31] Notably the issuance of telephone tapping and 'interference' warrants; see Ch. 2 above.

den territory—a strategy essential to protect the freedom and privacy of citizens. It may at the same time provide a firm basis for the development of respect for democratic values and legal procedures *within* the organization, so that the abuses would come to be regarded as illegitimate and objectionable by security service officers themselves. Internalization of democratic values is by far the most effective means of ensuring that they are respected—the inevitably *post hoc*, intermittent, and distanced processes of parliamentary and judicial control can never hope to come close to achieving equal effectiveness. We therefore start our analysis of the law and political practice governing security organizations with comparison and critique of their mandates. We then proceed similarly to consider their accountability and oversight systems.

14

The Legal Mandate

The idea that security agencies require any grounding in legality is of very recent vintage, and still has only partly gained acceptance.[1] Most owe their existence to the circumstances of war (and of the Cold War), as the British colloquial names 'MI5' and 'MI6' imply.[2] Like the conduct of all military matters, they were created and maintained under the royal prerogative. Consequently the range of their activities was limited solely by perceived necessity and political judgment. The movement toward open acknowledgement of the existence of internal security agencies, and their placement on a statutory footing, was a direct result of scandals which broke in the 1970s to reveal abuses of power. Scandal (which above all means embarrassment) has been the motor force for constitutional change in this area, to far greater effect than any principled concern for political freedom or constitutional propriety.[3] One illustration of this is that the communications intercept bodies and overseas intelligence agencies[4] maintained by the three countries studied here, which have less direct impact on the lives and liberties of their citizens, remain purely creations of the executive. Indeed, until the 1990s the British government tried to maintain the bizarre fiction that MI6 did not exist in peacetime. Though scandals of treason have tainted all components of the British intelligence machinery,[5] these have raised issues of competence rather than oppression, and hence there has been little active political movement to bring these bodies under some more visible and formal structure of control.[6]

---

[1] The sole exception is the USA, with its very different constitutional structure separating legislative and executive powers. There the CIA, which had its origins in the Second World War, was quickly given a statutory basis in peacetime, by means of the National Security Act of 1947.

[2] The 'MI' in MI5 and MI6 stands for 'military intelligence'. The two bodies grew out of the Secret Service Bureau first created in 1909. The latter began as the foreign section of the Bureau and worked closely with the Admiralty; the former was devoted to counter-espionage and staffed mostly by military officers. For details, see C. Andrew, *Secret Service* (London, 1986), 121 ff. However, governments in Britain (and even more on the Continent) had long engaged, rather erratically, in spying on domestic enemies. See further B. Porter, *Plots and Paranoia* (London, 1989), chs. 1–4. One of the few early legal recognitions of this activity is to be found in the Civil List and Secret Money Act 1782 (22 Geo. 3, ch. 82).

[3] See further below, p. 379. The galvanizing role of scandal in producing reform is explored more generally in A. Markovits and M. Silversten (eds.), *The Politics of Scandal* (New York, 1988).

[4] See List of Acronyms above. Canada alone has no equivalent of MI6, an external intelligence agency using human sources rather than intercepting signals.

[5] The famous agents and defectors were spread evenly: Philby and Blake in MI6, Blunt in MI5 (during the war), Burgess and Maclean in the Foreign Office, Vassall in the Admiralty. Only a generation later did GCHQ produce an equivalent in Geoffrey Prime.

[6] Somewhat ironically, and for no obvious political reason, the British government recently sharply changed tack. As this book goes to press it has introduced legislation to put both MI6 and GCHQ on a statutory basis. For discussion and critique see the Coda.

THE MAXWELL-FYFE DIRECTIVE

The Security Service (MI5) has, however, operated under a charter of sorts for decades. This was the Maxwell-Fyfe Directive, named after the Home Secretary in the Churchill administration who issued the document in 1952. He was acting in large measure in response to an initiative of the Cabinet Secretary, Sir Norman Brook, who insisted that a minister (and his or her Permanent Secretary) be responsible for the Security Service. The arrangement which had emerged from the war had given the Director-General of the Service virtual autonomy, for the Prime Minister, who was left in nominal charge, had little day-to-day (or even month-to-month), contact. The Maxwell-Fyfe Directive remained secret and only became public knowledge when Lord Denning unexpectedly quoted it in his famous Report on the Profumo Affair.[7] For convenience of reference, it is reproduced in Appendix I.

Several points about the Directive merit particular attention. The first is that the phrase 'Defence of the Realm as a whole' is used twice,[8] giving particular force to the idea that MI5 is not to serve sectional interests, nor concern itself with anything falling short of grave matters affecting the nation's safety. This is reinforced by the injunction to avoid both political bias and even the appearance of favouring one section of the community[9]—almost certainly a reference to the dangers of being seen to take the side of employers against trade unions. It is given practical effect by the prohibition on doing anything, even at the request of a government department, that does not involve an 'important public interest' connected with the Defence of the Realm.[10] This would seem to allow, indeed to require, the Director-General to refuse to permit his organization to be misused for partisan, selfish, or merely trivial purposes—one of the most important practical means by which a security agency can protect itself against its political masters.

However, although Defence of the Realm was the touchstone of the Service's activities, only the barest definition of that phrase was offered: it included espionage, sabotage, and activities 'which may be judged subversive of the State'.[11] The first two have generally been uncontentious,[12] but the concept of subversion has been the core issue of controversy about the legitimacy of security institutions throughout the world in the last decade. Indeed, it would not be too much to say that were it not for the subversion mandate and the use made of it by security services, it is very unlikely that their work and their position within

---

[7] Cmnd. 2152 (1963). On the background to the Directive, see D. Leigh, *The Frontiers of Secrecy* (London, 1980), 196–7.

[8] Paras. 2 and 4.   [9] Para. 4.

[10] Para. 5, which leaves a possible ambiguity where such a request comes from the Prime Minister rather than a government department.

[11] Para. 2.

[12] See further below, pp. 386–89.

government would even have entered public consciousness.[13] The history of the subversion mandate in the three countries is considered closely later in this chapter. All that need be said at present is that the Maxwell-Fyfe Directive treated the concept as either having a self-evident meaning or as best left undefined. The result, as was surely predictable to any student of bureaucracy, was a substantial expansion of both the working definition and the number of people engaged in dealing with it—and of the power of the Service over people's lives and the conduct of political life.

Giving evidence to the Franks Committee in 1971, the then Director-General of MI5, Sir Martin Furnival-Jones, described the Directive as 'a very un-English thing . . . certainly it is unusual in the Government service for an organisation to be given a specific directive as to what its functions are and what the limitations of its powers are'.[14] This was an illuminating comment, for it highlighted the constitutional status of the Security Service which was perhaps even more 'unusual' then than now. The more common alternatives were to rely on direct ministerial responsibility (as with the armed forces) or to create a statutory body.[15] Use of the Directive embodied a more 'hands-off' approach. It is not as detailed in its delineation of purposes and functions as a statute would be. Yet issuance of the Directive seems to have been viewed as discharging the Home Secretary's responsibility, for the Director-General was left to run the organization with virtually complete operational autonomy.[16]

However, Furnival-Jones's reference to 'limitations' on powers skates over an important ambiguity. The Director-General is adjured 'strictly' to do no more than is 'necessary' to protect the Defence of the Realm.[17] Yet whilst the *Concise Oxford English Dictionary* tells us that necessity imports the idea of indispensability, the question whether a particular action is in truth 'necessary' depends upon one's view of the relevant facts. The Service itself is likely to have, or can plausibly claim to have, greater factual knowledge of any particular secret matter than anyone else in government, and for reasons good and bad shares that knowledge as grudgingly as possible. Hence its judgment of necessity becomes virtually unchallengeable, short of some mistake so disastrous that it becomes a public scandal. Thus it becomes the effective judge of both the necessity and propriety of its own conduct.

· [13] Although in the UK various scandals relating to vanishing spies and penetration of security bodies by foreign agents would have ensured some public interest, mostly in sensationalist detail.

[14] Cmnd. 5104, iii. 243. Furnival-Jones gave his evidence anonymously. See Ch. 9 above for discussion of aspects of the Committee's Report.

[15] Though seldom considered in this light, the Security Service is in effect a very unusual variety of quango or, to use a more appropriate term, 'fringe organization'. Many of these, like the Parole Board or the Criminal Injuries Compensation Board, were also originally established under the royal prerogative and were subsequently placed on a statutory footing. A few, like the Arts Council, remain creatures of the prerogative. But none ever had the size, importance, manpower, or budget of any of the security and intelligence bodies. See also below, p. 414.

[16] The one exception related to warrants for telephone tapping, which required Home Office approval.   [17] Maxwell-Fyfe Directive, para. 3.

A related point, or rather a corollary, is that the limitations Furnival-Jones discerned were adminstrative, not legal, in character. Clearly no legislation could impose restrictions on an organization that until 1989 had no place on the statute book. Hence any legal limitations would have had to be found in the common law. And here we connect with a fundamental feature of the common law too often ignored: the deeply authoritarian character of prerogative powers. We have seen in Chapter 3 that invoking the royal prerogative has allowed governments, literally over a period of centuries and without judicial challenge, to operate a secret system of surveillance which expanded from letter opening to telephone tapping as technology allowed. The Security Service grew out of this same legal netherworld. This is not to suggest that it was allowed simply to run rampant. Peter Wright, one of the few insiders who has ever spoken about the process of interception, has stated that in the 1950s, 'Like the Post Office, the Home Office was always highly sensitive on the issue of interceptions, and they were always strictly controlled.'[18] However, this control was always purely discretionary, a characteristic that in a later era was to lead to condemnation in the European Court of Human Rights.[19] Moreover, it was also purely administrative, with no requirement of prior judicial approval—a practice upheld as a matter of common law in the *Malone* case.[20]

Though there are grounds for considerable doubt about the effectiveness of Home Office control of intercepts at various periods,[21] the existence of *some* system of external check has, in relation to intercepts, been a fact of life to which the Security Service has long had to adapt. The same cannot be said of other forms of activity which are simply illegal, but which neither the Maxwell-Fyfe Directive nor any other instrument effectively controlled at all. In what may be the most-quoted sentence in *Spycatcher*, Peter Wright reported that 'For five years we bugged and burgled our way across London at the State's behest, while pompous bowler-hatted civil servants in Whitehall pretended to look the other way.'[22] There was no pretence of legality about such exploits, and notwithstanding Furnival-Jones's view, one must remain profoundly sceptical about whether 'the very un-English thing' was in truth an effective limitation.

Strictly speaking the Maxwell-Fyfe Directive is part of constitutional history, superseded by the statutory provisions examined later in this chapter. None the less, it continues to exert influence on the minds of those who haved worked

---

[18] P. Wright, *Spycatcher* (New York, Viking, 1987), 46. The use of material from this book as evidence is controversial, but if one restricts its use to matters of which Wright had direct knowledge (and the quotation comes from a section describing various bugging and tapping activities), it is a valuable, indeed unique, source. For conflicting views on the value of Wright's account, see D. Watt, 'Fallout from Treachery: Peter Wright and the *Spycatcher* Case' (1988) 59 *Pol. Q.* 206–18, and L. Lustgarten, 'Learning From Peter Wright: A Response to D. C. Watt', (1989) 60 *Pol. Q.* 222–36.

[19] In *Malone* v. *UK* (1985) 7 EHRR 14, discussed above, p. 69.

[20] *Malone* v. *Metropolitan Police Commissioner* (*No. 2*) [1979] Ch. 344. This case then went to Strasbourg and produced the decision cited in the preceding note. As Ch. 3 has shown, exclusion of judicial scrutiny remains a feature of the present statutory regime of interceptions.

[21] Above, pp. 58–59.   [22] See (n. 18 above), 54.

under it. Our Security Service source emphasized the 'continuity of thinking: even though we are bound by the Act . . . we certainly would not reject light from the Directive.' Our critique of the Directive concerns its limited practical impact, not the principles laid down, which were wholly admirable and in certain significant respects superior to what has replaced them. Two such regressions are particularly worth noting. The first is the omission of any provision in the 1989 Act which would instruct the Director-General to ignore requests from a government department and rely upon his or her own judgment before embarking upon any enquiry.[23] Secondly, paragraph 4 of the Directive, which spoke of freedom from political bias or influence and avoidance of identification with any particular section of the community, has been replaced by a much narrower prohibition against taking actions 'to further the interests of any political party'.[24] This formulation does not bar harassment of pressure groups which, though in general terms left-wing are not part of the Labour Party and indeed may, like Militant, be deeply hated by its leadership. Especially with Cold War and nuclear disarmament issues removed from contention, the reality of contemporary British politics is that party political favouritism is a far less likely source of abuse than ideological bias.[25] The 1989 Act's retreat from Maxwell-Fyfe in this matter is inexcusable. The good news is that in working terms this may not matter, for the Service treats the present legislation as incorporating the principles of the Directive.

THE MOVEMENT TO A STATUTORY FOOTING

All three nations under study established agencies which, during or immediately after the First World War, were particularly concerned with 'the Red menace'.[26] However, it was in the Cold War era that internal security services achieved permanence, considerable standing within government, and political importance. And in all three countries there has been a strikingly similar trajectory of development. Creation by the executive in conditions of total secrecy; consequent absence of public debate about the purposes and methods of the organization; unreflective acceptance, with the onset of the Cold War, of an anti-communist

---

[23] Para. 5.   [24] SSA 1989, s. 2(2)(*b*); for the full text see App. II.

[25] Nor is it necessarily the case that the Security Service left to itself would be any more biased against Labour than the rest of Whitehall; our informant claimed that the political orientation of its members is not notably different from the civil service generally.

[26] For Canada, see G. Kealey, 'The Surveillance State: The Origins of Domestic Intelligence and Counter-Subversion in Canada, 1914–21' (1992) 7 *Int. & NS* 179. For Australia, see F. Cain, *The Origins of Political Surveillance in Australia* (Sydney, 1983). In Britain MI5, having achieved a separate existence during the First World War, went on to play a very active role against communists in its aftermath, and by 1931 had taken over from Special Branch responsibility for internal 'revolutionary' movements, and began to call itself the 'Security Service'. See Andrew (above n. 2), ch. 7 and 512–13.

ideology of a markedly right-wing character;[27] intervention in domestic politics by means animated by that ideology, leading to outcry—and hence for the first time intensive public debate—arising from revelations of harassment, political bias, and illegality. At this point the British trajectory begins to diverge from the others, for whilst in Australia and Canada the political reaction was strong enough to produce a statutory structure which imposes significant restrictions on the mandate,[28] in this country the response has been contained.[29] Consequently, whilst the Security Service does indeed now have a statutory basis, this has in no way restricted its sphere of operations. This can seen most clearly by examining the differences in the statutory mandates laid down in each nation; for ease of reference the key sections may be found in Appendix II. The analysis inevitably takes one deeply into some important issues of public policy.

THE MANDATES COMPARED

Perhaps the first point to make is a general one. It is that there is a significant difference in approach between Britain and Australia and Canada. Whilst Britain, in adopting the form of statutes has attempted to keep the mandate as unrestricted and open-ended as possible, the other two countries have attempted to specify the evils its services are to combat with as much precision as is possible.

In the definitional sections of the Australian and Canadian statutes, 'security' is defined in relation to a number of specific concepts or activities. By contrast, in Britain, 'The function of the Service shall be the protection of national security and, in particular, its protection against [enumerated threats]'.[30] These enumerated threats are clearly intended to be examples—to be sure, the most prominent examples—of national security, but the British approach is to leave this critical concept roaming free. This was made clear by the then Home Secretary, Douglas Hurd, when he resisted amendments designed to pin it down. He said,

The definition has to be comprehensive. The [House of Commons] would not want to establish a description of functions that did not cover all areas in which the Security

[27] In all English-speaking countries, the connection between Cold War anti-communism and right-wing political orientation in security personnel has been so strong as to seem an inherent feature of the Western security agenda. Yet it was not inevitable: throughout the 1940s the French Secret Service, the SDECE, was led largely by socialists. See R. Faligot and P. Krop, *La Piscine* (Oxford, 1989), pt. I, and esp. ch. 3.

[28] And also, and equally significantly, on the powers, procedures, and mechanisms of oversight, all of which are explored in Part V below.

[29] This difference is owing to a number of political factors. For a brief summary, see L. Lustgarten, 'Accountability of the Security Services in Western Democracies' (1992) 45 *Curr. L. Prob.* 145, 152–5. For a more detailed study, see R. Whitaker, 'The Politics of Security Intelligence Policymaking in Canada: I' (1991) 6 *Int. & NS* 649, 655–64. For Australia, see F. Cain, 'Accountability and the Australian Security Intelligence Organization: A Brief History', in S. Farson *et al.* (eds.), *Security and Intelligence in a Changing World* (London, 1991), ch. 8.

[30] SSA 1989, s. 1(2).

Service might, now or in the future, have to become involved. If [the House] did that, it could create an intolerable position, where the Security Service would be powerless to defend us or where there might be great pressure and, therefore, strains on the way the legislation was interpreted and understood.[31]

This viewpoint is not irrational, but at bottom it is literally authoritarian. The result of leaving the key concept of the mandate open-ended is to leave its effective definition to ministers or, perhaps equally likely, to the security agencies themselves. Either way the result is to legitimate arbitrary power in a way that is far more dangerous to the real security of a democratic Britain than the name-less horrors held out by the Secretary of State. To say this is not to depict all, or even most, security officials as would-be tyrants just waiting for the opportunity to oppress dissidents. It is simply to insist that it is too tempting to allow any official to define his or her own functions and powers, and further that the peculiar pressures and conditions of work prevailing in the field of security are more likely than most to lead to abuse of power.

Mr Hurd's approach would perhaps be justifiable during a war in which the nation was threatened with invasion, and it is certainly possible that, at a deep subconscious level, the experience of the last war has left a strong and continu-ing influence on the attitudes of officialdom in these matters. It is, however, very doubtful whether in an age in which human rights have become a central issue of world politics, and in which the consciousness of enjoying rights is increasingly a part of the outlook of at least the articulate public, the outlook he expressed will continue to command acceptance.

There may be another subtle difference between the British approach and that of the other two. As we have seen, the Security Service Act 1989 defines the function of the Service as 'protection of national security' and imposes the addi-tional function of 'safeguard[ing] the economic well-being' of the nation against the machinations of persons abroad.[32] In Australia and Canada, by contrast, the emphasis is on *information*. ASIO's function is defined primarily as 'to obtain, correlate and evaluate intelligence relevant to security'; ancillary to this is com-munication of information and advice to ministers and officials on security mat-ters.[33] CSIS is instructed to 'collect, by investigation or otherwise . . . and analyse and retain information and intelligence respecting security-threatening activities and report to and advise the Government'.[34]

Clearly MI5's 'protective' work will include receiving and analysing informa-tion to a major extent, and equally clearly ASIO and CSIS are not to be equated with university seminars in which analysis is undertaken for its intrinsic interest or the advancement of theory. Yet it seems appropriate to point out the differ-

---

[31] *HC Debs.*, vol 145, col. 214 (17 Jan. 1989).   [32] SSA 1989, s. 1(2) and (3).

[33] ASIO Act 1979 (as amended), s. 17(1).

[34] CSIS Act 1984, s. 12. One may note too that the Report of the Committee of the Canadian Parliament which conducted the five-year review of the CSIS Act described the organization's 'pri-mary mandate' as 'warning the government'. *In Flux—But Not in Crisis* (Ottawa, 1990), 15.

ence and to suggest that it implies a difference of emphasis, with MI5 being conceived as more action-orientated than its counterparts. It also seems unlikely that the way the mandate is expressed was entirely a technical decision of the parliamentary draughtsman.[35]

ELEMENTS OF THE MANDATE

Terrorism

The most topical and obvious threat with which MI5 is concerned, 'terrorism', might be thought to be the most straightforward conceptually, and the easiest to recognize in practice. However, British legislation is the only one of the three which uses the term. The Australian statute incorporates 'politically motivated violence' and 'promotion of communal violence' as elements of the 'security' ASIO is established to protect.[36] The CSIS Act refers to activities directed to or supporting the threat or use of 'serious violence . . . for the purpose of achieving a political objective within Canada or a foreign state'.[37] In Britain, moreover, the term remains undefined. This has a number of important consequences, some of which we have only discovered through correspondence with the Home Office. Unattributed quotations refer to this source.

One is that the definition of terrorism found in the Prevention of Terrorism Act (PTA) and incorporated in the 1984 Home Office Guidelines on Special Branch[38] is not identical to that used by the Security Service. The latter is restricted by the 1989 Act to acting against threats to 'national security'; hence only terrorism which rises to that level comes within its remit. In part this may be the functional equivalent achieved by the CSIS Act's requirement of 'serious' violence', the effect in both cases being to leave violence limited in scale and location entirely to the police. Beyond that, the 'Service is however well aware of the PTA definition'. Here questions of objective and organization of the violence seem to be crucial.

The obvious question which then arises is, on the basis of what criteria and information does the Service decide when this level is reached? This answer is usually treated as equally obvious, as no doubt it is in relation to Republican or

---

[35] As we have learned from our interviews, there is a great deal of interchange between officials in the three countries, who spoke knowledgeably about structures and practices in the others. Additionally, of course, since the UK was the last to introduce legislation it is likely that the comparable provisions had been carefully studied.

[36] ASIO Act, s. 4. These formulations were designed specifically to remove terrorism and especially 'subversion' from the ASIO mandate whilst keeping coercive acts unacceptable in a democratic society firmly within it. See below, pp. 406–7.

[37] CSIS Act, s. 2(*c*).

[38] The interpretation section, PTA 1989, s. 20, defines terrorism as 'the use of violence for political ends, and includes any use of violence for the purpose of putting the public or any section of the public in fear.' See above, pp. 72–74, on the Guidelines.

Loyalist paramilitary organizations, or to Khalistan separatists who have organized assassination attempts on Indian politicians visiting Britain and Canada.
However, the issue is more ambiguous and the scope for controversial value
judgment greater than perhaps is generally realized. Someone, or some kind of
information, has to alert the Service to consider whether it should become
involved. This leaves vast room for reasoning in a circle, in crudest form so that
national security becomes whatever the institution concludes in good faith that it
ought to be involved in. Just as it used to be said among police that 'you do not
have a drug problem until you have a drug squad', so the Security Service may
not uncover information about a particular activity until it decides to devote
resources to looking for it.[39] Institutional or, still worse, individual predilections
may influence the choice, and it is here that ideological bias or intolerance can
warp the decision.

An illustration of the difficulties only came to public attention as a result of
the trial in Caernarfon of three members of the Covenanters, a Welsh separatist
group supporting the aims of *Meibion Glyndwyr*.[40] Police in North Wales have
long believed the latter organization responsible for the burning of holiday
homes and other acts of violence against the property of 'outsiders', principally
though not exclusively English. Its activities have not caused personal injuries,
though that may owe much to luck since several persons over the years have
received letter-bombs. In a long and expensive trial which only began after the
defendants had been held in detention for more than a year, the role of the
Security Service was exposed when the presiding judge overruled a public interest immunity certificate[41] and four officers testified from behind a screen—the
first time MI5 officers have openly given evidence in a British court. Yet the key
question is why they were there at all.

The substantive offence was a serious one,[42] but that fact alone would not
justify the involvement of the Security Service. Its view was that 'the activities of
certain Welsh extremists engaged, for example, in arson and letter bomb campaigns, are clearly such as to constitute a threat to national security . . . [and]
also fall clearly within the terms of the PTA definition.' The first limb of this
statement may appear much less clear to many people in North Wales, but the

---

[39] The drug example is not one we have particularly in mind, though it has been discussed in
Parliament and the Press. Independently of each other, both our Home Office informants, one of
whom worked with the police and the other with the Security Service, insisted forcefully that the latter had no interest in straying into this territory. But the crudely self-serving phrase current in the
USA—'narco-terrorism'—epitomizes the danger.

[40] This trial did not receive the amount of media coverage and discussion its wider importance
merits. We have relied on the *Guardian* account, 'Welsh Activist Sent Letter Bombs', 10 Mar. 1993,
and P. Thomas, 'Secret Police on Trial' (1993) 98 *Planet* 3.

[41] Above, Ch. 11.

[42] Two of the defendants were charged only with conspiracy to cause explosions; both were
acquitted. The third, Sion Roberts, also acquitted of conspiracy, was convicted (by a bare majority of
10–2) of sending letter-bombs to four persons, including a Minister of State in the Welsh Office and
two local policemen prominently involved in the investigations into the incidents involving Meibion
Glyndwyr, said to number around 200 over more than a decade.

key word seems to be 'campaign': the organized and ongoing nature of the activities differentiating them from intermittent and opportunist violence. This interpretation is supported by the response to our query about whether the Service would treat the growing number of racist attacks—which unlike most of the incidents in Wales have frequently involved direct violence against individuals, including hundreds of cases of serious assault and several murders—as falling within their mandate, since they clearly satisfy the PTA test of 'putting . . . any section of the public in fear'.[43] The answer was no; for the reason that '[t]here is no evidence of systematic organised racial violence by any political group, and in the vast majority of cases of racial harassment reported to the police there is no evidence of the involvement of any political group'.

The emphasis on systematic organization by a political group seems right in principle: otherwise every act of violence with a political dimension would fall within the domain of the Security Service. This would wrongly erode the distinction between criminal conduct and threats to matters that are truly national in scope and significance; and as a practical consequence MI5 would take over the role of the police in such matters. This cannot be right, for two reasons. One is the constitutional dangers entailed in expanding the role of an organization granted greater powers and inevitably having far lower public visibility and less direct accountability than the police. The other is that it would require a major reorientation of the Service which, in gathering intelligence, is not limited or even primarily concerned with criminal prosecution, and whose officers are untrained in legal procedures (such as PACE Codes of Practice) or giving evidence in court.[44] Yet both in relation to the Caernarfon prosecution and the approach to racist violence, application of the principle raises serious doubts.

One hazard is the operation of another form of tautology: a number of incidents occur; there are political overtones; the police are unable to catch the offenders; *ergo*, this must amount to activity so 'organized' that it rises to a threat to national security. On this reasoning, so would Robin Hood and his merry men.[45] The ineffectiveness of the police may be due less to the existence of cleverly organized and concealed 'terrorist cells', than to the reluctance of people sympathetic to the grievances, though not the methods, of the activists to supply information. Equally, it may be owing to their own incompetence,[46] and clearly one way to camouflage such shortcomings is to present information to the Service so as to suggest the existence of a well-organized group with political aims. We should stress that we are not claiming that there was no basis for MI5's involvement with political violence in Wales. Obviously the evidence needed to satisfy a jury beyond reasonable doubt is very much greater than that

---

[43] See n. 38 above.   [44] Above, p. 370.

[45] More seriously, this outlook seems to have infected the prosecuting authorities, as seen in the jury's rejection of the conspiracy charges (above n. 42), which were the dominant element in the trial.

[46] There have been a number of instances in Wales of unsuccessful prosecutions or extended detentions of suspects against whom no charges were brought. See Thomas (n. 40 above), 4.

required to elicit inquiries by the Service; and the fact that inquiries fail subsequently to yield confirmation of terrorist activities does not invalidate the initial decision to probe. Ours is a more general point, which is that dependence on police information to establish the threshold condition for Service involvement has its own perils.

However, the trial raised another disturbing issue. Lack of police success in securing convictions may be due to the fact that their powers are subject to restrictions which do not apply to MI5. The only evidence against the convicted defendant came about after a burglary under warrant, apparently to place a concealed 'bug', led to the discovery of a package of bombs. This entry could not lawfully have been undertaken by the police, who do not have the power to enter private premises, let alone to bug them, merely under warrant from the Home Secretary.[47] Without this Security Service involvement there would have been nothing to convict any of the three defendants, since all the other charges failed. And it is hard to see what contribution the Service's extensive involvement made to this particular case, except to provide the otherwise unobtainable evidence.[48] There is no basis for suggesting that they were brought in specifically for the purpose of using their extraordinary 'property interference' powers, but this case does present a question which has never before been in issue, and which here we can do no more than state. It is whether material obtained by Service officers under powers not available to the police should be barred from use in any prosecution under the PACE provision designed to maintain the integrity of criminal justice.[49]

The treatment of racist violence raises a number of contrasting issues. One of the most important is that, as noted above,[50] the Service and Home Office require that a 'political group' be involved. This is an administrative gloss on the PTA definition, which requires only 'the use of violence for political ends',[51] saying nothing about the character of those undertaking it. This is a significant restriction, a discretionary policy choice adopted with no compelling justification. Indeed on policy grounds it seems quite wrong. Even more than when there is an undifferentiated risk affecting the public at large, violence targeted at a section of the public which may be socially isolated or unpopular and large enough to constitute a distinct group, demands to be treated as terrorism if the underlying purpose is 'political'. And there is no room for doubt that violence directed

---

[47] Above, Ch. 3. After this discovery the police were able to obtain a (judicial) search warrant and unearthed more equipment.

[48] It is, of course, possible that information gained during the operation but not used as evidence at the trial has been important in preventing future acts of political violence, but one would have to accept that conclusion wholly on faith.

[49] PACE, s. 78, which gives the trial judge discretion to exclude evidence where 'having regard to . . . the circumstances in which the evidence was obtained, the admission of the evidence would have such an adverse effect on the fairness of the proceedings that the court ought not to admit it'. A further question, even more difficult, is whether material evidence gained by the police directly in consequence of the Service's activities (see n. 47) ought also to be excluded.

[50] p. 383.   [51] See n. 38 above.

at making ethnic minorities feel psychologically insecure and not at home in Britain is political: it is part of a conflict about who counts as British—about citizenship and national identity.[52] Few questions are more quintessentially political.[53]

There are also important operational questions. Reliance upon the patterns emerging from cases of reported racial 'harassment' (which may include a range of offensive, frightening, and criminal activities which are not physically violent), would seem to be the wrong pool of incidents from which to draw conclusions.[54] They may conceal a smaller number of instances of serious violence which have some central point of co-ordination, or are being perpetrated by people connected with a movement or organization. Whilst it would be wrong deliberately to stretch the interpretation of the mandate to authorize Security Service involvement because the actions are hateful, the question of how it informs itself and takes decisions in these matters ought to involve much greater openness and public consultation. Representatives of those who feel under attack should be able to discuss openly with both the police and MI5 their perceptions of whether the attacks are political. Although victims may have exaggerated fears, they may also have information about the activities of racist groups not available to the authorities; and they may be able to put those activities in a context which officials have failed to understand. Senior police officials already engage in such consultations,[55] and there is no reason why some very senior person far removed from field operations, such as the Director-General or her Deputy, should not take part openly on behalf of the Service.[56]

Although we argue below that Britain should adopt the Australian definition of the Security Service mandate, which would explicitly include 'promotion of communal violence',[57] 'promotion' implies some sort of organized activity, so the change would not automatically give the Service a more active role in response to any particular incident. None the less, discussion of this topic has shown that what constitutes 'terrorism' may be a matter of dispute that raises important questions of policy (and correlative operational practice). The Service's working definition may be too wide as applied in some circumstances, and too narrow in others. This is not a question to be decided by courts on

---

[52] This is so over and above whether the violence succeeds in forcing some individuals or families to move to a different district or to emigrate.

[53] We do not know whether the Security Service has considered this point.

[54] See p. 383 above.

[55] We are not asserting that they they are unaware of the issue. The remarks of the new Metropolitan Police Commissioner, Mr Paul Condon, to a conference on 28 February 1993, in which he spoke of 'total intolerance of racially motivated attacks . . . and of those who indulge in racial abuse', are perhaps the most forceful statement made on the subject, and his predecessor, Sir Peter Imbert had also emphasized the issue publicly. But the attacks continue. More needs to be done and the question is whether the Security Service has a role to play, and how that decision is taken.

[56] A half-way house could be for a person of equivalent standing from the Home Office to participate, but only for a short transitional period whilst the Service prepared itself for the shock of contact with those whose 'security' it is supposed to protect.

[57] Below, p. 407.

judicial review, concerned with the reasonableness of administrative interpretation. It is a public and political issue in the widest sense of involving a choice among values and the interests of many citizens, and should be debated in public forums. In this sense mandate can never be detached from accountability and oversight.

Espionage and Sabotage

Perhaps the least controversial matter, and one common to all jurisdictions, is the inclusion of espionage and sabotage. Curiously, these terms are, strictly speaking, unknown to English criminal law. The main relevant provision is section 1 of the Official Secrets Act 1911, entitled 'Penalties for Spying', which in somewhat awkward but none the less comprehensible language covers collecting or communicating information in any form that might be 'directly or indirectly useful to an enemy'. This provision has not raised any controversial questions of interpretation in the major spy trials,[58] but one intriguing problem arising from the language of the section remains unresolved: who is an enemy?[59] However, definitions of espionage and sabotage do appear, not in an Act of Parliament, but in the Guidelines sent by the Home Office to all Special Branches of police forces in England and Wales.[60] Presumably these are also the definitions with which the Security Service works.

The Guidelines describe espionage as 'Covert or illegal attempts to acquire information or materials in order to assist a foreign power',[61] which would extend to an attempt on behalf of *any* state, regardless of the nature of its relations with the United Kingdom, to acquire information which the government wishes to keep to itself. Sabotage is defined as: 'An act falling short of a military operation, or an omission, intended to cause physical damage in order to assist a hostile foreign power or to further a subversive political aim.'[62]

Apart from the final clause, with its reference to the contentious issue of subversion,[63] the administrative definition of sabotage, like that of espionage, identifies conduct that it is right to guard against, defines it with reasonable precision, and does not interfere with political participation or other human rights.

It would be a serious error to confine one's mental picture of espionage to the activities of 'moles' in high places, false-bottom briefcases, and clandestine meetings in public lavatories. The grey, wet streets of a John Le Carré novel are

---

[58] The convictions of Fuchs, Vassall, the Portland spy ring, George Blake, Prime, and Bettaney produced no appeals on points of law. For a detailed, though not entirely reliable, study of s. 1, see R. Thomas, *Espionage and Secrecy* (London, 1991), critically reviewed by L. Lustgarten (1993) 33 *BJ Crim.* 302.

[59] See the discussion in the Ch. 9, TAN 16.   [60] Above, Ch. 3.   [61] Para. 20.

[62] Ibid. 'Espionage' does not appear in the Canadian Criminal Code (which received and has retained s. 1 of the OSA 1911), but 'sabotage' does. Its definition omits any reference to subversion, and penalizes destruction of property or impeding the working of military machinery for any 'purpose prejudicial' to public safety. RSC 1985, c. C-46, s. 52.

[63] 65. An extended critique is presented below, pp. 396 ff.

no longer the primary backdrop, having been replaced by the executive suites of weapons dealers and manufacturers, and the computer terminals of banks. In its Annual Report for 1988–9, SIRC devoted a chapter to 'Science and Technology'. This focused on 'clandestine, illegal transfers of goods and information to other countries', which it sees as part of CSIS's espionage mandate.[64] This new form of technological espionage takes place within the complex framework of export controls and classified research under government auspices which grew up during the Cold War.[65] Along with Canada, Britain is a member of COCOM, the Co-ordinating Committee for Multilateral Export Controls. In all, sixteen nations are members of this body, heavily dominated by the United States, which for years has tried with intermittent seriousness and mixed success to impose and enforce restrictions on transfer of sophisticated technology with possible military applications, especially to Soviet bloc countries.[66] The upheavals in Eastern Europe have led to growing ambivalence about these restrictions, but they have become of rapidly growing importance elsewhere, most obviously in relation to Iraq, which had purchased billions of pounds-worth of sophisticated military equipment from several COCOM members for many years.

Long and complex regulations, enshrining the COCOM rules, specify prohibited items and destinations.[67] They were supposed to apply to Iraq from the mid-1980s, and one of the major issues in the Inquiry headed by Lord Justice Scott is whether those rules were ignored by ministers and whether they misled Parliament about what they were doing.[68] The primary enforcement agency for this prohibition is the Department of Trade and Industry, whose commitment and competence, particularly where weaponry is concerned, have been much criticized, notably in relation to the so-called 'Supergun Affair'.[69]

Sanctions may, of course, be imposed for other purposes and by bodies other than COCOM. Most obviously, the United Nations embargo on all trade with Iraq, imposed after the invasion of Kuwait, requires monitoring of the commercial activities of many companies and transport facilities. Britain has perhaps more experience with the difficulties of implementing such measures than most, for sanctions—which were supposed to bring Ian Smith's Rhodesian 'rebels'

[64] SIRC, *Annual Report 1988–89* (Ottawa, 1989), ch. 6.

[65] Old-style espionage, attempting to gain access to knowledge of the design and manufacture of complex weaponry, has not disappeared. It seems, however, that the 'new frontier' of espionage is this more complex area of embargoes and the physical prevention of exports.

[66] Little has recently been written on COCOM. See esp. I. Anthony, *Arms Export Regulations* (Oxford, 1991), 208–11, and also S. Landgren, *Embargo Disimplemented* (Oxford, 1989), 7–8, 192–5; an earlier study is G. Adler-Karlsson, *Western Economic Warfare 1947–67* (Stockholm, 1968).

[67] Export of Goods (Control) Order 1989 (as amended), made under the Import, Export and Customs (Powers) Defence Act 1939. For a brief general account of the UK rules, see Anthony (n. 66 above), 175–82.

[68] See Ch. 17 below.

[69] A cogent and extremely critical account of the DTI's performance was broadcast on the BBC's *Panorama* (18 Feb. 1991), in a programme entitled 'Saddam Hussein's Supergun'.

quickly to heel—were the Government's primary response to Rhodesia's Unilateral Declaration of Independence in 1965. These proved singularly ineffective, as did the widely circumvented UN embargo against selling arms to South Africa, made mandatory in 1977.[70] All such policies require, as the SIRC Report noted, a significant contribution from the domestic security organization. To that must be added input from covert and open overseas intelligence (which thus would involve both MI6 and the Foreign Office directly), the Ministry of Defence, Customs and Excise, and the police. To be effective, all this effort must be well co-ordinated by some central body.

The Iraq example epitomizes a much deeper problem. Whether one considers the needs and interests of Britain alone, or takes account also of the wider concerns of political stability and avoidance of human slaughter and environmental catastrophe, one of the most important elements of national security policy in this decade and beyond will be the maintenance of various forms of embargoes and export restrictions. The most important, of course, concerns preventing the proliferation of nuclear weapons, but chemical and biological weapons are nearly as dangerous to Third World peoples whose governments lack the technology to support nuclear capability.

More generally, however, it will be imperative to control what has been called the 'arms bazaar', in which the weapons manufacturers of Western and Eastern Europe, and even more of the United States, have grown rich by contributing to the instability and violence in the Third World.[71] After the Gulf War, many pious words were spoken by Western leaders about the necessity to curb the arms trade. Yet press reports of the visits of those leaders to states which have the money to spend regularly include details of accompanying arms sales contracts. In such a climate, dominated by the most short-sighted economic expediency, it should surprise no one when those weapons are turned on ourselves or our allies at a later date; and the ensuing hand-wringing and search for scapegoats is as predictable as it is hypocritical.

Greater action may be expected in relation to the spread of nuclear capability, where the self-interest of Western states is most obvious, and here Britain, as Europe's senior nuclear power, will have a particularly important responsibility. Thwarting proliferation will demand vigilant enforcement of the prohibition on the transfer of the relevant technology—a highly profitable trade engaged in by those whom SIRC described as 'technobandits', who will need to be controlled. The task may well require the monitoring of their movements and telephone conversations, and possibly secret access to their financial records; a properly regulated security service is the organization most suited to such work. Indeed

---

[70] For details, see Landgren (above n. 67), chs. 1, 2, 14, and 15. The failure of the Rhodesian sanctions produced a report for the Foreign Office co-authored by the present Master of the Rolls: T. Bingham and S. Gray, *Report on the Supply of Petroleum and Petroleum Products to Rhodesia* (London, 1978).

[71] See further A. Sampson, *The Arms Bazaar in the Nineties: from Krupp to Saddam* (Sevenoaks, 1991) and J. Adams, *Trading in Death* (London, 1992) for two good accounts by journalists.

the monitoring and enforcement of embargoes and restrictions on transfer of weapons and military technology are among the most valuable contributions to real security that the intelligence agencies will be called upon to perform in the foreseeable future.

In line with general government practice, and in the absence of any independent authoritative body able to air such issues on behalf of the public, there has been no indication of the emphasis the Security Service gives to these problems, and whether recent years have seen any change. We were therefore particularly interested to pursue the question, and were somewhat surprised by the response.

The broad area of embargoes is now regarded as falling within the domain of national security, possibly but not necessarily under the head of espionage. The suggestion that this was a largely unexplored and critically important problem in which the Service could play a major role was not met with great eagerness or enthusiasm. It would have a role, but that would be relatively small and involve work with other agencies; the area is one which, like terrorism, illustrates the way in which the Service has necessarily become more closely involved with the rest of Whitehall. The idea that it could establish itself as a sort of watchman over weapons and sensitive technology transfer was dismissed as contrary to a basic principle of intelligence methodology: starting with the known, and proceeding to the unknown.[72] The only acceptable way to start is where one has good reason to believe a specific target should be investigated; in this context 'the known' would be potential purchasers: foreign states and arms dealers. The primary responsibility for this was said to lie elsewhere.[73] It is clear that MI5 cannot be accused of rushing into a new area as part of bureaucratic empire-building, although its increasing preoccupation with Irish terrorism obviously contributes greatly to this self-restraint.

SIRC has taken the view that, in so far as foreign intelligence officers are involved, these matters come within the mandate of espionage.[74] However, there is a much wider range of 'players' in the game, such as arms dealers and specialists in hidden financial transactions or in the obtaining of end-user certificates. It is at least possible that, for all sorts of readily imaginable reasons,[75] the Security Service might at some time take the view that at least some of the activities and issues we have discussed are outside its remit. It would therefore be desirable to preclude any dispute by amending the statutory mandate to encompass assisting the effectuation of sanctions or embargoes agreed to or imposed by the United Kingdom government.

---

[72] For another application of this principle, see below, p. 403.

[73] Presumably with those gathering intelligence overseas, though this was not stated.

[74] See n. 63 above, 39.

[75] Which could range from the admirable—a 'constitutionalist' objection that the issue does fall within the language of its mandate which it wishes to respect; to the bureaucratic—a decision that other activities have a more pressing claim on resources; to the objectionable—a wish to weaken the effectiveness of a particular embargo or sanction because of political opposition to it.

Economic Interests

As has been seen, the British statute specifies 'safeguarding the economic well-being' of the country as one of the functions of the Security Service.[76] The structure of section 1 makes plain that this is additional to, rather than part of, 'national security'. The only known legal source for the phrase is the European Convention on Human Rights, where it appears in one connection only: as a reason that may be used to curtail the right to privacy and family life found in Article 8. There is no parallel provision in Australia, though that has not stopped ASIO in certain instances from taking an interest in matters that would fall within this description.[77] The CSIS Act handles this issue with uncharacteristic ambiguity, but seems to leave some role for CSIS in this sphere.[78]

Nor is the boundary clear or unproblematic. Asked to elaborate on what this subsection was directed toward, the Home Secretary made quite plain that it was concerned with oil and other commodities on which the economy is dependent and over which foreign governments or companies can exercise considerable power.[79] But the constituents of our 'economic well-being' could readily be interpreted in much broader terms. In particular, as has been seen in Chapter 1, there may be pressure from some quarters to subsume certain economic interests under the rubric of security so as to bring them within the mandate of the 'intelligence community'.

One of the major advantages of the greater openness surrounding security matters in Australia and Canada is the role that oversight bodies can play in educating the public and stimulating intelligent debate about difficult questions. In its 1989–90 Annual Report, SIRC built upon its previous discussion of science and technology. It noted that, for the first time, the Cabinet had set public priorities, in the form of National Requirements for Security Intelligence.[80] One of these was 'economic security', which was amplified by the Solicitor-General (the minister responsible for the Service) to mean giving 'the government a strategic security intelligence assessment and advice in the area of clandestine technology transfer. We want an assessment of the extent of vulnerability of Canada's *high technology knowledge base*' (emphasis supplied).[81]

---

[76] Above p. 380. Note that this aspect of the mandate applies only to threats from persons 'outside the British Islands', a limitation which would seem to have been inserted to ensure exclusion of trade union activities or other internal economic conflict under this head.

[77] Below p. 392.

[78] There is no mention of economic matters in s. 2's definition of 'threats to the security of Canada'. However, s. 16 allows the Service, in relation to defence or the conduct of the nation's international affairs, to assist the relevant ministries in the collection of information or intelligence about 'capabilities, intentions and activities' of any foreign state or alien, even if resident in Canada. It has been suggested that this might extend to 'a broader range of military, political or commercial activities' (R. Atkey, 'Reconciling Freedom of Expression and National Security' (1991) 41 *U. Tor. LJ* 38, 45–6, although no information is available on activities undertaken under this provison.

[79] *HC Debs.*, vol. 145, col. 221 (17 Jan. 1989).

[80] SIRC, *Annual Report 1989–90* (Ottawa, 1990), 7.

[81] Quoted in ibid. 22. Note also the emphasis on 'advice' and 'assessment'; cf. p. 380 above.

The italicized phrase makes it clear that the focus no longer is limited to the traditional concerns of espionage. SIRC had earlier pin-pointed Canada's 'state-of-the-art technology' in areas far removed from the military sphere, such as information processing, food production, and development of natural resources.[82] Adding such matters to the mandate of a security service raises profound questions.

SIRC identified some of these.[83] One is possible interference with the 'free flow of ideas and information', particularly between scholars and researchers located in different states. Further, although the then Director of CSIS and other government officials had put primary emphasis on Eastern European states as the site of concern,[84] SIRC's consultation with a range of interested groups yielded a different analysis:

Industry seems more worried about domestic competitors than foreign governments. To the extent industry fears foreign competition, it is from the NICs (newly-industrialised countries) rather than the inefficient East Bloc [which is not seen] as having the know-how to pose a serious threat.[85]

The idea that South Korea or Taiwan could at least partly replace the Soviet Union or Czechoslovakia as the preoccupation of intelligence officers shows how profound are the implications of placing such matters in their domain. As SIRC concluded:

Another issue that needs thorough debate, inside and outside government, is whether CSIS has a proper role in providing intelligence for use in protecting commercial advanced technology as well as traditional national security secrets—better mousetraps that might boost Canadian exports as well as better lasers that might be used in bomber sights.[86]

We shall assume for purposes of discussion that there do truly exist areas in which Britain has developed non-military technology that would be worth pur-loining. Should the Security Service be given the task of protecting British mousetraps from the nefarious attention of Koreans? The question is best approached by considering the distinction between that task and protecting the secrecy of advanced military technology. The assumption in the latter case, which is certainly open to dispute,[87] is that all citizens of a state benefit from the development and deployment of the most advanced military technology when other states are similarly engaged. This justification would extend without undue strain to military-related research or production undertaken by private companies, or public but independent institutions such as universities under

---

[82] See n. 64 above, 37. [83] See n. 80 above, 22–3.

[84] Testimony of Mr Reid Morden, Director of CSIS, to the Special Parliamentary Committee on the Review of the CSIS Act (2 Nov. 1989), 19–20.

[85] See n. 80 above, 22. [86] Ibid., 22–3.

[87] Either by pacifists on grounds of principle, or by those who advocate a 'defensive defence' policy which would make possession of the most advanced weaponry unnecessary.

contract with a government department, since the fruits of such research and development accrue to the public.

Protection of privately owned assets used to generate private profit in a competitive market is a very different matter. As SIRC indicated, companies are most worried about industrial espionage conducted by other companies, so to admit a security service to a role in this field would require distinguishing between domestic and foreign industrial espionage; the former, assuming it involved theft, would be left to the police. The creation of such demarcation disputes is not, however, the main ground of objection. That relates to the interests which a security service is designed to protect. As we have argued, 'security' refers to interests that are as nearly as possible universal among citizens, central to which is protection of the democratic process and the integrity of public institutions; it does not extend to widely desired goals like greater economic prosperity.[88]

Moreover, in Western liberal democracies economic activity is seen as competitive, with rewards individualized and differentiated.[89] The role of repressive institutions of the state is therefore restricted to protecting possession of property, not its maximum profitability. Criminal law prohibits theft or fraud, but not competitors or employees seeking to gain relative advantage by other means, even if in an extreme case the result is the collapse of a particular enterprise. Consequently, although profitable high-tech industries clearly contribute to general social advantage in that they provide employment and foreign exchange earnings, they are no more entitled to protection of their property interests than a corner shopkeeper or any householder. This conclusion has particular force when one gives due emphasis to the extraordinary powers of intrusion on liberty and privacy that security services are granted—precisely because of the gravity and universality of the interests they are supposed to protect. Activities that accrue to the profit or employment of a limited number of individuals cannot meet this criterion without distorting it into meaninglessness.

It may be added that there is a clear distinction between the sort of economic interests cited in the parliamentary debate[90] and protection of privately owned assets. Decisions or negotiating positions taken by foreign governments can crucially influence the price of commodities that Britain must buy and which—as with oil—are both essential to virtually all productive economic activity and to the normal lives of most of the population. Moreover, in many instances foreign

---

[88] See above, Ch. 1 (and note the qualification for states which are the victims of economic warfare [n. 87]). The emphasis in the Maxwell-Fyfe Directive on 'Defence of the Realm as a whole' (above, p. 375) is in the same vein, and our Service informant, who emphasized the 'magnitude' of the interests connected to 'economic well-being', said he had never personally seen anything that could have come under that head in more than a decade before the 1989 Act was passed.

[89] This point is unaffected by the great differences in the degree of state intervention or adoption of policies aimed at economic redistribution, for competitive markets rather than state monopoly are in all cases the hallmark of the economy in these states.

[90] Above p. 390.

governments or companies at least partly influenced by their wishes will be taking decisions on matters like price or output with an eye to *national* advantage; in such circumstances Britain is fully entitled to take peaceful measures to safeguard its own. In some cases, as with oil again, output and price may be set by governments in formal agreement rather than in an open market. Somewhat ironically perhaps, the wholesale privatizations of the 1980s in Britain have removed what would otherwise have been a strong justification for a wider role for intelligence agencies: the need to protect the profitability of public investment in the commercial arena. In Australia, for example, there are centralized bodies, modelled on English marketing boards, which negotiate exclusively the overseas sale of commodities on behalf of thousands of farmers and ranchers. In other instances the Australian government negotiates directly with other governments over oil and gas contracts running into phenomenal sums. It became clear in one interview that ASIO would attempt clandestinely to learn as much as possible about the position to be taken by, for example, a Japanese delegation negotiating on large-scale purchase from the Wheat Board: a variation of a few cents would mean a difference of literally billions of dollars, and relatively few alternative purchasers exist. Similarly DSD, the Australian signals intercept body, was said to spend a great deal of its energies monitoring Japanese economic communications. By contrast, the logic of privatization and the dismantling of the public sector which has so altered the structure of the British economy is that profits accrue individually to those who flourish in competitive trading. Recourse to state aid of any character is illegitimate. Having forfeited the benefits which had been thought to derive from state ownership, it can hardly be right for the state to subsidize the security needs of private companies—which many private security companies are bidding in the marketplace to satisfy.

This conclusion runs parallel to the current law and practice governing the nearest analogous area, which is policing. As a matter of common law, the police owe all persons equally a duty to protect life, property, and the Queen's Peace.[91] If a person wishes to secure a higher level of individualized protection and the police in their operational discretion decide to provide it, under the Police Act 1964 he or she may be asked to pay the reasonable cost of 'special police services'.[92] As construed by the Court of Appeal in *Harris* v. *Sheffield Utd.*,[93] the factors determining whether services are 'special' or are part of normal police duties relate primarily to the public character of the activity. The key indices of what may be called 'publicness' are whether the activity occurs on private property, and whether it is undertaken primarily for the enjoyment or benefit of the public as a whole rather than merely a section of it, even if substantial.[94] We would suggest that this analysis applies *a fortiori* to security and

---

[91] *Glasbrook* v. *Glamorgan CC* [1925] AC 270.

[92] Police Act 1964, s. 15. For an extended discussion of this issue, see S. Weatherill, 'Buying Special Police Services' [1988] *PL* 106, *passim*.

[93] [1988] QB 77.　　　　　　　　　　　　　　　　[94] Ibid. at 91–92, per Neill LJ.

intelligence agencies, which enjoy greater powers and operate under cover of an intimidating but to some degree necessary secrecy.

We have probed the issue of economic interests far more deeply than is usual for two reasons. One is that it raises profound issues of principle: not only about the proper role of security agencies in a democratic state but also, and as a direct corollary, about the very character of that state.

The second is its practical significance. As the great ice sheets of the Cold War have unfrozen into a small puddle, various security institutions have been left with major surplus capacity. This has both coincided with and further stimulated a redefinition by policymakers at the highest level of national security interests, to give heightened emphasis to international economic competition. One obvious possibility is that security institutions will seek to increase their role in this field to avoid cutbacks. Whilst there is at present no sign that the Security Service in Britain has such designs, that could easily change with altered political circumstances.

Moreover, other agencies more directly involved in overseas intelligence have been highly active in this field for many years. This is particularly the case with GCHQ, as is confirmed both by published accounts[95] and disclosures by Robin Robison, who worked as a clerk in the Cabinet Office for five years during which time he saw 'sackloads' of economic material from GCHQ, passed to a subsection of the Joint Intelligence Committee.[96] It is also highly likely that the vast bulk of the telephone tapping authorized under the Interception of Communications Act 1985 for purposes of protecting 'economic well-being'[97] is carried out by GCHQ. When the latter achieves its promised statutory status, it would be astounding if this function were not included within its mandate.[98] This is the ideal occasion to open up to the British public a fundamental issue that has never been adequately debated, nor indeed debated at all: what are intelligence agencies for, and what principles should restrict the range of their inquiries? It is certainly possible to argue that obtaining information about foreign companies,[99] and about large enterprises rather than individuals, raises none of the human rights issues that would require prohibition on activities affecting domestic political or trade union activities. These are precisely the kinds of issues that require public argument, not executive decision by default. It is hoped that this chapter will persuade readers of the necessity for that debate to take place.

---

[95] P. Fitzgerald and M. Leopold, *Stranger on the Line: The Secret History of Telephone Tapping* (London, 1987), 50–4.

[96] Robison's account, which achieved considerable publicity in relation to surveillance of Robert Maxwell, appeared in the *Financial Times*, 15 and 16 June 1992. The quotation is taken from our subsequent discussion with him.

[97] ICA 1985, s. 2(2)(*c*).   [98] See Coda for discussion of the proposals.

[99] Though as pointed out in Ch. 1, in the age of multinational enterprises, subsidary relationships, and patterns of cross-ownership of shares, it may often be unclear what counts as a 'foreign' company.

Subversion

From a controversy of the future we must return to an issue of the present, important because of its long, inglorious past. Some readers may feel that this is indeed almost entirely a problem of the past, an issue which merits only the briefest attention today, and that our extended discussion will at best be the intellectual equivalent of flogging a dead horse. After all, did not the Interceptions Commissioner report that in 1991 there were *no* telephone tapping warrants relating to subversion in force throughout the entire country,[100] and this before the final disintegration of the Soviet Union and the transformation of its major constituent republics into food aid suppliants? However, it is our view that the issues, intellectual and political, have not vanished with the changed climate of international relations. Subversion remains part of the legal armoury of the Security Service and, as will be seen, the understanding of what constitutes 'subversion' has never been limited to organized communism and indeed considerably antedates the Cold War. Thus other unpopular political groups and movements may still be at risk from harassment and illegitimate interference by security agencies. Equally possible is that, as new folk-devils excite the official or popular imagination, the infinitely plastic category of subversion will be stretched to encompass them. Environmental activists are one possible target, particularly if they undertake organized civil disobedience. Another, with potentially more explosive implications, is the British Muslim community, whose outlook is already crudely misinterpreted in the Press and popular discussion as a primitive 'fundamentalism'.[101] This cultural stereotype could make it virtually impossible for security and intelligence officials working in an area of which they have little knowledge or training to distinguish between the rhetoric of outrage and the serious intention to carry out a *fatwa* or some other form of political violence.

To support the view that the subversion mandate grants excessive and unnecessary powers to security officials, we shall review the history of the official use of the concept of subversion in Britain. We shall also look at the divergent approaches taken in Australia and Canada in the 1980s, and consider whether developments in either nation provide a desirable model for reform. This involves careful comparison of the statutory mandates printed in Appendix II.

An entirely different level of critique would entail extensive documentation of the abuses of democracy that have been committed in the name of countering subversion. There would be little difficulty in doing so, but we have chosen not to plough this particular furrow, primarily because others have done so, deeply

---

[100] *Interception of Communications Act 1985: Report of the Commissioner for 1991*, Cm. 1942 (1992), para. 5. In 1990 there were only two such warrants in force: Cm. 1489 (1991), para. 5.
[101] This point is powerfully developed by T. Modood, 'British Asian Muslims and the Rushdie Affair' (1990) 61 *Pol. Q.* 143, *passim*.

and well.[102] It is, however, worth stating at the outset that the record of viola-tions is neither limited to Britain nor worse here than elsewhere. Quite apart from the odious history of McCarthyism in the United States, similar tales can be told about Australia and Canada.[103] This is not said in mitigation of Britain's record, but rather to emphasize the inseparable, causal connection between the subversion mandate and human-rights abuses everywhere it has existed.

'Subversion' in Britain

Although the Oxford English Dictionary provides numerous examples of the use of 'subversion' in literature and law reaching back as far as the fourteenth century, almost all have an active connotation of a physical overthrow, overturning, or visible ruin.[104] The idea of subversion as a sort of death-watch beetle eating away unseen at the timbers of society, or a mole steadily and secretly tunnelling under the pillars of the state so as to cause them to collapse without warning, is a much more recent notion, indeed a product of the twentieth century. As the historian Bernard Porter has argued in a series of studies which explore the ideas and institutions of political policing and security in modern Britain,[105] the Victorian governing élite was so confident of the superiority and rightness of English political institutions that it would have rejected out of hand any fears that the structure was vulnerable to dissent, whatever form it took. Hence the willingness to provide a safe haven for numerous refugees from 'Continental tyranny', a hospitality that began to be withdrawn with great reluctance around the turn of the century in the face of pressure from foreign governments, whose goodwill Britain felt compelled to court as its previously invulnerable interna-tional position began to come under threat.[106] The primary domestic enemy

---

[102] e.g., E. P. Thompson, *Writing by Candlelight* (London, 1980), 113–80; M. Hollingsworth and R. Norton-Taylor, *Blacklist: The Inside Story of Political Vetting* (London, 1988), ch. 5 and 6; D. Leigh, *The Wilson Plot* (London, 1988); R. Norton-Taylor, *In Defence of the Realm?* (London, 1990), 81–90. Critically important, because only an insider could overcome the secrecy which hid the abuses, were the disclosures of Cathy Massiter, a former Security Service officer. These are referred to at various places in this book: see pp. 28–29, 54, 244.

[103] For Canada, the authoritative point of departure is the McDonald Commission, *Inquiry into Certain RCMP Activities* (Ottawa, 1979–81), although a Quebec provincial inquiry published in the lat-ter year was even more critical. See also R. Whitaker, 'Left-wing Dissent and the State', in C. Franks (ed.), *Dissent and the State* (Toronto, 1989), 191–210; id., 'Fighting the Cold War on the Home Front: America, Britain, Australia and Canada' in *Socialist Register 1984: The Uses of Anti-Communism* (London, 1984), 25–67 and id., 'Canada: The RCMP Scandals', in (n. 4 above), 38–61. For Australia, see R. Hall, *The Secret State* (Sydney, 1978); F. Cain, (above n. 26); id., (above n. 29) 105–12; P. Grabosky, *Wayward Governance* (Canberra, 1989), ch. 7 ('Political Surveillance and the South Australian Police'); and the two critical official inquiries into the South Australian Special Branch: *Special Branch Security Records: Initial Report* (Adelaide, 1977) and *Royal Commission 1978: Report on the Dismissal of Harold Hubert Salisbury* (Adelaide, 1978).

[104] As in *Taylor's Case*, the origin of the law of blasphemy, discussed above, pp. 203–4.

[105] *Plots and Paranoia* (London, 1989) (hereafter *Plots*); *The Origins of the Vigilant State: The London Metropolitan Special Branch Before the First World War* (London, 1987) (hereafter *Origins*); *The Refugee Question in Mid-Victorian Politics* (Cambridge, 1979) (hereafter *Refugees*).

[106] Porter, *Refugees, passim* and *Origins*, chs. 8–12.

were the 'Fenians', but it was their bombs which caused concern, not their words or ideas. As Porter concludes in his most recent work:

A political police, properly so called, is one that is concerned with people's political opinions for their own sake: because they are considered to be in some way 'subversive' in themselves, rather than because they are likely to result in crime. Before 1910 the Special Branch was not like that at all. There may have been some exceptions . . . but usually the Branch took no interest in 'extremist' political opinions except when it had reason to believe that those opinions might give rise to violent crimes. This was why it left domestic British radical politics alone too, except on its wilder anarchist edges . . .[107]

Thus, although in particular disputes and at particular times anarchists, 'labour agitators', socialists and even suffragettes were regarded in some official quarters as threats to be dealt with severely, they were seldom regarded as permanent, long-term dangers. Nor, what is even more important, were they lumped together as manifestations or examples of a wider menace: enemies of the state or society who were plotting its destruction. This attitude of permanent suspicion grounded in insecurity (which can easily slide into that severe form of irrationality clinically known as paranoia), took root only with the coming of the First World War and its aftermath. The war itself produced 'spy-fever'— hysterical fears of wholly imaginary German spies or resident alien sympathizers roaming the land unearthing and betraying British military secrets to the Hun.[108] As the slaughter continued unabated it also produced pacifist and other critics of the conduct of the war. This put both the military authorities and the newly strengthened MI5 squarely into the business of—in the widest sense—policing opinion, since pacifism could easily be equated with pro-German views, and strikes over wages or working conditions were immediately suspected of being incited by German agents.[109] Critical speeches or pamphlets could be, and were, prosecuted under the Defence of the Realm Act.[110]

This atmosphere of insecurity, which produced repression of speech, strikes, and other forms of protest and not merely of espionage or sabotage, carried over into peacetime. Here the dominating factor was the Russian Revolution, one of the major international consequences of the war, which produced in reaction the great Red Scare. Widespread strikes (including those of police in Liverpool and London), unrest among soldiers facing long delays in demobilization, and demonstrations of sympathy for the new Soviet government in the face of British and French invasion, led the Cabinet to near-panic and the Special Branch particularly into unprecedented surveillance and infiltration of

---

[107] Porter, *Plots*, 119.

[108] Andrew (n. 2 above), ch. 2; D. French, 'Spy Fever in Britain' (1978) 21 *Hist. J.* 355.

[109] See further B. Weinberger, *Keeping the Peace?—Policing Strikes in Britain, 1906–26* (Oxford, 1991), ch. 6.

[110] Andrew (n. 2 above). 283–96; N. Hiley, 'British Internal Security in Wartime: The Rise and Fall of PMS 2' (1986) 1 *Int. & NS* 396.

the British political Left and trade unions.[111] The atmosphere of crisis abated after 1921, but left a permanent legacy: henceforth civil servants, police, and security officials would regard it as legitimate to maintain a permanent apparatus of spying on British citizens, and not merely suspect aliens. This view was shared, and at times encouraged, by politicians of virtually all shades of opinion, including the leaders of the first Labour government. The latter established a Cabinet Committee on Industrial Unrest which relied heavily on police and intelligence reports concerning the extent of communist influence on the outbreak of strikes that coincided with its accession to office early in 1924.[112]

None the less, official discourse did not produce a name for the permanent threat until the mid-1930s. Although in the memoirs of Sir Basil Thompson, the Special Branch chief from 1913 until his dismissal in 1920, the phrase is used once in this way,[113] 'subversion' does not appear in official documents regularly until the mid- or late 1930s.[114]

At the end of 1936, a three-man committee established to consider recommendations periodically emanating from MI5 that various naval or civilian defence industry employees be dismissed or disciplined for various activities, approved the sacking of four Devonport dockyard workers on the grounds that 'all four men have been actively engaged in dangerous subversive propaganda, and not merely in the doctrinaire preaching of Communism as a political creed'.[115] Shortly thereafter, an 'Ad Hoc Interdepartmental Committee' established during the Abyssinian crisis produced a Report on the form and content of future emergency legislation. In discussing anti-war propaganda, which it recognized might be 'actuated, not by sympathy with the enemy, but by "internationalist" affiliations or by disinterested opposition to the war', it concluded that all 'subversive activities of this kind' should be clearly proscribed.[116] Thus, even before the Second World War, the government had arrogated to itself the power to determine which views were acceptable and which 'subversive'; and the date is important because it preceded the Nazi–Soviet pact which led British communists to oppose the war at Moscow's bidding, thus in effect becoming Hitler's helpers whilst Britain stood alone. This habit of mind grew and became increasingly powerful during the Cold War. As has been seen,[117] the Maxwell-Fyfe

[111] Andrew (n. 2 above), ch. 7 ('The Red Menace at Home'); Porter, *Plots*, 142–50, 158–65; Weinberger (n. 109 above), Ch. 8.

[112] Andrew (n. 2 above), 425–30; T. Barnes, 'Special Branch and the First Labour Government' (1979) 22 *Hist. J.* 941.

[113] B. Thompson, *Queer People* (London, 1922), 275. We should like to thank Prof. Bernard Porter for this reference.

[114] Quite coincidentally—there is certainly no evidence to suggest that the authorities in the two countries were acting in concert—this is almost exactly the time that the term first appeared in American legal literature. See E. Grace and C. Leys, 'The Concept of Subversion and its Implications', in C. Franks (ed.), *Dissent and the State* (Toronto, 1989), 252, n. 9.

[115] Quoted in Andrew (n. 2 above), 519–20.

[116] N. Stammers, *Civil Liberties in Britain During the Second World War* (London, 1983), 9.

[117] Above, p. 375.

Directive included the term without amplification, and Lord Denning in his Report on the Profumo Affair offered the first public definition from an official source: 'contemplat[ing] the overthrow of the Government by unlawful means.'[118] But the legions of 'enemies' grew ever greater,[119] so that by 1975 Lord Harris of Greenwich, then a Home Office minister, enunciated a new definition in a House of Lords Debate, which was subsequently affirmed by the Home Secretary, Merlin Rees, in the Commons. The so-called 'Harris definition' described subversion as 'activities which threaten the safety or well-being of the State, and are *intended to undermine or overthrow parliamentary democracy by political, industrial or violent means*'.[120] The words we have italicized are now incorporated into the statutory mandate of the Security Service.[121]

No justification was ever offered for this immense expansion of the concept, nor is there any published information that might explain the change. However, we have had the benefit of discussion with one of the persons closely involved in the process, but under 'Chatham House rules' which preclude identification.[122]

The evolution and enlargement of the concept of subversion was but one chapter in the long history of sectarian feuding on the political Left in Britain. Historians have thoroughly documented the often bitter antagonism—far in excess of anything evinced toward the electorally dominant Conservatives—that successive Labour leaders have directed at those to their Left, most notably the communists and, in the 1930s, the Independent Labour Party.[123] Harold Wilson, Prime Minister of the government that took office in February 1974, was squarely in this tradition. Ever-quick to blame communist influence when confronted with trade union opposition, his response when Prime Minister during the Seaman's Union strike of 1966 was to order telephone tapping of its leaders.[124] Nor were dissidents within the Labour Party treated with greater tol-

---

[118] Cmnd. 2152 (1963), para. 230.

[119] For a particularly bizarre example, see G. Young, *Subversion and the British Riposte* (Glasgow, 1984) written in retirement by a former Deputy Director-General of MI6, who presumably had some practical influence in his many years in the Service.

[120] See *HL Debs.*, vol. 357, col. 947 (26 Feb. 1975) and *HC Debs.*, vol. 947, col. 618 (6 Apr. 1978). For one of the very few critical discussions at the time, see R. Spjut, 'Defining "Subversion"' (1979) 6 *JL & S* 254.

[121] SSA 1989, s. 1(2).

[122] We have no doubt whatever that our source would not accept the interpretation put forward here.

[123] See H. Pelling, *A Short History of the Labour Party* (8th edn., Basingstoke, 1985), 49–57, on the Party's decision to refuse admission to communists and its 'disaffiliation' of communist-dominated local parties in the early 1920s; and R. Dowse, *Left in the Centre—The Independent Labour Party, 1893–1940* (London, 1966), esp. chs. 12–13. In light of this history, the extended campaign against Militant Tendency in the 1980s, culminating in the expulsion of all of its members, was only the latest manifestation of a recurrent phenomenon.

[124] Leigh (n. 102 above), 105–6. See also B. Castle, *The Castle Diaries 1964–76* (London, 1990). On 6 May 1968 she wrote: 'One of my discoveries in my new job is that the Minister of Labour has always been furnished with security reports on the trade unions', and dismissed the material provided as 'always mighty thin' (314).

erance.[125] Indeed, given the historical connection between the Labour Party and the organized trade union movement, the greatest fear was of 'far-Left' influence in the unions, particularly since it would affect Party policy through the block vote at Conference. This obsession with infiltration reached its height in the 1970s as new or long-dormant Trotskyist splinter groups proclaimed a policy of 'entryism'.

The Conservative administration under Edward Heath had already steered the Security Service toward devoting much greater attention to trade unions, students, and other domestic radical groups.[126] But a review of the concept of subversion as a sort of legitimation exercise had to await the coming of a Labour government. Indeed, it is very doubtful whether the Conservative leadership of the early 1970s would have dared, or even felt it proper, to openly identify non-communist Left groups as legitimate targets. Only a Labour administration would feel the need to, or could do so with immunity from charges of ideological witch-hunting. One is reminded of the famous slogan of Ernest Bevin in the 1945 General Election, 'Left understands Left'.[127] In the words of the author and journalist Claud Cockburn, who had been an active communist in that election, 'the one sort of "Left" understands the other sort of "Left" so well that it fires from the hip on seeing just what sort of manoeuvre other comrades are up to'.[128]

It was singularly ironic that Lord Harris found himself in the position to enunciate the sweeping new definition of subversion, for Labour owed its return to office directly to the electorate's verdict on Mr Heath's repeated conflicts with the miners and accompanying three-day weeks, and therefore in considerable part indirectly to solidly organized and occasionally militant trade unionism. None the less, the new government undertook a review of subversion,[129] and broke out of the confines of Lord Denning's limited definition to incorporate activities of the kind which made it most fearful. No attempt was ever made to rein in subversion by tying it to illegal conduct, a position confirmed some years later when the Home Secretary stated that: 'Tactics which are not themselves unlawful could be used with the aim of subverting our democratic system of government.'[130]

---

[125] In an earlier era Sir Stafford Cripps and John Strachey, future Cabinet ministers, were expelled in 1939 and Aneurin Bevan, though practically apotheosized after his early death, shared their fate then and came close to a repetition in the mid-1950s.

.[126] This is one of the more valuable revelations found in Peter Wright's *Spycatcher* (New York, 1987), 359–61, but has been lost in the furore surrounding more sensational (and not always well-supported) material.

[127] The remark was widely understood to mean that Labour would get along more amicably than the Conservatives with Soviet Russia, then highly popular as a wartime ally against Hitler.

[128] C. Cockburn, *I, Claud* (Harmondsworth, 1967), 258.

[129] During a debate on the Interception of Communications Bill, Lord Harris confirmed that the new definition did not emerge off the cuff, but was the product of serious consideration within the Home Office: *HL Debs.*, vol 466, col. 143 (9 July 1985).

[130] *HC Debs.*, vol. 63, col. 483w (10 July 1984) (Leon Brittan QC).

Lord Harris's announcement emerged at the end of a seven-hour debate in the House of Lords on 'Subversive and Extremist Elements',[131] which illustrated with sharp clarity that allegations about subversion are not serious expressions of concern about illegal, violent, or intimidatory conduct, but rather a convenient form of Left-bashing. For the concept of subversion is never value-neutral, but contains an inherently right-wing bias.

It is important to understand why this is so. Perceptions of political opponents and the accompanying vocabulary are very different on the Right and the Left. Those who regard groups like the National Front or the British National Party as dangerous do not talk of them as 'subversive', but rather as racist and therefore insulting to the dignity of black people in Britain.[132] In so far as it is suggested that such groups are the proper objects of official surveillance or intelligence gathering, it is because many of their leaders and members have a history of involvement in racist *violence*, and not because of policies they advocate, however offensive. Subversion, on the other hand, is about ideas, or rather about peaceful political action in the furtherance of those ideas. To include it within the mandate of security agencies means that the governing élite has arrogated to itself the right to determine what the political system will tolerate as an 'acceptable' basis for opposition. Though doubtless advantageous to its maintenance of power, this is utterly incompatible with any pretensions to democracy.[133] And, to return to the assertion made in the preceding paragraph, a bias in the direction of the existing political, economic, and ideological order inevitably means, in the circumstances of contemporary Britain, a pronounced anti-Left tilt, though not one necessarily favouring the Conservative Party as such. For the dominant factions within the Labour Party also benefit when support for Left-wing groups is curtailed and their legitimacy placed in doubt. As we argued earlier, the problem of subversion is not one of party political favouritism but of ideological partiality.[134]

Our critique of subversion has so far centred on the inclusion of elements of relating to 'political' and 'industrial' means. Two other, more narrow, points which emerge from the current legal provision deserve further attention. The first is that 'undermining' imparts no limitation of immediacy or directness, and thus is dangerously elastic. A quick recall of the story of the House That Jack Built will make plain how, given a suitable frame of mind, there are few acts which could not be described, when seen in relation to W, and in the context of X, in the light of Y, and connected to Z, as 'undermining' the structure. The

---

[131] *HL Debs.*, vol. 357, cols. 820–955 (26 Feb. 1975).

[132] We are referring here to the thinking and terminology of politically active people, not officials of the Security Service or police Special Branch, who have long maintained surveillance of extreme Right groups under the head of 'subversion'. See e.g. R. Thurlow, 'British Fascism and State Surveillance, 1934–45' (1988) *Int. & NS* 77.

[133] Cf. the comment of Grace and Leys (above n. 114), at 63: 'the difficulty [with subversion] is not in giving it a definition, but that the definitions conflict with the principles of liberal democracy.'

[134] Cf. p. 378 above.

danger is compounded precisely because this frame of mind is too often found among politicians and officials. As two Canadian critics of subversion argue:

> State security agencies invariably take a broad view of their mandates. As a result they interest themselves not merely in 'subversive activity' but also in 'potential subversion'; in 'subversives' (i.e., people considered to be engaging in subversive activities, or thought liable to do so); [and] in 'subversive' beliefs and attitudes . . .[135]

Secondly, even 'parliamentary democracy' causes problems. In the Parliamentary Debate over the Security Service Act the Home Secretary declined repeated invitations to define it, whilst insisting that political dissent or challenges to government policy would not be considered dangerous to national security.[136] Apart from the fact that the interpretation of one particular Minister has no legal or even moral force—as CND activists discovered to their cost in the 1960s[137]— this assurance leaves all the hard questions unanswered. What of peaceful extra-parliamentary activity—less likely perhaps now than before the nearly simultaneous demise of the Cold War and the Poll Tax—such as mass demonstrations against nuclear power plants or other forms of state-sanctioned hazard, or the introduction of compulsory identity cards? It is easy to imagine officials—and in many ways easier to imagine ministers—treating 'parliamentary democracy' as the subject's opportunity to vote once every few years and the obligation to obey the rest of the time. Civil disobedience would thereby become subversive.

It is vital to emphasize that it is no part of our case against subversion that the Security Service is, at present, taking the stance or adopting the interpretations we have suggested are possible. In fact the reverse is true. A large part of one interview with an MI5 Assistant Director was devoted to refuting similar fears expressed in an article published earlier.[138] The response to a hypothetical question about the attitude that might be taken towards mass demonstrations against the Poll Tax made it quite clear that the Service considered this well outside its remit. Indeed, what emerged was an attitude of distinct caution, perhaps even of scepticism, about the whole area. This appears to be the result of several converging factors. One is a concentration on terrorism, which is regarded as of far greater importance. The second is a judgment, political in the broadest sense, that whilst there formerly existed a genuinely greater subversion threat, it began to recede in the mid- to late 1980s, thus justifying diminished efforts in this sphere. The third is a legal factor. As we have seen, the statute defines the

---

[135] (Above n. 114), 63.   [136] *HC Debs.*, vol. 145, cols. 180 ff. (17 Jan. 1989).

[137] The defendants in *Chandler* v. *DPP* [1964] AC 763, who had engaged in an attempt to obstruct peacefully the operation of an military airfield, were prosecuted under s. 1 of OSA 1911, which two previous Attorneys-General had assured Parliament would only be used in cases of espionage. However, the Attorney-General responsible for the prosecution told the House that: 'In considering whether or not to prosecute, I must direct my mind to the language and spirit of the Acts and not to what my predecessors said about them many years ago in an entirely different context.' *HC Debs.*, vol 657, col 611 (5 Apr. 1962). See further D. Thompson, 'The Committee of 100 and the Official Secrets Act' [1963] *Pub. L.* 201.

[138] I. Leigh and L. Lustgarten, 'The Security Service Act 1989' (1989) 52 *MLR* 801, 805–9.

function of the Service as protection of national security, expressed in terms of various 'threats', including actions which would constitute subversion.[139] The requirement that a given action constitute a 'threat' is taken as importing an objective test rather than leaving matters to individual officers' unfettered judgment. It is applied both when determining whether to proceed with an investigation and in examination of any application for a warrant.[140] Thus even an organization which declared an intention to undermine parliamentary democracy would not attract serious attention if its efforts were too feeble to constitute a 'threat', though clearly some degree of inquiry would be necessary to reach that conclusion. Finally, concerns about sweeping investigations into purported new threats such as Islamic 'fundamentalism' were dismissed as running counter to sound maxims of intelligence methodology: to start with the known, or the established and proven, and work toward the unknown. This is said to be an effective operational check on wide-ranging flights of fancy.

Readers will doubtless note that this picture fits very badly with the revelations of Cathy Massiter concerning the scope of domestic surveillance activities she and her colleagues undertook. When this objection was put, the response—a marvel of Civil-Servicespeak but also very candid—was that the Massister affair 'was one which everyone involved would wish to learn from'. Our informant also insisted that the Service takes a very critical approach to subversion: 'we know it is an area where one would not wish to do anything more than is necessary.' Perhaps, then, the most useful long-term effect of Miss Massiter's disclosures was to make the whole area far less vulnerable to future forays, either because it sensitized the Service to the abuses involved, or because it made the articulate public more alert to them. (An optimist would hope that both effects are present.) Either way, the whole episode stands as a powerful argument in favour of 'whistle blowing'.[141]

Moreover, this lack of enthusiasm for pursuing 'subversives' is mirrored in the Metropolitan Police Special Branch, by far the largest police organization concerned with national security.[142] Unlike public disorder or IRA violence, they only become involved at all with subversion at the request of the Security Service, and never without prior consultation and approval. Moreover, the 1984 Home Office Guidelines on Special Branch sent to all Chief Constables was accompanied by an unpublished covering letter which stated that universities, trade unions, and ethnic minority organizations were targets which should be

[139] See above. TAN 30.

[140] In this respect the statute merely codifies previous practice. In response to a letter from the Council of Civil Service Unions expressing concern about surveillance of trade unionists, the then Home Secretary, Leon Brittan QC, emphasized that the existence of a threat was a distinct element in the working definition of subversion (letter to Mr Peter Jones, Secretary of CCSU, 15 Aug. 1985; we thank Mr Jones for sending us a copy of this letter.) In view of past abuses in this particular area alone (see p. 399 above), the 'threat' requirement may not be much of a safeguard.

[141] Cf. above, pp. 257–59.

[142] This paragraph is based upon an interview with Sir Peter Imbert, then Metropolitan Police Commissioner, and Mr John Howley, Deputy Assistant Commissioner in charge of Special Branch.

approached with particular sensitivity, which appears to mean caution. And like the Security Service, Sir Peter Imbert also cited in explanation of the lessening emphasis on subversion 'the changing face of Europe', which has led to official visits to former Eastern bloc countries and requests for advice and assistance from their police forces.

It was a pleasant surprise and a great reassurance to be told of the Service's (and Special Branch's) approach to this matter which, particularly in light of corroborating indications,[143] seems entirely credible. None the less, in the end these institutional attitudes are irrelevant to whether it is right that subversion remain within the statutory mandate. The current lack of interest can be attributed to several contingent factors: the painful reality of political violence; the unprecedented—and doubtless entirely unwelcome—spotlight thrown upon security agencies by the *Spycatcher* controversy; quiescence in the labour movement for economic reasons entirely unconnected with wider developments in world politics; substantial change in the leadership since the early 1980s when Cathy Massiter (and others) found intolerable the demands made upon their loyalties; and a transformation in the Service's own interpretation of the external political world. Yet an alteration in leadership, political climate, or the former's perception of the latter could quickly put matters on a very different footing. Moreover, one would still not want to trust one's liberties to those who genuinely believed that CND ever constituted a threat to the British state, or that various obscure Trotskyist splinter groups threatened anything except the elegance of the English language. Above all, the range of objections to subversion grounded in democratic principle[144] retain their full force, regardless of whether a relatively benign situation exists at any particular moment.

There is also a particular objection to Special Branch involvement in the area. 'Subversion' is unknown to the criminal law. To make it a matter for the police is like telling them to gather information on 'immorality' or 'anti-social behaviour'. One essential characteristic of a police organization is surely that its mandate is confined to criminal conduct.[145] Special Branches may properly inquire into an individual or group's propensity to violence, since they are also responsible for public order in relation to demonstrations. This, however, is far removed from monitoring their beliefs and non-violent activities, and the tendency to stray into that realm is precisely what makes the concept of subversion a tool of oppression. It is particularly dangerous in police hands, because once identified as a 'subversive', and therefore undesirable, a person may become the target of inquiries about other criminal conduct which they would have otherwise escaped. This ability to undertake investigations for ulterior motives is almost

---

[143] Above TAN 100.   [144] Above, p. 401.

[145] This is not to deny that 'the central mandate of first-aid order maintenance' is 'the core of the police mandate' (R. Reiner, *The Politics of the Police* (2nd edn., Hemel Hempstead, 1992), 111–16). However, that 'order' is itself ultimately constituted by legal categories and definitions; see L. Lustgarten, 'The Police and the Substantive Criminal Law' (1987) 27 *BJ Crim.* 23, 23–5.

impossible to control, is not regarded as wrong in law, and is therefore one of the most oppressive forms of power exercised by the police.[146] Removing subversion entirely from the scope of the police mandate—which unlike that of the Security Service is not grounded in statute—can be done as a matter of administrative discretion, which should be exercised forthwith.

What, then, is the appropriate response in relation to the Security Service? One possibility which we would reject is adoption of the Canadian definition (found in Appendix II), as was proposed in an amendment moved by the libertarian Conservative back-bencher Richard Shepherd, MP during the Commons debates on the 1989 Act.[147] The purported advantage is that the CSIS Act specifically excludes 'lawful advocacy, protest or dissent' from the catalogue of threats to be countered (which include subversion). However, if these protected activities are 'carried on in conjunction with' any of the threats, they then fall within the Service's mandate.[148] The result, at least purely as a matter of statutory construction, is to authorize a very wide role for a security agency in the surveillance of dissent, since there are virtually no limits to what could be viewed as 'intended ultimately to lead to the destruction' of constitutional government. Of course this has not happened in Canada,[149] but not because CSIS has been reined in by its legal mandate. Thus the Canadian formulation, marred by this fatal ambiguity, would be no improvement on the present legislation in Britain. What then of the most straightforward and obvious course: simply abolish subversion whilst leaving the rest of the mandate unaltered? This has a powerful attraction, but there are a number of activities involving either attempts to advance the interests of foreign governments, or that are calculated to produce collective and politicized violence within this country, which genuinely merit monitoring and the collection of information in order to evaluate their seriousness and formulate effective counter-measures. Concentration upon these activities has been the hallmark of the approach taken in Australia, and it is to developments there that we now turn.

'Subversion' in Australia

Having served as a one-man Royal Commission on Intelligence and Security in the mid-1970s, Mr Justice R. M. Hope of the New South Wales Court of

---

[146] For further discussion of the issue, see L. Lustgarten, *The Governance of Police* (London, 1986), ch. 1.

[147] *HC Debs.*, vol 145, col. 180 ff. (17 Jan. 1989).

[148] A view confirmed by the decision in *Re Canadian Civil Liberties Association and Attorney-General of Canada* (1992) 91 DLR (4th) 38, which also upheld this provisions against a challenge under the Charter.

[149] As the text indicates, Canada has retained subversion but, by a series of administrative measures initiated over several years, has drastically pruned the scope of operations against it and imposed particularly rigorous operational controls not applicable in relation to other 'threats'. For a detailed account, see P. Gill, 'Defining Subversion: The Canadian Experience Since 1977' [1989] *Pub. L.* 617, supplemented by SIRC (n. 80 above), 43–50 ('the counter-subversion residue') and *Annual Report 1990–91* (Ottawa, 1991), 23–4.

Appeal was once again appointed in the same capacity when the Labor Party returned to office in 1983. His Report[150] covers a very wide range of issues, and strongly influenced the changes in the governance of ASIO which the government soon enacted.[151] He also considered in great depth the question of ASIO's mandate and—in what stands as the most comprehensive official examination of the question undertaken anywhere—devoted a chapter of nearly thirty pages to subversion.[152]

Justice Hope focused on the key issue, which is not the minutiae of definition but 'rather what activities, of a kind that may be regarded as subversive, are properly committed to a body such as ASIO for investigation, assessment and reporting to government'.[153] This reorientation in turn led him to the fundamental question: what reasons justify giving a security service responsibility for subversion? His answer, stated in language drawn from the Report of the McDonald Commission in Canada, was that its purpose is to 'preserve and maintain the democratic processes of government', thus ensuring that the country remains 'truly self-governing'.[154] Precisely because this bedrock constitutional structure is securely established in Australia,[155] he concluded that only activities involving present (rather than future or theoretical) violence should properly come within ASIO's purview.[156] For the basically healthy body politic can be relied upon to protect itself without recourse to extraordinary and potentially iatrogenic means:

It is possible to imagine lawful and unlawful acts which could create such an atmosphere [of revolutionary ferment] as, for example, by the organization of crippling strikes or the disruption of the country's economy in a way which creates a situation of chaos. However, unless accompanied by, or likely to lead to, violence these are matters which, within the Australian environment, should properly be dealt with through the ordinary political processes. These processes should be strong and flexible enough to withstand any such strains. Moreover, many of the activities which could be undertaken for such a purpose could be undertaken for much more limited purposes as, for example, the attainment of an industrial benefit or the ousting of the existing government, but by constitutional means. These activities, in themselves, should not attract the attention of ASIO.[157]

Hope's analysis was animated by awareness of the dangers to political freedom inherent in the subversion mandate. However, he was also careful to emphasize the difference between security agencies and the police, and to acknowledge the legitimate 'pre-emptive' role of ASIO in inquiring whether a

---

[150] Royal Commission on Australia's Security and Intelligence Agencies, *Report on ASIO* (Canberra, 1985).

[151] These are examined in detail below pp. 418 ff.

[152] See also the analysis presented by P. Hanks, 'National Security—A Political Concept' (1988) 14 *Mon. ULR* 114, 124–32.

[153] See n. 150 above, para. 4.13.

[154] Ibid., para. 4.14, quoting McDonald Commission Second Report, vol. I, para. 311.

[155] Cf. the discussion of strong and weak states in Ch. 1 above, pp. 3–4.

[156] See n. 150 above, paras. 4.49–54.   [157] Ibid., para. 4.41.

particular organization or person is engaged in activities which genuinely threaten constitutional government.[158] Though he accepted the term 'subversion' for purposes of his own analysis, he concluded that it should be abandoned in law and, with one exception considered below, replaced by what the ASIO Act now terms 'politically motivated violence'.[159] (See Appendix II.) Moreover, to emphasize that the new provisions mark a decisive break with the world-view that has historically accompanied subversion, a new section was added, making clear that: 'This Act shall not limit the right of persons to engage in lawful advocacy, protest or dissent and the exercise of that right shall not, by itself, be regarded as prejudicial to security, and the functions of the Organization shall be construed accordingly.'[160]

Justice Hope also supported the adaptation and retention of a curious histori-cal relic in the ASIO mandate. As we have seen,[161] the crime of sedition had long ago prohibited 'promoting hostility between different classes of Her Majesty's subjects'. Australian criminal law had imported this offence, which remains gathering dust in the Commonwealth statute book.[162] There is little doubt that, as the Report suggests, 'the classes to which it [sedition] referred presumably were primarily social or economic classes of persons'.[163] None the less, in the altered form of 'different groups within the Australian community'[164] it serves a valid and useful purpose when coupled with the threshold require-ment of promotion of violence.

Post-war Australia is a society of extraordinary ethnic heterogeneity, which does not always produce harmony. Some groups brought their hatreds with them, as with sporadic violence between Serb and Croat immigrants that prefig-ured what occurred after the dissolution of Yugoslavia. Others, such as Asian immigrants who came in substantial numbers after the 'White Australia' policy was eliminated in the early 1970s, were sometimes the target of organized local racists. Carefully distinguishing between hatred and violence, Hope endorsed the inclusion of 'promotion of communal violence' within the mandate.[165] Britain's 'cultural mosaic' is not as complex as that of Australia, but the reality of racist violence is every bit as serious. Our discussion of the terrorism mandate demon-strated the difficulties of trying to fit racist violence within that category;[166] and

[158] Ibid., paras. 4.15, 4.21 ff.

[159] See App. II. As noted on p. 000 above, PMV replaces both subversion and terrorism.

[160] ASIO Act, s. 17A. The language closely tracks the last subclause of s. 2 of the CSIS Act, also in App. II. [161] Above pp. 000–0.

[162] Crimes Act 1914, s. 24A(g)(Cth.) It also remains in force in those states which are still com-mon-law jurisdictions.

[163] See n. 150 above, para. 4.71.

[164] The change from 'classes' to 'groups' is meant to connote reorientation from economic or class conflict to ethnic divisions, which is made even clearer in the ASIO Act by the use of the expression 'communal violence'.

[165] See n. 150 above, paras. 4.70–74. It may be noted that this aspect of the mandate does not correspond to any criminal conduct. At Commonwealth level there is no legislation equivalent to the British provisions on incitement to racial hatred in ss. 17–27 of the Public Order Act 1986.

[166] Above, pp. 384–85.

Britain would therefore do well to follow Justice Hope's analysis and adopt his conclusion.

The one element of the mandate not relating to violence concerns foreign influence. Although Justice Hope may have been influenced in part by the circumstances attending his appointment in 1983,[167] the paramount concern for 'true self-government' would in any case dictate great emphasis on preventing foreign governments or organizations from influencing the processes or dictating the outcomes of democratic politics. Moreover, since the investigation of foreign interference would by definition not impinge upon the democratic rights of the nation's citizens—unlike any hunt for 'subversives'—the need for abstention until there appear clear indications of intended violence does not exist. Thus attempts at improper manipulation—with initial focus on the foreign end, that is, on those endeavouring to influence British political actors—is, uniquely, a form of non-violent political activity which is a legitimate subject of inquiry for a security service.

With its relatively small population and precarious economic condition owing to heavy dependence on primary agricultural and mineral products, Australia has good reason for concern about its vulnerability to the influence of both foreign governments and international companies. However, any notion that Britain can simply dismiss the problem is badly mistaken. As we have seen,[168] one key area of concern has already been addressed by giving the British Security Service the task of safeguarding the nation's 'economic well-being' from overseas threats. Another aspect of the problem is attempts by foreign governments, either directly through their own emissaries or through what are sometimes called 'agents of influence' among British citizens, to affect British policy towards them. It is in the nature of the activity that it is almost impossible for the ordinary citizen to identify those most active in this respect, but it would be astonishing if both Israel and the wealthier Arab states were not deeply involved.

There are difficult distinctions to be made here, because it is common practice, and certainly not unlawful, for foreign institutions, like any others, to engage public relations firms to advance their interests by means ranging from sumptuous lunches to preparation of well-researched briefings on particular issues. The contours of the line between legitimate 'lobbying' and illegitimate 'pressure' or 'undue influence' have not been charted and are hardly even sketched in Britain, which lacks any equivalent of the American legislation requiring registration, annual reports, and disclosure of activities by anyone acting as an 'agent' of a 'foreign principal', whether governmental or private.[169] The

---

[167] His most urgent task on appointment was to investigate politically charged allegations about dangers to security posed by the relations between a former Secretary of the Labor Party, David Coombe—a man with numerous contacts among members of the new administration—and a Russian diplomat. For a journalist's account of this episode, see D. Marr, *The Ivanov Trail* (Melbourne, 1984)

[168] Above, pp. 390 ff.

[169] The Foreign Agents Registration Act, passed initially in 1938 and amended several times since,

most important criterion is the one now found in the Australian legislation as a result of the Hope Report. It is the differentiation between open attempts—which, because they are visible, are readily counterable by political competitors and discountable by the independent-minded—and those which are 'clandestine or deceptive'.[170]

Even more pernicious are furtive attempts to influence, not merely particular official policies, but internal politics. It is highly debatable, for example, whether wealthy foreigners should be allowed to contribute to British political parties (as became an issue in the 1992 General Election and received heightened attention with the flight of Asil Nadir), but so long as such donations are open and legal, they are no business of security bodies. Unquestionably, clandestine payments or the establishment of 'front' organizations—those which do not admit whose bidding they do—corrupt the integrity of the democratic system. Two examples may suffice. One is the well-known story of secret CIA subsidies to *Encounter* magazine and the London news agency Forum World Features, funnelled through a front organization called the Congress for Cultural Freedom.[171] The other contains a neat irony. In the 1930s one of the great propaganda charges levelled against the British Communist Party was its purported dependence upon 'Moscow gold'. This was simply false, but became true two decades later, when the Party's membership plunged after it supported the Russian repression of the Hungarian Revolution of 1956. Unable to generate sufficient financial support to keep afloat, it began to receive secret funds from the Soviet Union, as records recently made public by its successor body reveal.[172]

Both episodes involved clandestine foreign-influenced activities which are legitimate objects of intelligence scrutiny. They were intolerable affronts to the democratic system, sorely aggravated in the first example by the fact that the news agency subsidy was undertaken with the knowledge and tacit approval of officials of the British government.[173] And given the constant surveillance of Russian officials and their communications, along with the thorough penetration by MI5 of the Communist Party,[174] it is virtually certain that the British govern-

---

imposes these requirements on any such agent who engages in political activities, consultancy, collection of funds, representation of the interests of the foreign principal (other than as a legal representative) before an American government agency, or who distributes 'political propaganda' on its behalf. See *Meese* v. *Keene*, 481 US 465 (1987).

[170] Hope discussed the issue in considerable depth in ch. 3 of the Report and paras. 4.75–80. The CSIS Act, s. 2(*b*), has responded to the same problem in almost identical fashion. Both are found in App. II.

[171] See e.g. W. Blum, *The CIA—A Forgotten History* (London, 1986), 114 and more generally ch. 15.

[172] A former treasurer of the Party revealed in 1991 that after the collapse of British membership after the 1956 repression—but not before—the KGB provided between £1–2 m. over the next twenty years. See '"Moscow Gold" Bankrolled Communists', *Guardian* (15 Nov. 1991), 4.

[173] This is not merely admitted but proclaimed with pride in B. Crozier, *Free Agent* (London, 1993), 63–71.

[174] Unless Peter Wright has manufactured a highly plausible fantasy, an MI5 burglary in 1955 yielded 55,000 files of CPGB members, giving 'total access to the Party organization'. This was over

ment knew of the Russian subvention, but apparently decided to let matters rest. Thus, quite extraordinarily, it colluded in attempts by both the Soviet and American governments to manipulate British public opinion. Whatever *realpolitik* calculations may have led to this response, they can never outweigh the betrayal of those who believed, however naïvely, that they were reading an independent periodical, or supporting a political party whose positions were based on philosophical conviction or its leaders' honest judgment. What we have termed the constitutional function of the Press[175] deserves greater respect.

It is unclear whether the fault lay with intelligence officials or with their political superiors who failed to act on available information. But whichever was the case, the conclusion most relevant to our subject is the same: the main task of security agencies is to gather and analyse information for the nation's political leadership. They discharge their responsibility by presenting that material without deliberate bias or selectivity. Beyond that, the choice of response, and the moral as well as constitutional responsibility for it, lies with ministers.

CONCLUSION

Our discussion of the Security Service mandate has ranged over an appropriately vast field—from the nature of a democratic political order to the legitimate interests of a nation in an international system that combines anarchy and cohesion in roughly equal measure. But for a strong state, more important than international concerns is the preservation of democratic freedoms and self-government. This requires careful and tight restriction on the range of matters to which security organizations are permitted to devote their attention, whilst enabling them to take effective counter-measures against activities which would negate democratic government.

In terms of legal formulations, it would be very difficult to improve upon the Australian definition of the mandate, which incorporates all these concerns whilst removing the potential for abuses associated with the term 'subversion'. The rest of the current UK definition, and particularly espionage and 'economic well-being' when limited to external threats, may prove to be of growing importance in the coming years in relation to weapons and military technology embargoes, as these become ever-more critical to the security of the British people as well as the British state.

A mandate strictly and carefully defined serves two important functions. Most obviously, it sets boundaries on the information the organization may legiti-

---

and above years of prior effort which had the result that 'the CPGB was penetrated at almost every level by technical surveillance or informants' (above n. 126), 55. The Security Service had begun intensive surveillance and infiltration of the British Communist Party in the 1920s and continued vigorously in the 1930s: C. Andrew (n. 2 above), chs. 10–11.

[175] Above, Ch. 10.

mately collect, and the activities it may take measures to deter or neutralize. The narrower the mandate, the more restricted the actions of individuals or groups that may come under examination; in concrete terms this means that no surveillance may be undertaken, or files kept, in relation to such conduct or the persons engaged in it. Since historically internal security agencies in Australia, Britain, and Canada have shown grossly excessive interest in political protest and dissent, particularly from the Left, it is essential that they be kept on a particularly tight rein to exclude them from such matters. Constricting the mandate is necessary to provide the breathing space that democratic principle demands for political dissent. To vary the metaphor, a mandate sensitive to democratic values marks off certain terrain where the agency's presence would be unacceptably dangerous.

Some readers may feel that this emphasis on legal limits is chasing a will-o'-the-wisp, that these are merely paper rules which have little practical effect. We believe this view to be mistaken. Our interviews in all three countries—not only with the limited number of officials but also with those engaged in oversight and with knowledgeable journalists—have yielded a strong and uniform impression: above all, security officials are bureaucrats. They live by rules and paper, and function by committee. Within this working ethos, a clear and limited mandate, though not sufficient of itself, is the essential point of departure. It provides the ground rules and thus plays a critical part in structuring the orientation of the bureaucracy. It can serve as an essential tool for leaders seeking to reorient their organization in a more constitutionalist direction from within, for it is the source of rules and procedures constraining what their subordinates may do.[176] And the organizational culture of bureaucracy, increasingly pervasive in internal security agencies, is a potent force for compliance.[177]

There is another side to the mandate, however, which should be borne in mind. It provides some necessary protection for the agencies themselves. Having internalized a commitment to democratic values, they may use the mandate as a shield when pressured by others, particularly ministers, to operate improperly. We shall see in the next chapter that in some statutory regimes, formal procedural protections are built in precisely to facilitate such a response. This is but one particular manifestation of a theme that recurs throughout this study: that whilst the public needs protection from security agencies, the agencies too need a strong measure of protection from the public's representatives.

[176] Both Alan Wrigley, formerly head of ASIO, and Mr Michael Boyle, assistant to his successor Mr John Moten, gave particular emphasis to the importance of the tightened statutory mandate (above, pp. 406–7) in this respect.

[177] It would, of course, be unsafe to rely on this factor entirely. The next step is to select leaders who are committed to following and enforcing those rules and then, as with any public institution, establishing a system of effective oversight to ensure among other things that this is done. The latter in particular is considered extensively in the next two chapters.

15

Executive Accountability

THE CONSTITUTIONAL FRAMEWORK

In this chapter the focus shifts to institutions, organizations, and structures. We consider how the various bodies which undertake activities in the field of security and intelligence have their tasks and operations defined and regulated—or not, as has often been the case.

There are a number of compelling reasons for comparing practices and developments in the three nations we have chosen to study. Most narrowly, their treatment of security matters has a great deal in common. British intelligence and security structures, principles of organization, and personnel have been the most influential in the Western world. They shaped the form and outlook of the much larger post Second World War American establishment,[1] and provided the model for the institutions established in Australia, Canada, and New Zealand, often directly under British guidance.[2] Moreover that model was based upon certain unspoken, and probably even unrecognized, political and constitutional assumptions—that is to say, assumptions about the relationships that would exist between the security agencies and key elements of the political and legal systems. Although those assumptions may not have been visibly influential to people working in the field, they in fact determined the framework of operations—the range of activities permitted, the degree and kinds of discretion enjoyed by security and intelligence officers, the extent and forms of accountability and oversight of their work, and the level of public scrutiny it would receive.

Secondly, as part of their imperial legacy, Australia and Canada inherited the élitism of British political culture, which they only began to shed in the 1970s.[3]

---

[1] A good description of British influence on American theory and practice, particularly in relation to counter-intelligence, is found in R. Winks, *Cloak and Gown: Scholars in America's Secret Wars* (London, 1987), Ch. 6.

[2] e.g. in relation to Australia, see J. Richelson and D. Ball, *The Ties That Bind*, (2nd edn. Sydney, 1990), 152–3, who point out that ASIS officers are often seconded to the British SIS and serve under British command. Moreover ASIO, the Australian equivalent of MI5, was established under the advice and guidance of Sir Roger Hollis, sent out on a special mission to oversee the process in 1948. Peter Wright's allegation that Hollis was a Russian agent—the obsession that led him to write *Spycatcher*—was thus of particular interest to the Australians, in whose courts the British government first sought to suppress publication.

[3] An apposite example is the analysis presented by the political scientist I. Galnoor in his comparative analysis of national variations in government secrecy. Writing in the mid-1970s, he identified Canada (along with Britain) as one of the 'less open' states (compared with Scandinavia and the USA), and listed as the main explanatory factors 'influence of the British approach' and 'oligarchical

Within this culture the conduct of government is seen as something for knowledgeable and well-intentioned (and often well-connected) initiates. The masses are let in on the act only so far as is good for them or is politically unavoidable. This ethos, though now attenuated, still pervades the entire administration, and is responsible among other things for the extreme secrecy of the British government, which virtually alone among Western democracies refuses to enact access or freedom of information legislation. And unrestricted executive discretion mixed with secrecy is a witches' brew, at its most potent in those areas where the 'mysteries of state'[4] are most jealously guarded by all governments: foreign relations, military matters, and 'national security'.

The paramount reason, however, is the underlying similarity of the form of government in all three states: the so-called 'Westminster model' of parliamentary democracy. The possible modes of effective accountability that may be created to oversee any aspect of government ultimately derive from the potentialities and constraints of constitutional structure. Though the given subject matter—whether security and intelligence or management of public expenditure—may raise specific problems, solutions can only be created within the framework established by the foundational model. Whilst this observation may occasion a yawn among specialists in constitutional law, the character of much public and media debate, in which examples drawn from the United States are regularly cited, makes it plain that the determinative influence of constitutional structure is not widely enough understood. It is therefore necessary to elaborate the point in some detail.

The Westminster system is characterized by a fusion of executive and legislature which results in all but the rarest cases in the domination of the legislature by the executive. Although parliamentary sovereignty is its theoretical underpinning, political reality has largely stood that doctrine (and even more importantly the doctrine of ministerial responsibility which derives from it) on its head. Colin Turpin has put it very well: 'It is, indeed, a paradoxical feature of the modern constitution that for the control and accountability of government we rely mainly upon an elected House in which a majority see it as their principal function to maintain the Government in power.'[5] This is perhaps not a novel observation, but it cogently makes the point that in an area which the executive has traditionally guarded as its own preserve, where secrecy is at least to some extent necessary, and where there is an extremely strong tendency for politicians to equate their interest in staying in power with the national interest, Parliament has very few reins indeed with which to restrain executive bodies.

Moreover, this relative impotence is compounded by an additional factor

political culture'. See his 'What Do We Know About Government Secrecy?', in I. Galnoor (ed.), *Government Secrecy in Democracies* (New York, 1977), 282, and more generally ch. 16.

[4] S. Bok, *Secrets* (Oxford, 1986), 171–5 notes the continuing sway of the idea of the sacred that formerly surrounded matters of state and rulers whose religious and secular responsibility were intermingled.

[5] C. Turpin, *British Government and the Constitution* (2nd edn., London, 1990), 424.

which bridles the executive branch as well. As will be seen, security and intelligence agencies are in varying degrees always kept insulated from direct ministerial dictation, in part precisely to prevent political manipulation. Hence all the well-known problems that democratic states have faced with the accountability of quangos or 'fringe organizations' are found and multiplied manyfold in this particular sphere.[6] Though there are obviously significant differences, the problems of governing security agencies have more than passing similarities to those surrounding nationalized industries, funding councils, and the increasingly large portion of public administration which has been transposed to 'Next Steps' executive agencies no longer headed by a minister directly responsible to Parliament.

When, in the late 1970s, Canada and Australia slowly began to grapple with the need to get some kind of grip on agencies and activities that seemed 'out of control' and 'a law unto themselves', there were simply no suitable or adaptable models available. For the one nation in the English-speaking world which has had any experience with formal legislative accountability structures was precisely the one source which could not provide a transplantable model.[7]

American practice and experience grows out of the distinctive features of the American Constitution. The separation of executive and legislative power does not necessarily, or even regularly, give Congress powers equal to the President in national security matters.[8] But it gives far greater potential scope for legislators to exert substantial influence than is possible for MPs within the Westminster system, primarily because of two factors. The first is the possibility (indeed for most of the post-war era the actuality) that the Executive and Congress will be in the hands of opposing political parties. Electoral competition, particularly in an atmosphere of partisan animosity, can provide a sharp spur to attempts to exert supervisory powers over security agencies independently of the President. This potential may often lie dormant (and indeed did so during the overwhelming anti-Communist consensus that lasted into the 1960s). None the less it is there, as it cannot be in parliaments which constitute, but are than dominated by, the executive; and on important occasions it has exploded into life.[9]

The second important difference is that the American Congress has an inde-

---

[6] For a discussion of some of the issues, see P. Craig, *Administrative Law* (2nd edn., London, 1989), 71–91.

[7] We need not consider the factual issue of whether the American system actually works effectively. The Iran–Contra affair must place a large question mark over it, to say the least.

[8] For an excellent exploration of these issues by an American scholar, see H. Koh, *The National Security Constitution* (New Haven, Conn., 1990), *passim*.

[9] Most notably in the 1970s, with the investigations of the Church Committee (Senate) and Pike Committee (House of Representatives). Much more than partisan wrangling is involved. Partly because an ethos of legislative independence has arisen from the constitutional creation of coequal branches of government, and partly due to the regional nature and weak party structure of American politics, legislators are far more willing to strike out on their own, and far less susceptible to political control by the executive, than in the Westminster democracies. (Canada may be moving to a point midway between Britain and the United States in this respect.)

pendent financial power unknown to parliamentary systems. With marginal exceptions, Congress must approve all expenditure. This power gives it not only the responsibility to inquire into the purposes for which it is being asked to authorize spending, and the effectiveness with which the money is used, but also the effective power—the threat to reject appropriations—to compel information and explanations. The executive and its agencies therefore can never ignore strong currents of Congressional opinion, and must consider relations with the legislature as a central feature of its operational world. Conversely, the Congress would never consider establishing a separate body to exercise oversight functions in its stead; that would be both an abnegation of power seldom seen in ambitious politicians, and a negation of its constitutional role. Thus many of the devices that parliamentary systems have been experimenting with in recent years, and which will be discussed in great detail in subsequent pages here, would be rejected out of hand in the United States.

Therefore when the call for reform in Westminster democracies became politically irresistible, it was necessary to invent the wheel before anything could roll. The attempt to ensure greater accountability over security agencies has also been a stimulus to creative constitutional innovation. Those designing these new institutions, particularly in Canada where the process started first,[10] had a quite sophisticated understanding of the problems of ensuring effective review within the conventions and conditions of the Westminster system. One of the models was the Comptroller and Auditor General in Britain,[11] and it is perhaps worth recalling that the 1980s saw the strengthening of the relationship between that office and Parliament, in response to similar feelings about the need to give the legislature a stronger position in a particular area which was thought to have been too much the domain of the executive.[12]

Accountability is multi-dimensional. In terms of formal structures which function as part of government, it may take two forms: executive and parliamentary. It is to these that most of the discussion in this and the following chapter is devoted. However there exists a third dimension, much more loose and informal—that of accountability directly to the public.[13] It has several diverse strands, held together by one common factor: all involve revelation of information that politicians or officials have decided to keep hidden. One strand, as has been seen, is the criminal trial.[14] Albeit infrequently, this can be a remarkable

---

[10] The Australians, who devised some innovations of their own, were none the less very well aware of the McDonald Commission Report and subsequent Canadian developments, which influenced their own Royal Commission and the legislation introduced in the mid-1980s.

[11] Below, p. 464.

[12] M. Elliott, 'The Control of Public Expenditure', in J. Jowell and D. Oliver (eds.), *The Changing Constitution* (Oxford, 1989), 177–8, and G. Drewry, 'The National Audit Act—Half a Loaf?' [1983] *PL* 531–7. Another view of these reforms would stress the desire of the Treasury to acquire parliamentary assistance in controlling public expenditure.

[13] R. Whitaker, 'The Politics of Security Intelligence Policy-making in Canada—I' (1991) 6 *Int. & NS* 649, 650, emphasizes this facet as well.

[14] Examples are given in on p. 355, n. 184 above.

source of otherwise deeply buried information: not surprisingly, perhaps, the prospect of lengthy imprisonment loosens tongues wonderfully. Another is the disclosures of 'whistleblowers'. Yet another is investigative journalism, with its peculiar dependence on preservation of confidentiality of sources. In all cases the key mechanism is the media, virtually the only means by which information can reach the public (or at least the elements among it prepared to take an interest). Hence our inclusion of an entire chapter devoted to freedom of the press, and our description of the issues involved as 'constitutional'.

Media dissemination of information, however, is only a means to an end: correction of behaviour, whether cessation of abuses or, more broadly, compliance with certain norms of conduct. Disclosures merely galvanize the attentive public to try to secure an official response. Indeed a strong empirical case can be made for the claim that public outcry, allied to victimization of people who later gained positions of power, has been far more important in initiating change in the security field than any principled concern for political freedom or constitutional propriety. As we have noted, this area has provided a particularly vivid example of what has been called 'the politics of scandal'.[15] Had the flow of information been stanched or public outcry silenced, it is highly unlikely that security institutions would ever have been openly acknowledged, placed on a statutory footing, or made subject to review bodies.

A troublesome question thereby arises. Which better serves the democratic purpose of ensuring the proper functioning of security agencies and preventing abuses of power: public exposure, or controls exercised within a structure of secrecy? In principle, the latter is more desirable as being more effective in two distinct senses. It should operate preventatively, and therefore suppress the possibilities of wrongdoing far more comprehensively than *post hoc* exposure. Though the latter provides greater excitement, it has not only proven remarkably ineffective in leading to punishment of wrongdoing,[16] but is also erratic and hence rather inefficient, being heavily dependent on journalists' luck or an individual's crisis of conscience. Secondly, in so far as the glare of publicity may to some extent disrupt the proper functioning of the agency, controls exercised behind what a British Home Secretary has called 'the barrier of secrecy'[17] do less damage to organizational efficiency.

The problem, of course, is that acceptance of such a regime, can only be a matter of trust:[18] of the public, in the governing classes. And though it is a matter of great regret, this seems an impossible pipe-dream in the Britain of the

---

[15] p. 374 above.

[16] In the end, despite voluminous documentation produced by federal and provincial Commissions of Inquiry, no one from the RCMP was ever convicted of any criminal offence. As has been noted (p. 304 above), the RUC officers involved in the Stalker and Sampson Inquiries were protected from prosecution by a decision of the Attorney-General.

[17] A phrase used by Douglas Hurd, MP in a succession of debates: e.g. *HC Debs.*, vol. 106, cols. 940–1 (3 Dec. 1986), and vol. 143, cols. 1114–15 (15 Dec. 1988).

[18] To borrow the title of a journalist's history of MI5: N. West, *A Matter of Trust* (London, 1982).

mid-1990s. There have been too many scandals, cover-ups, instances of crass incompetence, and revelations of misconduct and lowered ethical standards in public life (many far removed from the area under discussion here) to make this alternative acceptable. For it to be credible, the public would have to be willing to accept that any such internal oversight body, having seen all relevant information, had considered it fully and with no predisposition in favour of those in power, and had concluded without official pressure that no improper conduct had occurred. Simply to state these conditions is to indicate their unreality.

Thus there is an inescapable tension between attempts to design institutions of oversight which respect government standards of secrecy but purport to be effective, and a wider political perspective which both doubts the legitimacy in the public mind of such an exercise[19] and believes in the possibility of public disclosure as the ultimate safety valve. We think, however, that it is both possible and necessary to ride both horses together. Failure even to attempt to establish effective machinery that, under optimum conditions, might prove itself to the public would be tantamount to admitting that our present political malaise is a chronic condition. It would also consign us to reliance on a form of accountability which, though valuable when faced with spectacular wrongdoing, is of no use at all in day-to-day monitoring of organizational practices and the slow but persistent attempt to bring about change. Thus whilst at present it is essential to facilitate both forms of accountability and perforce rely excessively on the media, in the very long term one might be in the position to argue for a less welcoming approach to direct public accountability. However, that will depend upon more formal constitutional machinery proving itself; and the wait is likely to be a long one.

With these observations to set the scene, we shall describe and analyse critically first the executive and then the legislative mechanisms of oversight existing in all three nations.

EXECUTIVE ACCOUNTABILITY

Australia

General provisions

The particularly striking thing about the controls which have been established within the executive branch of government in Australia is the extent to which the legislation seeks to build in protection for the Director-General of ASIO. More particularly, it establishes procedures designed to make it very difficult for both the relevant Minister (Attorney-General) or the government generally to manipulate ASIO for political or personal self-interest.

---

[19] But not necessarily the effectiveness; ironically, it is possible that a body could discharge its duties conscientiously but without credit in the public mind.

The first provision requires the Prime Minister to consult the Leader of the Opposition before appointing a Director-General, which is presumably intended to ensure a broad consensus both on the general direction the Organization will take and on the standing of the person who will lead it.[20] The Director-General has a substantially more secure tenure of office than his counterparts in Canada and Britain. He or she is appointed for a period specified at the outset; the others serve at pleasure.[21]

Once in post, the Director-General, though subject both to specific ministerial directives, and to more general guidelines relating to the functions and powers of the agency,[22] is equipped with certain weapons for bureaucratic and political in-fighting. First, he or she may require that *any* direction be put in writing.[23] This is shrewdly calculated to prevent a minister from denying the existence of any direction that may be thought improper or be otherwise politically embarrassing; it is also a significant deterrent to any attempt at misuse of the Organization in the first place. Presumably any purported direction not put on paper upon request may be treated as a nullity. Responsibility is thus placed squarely on the shoulders of the Minister, where it belongs.

Secondly, and more precisely, the Director-General's opinion on whether collection or communication of intelligence about a person is justified on security grounds cannot be overridden except by a written direction from the minister setting out his or her reasons for so doing.[24] As with all written directions, a copy must be sent directly to the Inspector-General (of whom more below), but in this unique instance a copy must be sent to the Prime Minister as well.[25] The narrow aim here is clearly to prevent a politician from harassing political or personal antagonists. The broader one is to ensure the primacy of the non-political (in the partisan sense) judgment of the agency about what constitutes a security matter: statutory interference by a minister immediately becomes a matter for the review authority and his own political superior. The minister must therefore think long and hard, and feel himself on very firm ground, before intervening in this sphere. In both instances, protection of the agency's independence is sought by raising the political costs of interference, and particularly by preventing its occurrence in secrecy. Finally, the minister is simply forbidden from overriding advice given by ASIO to the Cabinet and other government ministers on security matters.[26]

The Inspector-General

Whilst the Australian system seeks to protect ASIO from interference by politicians, it also attempts to give the executive the capability of checking abuses by ASIO. In 1986, as part of the package of reforms growing out of the second

---

[20] ASIO Act, s. 7(2).   [21] Compare ibid., s. 9(1), with SSA, s. 2(1) and CSIS Act, s. 4(2).
[22] ASIO Act, ss. 8(2) and 8A. [23] Ibid., s. 8(3).   [24] Ibid., s. 8(5).
[25] Ibid., s. 8(6).   [26] Ibid., s. 8(4).

Royal Commission,[27] the Labor Government created the office of Inspector-General of Security. This official, whose appointment also requires consultation with the Leader of the Opposition,[28] has been granted the widest remit enjoyed by any oversight institution in the world. He or she is concerned with compliance with law and ministerial directives; with the 'propriety' of activities; with effectiveness and appropriateness of procedures in relation to legality and propriety; and with 'consistency with human rights'.[29] The objective of the Act is described as assisting *ministers* in oversight and review of these matters, and the primary audience for the Inspector-General's work, and the recipient of the reports that emerge from his or her inquiries, is the executive branch. Even where the report was triggered by an individual's complaint, all the complainant is entitled to receive is a written response which contains no material that either the Inspector-General or the minister believes would prejudice the nation's security, defence, or foreign relations.[30] Clearly the Inspector-General is no whistle-blower. Nor does the office possess remedial powers. The agency head is expected to act upon the report, and if the Inspector-General thinks the response is inadequate or inappropriate, he or she may discuss the matter with the minister and prepare a further report to be sent to the Prime Minister.[31] Ministerial pressure rather than public protest is envisaged as the main form of influence and correction.

The Inspector-General is not limited to responding to complaints; he or she is permitted to act on 'own motion'. This is particularly vital in relation to matters in which the minister personally participates, notably intrusive surveillance measures which, as in Britain, require only the authority of ministerial warrant.[32] What is most unusual is that this pro-active capability is not limited to ASIO: the Inspector-General's jurisdiction extends to the entire security and intelligence establishment, including the Defence Signals Directorate, the external intelligence service (ASIS),[33] the Office of National Assessments, and the Joint Intelligence Organization within the Department of Defence.[34] No other review agency anywhere has been granted such extensive jurisdiction. The Inspector-General is the nearest thing to a working example of functional rather than

---

[27] Other elements were narrowing the mandate of ASIO (above, Ch. 14), and creation of the Parliamentary Joint Committee discussed below, pp. 455–58.

[28] Inspector-General of Intelligence and Security Act 1986, s. 6.

[29] Ibid., ss. 4 and 8. The human rights jurisdiction must be activated by a reference from the Human Rights and Equal Opportunity Commission. A few other minor matters are also within the remit.

[30] Ibid., s. 23, which is headed 'advice to complainant', rather than a 'ruling' or 'determination'.

[31] Ibid., s. 24.   [32] ASIO Act, ss. 23–7; cf. Ch. 3 above.

[33] Thus creating a wonderful oxymoron, for the secrecy of the Australian Secret Intelligence Service becomes problematic when included in the Act.

[34] Inspector-General of Security and Intelligence Act 1986, s. 8. Various subsections impose slightly different restrictions on the review of each particular agency. There is less scope for review of the Office of National Assessments and the Joint Intelligence Organization, but neither of these collect intelligence and hence have little impact on the lives of individuals.

institutional review—key concepts which will recur throughout the chapters in this Part.

With such a wide range of matters to consider, and so many agencies under his superintendence, one would expect the Inspector-General to be extremely active. In the early years this was not so. The office's reported expenditure in 1987–8 was just over A$250,000; the Inspector-General had virtually no staff, and his initial public annual report was largely devoted to his problems in finding suitable office accommodation. His second report consisted of two and a half pages, of which only one paragraph discussed public requests or complaints. Apart from one complaint involving security assessment procedures in the public service, all were dismissed. The Inspector-General did not conduct any inquiries of his 'own motion'.[35]

Social scientists tend to denigrate the importance of the character and outlook of individuals in influencing the workings of institutions. Historians, more taken with the quirkiness and contingency of events, allow such idiosyncratic factors greater weight. There is an interesting contrast with the early history of oversight in Canada;[36] at present, all that need be said is that the initial inactivity of the Australian Inspector-General was in significant measure due to the approach taken by first appointee to the post.[37]

Mr Neil McInnes had an extensive background in intelligence and defence related matters as a government official—not the sort of background to encourage deep scepticism about security agencies. He also seemed markedly conservative, taking the view that the civil disobedience campaign of obstruction of logging in the Tasmanian wilderness, which involved some destruction of tractors and large-scale lying down in front of trucks, constituted 'politically motivated violence'. (It was reassuring to be told that ASIO itself resolutely refused to get involved.)

McInnes seemed very resistant to individual complaints about agency misconduct, and gave the impression that the complainant would have to present a very substantial case before he would take it seriously. He seemed untroubled by the obvious evidentiary difficulties this would entail. On the other hand, he placed great emphasis on what he called the 'monitoring procedures' he had established to satisfy himself that agencies were behaving properly. These were not mentioned at all in his annual report, and seemed to consist of looking at a random sample of files to determine whether they formed a satisfactory basis for the agency's conduct. This is very much like British Commissioners,[38] although Mr McInnes claimed that his own background in intelligence made him confident that he knew what to look for and how to find it. He also stated that

---

[35] *Annual Reports* for 1986–7 and 1987–8 (Australian Govt. Publishing Service, Canberra).

[36] In relation to the work of SIRC; below, Ch. 16.

[37] The succeeding paragraphs are based on an interview held on 30 March 1989 in Canberra with the Inspector-General, whose frankness is much appreciated.

[38] Below, pp. 430–33.

if he needed staff to assist him in an extended inquiry, he could obtain them from the equivalent of the Cabinet Office, or from another security agency. This would not, he asserted, lead to cosy complaisance; rather, the bureaucratic reality of inter-agency rivalry would ensure a thorough investigation.

Mr McInnes was not reappointed, and his successor, Mr Roger Holdich, has taken a notably more vigorous approach and has a higher public profile.[39] He has undertaken a number of full inquiries, for which statute grants him the powers of a Royal Commission, including right of access to any agency's premises and to compel testimony under oath and the production of documents.[40] His most noteworthy inquiry was undertaken in response to a matter that had raised substantial public disquiet. The Queensland Police Special Branch, tarred by its association with the discredited former state Premier and about to be abolished by the incoming state government, had reportedly passed its files to ASIO in order to circumvent an order that they be destroyed. The Inspector-General's inquiry, which involved reading hundreds of documents, produced a Report which concluded that, whilst fears of a mass transfer of politically charged files were groundless, and that ASIO had acted properly in the matter, there remained one unsatisfactory aspect. Over nearly ten years ASIO had received several hundred documents from the Queensland Special Branch which it had regarded as not relevant to its security mandate and not worth processing, but which it had retained.[41] The Inspector-General recommended that this irrelevant matter, and any such received from any source in future, should be destroyed.

Inspector-Generals are former civil servants, not lawyers or judges, and the difference in background[42] seems important to how Mr Holdich has approached the job. In his inquiry, legality and impropriety were considered together, with no attention paid to definitional nuances or technicalities. He treated the question of impropriety—the basis of almost all the complaints received—as a matter of 'reasonableness' of behaviour, understanding that term in its common usage, not in the specialized meaning it has acquired among administrative lawyers.[43] This has the advantage of allowing wide scope for criticizing actions which may, strictly speaking, adhere to the letter of the law but are ethically unsatisfactory. Conversely, it inevitably permits wide scope for subjective judgment, which means that an affirmation of the propriety of ASIO's conduct will be persuasive only if the Inspector-General personally has sufficient public standing. This is of great practical importance, for none of Mr Holdich's investigations have resulted in a finding of violation. We are unable to judge whether

---

[39] The ensuing paragraphs draw heavily on the *Annual Report 1990–91* (Canberra, 1991), and an unpublished lecture delivered by Mr Holdich, 'The Work of the Australian Inspector-General of Intelligence and Security' (1991); we are grateful for receipt of a copy from his office.

[40] Inspector-General of Security and Intelligence Act 1986, ss. 18–19.

[41] The ASIO Act provides in s. 19(1) for exchange of information between state police forces and the Organization.

[42] Contrast the statutory requirement for selection of the UK Commissioners, Ch. 3 above and p. 430 below. [43] See esp. p. 431 below.

this has affected his credibility. It is, however, interesting to note that on one occasion ASIS, the external intelligence service, consulted him about the propriety of an action it was contemplating. In so far as this suggests that the existence of the Inspector-General has assisted the agencies' internalization of statutory standards of conduct, the office can be said to have made a positive contribution.

The Inspector-General is a full-time official, whose workload has now risen sufficiently to have led him to seek an increase and upgrading of his small staff. One source of the increase is his function of hearing employment and related complaints from employees of the various agencies, some of which emerge during regular visits to central and regional offices; Holdich claims to have talked individually with virtually every ASIO and ASIS officer.[44] The job is clearly not one for an amateur, nor to be pursued as a sideline.

It is too early to attempt a thorough evaluation of the Australian Inspector-General. There has yet to be an occasion where his recommendations would have clipped the wings of any important institution or official; nor has he come into conflict with any of the institutions under his scrutiny. What is most remarkable is the design of the office itself. It is not limited to any one organization, though its ability to cut across organizational lines in the course of any one inquiry has yet to be tested. And the breadth of standards which may be applied to the various agencies shows a welcome advance on the legalism that, as will be seen, has so markedly afflicted the nearest equivalent in Britain.

Canada

The most comprehensive and complex set of mechanisms of executive accountability are those established in Canada. The Solicitor General's Department is given the explicit statutory role in two distinct ways. First, ministers are given power, which has been extensively used, to issue directions to the Director of CSIS. Though the CSIS Act does not impose explicit limitations, the fact that all such directions must be in writing and a copy forwarded to SIRC is intended to curb abuse and to limit them to general matters of policies and priorities.[45] Secondly, the Deputy Minister—the Department's senior civil servant—must be consulted by the Director on general policy matters and whenever the issuance of directions requires consultation.[46] Hence the Solicitor General's office has a Police and Security Branch employing several people who are engaged full-time in advising the Minister and also liaising with CSIS on matters ranging from operational policy to particular telephone tapping requests and reading 'correspondence flows'. Even more intensely involved, and the centre-piece of the new executive mechanisms, is the Inspector-General, whose office, though no

---

[44] Cf. the work of the Staff Counsellor in the UK; below, p. 430.
[45] CSIS Act, ss. 6(2) and 38(2); cf. the Australian provisions discussed on p. 418 above.
[46] CSIS Act, s. 7(1).

part of the McDonald Commission recommendations, was created by the CSIS Act.[47]

The Inspector-General does not exist to serve the public, which never sees his reports. Nor does he report to Parliament.[48] Rather, he serves as a sort of auditor for the minister, a function which is directly traceable to the scandals of the 1970s. 'The history of the security services in Canada is that they kept secrets from everyone, including Ministers.' Hence the Inspector-General's main task in a fundamental sense is to ensure that ministerial responsibility is real—that is, either that the minister is actually aware of what CSIS is doing and how it is doing it or, if something goes wrong and a public row ensues, that he or she can say: 'I know there is a problem and the Inspector-General is looking into it.'

There are two dimensions to the Inspector-General's work. One, which from a bare reading of the CSIS Act might seem predominant, but which emerged in interview as less important, is the issuance of a certificate covering two matters. The first is whether he or she is satisfied with the Director's statutorily required annual report to the minister. The second is whether in his or her opinion CSIS has engaged in any operational activities that are either unauthorized by the Act or ministerial directions, or have involved 'an unreasonable or unnecessary exercise by the Service of any of its powers'.[49] It requires the Inspector-General to make value judgements, and Mr Thompson recognised that: 'There is a great deal of grey, rather than black and white in "unreasonable and unnecessary".' This remit leads him to see himself as a sort of 'conscience of the Minister', urging the latter and the Deputy Minister to 'think hard' about any matter that might raise doubts.

The Inspector-General forms his judgments not simply by reacting to the director's report, but by a structured programme of research into CSIS's operations. This second dimension, the heart of his work, consists of six or seven major projects of 1,000 or more hours each, which are undertaken annually. These are based on a three-to-five-year work programme, worked out in conjunction with the Solicitor-General's office and SIRC,[50] a co-ordinated exercise

[47] Ibid., ss. 30–3. We are grateful to Mr Richard Thompson, then Inspector-General, and Mr Michael de Rosenroll, Deputy Inspector-General, for information provided in an extended interview, from which all quotations in the following paragraphs derive. The most comprehensive study of the office is J. Ryan, 'The Inspector General of the Canadian Security Intelligence Service' (1989) 9 *Confl. Q.* 33–51; unfortunately this periodical is very difficult to obtain in Britain.

[48] Indeed, he was extremely reticent in providing information to the Statutory Review Committee (n. 50 below), so much so that MPs from all three parties who served on the Committee expressed far greater irritation and dissatisfaction with the Inspector-General than with CSIS itself. Mr Thompson's attitude to the parliamentary body was very similar to that of a British civil servant who feels an overriding obligation of loyalty to his or her minister, in which is included a deep reluctance to reveal any information whose release the minister has not directly authorized.

[49] CSIS Act, s. 22(1) and (2).

[50] SIRC is discussed below, pp. 458 ff. For a list of the Inspector-General's review topics and priorities, see the Review Committee's Report, *In Flux But Not in Crisis* (Ottawa, 1990), 141–2. We need not explore the tangled relationships between the Inspector-General, SIRC, and CSIS, described by one participant as 'weird'.

designed to avoid repeating problems of duplication of directed 'tasking' which arose in the early years. The Inspector-General will pick a particular topic, for example use of human sources, and look at both policy and actual practice. This entails both reading files and interviewing officers. The Inspector-General is given a statutory right of access to all CSIS material relating to the scope of his jurisdiction.[51] Mr Thompson expressed confidence that his office had the capacity to 'go into the bowels of CSIS', and that it would be very difficult to conceal discreditable matters from him.

Thus the office of Inspector-General is neither a whistleblowing agency nor in any sense an avenue of public accountability. It is designed for monitoring compliance with statutory and ministerial standards, and for a policy evaluation of the Service's work. If the office functions effectively, it should avoid political embarrassment for the minister and possibly the government as a whole. It is impossible from the outside to judge how well the Inspector-General has carried out his task over the years, though it may be indicative that, whilst officials in the Solicitor General's office spoke quite critically of aspects of SIRC's work, they found little fault with the Inspector-General. What does seem clear, however, is that the Canadian system has placed the minister in a far more central role than in either Australia or (especially) Britain, and has also tried to give him or her the tools to do the job properly. In this sense, paradoxically, it has remained closest to the traditional Westminster concept of ministerial responsibility; but it has also tried to make that responsibility real.

Britain

To say that Britain relies most heavily on executive accountability is something of a tautology, since having rejected any form of legislative accountability it is left with nothing else. What also marks it off notably from the other two nations is its reliance on informality and bureaucratic consensus. Legal provisions play a role, but more in the background; they form the skeleton, but the flesh and blood are found not in books but in custom and practice.[52] As such it is a faithful reflection of the culture of British public administration. Paradoxically, the only exception does indeed prove the rule: the stunted version of an Inspector-General which Britain has created has been given a narrowly legalistic task.

The brevity of the British statute reflects the fact that it is largely a cloak draped over an unchanged figure, not intended significantly to disturb existing working relationships. The Director-General, appointed by the Home Secretary,

---

[51] CSIS Act, s. 31(1). This is extremely wide, and would exclude only Cabinet documents held by CSIS (s. 31(2)).

[52] One sees this graphically in the fact that, whilst the two comparable Australian statutes comprise in all about 150 sections occupying nearly eighty pages and the CSIS Act contains about seventy sections, the Security Service Act 1989 (SSA) consists of seven section and two Schedules, amounting in all to less than eight pages.

is placed in 'control' of the 'operations' of the Service.[53] This seems a deliberate attempt, by analogy to what has become the twentieth-century constitutional orthodoxy about policing, to grant the Director-General a similar degree of 'operational' independence as is provided for chief constables outside London, who are given 'direction and control' of their forces.[54] However, the matter is not so clear-cut. Quite apart from the shadowy role of the Prime Minister,[55] the Act also speaks of the Service being under the 'authority' of the Home Secretary, which at the very least could provide a basis for leadership in matters of policy.[56] Though in one sense Britain pioneered the use of this technique with the Maxwell-Fyfe Directive, unlike Canada and Australia there is no provision for any ministerial directions save in relation to disclosure of information relating to employment security vetting.[57] This raises an important issue, best explored by comparing the British and Canadian approaches.

One of the main issues which confronted the McDonald Commission was whether the RCMP, principally a law enforcement agency, should continue to perform security and intelligence work as well. The Commission recommended complete separation,[58] on the ground that whilst policing required independence from the executive, security had to be under its control in order to prevent abuses, and also to ensure that its efforts were devoted to generating intelligence useful to policymaking.[59] The conclusion in favour of executive control was based on the lessons drawn from the preceding experience of agencies out of control. The British experience has been more complex, the full history more concealed, and the extent of public reaction more muted. Certainly no strong consensus has emerged about the necessity to place the Service under much closer ministerial control. It could of course be argued that consequently there is less danger of politicians abusing the Security Service for their own purposes, but this assumes that the protections built into the Australian and Canadian statutes are not as effective. It can certainly be said that the British system is sensitive to the need to protect security officials from politicians; what remains in question is whether it is lopsided in its failure to make formal provision to prevent the converse.

In terms of legal duties, the Director-General must deliver an annual report to the Home Secretary and Prime Minister, which remains secret.[60] He or she is

[53] SSA, s. 2(1). It may be recalled, however (see p. 418) that the Director-General lacks the security of tenure of his or her Australian counterpart.

[54] Police Act 1964, s. 5; for discussion, see L. Lustgarten, *The Governance of Police* (London, 1986), 74–5.

[55] Below, pp 428–29.

[56] SSA, s. 1(1). This assumes that a distinction between 'operations' and policy is coherently maintainable; for doubts, see Lustgarten (n. 54 above), 20–2.

[57] SSA, s. 2(3).

[58] This combination seems to have been virtually unique in post-war Western democracies.

[59] For discussion of the Commission's approach to this matter, see S. Farson, 'Restructuring Control in Canada: The McDonald Commission of Inquiry and its Legacy', in G. Hastedt (ed.), *Controlling Intelligence* (London, 1991), 157–60.

[60] SSA, s. 2(4).

also put under a duty to ensure that the organization does not further the interests of any political party, and that it does not gather or disclose information save
as is necessary for security purposes.[61] Beyond this the Act leaves the Service on
its own. This is where the strange culture of Whitehall becomes important.
Officials insist that they are aware of the dangers emphasized throughout this
book. The key check is said to be that security and intelligence matters are continually being negotiated and talked through at quite a high level, in what is actually
a very small community—a secretive quarter of 'the Whitehall village'. This occurs
both formally within the Joint Intelligence Committee,[62] and informally between
people at assistant director level, within the various ministries. Outsiders are in no
position to know how effective that co-ordination is, but in one Home Office
person's view: 'Ninety five per cent of the time we reach agreement. There may
be a difference of five per cent.' The key phrase that emerged in a three-way discussion with that official and her MI5 counterpart[63] was 'the common mind of
British administration'. Their view was that, unlike many fringe organizations
which are given a budget but not a ministerial home and told to get on with a
specific job, the Service deals with issues of almost daily relevance to senior ministers and civil servants. It is therefore continually under a spotlight within
Whitehall, and the constant give and take ensures both that it does not go off the
rails operationally, and that it influences and is influenced by the climate of consensual opinion about policies and priorities. This is the administrative setting
within which strong resistance to the notion of issuing or accepting directions was
expressed. Both participants were at one in regarding this practice as an improper
infringement on the independence of the Service.

Since such great emphasis is placed on collegiality and co-ordination within
the executive as a means of control, it becomes particularly important to learn
what occurs in practice. The working relationship between MI5 and the Home
Office[64] has not received attention from either journalists or scholars in Britain,
in part because of the tradition of general administrative secrecy. We are therefore entirely reliant on interview material.

What emerged from the discussions was both unexpected and rather alarming.
First, the legal ambiguity has permitted officials to take a very limited view of
the scope of Home Office responsibility. Apart from the Home Secretary's
explicit statutory responsibility for 'warrantry', the function of the Home Office

---

[61] SSA, s. 2(2).

[62] About which officials are remarkably close-mouthed, as is also true of the office of the Intelligence
Co-ordinator. Whether this reticence is necessary must be considered doubtful; Australia put its entire
intelligence analysis structure on a statutory footing in the Office of National Assessment Act 1977,
which reads like an organizational chart and lays out diverse functions in great detail. ONA 'product' is
generally held in high regard. In any case, information is publicly available: see the extensive description
in R. Norton-Taylor, *In Defence of the Realm?* (London, 1990), ch. 5. A change of attitude occurred in
1993, and we were able to interview the Intelligence Co-ordinator. See Coda, pp. 493 ff.

[63] The Home Office informant was twice interviewed separately, but was also present and participated in a secondary role during two interviews with the Security Service official.

[64] Discussed in relation to 'warrantry' in Ch. 3.

is seen as assisting the exercise of the latter's statutory 'authority'—whose undefined extent and quality thus can be, and is, interpreted quite narrowly. Certainly there is formalized contact between Home Office civil servants and their Security Service equivalents, and they will talk in general terms about priorities and the 'operational landscape', but no attempt is made to exercise day-to-day supervision, let alone control, over the Service.

What came over very strongly in interviews is that the mainspring of this reticence is not the legal ambiguity—which is more of a supporting rationalization—but an open and admitted attitude that might be called 'the presumption of regularity'. In the words of our informant, MI5 is not seen as a 'wild tiger that needs to be caged' but rather as an organization 'disposed to carry out its statutory functions in a legal and honest way'. Officials also feel restricted by the 'need to know' principle, and equally by a view that 'our own natural curiosity might lead us further in than is necessary'. Indeed, 'there is greater reluctance on our part to ask questions, than of the Service to answer them'.

This orientation towards the relationship with MI5 is not imposed by it on a cowed civil service, nor dictated by ministers, who indeed vary considerably in the interest they take in security matters. Rather, it flows from what may be called a 'collegial view'—one official's respect for the professionalism of another. If she 'burrowed around' too insistently in the files, she feared 'demoralizing' people who 'are genuinely trying to protect the interests of the state'. Just as she would not welcome others browsing through her files, so is she reluctant, in the absence of clear justification, to treat another official in that fashion.

The nub of the matter came when our informant expressed confidence that there was no propensity for MI5 to 'run wild'. Asked to substantiate this confidence she could—inevitably in view of the unwillingness to 'burrow around'—offer no supporting evidence except personal contact with the Director-General and perusal of the latter's Annual Report. And there is both the nub and the rub. To reuse a phrase borrowed earlier,[65] the relationship between the Home Office and the Security Service is a matter of trust. To an outsider it seems more akin to religious faith than empirically based judgment. And even if this faith turns out to be rewarded (by means miraculous or otherwise), that would hardly constitute a basis for the conduct of government in a democratic society. In the words of a Canadian official who has liaised with Whitehall, in the British system there is 'a strong element of paternalism', of a belief that 'we are good people who know what is best'. But as the emphasis on 'the common mind of British administration' suggests, this ethos is not something peculiar to the field of security. Nor is it likely to vanish from the security field whilst it pervades the rest of Whitehall. The foremost prerequisite for greater accountability of security is a much wider democratization and openness in the conduct of government generally.

---

[65] See n. 18 above.

There is a related problem, of which a glimmer appeared fleetingly in discussion. Entirely in passing, Peter Wright's account of the 'molehunts'—the search for a Soviet agent within MI5, which resulted in the formation of a high-level committee which met for several years and interrogated, among many others, the previous Director-General, his deputy, and a future Director-General[66]— happened to be mentioned. In response to incredulity that such organizational turmoil and allocation of resources was successfully concealed from ministers, our Home Office informant doubted whether the Service had a constitutional responsibility to report the matter to them. Her view was that there could not be an automatic duty to inform ministers of everything, given their numerous other responsibilities and the fact that many matters, seemingly vital at the time, later prove false or of exaggerated consequence. Only matters of 'intrinsic importance' should be raised with ministers, and what seemed to be the paramount element in this amorphous concept was the potential to embarrass the government.

One obvious objection to this view is that matters which embarrass the Service will stay buried within it if they can be interred deeply enough to prevent embarrassment to its political masters. It is surely a matter of constitutional necessity that ministers be made aware of the existence of a strong suspicion of espionage within a security agency. They need to know whether there is any likelihood that the information they are receiving and upon which they may act is untrustworthy. That need is compounded when corresponding officials of foreign agencies are well aware of the problem and regard this unreliability as a reason for threatening to withdraw co-operation,[67] thus, presumably, impairing the organization's effectiveness. Unless our informant, a highly conscientious senior official, happened to be wildly out of sync with the 'common mind' on this one particular point, there must be concern that information may, for reasons that (to put it no higher) are constitutionally questionable, be withheld by the Service and its Home Office counterparts from ministers who are in no position even to suspect what is occurring. In these circumstances the gap left by the absence of an Inspector-General on the Canadian model—acting on behalf of the minister—is particularly wide and visible.

The role of the Prime Minister

The ambiguous and flexible relations between the Home Office and the Security Service are further complicated by the possibility of prime ministerial intervention. Historically, the Director-General has enjoyed by convention a right of

---

[66] P. Wright, *Spycatcher* (New York, 1987). This episode is so incredible that one would be disinclined to believe Wright's version were it not for corroboration elsewhere, e.g. N. West, *Molehunt* (London, 1987), *passim* (though his conclusions about the purported 'mole' are radically different.)

[67] As, according to Wright (previous note), the Americans did in the mid-1960s. There is also a question of self-government, if not quite nationhood: it seems wrong in principle for the CIA to know more about MI5 than British ministers.

direct approach to the Prime Minister.[68] This access, unique among civilian officials and indeed shared only with the Chiefs of Staff of the armed forces, has now been incorporated into statute[69]—one of the very few examples in the British constitution in which the Prime Minister's relations with an official are formally prescribed.

The blurring of responsibility between the Prime Minister and the Home Secretary reflects the fact that prior to 1952 responsibility for the running of the Service lay with the former. The rationale for the transfer of function was that the Security Service's task of defending the realm was more analogous to the Home Office's role of keeping law and order and preventing subversion than the military task of preserving physical territorial integrity. Despite the Home Secretary's new role, the dominance of the Prime Minister in security matters has in more recent years been enhanced by the creation within the Cabinet Office of a Joint Intelligence Secretariat reporting to the Cabinet Secretary, and the posts of the Intelligence Co-ordinator and the Chairman of the Joint Intelligence Committee, in effect the senior figures in the intelligence community. Furthermore, it is the Prime Minister who chairs the MIS (the Ministerial Committee on the Intelligence Services), the Cabinet committee responsible for policy on the security and intelligence services.[70] Likewise the Prime Minister has exclusive authority for the making of a discretionary reference of any matter to the Security Commission, or establishing a special inquiry.[71] This personal responsibility is also demonstrated in the answering of Parliamentary Questions and the making of ministerial statements on security matters. Even where these directly touch the conduct of the Security Service, it has been the Prime Minister rather than the Home Secretary who has invariably assumed responsibility.

Given that the Act is devoted to only one piece of the security and intelligence machinery, the failure to acknowledge the unique place of the Prime Minister at the centre of its workings is not surprising. The office is mentioned only in relation to formal powers or functions in relation to the Service: receiving the Annual Reports which the Director-General (section 2(4)) and the Commissioner (section 4(6)) are obliged to make under the Act and in appointing the Commissioner (section 4(1)). The statutory silence about the role of the Prime Minister is as it were echoed in relation to a vital matter in which he or she may be presumed to have a determining voice: money. This is discussed in the following chapter.

---

[68] Recognized and preserved in para. 1 of the Maxwell-Fyfe Directive (see App. I) even as the transfer of responsibility to the Home Secretary described below was initiated.

[69] SSA, s. 2(4).

[70] For details of the co-ordination of intelligence at Cabinet level, see the official booklet, *Central Intelligence Machinery* (London, 1993); *Falkland Islands Review*, Cmnd. 8787 (1983); P. Hennessy, *Cabinet* (London, 1986), 26–9; and Richelson and Ball (n. 2 above), 26–9.

[71] Below, Ch. 17.

The Security and Intelligence Services Staff Counsellor

In 1987 the Prime Minister announced the appointment of a Staff Counsellor who would be available to be consulted by intelligence officers concerned about any aspect of their work.[72] The clear purpose was to provide an alternative outlet to damaging public disclosure by the disaffected. This impression was confirmed when, by a later announcement, the reconsideration of refusals to allow the publication of Security Service officials' memoirs was added to his job description.[73] The person appointed, Sir Philip Woodfield, is known to hold surgeries around the country to make himself available for these kinds of discussions. He is no stranger to security work, having formerly been Permanent Secretary at the Northern Ireland Office. In view of this background it is hard to have great confidence in the detached impartiality of the office, despite the fact that it is formally external to the services and has access to all documents, to all levels of management, and to the Cabinet Secretary. The credibility of the Counsellor was further undermined by the semi-public announcement that he had been asked to conduct an internal review of MI5 performance over the handling of the Gulf War detentions,[74] and had reported clearing the Service of allegations of ineptitude.[75] The Staff Counsellor produces an unpublished report at least annually for the Prime Minister, Home Secretary, and Foreign Secretary. The office is a safety-valve for conscience-troubled officials, rather than a form of oversight. Unlike the Canadian and Australian Inspector-Generals, the Counsellor is entirely reactive, and has in any event a much narrower brief. Indeed it may be said that on the rather crowded stage of executive accountability he is an actor cast in a bit part. Before the Staff Counsellor could be viewed as a safe and reliable means for airing grievances—for instance, over illegal or unconstitutional behaviour by the Service—or even as an effective early warning system for troubles which might explode in ministers' faces, it would be necessary to know how such complaints are handled and what safeguards exist for protecting complainants from disciplinary sanctions. No details of these, or of the Staff Counsellor's performance, have been made public.

The Commissioner

The 1989 Act makes one concession to the need for independent oversight, though none at all to openness. It creates the office of Commissioner, a part-time post to be occupied by a former or sitting judge of High Court rank.[76] The office is modelled directly on the Interceptions Commissioner, whose work has been discussed in Chapter 3. The Security Service Commissioner has two func-

---

[72] *HC Debs.*, vol. 121, col. 512 (2 Nov. 1987); P. Birkinshaw, *Freedom of Information: The Law, the Practice and the Ideal* (London, 1988), 26; K. Ewing and C. Gearty, *Freedom Under Thatcher* (Oxford, 1990), 171–4.

[73] *HC Debs.*, vol. 144, cols. 537–8 (21 Dec. 1988). [74] See Ch. 7.

[75] *Independent*, 10 Dec. 1991. [76] SSA 1989, s. 4(1).

tions. The first is to review the Home Secretary's issuance of property intrusion warrants,[77] and make an annual report to the Prime Minister. This is made available to Parliament (and only thence to the public), subject to deletion of matters the Prime Minister believes would be prejudicial to the organization's functioning.[78] The post has from its inception been occupied by Lord Justice Stuart-Smith of the Court of Appeal; our account of it derives from his annual reports and information obtained in interview.

In his oversight of intrusion warrants, the Commissioner has interpreted his task as applying principles of judicial review, based on a rather convoluted piece of legal reasoning. As he has recognized, section 4(3), which instructs him to 'keep under review' the Home Secretary's use of his warrant powers, 'does not lay down the nature of the review that I am to undertake'.[79] None the less, since a subsequent provision instructs him to apply principles of judicial review when considering a complaint, he applies those principles when considering all warrant matters.[80]

One can see how such an approach would seem naturally and obviously correct to a common lawyer with no experience of security or indeed of government service, but who had done Crown Office litigation and felt himself particularly at home in matters of judicial review.[81] None the less it seems unjustifiably narrow. The handling of an individual complaint is by no means the same thing as the exercise of 'review' by the sole person in Britain given access to the necessary information. A strong case can be made that something very like the Australian idea of propriety ought to be included, as well as adherence to the nation's obligation in international law to comply with the European Convention on Human Rights. There is nothing inconsistent or incoherent in applying the laxer standard mandated by statute in the case of an individual complaint, whilst as a matter of general superintendence pressing for compliance with higher standards. Indeed such an approach would go far to vindicate the worth of the office which, as it currently stands, is questionable.

The Commissioner has described his judicial review approach as follows:

provided that I am satisfied that the [warrant] application falls within the functions of the Service, it is not for me to substitute my judgement for that of the Secretary of State, but to consider whether the Secretary of State could properly have come to the conclusion which he did.[82]

---

[77] But not telephone intercepts, which are reviewed by the Interceptions Commissioner.

[78] SSA, s. 4(5)–(7).

[79] *Security Service Act 1989, Chap. 5—Report of the Commissioner for 1990*, Cm. 1480 (1991), para. 12.

[80] Ibid.; the relevant provision is SSA 1989, sch. 1, para. 4, discussed at p. 433 below.

[81] Although he disclaimed any knowledge of the reasons for his appointment, Lord Justice Stuart-Smith pointed out that there are only twenty-seven members of the Court of Appeal, half of whom are specialists in chancery, family, or other matters well removed from common law. 'If one eliminates recent appointees and really senior people who consistently preside', that did not leave many people to choose from. Whatever the actual reasons for his selection, the explanation is revealing of his conception of the task involved.

[82] See n. 79 above, para. 12.

This standard, immediately recognizable to administrative lawyers as 'the *Wednesbury* test',[83] grants very wide leeway to government officials, whose judgments it serves to uphold unless they can be described as 'irrational'.[84] Indeed flaccidity of the test may be seen in the Commissioner's application; he requires only that the Service makes 'a sufficient factual case to satisfy the Secretary of State . . . that there are *grounds* for believing that national security interests are involved' for the issuance of a warrant to be justified.[85] This is a very low standard,[86] and it is hardly surprising that the Commissioner has yet to find that a warrant has been issued illegally, though his unpublished report does provide guidance as to good practice.[87]

In interview, however, his approach seemed somewhat more trenchant. He described it as 'a form of inquisitorial judicial review, almost as though I were presiding in the High Court', permitting the Service no more discretionary leeway than would be allowed the Milk Marketing Board. He also makes a point of looking at the 'product'—that is, the information obtained—of some of the warrant applications since, especially where there is an application for renewal, it 'is probably the best evidence that the [statutory] criteria are satisfied'.[88]

Asked about the 'techniques' he employs, the Commissioner said he would not 'glorify' his approach with that description: 'I try and ask embarrassing questions.' The Act requires all MI5 officers and civil servants to provide him with whatever information he requires,[89] and he makes several visits annually to Security Service offices, questioning both those who have requested warrants and case officers. The number of warrants issued each year is 'comparatively small',[90] allowing him at least in his first year to examine all applications. However, the office is very much a part-time activity. Lord Justice Stuart-Smith continues to carry almost a full load in the Court of Appeal, taking only about two weeks leave from court work; the rest of the work is done in his 'own time' and during vacations. As he readily admitted, he could not do the job of the Australian Inspector-General: he has no staff whatever. This is in a sense part of the design of the office, for, apart from a limited involvement in the handling of

---

[83] From *Associated Provincial Picture Houses* v. *Wednesbury Corporation* [1948] 1 KB 223.

[84] A term of art meaning, among other things, taking account of irrelevant considerations, failing to take account of relevant ones, acting for improper purposes, and a decision so unreasonable that no reasonable body could have taken it. For discussion see Craig (n. 6 above), 281 ff.

[85] See n. 79 above, para. 12 (emphasis added).

[86] By contrast, the test for issuance of warrants by ministers under the ASIO Act (ss. 25–7) and by judges under the CSIS Act (s. 21 ff.) in all cases requires the existence of 'reasonable grounds'.

[87] The unpublished parts of the report to the Prime Minister provide a regular opportunity to go into particular matters in necessary detail. The Commissioner said that he prepares the report in two parts, one for public, the other for prime-ministerial consumption; and it is 'perfectly obvious' what should appear only in the latter, including anything involving operational matters.

[88] *Report of the Commissioner for 1991*, Cm. 1946 (London, 1992), para. 2, reiterating a point made the previous year (above n. 79, para. 13).

[89] SSA, s. 4(4).

[90] A phrase appearing in both reports, though it is not clear what the standard of comparison is. See also Ch. 3 above.

complaints,[91] he is essentially a bugging and break-in commissioner, checking for legal compliance.

At its best, it may well be useful for ministers and senior civil servants to have a respected individual able to probe freely into these distasteful operations in a way that they could not; and the existence of the office may help keep wayward tendencies within the Service under restraint. It is no reflection at all on the work of any individual to say that this can hardly be regarded as adequate assurance to the public, especially since (presumably owing to his view of the requirements of secrecy) the Commissioner's reports have been liberally strewn with 'I am satisfieds' without supporting reasons.[92] The office of Commissioner is so narrowly focused, and so limited in resources, that any criticisms of its 'product' must ultimately trace the source of the problem to design flaws. Whilst it is right to single out various forms of intrusions on privacy for special attention, they are only a small proportion of what the Service does; and since, as has been seen, other serious intrusions, notably use of informers, are not subject to warrant,[93] they are not reviewed by any Commissioner. The remainder of the Service's activities have been kept outside any formal mechanism of executive accountability. Though it may be accepted that the constant interaction within Whitehall does impose considerable restraints, it is difficult to regard current practice as satisfactory from the point of view of control. Nor, in the absence of anything like a 'devil's advocate'[94] or other internal protection for proposed targets, can the office and function of Commissioner possibly be regarded as an effective guardian of individuals' rights.

Complaints against misconduct

Before the enactment of the Security Service Act 1989, the sole exception to the Service's effective immunity from legal review was the procedure for investigating complaints of telephone tapping under the Interception of Communications Act 1985. This measure has provided the model for complaints under the present Act. As such it faithfully replicates all the substantial flaws therein. We begin with a skeletal account elucidating the statutory framework before discussing the little available material about the working of the system.

The Act establishes a Tribunal of three to five members, all of whom must be lawyers of at least ten years standing, who are appointed for a five year term with protected tenure.[95] This Tribunal adjudicates upon all complaints, with one important exception. Where the complainant contends that any property of his has been affected by the Service in any way, the complaint must be funnelled to the Commissioner, who then must determine (*a*) whether a warrant has been

---

[91] Below, pp. 434–35, 437.

[92] e.g., *Report for 1990* (n. 79 above), paras. 15, 16; *Report of 1991* (n. 88 above), paras. 4, 5. One honourable exception was presentation of a reasoned explanation of his belief that the Security Service does not undertake warrantless—that is, illegal—bugging and burglary operations. *Report of the Commissioner for 1992*, Cm. 2174 (1993), para. 8.

[93] Above, Ch. 4.   [94] Above, p. 83.   [95] SSA, sched. 2, para. 1.

issued under section 3 and, if so, (*b*) applying principles of judicial review such as would be applied by a court, whether the Secretary had properly issued the warrant.[96] Thus the Tribunal is excluded from considering anything to do with warrants, and the Commissioner's general superintendence over them is reinforced by his authority to deal with complaints involving them. This division of labour makes sense, particularly in light of the Commissioner's judicial status and the statutory command that he or she apply the standards of judicial review. However, it leaves a great void, namely the problem of burglaries or bugging not done pursuant to any warrant. The Act simply ignores this problem, presumably on the grounds that such conduct, if unauthorized, would be both a criminal offence and a civil trespass. In reality, of course, a complainant will have no way of proving whether such conduct even occurred, let alone who carried it out, and the prohibition on the Tribunal revealing any information placed before it to a complainant without the provider's consent[97] denies access to the most reliable potential source of proof. The Act fails to redress this unhelpful treatment of individual victims by an administrative alternative; for example, by requiring that any evidence of illegal conduct by members of the Service be reported to the Home Secretary, Commissioner, or the police.[98]

All complaints not involving warrant remain within the Tribunal's jurisdiction. Access to it is not limited to individuals; organizations and associations may also complain.[99] But the questions to which it must address its collective mind are restricted, and in some respects odd. Where the Service had made or is presently making inquiries about the complainant, the Tribunal is to determine whether there were 'reasonable grounds' for initiating or continuing those inquiries.[100] This is straightforward enough in relation, say, to a person suspected of selling information to a foreign government. Much less satisfactory is where a person becomes a target of investigation because he is active in an organization which the Service deems to require scrutiny. A very awkwardly worded provision[101] mandates that, where the Tribunal finds that the inquiries were based on the 'ground of his membership of a category of persons regarded by the Service as requiring investigation in the discharge of its functions', it shall treat the grounds as reasonable if it considers that the Service reasonably believed him to be 'a member of that category'. Thus if the Service deems, say, the Campaign for Nuclear Disarmament to be engaged in subversive activities and the complainant was investigated because of his participation in that organization, the Tribunal must determine whether CND activists are a 'category' of subversive persons. It may conclude that they are and reject the complaint; but in addition it may refer to the Commissioner the question of whether all persons in that 'category' are

---

[96] Ibid., sched. 1, para. 4.   [97] Ibid., sched. 2, para. 4(2).

[98] The CSIS Act, s. 20(2), imposes a duty on the Director to submit a report detailing any evidence of illegal conduct by a CSIS officer to the responsible minister; copies must be sent to the Solicitor General and to SIRC.

[99] SSA, sched. 2, para. 8.   [100] Ibid., sched. 1, paras. 2(2) and (3).

[101] Ibid., sched. 1, para. 2(4).

properly targets for investigation; for example, whether all CND members or only high level officials should be investigated.[102] A reference of this kind, which would require the Commissioner to make an explicit value judgment, has yet to be made.

The Tribunal is master of its own procedure, subject to the important prohibition on disclosure on information.[103] In effect this means that it is enjoined to absolute secrecy, with the complainant barred from sight of any documents or evidence and obviously incapable of cross-examination, confrontation, or even refutation of adverse allegations. There is little doubt that United Kingdom domestic courts would uphold this procedure,[104] but whether it will pass muster in Europe is more dubious. Members of the Service are required to furnish the Tribunal or Commissioner with all documents and information they require to carry out their functions,[105] so the adjudicating body should have all the relevant evidence before it. In order to know what is required, it may be necessary to examine a range of files or interview several officers. The Tribunal will need staff for this purpose, but their numbers are to be determined by the judgment of the Home Secretary, not the Tribunal's assessment of its requirements.[106] Given both that the Secretary may have an interest in the matter as the Minister responsible for the Service, and the present government's obsession with cutting public spending, those concerned about prompt and effective investigation will not be reassured.

The final subject matter to come under the Tribunal's purview is disclosure of information relating to the complainant's suitability for employment. The Service is prohibited from such disclosure except in accordance with 'provisions' made by the Secretary of State, which have never been made public. The bare statutory language might suggest that the Tribunal is not empowered to determine compliance, but is limited to inquiring whether the Service reasonably believed the information to be true.[107] Assuming the Secretary imposes any restrictions on the disclosure of such potentially damaging material beyond belief in its accuracy, this will be a much more limited question. However, we were informed that the Tribunal has received a copy of these provisions, and regards it as within its remit to consider whether any disclosure had breached them. If so, the matter would be referred to the Commissioner.

One important matter casts a broad shadow of doubt over the effectiveness of the complaints mechanism. How will a person know if he or she has been bugged, burgled, or investigated? The Security Service does not leave calling cards. Tell-tale traces, for example, of papers missing or disturbed, might raise suspicion, and it is possible accidentally to uncover a room 'bug'. It is also possible, though expensive, to 'sweep' a room electronically, that is, to search for

---

[102] Ibid., sched. 1, para. 7(1).   [103] Above, n. 97.

[104] The Court of Appeal upheld a similar procedure, used in deportation cases where national security is claimed as justification, despite the denial of natural justice: *R.* v. *Secretary of State for Home Department, ex p. Hosenball* [1977] 1 WLR 766.

[105] SSA, sched. 2, para. 4.   [106] Ibid., sched. 2, para. 6.

[107] Ibid., sched. 1, para. 3.

hidden transmitters. In the absence of these unlikely possibilities, there is a nasty catch-22. A generalized suspicion or fear is not evidence, and is only too readily dismissable as paranoia; and the Tribunal is empowered to dismiss frivolous or vexatious complaints, a power laid down with ominous symbolism in the very first provision governing its work.[108] In fact the Commissioner has reported that during the first two years all complaints, even if they were thought to fit this category, have been accepted and looked at.[109] Yet it is difficult to see how the complaint will be able to give the Tribunal anything to work on, except to point to odd coincidences and unexplained happenings. And one door has been firmly shut, not to say slammed: we have seen in Chapter 9 that present and former members of the Service are now under a lifelong duty of confidentiality with respect to information obtained in the course of their employment. Since revelation of such information may lead to criminal prosecution and up to two years imprisonment, the price of whistleblowing has been set high, perhaps too high for most people to contemplate it. And should an MI5 employee suffering a crisis of conscience leak the information to the victim, it is possible that the latter would be asked by the Tribunal to identify the source, under threat of dismissal of the complaint for failure to comply. Such a stance would do little for the Tribunal's credibility, however. Thus though the duty of confidentiality is abrogated for officials who, as has been seen, may be required to give evidence to the Tribunal, they must first be asked; and that seems unlikely to occur.

One way out of the impasse would be to allow Service personnel who feel they are being asked to behave improperly, themselves to complain directly to the Commissioner or Tribunal. No such facility is provided by the Act. But an extra-legal mechanism of this type does exist.[110] The Staff Counsellor may uncover improper activities, but will also stop knowledge of them from reaching the public. Achieving the former is greatly to the public benefit, and it may well be argued that prevention or termination of improper activities is of greater importance than individual redress. But the price is that victims of abuse of power are left out in the cold.

Complainants may also find equally chilly comfort even when their complaints are upheld. The Tribunal is explicitly barred from giving any reasons for its decisions.[111] All it can do is give notice, yea or nay, to the complainant of its determination.[112] Even a successful complainant may regard this as unsatisfactory, since he will remain in the dark about why, and even to what extent, he has been mistreated, but the rejected complainant will feel a justified bitterness. Prevented from contesting any of the allegations of the material presented by the Service, and left in the dark about the basis of the Tribunal's determination, he can be pardoned if he regards the whole procedure as designed to cover up misconduct or oppression.

---

[108] SSA, sched. 1, para. 1.   [109] See n. 88 above, para. 7.
[110] See p. 430 above.   [111] SSA, sched. 2, para. 4(2).
[112] Ibid., sched. 1, para. 5.

Where the complaint is upheld, the Tribunal can order termination of any inquiries and destruction of records relating to it, and order any sum it deems appropriate to be paid in compensation.[113] Where the Commissioner on reference from the Tribunal considers that a warrant was improperly issued, he may quash it and order compensation; the Tribunal gives effect to these decisions.[114] Moreover, in cases where it rejects the specific complaint but believes it appropriate for there to be an investigation into whether the Service has in any other way acted improperly toward the complainant, the Tribunal is to refer the matter to the Commissioner.[115] Unfortunately, the Commissioner himself then has no power to investigate, but *may* report the matter to the Home Secretary.[116] The latter enjoys unrestricted remedial powers but is under no compulsion to take the matter further. To leave the final decision about misconduct by officers of the executive to a minister, particularly the minister nominally in charge, makes nonsense of the rule of law. This might cut very little ice with the Home Office, but could possibly reach a more receptive audience in Strasbourg. Perhaps more important in the long run, it seriously detracts from the legitimacy of the Act, bringing its grievance machinery into disrepute and encouraging people who believe themselves victimized to bring the matter into the public domain—precisely what the government sought to avoid by establishing the complaints mechanism.

What of the complainant who is dissatisfied with the handling of his or her case? The Act attempts to answer that question in no uncertain terms: decisions of the Tribunal and Commissioner, '*including decisions as to their jurisdictions* shall not be subject to appeal or liable to be questioned in any court'.[117] Apart from the italicized phrase, this is the standard ouster clause, which since *Anisminic*[118] has not prevented the courts from quashing errors they characterize as jurisdictional. None the less that phrase is as clear an expression of Parliamentary intention as language can convey. It is lifted directly from section 7(8) of the Interception of Communications Act 1985, of which Professor Wade has written: 'This is scarcely different from the clause which failed in the *Anisminic* case, but it may be at this point that the judges will accept the unambiguous instructions of Parliament.'[119] Purely as a behavioural prediction, this is likely to be correct, particularly because the Commissioner is a senior judicial colleague required to apply precisely the same standard he would use when wearing his judicial robes.

---

[113] Ibid., sched. 1, para. 6(1).   [114] Ibid., sched. 1, para. 6(2).

[115] Ibid., sched. 1, para. 7(2). It is under this provision that the question of compliance with the rules governing disclosure of information could be referred: above, p. 435.

[116] Ibid., sched. 1, para. 7(3). Though the statutory language is not mandatory, our Security Service source insisted that the matter would be both looked into and forwarded to the minister.

[117] Ibid., s. 5(4). However the effect of this provision was left undecided in *R.* v. *Security Service Tribunal, ex p. Harman and Hewitt*, QBD, 14 Feb. 1992.

[118] *Anisminic Ltd.* v. *Foreign Compensation Commission* [1969] 2 AC 147.

[119] H. Wade, *Administrative Law* (6th edn., Oxford, 1988), 728.

The complaints machinery—an evaluation

In its first two years of existence the Tribunal made determinations in eighty-one cases and rejected all of them.[120] The obvious credibility problem[121] elicited an explanation from the Commissioner involving several reasons, some of which reflect deliberate decisions taken when the legislation was framed.[122] Although his view is not wholly persuasive, it correctly identifies the main problem as flaws in the design of the architects, rather than in the competence of the workmen.

The gravest defect is that the Act does not apply to anything done before its commencement at the end of 1989.[123] This is normal practice when a novel law is enacted, but the limitation causes a peculiar but grave problem in relation to any intelligence and security body. It means not only that actions before that date cannot be investigated, but also that information gained thereby may continue to be held. Retention of previously acquired information—involving no further 'inquiries'[124]—is simply outside the Act entirely; put another way, the fact that the Service is keeping a file on someone is not of itself a ground for complaint under the Act. Since this is precisely what most concerns many people whose anxieties about the power of the Security Service are directly personal rather than more broadly constitutional, the Act contributes nothing towards resolving one of the major issues in the field. Presumably this was intentional.

What was certainly intentional is the inability of citizens to use the Act as a substitute for freedom of information legislation in this particular sphere. Several complainants have simply asked whether a file has been kept on them, and to be told its contents or given access to it. That is not within the jurisdiction of the Tribunal either. It is worth noting that if, as is desirable in principle, such access legislation were enacted, experience elsewhere has been that such files as are made available to applicants often are subject to heavy deletion of 'national security' or other exempt material.

Another important limitation on the Tribunal's remit has been referred to in Chapter 6 on employment vetting. Because it is limited to certain actions taken by the Security Service only, it cannot investigate vetting decisions *per se* (which may be based on information emanating from other sources), but is limited to looking at the Service's role in relation to them. Thus a request to determine

---

[120] See n. 84 above, para. 6.

[121] Which was enhanced by the figures subsequently published for 1992, showing that a further twenty complaints had been rejected whilst none had succeeded (n. 92 above), para. 6. To mix sporting metaphors, at the close of play the score was Complainants 0, Security Service 101.

[122] Ibid., paras. 7–12. All factual statements in the following paragraphs derive from this reference.

[123] SSA, sched. 1, para. 9(1).

[124] The phrase used in ibid., sched. 1, para. 2(1) as the initial criterion for those matters the Tribunal may investigate.

why an applicant was refused government employment cannot be taken up. We suggested earlier[125] that this restriction is one reason why decisionmaking practices in this area may not comply with the European Convention on Human Rights. It is also one more illustration of the difference between a functional rather than an institutional approach; the latter is needed in relation to individual complaints as much as for more general oversight.

The other factor cited by the Commissioner is that a substantial number of complainants suffer from delusions. This view is supported by the statistics presented in his third Report, which clearly has been written with the aim of preventing the complaints process from falling into public disrepute. The overwhelming number of complaints (99 of 124) over the three years have involved an allegation that the person had been the subject of inquiry, where no inquiry had in fact been made.[126] Some of the complainants are repeaters who, as the Commissioner expressed it informally, are 'plain barmy'; the existence of this problem was confirmed from the other side by Mr John Wadham, Legal Officer of Liberty (NCCL). It is apparently a difficulty common to complaint systems in this field, for the same opinion was expressed by the Australian Inspector-General.[127]

Even granting this, and coupling it with the statutory fetters, there are still strong grounds for dissatisfaction with the Tribunal's operations, which will come to the fore if factually stronger cases are received. In particular, Wadham's sharp criticism of the Tribunal's procedure is highly pertinent. As he pointed out,[128] it excludes the complainant entirely, does not permit adequate refutation of adverse evidence, since neither he nor his adviser is told what it is, and indeed makes no pretence to be a fair adversarial hearing. In effect it is an inquisitorial proceeding in which decisions are taken on the papers. He described the Tribunal as 'useless', and looks to Strasbourg as the sole forum for possible redress.[129] Under such circumstances, it would be entirely premature to conclude that the failure of any complainant to prevail before the Tribunal is reliable evidence of the Security Service's good conduct. This is less a reflection on the Service than an illustration of a more general point: failure to establish a fair and trustworthy means to investigate complaints may taint an organization in circumstances in which a credible system might have vindicated it and even enhanced its legitimacy in the public mind.

More concretely, in so far as the government believed that by creating these new structures it would reassure the public that all is well, it seriously miscalculated. It began with a Staff Counsellor acting as internal confessor and conduit

---

[125] pp. 153–56 above.   [126] Above n. 92, para. 7.
[127] *Annual Report 1990–91* (n. 39 above), 6.   [128] See also above, p. 434.
[129] None the less an aggrieved person must utilize the Tribunal, for the Convention (Art. 26) requires that domestic remedies be exhausted. Reliance on the Convention may be optimistic: we are grateful to Mr Wadham for the information that a further complaint brought by Harman and Hewitt following their unsuccessful applications to the Tribunal and to the High Court (n. 117 above) was declared inadmissable by the Commission of Human Rights in October 1993.

to higher ministerial authority, whose existence remains obscure. It then added the combination of Commissioner and Tribunal for, in the Home Secretary's unwittingly revealing phrase, 'aggrieved outsiders'.[130] As to them, Gill's conclusion seems irrefutable: 'It is clear that this structure . . . has been constructed neither for elegance nor for impact.'[131] Nor, *a fortiori*, for allaying concern.

The executive branch, though dominant (especially in Britain), does not have the field entirely to itself, however. Significant developments of models of accountability to the legislature have also occurred. We examine these in the following chapter.

[130] Douglas Hurd, MP, quoted in P. Gill, *Policing Politics* (London, 1994), 291. Mr Hurd was referring to those not permitted access to matters classified secret, but the reference to ordinary citizens as 'outsiders' none the less speaks volumes about the outlook of the political élite.

[131] Ibid., 295.

16

Legislative Accountability

BRITAIN

The democratic instinct is to look to Parliament and especially to the House of Commons—the eighteenth century 'grand inquest of the nation' and the twentieth century forum for popular representation—to take on the task of superintending the Security Service and other government bodies whose actions may threaten citizens' freedoms. After all, the argument runs, if Parliament cannot protect what used proudly (if xenophobically) to be known as 'English liberty', who can, or indeed would have the desire to? Though we share the impulse behind it, we must question whether this instinct is misdirected. At the deepest level, it may mistake the fundamental purpose of Parliament, which David Judge has persuasively argued is representation of opinion—'the transmission of opinion between "the political nation" and the governors'—and thereby the legitimation of executive power.[1] The idea of Parliament as a 'check' on the executive may therefore be simply misconceived.[2] However, even if it be assumed that in a professedly democratic era Parliament can to any significant extent maintain the adversary relationship to the executive that the notion of 'checking' implies, there are other, more mundane, reasons to doubt the effectiveness of a Parliamentary body as an institution of direct oversight.

Perhaps the most traditional method is by debate and questions on the floor of the House of Commons. However, dissatisfaction with the Parliamentary treatment of intelligence and security matters is long-standing. Recent years, though, have seen a discernible loosening of attitudes in Parliamentary debate of security matters. Whereas Sir Anthony Eden claimed to be 'appalled' that a debate on a motion to reduce the Navy estimates should have been held following the disappearance of Commander Crabbe on an unauthorized surveillance mission in 1956,[3] Mrs Thatcher broke new ground in not only making statements on the Blunt, Hollis, and Oldfield cases but also, in the first two instances, in answering questions.[4] This trend has been continued under Mr Major's administration, not only with the public naming of the Director-General of MI5, but also with Parliamentary statements about MI5 responsibility for

[1] D. Judge, *The Parliamentary State* (London, 1993), 6 and more generally ch. 1.
[2] Judge also emphasizes (ibid. 27) that 'since the 13th century the British state has favoured a strong executive'—a tradition established longer than anywhere else in Europe.
[3] *HC Debs.*, vol. 552, col. 1751, 1764 (14 May 1956).
[4] Ibid., vol. 973, col. 1679 (15 Nov. 1979); vol. 20, col. 1079 (26 Mar. 1981).

counter-terrorism[5], and acknowledging the existence and role of MI6.[6] Nevertheless, Parliamentary Questions on security matters may still be out of order for one of two reasons. Erskine May records that 'there are certain matters, of their nature secret, relating to the secret services and to security, and questions on these matters are not in order'.[7] However, the Clerk of the House of Commons has indicated that 'in practice questions which mention the security or intelligence services but which do not seek information about individuals or operations are allowed'.[8] Questions are now regularly accepted by the Table Office under this more relaxed view.[9] Questions may also be debarred if they 'fall within a class of questions which a Minister has refused to answer'.[10] The list includes many defence and security related issues and traditionally MPs have been allowed a single attempt in each Parliament to loosen the ministerial tongue on such long-standing 'undiscussables'. Even if a particular question passes these hurdles, Ministers have unfettered discretion in deciding how to reply. Consequently, and despite recent moves to greater openness, it is all too easy for ministers to slip back behind the national security shield to cover political embarrassment: as the Prime Ministerial refusals to answer questions during the 'Spycatcher' affair[11] and over the Matrix Churchill case[12] well illustrate.

Accountability to Parliament as a whole (that is, apart from the committees discussed later in this chapter) is more comprehensive in both Canada and Australia due to the greater information about the CSIS and ASIO made available, either under statutory provisions or by administrative practice. The relevant reports are more informative in every way than the terse documents tabled in Britain each year by the Commissioners under the Interception of Communications Act 1985 and the Security Services Act 1989.[13] In Australia the legislation requires an annual report from ASIO to be tabled in Parliament by the Attorney-General (after deletions on security grounds), with an unedited version being shown to the Leader of the Opposition.[14] The bare statistics speak for themselves: the published report for 1990–1 runs to 121 pages and, after describing the constitutional framework, discusses the organization's management structure and recent management initiatives, strategic issues which occu-

---

[5] *HC Debs.*, vol. 207, cols. 297–8 (8 May 1992).   [6] Ibid., vol. 207, col. 65 (6 May 1992).

[7] Erskine May, *Parliamentary Practice* (20th edn., London, 1983), 343.

[8] See *First Report from the Committee of Privileges, Session 1986–87*, HC 365, paras. 37–9 and Annex D.

[9] *First Report from the Home Affairs Select Committee, Accountability of the Security Service*, HC (1992–3) 265, paras. 6 and 7.

[10] Erskine May (n. 7 above), 342.

[11] See esp. *HC Debs.*, vol. 105, col. 436 (18 Nov. 1986) and vol. 115, col. 163 (28 Apr. 1986).

[12] e.g. refusing to comment on how many of the defendants were assisting MI5 and MI6 on the grounds that 'it would be contrary to normal practice to comment further on intelligence matters' (*HC Debs.*, vol. 214, col. 746 (26 Nov. 1992)), despite the evidence given about these contacts in open session the trial (see further Ch. 11 above).

[13] Each Act provides for deletions on security grounds from the published versions: ICA, s. 8(8); SSA, s. 4(7).

[14] ASIO Act 1979, s. 94; before this provision was amended in 1986 it merely required the report to be shown to the Leader of the Opposition, who was then duty-bound to keep it secret.

pied its time in the preceding year, the types of measures taken to fulfil different aspects of its mandate (including statistics on responses to requests for threat assessments, security assessments on individuals for migration and employment purposes, and other types of protective security advice), budget, and staffing details. In Canada much of same detail has been available on CSIS since 1985 indirectly through SIRC's published annual reports.[15] The Canadian Parliament has also attempted to achieve more direct accountability to it on security matters and, despite the opposition of the government, has won some concessions.[16] The Parliamentary Committee conducting the statutory five-year review of the CSIS Act recommended that a permanent subcommittee of the House of Commons Standing Committee on Justice be established to deal with security and intelligence matters,[17] with the intention both of going behind SIRC reports (it proposed that a version of the annual report of CSIS to the Solicitor General be tabled in Parliament)[18] and of examining agencies other than CSIS. In response the government argued that it would be premature to establish the subcommittee but, nevertheless, offered to make available an annual statement on security issues together with an annual report from CSIS.[19] The Canadian Parliament refused to be deflected and established the subcommittee in 1991, with the intention of reviewing not merely CSIS, but also the CSE, and the security aspects of the RCMP's role. The subcommittee will attempt to follow up aspects of the five-year review, and will examine the annual reports from SIRC and CSIS and the annual security statement. It is too early to assess its performance, but both the determination and the government's willingness to give ground might well be borne in mind in Britain as Parliament once again faces up to the government in the debates over the proposed Secret Intelligence Service legislation.[20]

There are also several reasons to doubt the 'checking' capability of Parliament; reasons unconnected with the demands of security and intelligence, but deriving rather from the nature of parliamentarians as active politicians or political animals. As one Canadian MP said, 'there are no votes in security',[21] meaning that it is not an area from which party advantage or personal recognition can be gained.

[15] As required under the CSIS Act 1984, s. 53; SIRC must consult with the Director of CSIS about security deletions: ibid., s. 55.

[16] S. Farson, 'Oversight of Canadian Intelligence: A Revisionary Note' [1992] *PL* 377, 379–83.

[17] Report of the Special Committee on the Review of the CSIS Act and the Security Offences Act, *In Flux But Not in Crisis* (Ottawa, 1990), ch. 14.

[18] Ibid. 91. The review committee had been generally unhappy about its inability to obtain certain categories of information on CSIS. See S. Farson, 'Problems of Political Oversight: Difficulties Encountered by the Special Committee During Parliament's Five-Year Review of the CSIS Act' (unpublished paper prepared for the annual conference of the Canadian Association of Security and Intelligence Studies, 1991).

[19] Solicitor General Canada, *On Course: National Security for the 1990s* (Ottawa, 1991), ch. 10.

[20] See Coda.

[21] These comments, and other remarks attributed to MPs, emerged in interviews with Blaine Thacker, Chairman of the Review Committee and a Progressive Conservative; Derek Lee, Liberal; and John Brewin of the NDP.

Hence when compared with analogous matters like defence or foreign policy, it is relatively low in the pecking order and unlikely to engage the long-time attention of an able and/or ambitious MP. This exacerbates the normal problem of turnover which afflicts parliamentary committees generally, depriving them of the expertise which members gain only after several years of immersion in the subject. There is also an unfortunate tendency—to which MPs will admit in private discussions, but which seems to be an occupational affliction—towards 'playing to the gallery' or 'grandstanding': saying or doing things with an eye to media publicity rather than in an effort to make a genuine contribution. Two political scientists who have studied earlier attempts at parliamentary accountability in the field of defence have noted the related phenomenon that 'British legislators tend to prefer the role of the political magpie . . . prefer[ring] to be free to jump from one issue to another as it enters the political agenda and win popular and peer support by appearing to be all things to all men'.[22]

A closely related problem is that of partisan point-scoring and rigidity, both of which derive from the need to maintain the Government's, Opposition's, or an individual MP's hold on or chance for office by discrediting those on the other side. In such an atmosphere, changing one's mind on the basis of new information or simply taking a fresh look is more readily portrayed as being indecisive rather than thoughtful. Members from all three parties of the CSIS Act Review Committee [23] emphasized that their effort, which produced a large number of recommendations which were almost all unanimous, was unusual in avoiding these problems. Lack of political pressure, absence of members with highly polarized or high-profile views, and a deliberate effort to achieve consensus in order to maximize the impact of the Report were offered as explanations. These factors are unlikely to be ever-present when a body with a shifting membership exists on a permanent basis. And even this Committee found that there are a variety of means which can be used to frustrate a parliamentary body's work. Much the most important are control over time and over information; parliaments remain critically dependent on the willingness of those they seek to hold accountable to make themselves and information about their activities available to them.[24]

Finally, it should be emphasized that the 'expertise' of parliamentarians can be too readily exaggerated, because their job allows them only a limited time to devote to any particular subject, even if they are given that brief for an extended period. The only practical answer is to ensure the provision of adequate support staff. With one significant exception,[25] this has been denied to the select com-

[22] A. Cox and S. Kirby, *Congress, Parliament and Defence* (Basingstoke, 1986), 299.

[23] This body was established pursuant to a provision written into the Act requiring review of its workings after five years, to report within one year (s. 56). Its Report was that cited in n. 17 above.

[24] We draw here on the account and reflections of the Research Director of the Review Committee: S. Farson, 'Parliament's Capacity to Conduct a Comprehensive Review: Weak Link in the Chain of Accountability?' (unpubl., 1991). We thank Dr Farson for providing a copy of this paper.

[25] This is the Public Accounts Committee, discussed below, pp. 464–65.

mittees of the British Parliament, which have had to make do with a tightly rationed number of permanent staff and to rely on the interest and goodwill of academic and other expert contributors on particular subjects. This is one of the most important practical means by which the executive keeps parliament at bay, and is not an advantage it will surrender lightly.

A committee on security matters raises particular difficulties, because the agencies will be chary of co-operating unless their fears about leaks can be allayed. In Australia and the United States, where legislative committees do exist, vetting elected representatives is regarded as unacceptable in principle, but there is a corresponding insistence on careful scrutiny of committee staffers. Also telling is the view that membership on such a committee could compromise the work of an MP. Participation entails respect for the secrecy of the information received, and the MP who is dissatisfied with the picture that emerges is placed in an impossible position. He or she cannot offer public criticism supported by reasoned argument without violating that condition; and this silence can then be readily misinterpreted, or deliberately misrepresented, as approval. And if criticisms or dissatisfaction aired *in camera* are ignored by the security agency, the MP lacks the normal means of generating pressure by means of public campaigning and media publicity. These restrictions may be acceptable for a priest hearing confession, but they negate the function of a public representative. They can become co-optation with a vengeance.

Britain has had considerable experience with parliamentary select committees in other fields, and the results do not provide much basis for optimism about what they can be expected to accomplish. In the immediate aftermath of their reform in 1979 they generated a great deal of interest, but as the novelty wore off they came to be seen as having a very modest impact on government policy, with perhaps somewhat more on administrative practices.[26] Their reports have also made available to the public considerably more information about certain matters than government had been willing to surrender previously; however, this is the one function it is certain they cannot serve in the field of security and intelligence. Indeed the first committee inquiry that even came close to this area—into police Special Branches—resolved not to hear what it could not publish, held public hearings only, and produced an unilluminating and anodyne Report.[27]

Moreover, and again with the Public Accounts Committee as the exception, the reconstituted committees all track the departmental organization of Whitehall, shadowing one particular ministry. This raises allocation difficulties in relation to any fringe organization (and perhaps also the new 'Next Steps' Agencies) for which no minister is, in the classic sense, responsible. These can be surmounted by *ad hoc* decisions, but more intractable is the problem of

[26] See G. Drewry (ed.), *The New Select Committees* (2nd edn., Oxford, 1989); D. Englefield (ed.), *Commons Select Committees: Catalysts for Progress?* (Harlow, 1984).

[27] 'Special Branch', *Home Affairs Committee, Fourth Report*, HC 71 (1984–5).

activities which cross organizational boundaries. Different aspects of security and intelligence—severable to make them operationally manageable but ultimately requiring to be kneaded together—regularly involve the Home Office, Foreign Office, Treasury, and the Ministry of Defence (and, increasingly, others such as the Department of Trade and Industry); the Prime Minister; and the three main agencies. A departmentally based committee simply cannot come to terms with this structure. The best that can be expected is a committee limited to MI5, MI6, and GCHQ, but even that approach—treating a subject as a whole (functionally) rather than by organizational demarcation—would be radical indeed.

Yet there is reason to believe that even such a step, undertaken by a parliamentary committee, is likely to be of limited effect. A detailed study of parliamentary scrutiny of defence came to a number of depressing conclusions, which require consideration at some length. It examined the experience of the late 1960s and 1970s, when the Defence and External Affairs Select Committee (DEASC) was able to combine consideration of both foreign threat and the means used to counter it—a synoptic view denied its successors, which are divided between foreign relations and defence with the twain seldom meeting.[28]

The DEASC, they argue, failed to scrutinize value for money effectively, and also failed in the more ambitious aspiration of controlling executive policymaking. Although it provided more information to Parliament and the public, it had access only to material the executive wished to make available.

Overall, however, the committee appeared to have had little impact in those areas of scrutiny and control of the Executive which generated the demand for the parliamentary reforms in the first place—perhaps the perfect example of this was the complete failure of the DEASC to notice [*sic*] the £1 billion programme being undertaken on the Chevaline enhancement of Polaris.[29]

Among the most important reasons for this failure were 'lack of independent information and dependence on MOD "goodwill"',[30] along with the almost complete absence of support staff. Moreover, there were determined and successful efforts by the Whips to control membership on the DEASC. Labour in particular were at pains to exclude those on the Left who might challenge the strongly consensual, bipartisan orientation of the Committee. This even took the extreme form of vetting prospective members,[31] a treatment of elected representatives that would not be tolerated elsewhere.[32] It is virtually certain that a similar attempt to exclude potential 'troublemakers' would, at least initially, ensure a

---

[28] Cox and Kirby (n. 22 above), 169–170. A subsequent review of the performance of the reconstituted Defence Committee in 1979–83 did nothing to disturb the conclusions of this more intensive study. See R. Borthwick, 'The Defence Committee', in Drewry (above n. 26), Ch. 4.

[29] Cox and Kirby (n. 22 above), 165. See also Ch. 1, n. 102.

[30] Ibid. 169. The parallel between this analysis and that of Stuart Farson (above n. 24) based on Canadian experience is very striking.

[31] Ibid. 168, 297–8. This vetting was undertaken in collaboration with the MOD, Cabinet Office, Whips' Office and the Chief Clerk's Office in the Commons.

[32] See preceding page.

bland conformity in any parliamentary committee established in the security field. It is difficult to fault the conclusion that 'creating new committees in Parliament without transforming the relationship betweeen executive and legislature is an exercise in futility'.[33]

Parliamentary committees have been described as having three possible roles. These are legal and managerial, which together concern themselves with aspects of expenditure, and strategic, which concerns policy.[34] We have doubted their effectiveness in discharging the latter. And the history of Parliament's efforts to exercise oversight of expenditure of security agencies is a tale of even more demonstrable failure.

Financial Control[35]

Although the House of Commons has prided itself on pre-eminent control of the public finances this is more a statement of its dominance over the unelected House than over the executive. Controls over the executive in this realm are weak and can be summarized in the cursory exercise in approving the raising of revenue (the budget), approval of estimates for expenditure on government service, and, after the event, the more thorough scrutiny of the Public Accounts Committee and the Comptroller and Auditor General. Where security-related expenditure is concerned even these controls are further diluted.[36]

The importance of control over expenditure is shown by the history of the secret vote.[37] The historical evidence now released for the period up to the end of the nineteenth century strikingly demonstrates both the advantages (to the authorities) and the dangers (to the public) in the lack of independent scrutiny. The history of the Secret Service Fund is one of scandal and abuse: with the fund being used for bribery in the eighteenth century, especially of both domestic and foreign politicians, and for the payment of informants, both at home and abroad.[38] The abuses were such that Parliament legislated against them in the Civil List and Secret Service Money Act 1782.[39] The Act limited domestic expenditure from the Civil List for the purposes of the secret service to £10,000

---

[33] n. 22 above, 309. [34] Ibid. 40–1.

[35] For an extremely valuable survey of the control of the finances of the intelligence agencies in the period 1900–45 see E. O'Halpin, 'Financing British Intelligence: The Evidence up to 1945', in K. Robertson (ed.), *British and American Approaches to Intelligence* (London, 1987).

[36] For a general account, see C. Turpin, *Government Procurement and Contracts* (London, 1989), ch. 2, esp. in this context 32–5.

[37] See O'Halpin (n. 35 above); C. Andrew, *Secret Service* (London, 1986), 22–7; J. F. McEldowney, 'Legal Aspects of the Irish Secret Service Fund' (1986) 25 *Ir. Hist. Studs.* 129.

[38] Andrew (previous note), 22–4. Fresh evidence of abuses was revealed when files including a ledger entitled 'Secret Service Accounts' (dealing with payments from 1826 to 1882) were released in July 1993; these included an agreement to pay Reuters news agency £500 p.a. from 1894 to 1898 in return for intelligence: *The Times*, 16 July 1993.

[39] 22 Geo. III. c. 82.

per annum.[40] The continued charging of this money to the Civil List rather than to the Consolidated Fund was perhaps symptomatic of early royal abuse: Charles II's mistresses were maintained on Secret Service money, and in the next century the King used it as a way of buying support among MPs', with the Prime Minister as chief paymaster. However, the Civil List stratagem succeed in deflecting political controversy, which may explain why the charge was not transferred to the Consolidated Fund until 1837. Foreign Secret Service money was not cash-limited, but the Act tightened the procedures for accounting back to the Treasury on its use:[41] ambassadors, consuls, and army and naval officers were obliged to swear an oath of the proper use of the money on their return to the realm. In the case of money expended on 'detecting, preventing or defeating treasonable or other dangerous conspiracies' at home, the controls were looser, no doubt because of the sensitivity of the topic, it being sufficient that a minister swear an oath that the money had been used for this purpose.[42]

Freedom from financial scrutiny has enabled the authorities to create new intelligence agencies without Parliamentary sanction or knowledge. This was the case with the embryonic code-breaking agency (the Decyphering Branch) run from 1703 to 1844 and financed from the Secret Service Fund.[43] The same facility proved useful at the foundation of the Special Branch.[44] When the full papers are available, no doubt the same will prove true of the other current intelligence agencies. On a more contemporary note, Colonel Oliver North proved the usefulness to an intelligence agency of having access to funds beyond the reach, control, or knowledge of its legislative masters in mounting covert operations in El Salvador (circumventing an express Congressional veto), financed by secret arms sales to Iran.[45] The same desire to be free of political restraint is shown by the First World War plan, unearthed by O'Halpin, to invest a million pounds in trust as an endowment for the secret services against feared reductions in budget in the event of a post-war Labour government being returned.[46]

Some security related expenditure is disclosed in the Secret Service Vote, which since 1797 has been included in the annual estimates. In 1992/3 this

[40] 22 Geo. III. c. 82 s. 24. The charge was transferred to the Consolidated Fund by the Civil List Act 1837 (1 and 2 Vict., c. 2), s. 15. With the repeal of the latter provision by the Civil List Act 1901 (1 Edw. 7, c. 4), all mention of a Home Secret Service Fund disappears—several years before the formation of MI5. The heading surviving in the Supply Estimates (see nn. 47 ff. below) derives from the Foreign Secret Service Fund.

[41] S. 26. A modern reference to Secret Service Money appears in the Government of Ireland Act 1920 (10 and 11 Geo. 5, c. 67), sched. 6, which treats it as a part of the expenses of the Foreign Office, to which Northern Ireland is to contribute.

[42] S. 27.   [43] Andrew (n. 37 above), 24–6.

[44] B. Porter, *Origins of the Vigilant State: The London Metropolitan Special Branch Before the First World War* (London, 1987), 18, 41, 85–6.

[45] House Select Committee to Investigate Covert Arms Transactions with Iran and Senate Select Committee on Secret Military Assistance to Iran and the Nicaraguan Opposition, *Report of the Congressional Committees Investigating the Iran–Contra Affair*, S. Rep. No. 216, H. Rep, No. 433 (1986).

[46] See n. 35 above, 208–9 and 212; it is unclear whether the proposal was executed.

stood at £185 million.[47] Estimates do not give other information of finanace expended on intelligence agencies, nor do they explain what the Secret Service money is used for. Although the sum is large, presumably it accounts for only a small proportion of the costs of running GCHQ, MI5, and MI6. It is presumed that other votes are either not declared or are hidden elsewhere in the estimates. Parliament has turned a blind eye to deception in tolerating these practices: traditionally the Secret Service Vote is not debated. Where direct questions have been asked ministers have either feigned ignorance of the use to which the money is put,[48] or more rarely have simply refused to give an account of intelligence expenditure.[49] Our Home Office and Security Service informants also remained silent about the budgetary process, on the constitutionalist ground that, since ministers have thus far refused to say anything, it was not for them 'to break new ground'. Although, judging from the growth (well above inflation) of the Secret Service Vote under the Conservative administrations of 1979–92 the intelligence agencies' budgets did rather well in this period,[50] it is unlikely that they entirely escaped other aspects of the discipline of financial control, but these details are not publicly available. Such scrutiny of their budgets as does take place is by ministers and the Security and Intelligence Secretariat within the Cabinet Office.[51]

The Comptroller and Auditor General is the statutory watchdog over expenditure of government departments, ensuring both that money is spent on the purposes for which Parliament granted it and that value for money has been obtained. The office is an independent one and works hand in hand with the Public Accounts Committee of the House of Commons, which considers the resulting reports. However, this system is circumscribed in the security realm: the Comptroller's jurisdiction does not run to the budgets of the intelligence agencies (nor does the PAC consider these) or the use of the Secret Service

[47] *Supply Estimates*, 1992/3, HC 273–xix, Class XIX, Vote 3. Until 1984–5 the Supply Estimate in which the Secret Service Vote appeared was entitled "Other External Relations: Secret Service (Cabinet Office)'. It now appears as 'Cabinet Office: Secret Service'. What the change signifies is hard to discern: it may simply reflect the fact that the Cabinet Office is responsible for accounting for the vote in practice.

[48] O'Halpin (n. 35 above), 192–5; T. Bunyan, *The Political Police in Britain* (London, 1977), 158.

[49] e.g. during the Zircon affair, *HC Debs.*, vol. 109, cols. 130–2w (26 Jan. 1987).

[50] One former Chancellor of the Exchequer has written: 'in general the security services escaped the rigours of the Thatcher era': N. Lawson, *The View From No. 11* (London, 1993), 314.

[51] The process is described in a recent official publication: *Central Intelligence Machinery* (London, 1993), 17. Initial scrutiny of the intelligence agencies' Expenditure Forecasts is by civil servants. An advisory committee ('the Preliminary Committee'), chaired by the Intelligence Co-ordinator, makes recommendations to the Permanent Secretaries' Committee on the Intelligence Services ('PSIS'), which in turn examines the proposals as part of the annual Public Expenditure Survey. The agencies' plans, together with PSIS comments, are submitted to ministers for approval. Bearing in mind the arrangements for defence expenditure, it seems unlikely that the full Cabinet has access to the figures. Lord Lawson claims that prior to 1986 only the 'block budget' for the MoD rather than the detail was made known to the Chancellor, and that after 1986 only six civil servants and ministers knew the details: ibid. 313–14. This suggests that similar arrangements would apply to the intelligence and security budgets.

Vote. In 1887 the Comptroller and Auditor General refused to certify expenditure on the Secret Service Vote, having no means of checking its accuracy. Accordingly, the PAC agreed that in future the responsible minister should submit a certificate that the monies had been properly expended 'in the interests of the public service'. The Committee considered that such a certificate 'answers all reasonable Parliamentary requirements . . . considering the nature of the service on which expenditure is incurred'.[52] Even where the Comptroller has power to investigate and report—for instance, in relation to defence projects—he has exercised self restraint about publishing details in the interests of national security, although not formally required to do so.[53]

O'Halpin's conclusion on the period up to 1945 could stand unchanged today:

Because of the secrecy surrounding intelligence finance, prevention of abuses was the responsibility of civil servants, upon whose probity and sense of constitutionality parliament had to rely absolutely . . . However it is clear that civil servants could exercise only very limited control over the use to which money given to the intelligence services was put.[54]

What are the alternatives to blind trust of this kind? In Britain scrutiny of sensitive expenditure has been developed furthest in the field of defence research and procurement, which shares many of the same problems of accountability as expenditure on intelligence. The dilemma was summarized by the Defence Select Committee:

Public expenditure on defence poses particular problems for Parliamentary accountability. On the one hand, the sums of money involved are very large; on the other hand, the effectiveness of the expenditure may depend on a degree of secrecy. Major programmes whose very existence should be kept secret are rare. However, there can be no doubt that detailed information about defence spending plans, particularly in respect of development and purchase of new equipment, gives indications of capability and intentions which could be of great assistance to a potential aggressor.[55]

Earlier arrangements for reporting expenditure had allowed a project totalling £1,000 million over seven years (the Chevaline improvements to the Polaris missile system) to go unreported to Parliament, hidden in global figures on defence expenditure appearing in the estimates. Following this episode, agreement was reached with the Ministry of Defence for notifying the Defence Select

---

[52] *Epitome of the Reports from the Committee of Public Accounts, 1857 to 1937*, HC 154 (1938), 203. The Comptroller accordingly now merely certifies of money expended under the Secret Service Vote that 'the amounts shown in the above account to have been expended are supported by certificates from the responsible Ministers of the Crown'. This is in place of the normal wording, applicable to other votes, that in his opinion 'the sums expended have been applied for the purposes authorised by Parliament and the Account properly presents the expenditure and receipts . . . for the year.'

[53] *Ninth Report of the Public Accounts Committee*, 1981–2, HC 269, app. 1, para. 11.

[54] See n. 35 above, 212.

[55] *First Report from the Defence Committee for 1986–87*, HC 340, para. 1.

Committee and the Public Accounts Committee of major research and development projects under the so-called Chevaline guidelines.[56] These require projects where the anticipated costs are £250 million or the project definition costs are £10 million to be disclosed in the annual Major Projects Statement (MPS) to the Committees. The MPS is classified as 'Confidential/Commercial in Confidence'. However, it contains only bland details of overall sums and not of the phasing of expenditure

Where the existence of a defence project is itself a secret, accountability is more problematic. There was an understanding that details could be withheld from the PAC for reasons of national security, but that the Comptroller and Auditor General would consult with the chairman of that Committee about the making of a report.[57] The difficulties were highlighted by the public debate over the (now cancelled) Zircon satellite project which, despite estimated development costs of £500 million, was not included in the MPS, nor was the Chairman of the PAC informed of its existence. Following a confidential briefing from the Ministry of Defence, the Defence Committee decided, for undisclosed reasons, that the Chevaline guidelines had not been broken. Nevertheless, following this episode agreement was reached for more detailed notification about defence projects in a Defence Equipment Project Report. In view of the more detailed information, problems over secrecy were anticipated. The Ministry of Defence's proposal that highly classified projects should, exceptionally, not be declared in the Report was rejected by the PAC. The Committee, nevertheless, claimed to be 'prepared to consider sympathetically requests for deletions on grounds of national security or commercial sensitivity; or, wherever possible, the rounding of figures to achieve the same end'.[58] The Committee proposed that the requirements of formal parliamentary accountability and secrecy could be reconciled by the reporting of top secret projects to the Chairman and two other members: this would formally constitute declaring the projects to a quorum of the Committee under the rules of the House of Commons.[59] Administrative procedures for ensuring secrecy (for instance, the retention of all papers within the Ministry of Defence), could be made, consistent with these arrangements.[60]

According to a report which was transparently the result of official briefing and which appeared in the *The Times*[61] at the height of the 1993 'silly season', new arrangements are to be announced for scrutiny of the budgets of MI5, MI6, and GCHQ. The purpose is an attempt to ensure 'value for money'. This (non-statutory) arrangement will involve the Comptroller and Auditor General being given access to the agencies' general accounts: this access will exclude detail on

---

[56] For the background to the adoption of this procedure see *Ninth Report* (n. 53 above), paras. 15–20.

[57] Ibid., app. 1; Turpin (n. 36 above), 34.   [58] *First Report* (n. 55 above), para. 28.

[59] Consequently, a member who leaked details could be disciplined by the House of Commons for contempt of Parliament.

[60] *First Report* (n. above), paras. 29–33.   [61] *The Times*, 23 Aug. 1993.

particular operations and techniques. It appears that the fiction of the Secret Vote is also to be ended, suggesting that the government intends publicly to declare overall figures for expenditure on security and intelligence in the Estimates, although the newspaper report gave no details of proposals for Parliamentary scrutiny of the budgets.[62] This (non-)announcement followed signs of growing discontent in Parliament. The Home Affairs Select Committee cited the inadequacy of parliamentary scrutiny of intelligence budgets in support of its claim to scrutinize MI5.[63] The Foreign Affairs Select Committee has been critical of expenditure on the new headquarters for MI6.[64]

In Canada, where Parliament's knowledge of intelligence expenditure has been only slightly fuller (CSIS's budget is disclosed in the Estimates but only as an overall figure),[65] a Special Parliamentary Committee has recommended that among the functions of a security and intelligence subcommittee should be review of intelligence and security budgets.[66] In Australia slightly fuller accounts appear as part of ASIO's Annual Reports to Parliament.[67] In the climate of increased openness surrounding the intelligence services, financial acountability is a topic which deserves urgent attention in Britain also.

Parliament and Operational Review

To this dismal record in matters of management and policy, in recent years British parliamentary committees have added an attempt a new form of oversight: that of investigating a particular episode, in an attempt to reach a factual determination and allocate responsibility. The much-analysed Defence Select Committee investigation into the government's actions during the Westland affair underscored their abject position in the face of a determined executive: testimony of civil servants who might have contradicted ministers' accounts was withheld; those who did appear refused to provide much of the information requested.[68] More recently, however, the Trade and Industry Select Committee

---

[62] The Labour Party has proposed that the Public Accounts Committee should have access to the accounts of the intelligence agencies: Labour Party, *Freedom and the Security Services* (London, 1983), 68.

[63] First Report from the Home Affairs Committee, *The Accountability of the Security Service*, HC (1992–3) 265, para. 13; the Home Secretary suggested in evidence that he had no objection to the PAC examining individual items of expenditure 'from time to time': ibid., Minutes of Evidence, p. 8.

[64] Foreign Affairs Committee, *Fourth Report for 1992–93*, HC (1992–3) 562, paras. 5–7; and see the *Independent*, 26 and 27 July 1993.

[65] *In Flux But Not in Crisis* (n. 17 above), 191.

[66] Ibid. 193–4. The proposal to establish a subcommittee was rejected in the Government's response (*On Course* (n. 19 above), ch. 10).

[67] See n. 14 above.

[68] *'Westland plc: The Government's Decision-making'*, Defence Committee, Fourth Report, HC 519 (1985–6); see R. Austin and D. Oliver, 'The Westland Affair' (1987) 40 *Parl. Aff.* 20. Note also the remarks of the subsequent Defence Committee Inquiry about 'the constraints on the Select Committees seeking to inquire into matters of this kind, [due to] the absence . . . of papers, and as a result of the current conventions on scrutiny of the intelligence services' (Defence Committee Third Special Report, Papers Relating to the Administration and Policy of the Ministry of Defence in the Case of Colin Wallace, HC 261 (1992–3), 1).

investigation into the state of government knowledge about the Iraqi 'Supergun'[69] came closer than has any previous inquiry[70] to probing a specific intelligence operation. As such it contains a number of lessons of more general application.

Although the Committee did not divide along party lines its work was, nevertheless, subject to stringent outside political pressures: the whole of its investigation was conducted in the shadow of an imminent General Election, although as it transpired that event came later than expected. However the result was severely to curtail the extent of the investigation, with the overriding criterion being to publish *some kind* of report, even if many leads remained uninvestigated, before the election. A minority of members wished to postpone publication of the report in order to explore fresh evidence, but it is by no means clear that it would have resurfaced in the next Parliament had they been successful. A minority of the Conservative members would, perhaps, have liked to have obstructed publication of the report entirely in view of the obvious discomfort it would cause the government. Some horse-trading was necessary on the Committee's internal priorities (for instance, agreeing to an unrelated overseas visit for some members) in order to ensure overall, if slower, progress.

The Committee suffered several difficulties over getting access to appropriate evidence. First, it was denied direct access to intelligence officers serving in the principal intelligence agencies. Since one key allegation was that these agencies had knowledge of Iraqi intentions even while other departments were granting export licences, this necessarily inhibited the investigation. As a substitute, it was agreed that the Committee would be allowed to interview an intelligence specialist, who was a Ministry of Defence metallurgist. He appeared before the Committee under what was possibly an assumed name and parts of his evidence were given with 'strangers' excluded. In addition, one of the other witnesses the Committee interviewed (Stephan Kock), ostensibly because of his involvement in the complicated commercial arrangements surrounding the Supergun order, was known to have intelligence connections.

Evidence was also denied from two other major sources. An MP (Sir Hal Miller) who had alleged on the floor of the House of Commons that he had contacted government departments and an intelligence agency with details of the orders, inexplicably refused to give evidence. This presented the Committee with a tactical difficulty to which much (private) discussion was devoted—the allegation was the reason why the investigation had commenced in the first place, but a House of Commons resolution would be required in order to compel the

---

[69] Trade and Industry Committee, Second Report, *Exports to Iraq: Project Babylon and Long Range Guns*, HC 86 (1991–2); we are grateful to Jim Cousins, MP for an interview on the Committee's work. See also I. Leigh, 'Matrix Churchill, Supergun and the Scott Inquiry', *PL*, Winter 1993.

[70] See also M. Phythian and W. Little, 'Parliament and Arms Sales: Lessons of the Matrix Churchill Affair' (1993) *Parl. Aff.* 293. For surveys of earlier reports of select committees in the security realm, see G. Drewry [1984] *PL* 370; I. Leigh and L. Lustgarten, 'The Security Service Act 1989' (1989) 52 *MLR* 801, 818–9.

attendance of an MP. The decision not to attempt to compel attendance was taken because it was felt that a motion of this kind would be defeated by the Government, while the debate on the motion would pre-empt and dilute the force of the Committee's final report. Customs and Excise also refused to give details of what their investigation had uncovered, although in the light of subsequent events in the Matrix Churchill affair[71] this is perhaps more readily explicable as a genuine assertion of prosecutorial independence than as anything more sinister.

In view of the much greater detail about the extent of government knowledge that became available through release of documents at the Matrix Churchill trial, it would be easy to claim that the Select Committee was a signal failure in exposing the evidence. This comment should, however, be qualified in two respects. First, many of the later revelations were made possible because of the earlier work of the Committee, especially in amassing unglamorous evidence about the treatment of hundreds of export licence applications. Secondly, some of the more politically damaging evidence had been released to the Committee, but its significance was apparently not appreciated.[72] It should also be noted, although the details cannot be catalogued, that at least some members of the Committee were given private information and drew on work of investigative journalists as a source of lines of inquiry.

The process of drawing up the Report was also heavily tactical. A bare reading of it suggests conclusions which were muted in view of some of the evidence. It is clear, though, that Opposition members compromised on the wording they would have preferred in order to achieve a majority for a report that could be agreed and published. The Committee confined itself to stating its serious concerns over the accountability of the intelligence services to Parliament. What subsequently appeared as wilful deception in the execution of government policy over export licences was attributed to lack of co-ordination between the different departments. Departments were criticized for failing fully to inform mininsters.[73] The record of the Committee's proceedings clearly shows a political battle (although not always exactly on party lines) over the inclusion of each critical comment in the final Report. However, even where wording apparently consistent with the evidence was omitted, members of the

---

[71] Where the Customs and Excise decision to prosecute inevitably led other government departments into acute public embarrassment over their knowledge of the true purpose of exports to Iraq in the same period.

[72] For instance, evidence from the Foreign Office detailed the revision of the 'Howe Guidelines' on the export of equipment following the cease-fire in the Iran–Iraq war, but because the Committee was primarily concerned with lethal weapons (rather than dual technology machinery, such as machine tools) it failed fully to explore this.

[73] Ironically this arose from an exchange in which Alan Clark, the Defence Procurement Minister, expressed himself 'not entirely' satisfied that he had been kept fully informed: (n. 69 above), para. 109. It was Mr Clark's own evidence at the Matrix Churchill trial of his connivance at relaxation of the Howe Guidelines which led to the abandonment of the prosecution: see D. Leigh, *Betrayed: The Real Story of the Matrix Churchill Trial* (London, 1993), ch. 11.

Committee were working on the understanding that this part of their discussions would also be published. Hence, one tactic was to 'get material on the record' and, therefore, published, even if not endorsed by the majority, without lessening the impact of the Report as a whole by formally producing minority recommendations. The publication of the Report was itself constrained by a highly unusual set of circumstances: Parliament had been prorogued and members of the Committee were inhibited in commenting because they had been informed that they were no longer protected by Parliamentary privilege.

The most obvious conclusion from this experience is that short term political considerations may decisively impinge on a Select Committee's work to the detriment of effective scrutiny and accurate reporting. The Supergun inquiry was unusual because of the proximity of the election, but party pressures of one type or another are not merely symptomatic of Westminister, but dominant within it. Despite the obvious appeal of Select Committees from an idealized democratic perspective, when taken together with the limitations on obtaining evidence, we regard this objection as compelling.

We began this extended analysis of legislative accountability in Britain by expressing some theoretically grounded doubts about the value of primary reliance on Parliament and its committees as the forum for oversight of executive institutions generally, and of security agencies *a fortiori*. A review of actual experience has done little to alleviate them. At the end of 1992 the House of Commons Home Affairs Committee recommended that it take over responsibility for scrutiny of the Security Service.[74] The government's response, understandably enough, was to remain wholly non-committal and put the matter in suspension until it tables the long-promised Bill to put SIS and GCHQ on a statutory footing, when the 'the opportunity for full debate of all these issues will arise'.[75] Our analysis of the Bill appears in the Coda, in which any developments with respect to the Security Service will also be addressed. Meanwhile, the only example of a working committee in the security field is that found in Australia, to which we now turn.

AUSTRALIA[76]

The establishment of a legislative oversight committee was described independently by interviewees inside and outside government as 'a sop to the Labor Left'. In other words, the Labor Government as a whole was not committed to the idea, which indeed had been explicitly rejected by the Royal Commission

---

[74] 'Accountability of the Security Service', *Home Affairs Committee, First Report*, HC 265 (1992–3).

[75] *Accountability of the Security Service*, Cm. 2197 (1993), para. 8.

[76] See also H. Lee, 'The Australian Security Intelligence Organisation—New Mechanisms for Accountability' (1989) 38 *ICLQ* 890, and F. Cain, 'Accountability and ASIO: A Brief History' in S. Farson *et al.* (eds.), *Security and Intelligence in a Changing World* (London, 1991), 104–25.

whose recommendations strongly influenced the reforms introduced in 1986.[77] However, there was a long history of distrust of ASIO within the Labor Party— which came within one vote of adopting abolition of the Organization as official policy in 1971—fuelled by the publication of a secret annex to Mr Justice Hope's Report revealing that ASIO had been supplying intelligence material about Labor politicians and other Left figures to a right-wing pressure group.[78] Perhaps uniquely in parliamentary democracies, the Australian Labor Party is organized into identified factions, so that a particular MP will be described as of 'the New South Wales Right' or the 'Victorian Left'. The Left faction secured the creation of a Parliamentary committee in the 1986 legislation, but one hedged about with major restrictions on its jurisdiction and powers. Though rare, joint committees (whose members are drawn from the House of Representatives and Senate) have a considerable pedigree in Australia: the Joint Committee on Foreign Affairs and Defence was established in 1952, and one on the National Crime Authority in 1984.[79] The inclusion of Senators allows representation of the Australian Democrats, a small centre party which has never been able to elect any MPs; it also removes some of the discipline of the Whips, which operates much more tightly on MPs than on Senators.

The Committee operates under two major kinds of restriction. The first is that it cannot initiate inquiries on its own. It can act only upon a reference from the Attorney-General (the Minister responsible for ASIO) or upon a motion by either House.[80] The latter is highly unlikely to be passed over government opposition,[81] so essentially the Committee can only act with executive approval.

Secondly, it is forbidden to inquire into certain crucial matters, notably anything that is 'operationally sensitive', which specifically includes anything 'that relates to intelligence collection methods or sources of information'.[82] Hence infiltration, telephone tapping, or other forms of intrusion on privacy, and virtually anything concerning current projects, will be beyond its scope. It is also excluded from examining anything relating to the obtaining or communicating of foreign intelligence by ASIO, which would exclude significant aspects of relations with foreign intelligence organizations.[83]

A cynical view is that these restrictions were included by the Government to

[77] This was the one-man Commission consisting of Mr Justice Hope, whose analysis of mandate was discussed in Ch. 14 above. For his views on a parliamentary committee, see Royal Commission on Australia's Security and Intelligence Services, *Report on ASIO* (Canberra, 1985), ch. 17.

[78] This annex was leaked and published in the *National Times*, a small journal edited by Brian Toohey, a journalist who has long specialized in security matters. See D. Marr, *The Ivanov Trial* (Melbourne, 1984), 15–16, 269.

[79] K. Sibraa, 'Parliamentary Scrutiny of Security and Intelligence Services in Australia', 68 *The Parliamentarian* (1987) 120. The author was then President of the Australian Senate and former Chairman of the Joint Committee on Foreign Affairs and Defence.

[80] ASIO Act, s. 92C(2).

[81] The Government only governs because it commands a majority in the House of Representatives, but it does not necessarily have a majority in the Senate. It is therefore remotely possible that the latter could activate the Joint Committee over the opposition of those in office.

[82] ASIO Act, s. 92C(4)(*c*).   [83] Ibid., s. 92C(4)(*a*).

hobble and/or nobble the Joint Committee at the outset. However, the Opposition fought its creation strongly, and such concessions may have helped to ensure its survival in the long term.[84] In any case a combination of difficulties in obtaining physically secure premises and security clearance for the Secretariat, and the disruption of membership caused by retirements and two federal elections, meant that the Committee was not launched until May 1990. It had to manage without a full-time Secretariat until July 1991. This may in some measure explain why its first inquiry took nearly two years to complete,[85] with public hearings spread out over eleven months. An extended range of individuals and institutions, including ASIO, presented submissions.

The subject was the narrow but important one of how ASIO has been affected by legislation enacted in 1983 requiring that all records of government agencies be lodged in the Australian Archives; the underlying problem being whether this requirement, which is linked to the public access provisions of the Freedom of Information Act, jeopardizes necessary secrecy of ASIO-held material. The Committee produced a unanimous Report,[86] which is well-informed and reflects awareness of the breadth of opinion and information made available to it. Although its first three recommendations were in line with ASIO's position, a number of subsequent ones took a contrary view; there seems no question of it functioning as a rubber-stamp. However, its dependence on the executive was made plain by the fact that the Committee's Presiding Member had to request permission of the Attorney-General to hold public hearings. Approval was granted, but subject to certain conditions.[87] Most of the Report's recommendations were accepted in detail or in principle by the government some months later. The Committee was then asked by the Attorney-General to inquire into the operation of ASIO's security assessment procedures. Prominent issues will include the criteria that are appropriate with the ending of the Cold War, and the entire appeals process, particularly in light of virtual cessation of cases going to the Security Appeals Tribunal.[88]

It clearly would be premature to attempt an evaluation of the work of the Joint Committee. It may serve as a useful forum for gathering and gauging opinion among interested parties, and for developing consensus on matters about which the executive is undecided and which it does not view as vital to any of

[84] For statements from the Opposition, see Sibraa (n. 79 above). Although the policy of abolishing the Joint Committee if elected to office has not been abandoned, Liberal and National Party members are now participating on the Committee.

[85] During this period it also received (and continues to do so) periodic private briefings from ASIO and discussed public issues such as the Queensland Special Branch files (see above, p. 42) with the Acting Director-General. (Information supplied by Ann Hazelton, then Secretary to the Joint Committee, to whom thanks are also due for all the material cited in this section.)

[86] Report of the Parliamentary Joint Committee on ASIO, *ASIO and the Archives Act* (Canberra, 1992); the substance of the recommendation is discussed in Ch. 5 above.

[87] See ibid., app. C, containing the Attorney-General's letter.

[88] Parliamentary Joint Committee, Media Release, undated (Autumn 1992). It is anticipated that the Report will be tabled in November 1993.

its policies or interests. Its major and irremediable weakness, present by design, is its lack of independence from the executive. It cannot take up a matter, regardless of the extent of public dissatisfaction, if the executive wishes to play it down or to cover up misconduct. Moreover, and in notable contrast to the Inspector-General, the Committee can only look at ASIO; none of the other security institutions have been placed within its purview.

If Parliament, for reasons of institutional competence as well as constitutional constraint, cannot provide an effective forum for review, where else can one look? A novel experiment, the product of an unusual and fortunate confluence of circumstances, which has broken new ground both in design and achievement, has occurred in Canada with the creation of the Security Intelligence Review Committee (SIRC). This body has no parallel elsewhere. It demands detailed study because it is one of the few examples of a body whose operations, though immersed in and hedged about with secrecy, may still act in the service of parliament and public, significantly but not exclusively with an eye to protecting human rights.

CANADA

SIRC consists of five members who do the work part-time but are supported by a full-time staff of about a dozen which includes six or seven researchers. The members are people of stature in public and professional life, most of whom have experience of politics or administration. They cannot be serving members of Parliament, and must be Privy Councillors, a requirement presumably intended to bind them to secrecy by means of the Privy Councillor's oath.[89] However, this requirement does not limit potential membership to a small group of Establishment-minded people, for some members have been made Privy Councillors in consequence of their appointment to SIRC. They are appointed by the Prime Minister, who must consult with the leaders of opposition parties with substantial representation before any appointment. This statutory rule[90] has been supplemented by the practice of appointing a member of each of the two main opposition parties to the Committee. Though not outsiders or considered 'extreme', neither are they so locked into the Ottawa establishment that they can be counted upon to be 'tame'. This is true partly because they have independent provincial or professional bases, and partly because the original five members took a deliberate decision early on to assert their independence quite boldly in order to build up the credibility of the Committee, about which there was initially considerable scepticism. In this they were led by their Chairman, Mr Ronald Atkey, who began his career as a teacher of constitutional law. A Conservative, he had been a Minister during their brief period of office at the

[89] CSIS Act. s. 34 (1).   [90] Ibid.

end of the 1970s, but (*sic*) also enjoyed a high profile as an active civil libertarian.[91] Atkey and his colleagues took their responsibilities very seriously.

SIRC has a statutory power of access to any information held by CSIS or, where relevant, by a government department. Cabinet documents alone are excluded,[92] but a compromise was agreed under which Cabinet decisions are put in the form of ministerial directions, which are unequivocally within SIRC's superintendence and copies of which it receives as a matter of course. Its inquiries are conducted in secret, and therefore CSIS has no need to be fearful about protection of sources or similar information. SIRC is entitled to line-by-line budgetary breakdown, in marked contrast to Parliament which receives only a one-line statement of the annual total CSIS expenditure.

SIRC has been given a wide range of tasks, combining what British lawyers would regard as an odd combination of 'judicial' and 'administrative' functions. Of the latter, perhaps the most important are reviewing ministerial directions (a power which creates a check on manipulation by ministers), reviewing the Annual Report of the Director of the Service, reviewing dissemination of information held by CSIS under agreements with foreign governments or with government and police bodies at provincial or federal level within Canada, and undertaking a statistical review of operations.[93] The importance of this last, as the Director of Research explained, is that if repeated checks of files reveal variations over time in the use of specific powers or in the allocation of resources for particular purposes, SIRC can determine whether or not there have been unexplained shifts in agency activities. A statistical analysis is quite important for understanding what the organization is doing—for example, of the number of intercepts applied for in a given region or period of time.

SIRC has the power to conduct an inquiry and produce a 'special report' to the Minister at any time.[94] This is connected to, but not subsumed within, its powers to conduct reviews to determine not only legality and compliance with ministerial directions, but also 'that the activities do not involve any unreasonable or unnecessary exercise by the service of any of its powers'.[95] Thus, whilst a number of these reports concern serious human rights issues, others have focused on competence and management, or more generally on questions of efficacy. SIRC has also considered security breaches of the sort that in Britain might have been referred to the Security Commission.[96] Since our discussion lays particular emphasis on issues of legality, propriety, and broad policy, this perhaps gives an unbalanced picture of SIRC's activities. It is actively concerned with all aspects of efficacy as well.[97]

---

[91] See further below, p. 465.   [92] CSIS Act, s. 39(3).
[93] Ibid., s. 38(*a*).   [94] Ibid., s. 54.   [95] Ibid., s. 40
[96] A list of SIRC Reports up to mid-1990 may be found in the Review Committee Report (n. 17 above), at 157–8. A number of them are both s. 54 and s. 40 Reports. See also Farson (n. 16 above). The Security Commission is discussed below, Ch. 17.
[97] See further P. Gill, 'The Evolution of the Security Intelligence Debate in Canada Since 1976', in Farson *et al.* (n. 76 above), ch. 6; and S. Farson, 'Restructuring Control in Canada: The McDonald

A critical feature of SIRC's operations is its pro-active capability. It need not wait until someone brings a complaint, and indeed relatively few of its reviews seem to have originated in that way. It can initiate review on the basis of its own perception of what seems to be important, drawing upon its developing expertise to decide what area or problem needs inquiry. In the first six years of operation it produced Annual Reports and some twenty special reports, some of great length. Many were in secret form, though in some cases an edited public version was made available.[98] Among the key issues it has tackled have been counter-subversion and the whole question of how subversion has been handled; CSIS activities with respect to the labour movement and the Canadian peace movement; and evaluation of the Service's counter-terrorism and counter-intelligence programmes.

SIRC has also done extensive checking of warrant files, which is very important because all that is seen by the courts is a summary of the reasons supporting the application. It is able to see the entire file and check whether the summary given the Judge is actually a fair representation of the background information and material held by CSIS when it sought the warrant.[99] A related function is the ability to look at the quality of intelligence generated by the various forms of intrusive activities the Service uses, which serves as a yardstick in determining whether the intrusions are excessive.[100]

SIRC staff see their role, in the words of one of them, as that of a 'power auditor'—checking on whether CSIS's powers are being used properly, for the right purposes, and in a way that is not abusive. And they seem to get results, a claim not limited to the organization itself, but supported by both independent evaluation[101] and the views of the Parliamentary Review Committee whose report on the first five years of the working of the CSIS Act was required by the legislation itself.[102] Members interviewed were generally satisfied with its performance, and in particular felt confident that SIRC was getting inside CSIS sufficiently to be able to satisfy the public that the oppressive activities and 'dirty tricks' that had caused alarm were no longer taking place. Indeed the Committee thought highly enough of its work to recommend substantial enlargement of its functions and budget.[103]

Perhaps foremost among these achievements is the radical reduction of attention and resources devoted to subversion. Whilst the statutory mandate remains, CSIS has actually closed down its counter-subversion branch, partly (though not

---

Commission of Inquiry and its Legacy', in G. Hastedt (ed.), *Controlling Intelligence* (London, 1991), esp. 159–66.

[98] See n. 96 above.　　　　　　　　　　　　　　　　[99] See pp. 82–84 above.

[100] The British Commissioner looks at 'product' for the same reason: above, p. 432.

[101] See e.g. M. Rankin, 'The Security Intelligence Review Committee: Reconciling National Security with Procedural Fairness,' 3 *Can. J. Admin. L. & Prac.* 173 (1990); and P. Gill, 'Symbolic or Real? The Impact of SIRC, 1984–88', 4 *Int. & NS* 550 (1989). Canadian academics interviewed shared this view.

[102] Above n. 17, published in September 1990.　　　　　　　[103] Ibid., ch. 11

entirely) as a result of pressure from SIRC.[104] Secondly, it has pushed CSIS into what was described as 'pre-emptive change'. That is, CSIS has done things it probably would not have done, sometimes in more radical fashion than SIRC itself might have suggested. The very existence of a review body pushed the Service into integrating into its own decision-making the kinds of considerations SIRC exists in order to voice publicly.

Thirdly, SIRC has raised issues for consideration by all those, in and outside government, concerned with security and intelligence matters. A leading example is its attempt to launch a debate within Canada about the proper range or realm of activity for a domestic security and intelligence agency in the aftermath of the Cold War.[105]

Finally, SIRC has raised public consciousness and concern, particularly where human rights are involved. In its early years it adopted a high public profile as gadfly to CSIS and deliberately courted (indeed, to some extent fostered) a civil liberties constituency which has taken an interest in security matters unparalleled elsewhere.[106] The early Annual Reports were written in an unusually combative, quite unworshipful tone. This was part of a deliberate strategy, which included establishing a certain amount of 'street cred' for the new body, particularly with the interested public. It was also intended to get CSIS to take it seriously by dispelling any notion that SIRC was either a public relations exercise or a body mostly of retired politicians content to make a few headlines and then fade away. The strategy seems to have proven successful, in that SIRC became an effective force and was perceived by those who take the issues seriously as a useful innovation. The only discordant notes were expressed by certain officials in the Solicitor General's department who criticized some of its work as 'shallow' and 'headline-grabbing'. However these critics emphasized that they supported the existence of SIRC as an institution, despite being unhappy with some aspects of its performance.

If this consensual verdict is correct, and SIRC has performed its review functions effectively, it may be possible to identify the institutional characteristics most important to that success. Eight in particular may be cited:

(1) *independence from the executive;*

---

[104] SIRC's efforts in this direction were strongly reinforced by the recommendations of an Independent Advisory Team composed of very senior ex-civil servants, which endorsed its recommendations. See further P. Gill, 'Defining Subversion: The Canadian Experience Since 1977', [1989] *PL* 617, 626–36. SIRC kept up the pressure: see its *Annual Report 1989–1990* (Ottawa, 1990), ch. 6, on 'the counter-subversion residue'. It has also recommended deletion of subversion from the CSIS mandate which, however, the government has rejected.

[105] Ch. 14, pp. 390–92.

[106] For example, SIRC has supported two conferences which elicited contributions from scholars, security practitioners, and lawyers, and have led to two good books: C. Franks (ed.), *Dissent and the State* (Toronto, 1989) and P. Hanks and J. McCamus (eds.), *National Security: Surveillance and Accountability in a Democratic Society* (Cowansville, Que., 1989). There can be little doubt that there is more interest in, and interesting writing about, security governance and accountability issues in Canada than anywhere else. This includes the USA, which has a far greater need for it.

(2) *proactive capacity*;

(3) *membership representative of the spectrum of political parties*, but acting in a non-partisan manner;

(4) *full access to information* about all aspects of the agency's activities;

(5) *the ability to maintain secrecy where necessary*;

(6) *institutional expertise*, a matter intimately tied to

(7) *adequate support staff*—people working full time, and in post long enough to find out what they were doing.

This last point requires some elaboration. It was estimated that there is a learning curve of twelve to eighteen months before SIRC staff can do their job properly. This means above all asking the right questions, and making sure that the answers received are not mere evasions. It is not something that one could just walk in and do: even though SIRC employees had been recruited from other departments of government and were not strangers to the Ottawa bureaucracy, they still found that there were peculiarities about the working of security and intelligence agencies which required quite a long time to understand.[107] Finally (8) *the capacity to campaign*—that is, to use the media to build up support for the review body's position if it finds itself at loggerheads with the agency.

SIRC, then, is generally accounted a success. It is important to specify what this means. Success for an institution of accountability is not easily measurable; indeed is not susceptible to precise measurement. It entails having significant impact on an organization whose operations are perforce hidden from public view, and altering the climate of public opinion and interest within which the organization functions. Perhaps its most important elements are:

1. Ensuring compliance with legal restrictions and norms of respect for democracy and human rights. Public censure and reversal of decisions will have some effect in this direction, but greater long-term impact will be achieved if the organization is helped to respond positively and begin to internalize those norms, rather than responding defensively by either rejecting the criticism or looking for ways round the standards.

2. To achieve sufficient public authority and credibility so that when it concludes that the organization is behaving creditably, that conclusion is believed and rational people abandon their fears and suspicions about what it being done (to themselves or to others).[108] This function of reassurance is also valuable politically to the organization, since it should increase support, or at least minimize opposition, when it seeks greater resources.

In order to achieve this credibility, it is probably necessary for the review body to 'take on' the organization publicly and be seen to defend human rights aggressively. This point, fully appreciated by SIRC, underpinned its early strat-

---

[107] This fact makes one particularly doubtful about the British practice of using part-time judges with no relevant experience in an oversight capacity, even granted that the range of what they look at is much narrower

[108] Cf. p. 86, n. 203 above.

egy, and the acerbic tone of the reports, coupled with its Chairman's critical comments made during appearances on television, helped it achieve credibility with unusual speed.

3. To stimulate greater public interest in the problems surrounding the activities of the agency it covers—in this case, of bringing security and intelligence issues more visibly on to the public agenda. It should stimulate increased and better-informed debate and alert the interested public to new developments and trends. In parallel, it should encourage and bring fresh thinking from other sources into the often closed systems of bureaucracy. An important spin-off of this last contribution is to stimulate the agency's leadership to rethink and review its main activities and their rationales.

4. Finally, to take seriously and make useful contributions to the agency's effectiveness. This is both desirable in itself[109] and politically necessary. If an oversight body is perceived to be indifferent or (worse) hostile to the organization's primary aims, its human rights concerns will be resisted internally. It will also be vulnerable to attack from the authoritarian minded who assert that there is an inevitable conflict between efficacy and human rights, and that the former must prevail. SIRC has managed to avoid this trap; there was a notable absence of calls for its disbandment or even serious curtailment in the evidence to the Parliamentary Review Committee.

SIRC as a Constitutional Innovation

SIRC is a constitutional innovation which stands in unusual relation to both executive and legislative branches of government. It is independent of the executive, which cannot withhold any information SIRC requests. It provides the minister with secret reports which it has refused to make available to Parliament without the latter's consent.[110] Yet it has also been described as 'Parliament's surrogate',[111] which may mean a number of different things. Most obviously it takes Parliament's place as the forum in which the hard day-to-day work of accountability is undertaken. More fundamentally this phrase may mean that it acts on behalf of Parliament—and through it, of the public—to ensure that matters of public concern are pursued. For SIRC to fulfil this role it must of course retain Parliament's confidence; this, to judge from the Review Committee's Report, it has done. The latter's complaint about its inability to gain access to section 54 reports grew out of its wish to reach a fully informed evaluation of SIRC, which required analysing its product. In its words,

---

[109] This conclusion seems inevitable once it is accepted that there are genuine national security values requiring protection, and that some forms of special powers must be granted the agency charged with protecting them. As with any organized activity, once purpose and legitimacy are established, attention progresses to efficacy.

[110] The Parliamentary Review Committee, (n. 17 above), 155–60, expressed great frustration at this refusal but could do nothing. For a more detailed account, see Farson, above n. 24.

[111] A phrase apparently coined by the Review Committee (ibid.), at 156.

The Committee believed that it had to be able to assure itself that SIRC's research techniques were effective and that there was no indication of [it] having been captured by either the executive branch of government or by the intelligence community. Furthermore, the Committee considered that it had to have hard evidence for this. It could not simply take SIRC's word for it.[112]

This problem was never satisfactorily resolved. The Review Committee recommended that a permanent subcommittee be established to deal exclusively with security and intelligence.[113] This was rejected by the government; instead, such a body was set up to last only for the duration of the Parliament which expired in 1993. Its chairman had also chaired the Review Committee; and interestingly it was decided not to seek access to classified information, for fear of being compromised. This entailed accepting reliance on SIRC in this respect.[114]

Scope does seem to remain for one reform which would not involve drastically upsetting various institutional relations and seems desirable on constitutional grounds. Whilst accepting that for many reasons it is right to retain SIRC's role as the prime mover in relation to review, it would enhance responsiveness to public opinion and thus democratic legitimacy if Parliament, through the subcommittee, were given the power to 'task' SIRC when a matter arises and causes concern. The need should not come about frequently, but it seems wrong in principle for Parliament to be unable directly to require that its surrogate delve into a subject it deems important.

Although the McDonald Commission had recommended the establishment of SIRC, it had envisaged a smaller body with a narrower range of competence. SIRC's present form is the result of the report of a committee chaired by Senator Michael Pitfield, set up after the Government's initial proposals met a storm of criticism, whose recommendations heavily influenced the final structure of the CSIS Act. Senator Pitfield, who had previously held the post equivalent to the British Cabinet Secretary, described himself in interview as a disciple of Sir Burke (later Lord) Trend, who occupied that office from 1962 to 1973. He cited the Comptroller and Auditor General as the model which he drew upon in designing SIRC. There are some important similarities, notably independence from the executive (especially since the National Audit Act 1983 made the Comptroller an officer of the House of Commons), and the fact that it has both a large and expert staff and the power to acquire whatever information it wishes.

However, there are significant differences. The Comptroller and Auditor General does not displace the Public Accounts Committee, to which he reports, in the sense of precluding it from questioning ministers and civil servants. Indeed the PAC enjoys 'the enviable reputation . . . as the one select committee before which even the most exalted permanent secretary can be made to trem-

---

[112] A phrase apparently coined by the Review Committee (ibid.), at 156.
[113] Above, p. 443.
[114] Information received from Prof. Reg Whitaker, letter of 21 June 1992; cf. above, p. 445.

ble'.[115] Yet when the CSIS Act structure emerged in 1984, it did not include a standing review body in Parliament. Moreover, the PAC relies on the Treasury, which has its own institutional interest in public expenditure control, to effect its recommendations.[116] By contrast, SIRC does not rely on another government department to play the role analogous to the Treasury in public expenditure, but works simultaneously with the minister responsible whilst seeking to generate interest and support by direct communication to the public through the media. It is a unique and fascinating invention, and one which may provide a valuable model for the assertion of greater parliamentary influence and accountability over policy-making and administration in areas far removed from that which gave it birth.

The eight features identified earlier[117] may be necessary conditions for the success of a review body, but are they sufficient? One of the points emphasized repeatedly by people interviewed—whether officials, academics, or those associated with SIRC itself—was the importance of individual personalities and political attitudes. SIRC began its operations quite coincidentally with the arrival of the first Progressive Conservative government in over two decades.[118] The PCs as a party, therefore, did not have the kind of Establishment mentality, including a close psychological identification with the security apparatus, that one would find among their British counterparts. Ronald Atkey, the first Chairman and moving figure, is a 'Red Tory' and a member of the Board of Directors of the Canadian Civil Liberties Association. His successor, whose political image is very different, also described himself in interview as a 'Red Tory'.[119] Thus the government made no attempt to pack the Committee with people predisposed to acquiescence in CSIS's outlook. Moreover, Atkey placed great emphasis on proceeding consensually and avoiding partisan division. Partly under his influence, and partly as a matter of self-education, some other members altered their views.[120] Good collegial relations have prevailed. There is no way that this chemistry could have been predicted, and it certainly cannot be created by statute. A body split by rancorous relationships and ideological differences would have had little practical impact or public respect. To an immeasurable but

---

[115] G. Drewry, 'Select Committees and Back-bench Power' in J. Jowell and D. Oliver (eds.), *The Changing Constitution* (2nd edn., Oxford, 1989), 157.

[116] Ibid.   [117] Above, pp. 461–62.

[118] The CSIS Act was the last piece of legislation enacted by the Trudeau administration before its electoral defeat.

[119] 'Red Tories' are a well-recognized stream within the Progressive Conservative Party. They may support policies of deregulation and market economics (and hence are not 'wets' in English parlance), but also take a strong position in favour of legal protection of civil liberties. There are very few people among current British Conservatives who could be characterized in the same way; perhaps the best known is Richard Shepherd, MP, whose exertions in favour of freedom of information and greater accountability of the Security Service have ensured him a long career on the backbenches.

[120] Mr J.-J. Blais, formerly Solicitor General in the Liberal government, was particularly frank about his own liberalization of outlook and emphasized the role of Mr Atkey in this respect.

important extent, Canada has been lucky.[121] And it is only too easy to envisage a British government, compelled by public pressure to establish a review body, packing it with people content with the *status quo* and to whom human rights considerations were decidedly secondary. There is no magic in institutions, although badly designed institutions will predictably fail.

CONCLUSION

Views on the most desirable models of accountability are initially based on what aims are intended and what problems are being addressed in the specific field. Ultimately they should also be grounded in a deeper conception of constitutional principle. Either perspective leads directly to a clear sight of one major failing in the current British system: its legalism. No one has been given the task of looking, as in Australia, at propriety and compliance with certain human rights standards or, as in Canada, at 'unreasonable or unnecessary exercise of powers'.[122] It is, to use a well-known phrase, unsafe and unsatisfactory to leave these concerns to the organization itself or to ministers; and legal compliance, though critically important, does not exhaust the range of legitimate concern.

Turning to the process of oversight specifically, we believe that to confine accountability of a government agency wholly within the executive branch can never be acceptable in a democratic state. There must exist mechanisms independent of the executive which relate in some way to the legislature, and ultimately to the people. Only then can citizens be confident that the values embedded in what we have called the democratic conception of national security are being protected, not imperilled, by security institutions and their political masters. At the moment, the working machinery with the most promising record of demonstrable effectiveness is SIRC. However, though there is an attractive simplicity to recommending the establishment of a British SIRC and then concluding this chapter, that would unfortunately not meet the case.

SIRC shares the serious defect common to all the institutions of accountability discussed in this Part, with the sole exception of the Australian Inspector-General. To recall terms introduced earlier, its review is *institutional*, rather than *functional*. That is to say, a particular service is made the subject of attention by a particular oversight body. However, if activities of a kind similar to those which led to the formation of the review structure are undertaken by another agency, they will escape review entirely because they occur within a different institutional framework. This may happen because the second agency independently decides

---

[121] Also, and again fortuitously, the reform of security and intelligence coincided with the patriation of the Constitution and the inclusion of the Charter of Rights and Freedoms. The heightened 'rights consciousness' which this produced has strongly influenced the culture of public administration in Canada, and CSIS and its oversight bodies were not exempt.

[122] Above, p. 419 and 459, respectively.

to act in that way, but more sinister is the possibility that the work is shunted to it to avoid review, or that it is created specifically for that reason. Awareness of this problem underlay the recommendation of the Parliamentary Review Committee into the CSIS Act that the Communications Security Establishment—Canada's GCHQ, which has the technical capacity to monitor vast amounts of telephone traffic—be put under SIRC's review jurisdiction. At the moment, said the Committee, 'to all intents and purposes [it] is unaccountable'.[123] This, of course, has also been the position with GCHQ, for which the Foreign Secretary has had an ill-defined responsibility which will only be clarified when the government unveils its promised legislation. The sole exception in this respect is Britain's one example of institutional review—the Interceptions Commissioner, who looks at all telephone tapping regardless of which agency carries it out and which of four possible Secretaries of State has authorized it. Although the performance of those who have held this particular office may be open to criticism, the design of subjecting all practitioners of activity in a particular field to oversight by the same scrutineer is an excellent model. The essential next step is to generalize its logic and create a review committee to cover all activities within the security and intelligence field. Detailed discussion is best postponed to the Coda.

[123] See n. 17 above, 153.

17

Inquiries and Investigations

The purpose of this chapter is to consider one recurrent theme in security governance—the use of inquiries to delve into scandals and matters of public concern. Their history extends from the Committee of both Houses of Parliament established in 1844 to inquire into the Mazzini letter-opening affair[1] to the recent announcement of the Scott Inquiry into exports to Iraq in 1992.[2]

Doctrinally neat categorization is hardly the distinctive feature of the British Constitution, but when it comes to committees of inquiry even by these standards the picture is extraordinarily confused.[3] The series of Cold War spy scares, from the late 1940s to the early 1960s (Nunn May, Fuchs, Pontecorvo, Burgess, Maclean, Philby, Vassall, and Blake) led in each case to public calls for independent (usually judicial) investigation. By the early 1960s the response to spy scandals was more or less ritualized, although in constitutional terms there were subtle differences in the chosen means of investigation. Internal inquiries, departmental inquiries, committees of Privy Councillors, judicial inquiries, and tribunals under the Tribunals of Inquiry (Evidence) Act 1921 have all played some part in investigating security scandals in Britain.[4] To these should be added Britain's peculiar contribution to the list: the Security Commission.[5] The only notable omission in Britain from the taxonomy of investigative devices is the refusal (to date) to resort to a Royal Commission.[6]

There are three main distinctions of practical importance between these investigatory bodies: their composition and appointment, powers and method of investigation, and the ultimate form of the report. Each of these is likely to

[1] *Report of the Secret Committee on the Post Office* (PP 1844, xiv).
[2] Discussed at pp. 471 ff. below.
[3] T. Cartwright, *Royal Commissions of Inquiry* (London, 1975), esp. ch. 2. See also R. Brazier, 'The Machinery of British Constitutional Reform' (1990) 41 *NILQ* 227.
[4] P. Gill, *Policing Politics: Security Intelligence and the Liberal Democratic State* (London, 1993), ch. 9.
[5] See pp. 476 ff. below.
[6] The device has been used several times in Canada and Australia in the security domain. In 1969 there had been a Royal Commission report: *Report of the Royal Commission on Security* (Ottawa, 1969). An earlier Royal Commission had been established following the Gouzenko defection in 1945. The McDonald Commission, though most noteworthy for its constitutional analysis and proposals for reform, also produced a volume on misconduct by the RCMP, which had been the activating cause for its creation. In Australia a Royal Commission had been established following the Petrov defection in 1954. Mr Justice Hope's two reports, in 1977 and 1984, were both formally Royal Commission documents. Mr Justice Hope of the Supreme Court of New South Wales was appointed sole commissioner of a Royal Commission established in 1977 by the Whitlam government. The Commission produced a series of reports on different agencies: *Royal Commission on Intelligence and Security* (1977). Mr Justice Hope was asked to carry out further reviews in 1984, producing several reports (above, Ch. 13).

affect a critical fourth ingredient, namely, the extent to which the investigation is seen to be impartial, effective, and to allay public disquiet. On an imaginary scale of impartiality the internal inquiry comes at the bottom end. In such cases the public and parliament are essentially asked to take on trust assurances based on a report which is typically not published and an investigation carried out by those already close to the events or policy in question. Marginally more credible is an inquiry carried out by a retired civil servant with relevant experience but not directly implicated in the events: examples would include the review of the Roger Hollis case[7] and the review of the performance of MI5 over the Gulf War detentions.[8] A departmental inquiry conducted by a senior lawyer is more impartial still, even if it is conducted without formal powers and, in private, and the report is unpublished.[9]

If an inquiry is expected to produce a public report or involve political representation its composition becomes more delicate. Governments have usually resisted calls for direct investigation by committees comprising elected members, but where some sort of cross-party investigation is unavoidable they have resorted to another constitutional anachronism, Privy Councillors. Two characteristics make them suitable. The first is the breadth of the composition of the Privy Council, which includes senior statesmen and women and judges. The second is the oath sworn by all members: 'to keep secret all matters regarded or treated in the Council; not to discuss matters so treated or touching any of his colleagues without the consent of the sovereign or the Council; to bear faith and allegiance to the Crown and to defend its jurisdiction and powers against all foreign princes, powers, prelates, states or potentates.'[10] Thus a Conference of Privy Councillors was established in 1955 in the aftermath of the Burgess and Maclean defections, to consider the adequacy of the security arrangements in the public service.[11] The membership comprised three members of the Conservative government of the day, three former Labour ministers, and the Head of the Civil Service: the essentially political (but non-partisan) nature of the investigatory body was a result partly of the need to maintain a cross-party consensus on security and partly for the practical reason that the actions of different administrations were to be investigated.[12] Its Report to the Prime Minister was

[7] Conducted by the former Cabinet Secretary, Lord Trend: *HC Debs.*, vol. 1, cols. 1079–85 (26 Mar. 1981).

[8] Conducted by Sir Phillip Woodfield, Security and Intelligence Services Staff Counsellor but unpublished and definitely not the subject of comment by our interviewees. See the *Independent*, 10 Dec. 1991.

[9] As in David Calcutt, QC's investigation into aspects of the Colin Wallace affair: see P. Birkinshaw, *Reforming the Secret State* (Milton Keynes, 1990), 69.

[10] *Halsbury's Laws of England* (4th edn.), vol. 8, para. 1149.

[11] For the background to the establishment of the inquiry see *HC Debs.*, vol. 545, col. 1609 (7 Nov. 1955) and vol 546, col. 1462 (23 Nov. 1955). The reason for terming it a 'Conference' is unclear but may, perhaps, be by analogy to a Speaker's Conference.

[12] See the comments of the former Private Secretary to the Cabinet Secretary of the day: *HL Debs.*, vol. 483, col. 185 (17 Dec. 1986) and P. Hennessy, *Whitehall* (London, 1989), 543 on the discussions in Cabinet.

not published, but the government did issue a statement summarizing some of the Report's recommendations.[13] The precedent for an inquiry of this kind was revived when the Franks Committee was established following the Falklands War.[14] Particular stress was laid on that occasion on the need for a body which could be shown intelligence assessments, Cabinet minutes, and the papers of previous administrations in secrecy.[15]

Judicial inquiries are another favourite.[16] In 1961, following the Portland spy cases and the conviction of George Blake, an independent inquiry was established, chaired by Lord Radcliffe.[17] Like the 1955 Conference of Privy Councillors, its purpose was to review security practices and procedures. However in this instance the resulting Report was published, but with the excision of passages which would compromise security.[18] The inclusion of judicial personnel (Lord Radcliffe was a Law Lord)[19] was soon to become established as a pattern. Within months a second spy scandal in the Admiralty (following the conviction of John Vassall) led to the government establishing a further inquiry. On this occasion, however, since ministerial conduct was in issue,[20] the rare step was taken of instituting a tribunal under the Tribunal of Inquiry (Evidence) Act 1921, chaired once again by Lord Radcliffe. The procedure under the 1921 Act is unusual in several respects that distinguish it from the forms of investigation already discussed: formal powers of subpoena and to deal with perjury and contempt are available under the Act, the Attorney-General is responsible for presenting evidence, hearings are to be held in public subject to a discretion in the tribunal to exclude the public 'for reasons connected with the subject matter of the inquiry or the evidence given',[21] and a resolution of both Houses of Parliament is required before the tribunal may be established.[22]

The final *ad hoc* inquiry from this era to be mentioned is the most famous, Lord Denning's Report,[23] following the Profumo affair. Compared with its predecessors, the format was unusual. Lord Denning himself interviewed those he decided to take evidence from in private and without either cross-examination or giving them details of the evidence of any other witnesses. In an introductory passage, after reviewing the possiblity of investigation by a tribunal or by a select committee, Lord Denning wrote of the disadvantages of a one-man tribunal: 'It has the advantage that there can be no dissent, but it has two great

---

[13] Cmnd. 9715 (1956).   [14] Cmnd. 8787 (1983).

[15] *HC Debs.*, vol. 27, cols. 469 ff. (8 July 1982).

[16] For a critical discussion on the use of judges in this role see nn. 112 ff. below.

[17] An earlier Departmental Inquiry under Lord Romer had been established to examine such procedures in the Admiralty.

[18] *Security Procedures in the Public Service*, Cmnd. 1681 (Apr. 1962).

[19] In an illuminating pen portrait of Lord Radcliffe's non-judicial public career Peter Hennessy (n. 12 above), 568, asserts that in addition to those inquiries officially acknowledged he had also conducted an inquiry into recruitment to MI6.

[20] It was alleged that the First Lord of the Admiralty had failed to take action, despite having been informed of the existence of a spy ring some months earlier.

[21] S. 2.   [22] Ibid., s. 1.   [23] Cmnd. 2152 (1963).

disadvantages: first being secret it has not the appearance of justice; second in carrying out the inquiry, I have had to be detective, inquisitor, advocate and judge and it has been diffcult to combine them.'[24] The commissioning of Lord Denning's report may have given the government of the day a temporary stay of execution, but its publication proved a deep embarrassment. Reports of judicial inquiries are not supposed to be racy reading. More seriously, by leaving no stone unturned and no rumour unconsidered, many MPs considered that Lord Denning's 'one man inquisition' had seriously harmed reputations.[25] Despite describing the Denning report as 'a brilliant exception', the Royal Commission on Tribunals of Inquiry was later to recommend that this type of inquiry should never again be established.[26]

Although the habitual response of setting up inquiries is partly explicable by the tendency of most governments to turn to the Great and the Good in moments of crisis,[27] there are also features of security crises which make this a particularly appealing option. Paramount is the perceived need to stifle public debate on potentially damaging security matters as quickly as posssible by entrusting investigation to trustworthy hands who can carry out investigation away from the political arena. The establishment of the Security Commission in 1964 was, in this spirit, hailed as the installation of a permanent 'lightning conductor'.[28]

As we shall see later, it has been so successful in this role that for over a quarter of a century most security-related scandals have been dealt with (if at all) by this route. Were it not for recent events, the earlier examples of security investigations could be safely despatched to the museum of constitutional curiosities. However, the old debates were abruptly and unexpectedly revived in 1992 with the setting up of the Scott Inquiry. Although at the time of writing the inquiry has yet to report, it nevertheless provides a useful contemporary case study of the use of inquiries in this field.

THE SCOTT INQUIRY[29]

The establishment of the Inquiry followed the collapse in November 1992 of the trial of executives from the machine tools company Matrix Churchill,

---

[24] Ibid., para. 5 and see also *HC Debs.*, vol. 679, col. 801 (21 June 1963).

[25] For his own acccount see Lord Denning, *Landmarks in the Law* (London, 1984), pt. 13 where he describes it as 'my most important case'. Controversy over the report's findings lingers on. For two accounts alleging either that Lord Denning was misled or that the report was selective, see P. Knightly and C. Kennedy, *An Affair of State* (London, 1987) and A. Summers and S. Dorril, *Honeytrap* (London, 1988).

[26] *Royal Commission on Tribunals of Inquiry*, Cmnd. 3121 (1966), paras. 21 and 42.

[27] This was less pronounced during the Thatcher years: Hennessy (n. 12 above), 574–86.

[28] *The Times*, 24 Jan. 1964 (cited by D. Williams, *Not in the Public Interest* (London, 1965), 169).

[29] A detailed account of the Matrix Churchill case, quoting many of the documents and much of the testimony, can be found in D. Leigh, *Betrayed: The Real Story of the Matrix Churchill Trial* (London, 1993). See also: I. Leigh, 'Matrix Churchill, Supergun and the Scott Inquiry', [1993] *PL*, 630.

charged with deception in obtaining export licences. The terms of reference cover both the prosecution conduct at the trial, the issuing of the public interest immunity certificates, the Supergun affair, and government actions and policy on exports to Iraq.[30] They thus embrace the export of arms and of dual use technology to Iraq (such as machine tools), the information made public and given to Parliament, and the conduct of the Matrix Churchill case. One significant omission is the lack of explicit reference to the security and intelligence agencies. An investigation of their role will be an essential part of the Inquiry's amassing of evidence on the state of government knowledge, and of the conduct of the prosecution. This will be hard to divorce from questions about the control and accountability of the intelligence agencies. When the Trade and Industry Select Committee investigated the Supergun affair they were troubled by the lack of parliamentary accountability.[31] It is to be hoped that Lord Justice Scott will interpret the terms of reference liberally at this point and make recommendations.The initial indications suggest that the ultimate report might be confined to historical events about the cases in question and future policy on export licences and public interest immunity certificates. Between these concerns stand significant questions about the use by the intelligence agencies of human sources of information, and potential conflicts between such use and the administration of justice, which deserve investigation.[32]

When the Scott Inquiry was announced some criticism of the choice of investigation by a judge rather than Parliament was made. The spectre of Profumo stalked: it was Harold Wilson, then leader of the Opposition, who complained in the Profumo debates about the government 'shuffling off' its responsibilities to a judge. There were calls then, too, for investigation by a Select Committee or Parliamentary Commission of Inquiry. But the history of Parliamentary investigations of this kind in the late nineteenth and early twentieth centuries is an unhappy one: both the Parnell and Marconi commissions fell into deep, partisan controversy, and it was precisely because of the disadvantages of this method of investigation that the Tribunals of Inquiry Act 1921 and its predecessors were passed.[33]

A year before the Matrix Churchill trial the Trade and Industry Select Committee had conducted an investigation into the state of government knowledge about the Iraqi Supergun.[34] Comparing that investigation with the Scott

---

[30] The terms of reference are: 'Having examined the facts in relation to the export from the United Kingdom of defence equipment and dual use goods to Iraq between December 1984 and August 1990 and the decisions reached on the export licence applications for such goods and the basis for them, to report on whether the relevant Departments, Agencies, and responsible Ministers operated in accordance with the policies of Her Majesty's Government; to examine and report on decisions taken by the prosecuting authority and those signing public interest immunity certificates in *R* v. *Henderson* and any other similar cases that he considers relevant to the inquiry; and to make recommendations' (*HC Debs.*, vol. 214, col. 74w (16 Nov. 1992)).

[31] Above, pp. 452–5.   [32] See Ch. 4 above.

[33] See G. Keeton, 'Parliamentary Tribunals of Inquiry' (1959) 12 *Curr. L. Prob.* 12.

[34] *Trade and Industry Committee, Second Report, Exports to Iraq: Project Babylon and Long Range Guns*, HC 86 (1991–2); we are grateful to Jim Cousins, MP for an interview on the Committee's work.

Inquiry, one need look no further to see the limitations of a Select Committee to conduct this kind of investigation. As we have seen, lack of access to key witnesses and short-term political pressures hampered its work.[35] Despite the obvious appeal of Select Committees from the standpoint of the democratic ideal, these are serious and deep-seated objections.

The Scott Inquiry has been established under the prerogative, rather than specific statutory authority, and will report to the Board of Trade. The irony of the latter requirement will not be lost on those in the Foreign Office, like the then Minister of State William Waldegrave, who insisted as the price of their acquiescence in granting the licences that the Department of Trade and Industry should handle any embarrassing parliamentary questions.[36] The DTI is the lead Department for the granting of export licences (although it would be premature to assume that it will remain so), but many of the fateful decisions were taken by an interdepartmental committee of ministers, including ministers from the Foreign Office and the Ministry of Defence. Ministers from all three departments, and the Prime Minister, gave at various times highly selective or downright misleading responses to parliamentary questions about exports to Iraq. The Attorney-General advised on the public interest immunity certificates. The Home Secretary, Foreign Secretary, and ultimately the Prime Minister carry responsibility for the role of the intelligence and security agencies. This is a collective affair touching the whole administration. The point is worth emphasizing because of early attempts by the government to shift the blame on to a single individual, Alan Clark, the former Trade and Industry and Defence Procurement Minister.[37] Although that may account for the final decision to abort the prosecution,[38] the involvement of other departments is obvious, and it makes the establishment of the Inquiry on a departmental basis questionable.

The form of the Scott Inquiry occasioned some controversy when it was announced.[39] The Opposition called for the Inquiry to be established under the Tribunal of Inquiry Act 1921, so that it would have statutory powers to *subpoena* evidence. Although the Prime Minister made it clear that serving ministers and civil servants would be required to give evidence, this left in doubt the position of former ministers such as Baroness Thatcher and Alan Clark, retired MPs such as Sir Hal Miller (who refused to give evidence to the Trade and Industry Select Committee), and former officials such as the previous Director-Generals of MI5 and MI6, and the head of Customs and Excise. Although Lord Justice Scott issued 'invitations' to both former ministers,[40] the government was also publicly committed to giving his Lordship powers under the Tribunal of Inquiry Act 1921 if necessary. Lord Ridley is beyond the reach of any summons: his,

---

[35] See pp. 452–5 above. [36] See D. Leigh (n. 29 above), 194.

[37] e.g. the Prime Minister's reply at *HC Debs.*, vol. 213, col. 987 (12 Nov. 1992).

[38] Following his quite candid answers in cross-examination to Geoffrey Robertson, QC, Henderson's counsel at the trial: excerpted at length in D. Leigh (n. 29 above), ch. 11.

[39] See the debate at *HC Debs.*, vol. 214, cols. 631 ff. (23 Nov. 1992).

[40] The *Independent*, 1 Apr. 1993.

potentially useful, testimony died with him. Does it matter then that the inquiry is a non-statutory one? The chief consequence of the lack of statutory powers is that evidence before the inquiry will not be taken on oath nor be subject to perjury itself. In the light of all that has gone before, one cannot lightly rely on the high standards in public life and dismiss this as a mere technicality.

Although 1921 Act tribunals of inquiry were the normal method by which allegations of scandal against politicians and public officials were investigated for much of this century, the procedure has fallen into disuse. The Salmon Commission recommended in 1966 that the Act be amended to provide greater protections for people coming before the tribunal, in view of the inquisitorial form of the proceedings. They also said that, although such tribunals should be used sparingly and reserved for times when there was a national crisis of confidence, they were appropriate where the conduct of ministers was impugned.[41] It would be hard to identify a more suitable candidate for this treatment than the Matrix Churchill débâcle. It was because of the disadvantages in the procedure that the government chose not to use it.[42]

The first of these, as the government itself was quick to assert when pressed to alter the basis of the Inquiry, is that a tribunal under the 1921 Act would have invoked the parliamentary *sub judice* rule and thus stifled Parliamentary discussion further. This is a real concession. At various times imminent or active proceedings in the Matrix Churchill and other prosecutions did indeed curtail parliamentary debate, especially when Customs investigating officers refused to give evidence to the Supergun inquiry. One should not, however, overdo the praise: since announcing the Inquiry ministers have given further information strictly on their terms and refused to answer a number of parliamentary questions on the basis that the relevant material would be inquired into by the Scott Inquiry.[43]

A further disadvantage is that because witnesses are compelled to answer before the statutory tribunal on fear of being found in contempt, it has been customary to give them immunity in advance against subsequent criminal proceedings for any self-incriminating testimony. Ministers were, perhaps, mindful of continuing investigation into alleged perjury against Mr Clark and were anxious not to prejudice any possible prosecution. In the event the Director of Public Prosecutions decided that prosecution was impossible since it could not

---

[41] *Royal Commission on Tribunals of Inquiry*, Cmnd. 3121 (1966), para. 27.

[42] These were extensively explored by the Royal Commission (ibid.). The proposals, mostly designed to protect individuals appearing before a tribunal of inquiry, remain unimplemented in legislation, despite the government's acceptance (see Cmnd. 5313 (1975)). They have, however, borne fruit in Israel: Z. Segal, 'Tribunals of Inquiry: A British Invention Ignored in Britain' [1984] *PL* 206.

[43] e.g. *HC Debs.*, vol. 214, col. 857 (25 Nov. 1992). The Prime Minister has refused to comment on how many of the Matrix Churchill defendants were assisting MI5 and MI6 on the grounds that 'it would be contrary to normal practice to comment further on intelligence matters' (*HC Debs.*, vol. 214, col. 746 (26 Nov. 1992)), despite the evidence from intelligence officers about these contacts in open session at the trial. Similarly a parliamentary request for government documents produced to defence counsel in the case has been refused: ibid., col. 217.

be decided which of Mr Clark's apparently contradictory statements might have been false.

One disadvantage of a statutory tribunal not emphasized by the government, but real none the less, is the further embarrassment it would have caused to the Attorney-General. For it has been customary in the past for the Attorney-General to act as counsel to a 1921 Act tribunal, or at least to appoint counsel. On occasion this has put the Attorney-General in the position of cross-examining ministerial colleagues.[44] Here in view of the terms of reference he would plainly have had to refuse. In the event although the Inquiry was serviced by staff from the Treasury Solicitor's department, independent counsel (Presiley Baxendale, QC) was appointed.

Notwithstanding the disadvantages, in eschewing the statutory format and appointing a single judge with discretion to inquire upon his own terms into a matter vital for the government's continued existence, the Prime Minister was retracing the steps of Harold MacMillan thirty years earlier in the Profumo affair.[45] Although Lord Justice Scott has been given much the same freedom as was Lord Denning over how to conduct the investigation and report, he has approached the task quite differently: a one-man investigation behind closed doors in Whitehall would not now satisfy public or parliamentary opinion. Lord Justice Scott has decided on a presumption of open testimony and, furthermore, has published the Cabinet Secretary's correspondence attempting to secure greater confidentiality.[46]

Witnesses were given immunity from prosecution for their evidence to the Inquiry by an undertaking given to Lord Justice Scott by the Attorney-General.[47] The government has also given lawful authority to disclose official information to the Inquiry for the purposes of the Official Secrets Acts. The immunity did not extend to civil proceedings, but the Cabinet Secretary undertook that no civil servant would be disciplined for evidence given. Nevertheless, *The Times* reported a fear among civil servants at the outset of the Inquiry that their careers could be prejudiced as a result.[48]

The Inquiry has had made available to it a mass of documentation, including the evidence and transcripts of the Matrix Churchill prosecutions.[49] It has also been given evidence submitted to the Trade and Industry Select Committee and material about the Supergun affair which was not made available to the Committee. Witnesses were selected by the judge after considering written evidence, mainly on the basis of the need to elucidate that evidence, but they could

[44] Keeton (n. 34 above), 25–6 and 31; and see J. Edwards, *The Law Officers of the Crown* (London, 1964), 295 ff.

[45] See p. 470 above.

[46] *Inquiry into Exports of Defence Equipment and Dual Use Goods to Iraq*, Press Release, 31 Mar. 1993.

[47] For the terms see ibid., 'Proposed Procedure for Hearings before Lord Justice Scott', para. 4(*a*).

[48] *The Times*, 4 May 1993.

[49] After requesting more than 85,000 pages of documents, the public hearings began on 4 May 1993.

also be called where their conduct had been or might have been called into question. The Inquiry announced that when oral evidence is given it will be given in public unless it was satisfied that 'the public interest in an open hearing is outweighed by the public interest in protecting from disclosure in public the documents or information in question'.[50] Perhaps not surprising, but ironic none the less, is the similarity to the test applied in considering whether to uphold a public interest immunity certificate.[51] Witnesses could be legally represented but their representatives would not normally play a part in the proceedings; instead, questions will be asked by the Counsel to the Inquiry.

It is a matter of debate whether inquiries are established to delay scrutiny, or to investigate and allay public fears. Nevertheless, the Scott Inquiry has the potential for allowing sunlight into parts of Whitehall never before subjected to public critical inquiry. In other countries public investigation of intelligence scandals has been a major catalyst for reform. It may yet prove so in Britain provided the report is not merely a technical treatise on the reform of export licences and public interest immunity certificates. Much will depend on how much detail is ultimately published, a matter over which Lord Justice Scott himself will have control.

It might seem premature to discuss what action should be taken following an inquiry that has yet to report, but it is here that Parliamentary scrutiny can be made to count. Although we have argued that investigation by Select Committee is inappropriate, once the report is available there is a very strong case for the Trade and Industry Select Committee conducting its own follow-up investigation into the policy issues raised by the supply of weapons and dual use technology to countries like Iraq, and the related intelligence questions arising from the case. At that point its own hurried and inadequate investigation would have been supplemented by the Scott Inquiry, problems of access to evidence would have been overcome, and there could be detailed and mature Parliamentary discussion of any proposals emanating from the report, rather than the instantaneous and partial response which is more normal in these cases. It would also be a way of maintaining Parliamentary pressure on the executive to take subsequent action. If Parliament allows itself to be deterred from increased intelligence scrutiny and a more probing role for Select Committees generally it will only have itself to blame.

THE SECURITY COMMISSION[52]

One result of the lingering dissatisfaction with the investigation of the Profumo affair[53] was the birth of the Security Commission—a standing body to which

---

[50] Letter of 23 Mar. 1993 from Sir Richard Scott to Sir Robin Butler.

[51] See pp. 313–19 and 334–8 above.

[52] This section is based in part on an extended interview with Mr Hugh Taylor, Head of the

future security scandals could be referred. The Security Commission celebrated its twenty-fifth anniversary in 1989 and has produced fourteen reports.[54] It may be best to begin by clarifying what the Security Commission is not. It is not an oversight body, an inspectorate, nor an appeal tribunal. It does not sit continuously, is not pro-active, has no links with any department or ministry, and has no adjudicative function. The Commission may venture on any terrain where security may be said to be involved. The problem of definitional tautology[55] is solved by pure political power: the Prime Minister alone may activate the Commission, and it may go wherever he or she directs. Thus, the Commission can and has reported on the conduct of Ministers,[56] of members of the Forces,[57] of a person in the Diplomatic Service,[58] and of an employee of GCHQ,[59] as well as those working in the Security Service.[60] In principle the activities of those working for MI6, the Secret Intelligence Service, would also come under its purview. However, the absurd Whitehall convention that the Service dare not speak its name in time of peace—only recently discarded[61]— would logically require that any such investigation be conducted in secret and that no report be published. Whether for this reason or because the Commission has never been asked to examine any matter relating to MI6, none of its published reports have dealt with that organization.

The Commission's main purpose is to investigate known or possible breaches of security; indeed its terms of reference might have been taken from *Henry V*— 'once more unto the breach, dear friends'—for only rarely has it been given any other task. This function was first outlined by the Prime Minister, Sir Alec Douglas-Home, in the aftermath of the Profumo affair,[62] and was slightly

Security Division, Office of the Minister for the Civil Service and Secretary to the Security Commission and Mr Rex Davie, who previously held that position and is presently Principal Establishment and Financial Officer, Cabinet Office. All direct quotations are taken from this interview. We are similarly grateful to a senior figure closely associated with the Commission who agreed to be interviewed but wished to remain anonymous.

[53] See n. 23 above.

[54] It is briefly discussed in Williams (n. 29 above), 167–9, and P. Birkinshaw, *Freedom of Information: The Law, the Practice and the Ideal* (London, 1988), 24.

[55] i.e. a matter becomes one of security because the Security Commission is involved; the Security Commission becomes involved because the matter is one of security.

[56] (Earl Jellicoe and Lord Lambton) Cmnd. 5367 (1973).

[57] e.g. (Sq. Ldr. P. J. Reen) Cmnd. 3151 (1966); (Ch. Technician Britten) Cmnd. 3856 (1968); and (Lance Corporal Aldridge), Cmnd. 9212 (1984).

[58] (Miss R. J. M. Ritchie) *HC Debs.* vol. 46, cols, 517–23 (28 July 1983).

[59] (G.A. Prime) Cmnd. 8876 (1985).   [60] (M. J. Bettaney) Cmnd. 9514 (1985).

[61] See Coda.

[62] The initial terms of reference of the Commission announced to the House of Commons were: 'If so requested by the Prime Minister, to investigate and report upon the circumstances in which a breach of security is known to have occurred in the public service, and upon any related failure in Departmental security arrangements or neglect of duty: and, in the light of any such investigations to advise whether any change in security arrangements is necessary or desirable'. (*HC Debs.*, vol. 687, col. 1271 (23 Jan. 1964)).

widened by his successor, Harold Wilson, in 1965.[63] Four years later Mr Wilson revised the reference procedure, making it clear that not only the Leader of the Opposition but also the Chairman of the Commission would be consulted before any matter would be referred to the Commission. No further Prime Ministerial announcements on the subject have been issued.[64] However subsequently the Commission's operational sphere was widened. In 1973 it undertook an investigation into whether the lifestyle of two former ministers might have presented a security threat although it was already known that no breach of security had in fact occurred.[65] An investigation which began when the 'Cyprus Eight' were charged was subsequently continued under revised terms of reference even after their acquittal as an investigation into security in Static Signals Units generally.[66]

The most wide-ranging, and perhaps the most important, of Security Commission reports is one that remains unpublished—a general review of security practices and procedures announced in the Prime Minister's statement on Sir Roger Hollis.[67] The government argued that to publish the report would have been seriously misleading in view of the number of passages which would have had to have been deleted on security grounds. Instead a statement was produced detailing the action which had been taken on such of the recommendations as could be published.[68]

The Commission is thus a device at the service of the Prime Minister, owing its existence to successive occupants of that office, and acting only at the summons of, and under the terms of reference laid down by the incumbent. Moreover the Commission's reports are advisory only, the Prime Minister retaining complete discretion as to whether and what action should be taken subsequently. However the practice of consulting with the Leader of the Opposition over the making of a reference and over the action to be taken on any report is intended to remove security issues from partisan controversy.

Who serves in this capacity, and how do they undertake their tasks? The term 'Establishment' has fallen into disuse and some disrepute in recent years, perhaps through excessive and sloppy use. None the less it would be difficult to find a group more deserving of the description. The seven members consist of five knights, a Dame, and—sign of the times—one Peer, the first industrialist to be appointed.[69] Following long practice, the chairman is a senior judge—Lord

---

[63] *HC Debs.*, vol. 712, col. 34 (10 May 1965).

[64] Ibid., vol. 780, col. 311 (26 Mar. 1969). In all cases of official secrets prosecutions involving a breach of security the chairman automatically receives a statement of facts outlining the case and will be asked to give his opinion on whether an investigation 'would be likely to serve a useful purpose'.

[65] (Earl Jellicoe and Lord Lambton) Cmnd. 5367 (1973).

[66] (9th Signals Unit and Other Static Communications Units) Cmnd. 9923 (1986), para. 1. 9. The circumstances of the acquittal gave rise to a quite separate investigation by David Calcutt, QC into the interrogation procedures used: Cmnd. 9781 (1986) (for discussion see A. Bradley, 'The Cyprus Eight and the Rule of Law' [1986] *PL* 363).

[67] *HC Debs.* vol. 1, col. 1079–85 (26 Mar. 1981).   [68] Cmnd. 8540 (1982).

[69] Lord Tombs, formerly Chairman of Rolls-Royce.

Lloyd, who has been at the epicentre of security and intelligence matters since he also sat as a member of the Advisory Panel to the Home Secretary reviewing cases of deportation on grounds of national security and was for six years the Commissioner under the Interception of Communications Act 1985.[70] The other current members, all of whom are retired from their positions in the public service, include a General, an Air Chief Marshall, a former Permanent Under-Secretary of State in the Home Office, a former Head of the Diplomatic Service, and a former Scientific Adviser to the Government and member of the UK Atomic Energy Authority.

Not all are Privy Councillors; unlike the members of SIRC, it is felt unnecessary to make them Privy Councillors on appointment. They are not positively vetted, but the public servants will all have successfully undergone the highest level of vetting whilst in office. The judicial members uniquely are taken on trust—an extraordinary testament to the perception of judges and their role in the British system of government. Why particular judges receive the Prime-Ministerial letter of invitation remains a mystery,[71] but it may be not irrelevant to the process that the first Chairman, Winn J, had served in naval intelligence and that both he and Lord Bridge (member of the Commission 1977–85 and Chairman 1982–5) had before their elevation been Treasury Counsel. No formal criteria govern the appointment of the other Commissioners. The idea is to cover the full range of the public sector by picking people with experience in all areas relevant to the Commission's work at the very highest level of government. Although the Commission's reports may have important implications for their conditions of service, no attempt has been made to include a member of a trade union or association representing public sector employees on the Commission. The objective is not to ensure representativeness or consensus, but to reach conclusions and advise the Prime Minister on correction or prevention of breaches of security.

Only three or four members will work on a particular investigation; the breadth of experience is expected to ensure that at least one or two of them will be familiar with any area or subject which requires scrutiny. They are assisted by a Secretary and a very small support staff, drawn from the Cabinet Office, all of whom will have been previously fully vetted. The key person in the whole process is the Chairman. He will be briefed at the outset by the Cabinet Secretary in person and thereafter by the Commission's Secretary.[72] The

---

[70] See Ch. 3 above.

[71] The following judges have been Security Commissioners: Winn LJ (chairman 1964–71), Lord Simon of Glaisdale (1965–77), Lord Diplock (Chairman 1971–82), Lord Bridge of Harwich (1977–85; Chairman 1982–5), Lord Griffiths of Govillon (1982–92; Chairman 1985–92), and Lord Lloyd (1985– ; Chairman 1992–); Butler-Sloss LJ (1992–) was appointed as the first female member of the Commission.

[72] It should be noted that this office is not a full-time post; the present incumbent and his successor have combined it with responsibility for security vetting throughout the Civil Service, which is far more time-consuming. With the abolition of the Civil Service Department, the Secretary has been located in the Cabinet Office.

Chairman conducts the hearings and undertakes most of the questioning of witnesses. Chairmen can range as widely as they choose and, although advised by the Secretary, are not constricted by the guidance they receive. Each inquiry begins from scratch and in certain cases the Chairman's approach has made it clear that in his view the exercise was of doubtful value. The relative inactivity of the members—for example, they did not meet at all in 1989 or 1990—gives little opportunity for a learning curve to develop, although the Chairman will acquire greater experience.

The primarily inquisitorial function of the Commission reflects the circumstances which led to its creation and is demonstrated in its powers and procedures. As a substitute for *ad hoc* tribunals of inquiry, in practice it commands the same respect as a tribunal instituted under the 1921 Act.[73] The Commission may interview anyone it chooses; rank or organizational attachment does not provide exemption. For instance, in the inquiry after the conviction of Geoffrey Prime for espionage, the Commission began by interviewing the Director of GCHQ, where Prime worked, and then talked with 'anyone else who might help decide what went wrong, including junior co-workers'.[74] Lists of those interviewed are usually published with the subsequent report.[75] Although it has free rein over witnesses anywhere in the public service (intelligence officers regularly appear), the Commission primarily relies on calling for papers; it has unrestricted access to all files and will have before it the transcripts of any relevant official secrets trials arising from the facts of the reference. Since it is convened to investigate some breach of security its members start with a clear idea of what they are looking for and what papers they wish to see, or at least what questions to ask. Usually the ground will have been prepared in advance by investigations into the breach of security by officers of the Security Service.[76] Whether this method of operation can be equally effective in the rare instances where the Commission's task is more open-ended[77] must be at least questionable, though imposssible to determine. New lines of inquiry may be pursued as the investigation develops, and the Commission has never yet been dissatisfied with the co-operation it has

[73] For comparison between the two procedures see pp. 481–2 below.

[74] The investigation was unusual in that, in formulating proposals for the trial introduction in the UK of the polygraph (lie detector), the Commission interviewed US officers working with NSA (the equivalent body to GCHQ): Cmnd. 8876 (1983). Although the incident is a rare public acknowledgement of the international context in which security restrictions operate, it appears that the purpose of these interviews was purely fact-finding, not consultative.

[75] The names of intelligence officers are omitted from the published version of the reports. In the report on the Bettaney Case (see n. 60 above) two Security Service officers agreed to give evidence in return for a promise of anonymity and their names were accordingly omitted from the pre-publication version of the report.

[76] To this extent there may often be a close working relationship with the Security Service. The Commission felt unable to rely on this method in the one instance where it was called upon to investigate the Security Service itself (the Bettaney case, n. 60 above) and accordingly relied in that, investigation more than normally upon oral testimony.

[77] As in its general review of security procedures (see nn. 67 and 68 above).

received.[78] The responsiveness of such normally secretive institutions as MI5 may, perhaps, be attributed less to the stature of the the Commission and its members than to the fact they are known to be acting on behalf of the Prime Minister.

There are dangers here, which in fact were one of the mainsprings of the establishment of the Commission. It is necessary to protect the reputation of innocent participants; there was great concern at the time that the Profumo investigation had done unnecessary damage to reputations.[79] Interviewees enjoy neither legal representation nor immunity and it is very unclear what range of penalties might be threatened or imposed on someone who refuses co-operation, although in the case of civil servants loss of employment would seem to be a serious possibilty. None the less, the former Secretary recognized that it was 'not inconceivable' that lack of representation could become a problem in future, and that inquiries might in consequence take on a more judicial mode. A further problem area also left unclear under the existing arrangements is the relationship between Commission investigations and internal civil service disci-plinary procedures: in some reports the conduct of named officers has been commented on, although they themselves were not directly responsible for the breach of security.

The Bettaney case,[80] whilst in many ways unique, stands as a spectacular example of these problems. What began as a probe into the misconduct of one Security Service employee broadened out into a wider inquiry into the efficiency, morale, and personnel policy of the Service. A large part of the Report remains secret, but it is has been noted that the then Director-General retired prema-turely soon afterwards.[81] It is not known, but seems highly unlikely, that natural justice in the *Ridge* v. *Baldwin*[82] sense significantly constrained those determining the organization's future and leadership.

One apparent way of resolving some of these difficulties would be if the Commission were to receive evidence under the Tribunals of Inquiry (Evidence) Act 1921. Indeed this was envisaged as a possibility in cases of difficulty by the Prime Minister, when announcing the establishment of the Commission.[83] However the Royal Commission on Tribunals of Inquiry in 1966 recommended

---

[78] However in its investigation of a peripheral matter raised during the Bettaney case, the Commission encountered an outright refusal by the Press Association to reveal the source of a story. The Commission acquiesced, stating only that to have invoked the procedure under the Tribunal of Inquiry (Evidence) Act 1921 would have been 'a cumbersome and profitless exercise' (see Cmnd. 9514 (1985), app. 1, para. 5). The experience of the Committee of Privy Councillors established to investigate the 'D Notice Affair' (Cmnd. 3309 (1967)) in failing to identify the source of a leak in similar circumstances was, perhaps, salutary.

[79] *HC Debs.*, vol. 686, col. 859 (16 Dec. 1963). [80] See n. 60 above.

[81] N. West, *Molehunt* (London, 1987), 200–2. The author is Rupert Allason, MP, whom we must also thank for an informative interview.

[82] [1964] AC 40.

[83] *HC Debs.*, vol. 686, col. 1272 (23 Jan. 1964). If the Security Commission were ever to be vested with powers under the 1921 Act the report would go instead to the Home Secretary, who would similarly consult.

that the powers under the Act should not be made available to the Security Commission, as proposed, because investigations by the Commission were of a fundamentally different character and purpose.[84] The Royal Commission saw inquiries under the 1921 Act as concerned with resolving matters of acute public disquiet; in such cases the extraordinary powers to obtain evidence in what are normally public proceedings required special protections for witnesses.[85] Security Commission investigations were private and were concerned, in the Royal Commission's view, with establishing the cause of a breach of security in the interests of efficiency.[86]

Although this appears to come close to saying that the procedural deficiencies are unavoidable in the Security Commission procedure, the Royal Commission proposed that if 'teeth' were required a seperate statutory scheme could be created to put the Security Commission's powers on to a formal basis.[87]

A connected issue is the relationship between the courts and the Commission where someone is charged with a criminal offence (notably under section 1 of the Official Secrets Act 1911).[88] The widening of the terms of reference to include cases where there was good reason to think that security had been breached[89] avoided the necessity of postponing investigation until the trial had been concluded. The obvious possibility of prejudice to a fair trial in such circumstances is countered by two precautions. First, no announcement of the investigation is made until later, and secondly, whilst the the matter is before the courts the Commission does not take evidence from persons outside government service. On occasion defendants have been interviewed by the Commission following conviction.[90] Several investigations have begun in this way, with the report being delivered after conviction. Until 1986 this procedure had presented no problems. However, the acquittal of all the defendants in the 'Cyprus Secrets' trial resulted in the terms of reference of the Security Commission investigation already in motion being amended to broaden the inquiry by replacing reference to the men acquitted with a general one to their unit and similar ones.[91]

Completed reports go directly to the Prime Minister. They are produced in a

[84] Cmnd. 3121 (1966), paras., 45 and 46.

[85] Ibid., para. 45. The Royal Commission conceded that, although the two forms of investigation were not alternatives, exceptionally there might be some overlap between them, citing the Vassall inquiry (Cmnd. 2009 (1963) and see p. 470 above, which was held under the 1921 Act and received evidence *in camera* using s. 2(*a*), as an example. The Royal Commission's advice (para. 41) that any future allegations of security risks associated with Ministers should be dealt with under the statutory procedure (and, therefore, by public hearing) was disregarded when the Security Commission was asked to investigate the cases of Earl Jellicoe and Lord Lambton (n. 65 above).

[86] Ibid., para. 46.

[87] Ibid.; see discussion below at p. 486.

[88] Not all security breaches where the Commission has been asked to investigate have involved espionage charges. For instance, in the Ritchie case (n. 58 above) the charge was one of passing information, brought under the old s. 2 of the 1911 Act.

[89] See n. 66 above. Investigation was no longer confined to cases of proven breach.

[90] e.g. Bettaney (n. 60 above.).   [91] See n. 66 above.

form intended to permit publication: classified material is confined to annexes which can be omitted from the published version if thought necessary. The rather vague notion of 'national interest' governs decisions about deletion. Officials have stated that 'there is a great presumption in favour of publication', and indeed a reading of the reports suggests that more appears in print than if the excessively wide classification categories[92] were strictly adhered to. Whereas the published reports are relatively informative on the mechanics of security procedures in the particular case, as one would expect, they are silent on operational details.

Reports always include recommendations, which the Prime Minister may or may not choose to implement. The main purpose of the investigation is seen as organizational—to propose changes to prevent future mistakes, rather than as pin-pointing individuals' poor performance (and still less to identify criminal conduct). It was described as 'a constant process of challenging management to justify their decision'. Moreover, occasional 'follow up' investigations have taken place at the behest of government to assess the implementation of the Commission's recommendations. Yet, however effectively the Commission may function in any particular instance, the process can hardly be described as 'constant'. This observation leads us to an overall evaluation of the Commission and its work.

We began by identifying a number of characteristics which the Commission might, but did not, possess.[93] More positively it may be described as an independent, standing advisory body, non-statutory, specialist in its composition, reporting on an *ad hoc* basis, and recommendatory in method. Above all it is a body of limited purpose, which accounts for its greatest strengths and weaknesses. It is well equipped, as one might expect in view of its close similarity to other tribunals of inquiry[94] to investigate a particular set of events with limited parameters. It can preserve secrecy where nececessary, move sure-footedly in the corridors of power, and obtain information and co-operation where others may meet a brick wall.

On the other hand, because it is so tightly fettered to the Prime Minister, it cannot undertake any inquiries on its own, nor even suggest that one be initiated. Nor is it consulted on policy matters, even where it might be expected to have accumulated expertise. Thus, although many of the Commission's reports have involved consideration of Positive Vetting (including its major review of 1981–2),[95] its views were not sought when the government was preparing the extensive revision of the system it announced in July 1990.[96] This seems a waste of talent, but is perhaps best understood as a result of the determination of

[92] See Ch. 5 above. For contrasting judicial treatment of the classification system see the judgments of Lord Diplock (who had chaired the Security Commission investigation which, *inter alia*, considered the categories) and the unusually sceptical dissent of Lord Scarman in *Secretary of State for Defence* v. *Guardian Newspapers* [1984] AC 349, 354 ff. and 364–6 respectively.

[93] p. 477 above.   [94] See nn. 84–6 above.   [95] See n. 68 above.

[96] *HC Debs.*, vol. 177, cols 159–61w (24 July 1990).

successive Prime Ministers not to share power over security matters with any-one, however impeccably Establishment their credentials.

Outsiders like ourselves are in no position to judge whether the Security Commission has produced significant improvements in security or indeed has always succeeded in getting at all the salient facts. However, it is worth record-ing the view of Rupert Allason, MP, whose perspective on security matters—based as it is on numerous contacts within the Security Service—is both unusual and astringent.[97]

During the debate over the Security Service Bill, Mr Allason, describing him-self as 'a very late convert to the introduction of some kind of oversight or scrutiny', said:

We have heard glowing tributes to the Security Commission. However why was the Security Commission created in the first place? It was because a series of monumental blunders had occurred . . . However that organisation is treated with derision within the Security Service. The Security Commission has been described to me as 'a stable door operation'. On occasions the Security Commission has been completely misled. Should any of my colleagues say that is disgraceful and take the Security Commission quite seri-ously, can they tell me why the Government has consistently ignored its recommenda-tions? . . . There are numerous other examples of the Security Commission being misled. Perhaps the most recent example was over the Michael Bettaney case . . .[98]

These comments were supplemented in an informal discussion. Allason's view is that the Commissioners can be readily led in the direction that the Security Service and their own secretariat wish to lead them. Their lack of expertise means that they do not know what questions should be asked; and they only receive the information they request. Not only are their recommendations not taken up, he argued, but the Service itself would undertake its own parallel analysis of matters which concerned it directly, and this would be both 'fuller and harsher'.

It will come as no surprise that the picture painted by other sources[99] was very different. We cannot judge between them in general terms. However, there are certain specific points it is possible to comment upon with some assurance. One is that although its detailed proposals for the Positive Vetting system have frequently been adopted, some of the Commission's other major recommenda-tions in recent years have been rejected. It has proposed more than once, as a measure of tightening physical security of government premises, the random searching of employees for highly classified documents as they leave.[100] This proposal remains unimplemented. Another even more controversial instance concerns use of the polygraph, or lie detector, as part of the security vetting process. In its report on Geoffrey Prime,[101] the Commission had strongly urged its adoption, in line with common practice in the United States. The recommen-

---

[97] See n. 81 above.   [98] *HC Debs.*, vol. 145, cols. 64–5 (16 Jan. 1989).
[99] See n. 53 above.   [100] Cmnd. 8876 (1983), paras. 8.3–8; Cmnd. 9514 (1985), para. 4.7.
[101] See n. 60 above.

dation met extraordinary resistance, not least from the Civil Service, but the Government agreed to a pilot study. However, it was eventually decided not to incorporate polygraph testing as standard British practice. This was announced as a written answer to what was obviously an 'inspired' Parliamentary Question, but only after an 'informal consultation' with the Commission during which the decision was explained.[102] In both instances those who value human rights have cause to thank the Government, rather than the Commission.

However other functions of the Commission, political in the widest sense, are more readily assessable. For over twenty years, from the Profumo scandal until the Spycatcher affair, a broad political consensus on security matters prevailed, assisted in part by the superconductivity of Security Commission references. Even a scandal in the mid-1970s involving government ministers[103] barely disturbed the peace. As a lightning conductor the Security Commission appears to have been largely effective. The more recent disintegration of an all-party approach to security is due very largely to the refusal to allow allegations made by former intelligence insiders such as Peter Wright, Cathy Massiter, and Colin Wallace[104] to be investigated independently. None of these cases would in fact have fallen squarely within the terms of reference of the Security Commission, but the terms of reference have been used flexibly on previous occasions. On the other hand, the Blunt case (which was discovered after the creation of the Commission but did not become public knowledge until 1979)[105] is an example of a case indisputably falling within the Commission's remit where it was not asked to investigate. Indeed, despite abundant opportunity no case has been referred to the Security Commission since 1985[106].

One cannot help but wonder to what extent narrow political calculations are responsible for this reticence. There is little incentive to refer a hitherto undisclosed security failure to the Commission, since this will necessarily result in it becoming public. It has also been suggested that a desire not to inform the Leader of the Opposition of the details of a case might prove influential as a reason for not invoking the procedure.[107] In practice the result appears to have been that the most serious security allegations of all are not referred, with consequently more controversy when they become uncovered. If this analysis is

---

[102] *HC Debs.*, vol. 143, cols. 268–9w (8 Dec. 1988). See also n. 74 above. This 'informal consultation' is not standard practice, but is not precluded by the standing terms of reference (above, text at nn. 62–4 above). This procedure avoids the necessity of consulting the Leader of the Opposition, but there are no grounds whatever for suspecting the presence of that motive in this particular instance.

[103] The Jellicoe and Lambton affairs, n. 65 above.

[104] Limited aspects of the Wallace case have been investigated by David Calcutt, QC (see *HC Debs.*, vol. 166, col. 112 (30 Jan. 1990), but requests for a full investigation of Wallace's allegations of a plot ('Operation Clockwork Orange') to smear politicians, including those of the then Labour government, have been rejected.

[105] See the Prime Minister's statement at *HC Debs.*, vol. 973, col. 1679 (15 Nov. 1979).

[106] The revision to the terms of reference to the 'Cyprus Signals' investigation was announced on 12 Nov. 1985: see Cmnd. 9923 (1986), 1 and 2.

[107] As has been alleged of the Blunt case (n. 105 above).

correct it leaves the Commission as essentially outside the intelligence and security establishment, but occasionally invited to step in as a guest for a limited purpose. The abiding impression is that the invitations are issued more for the sake of decorum than hospitality.

In the light of the foregoing analysis, what would be the most appropriate role for the Commission in the 1990s and beyond? In its narrow and specific sphere of operation it has shown itself capable of performing a useful function. Much of our disquiet concerns failure to make use of it as distinct from incompetence, over-zealousness, or political bias—the main grounds of complaint often aired against the Security Service particularly. The Commission has shown itself worthy of a permanent status and enlarged brief, both of which should be derived from an Act of Parliament. Perhaps the most obvious reform would be to give the statutory body responsibility for periodic reviews of security arrangements, not, as at present, by Prime-Ministerial fiat, but at its own initiative and at specified intervals. It would then have further opportunity to build up continuing expertise in security matters (indeed, we envisage it becoming more 'expert' than at present), but from a perspective wholly detached from ministerial self-interest. A reform of this kind would be the natural concomitant of the long overdue need to place security vetting on a statutory basis.[108]

If such a reform was adopted the opportunity could then also be taken to give the Commission explicit powers to obtain information, balanced with procedural protections for witnesses, appropriate to the forum. Imaginative attempts have been made in the Canadian procedures for dealing with interception warrants and reviews of refusal of security clearance to provide procedural protection without compromising security, through the use of vetted 'devil's advocates'.[109] Although less satisfactory than formal cross-examination, this nevertheless enables objections to be made to sensitive evidence on an individual's behalf, without breaching security by disclosing it to him or her in the course of a hearing.

A statutory Security Commission with a power of independent investigation and a duty of periodic review need not be composed very differently from at present. There would still be a need for a cross-section of informed opinion with experience of public service. If, however, it was also periodically to give its general advice on aspects of security procedures, there would be a case for including a member with public sector union experience, if not formal staff representation. There would also still be a place for judges in such a Commission but, arguably, it should be a less prominent one than at present. Where a report requires the impartial investigation of a referred set of facts the argument for inclusion of members of the judiciary is at its strongest. However judges are less obviously specially qualified to deal with more diffuse questions of the merit of one proposed security practice as against an alternative. The need for continuity

---

[108] See Ch. 6 above.   [109] See Chs. 6 and 7 above.

of membership and the artificiality of divorcing 'policy' investigations from 'breach of security' investigations would militate against the exclusion of judicial members from the Commission's wider activities, but there would be no need for them to take the central role in these cases.

The Commission could be given statutory authority without any change in the present governance of security matters, under which the Executive, and particularly the Prime Minister, are virtually in complete control and Parliament is excluded. The more intriguing question is what place the Commission might occupy if, as we advocate, Britain adopts a more democratic structure of governance. The answer, perhaps surprisingly, is that such change need make little difference in this respect. If a structure of institutional oversight were to emerge, the Security Commission would continue to enjoy the unique flexibility of transcending such rigid lines of demarcation, which it would be a serious error to sacrifice.[110] And even if, much against the odds, functional review were established, the initial period of adjustment and learning will be difficult and controversial, and it would be as well to leave this aspect undisturbed at least for the moment. At present and in the likely future, the Security Commission occupies a unique niche, because of its concentration on security breach and management issues, and would continue to be useful even in a structure in which considerations of democracy and human rights finally received their due weight in the security context. Its limited but useful specialism should guarantee it a continuing existence, albeit in altered form.

THE USE OF JUDGES

One key aspect of the inquiries considered which invites critical consideration is the continuing involvement in them of senior members of the judiciary.[111] The use of judges in this kind of extra-judicial duty is long-standing. Examples from the security field go back to the Second World War when Norman Birkett, then a leading King's Counsel, chaired the Advisory Committee which reviewed the cases of wartime internees; his elevation to the High Court judiciary in 1941 may have been not entirely unconnected with this service.[112] In the 1950s it was Birkett again, by then a retired Lord Justice of Appeal, who chaired a Privy Counsellor's Committee into telephone tapping.[113] Lord Radcliffe was another favourite choice of the government for such tasks:[114] among several other

---

[110] As our sample listing of reports indicates (nn. 56–60 above), the Commission has investigated the activities of individual Ministers, and personnel from the military, the Foreign Office, GCHQ, and the Security Service. In Canada, SIRC looks at security breaches in respect of CSIS only. See S. Farson, 'Oversight of Canadian Intelligence: a Revisionary Note', [1992] *PL* 377.

[111] See n. 71 above on judicial members of Security Commission.

[112] A. Simpson, *In the Highest Degree Odious: Detention Without Trial in Wartime Britain* (Oxford, 1992), 265 and 379.

[113] Cmnd. 283 (1957). [114] See Hennessy, *Whitehall* (n. 12 above), 565–8.

public duties he chaired a Committee on Security Procedures in the Public Service,[115] a 1921 Act tribunal on the Vassall case,[116] a committee on recruitment to the secret intelligence service,[117] and Privy Councillors' Committees on D Notices[118] and on ministerial memoirs.[119]

Lord Denning, of course, inquired into the Profumo affair.[120] In recent years the standing involvement of individual judges in this area has grown and become more formalized. It began with the successive appointments of Lord Diplock and Lord Bridge, while each was Chairman of the Security Commission, as judicial monitor for the interception of communications.[121] Subsequently Lord Justice Lloyd, having been appointed Deputy Chairman of the Commission, became statutory Interceptions Commissioner, to be suceeded as Commissioner by Sir Thomas Bingham, Master of the Rolls, in 1992;[122] Lord Justice Stuart-Smith occupies the analogous position under the Security Service Act 1989. Judges have also been appointed to the tribunals established to hear complaints under these Acts.[123]

Judges have also featured prominently in similar investigations in Canada and Australia. The McDonald and Hope Commissions[124] both comprised senior members of provincial appeal courts, and judges have also investigated further scandals in Australia.[125] Indeed it is notable that the ASIO Act specifically provided that a judge could be appointed as Director of ASIO.[126]

General concern about the extra-judicial use of judges has tended to focus on the questions of whether the tasks are always appropriate for a judge and on the dangers of involvement in party political controversy.[127] So far as the first is concerned judicial involvement seems most justified where a major part of the exercise is to determine the facts in an impartial fashion. Most of the instances cited above would fall into this category, but equally often the terms of refer-

---

[115] Cmnd. 1681 (1962). [116] Cmnd. 2009 (1963).

[117] Not officially acknowledged but recorded in Hennessy (n. 12 above), 568; presumably the occasion was the Blake case.

[118] Cmnd. 3309 (1967). When the government rejected the findings of the report Lord Radcliffe spoke in a debate in the House of Lords criticizing its White Paper (Cmnd. 3312 (1967)): Hennessy (n. 12 above), 566.

[119] Cmnd. 6386 (1976). [120] Cmnd. 2152 (1963).

[121] See the announcement of these arrangements (*HC Debs.*, vol. 982, cols. 205, 208 (1 Apr. 1980)); see further Ch. 3 above.

[122] Bingham LJ had previously conducted two inquiries with security implications: T. H. Bingham and S. M. Gray, *Report on the Supply of Petroleum and Petroleum Products to Rhodesia* (HMSO, 1978); *Return to an Address of the Honourable House of Commons dated 22 October 1992 for the Inquiry into the supervision of the Bank of Credit and Commerce International*, HC (1992–3) 198 (with an unpublished app. 8, on the involvement of the intelligence agencies, omitted).

[123] Simon Brown J is President of the Interception of Communications Tribunal.

[124] See n. 6 above.

[125] An investigation was conducted by acting Justice White in 1976: *Special Branch Security Records: Initial Report to the Honourable Donald Allen Dunstan Premier of South Australia* (Adelaide, 1977); see R. Fox, 'The Salisbury Affair: Special Branches, Security and Subversion' (1979) 5 *Monash LR* 251.

[126] ASIO Act 1979, s. 15.

[127] S. Shetreet, *Judges on Trial* (Amsterdam, 1976), 354–63; G. Zellick, [1972] *PL* 1.

ence invite the Committee or whatever the body is to make recommendations. Some of these exercises have been purely policy-oriented, for instance, the Radcliffe and Security Commission reports on security procedures. Here the exercise is more executive than judicial, and there will always remain at the end a political choice whether to implement the recommendations. As to the second concern, there is a danger that a government faced with some pressing crisis may deflect criticism and buy time by sheltering behind the appointment of a figure with an appearance of impartiality. Whatever the merits of this criticism in some fields where judges have been asked to conduct inquiries, the broadly bipartisan nature of security policy means that it applies less stringently here. Nevertheless the danger that involvement in such work might compromise a judge's reputation was amply demonstrated by the controversy surrounding Lord Bridge's report reviewing the issue of warrants for telephone tapping in 1985.

This episode stands as a cautionary tale. Cathy Massiter, the MI5 officer in charge of the investigation of CND as an allegedly subversive organization, resigned and gave a televised interview in which she alleged that the Service had engaged in a number of politically-motivated improper acts, including telephone tapping, infiltration, and surveillance of other campaign groups like Friends of the Earth.[128] These allegations provoked a public outcry, and Lord Bridge— apparently in his capacity as judicial monitor of interceptions and not as Chairman of the Security Commission—was asked to investigate. When it was known that that his inquiry had been completed in five days, including a week-end, he was attacked by Roy Jenkins MP (then Leader of the SDP), in a letter to *The Times* as 'a poodle of the executive'.[129] The publication of this letter coincided with the House of Commons Second Reading debate on the Interception of Communications Bill, which was opened with a speech by the Home Secretary, Leon Brittan, including a statement on Lord Bridge's inquiry. In language that would have done credit to Charles Dickens's Circumlocution Office, Mr Brittan stated that Lord Bridge had been asked to look at: 'whether the authorisation of interceptions over the whole period covered by the recent allegations named the individuals in question and, if so, whether the authorisations were sought and given in accordance with the procedures and criteria . . .'[130] Uncoiling this prose, all Lord Bridge had done was to look at the files of the individuals named by Massiter—approximately a dozen—and to determine only that the existing (and at that point non-statutory) criteria for interceptions had been followed in those cases.

[128] See Ch. 3.

[129] 12 Mar. 1985; for a letter in reply from Lord Bridge see *The Times*, 14th Mar. 1985. Mr Jenkins (now Lord Jenkins of Hillhead) has acquired something of a proprietary interest in the phrase, which appeared in the title of a historical study he had written some years earlier: R. Jenkins, *Mr Balfour's Poodle: An Account of the Struggle Between the House of Lords and the Government of Mr Asquith* (London, 1954). The comment was later to be retracted following Lord Bridge's dissent in *A-G* v. *Guardian Newspapers* [1987] 1 WLR 1248. On the whole incident see K. D. Ewing and C. Gearty, *Freedom under Thatcher: Civil Liberties in Modern Britain* (Oxford, 1990), 54–5.

[130] *HC Debs.*, vol. 75, cols. 151–4 (12 Mar. 1985).

No one emerges from this affair with much credit. One cannot say whether the government deliberately presented matters so as to give the false impression—which undoubtedly emerged—that a judicial stamp of approval had been embossed on all MI5's activities in relation to domestic dissent. Certainly the public version of Lord Bridge's Report, which was heavily edited, was highly ambiguous on the point and ministers did nothing to correct the impression. The critics seem to have been over-hasty or careless; and indeed years later the criticism is still repeated that Lord Bridge's inquiry had covered thousands of warrants wholly inadequately.[131]

Most important, however, is that the end result was to cover all the issues raised in a fog of confusion. The Massiter allegations—which went well beyond abuses related to telephone tapping—have never been properly investigated. Complaints by others of victimization by the Security Service in this period have been met by governmental stonewall. It is very doubtful whether Lord Bridge appreciated that he had been cast into a political snake-pit, a treatment undesirable for any public servant, but especially so for the current holder of high judicial office.

An equally serious danger is to the appearance of impartiality when judges with inside experience of reviewing intelligence matters subsequently sit to hear cases involving questions of national security. Although apparently unnoticed at the time, Lord Radcliffe sat in the House of Lords' appeal in *Chandler* v. *DPP*[132] immediately after completing his review of security procedures in the public service.[133] It is difficult to read Lord Denning's judgment in the *Hosenball* case[134] or Lord Griffiths's speech in the second House of Lords decision in *Spycatcher*[135] without forming the impression that the tone was influenced by their extra-judicial experiences. Similarly, it would be natural to expect that Lord Diplock's approach to questions of secrecy and the classification of documents in the *Guardian Newspapers* case[136] might have been influenced by his chairmanship two years earlier of the Security Commission investigation into security procedures, which, among other things, reviewed the classification categories.[137] Indeed the Security Service Commissioner, Lord Justice Stuart-Smith, admitted to us that his judgment in one instance, a case concerning the handling of applications for access on security grounds to material held by the press,[138] had been directly so influenced—in his view to the good, since it gave him experience which the remainder of the court lacked.

[131] e.g. by R. Norton-Taylor, *In Defence of the Realm?* (London, 1990), 80.

[132] [1964] AC 763 (hearings during May, June, and July 1962).

[133] Cmnd. 1681 (Apr. 1962); ch. 8 of the report dealt with physical security at government premises—substantially the issue in the *Chandler* appeal.

[134] [1977] 1 WLR 766, esp. at 782 (where he makes explicit reference to the Profumo report) and 783.

[135] *A-G* v. *The Observer* [1988] 3 WLR 776, 793 (esp. at 800).

[136] *Secretary of State for Defence* v. *Guardian Newspapers* [1984] AC 349, 354 ff.; contrast the approach of Lord Scarman, ibid. 364–6.

[137] See n. 68 above. [138] *R.* v. *Guildhall Crown Court ex p. Sallinger, The Times,* 30 Mar. 1992.

We are not, of course, alleging judicial impropriety in any of these instances. Each of them and others[139] can be justified by application of the narrow principle that the judge was not dealing in court with the particular facts investigated extra-judicially. However whether it is wise for judges publicly associated with extra-judicial investigations to continue to sit thereafter in cases arising in the same field is at least debatable.[140] This point has nothing in particular to do with security, but the argument can be made more strongly in that area, because of the presumption that the court will not enquire into the evidence of the government's assertion of national security interests:[141] a judge publicly known to have been party to state secrets is (although they may be wholly unrelated) in this sense one of the initiated. Overall there is a curious paradox between the self-denying judicial ordinance on substantive consideration of issues of national security in court and the preparedness to use the judiciary to consider identical issues extra-judicially. If judges are to continue to serve as Security Commissioners (and in the other roles mentioned) the appearance of justice would be better served if they declined to sit in all cases associated with official secrecy and national security. A strong case can be made for such a practice in cases even when the judge has no direct knowledge of the facts in issue, since if the theory is that the executive is the judge of what national security requires and the court is merely reviewing whether some evidence exists for the assertion, this task is best performed from a fully detached and uninformed position.

CONCLUSION

There is a strange inevitability about the cycle of scandal, investigation, report, and fresh scandal which litters the history of investigations into security matters and ought to make one sceptical about any suggestion that the need for such *ad hoc* devices would disappear if a permanent, independent oversight body for security and intelligence were established. At best such an institution might prove a safety-valve, preventing such frequent resort to inquiries and committees. To some extent the Security Commission has already played this role, although in view of the inactivity of that body in recent years its future must be in doubt. Two factors are likely to guarantee a future place for investigations of this kind.

First is the complexity of some scandals. An affair like that of Matrix Churchill, crossing departmental and institutional boundaries, demands an exceptional response outside a framework of scrutiny set up to shadow the

---

[139] e.g. Lord Bridge also sat in *Secretary of State for Defence* v. *Guardian Newspapers* [1985] AC 349; Lord Diplock sat in *CCSU* v. *Minister for the Civil Service* [1985] AC 374; Lord Bridge sat (and dissented) in *A-G* v. *Guardian Newspapers* [1987] 1 WLR 1248; and Lloyd LJ sat in *A-G* v. *Newspaper Publishing plc* [1988] Ch. 33.

[140] Cf. J. Griffith, *The Politics of the Judiciary* (4th edn., London, 1991), ch. 2.

[141] See Ch. 12 above.

work of particular agencies. The second is that the failure of the regular means of oversight may itself be part of what is to be investigated in any future *cause célèbre*.

However, we have identified a number of difficulties about the range of existing practices concerning the gathering and publication of evidence and the use of judges. To these should be added a final problem which may be unresolvable. In the climate of international intelligence co-operation which has prevailed in the West since the Second World War it has become increasingly apparent that many security investigations have international dimensions. The recent investigations into the Bank of Credit and Commerce International and arms sales to Iraq pursued independently on both sides of the Atlantic illustrate the point. Unless the respective legislatures develop some way of at least taking account of evidence received within a different constitutional system, it is hard to see how investigation and scrutiny of these complex international scandals can ever be comprehensive.[142]

---

[142] For a proposal for Commissions of Inquiry to be able to adopt evidence received abroad in this way, see Law Reform Commission of Canada, *Commissions of Inquiry: A New Act* (Ottawa, 1977), 60.

Coda

The Intelligence Services Bill, the very first piece of legislation introduced by the government in the House of Lords in the 1993/4 parliamentary session, is the culmination of an extraordinary change of tack. Britain was the last of the parliamentary democracies to put any of its security and intelligence services on a statutory footing, and into the 1990s it obdurately attempted to maintain the bizarre fiction that the Secret Intelligence Service (SIS, or MI6), having been valiantly active in war, had magically disappeared with the coming of peace. And even as it began the process of concession with the introduction of the Security Service Act 1989, the Conservative government adamantly insisted that Parliament could not be granted any role in the oversight of these agencies. Now, however, there has been a remarkable turnabout. SIS and GCHQ, the signals intercept body, have been brought, if not into the limelight, at least in from the cold. As with MI5, they are to be given a statutory existence,[1] mandate, powers, and formal relationship to its political superiors. They will also be made subject to the same structure of executive accountability, and to the complaints procedure, which have been described in Chapter 15. Morever, though to an extent that remains controversially unclear, all three services are to be subject to scrutiny by a new parliamentary committee. To borrow a phrase from the great constitutional historian F. W. Maitland, we have been living very fast.

The Bill is almost certain to be enacted without significant change, as was the 1989 Act.[2] And like that legislation, it was not preceded by any White Paper or explanatory document, though it was accompanied by a useful if somewhat bland document describing the organization of intelligence gathering and analysis in Britain.[3] Nor, as we write at the end of 1993, has it received any parliamentary discussion save the inevitably highly general Second Reading debate in the Lords. Our analysis and critique of the Bill therefore draws largely upon scholarly and unofficial sources. However, we have had the benefit of a long interview with Mr Gerald Warner, the Intelligence Co-ordinator, who is based in the

---

[1] Formerly MI6 was governed by a Directive to 'C' (the title traditionally given to its Chief). ASIS remains the subject of a similar non-statutory Charter, the 'Directive For Director, Australian Secret Intelligence Service', an earlier version of which can be found published in B. Toohey and W. Pinwill, *Oyster* (Port Melbourne, Victoria, 1990), 291–5. The CIA is, by comparison, a veteran of the statute book, having been created under the National Security Act of 1947.

[2] Hence most of our citations to particular clauses of the Bill are likely to be equally applicable to sections of the Act when it comes into force. All references are to clauses in the Bill as first published in the House of Lords in November 1993.

[3] See the official booklet *Central Intelligence Machinery* (London, 1993). Note also the booklet *MI5: The Security Service* (London, 1993).

Cabinet Office and occupies a critical role in determining intelligence requirements and the allocation of responsibilities among the three agencies. Also present was a member of the Foreign Office legal team working on the Bill, who
requested anonymity.

Our survey of the Bill begins with consideration of the mandates of SIS and
GCHQ. This is integrated where necessary with exposition of the provisions
which enable ministers to authorize (and in effect grant immunity for) a range
of activities that would otherwise be criminal acts or civil wrongs. Following discussion of the remaining warrant clauses, we look at mechanisms of executive
accountability. The analysis concludes with a survey of the composition, jurisdiction, and powers of the parliamentary committee.

THE MANDATE OF SIS

Analysis of the statutory mandate is most conveniently divided between
functions—what the organization does—and the *purposes* for which it is permitted
to act.

Functions

These are stated in clause 1 (1) to be (a) 'to obtain and provide information
relating to the actions or intentions of persons *outside the British Islands*, and
(b) to perform *other tasks* relating to the actions or intentions of such persons'
(emphasis supplied). Behind this bland facade lie some major political and moral
issues, as well as more narrow operational ones.

The restriction of the Service's attentions to persons outside the country is of
course a reflection of its historic role, which—like that of its counterparts everywhere else—is to gather information by and from human officers, agents, and
sources[4] about foreign governments, companies, and persons. The means by
which such information is to be gathered may often be mundane and straightforward, such as conversations with officials, businessmen, or journalists, or
careful reading of government documents, newspapers, or other open sources.
However, secret means of obtaining information, the stuff of a thousand novels
and which evokes names ranging from Mata Hari, through Klaus Fuchs and
George Blake, to Oleg Gordievsky, is equally a method of acquiring hidden
knowledge accepted and employed by governments everywhere. This observation is worth making at the outset as a caution against hypocrisy. MI6 is, in part,
an organization devoted to espionage. This involves, among other things,
recruiting people to provide information whose disclosure is illegal under the

---

[4] Canada is virtually alone among major nations in not having an organization devoted to human
intelligence gathering. It does, however, have a signals intercept body, the Communications Security
Establishment (CSE).

laws of another state, and is regarded by that state as extremely damaging to its interests. Other nations direct similar efforts at Britain and it should come as no surprise when they enjoy some successes. We argued in Chapter 9 that it is legitimate to impose criminal penalties for such activities, to try to prevent their consequences and punish those who have been involved. It is, however, impossible to regard them as having acted especially immorally when those acting in our name are assiduously trying to achieve the same result elsewhere.

Though MI6 may only target individuals outside Britain, that restriction does not entirely preclude operations on British soil. Relevant information about their actions or intentions may be found in this country, and individuals may visit or temporarily reside here. (This applies particularly to the activities of citizens of the Irish Republic in relation to Northern Ireland.) However, the traditional notion that SIS works overseas remains largely vindicated. Provisions in clause 5, described in greater detail below, allow the Security Service to apply for a warrant to the Home Secretary to carry out actions on behalf of MI6. The intention seems to be to maintain to the greatest possible extent the home/overseas division of labour between the two organizations and, subject to one exception (also described below) where the SIS mandate is broader than that of MI5, the latter will act as agent for the former when operations on British soil are required.

If the means used to obtain information may be controversial, far more troubling moral and political questions are raised by the 'other tasks' that any overseas intelligence service may be called upon to perform. Oscar Wilde wrote that hypocrisy is the tribute vice pays to virtue; nothing better illustrates this than the language used by governments everywhere when discussing illegal and violent acts committed on foreign soil in defence of supposed national interests. 'Wet affairs', the Russian term for assassination, is perhaps the crassest euphemism, but the standard phrases 'special operations' and 'covert action' are used to cover an enormous range of activities that no government wishes to acknowledge publicly. Perhaps the greatest defect of the Bill is its failure to address the question of limitation: what kinds of conduct do we as a society wish to declare off-limits to those who act on our behalf? We offer an extended discussion in the hope that it will raise awareness of the importance of what is involved.

There will always be limits dictated in particular circumstances by considerations of prudence: fear of embarrassment in the event of failure, or of retaliation in kind.[5] More fundamental are those which would constitute a moral statement: that a nation does not wish to be tainted by its involvement in and responsibility for certain kinds of conduct. Such practical idealism, the very opposite of wordy utopianism, could only have a beneficial effect on the conduct of government generally, including its treatment of its own citizens, for it would amount

---

[5] Fear of retaliation and of setting a bad precedent were officially offered at the time of the Gulf War as reasons for not assassinating Saddam Hussein.

to a statement that whatever the supposed short-term benefits, it is better for the society in the longer term to respect certain moral imperatives.

This notion has already achieved a limited recognition in the acceptance by all European states of restraints in dealing with persons within their borders. Whilst most of the rights contained in the European Convention on Human Rights are expressly subject to curtailment when certain important public interests are implicated,[6] Article 3 simply forbids torture or inhuman or degrading treatment in all circumstances. Yet one can readily imagine circumstances where a simple utilitarian calculus would suggest that torture would be permissible, for instance the extracting of information from an admitted terrorist about the location of the bomb might be justified to save lives. None the less the absolute prohibition on torture is surely right (among other reasons) because once the possibility of torture is admitted in any circumstances, however seemingly compelling, in future those under pressure to prevent a disaster will be increasingly prone to offer, or to accept when others offer, specious arguments for its use. The 'exception' would insidiously become part of the norm.[7] The only safe way to proceed is to rule some tactics out of bounds at the start.

There is no sign at all that the Government understands the need for talking through the issues involved, let alone that it wishes to stimulate public interest in them. Nor have the Opposition parties shown any immediate indication that they intend to seize the opportunity to bring them to the fore. And one cannot expect pressure from below for opening up debate, because years of exclusion from what has been treated as a super-secret area of executive discretion have ensured an almost complete lack of awareness among the general citizenry that there are issues to be discussed. Journalists and academics have contributed little to informing the public, in significant part because with very few exceptions they too have respected the government's claim of dominion and remained ignorant in consequence. The situation is very different in the United States, where some of the acts committed by the CIA were so outrageous that they could no longer be ignored, and the absence of the English culture of deference meant that the identical official unwillingness to talk about such matters was relatively easily overcome. In relation to other aspects of this study we have argued that American experience is largely irrelevant because of the constitutional differences, and this is equally true of discussions of covert action as they relate to the relative responsibilities of the President and the Congress. However, it is helpful, indeed necessary, to draw upon the conceptual analyses offered by American writers, since virtually nothing has been written anywhere else. Moreover, it is only in the United States that a definition of covert action has been enacted into law.

---

[6] See, e.g., the discussion in Ch. 3 of the right to privacy (Art. 8) and in Ch. 10 on freedom of expression (Art. 10).

[7] Cf. the discussion of the work of Carl Schmitt; above, pp. 19–20.

The American statute[8] defines covert action as government activities undertaken 'to influence political, economic or military conditions abroad, where it is intended that the [American government's] role . . . will not be apparent or acknowledged publicly'. Two major recent studies[9] have included catalogues of the activities that come under this head. The range is vast, and many would be carried out by agencies other than an intelligence service, but even a partial list would include several different types of strategy under the heads of military/ paramilitary; economic; ideological; and diplomatic/political. Examples from within these broad categories include currency destablization; open broadcasting; false flag propaganda;[10] support for internally mounted coups; break-ins and sabotage; aerial drops of supplies to insurgents; organizing strikes, demonstrations, or riots; supporting political parties, candidates, or newspapers; bribing or blackmailing politicians; assassination; and arms sales or training of military or secret police.[11] All of these activities involve interference in the internal politics of a foreign state which would be regarded as intolerable if attempted in Britain by another state; some, such as the last example, may involve maintaining a brutal but friendly regime in power and the covert aspect is necessitated by the attempt to conceal the activity from the British public, not from the only-too-happy recipient government.

Before discussing whether and when it might be appropriate for the British government to engage in covert action, we must first consider a point put forward by the Intelligence Co-ordinator. Asked about the absence of any standards or controls in the Bill, he suggested that they would be inappropriate, for SIS is not a 'self-tasking' body. That is, it is closely controlled by its parent department, the Foreign and Commonwealth Office, and requires the latter's approval before it may undertake anything of significance, not just covert operations. The process is surprisingly formal: a written 'presentation' is required, setting out the proposal, the intended result, and an assessment of the risks involved. Anything 'politically sensitive' would require the Foreign Secretary's personal approval. In addition, a detailed internal administrative rule-book governs intelligence officers.[12] This tight ministerial and departmental control, Mr Warner argued, makes unnecessary and undesirable any external statutory 'methodological limits'. The controls ensure that the organization never goes off the rails, setting its own priorities, or taking risks its political masters would find unacceptable; and the ultimate choice as to whether a particular method is acceptable remains with ministers.

---

[8] Intelligence Authorization Act of 1991, PL 102–88.

[9] J. Reisman and J. Baker, *Regulating Covert Action* (New Haven, Conn., 1992); and A. Goodman and B. Berkowitz, *The Need to Know* (New York, 1992). See also G. Treverton, *Covert Action: The Limits of Intervention in the Post-War World* (New York, 1987).

[10] A term meaning action or information purporting to come from a source other than the real one.

[11] Reisman and Baker, *Regulating Covert Action*, 4–5; Goodman and Berkowitz, *The Need to Know* 11–13.

[12] The Commissioner acting under the Interception of Communications Act 1985 and the Staff Counsellor are given access to these rules.

Though attractive in that it suggests that the classic model of ministerial responsibility actually works in this area, the argument is still badly flawed. It ignores entirely three central points. First, implicit in our previous discussion, is that although in a narrow legal sense the legislation is addressed to the Service, the wider political dimension is that this law will provide one of the primary statements about how our society believes international dealings ought to be conducted. It therefore serves a function every bit as important as that of providing a legal charter for the Service: that of educating the public about the issues involved. Assuming that there are certain ethical limits which ought to be respected, defining those boundaries is a particularly important form of societal self-definition, a process which should engage as many interested people as possible (which quite definitely should include those with experience within SIS).

Secondly, reliance on ministerial control ignores the lesson that has fully and profitably been learned by the Australians and Canadians:[13] that in addition to restraining the services, an equally compelling reason for creating formal mandates and a requirement of written instructions is to protect security and intelligence services from their political masters. Although those restraints have been erected for the different purpose of preventing ministerial abuse of the services at home (a point which is separately acknowledged in the Bill in relation to SIS and GCHQ[14]), the principle is equally applicable where domestic politics are not at stake. In so far as ministers may be tempted to use certain unacceptable methods, members of the Service would be on far firmer ground if they could base their refusal on grounds of illegality, rather than upon moral opposition which could be dismissed as mere personal squeamishness or as constitutionally inappropriate for a public official. The double-edged character of legal norms when used in this realm is one of their main advantages.

Finally, the Commissioner and parliamentary committee created by the Bill have been left entirely at sea in their oversight of this aspect of SIS activities. Statutory standards of propriety would give them at least some specific measure of evaluation to work with. In this limited context, the American discussions and legislation about when the President must inform the congressional Intelligence Committee (which meets in secret) of any proposed covert action are relevant to the Bill, if only as a contrast. For the parliamentary body has been explicitly barred from receiving information about any particular operation, past, present, or contemplated.[15]

In any such debate, those in favour of engaging in some forms of covert action would have several strong arguments on their side. In dealing with hostile states that are at least as secretive as our own and perhaps much more so, it is necessary to gain reliable information about their intentions and capabilities. The persons most likely to possess such knowledge are those who are part of or

---

[13] Above, Chs. 14 and 15.

[14] Restrictions on furthering the interests of any United Kingdom political party appear in cl. 2 (2)(b) and 4 (2)(b) respectively.   [15] Sched. 3, para. 4(b).

close to the apparatus of government, all of whom—like their British counterparts—are subject to rigorous norms of secrecy. In such circumstances, if the information were sufficiently important—for example, if it concerned the state of development of nuclear or chemical weapons in any one of a dozen countries one could name—should clandestine payments, or a promise of resettlement and British citizenship, in exchange for that material be forbidden? Are inducements of that kind acceptable, whilst blackmail is not on the ground that it is 'dirtier' than bribery? Are ethical distinctions of that kind sustainable? For those who believe they are not, what is the corollary: that there are no ethical limits, only prudential ones (it might not work; if we are caught out, British interests will suffer too much to justify the risk)? Or is it that only activities which are legal (in which system—a dictator's?; ours?) are permissible?

To take a second and unfortunately realistic example, if there exists a highly unstable political situation in a country which is militarily so strong that its antagonism would be a matter of serious concern, and a leader regarded as hostile to British security interests begins to emerge, would it always be wrong to assist his opponents in their attempts to defeat him electorally? Put concretely, should we be secretly backing some alternative to Mr Zhirinovsky before he comes to dominate the Russian parliament? This is of course a very different question from whether we should assist those who might wish to mount a *coup d'état* against such a leader after he has been fairly elected. It may also be critically dependent upon circumstances: an antagonistic Russia can reasonably be said to present a threat to our national security, whereas a militarily weak Asian or African country could not, however much its hostility might threaten the economic interests of some British companies.

Finally, although like most major powers Britain has shown scant concern for the human rights record of those whose friendship it has regarded as politically or economically desirable—the arming of Saddam Hussein while he was gassing Kurdish secessionists is only the most despicable example—one may hope, however faintly, that this attitude will not endure forever. If opposition to particularly violent and autocratic regimes were to become part of British foreign policy, what forms may it properly take? Some activities, such as food or humanitarian aid to areas threatened with ethnic cleansing, would seem relatively uncontroversial. This is much less true of political, educational, or military assistance to resistance forces. Does the scope for intervention disappear if a government preserves the forms of law and electoral democracy, but systematically gaols or exiles its opponents (as occurs in many African countries), or is it legitimate to offer surreptitious support for democratic forces, financially or in other ways? Given that there are complex norms of international law concerning the right of states to intervene in each other's internal affairs, how would these affect the legality and propriety of various forms of covert action?[16]

[16] Ch. 3 of Reisman and Baker, *Regulating Covert Action* presents an extensive discussion of what they call 'international legal regulation of proactive covert operations'; ch. 4 is devoted to

These are only a sampling of the matters that ought to be central to parliamentary and public debate over the functions of SIS. With one exception, the sole purpose of the discussion here is to demonstrate that important and difficult questions exist, not to suggest answers. The exception arises from the paramount consideration of maintaining democracy. The involvement of the British government in an operation may be concealed for three reasons: to maximize the chances of success, to avoid political or other retribution by the target state if it fails, or to prevent an outcry at home. The first two may generally be accepted; but there must be severe limits on the circumstances in which the final justification can be. One important reason for bringing these issues to greater prominence is that once a decision that certain types of activities are unacceptable has been taken democratically, others not thus excluded can proceed secretly, because the criterion then becomes efficacy within an agreed moral framework. However, what can never be tolerable is taking any action, regardless of its nature, in pursuance of a policy that has been hidden from the electorate. The classic example is the focal point of the Scott Inquiry: did the government secretly alter the guidelines on arms sales to Iraq while adopting a different overt stance in its pronouncements to Parliament and the public? Whatever one's views about the arms bazaar, all governments have avowedly, indeed avidly, sought to promote export of lethal weapons. The practice becomes unacceptable on *democratic* grounds only when the sales are made or permitted covertly because revelation of the purchaser's identity would generate a political furore.

Our concern that the issues be addressed does not derive from a view that MI6 has been notable for the commission of abominable acts.[17] There is in fact surprisingly little written about its recent activities (possibly reflecting successful concealment as well as a record of treading the straight and narrow). Perhaps the most critical book published about the organization, Bloch and Fitzgerald's *British Intelligence and Covert Action*,[18] devoted most of its pages to events of the 1950s and 1960s; the most recent episode which they found objectionable— helping the brutal Sheikh of Oman to remain in power, then assisting the coup by which his son overthrew him—took place in the early 1970s, and it is not even clear from their account whether the main actors on the British side were from SIS or other organizations.[19] It is notable too that Fred Holroyd's disillusioned attack on Britain's conduct of the war in Northern Ireland directs its account of murder and various dirty tricks at MI5 and its allies in the RUC and

---

international regulation of the reactions to covert operations. See also J. Moore, F. Tipson, and R. Turner, *National Security Law* (Durham, NC, 1990), ch. 9.

[17] Indeed as the example in the previous paragraph suggests, covert actions may be taken by many government or military agencies other than the intelligence services. The tabling of the Intelligence Services Bill is simply the most convenient, if not the only, occasion Parliament has had to air such matters in many years.

[18] J. Bloch and P. Fitzgerald, *British Intelligence and Covert Action* (London, 1983).

[19] Ibid. 134–9.

special army units; MI6, with whom he was initially assigned to work, emerges quite creditably.[20] Thus, whilst there may well have been disreputable episodes which have been successfully concealed, the need to address the wider issues derives not from scandal, but from democratic principle. Indeed the Intelligence Co-ordinator stated that the timing of the legislation's appearance derives in part from a wish to do something before a scandal erupted, unlike everywhere else: to 'proceed in a calm atmosphere'. This is precisely why consideration of the limits of 'special operations' should take place now.

The government was not entirely unaware that actions by its agents might be problematical. Its conception of the difficulties and its method of handling them, however, are both extraordinary. It defined its concern in terms of illegality (civil or criminal), thus ignoring ethical and constitutional dilemmas presented by activities that may not be unlawful. Even more important, 'legality' is not understood in terms of the law of the state in which an operation takes place.[21] It refers only to conduct for which 'a person would be liable in the United Kingdom for any act done outside [it]' (clause 7(1))—not the whole of the criminal law, but only that small (though growing) portion of it which applies extra-territorially.[22] Among the many offences this does not include are bribery and grievous bodily harm. Those which would be covered are bigamy (which conjures up all sorts of bizarre scenarios), genocide, murder, several terrorist-related offences over which British courts were granted extra-territorial jurisdiction by the Suppression of Terrorism Act 1978,[23] and those treated in the same manner under the Criminal Justice Act 1993.[24]

Having identified the problem, the government's response was to treat it predominantly as a matter of licensing. Clause 7 provides that if the Secretary of State formally and personally authorizes the conduct,[25] those who engage in it are absolved of all liability. The legal constraints are imposed, not on officials, but on the Foreign Secretary who, before he approves the action, must be satisfied that it is 'necessary for the proper discharge' of one of the Service's statutory functions and that there are 'satisfactory arrangements' in place to ensure that nothing will be done under the authorization beyond what that necessity

---

[20] F. Holroyd and N. Burbridge, *War Without Honour* (Hull, 1989). Holroyd was a career army officer whose posting to Northern Ireland exposed him to actions he could not stomach; he claims that his reaction led among other things to confinement to a military psychiatric hospital on trumped-up grounds.

[21] Nor is the criterion that of international law: n. 16 above.

[22] It would also include aspects of civil law, notably certain torts, but these are not sufficiently important to merit attention here.

[23] See s. 4 and Sched. 1 of the Act. Included are manslaughter, kidnapping, hostage-taking, and various explosives and firearms offences. We should note, though, that Mr. Warner stated that it would be 'unthinkable' for SIS officers to be authorized to use violence in peacetime, and that they do not carry weapons.

[24] Which include: theft, blackmail, fraud, forgery, and conspiracy, incitement, or attempt to commit any of them: Criminal Justice Act 1993, Pt.1.

[25] It is permissible in an 'urgent case' for the authorization to be made by a 'senior official': such warrants remain in force for only a maximum of two days.

requires. Additionally, he must determine that the 'nature and likely consequences' of the acts authorized will be 'reasonable' in light of their intended purposes.[26]

This approach conforms to the pattern of close ministerial control emphasized by the Intelligence Co-ordinator. In constitutional terms it is admirable; in
policy terms, there remain doubts. The first concerns the reasonableness criterion. This is obviously intended, as our interview confirmed, to import the
notion of proportionality into the process of decision. Yet it includes no boundaries, restrictions, or guidance. How is a conscientious Secretary of State, or officials advising him or her, supposed to apply the concept? Even if one leaps over
a large philosophical argument and accepts as valid a utilitarian approach which
would permit taking or endangering a lesser number of lives in order to save a
greater number,[27] how is one supposed to weigh, for example, relatively low risk
to lives against the achievement of a political objective like helping overthrow a
politically hostile, but not militarily dangerous, regime? It is misleading to talk of
'proportionality' in this context, because one is weighing incommensurables:
there are simply no common values that would permit a true equation. Although
it is possible that inclusion of this provision will, as a matter of practice, have
the salutary effect of making the process of decision more deliberate, and of
ensuring that the damage done to others is forced to the forefront of decision-
makers' minds, the parameters of the evaluation have been left so undefined
that in legal terms what these provisions achieve is casting an essentially unbri-
dled discretion into statutory form.

The corollary of the system of authorization is that any acts which do not
receive the ministerial imprimatur remain unlawful in British law. The unanswered question is whether those who engage in them will ever be prosecuted.
This seems unlikely in the extreme. Any such trial would involve public exposure, not only of this particular wrongdoing, but of similar though properly
authorized acts. Equally important from the government's point of view, it
would inevitably disclose aspects of operational methods and possibly even identities of sources: precisely the kinds of material to which even the parliamentary
committee may be denied access.[28] The information necessary to achieve a conviction could in most instances come only from fellow members of the Service,
colleagues of the accused; for many obvious reasons it is highly improbable that
they will come forward. Thus in hard practical terms, the distinction between
authorized and unauthorized crimes verges on the meaningless.

There is a final point, unconnected to any of the others. Although clause 7
appears in legislation concerning the intelligence services, it is phrased in terms
of 'a'— meaning any—person. Its extension beyond officers of the various ser-

---

[26] Cl. 7 (3) (a) and (b).

[27] This would assume, at the very least, that the threat was both so grave and immediate that the
likelihood that the lives would be lost was close to 100 per cent.

[28] Below, p. 513.

vices not only raises questions about 'sub-contracting' and deniable operations, worrisome as those are. Its plain meaning would include all military personnel. This seems entirely right, since their activities are the most obviously likely to result in risk to or loss of life. If this reading is correct, it follows that SAS operations involving assassination of potential terrorists, if authorized by the responsible minister, would become lawful. This provision would *not* have avoided the need for the inquest in Gibraltar after the killing of the three members of an IRA active service unit[29], for the immunity would extend only throughout the United Kingdom, and not to Gibraltar's separate legal system.

However, had clause 7 then been in force, it might have substantially altered public perception of the issues. Had the government admitted authorization, Parliament could have debated the propriety of that decision. If authorization had been disclaimed but no prosecution followed, the Attorney-General would eventually have had to justify that decision in the same forum. And had the government simply refused to comment, the press and MPs would have been alerted to what would rightly be seen as evasion of constitutional responsibility. The very broad sweep of clause 7—the only provision of the Bill to affect those outside the three intelligence services—is thus to be welcomed, although its presence may well have escaped attention, and deserves to receive greater prominence.

Purposes

SIS may conduct its activities only in pursuance of certain specified ends. As set out in clause 2, they are (a) 'the interests of national security, with particular reference to defence and foreign policies'; (b) the interests of the nation's 'economic well-being'; and (c) assisting in 'the prevention or detection of serious crime'. The first merely states what one would expect and requires no further comment. The other two raise more interesting issues.

We have seen that in the parliamentary debate in 1989, the Home Secretary identified 'economic well-being' with commodities on which the economy is dependent, and over which foreign government or countries have a powerful influence on availability or price.[30] However, the Intelligence Co-ordinator understood the term more widely, connecting it to general economic interests. He described the SIS role under this head as helping to maintain a stable world order, a political framework within which Britain, as a trading nation, would most effectively prosper. The emphasis upon stability and trading opportunities is squarely within the dominant tradition of British foreign policy, and largely accounts for the support that governments of all political stripes consistently

---

[29] The European Commission on Human Rights has declared admissible a complaint alleging (*inter alia*) that the failure to lay down clear and detailed rules on the use of force violated Art. 2 (the right to life) of the Convention: *McCann and Others* v. *UK*, Application No. 18984/91.

[30] Above, p. 390.

gave to South Africa, and to other regimes where brutality and autocracy were not grounded in racism. Political turmoil is, almost by definition, bad for commercial activity, and Britain has therefore tended to back whatever regime happens to be in control until its grip shows clear signs of weakening. In this respect, as in several others of great importance, questions of the proper role of any one of the security and intelligence services cannot be divorced, and indeed flow directly, from the view one takes of wider foreign or internal policy.

The other point on which Mr Warner was firmly insistent is that pursuance of economic well-being does not encompass spying on behalf of British companies, bribing foreign officials on behalf of British interests, or even carrying money provided by private interests to be used for that purpose. 'We are not businessmen', he emphasized, and in any case such activities are 'not the right way' to go about advancing British industry. Since it is notorious that in several lucrative markets bribing officials is virtually the only way to gain contracts, his attitude may reflect some attenuated influence of ethical restraint (which he disclaimed), or perhaps merely a feeling that such behaviour would be beneath the dignity of an SIS officer.

The great novelty in the list of purposes is the last. 'Serious crime' is left undefined in the Bill, but is understood by those who will work with it to mean terrorism, drugs, and money-laundering.[31] The Service's interest in drugs seems to arise not so much as part of the government's policy of prohibition on their use, but from the wider political dimension: 'Narcotics is a world-wide phenomenon and small countries are particularly vulnerable', in Mr Warner's words. The profits that arise from prohibition are so vast and can finance corruption on such a pervasive scale that drug traffickers can purchase effective immunity if the number of people who need to be bought is small. The effect on the integrity of the government is a concern when the country is one for which Britain has responsibility, such as the Cayman Islands, but at least as important is that a country in which drugs may be moved and stored with minimal interference quickly becomes a transit centre for export elsewhere, including of course to Britain. Operating overseas, SIS is the only one of the intelligence services able to gain information that will link with that held by police and Customs, who are concerned with importation.

The emphasis on money-laundering flows from the concern with drug and terrorist organizations.[32] This is squarely in line with recent legislation, which seeks to attack these bodies by seizing their profits, or donations and extortions,

---

[31] The term is defined in the Interception of Communications Act 1985, s. 10 (3) to include offences involving the use of violence, substantial financial gain, or a large number of persons acting in common, or where a three-year or more prison term might be expected to be imposed on a defendant with no previous convictions. The working definition offered by the Intelligence Co-ordinator is obviously much narrower.

[32] In so far as it affects the integrity of financial institutions, large-scale money-laundering may be a threat to economic well-being in its own right.

and choking off their ability to buy weapons.[33] The intelligence services are not interested in fraud as such, but only in the financial dealings of people or organizations who are regarded as threats to British interests for other reasons. This must surely be the right approach, for otherwise they would become an international adjunct of the Serious Fraud Office. There may well be strong arguments for strengthening that body, and for greater co-operation between states in breaking down barriers of financial secrecy and otherwise facilitating the enforcement of criminal laws against fraud which has an international dimension. None the less, this should remain a matter for the normal machinery of criminal justice, and not for secret bodies from whose oversight the courts have been carefully excluded.[34]

The serious crime mandate has had one important implication for the criminal justice system, and for all three services. The head of each is under a duty to establish arrangements ensuring that no information is 'obtained or disclosed' by officers of the organization except as is necessary for certain specified purposes; these now include 'the purpose of any criminal proceedings'.[35] One obvious aim of this addition is to remove any obstacles to intelligence officers giving testimony in criminal prosecutions. This merely gives effect to what has already occurred.[36] However, as has been seen, the function of SIS is limited to gathering information in relation to 'prevention or detection of serious crime' not 'for the purpose of criminal proceedings'.[37] This apparently trivial distinction in fact reflects an important, and extremely valuable, principle of English criminal justice. In many legal systems, material gathered by means of lawful telephone tapping or bugging is itself capable of being introduced into evidence against the accused. That has never been the case in Britain, where such material is only used to provide leads for the police to uncover further evidence. Indeed, as the House of Lords has recently affirmed,[38] section 9 of the Interception of Communications Act 1985 explicitly enacts this principle, though in language whose rather opaque expression had caused some confusion in the lower courts.[39] By including both these phrases in clause 2(2)(a), the Bill permits material obtained by virtue of a secret and purely administrative warrant to be used

---

[33] Both the Prevention of Terrorism (Temporary Provisions) Act 1989, Part III and the Northern Ireland Emergency Provisions Act 1991 create several offences relating to financial assistance for terrorist activities or organizations. These have been strengthened by the Criminal Justice Act 1993, which makes money-laundering and related acts (such as 'tipping off') offences, regardless of the specific purpose (ss. 29–32).

[34] See above, pp. 368–72 and 393–4.

[35] Clauses 2 (2) [SIS]; 4 (2) [GCHQ]; and SSA 1989, s. 2 (2), supplemented by Sched. 4, para. 1 (1) of the Bill [MI5].

[36] Above, p. 382 (Meibion Glyndwr prosec.). SIS evidence was received in the Matrix Churchill case: see above, Ch. 11.

[37] And correspondingly, warrants for property 'interference' may only be granted for the former purpose, not the latter: cl. 5 (2)(a)(2).

[38] *R* v. *Preston* [1993] 4 All ER 638.

[39] Notably in *R* v. *Effik* (1992) 95 Cr App R 427, CA.

as evidence in a British court for the first time. The real worry is that this provision may be the first step of a government attack on the exclusion principle itself, which plays a vital, if not adequately recognized, role in protecting human rights in Britain.[40]

THE MANDATE OF GCHQ

By placing GCHQ on to a statutory footing the British government has broken ranks with Australia and Canada where the equivalent bodies, the Defence Signals Directorate and the Communications Security Executive respectively, remain creatures of the prerogative. In making GCHQ subject to a complaints procedure for the whole of its activities rather than merely, as before, interception authorized under the Interception of Communications Act 1985, the legislation goes further than that of any comparable nation.[41] Ironically, this development is occurring at a time when the government is also moving inexorably towards final condemnation under the International Labour Organization machinery for the ban on membership of trade unions imposed upon GCHQ employees in December 1983.[42]

GCHQ is the post-war successor to the acclaimed Government Code and Cipher School.[43] The mandate of GCHQ in clause 3 of the Bill reflects its varied tasks—both offensive and defensive—grouped around the specialism of signals. On the defensive side GCHQ is charged with linguistic and technical

---

[40] This is particularly true because in states like Canada or the United States where such evidence is permitted, potential defendants have two protections not provided by the legal system in any of the British jurisdictions. The first is that the warrant is not merely issued by a minister, but must be approved by some judicial authority, Secondly, there are provisions for the exclusion of improperly obtained evidence which are substantially stronger than would apply to non-confession material under the Police and Criminal Evidence Act 1984.

[41] The United States National Security Agency was created in 1952 by a still-classified Executive Order of the Truman administration. Subsequent Congressional legislation acknowledging the Agency relates to personnel questions only. Indeed sect. 6(a) of the National Security Agency Act 1959 states that 'nothing in this Act or any other law . . . shall be construed to require the disclosure of the organization or any function of the National Security Agency, or any information with respect to the activities thereof . . .'. See J. Moore, F. Tipson, and R. Turner, *National Security Law*, ch. 9.

[42] The ban was found to violate ILO Convention No. 87 (Freedom of Association and Protection of the Right to Organize, 1948), Art. 2 of which states: 'Workers and employers, without distinction whatsoever, shall have the right to establish and, subject only to the rules of the organization concerned, to join organizations of their choosing without previous authorization.' The ILO recommended that an attempt be found to resolve the dispute short of an outright ban, for instance, by accepting the trade unions' offer of a 'non-disruption' agreement. Although the government reopened formal contact with the civil service unions on the matter in late 1993 no agreement has been reached: *The Independent*, 11 and 21 Dec. 1993. For accounts of the various applications see: S. Fredman and G. Morris 'Union Membership at GCHQ' (1988) 17 *Ind LJ* 105; B. Napier 'The International Labour Organization and GCHQ' (1989) 19 *Ind LJ* 255; K. Ewing, *Britain and the I.L.O.* (London, 1989), ch. 2. For discussion of the domestic legal proceedings see Ch. 12.

[43] Many books have been written about and by participants in the wartime code-breaking activities of GC&CS. General overviews may be found in C. Andrew, *Secret Service* (London, 1986) and N. West, *GCHQ* (London, 1986).

advice and assistance to government departments and the armed forces on communications and information technology security.[44] Offensively its function is the monitoring and interference with 'electromagnetic, acoustic and other emissions and any equipment' and the obtaining, supply, and decrypting of information so obtained.[45]

This wording covers operations falling outside those authorized under warrants and certificates issued to GCHQ under the Interception of Communications Act 1985. The latter applies only where one party to the communication is in Britain and where the communication is intercepted in the course of transmission on a public telecommunications system. Interception of diplomatic communications from or to Britain and satellite communications generally are within the monitoring remit. So too are measures to disrupt such communications by signals jamming or other technical interference with the equipment concerned.[46] The exact interrelationship between the 1985 Act powers and these provisions will inevitably remain shrouded in some technical mystery unless, now that more has been publicly acknowledged of GCHQ's role, the Interceptions Commissioner and the new Commissioner to be appointed under this Bill provide elucidation in their annual reports. The controversial question of whether GCHQ is involved in signals monitoring of people in Britain beyond that authorized under the 1985 Act can be answered (if hesitantly) in the affirmative, since only in the case of activity directed towards the economic well-being ground is there any limitation to its use 'in relation to the acts or intentions of persons outside the British Islands'.[47] The mandate in relation to national security and the prevention and detection of serious crime is not restricted in this way: in this the Bill follows the scheme of the 1985 Act.[48]

The question of executive accountability is dealt with through a clause providing for the continuation of the office of Director of GCHQ responsible to the Foreign Secretary for the efficiency of the agency.[49] The current incumbent , Sir John Adye,[50] has been officially named and appeared with Sir Colin McColl (Chief of the SIS) at a press conference on publication of the Bill to welcome the new mood of openness. Like the agency heads of MI6 and MI5, the Director is given a right of access to the Prime Minister and is subject to duty to submit an annual report.[51] The enthuasiasm of one Prime Ministerial forebear

[44] Cl. 3 (1) (b). The work of the Communications Electronics Security Group of GCHQ also involves collaboration with industry (presumably defence contractors) and the Security Service: *Central Intelligence Machinery*, 21.

[45] Cl. 3(1).

[46] The latter was offered by officials as an example of where GCHQ might want to use interference warrant powers under cl. 5.

[47] Cl. 3 (2) (b). Even this wording carefully stops short of precluding domestic monitoring outright since one of the parties could be on British soil, or both could be if discussing the involvement of a third (non-British) commercial partner.

[48] ICA, s. 2.   [49] Cl. 4.   [50] *Central Intelligence Machinery*, 21.

[51] Cl. 4 (4).

for wartime signals intelligence is legendary[52] but most ministerial consumption of intelligence takes place at some remove in the Red Book material produced by the JIC, to which signals intelligence is a key contributor.[53]

Officials emphasized that like the Secret Intelligence Service, GCHQ is a 'tasked' service: it operates in response to politically approved instructions to obtain intelligence, in contrast to the Security Service which is 'self-tasking', that is largely responsible for assessing where its own priorities should lie. The difference in approach arises partly because the convention of ministerial restraint in security matters does not apply to the collection of overseas intelligence, where the political dangers are recognized to be less than in the domestic realm. It is also a question of prioritizing use of resources. The technical capability of GCHQ to monitor communications greatly exceeds the resources available to analyse the material collected, so it is necessary to concentrate effort on monitoring only signals which might relate to a recognized security, defence, foreign, or economic policy objective. In practice this is achieved by GCHQ, in conjunction with the Foreign and Commonwealth Office, particularizing the sub-headings appearing in the annual 'United Kingdom Intelligence Requirements'—the ministerially approved planning document produced through the Joint Intelligence Committee—to generate the 'unique designators' recognized by GCHQ's computer-searching facility.[54] Thus, to take an example offered by officials, a requirement to collect information on Iranian-sponsored terrorism will be particularized until it relates to particular known groups, individuals, names, and names of potential targets. The statutory language reflects this political and administrative process of 'tasking' GCHQ when it refers to its functions being exercisable 'in the interests of national security, with particular reference to the defence and foreign policies of *Her Majesty's Government*',[55] i.e. the government in office rather than the continuing interests of the state.

Like the Interception of Communications Act before it, the Bill is silent on international signals co-operation, despite the highly formalized arrangements which are known to exist with GCHQ's cousin agencies under the UKUSA treaty.[56] No doubt this is because of continued political and diplomatic sensitivity about the scale and siting of the relevant installations, not least the National Security Agency installation at Menwith Hill in North Yorkshire. International co-operation must be deduced from the deep silences of the statutory language. The references in clause 3 (2) (a) to the defence and foreign policies of Her

---

[52] On Churchill's immersion in this material, see Andrew *Secret Service*, 627 ff. Mrs Thatcher is also said to be have been an enthusiast, according to one of our informants.

[53] *Central Intelligence Machinery*, 11.

[54] For a historical perspective on the process of prioritizing signals and intelligence requirements, reprinting some relevant official documents see: R. Aldrich and M. Coleman, 'The Cold War, the JIC and British Signals Intelligence' (1989) 4 *Int. and Nat. Sec.* 535.

[55] Cl. 3 (2) (emphasis added).

[56] See further Ch. 3; in addition to the materials cited there valuable historical material can be found in : C. Andrew, 'The Growth of Australian Intelligence and the Anglo-American Connection' (1989) 4 *Int. and Nat. Sec.* 213, esp. 223–6.

Majesty's Government are broad enough to encompass such co-operation. GCHQ actions in support of the prevention or detection of serious crime[57] are not limited by any reference to the United Kingdom. Another sub-clause[58] allows the lending of linguistic and cryptanalytical assistance 'to any other organisation determined for the purpose of this section in such manner as may be specified by the Prime Minister'.[59] When asked about the practice of authorization of contact with foreign intelligence agencies, officials stated that this was authorized in general by ministers—for instance ministers have specifically approved contact with the intelligence agencies of the new East European republics following the end of the Cold War. Arrangements for disclosure of information are envisaged relating to the functions of GCHQ:[60] obligations under international treaties for mutual disclosure of signals intelligence would therefore not conflict with these provisions.

Our analysis of the mandates of SIS and GCHQ has inevitably spilled over in places to discussion of ministerial authorization, as part of the process by which the mandate is actually carried. However, clause 7 (discussed earlier) is part of a trilogy dealing with ministerial approval, a subject meriting specific attention, and to which we now turn.

WARRANTS AND COMPLAINTS MACHINERY

Whereas clause 7 speaks of 'authorizations', clauses 5 and 6 refer to 'warrants', as the means by which the Secretary of State must 'authorize' various actions under them.[61]

An important preliminary point is that all references in the main text to section 3 of the Security Service Act 1989 have been superseded. It has been repealed (clause 6 (6)(b)), and replaced by clauses 5 and 6, which apply equally to MI6 and GCHQ as well. The procedural requirements described above[62] have however remained entirely unaltered, though there have been changes of substance. There are also new provisions concerning the relationship between MI5 and the other two agencies.

For all three services, the scope of the warrant has been slightly expanded: it now includes interference with 'wireless telegraphy' as well as with property.[63]

---

[57] Cl. 3(2)(c).   [58] Cl. 3(1)(b).

[59] Note, not the Foreign Secretary, who is more generally responsible for GCHQ under cl. 3 and 4. The Prime Minister is presumably involved because of the extreme sensitivity and importance of foreign intelligence liaison.

[60] Cl. 4(2)(a).

[61] The difference in terminology would appear to be that the latter are limited to specific forms of action—'interference' with property and wireless telegraphy—which may be taken by members of the three services. By contrast cl. 7, as we have seen, is neither limited as to any particular kind of conduct, nor to members of the intelligence services. It is, however, limited as to place: it can only apply to acts done outside the United Kingdom. Outside these islands, there are no holds barred.

[62] Pp. 55 ff. above.   [63] Cl. 5 (1).

This is intended to remove any doubts about the legality of 'jamming' communications—for example, between two suspect terrorists conversing by radio sets or cellular telephones.[64] Much more important, the purposes for which an interference warrant may be granted have been enlarged. Under the 1989 Act, MI5 could only obtain a warrant in order to obtain information likely to be of substantial value in assisting it to do its work. Under the Bill, all three agencies may be granted a warrant for acts which directly assist them in carrying out their statutory functions: the limitation relating to seeking information no longer applies.[65] This seems to imply a more activist approach: whereas previously a burglary by MI5 might have been approved in order to copy an organization's membership list,[66] now it might be endorsed if its aim is surreptitiously to replace membership or financial records with inaccurate ones, or to leave false papers that purport to prove that its leader has been abusing young boys. Legalizing dirty tricks of this kind by means of a highly technical reformulation of powers when the implications have been kept deliberately obscure is simply dishonest, and destroys the credibility of the government's claim that the Bill is one demonstration of its commitment to open government.[67]

Since active SIS officers work almost entirely overseas, the question may arise as to the practicality of keeping track of a targeted person, such as a foreign intelligence official, or a resident of the Irish Republic thought to be involved in terrorist activities, when he or she enters British territory. This is covered in clause 5, which empowers the Security Service to seek warrants on behalf of the others. However, this agency relationship cannot be used to allow SIS (or GCHQ) to go beyond the limits of their functions.[68] Conversely and of great importance, MI5 is forbidden to act as agent where the serious crime function is involved.[69] Coupled with the restriction noted earlier that interference warrants may not relate to property within the United Kingdom under any circumstances,[70] the result is to exclude the Security Service from any role in relation to serious crime. This seems both correct in principle—criminal offences, whatever their seriousness, should remain matters for the police—and welcome as a practical demonstration of repeated government protestations in recent years that there are no plans for MI5 to expand its activities into the area of drugs.

To review the exercise of these powers and deal with complaints the Bill provides for a Commissioner[71] and a Tribunal[72] with jurisdiction over matters

[64] It was thought that under the Wireless Telegraphy Act 1949, jamming might be illegal.
[65] Cl. 5 (2)(a). All the other requirements outlined in Ch. 3 continue to apply to all warrants.
[66] Peter Wright describes a burglary exactly like this, committed by MI5 against the Commmunist Party in 1955: *Spycatcher* (New York, 1987), 54–6.
[67] See White Paper, *Open Government*, Cm 2290 (1993), para. 00.   [68] Cl. 5 (5)(a).
[69] Cl. 5 (5)(b). Subject to this primary restriction, however, MI5 may undertake activities not ordinarily within its functions when acting in this agency capacity: cl. 5 (4).
[70] Cl. 5 (3); above, p. 495.   [71] Cl. 8 and sched. 1.
[72] Cl. 9 and scheds. 1 and 2.

relating both to SIS and GCHQ. The pattern of the Security Service Act is followed closely.[73] Accordingly the criticisms already made of the equivalent bodies in Chapter 15 apply in substance to these provisions also. Although there is a certain symmetry to the arrangements it is hard to see why they have been so closely followed in the case of SIS, since its main actions affecting individuals either concern people outside Britain or occur abroad. In these circumstances it is not clear why the government felt impelled to provide a complaints machinery at all, except in the case of actions occurring under ministerial warrant. As the Bill stands, the quite remarkable position (apparently intentional) is that members of foreign governments will be able to complain to a British statutory tribunal about the reasonableness of the actions of Britain's espionage agency. While this must say something about the government's confidence in SIS or the tribunal, or both, it is also surely an exercise in futility.

From the complainant's point of view one possible outcome of the new arrangements is confusion, since the new Tribunal will inevitably partially overlap the functions of the existing bodies under the earlier legislation. This is the inevitable result of the similarity and overlap in the mandates of the agencies themselves. While the respective spheres of influence may be apparent to an insider, these are less a matter of legal necessity than of operational and territorial convenience. As a result, a complainant who suspects that his or her communications have been interfered with in some way may be unclear which Tribunal to complain to since the complainant will not have the benefit of knowing which agency (if any) is responsible, and, in any event, there is some overlap where the actions of GCHQ are concerned with the jurisdiction of the Interception of Communications Tribunal. Similarly a complainant who suspects that some other action has been taken by an (unidentified) intelligence agency will have the new benefit of a potential remedy against GCHQ or SIS but at the cost of having to make two separate complaints—to both the Security Service Tribunal and the Intelligence Services Tribunal. The Bill contains no power of cross-referral should it become obvious to a Tribunal that the wrong forum has been selected by a complainant. Organization of the Tribunals and the Commissioners on a wholly functional basis would have been preferable to the resulting position where no fewer than six institutions compete for jurisdiction on a partially functional and a partially institutional basis.

THE NEW COMMITTEE

The new Intelligence and Security Committee created under the legislation[74] has some unique features from the perspectives of both the British constitution and

---

[73] The Tribunal and Commissioner have similar powers to those under the 1989 Act. Complaints relating to alleged interference with property (including for this purpose wireless telegraphy) are routed via the Commissioner, as are questions possibly involving a cl. 7 authorization.

[74] Cl. 10 and sched. 3.

of security oversight. From the constitutional viewpoint it is a curious body: it is neither a Select Committee nor a Privy Councillors' committee, yet it will comprise six members drawn from both Houses of Parliament. However, as a statutory body its jurisdiction and powers are not derived from the Standing Orders of the House of Commons. As we shall see this does not imply that its powers are enhanced, since the Bill states in some detail when information can be withheld from the Committee. By its statutory basis the Committee will be protected from speedy abolition and from the vagaries of the Party system which have sometimes put the Select Committee machinery into abeyance while some outstanding dispute is settled.

Individual members will be appointed by the Prime Minister after consultation with the Opposition but there is no requirement to try to achieve balance of representation between the parties. Bearing in mind the freedom of appointment granted, the government is unlikely to need to resort to the uncouth formalities of vetting committee members or serving them with notices under section 1 (6) of the Official Secrets Act 1989. The Prime Minister also has an unlimited power of dismissal.[75] The statutory basis may lend a façade of dignity and political detachment, but whether it can be translated into independence from party politics will depend to a large degree on the stature of the individuals chosen. From the government side, ministers are excluded and, in view of this, opposition front-benchers are unlikely to be put forward or chosen. If politically ambitious parliamentarians are discounted the most likely candidates are party elder statesmen and women (less generously described to us by one MP as 'old lags'), who, given the availability of peers of the realm, could include former Prime Ministers, Home Secretaries, and Foreign Secretaries. Another group, independent-minded back-benchers and their Lords' equivalents, would satisfy the criteria but are unlikely to be called upon in view of their natural curiosity and unpredictability.

The Committee will meet in Whitehall, not in Westminster, and in private, within the secure surroundings of the Cabinet Office. The symbolism and psychological effect are more potent than the quarter-mile distance might suggest: the world looks subtly different from behind the bomb-proof doors at 70 Whitehall, threats seem more real and secrecy more credible. In footballing terms, the intelligence services will have the home advantage. The Bill provides only a generalized duty (subject to exceptions discussed below) for officials to arrange to meet the Committee's requests for information '*subject to and in accordance with arrangements approved by the Secretary of State*'.[76] In the unlikely event of the Committee catching some exotic form of the open-government virus, involving public hearings, presumably the government would simply impose quarantine.

The Committee is 'to examine the expenditure, administration and policy'[77] of

---

[75] Sched. 3, para. 1 (d).   [76] Sched. 3, para. 3 (1) (a).   [77] Cl. 10 (1).

the Security Service, the Secret Intelligence Service, and GCHQ. 'Operations' have been deliberately omitted.[78] This represents an implicit abandonment of the government's earlier position, that it would be impossible to separate policy and operations meaningfully,[79] a view which was unsustainable in the light of experience in other countries.[80] Officials admitted that the policy/operations distinction would need to be worked out pragmatically as the Committee proceeds with its work. The solution arrived at will greatly influence the effectiveness of the Committee's scrutiny. Too wide a definition of operational matters will prevent the Committee from inquiring into the efficiency and value for money of the services. Too insistent demands for information about operational detail (especially if they come early in the Committee's history) will make the services fearful of full co-operation. For the Committee to arrive at a sensitive appreciation of legitimate operational secrecy without having been co-opted entirely to the services' worldview will require vigilant detachment and constructive scepticism. It was stressed by officials that the agencies are looking forward to the challenge of putting their case to 'a new constituency'.

No blueprint exists for what the Committee should examine within its remit or how it should approach the task.[81] However it will be given access to the annual 'United Kingdom Intelligence Requirements', the key policy document establishing intelligence priorities. It is to be anticipated that early in the Committee's life it will meet the key intelligence heads and Cabinet Office intelligence offiicials and it will be invited to visit the premises of the MI5, MI6, and GCHQ. Whether access is granted to officers below agency-head level remains to be seen. Nevertheless, for parliamentarians to be allowed to come face to face with intelligence officials in a formal (if not parliamentary) setting is a significant new departure. To carry out examination of the expenditure of the services the Committee will require fairly detailed access to their budgets, in conjunction with the new arrangements for scrutiny of them by the Comptroller and Auditor-General.[82] It is unclear whether the Committee will have access to

[78] Operational matters of various kinds feature among the categories of 'sensitive information' specified in sched. 3, para. 4 (and see discussion below).

[79] As recently as Dec. 1992 the Home Secretary doubted if the distinction could be drawn: *First Report from the Home Affairs Select Committee, Accountability of the Security Service (1992–93)* (HC 265), Minutes of Evidence, 7 Dec. 1992, 8–9.

[80] The Australian Parliamentary Joint Committee on ASIO is precluded from investigating (*inter alia*) matters relating to intelligence collection, methods, or sources where these are 'operationally sensitive' (ASIO Act, s. 92 (4) (c)): see further, Ch. 16 above.

[81] Lord Callaghan suggested that early items for its agenda might include: changes in the services' priorities since the end of the Cold War; intelligence concerning the current position of Russia and North Korea; international terrorism; as well as intelligence requirements connected with the negotiations of international treaties: *HL Debs.*, vol. 550, cols. 1039–40 (Dec. 9 1993).

[82] Reference is made to these in the provisions permitting disclosure of information by all 3 agencies to the Comptroller and Auditor-General: Cl. 2 (3) (b), 4 (3) (b), and sched. 4, para. 1 (2). See further Ch. 16 above. Note also that the government has published a unified budget for the intelligence agencies totalling £900m., comprising allocations of £150m. to MI6, £200m. to MI5, and £550m. to GCHQ: *Guardian*, 1 Dec. 1993.

the detailed internal manuals governing the work of intelligence officers. One source the Committee is unlikely to have access to is unauthorized whistleblowing: where disclosures to the Committee are unauthorized they will attract criminal liability under the Official Secrets Act 1989.[83]

The statutory form also gives the government the advantage in laying down clearly in advance when the Committee may be denied information. The qualified duty on the intelligence and security services to provide information[84] is noticeably weaker than the corresponding duties owed to the Tribunal[85] and to the Commissioner.[86] Crucial in this respect is the definition of 'sensitive information'[87] which the agency heads may withhold. Three categories are listed. First is information which might lead to the identification of sources, other forms of assistance to the agencies, or of operational methods. The second is information about particular operations, whether past, present, or future.[88] Thirdly, information may be withheld where it was provided by a foreign government which does not consent to its disclosure.

It was stressed by officials that much careful thought had been given to drafting these categories as narrowly as possible. Nevertheless they could easily be manipulated to emasculate the Committee. Operational *methods* rather than particular operations are intimately linked to policy questions, as is obvious from our earlier discussion of covert action. The need for an indefinite embargo on details of actual operations is questionable also, bearing in mind that what is under discussion here is not publication but very limited disclosure to an oversight committee. The 'foreign government' exception is capable of creative collaborative misuse, since similar exemptions apply to other agencies within their jurisdictions. The danger is that effective scrutiny of intelligence co-operation may become a constitutional no-go area in each of the co-operating states, because of the alleged objections of each of the others.

The withholding of sensitive information is discretionary rather than mandatory. The agency heads are permitted to disclose it where they consider it would be safe to do so.[89] In addition an intriguing provision allows the Secretary of State to override a refusal to disclose sensitive information in the public interest.[90] The use of this power is not readily imaginable and its inclusion seems largely a matter of constitutional propriety.

The minister is also given power to withhold 'non-sensitive' information. The

---

[83] Ch. 9 above. Sched. 3, para. 3(5) of the Bill states that disclosures will be within the functions of the relevant agency only if the other provisions of sched. 3 are complied with. In cases falling outside such authorization s.1 of the Official Secrets Act 1989 would apply.

[84] Sched. 3, para. 3 (1) (a).   [85] Sched. 2, para. 4.
[86] Cl. 8(4).   [87] Sched. 3, para. 4.

[88] Contrast the United States' Intelligence Oversight Act of 1980 50 U.S.C.A. 413 which requires the Congressional intelligence committees to be 'fully and currently informed of all intelligence activities . . . including any significant anticipated intelligence activity'. This is not, however, a precondition to authorization and exceptions allow for prior notice to be restricted on presidential authority: Moore, Tipson, and Turner, *National Security Law*, 927.

[89] Sched. 3, para. 3 (2).   [90] Sched. 3, para. 3 (3).

Bill equates this directly with the circumstances in which information may be withheld from a Select Committee.[91] Asked about the circumstances in which this power might be used, officials volunteered the hypothetical example of personal information about members of the royal family. If the intention was simply to exempt information of this kind, the drafting is seriously over-inclusive because the list of situations in which a minister might refuse to answer questions before a Select Committee cover a variety of other potential political embarrassments. Furthermore, these are precisely the types of reasons which ought *not* to be relevant if the Committee is not intended to behave as a substitute Select Committee in the first place.

The demarcation lines between the Committee and the Commissioner and Tribunal system are somewhat unclear. Plainly the latter two will be primarily concerned with operational matters in dealing with complaints and in reviewing warrants. The legislation contains no formal link between Commissioner and the Tribunal and the Committee. A power to refer matters with policy implications to the Committee would be a useful adjunct to the powers of each of the Commissioners and the Tribunals, and a safety valve on the closed world of ministerial control. As it stands there is no guarantee that the Committee will even be shown the unedited versions of the Commissioners' reports.

The Committee is to produce an annual report, which, as with the reports of the various Commissioners, will be published in an edited form.[92] However for the Prime Minister to have such control over the published findings of a group of parliamentarians puts the Committee in a markedly weaker position than either a Select Committee or a Privy Councillors' committee (which would be more trusted). This is the price of privileged access to information, but as we have seen, the extent to which the Committee will be granted such access will be dependent on continued executive largesse. If Parliament is to be better informed about intelligence matters the reports will need to be considerably less edited than the Commissioners' reports under the existing legislation. Otherwise demands for Select Committee access to intelligence officers will continue unabated.

CONCLUSION

Clearly any comparison of the new mechanisms with those operating in Canada and Australia has to be on the basis of the overall package, rather than individual

---

[91] Sched. 3, 3 (4); for these categories see 'Memorandum of Guidance for Officials Appearing Before Select Committees', C. Turpin, *British Government and the Constitution* (2nd edn., London, 1990), 466–7 .

[92] Cl. 10 (6) and (7).

elements[93]—a point robustly made by officials in interview. Strong scepticism was expressed about the value of SIRC[94] in particular and the claim made 'we would gave been delighted' to have introduced a similar Privy Councillors' committee in Britain 'if we thought we could have got away with it'. However, the (apparently sincere) official belief that the reformed British oversight system would be the most rigorous in the Western world seemed to rest more upon the role of the Commissioner and the Tribunal than upon the Committee. There is an air of complacent superiority about this state of mind, and some anti-democratic leanings. It bears an unpleasant resemblance to the dominant attitude in the 1970s and 1980s towards those who campaigned against police misconduct and miscarriges of justice: stop making so much fuss, our police are the best in the world. And, as also with the denigration of SIRC, this attitude was underpinned by a greater official respect for the abilities of judges than for those of politicians. Much play was made of the abilities of the Commissioners appointed under the earlier legislation. It will be apparent that on the whole we disagree with the exaggerated claims made for judicial involvement, especially where it occurs on the basis of a narrow jurisdiction. A final assessment on the respective merits of the systems will in our view have to await several years' operation of the new Committee.

[93] Of all foreign models, the new British Committee most resembles the Australian Parliamentary Joint Committee (see Ch. 16 above) but with fewer formal powers. However, other elements of the British mechanisms remain markedly different.

[94] A view mirrored expressly or impliedly by several speakers (but without reasoned explanation) in the House of Lords' Second Reading debate: see *HL Debs.* vol. 550, col. 1037 (Lord Hunt of Tamworth), col. 1039 (Lord Callaghan), and col. 1046 (Lord Chalfont).

Appendix I. The Maxwell-Fyfe Directive

1. In your appointment as Director-General of the Security Service you will be responsible to the Home Secretary personally. The Security Service is not, however, a part of the Home Office. On appropriate occasion you will have a right of direct access to the Prime Minister.

2. The Security Service is part of the Defence Forces of the country. Its task is the Defence of the Realm as a whole, from external and internal dangers arising from attempts at espionage and sabotage, or from actions of persons and organisations whether directed from within or without the country, which may be judged to be subversive to the State.

3. You will take special care to see that the work of the Security Service is strictly limited to what is necessary for the purposes of their task.

4. It is essential that the Security Service should be kept absolutely free from any political bias or influence and nothing should be done that might lend colour to any suggestion that it is concerned with the interests of any particular section of the community, or with any other matter than the Defence of the Realm as a whole.

5. No enquiry is to be carried out on behalf of any Government Department unless you are satisfied that an important public interest bearing on the Defence of the Realm, as defined in para. 2, is at stake.

6. You and your staff will maintain the well-established convention whereby Ministers do not concern themselves with the detailed information which may be obtained by the Security Service in particular cases, but are furnished with such information only as may be necessary for the determination of any issue on which guidance is sought.

Issued by the Home Secretary, Sir David Maxwell-Fyfe, to the Director-General MI5 in 1952.

Appendix II. The Legal Mandates of Security Services

I. THE UNITED KINGDOM

Security Service Act 1989

S. 1

(1) There shall continue to be a Security Service . . . under the authority of the Secretary of State.

(2) The function of the Service shall be the protection of national security and, in particular, its protection against threats from espionage, terrorism and sabotage, from the activities of foreign powers and from actions intended to overthrow or undermine parliamentary democracy by political, industrial or violent means.

(3) It shall also be the function of the Service to safeguard the economic well-being against threats posed by the actions or intentions of persons outside the British Islands.

II. AUSTRALIA

Australian Security Intelligence Organization Act 1979 S. 4

Interpretation

In this Act, unless the contrary intention appears—

'activities prejudicial to security' includes any activities concerning which Australia has responsibilities to a foreign country as referred to in paragraph (b) of the definition of 'security' in this section;

'acts of foreign interference' means activities relating to Australia that are carried on by or on behalf of, are directed or subsidised by or are undertaken in active collaboration with, a foreign power, being activities that—

    (a)   are clandestine or deceptive and—

        (i)   are carried on for intelligence purposes;

        (ii)   are carried on for the purpose of affecting political or governmental processes; or

        (iii) are otherwise detrimental to the interests of Australia; or

    (b)   involve a threat to any person;

'foreign power' means—

    (a)   a foreign government;

    (b)   an entity that is directed or controlled by a foreign government or governments; or

    (c)   a foreign political organisation;

'politically motivated violence' means—

    (a)   acts or threats of violence or unlawful harm that are intended or likely to achieve a political objective, whether in Australia or elsewhere, including acts or threats carried on for the purpose of influencing the policy or acts of a government, whether in Australia or elsewhere;

    (b)   acts that—

        (i)   involve violence or are intended or are likely to involve or lead to violence (whether by the persons who carry on those acts or by other persons); and

        (ii)   are directed to overthrowing or destroying, or assisting in the overthrow or destruction of, the government or the constitutional system of government of the Commonwealth or of a State or Territory;

(c)   acts that are offences punishable under the *Crime (Foreign Incursions and Recruitment) Act 1978*, the *Crime (Hijacking of Aircraft) Act 18972* or the *Crimes (Protection of Aircraft) Act 1973*; or

(d)   acts that—
  (i)   are offences punishable under the *Crimes (Internationally Protected Persons) Act 1976*; or
  (ii) threaten or endanger any person or class of persons specified by the Minister for the purposes of this sub-paragraph by notice in writing given to the Director-General;

'promotion of communal violence' means activities that are directed to promoting violence between different groups of persons in the Australian community so as to endanger the peace, order or good government of the Commonwealth;

'security' means—

(a)   the protection of, and of the people of, the Commonwealth and the several States and Territories from—
  (i)   espionage;
  (ii)   sabotage;
  (iii) politically motivated violence;
  (iv)   promotion of communal violence;
  (v)   attacks on Australia's defence system; or
  (vi)   acts of foreign interference,

  whether directed from, or committed within, Australia or not;

Functions of Organization

S. 17. (1) The functions of the Organization are—

(a)   to obtain, correlate and evaluate intelligence relevant to security;

(b)   for purposes relevant to security and not otherwise, to communicate any such intelligence to such persons, and in such manner, as are appropriate to those purposes;

(c)   to advise Ministers and authorities of the Commonwealth in respect of matters relating to security, in so far as those matters are relevant to their functions and responsibilities.

(d)   to advise Ministers, authorities of the Commonwealth and such other persons as the Minister, by notice in writing given to the Director-General, determines on matters relating to protective security; and

(e)   to obtain within Australian foreign intelligence pursuant to section 27A of this Act or section 11A of the *Telecommunications (Interception) Act 1979*, and to communicate any such intelligence in accordance with this Act or the *Telecommunications (Interception) Act 1979*.

Act not concerned with lawful dissent, &c.

S. 17A. This Act shall not limit the right of persons to engage in lawful advocacy, protest or dissent and the exercise of that right shall not, by itself, be regarded as prejudicial to security, and the functions of the Organization shall be construed accordingly.

Note: Although the statute carries the date of its initial enactment in the title, all subsequent amendments have been incorporated into the text.

III. CANADA

Canadian Security Intelligence Service Act S. 2

Interpretation

'threats to the security of Canada' means

(*a*) espionage or sabotage that is against Canada or is detrimental to the interests of Canada or activities directed toward or in support of such espionage or sabotage,

(*b*) foreign influenced activities within or relating to Canada that are detrimental to the interests of Canada and are clandestine or deceptive or involve a threat to any person,

(*c*) activities within or relating to Canada directed toward or in support of the threat or use of acts of serious violence against persons or property for the purpose of achieving a political objective within Canada or a foreign state, and (*d*) activities directed toward undermining by covert unlawful acts, or directed toward or intended ultimately to lead to the destruction or overthrow by violence of, the constitutionally established system of government in Canada,

but does not include lawful advocacy, protest or dissent, unless carried on in conjunction with any of the activities referred to in paragraphs (*a*) to (*d*).

Duties and Functions of Service

S. 12. The Service shall collect, by investigation or otherwise, to the extent that it is strictly necessary, and analyse and retain information and intelligence respecting activities that may on reasonable grounds be suspected of constituting threats to the security of Canada and, in relation thereto, shall report to and advise the Government of Canada.

Note: Enacted in 1984, the CSIS Act is presently cited as R.S., 1985, c. C-23.

Bibliography

Books and Articles.

ADAMS, J., *Trading in Death* (London 1992).

ADLER-KARLSSON, G., *Western Economic Warfare 1947–67* (Stockholm, 1968).

ALDRICH, R., and COLEMAN, M., 'The Cold War, the JIC and British Signals Intelligence' (1989) 4 *Int. and Nat. Sec.* 535.

ALLAN, T., 'Public Interest Immunity and Ministers' Responsibilities' [1993] *Crim. LR* 660.

ALLEN, C., *Law and Orders* (3rd edn., London, 1965).

ALLEN, M., 'The Law and Practice Relating to Agent Provocateurs in the United States, United Kingdom and Commonwealth Jurisdictions' (LL M thesis, Queen's University of Belfast, 1981).

AMERY, L., *My Political Life*, 3 vols. (London, 1951–5).

ANDERSON, L., 'Antiquity in Action—Ne Exeat Regno Revived' (1987) 103 *LQR* 246.

ANDREW, C., *Secret Service* (London,1986).

—— 'The Growth of Australian Intelligence and the Anglo-American Connection' (1989) 4 *Int. and Nat. Sec.* 213.

ANDREWS, J., 'Public Interest and Criminal Proceedings' (1988) 104 *LQR* 410.

—— and HIRST, M., *Criminal Evidence* (London, 1987).

ANTHONY, I., *Arms Export Regulations* (Oxford, 1991).

ARMSTRONG, M., BLAKENEY, M., and WATTERSON, R., *Media Law in Australia* (2nd edn., Melbourne, 1988).

ARONSEN, M., and FRANKLIN, N., *Review of Administrative Action* (Sydney, 1987).

ASHWORTH, A., *Sentencing and Criminal Justice* (London, 1992).

—— *Principles of Criminal Law* (London, 1991).

ASKIN, F., 'Secret Justice and the Adversary System' (1991) 18 *Hastings Constitutional LQ* 745.

ATKEY, R., 'Reconciling Freedom of Expression and National Security' (1991) 41 *U. Tor. LJ* 38.

AUBREY, C., *Who's Watching You?* (London, 1981).

AUSTIN, R., and OLIVER, D., 'The Westland Affair' (1987) 40 *Parl. Aff.* 20.

BAILEY, S., HARRIS, D., and JONES, B., *Civil Liberties: Cases and Materials* (3rd edn., London, 1990).

BAKER, C., *Human Liberty and Freedom of Speech* (New York, 1989).

BALDWIN, J., and McCONVILLE, M., *Jury Verdicts* (Oxford, 1979).

BALDWIN, R., and HOUGHTON, J., 'Circular Arguments: The Status and Legitimacy of Administrative Rules' [1986] *PL* 239.

BARENDT, E., *Freedom of Speech* (Oxford, 1987).

BARNES, T., 'Special Branch and the First Labour Government' (1979) 22 *Hist. J* 941.

BARNET, R., and MULLER, R., *Global Reach* (New York, 1974).

BARNETT, C., *The Collapse of British Power* (London, 1972).

BAXTER, J., *State Security, Privacy and Information* (London, 1990).

BAYNE, P., *Freedom of Information* (Sydney, 1984).

BENDERSKY, J., *Carl Schmitt: Theorist for the Reich* (Princeton, NJ, 1983).

BERKI, R., *Security and Society: Reflections on Law, Order, and Politics* (London, 1986).

BERLIN, SIR ISAIAH, 'The Hedgehog and the Fox', in *Russian Thinkers*, H. and A. Hardy (eds.) (Oxford, 1978).

BIRKINSHAW, P., *Freedom of Information: The Law, the Practice and the Ideal* (London, 1988).

—— *Reforming the Secret State* (Milton Keynes, 1990).

—— *Freedom of Information: The US Experience* (Hull, 1991).

—— HARDEN, I., and LEWIS, N., *Government by Moonlight* (London, 1990).

—— '"I only ask for information"—the White Paper on Open Government', [1993] *PL* 557.

BLACK, JUSTICE HUGO, 'The Bill of Rights' (1960) 35 *New York University LR* 865.

BLOCH, J., and FITZGERALD, P., *British Intelligence and Covert Action* (London, 1983).

BLUM, W., *The CIA—A Forgotten History* (London, 1986).

BOASBERG, J., 'Seditious Libel and Incitement to Mutiny' (1990) 10 *Ox. JLS* 106.

BOK, S., *Secrets* (Oxford, 1986).

BONNER, D., *Emergency Powers in Peacetime* (London, 1986).

—— 'Combating Terrorism: Supergrass Trials in Northern Ireland' (1988) 51 *MLR* 23.

—— 'Combating Terrorism in the 1990s: The Role of the Prevention of Terrorism (Temporary Provisions) Act 1989' [1989] *PL* 440.

BOTTOMS, A., and BROWNSWORD, R., 'The Dangerousness Debate after the Floud Report' (1982) 22 *Brit. J. Crim.* 229.

BOYLE, A., *The Climate of Treason* (London, 1978).

BRADLEY, A., 'Justice, Good Government and Public Interest Immunity' [1992] *PL* 514.

—— 'The Cyprus Eight and the Rule of Law' [1986] *PL* 363.

—— 'The Judge Over Your Shoulder' [1987] *PL* 485.

BRAUNTHAL, G., *Political Loyalty and Public Service in West Germany* (Boston, 1990).

BRAZIER, R., *Constitutional Reform* (Oxford, 1991).

—— 'The Machinery of British Constitutional Reform' (1990) 41 *NILQ* 227.

BREWER, J., and STYLES, J. (eds.), *An Ungovernable People* (London, 1980).

BRIDGE, J., 'The Case of the Rugby Football Team and the High Prerogative Writ' (1972) 88 *LQR* 83.

BRIGGS, A., *Governing the BBC* (London, 1979).

—— *The War of Words: The History of Broadcasting in the United Kingdom, Volume III* (Oxford, 1970).

BRINKMAN, G., 'Militant Democracy and Radicals in the West German Civil Service' (1983) 46 *MLR* 584.

BROWNLIE, I., and WILLIAMS, D., 'Judicial Legislation in Criminal Law' (1964) 42 *Can. Bar Rev.* 561.

BUNYAN, T., *The Political Police in Britain* (London, 1977).

BUZAN, B., *People, States and Fear* (2nd edn., London, 1991).

CAIN, F., *The Origins of Political Surveillance in Australia* (Sydney, 1983).

—— 'Accountability and the Australian Security Intelligence Organization: A Brief History', in S. Farson, *et al.* (eds.), *Security and Intelligence in a Changing World* (London, 1991).

—— 'The Right to Know: ASIO, Historians and the Australian Parliament', (1993) 8 *Intelligence and National Security* 87.

CAMERON, I., 'Telephone Tapping and the Interception of Communications Act 1985' (1986) 37 *NILQ* 126.

CAMPBELL, D., and CONNORS, S., *On the Record: Surveillance, Computers and Privacy* (London, 1986).

CARR, E., *The Twenty Years' Crisis, 1919–1939* (London, 1939).

CARTWRIGHT, T., *Royal Commissions of Inquiry* (London, 1975).

CASTLE, B., *The Castle Diaries 1964–76* (London, 1990).

CHAPMAN, R. (ed.), *Ethics in Public Service* (Edinburgh, 1992).

—— and HUNT, M. (eds.), *Open Government* (Beckenham, 1987).

CHITTY, J., *A Treatise on the Law of the Prerogatives of the Crown* (London, 1820).

CHOO, A., 'A Defence of Entrapment' (1990) 53 *MLR* 453.

COCKBURN, C., *I, Claud* (Harmondsworth, 1967).

COCKERELL, M., *Sources Close to the Prime Minister* (London, 1984).

COOPER, T., *Crown Privilege* (Aurora, Ont., 1990).

COX, A., and KIRBY, S., *Congress, Parliament and Defence* (Basingstoke, 1986).

COX, N., 'The Thirty Year Rule and Freedom of Information', in G. Martin and P. Spurford (eds.), *The Records of the Nation* (Woodbridge, 1990).

CRAIES, W., 'The Right of Aliens to Enter British Territory' (1890) 6 *LQR* 27.

CRAIG, P., *Administrative Law* (2nd edn., London, 1989).

CRIPPS, Y., 'Disclosure in the Public Interest: The Predicament of the Public Sector Employee' [1983] *PL* 600.

—— 'Breaches of Copyright and Confidence: The Spycatcher Effect' [1989] *PL* 13.

CRITCHLEY, T., *A History of the Police in England and Wales* (2nd edn., London, 1978).

CROZIER, B., *Free Agent* (London, 1993).

DAINTITH, T., 'Regulation By Contract: The New Prerogative' [1979] *Current Legal Problems* 41.

DARBYSHIRE, P., 'The Lamp That Shows That Freedom Lives—Is it Worth the Candle?' [1991] *Crim. LR* 740.

DASGUPTA, P., *An Inquiry into Well-being and Destitution* (Oxford, 1993).

DENNING, Lord, *Landmarks in the Law* (London, 1984).

DENNIS, I., 'The Rationale of Criminal Conspiracy' (1977) 93 *LQR* 39.

DE SMITH, S., and BRAZIER, R., *Constitutional and Administrative Law* (6th edn., London, 1989).

DEVLIN, P., *The Judge* (Oxford, 1979).

DICEY, A., *The Law of the Constitution* (10th edn., London, 1965).

DREWRY, G. (ed.), *The New Select Committees* (2nd edn., Oxford, 1989).

—— 'The National Audit Act—Half a Loaf' [1983] *PL* 531.

—— 'The House of Commons and the Security Services' [1984] *PL* 370.

—— 'Select Committees and Back-bench Power' in J. Jowell and D. Oliver (eds.), *The Changing Constitution* (Oxford, 1989).

DUMMET, A., and NICOL, A., *Subjects, Citizens, Aliens and Others: Nationality and Immigration Law* (London, 1990).

DUNLEAVY, P., and O'LEARY, B., *Theories of the State* (2nd edn., London, 1992).

DURKHEIM, E., *The Division of Labour in Society* [1893] (New York, 1933).

DWORKIN, R., *Law's Empire* (London, 1986).

—— *Taking Rights Seriously* (London, 1977).

—— 'Principle, Policy, Procedure', in C. Tapper (ed.), *Crime, Punishment and Proof: Essays in Memory of Sir Rupert Cross* (London, 1981).

DYSON, K., *The State Tradition in Western Europe* (Oxford, 1980).

EAGLES, I., 'Evidentiary Protection for Informers—Policy or Privilege?' (1982) 6 *Crim. LJ* 175.

EAST, R., 'Jury Packing: A Thing of the Past?' (1985) 48 *MLR* 518.

EDWARDS, J., *The Law Officers of the Crown* (London, 1964).

—— *The Attorney-General, Politics and the Public Interest* (London, 1984).

ELIFF, J., *The Reform of FBI Operations* (Princeton, NJ, 1972).

ELLIOTT, M., 'The Control of Public Expenditure' in J. Jowell and D. Oliver (eds.), *The Changing Constitution* (Oxford, 1989).

EMERSON, T., *The System of Freedom of Expression* (New York, 1970).

ENGLEFIELD, D. (ed.), *Commons Select Committees: Catalysts for Progress?* (Harlow, 1984).

ENRIGHT, S., and MORTON, J., *Taking Liberties: The Criminal Jury in the 1990s* (London, 1990).

ERSKINE MAY, T., *Constitutional History of England* (2nd edn., London, 1866).

—— *Parliamentary Practice* (20th edn., London, 1983).

EVANS, P., *et al.* (eds.), *Bringing the State Back In* (Cambridge, 1985).

EVANS, E., *The Great Reform Act of 1832* (London, 1983).

EWING, K., *Britain and the I.L.O.* (London, 1989).

—— and GEARTY, C., *Freedom Under Thatcher: Civil Liberties in Modern Britain* (Oxford, 1990).

FAIRLEY, D., 'D Notices, Official Secrets and the Law' (1990) 10 *OJLS* 430.

FALIGOT, R., and KROP, P., *La Piscine* (Oxford, 1989).

FARSON, S., 'Restructuring Control in Canada: The McDonald Commission of Inquiry and its Legacy', in G. Hastedt (ed.), *Controlling Intelligence* (London, 1991).

—— 'Oversight of Canadian Intelligence: A Revisionary Note' [1992] *PL* 377.

—— 'Problems of Political Oversight: Difficulties Encountered by the Special Committee During Parliament's Five-Year Review of the CSIS Act' (unpub. paper prepared for the annual conference of the Canadian Association of Security and Intelligence Studies, 1991).

—— 'Parliament's Capacity to Conduct a Comprehensive Review: Weak Link in the Chain of Accountability?' (unpublished, 1991).

—— 'Security Intelligence versus Police Intelligence' (1991) 2 *Pol. & Soc.* 65.

—— 'Propriety, Efficiency and Balance: "A Preliminary Appraisal of Canada's 'New', 'Improved', Administrative Secrecy Program"', in P. Hanks, and J. McCamus (eds.), *National Security, Surveillance and Accountability* (Cowansville, Que., 1989).

FELDMAN, D., *Civil Liberties and Human Rights in England and Wales* (Oxford, 1993).

FINLAY, M., and DUFF, P., 'Jury Vetting—the Ideology of the Jury in Transition' (1982) 6 *Crim. LJ* 138.

—— 'Jury Vetting—the Jury Under Attack' (1983) 3 *Legal Studies* 159.

—— *The Jury Under Attack* (London, 1988).

FINN, J., *Constitutions in Crisis: Political Violence and the Rule of Law* (Oxford, 1991).

FITZGERALD, P., and LEOPOLD, M., *Stranger on the Line: The Secret History of Telephone Tapping* (London, 1987).

FLOUD, J., and YOUNG, W., *Dangerousness and Criminal Justice* (London, 1981).

FOOT, P., *Who Framed Colin Wallace?* (London, 1989).

FOX, R., 'The Salisbury Affair: Special Branches, Security and Subversion' (1979) 5 *Monash LR* 251.

FORSYTH, C., 'Judicial Review, the Royal Prerogative and National Security' (1985) 36 *NILQ* 25.

FRANKS, C., *Dissent and the State* (Toronto, 1989).

FREDMAN, S., and MORRIS, G., 'Union Membership at GCHQ' (1988) 17 *Ind. LJ* 105.

—— —— *The State as Employer* (London, 1989).

FREIBURG, A., 'Confiscating the Literary Proceeds of Crime' [1992] *Crim. LR* 96.

FRIEDLAND, M., *National Security—The Legal Dimensions* (Ottawa, 1980).

FRENCH, D., 'Spy Fever in Britain' (1978) 21 *Hist. J* 355.

GADDIS, J., *Strategies of Containment* (New York, 1981).

GAGE, B., and JONES, M., *Law, Liberty and Australian Democracy* (Sydney, 1990).

GALANTER, M., 'Why the Haves Come Out Ahead' (1974) 9 *Law & Soc. Rev.* 115.

GALE, A. (ed.), *The Polygraph Test: Truth, Lies and Science* (London, 1988).

GALLIVAN, T., and WARBRICK, C., 'Jury Vetting and the European Convention on Human Rights' (1980) 5 *Human Rights Rev.* 176.

GALNOOR. I. (ed.), *Government Secrecy in Democracies* (New York, 1977).

GAMBLE, A., *The Free Economy and the Strong State* (Basingstoke, 1988).

GANZ, G., 'Matrix Churchill and Public Interest Immunity' (1993) 56 *MLR* 564.

—— *Quasi-Legislation* (London, 1986).

GERMER, P., 'Administrative Secrecy under the European Convention on Human Rights', in *Secrecy and Openness: Individuals, Enterprises and Public Administrations, Proceedings of the Seventeenth Colloquy on European Law* (Strasbourg, 1988) .

GERTH, H., and MILLS, C., *From Max Weber: Essays in Sociology* (New York, 1958).

GIBBONS, T., *Regulating the Media* (London, 1991).

GIFFORD, T., *Supergrasses: The Use of Accomplice Evidence in Northern Ireland* (London 1984).

GILL, P., ''Allo, 'Allo, 'Allo, Who's in Charge Here Then?' (1987) 9 *Liverpool LR* 189.

—— 'Symbolic or Real? The Impact of SIRC, 1984–88' , 4 *Intelligence and National Security* 550.

—— 'Defining Subversion: The Canadian Experience Since 1977' [1989] *PL* 617.

—— *Policing Politics: Security Intelligence and the Liberal Democratic State* (London, 1994).

GILLMAN, P, and L, *'Collar the Lot!': How Britain Interned and Expelled its Wartime Refugees* (London, 1980).

GOBERT, J., 'Peremptory Challenge—An Obituary' [1989] *Crim. LR* 528.

GOODMAN, A., and BERKOWITZ, B., *The Need to Know* (New York, 1992).

GORDON WAKER, P., *The Cabinet* (rev. edn., London, 1972).

GORLICK, B., 'The Exclusion of "Security Risks" as a Form of Immigration Control: Law and Process in Canada and Nationality' (1991) 5 *Immigration Law and Practice* 76 and 109.

GRABOSKY, P., *Wayward Governance* (Canberra, 1989).

GRACE, E., and LEYS, C., 'The Concept of Subversion and its Implications', in C. Franks (ed.), *Dissent and the State* (Toronto, 1989).

GREER, S., 'Supergrasses and the Legal System in Britain and Northern Ireland' (1988) 102 *LQR* 189.

GRIFFITH, J., 'The Official Secrets Act 1989' (1989) 16 *JLS* 273.

—— *The Politics of the Judiciary* (4th edn., London, 1991).

GUEST, S., *Ronald Dworkin* (Edinburgh, 1982).

HALL, R., *A Spy's Revenge* (Harmondsworth, 1987).

—— *The Secret State* (Sydney, 1978).

HAMBURGER, P., 'The Development of the Law of Seditious Libel and Control of the Press' (1985) 37 *Stan. LR* 661.

HANKS, P., 'National Security—a Political Concept' (1988) 14 *Monash LR* 114.

—— and McCAMUS, J. (eds.), *National Security: Surveillance and Accountability in a Democratic Society* (Cowansville, Que. 1989).

HANNANT, L., 'Inter-war Security Screening in Britain, the United States and Canada' (1991) 6 *Int. and Nat. Sec.* 711.

HARRIS, B., 'The "Third Source" of Authority for Government Action' (1992) 108 *LQR* 626.

HAZELL, R., *Conspiracy and Civil Liberties* (London, 1973).

HENNESSY, P., *Cabinet* (London, 1986).

—— *Whitehall* (London, 1989).

—— and BROWNFIELD, G., 'Britain's Cold War Security Purge: The Origins of Positive Vetting' (1982) 25 *Hist. J* 965.

HEPPLE, B., 'Aliens and Administrative Justice: the Dutschke Case' (1971) 34 *MLR* 501.

HEUSTON, R., 'Liversidge v Anderson in Retrospect' (1970) 86 *LQR* 33.

—— 'Liversidge v Anderson; Two Footnotes' (1971) 87 *LQR* 161.

HEYDON, J, 'The Problems of Entrapment' [1973] *Camb. LJ* 268.

HILEY, N., 'British Internal Security in Wartime: The Rise and Fall of PMS 2' (1986) 1 *Intelligence and National Security* 396.

—— and PATOWSKI, J., 'A Postscript on PMS2' (1988) 3 *Int. and Nat. Sec.* 326.

HINSEY, F., *British Intelligence in the Second World War* (London, 1979).

HIRST, P., *Representative Democracy and its Limits* (Cambridge, 1990).

HOBBES, T., *Leviathan* [1651] (Harmondsworth, 1981).

HOGAN, G., and WALKER, C., *Political Violence and the Law in Ireland* (Manchester, 1989).

HOLDSWORTH, W., *A History of English Law* Vol. 3 (London, 1923); Vol. 10 (London, 1938).

HOLLINGSWORTH, M., and NORTON-TAYLOR, R., *Blacklist: The Inside Story of Political Vetting* (London, 1988).

HOLROYD, F., and BURBRIDGE, N., *War Without Honour* (Hull, 1989).

HOOPER, D., *Official Secrets—The Use and Abuse of the Act* (London, 1977).

HOWARD, M., CRANE, P., and HOCHBERG, D., *Phipson on Evidence* (14th edn., London, 1990).

HOWARD, C., *Australian Federal Constitutional Law* (3rd edn., Sydney, 1985).

HUNTINGTON, S., 'American Ideals versus American Institutions' (1982) 97 *Pol. Sci. Q* 1.

INGMAN, T., '"Interfering With the Proper Administration of Justice": Some Recent Developments' (1992) *Civil Justice Quarterly* 175.

—— *The English Legal Process* (4th edn., London, 1992).

IPPR (Institute of Public Policy Research), *The Constitution of the United Kingdom* (London, 1991).

JACOB, J., 'From Privileged Crown to Interested Public' [1993] *PL* 121.

JACONELLI, J., 'The "D" Notice System' [1982] *PL* 37.

JEFFERSON, T., and GRIMSHAW, R., *Controlling the Constable* (London, 1984).

JORDAN, S., 'Classified Information and Conflicts in Independent Counsel Prosecutions: Balancing the Scales of Justice After Iran–Contra' (1991) 91 *Colum. LR* 1651.

JOWELL, J., and OLIVER, D., *The Changing Constitution* (Oxford, 1985; 2nd edn., Oxford, 1989).

JUDGE, D., *The Parliamentary State* (London, 1993).

'Justice', *Going Abroad: A Report on Passports* (London, 1974).

KAMISAR, Y., *et al.*, *Modern Criminal Procedure* (7th edn., St. Paul, Minn., 1990).

KEALEY, G., 'The Surveillance State: The Origins of Domestic Intelligence and Counter-Subversion in Canada, 1914–21' (1992) 7 *Int. & NS* 179.

KEETON, G., 'Parliamentary Tribunals of Inquiry' (1959) 12 *Current Legal Problems* 12.

KELLEHER, J., 'The Counter-Terrorism Program of the Government of Canada: Some Recent Developments', in P. Hanks, and J. McCamus (eds.), *National Security: Surveillance and Accountability in a Democratic Society* (Cowansville, Que., 1989).

KENNEDY, G., *The Economics of Defence* (London, 1975).

KENNEDY, P., *The Rise and Fall of the Great Powers* (London, 1989).

KENNY, 'The Evolution of the Law of Blasphemy' (1922) 1 *Camb. LJ* 127.

KNIGHTLEY, P., *The First Casualty: From Crimea to Vietnam the War Correspondent as Hero, Propagandist and Myth Maker* (New York, 1975).

KNIGHTLEY, P., and KENNEDY, C., *An Affair of State* (London, 1987).

KOH, H., 'Why the President (Almost) Always Wins in Foreign Affairs', 97 *Yale LJ* 1255 (1988).

—— *The National Security Constitution* (New Haven, Conn., 1990).

KORTHALS ALTES, W., 'Protecting Journalists' Sources—A Dutch Proposal for Legislation' [1992] *PL* 73.

LACEY, N., *State Punishment* (London, 1988).

LAFITTE, F., *The Internment of Aliens* (London, 1940).

LANDGREN, S., *Embargo Disimplemented* (Oxford, 1989).

LAWS, J., 'Is the High Court the Guardian of Fundamental Constitutional Rights?' [1993] *PL* 59.

LAWSON., N., *The View From No. 11* (London, 1992).

LEE, H., 'The Australian Security Intelligence Organisation—New Mechanisms for Accountability' (1989) 38 *ICLQ* 890.

—— *Emergency Powers* (Sydney, 1984).

LEFLER, M., 'The American Concept of National Security and the Beginning of the Cold War' (1984) 89 *AHR* 346.

LEGOMSKY, S., *Immigration and the Judiciary* (Oxford, 1987).

LEIGH, D., *The Frontiers of Secrecy* (London, 1980).

—— *The Wilson Plot* (London, 1988).

—— *Betrayed: The Real Story of the Matrix Churchill Trial* (London, 1993).

—— and LINKLATER, M., *Not With Honour* (London, 1986).

LEIGH, I., 'Not To Judge But To Save?' (1977) 8 *Cambrian LR* 56.

—— 'Spycatcher in Strasbourg' [1992] *PL* 200.

—— 'Matrix Churchill, Supergun and the Scott Inquiry' [1993] *Public Law* 630.

—— and LUSTGARTEN, L., 'The Security Service Act 1989' (1989) 52 *MLR* 801.

LEIGH, L., 'Law Reform and the Law of Treason and Sedition' [1977] *PL* 128.

LESTER, A., 'Fundamental Rights: The United Kingdom Isolated' [1984] *PL* 46.

—— and BINDMAN, G., *Race and Law* (Harmondsworth, 1972).

LEWIS, G., *Lord Atkin* (London, 1983).

'Liberty', *A People's Charter* (London, 1991).

LINN, I., *Application Refused: Employment Vetting by the State* (London, 1990).

LOBBAN, M., 'From Seditious Libel to Unlawful Assembly: Peterloo and the Changing Face of Political Crime *c.*1770–1820' (1990) 10 *Ox. JLS* 307.

LOCKE, J, *Second Treatise of Government* [1692] (Harmondsworth, 1981).

LOMAS, O., 'The Executive and the Anti-Terrorist Legislation of 1939' [1980] *PL* 16.

LUSTGARTEN, L., 'Common Law Crimes and Trade Union Activities' (1976) 27 *NILQ* 216.

—— *The Governance of Police* (London, 1986).

—— 'The Police and the Substantive Criminal Law' (1987) 27 *BJ Crim.* 23.

—— 'Learning From Peter Wright: A Response to D. C. Watt' (1989) 60 *Pol. Q* 222.

—— 'Accountability of the Security Services in Western Democracies' (1992) *Current Legal Problems* 145.

LYKKEN, D., *A Tremor in the Blood* (New York, 1981).

LYON, N., 'Constitutional Validity of Sections 3 and 4 of the Public Order Regulations, 1970' (1972) 18 *McGill LJ* 136.

McBARNET, D., *Conviction: Law, the State and the Construction of Justice* (London, 1981).

McELDOWNEY, J., 'Legal Aspects of the Irish Secret Service Fund' (1986) 25 *Ir. Hist. Studs.*

—— 'Stand By For the Crown' [1979] *Crim. LR* 272.

McINTOSH, M., *Managing Britain's Defence* (Basingstoke, 1990).

MAITLAND, F., *The Constitutional History of England*, ed. H. A. L. Fisher (Cambridge, 1908).

MANSELL, G., *Let Truth Be Told* (London, 1982).

MARKOVITS, A., and SILVERSTEN, M. (eds.), *The Politics of Scandal* (New York, 1988).

MARR, D., *The Ivanov Trail* (Melbourne, 1984).

MARSHALL, G., 'Press Freedom and Free Speech Theory' [1992] *PL* 40.

MARX, G., *Undercover: Police Surveillance in America* (Berkeley, Calif., 1988).

MASTERMAN, J., *On the Chariot Wheel* (Oxford, 1975).

MATHEWS, A., *The Darker Reaches of Government* (Berkeley, Calif., 1978).

MAY, C., *In the Name of War: Judicial Review and the War Powers Since 1918* (Cambridge, Mass., 1989).

MENKHAUS, D., 'Graymail: Constitutional Immunity From Justice?' (1981) 18 *Harv. J. on Legis.* 389.

MERCER, D., MUNGHAM, G., and WILLIAMS, K., *The Fog of War* (London, 1987).

MICHAEL, J., 'Malone and Police Use of Metering Information' (1984) *New Law Journal* 646, 669, and 710.

MILLER, C., *Contempt of Court* (2nd edn., Oxford, 1989).

MILNE, A., *DG: The Memoirs of a British Broadcaster* (London, 1988).

MOCKLER, A., *Lions Under The Throne* (London, 1983).

MODOOD, T., 'British Asian Muslims and the Rushdie Affair' (1990) 61 *Pol. Q* 143.

MOORE, J., TIPSON, F., and TURNER, R., *National Security Law* (Durham, NC, 1990).

MORGAN, K., *Labour in Power 1945–51* (Oxford, 1985).

MORRIS, P., 'Sex Discrimination, Public Order and the European Court' [1987] *PL* 334.

MUNRO, C., *Television, Censorship and the Law* (London, 1979).

NAPIER, B., 'The International Labour Organisation and GCHQ' (1989) 19 *Ind. LJ* 255.

National Council for Civil Liberties Trade Union Liaison Committee, *The Purging of the Civil Service* (London, 1985).

NETTHEIM, G., 'Open Justice and State Secrets' (1985–6) 10 *Adelaide LR* 281.

NEWDICK, C., 'Deportation and the European Convention' (1982) 2 *Ox. JLS* 151.

NICOL, A., 'Official Secrets and Jury Vetting' [1979] *Crim. LR* 284.

NORTON-TAYLOR, R., *In Defence of the Realm?* (London, 1990).

Note, 'Conspiracy and the First Amendment', 79 *Yale LJ* 872 (1970).

O'CONNOR, P., 'Prosecution Disclosure: Principle, Practice and Justice' [1992] *Crim. LR* 464.

O'HALPIN, E., 'Financing British Intelligence: The Evidence up to 1945', in K. Robertson (ed.), *British and American Approaches to Intelligence* (London, 1987).

O'HIGGINS, P., 'Disguised Extradition: the Soblen Case' (1964) *MLR* 521.

OSBOURNE, C., 'Hearsay and the European Convention on Human Rights' [1993] *Crim. LR* 255.

OSCAPELLA, I., 'A Study of Informers in England' [1980] *Crim. LR* 136.

PALMER, S., 'Tightening Secrecy Law: The Official Secrets Act 1989' [1992] *PL* 61.

PALMER, A., 'The History of the D Notice Committee', in C. Andrew, and D. Dilks (eds.), *The Missing Dimension: Governments and Intelligence Communities in the Twentieth Century* (London, 1984).

PANNICK, D., 'Spycatcher: Two Years of Legal Indignations', in D. Kingsford-Smith, and D. Oliver (eds.), *Economical With the Truth: The Law and Media in a Democratic Society* (Oxford, 1990).

PELLING, H., *A Short History of the Labour Party* (4th edn., London, 1985).

PHILBY, K., *My Silent War* (London, 1968).

PHYTHIAN, M., and LITTLE, W., 'Parliament and Arms Sales: Lessons of the Matrix Churchill Affair' (1993) *Parl. Aff.* 293.

PINCHER, C., *Their Trade is Treachery* (London, 1981).

PLENDER, R., *International Migration Law* (2nd edn., Dordrecht, 1988).

POLLOCK, F., and MAITLAND, F., *The History of English Law* (2nd edn., Cambridge, 1968).

PONTING, C., *The Right to Know* (London, 1985).

PORTER, B., *The Refugee Question in Mid-Victorian Politics* (Cambridge, 1979).

—— *Britain, Europe and the World 1850–1982: Delusions of Grandeur* (London, 1983).

—— *The Origins of the Vigilant State: The London Metropolitan Special Branch Before the First World War* (London, 1987).

—— *Plots and Paranoia* (London, 1989).

RANDLE, M., and POTTLE, P., *The Blake Escape* (London, 1989).

RANKIN, M., 'National Security: Information, Accountability, and the Canadian Security Intelligence Service' (1986) 36 *U. Tor. LJ* 248.

—— 'The Security Intelligence Review Committee: Reconciling National Security With Procedural Fairness' (1990) 3 *Can. J. Admin. L. & Prac.* 173.

REINER, R., *The Politics of the Police* (Brighton, 1985).

—— and SPENCER, S. (eds.), *Accountable Policing—Effectiveness, Empowerment and Equity* (London, 1993).

REISMAN, W., and BAKER, J., *Regulating Covert Action* (New Haven, Conn., 1992).

RICHELSON, J., and BALL, D., *The Ties that Bind* (2nd edn., Sydney, 1990).

ROBERTSON, G., *Whose Conspiracy?* (London,1974).

—— *Reluctant Judas* (London, 1979*a*).

—— *Obscenity* (London, 1979*b*).

—— *Freedom, the Individual and the Law* (London, 1989).

ROBERTSON, K., *Public Secrets* (Basingstoke, 1982).

ROBILLIARD, ST. J., *Religion and the Law* (Manchester, 1984).

ROPER, M., 'Access to Public Records', in R. Chapman, and M. Hunt (eds.), *Open Government* (Beckenham, 1987).

RUBIN, G., 'The Royal Prerogative or a Statutory Code? The War Office and Contingency Planning, 1885–1914', in R. Eales, and D. Sullivan (eds.), *The Political Context of Law* (London, 1987).

RUBIN, G., *War, Law and Labour* (Oxford, 1988).

RUDÉ, G., *Wilkes and Liberty* (Oxford, 1962).

RYAN, J., 'The Inspector General of the Canadian Security Intelligence Service' (1989) 9 *Conf. Q.* 33.

SALGADO, R., 'Government Secrets, Fair Trials, and the Classified Procedures Act' (1989) 98 *Yale LJ* 427.

SAMPSON, A., 'Secrecy, News Management and the British Press', in T. Franck, and E. Weisband (eds.), *Secrecy and Foreign Policy* (New York, 1974).

—— *The Arms Bazaar in the Nineties: From Krupp to Saddam* (Sevenoaks, 1991).

SARGANT, T., and HILL, P., *Criminal Trials: The Search for Truth*, Fabian Research Series 348 (London, 1986).

SAYER, F., 'Criminal Conspiracy' (1922) 35 *Harv. LR* 393.

SCHAUER, F., *Free Speech: A Philosophical Enquiry* (Cambridge, 1982).

SCHMITT, C., *The Concept of the Political*, trans. G. Schwab (New Brunswick, NJ, 1976).

—— *Political Theology*, trans. G. Schwab (Cambridge, Mass., 1985).

SEGAL, Z., 'Tribunals of Inquiry: A British Invention Ignored in Britain' [1984] *PL* 206.

—— 'Security Censorship: Prior Restraint (After the Schnitzer Decision)', in S. Shetreet (ed.), *Free Speech and National Security* (Dordrecht, 1991).

SHARPE, R., *The Law of Habeas Corpus* (2nd edn., Oxford, 1989).

SHETREET, S., *Judges on Trial* (Amsterdam, 1976).

—— (ed.), *Free Speech and National Security* (Dordrecht, 1991).

SHILS, E., *The Torment of Secrecy* (London, 1956).

SHORT, K., *Western Broadcasting Over the Iron Curtain* (London, 1986).

SIBRAA, K., 'Parliamentary Scrutiny of Security and Intelligence Services in Australia' (1987) 68 *The Parliamentarian* 120.

SIEPP, D., 'Judicial Recognition of the Right of Privacy' (1980) 5 *Ox. JLS* 325.

SIMPSON, A., *In the Highest Degree Odious: Detention Without Trial in Wartime Britain* (Oxford, 1992).

SMITH, A., 'Judicial Lawmaking in the Criminal Law' (1984) 100 *LQR* 46.

—— 'Immunity From Prosecution' (1983) 42 *Camb. LJ* 299.

—— 'Public Interest Immunity in Criminal Cases' [1993] *Camb. LJ* 1.

SMITH, J., and HOGAN, B., *Criminal Law* (7th edn., London, 1992).

SMITH, K., 'Sampling and Selection: Current Policies', in G. Martin, and P. Spurford (eds.), *The Records of the Nation* (Woodbridge, 1990).

SNYDER, F., and HAY, D. (eds.), *Labour, Law and Crime* (London, 1987).

SPJUT, R., 'Defining "Subversion"' (1979) 6 *JL & S* 254.

SPENCER, S., *Called to Account* (London, 1986).

SPICER, R., *Conspiracy: Law, Class and Society* (London, 1981).

STALKER, J., *Stalker* ,(London, 1988).

STAMMERS, N., *Civil Liberties in Britain During the Second World War* (London, 1983).

STENT, R., *A Bespattered Page?—The Internment of His Majesty's 'Most Loyal Enemy Aliens'* (London, 1982).

STEPHEN, J., *History of the Criminal Law of England*, Vol. 2 (London, 1883).

STEWART, P., 'Or of the Press' (1975) 27 *Hast. LJ* 631.

STOPFORD, J., and STRANGE, S., *Rival States, Rival Firms* (Cambridge, 1991).

STREET, H., *Freedom, the Individual and the Law* (4th edn., Harmondsworth, 1977).

SULLIVAN, K., 'Unconstitutional Conditions' (1989) 102 *Harv. LR* 1413.

Summers, A., and Dorril, S., *Honeytrap* (London, 1988).

Supperstone, M., *Brownlie's Law of Public Order and National Security* (2nd edn., London, 1981).

Swan, K., 'Whistleblowing and National Security' in P. Hanks, and J. McCamus (eds.), *National Security: Surveillance and Accountability in a Democratic Society* (Cowansville, Que., 1989).

Thomas, D. (ed.), *State Trials*, Vol. 1 (London, 1972).

Thomas, P., 'Secret Police on Trial' (1993) 98 *Planet* 3.

Thomas, R., 'The British Official Secrets Act 1911–39 and the Ponting Case' [1986] *Crim. LR* 491.

—— 'The Experience of Other Countries' in R. Chapman, and M. Hunt (eds.), *Open Government* (Beckenham, 1987).

—— *Espionage and Secrecy* (London, 1991).

Thompson, B., *Queer People* (London, 1922).

Thompson, D., 'The Committee of 100 and the Official Secrets Act 1911' [1963] *PL* 201.

Thompson, E. P., *The Making of the English Working Class* (Harmondsworth, 1968).

—— *Writing by Candlelight* (London, 1980).

Thompson, L., 'The Press and the Pentagon: Old Battles, New Skirmishes' (1992) 3 *The American Enterprise* 14.

Thornberry, C., 'Dr. Soblen and the Alien Law of the United Kingdom' (1963) *ICLQ* 414.

Thurlow, R., *Fascism in Britain: A History, 1918–1985* (Oxford, 1986).

—— 'British Fascism and State Surveillance, 1934–45' (1988) 3 *Int. & NS* 77.

Tomkins, A., 'Public Interest Immunity After Matrix Churchill' [1993] *Public Law* 650.

Toohey, B., and Pinwill, W., *Oyster* (Port Melbourne, Victoria, 1990).

Trager, F., and Simonie, F., 'An Introduction to the Study of National Security' in F. Trager, and P. Kronenberg (eds.), *National Security and American Society* (Lawrence, Ka., 1973).

Treverton, T., *Covert Action: The Limits of Intervention in the Post-War World* (New York, 1987).

Tunstall, J., *The Westminster Lobby Correspondents* (London, 1970).

Turnbull, M., *The Spycatcher Trial* (Richmond, Victoria, 1988).

Turpin, C., *Government Contracts* (Harlow, 1972).

—— *Government Procurement and Contracts* (London, 1989).

—— *British Government and the Constitution* (2nd edn., London, 1990).

Urban, M., *Big Boys' Rules: The Secret Struggle Against the IRA* (London, 1992).

van Alstyne, W., 'The Demise of the Right–Privilege Distinction in Constitutional Law' (1968) 81 *Harv. LR* 1439.

van Dijk, P., and van Hoof, G., *Theory and Practice of the European Convention on Human Rights* (2nd edn., Deventer, 1990).

Vennard, J., and Riley, D., 'The Use of Peremptory Challenge and Stand By of Jurors and their Relationship to Trial Outcome' [1988] *Crim. LR* 731.

Vercher, A., *Terrorism in Europe: An International Comparative Legal Analysis* (Oxford, 1992).

Verrier, A., *Through the Looking Glass* (London, 1983).

Vincenzi, C., 'Aliens and the Judicial Review of Immigration Law' [1985] *PL* 93.

—— 'Extra-Statutory Ministerial Discretion in Immigration Law' [1992] *PL* 300.

von Hirsch, A., and Ashworth, A., *Principled Sentencing* (Edinburgh, 1993).

WACKS, R., *The Protection of Privacy* (London, 1980).

WACKS, R., *Personal Information: Privacy and the Law* (Oxford, 1989).

WADE, H., 'Procedure and Prerogative in Public Law' (1985) 101 *LQR* 180.

—— *Administrative Law* (5th edn., Oxford, 1980; 6th edn., Oxford, 1988).

WALKER, C., 'Police Surveillance by Technical Devices' [1980] *PL* 184.

—— 'Review of the Prerogative: the Remaining Issues' [1987] *PL* 62.

—— *The Prevention of Terrorism in British Law* (2nd edn., Manchester, 1992).

WALLACE, J., 'The Canadian Access to Information Act 1982', in N. Marsh (ed.), *Public Access to Government-Held Information* (London, 1987).

WALLINGTON, P., and MERKIN, R., *Essays in Memory of Professor F. H. Lawson* (London, 1986).

WALTON, J., *The Second Reform Act* (London, 1987).

WATT, D., 'Fallout from Treachery: Peter Wright and the *Spycatcher* case' (1988) 59 *Pol. Q.* 206.

WEATHERILL, S., 'Buying Special Police Services' [1988] *PL* 106.

WEDDERBURN, K., *The Worker and the Law* (3rd edn., Harmondsworth, 1986).

WEST, N., *A Matter of Trust* (London, 1982).

—— *GCHQ: The Secret Wireless War 1900–86* (London, 1986).

—— *Molehunt* (London, 1987).

WHISH, R., *Competition Law* (3rd edn., London, 1993).

WHITAKER, R., 'Origins of the Canadian Government's Internal Security System, 1946–52' (1984) 65 *Can. Hist. Rev.* 154.

—— 'Fighting the Cold War on the Home Front: America, Britain, Australia and Canada' (1984) *The Socialist Register* 23.

—— *Double Standard: The Secret History of Canadian Immigration* (Toronto, 1987).

—— 'Left-wing Dissent and the State' in C. Franks (ed.), *Dissent and the State* (Toronto, 1989).

—— 'The Politics of Security Intelligence Policy-Making in Canada' (1991) 6 *Intelligence and National Security* 649 and (1992) 7 *Intelligence and National Security* 53.

—— 'Apprehended Insurrection? RCMP Intelligence and the October Crisis' (1993) 100 *Queen's Qu.* 383.

WHYTE, J., and MACDONALD, A., 'Dissent and National Security and Dissent Some More', in C. Franks. (ed.), *Dissent and the State* (Toronto, 1989).

WILLIAMS, D., *Not in the Public Interest* (London, 1965).

—— 'Official Secrecy and the Courts', in P. Glazebrook (ed.), *Reshaping the Criminal Law* (London, 1978).

WINDLESHAM, Lord, and RAMPTON, R., *Death on the Rock* (London, 1989).

WINKS, R., *Cloak and Gown: Scholars in America's Secret Wars* (London, 1987).

WINTERTON, G., 'The Significance of the Communist Party Case' (1992) 18 *Melbourne University LR* 630.

WOLFERS, A., *Discord and Collaboration* (Baltimore, 1952).

WRIGHT, P., *Spycatcher* (New York, 1987).

WYDRZNSKI, C., *Canadian Immigration Law and Practice* (Toronto, 1983).

WYNDHAM-GOLDIE, G., *Facing the Nation: Television and Politics, 1936–76* (London, 1977).

WYNES, W., *Legislative, Executive and Judicial Powers in Australia* (5th edn., Sydney, 1976).

YERGIN, D., *Shattered Peace* (Harmondsworth, 1980).

YOUNG, G., *Subversion and the British Riposte* (Glasgow, 1984).

ZANDER, M., *The Police and Criminal Evidence Act 1984* (2nd edn., London, 1990).

ZELLICK, G., 'Comment'. [1972] *PL* 1.
—— 'Government Beyond Law' [1985] *PL* 283.
ZINES, L., *The High Court and the Constitution* (2nd edn., Sydney, 1986).
ZUCKERMAN, A., 'Privilege and Public Interest', in C. Tapper (ed.), *Crime, Proof and Punishment: Essays in Honour of Sir Rupert Cross* (London, 1981).

Official Publications

UNITED KINGDOM

Command Papers
Report of the Royal Commission on Police Powers, Cmd. 3297 (1929).
Report of the Committee on the Political Activities of Civil Servants, Cmd. 7718 (1949).
The Political Activities of Civil Servants, Cmd. 8783 (1953).
Report Concerning the Disappearance of Two Former Foreign Office Officials, Cmd. 9577 (1955).
Statement on the Findings of the Conference of Privy Councillors on Security, Cmd. 9715 (1956).
Report of the Committee of Privy Councillors Appointed to Inquire into the Interception of Communications, Cmnd. 283 (1957).
Security Procedures in the Public Service, Cmnd. 1681 (1962).
Interim Report by the Committee of Enquiry into the Vassall Case, Cmnd. 1871 (1963).
Report of the Tribunal Appointed to Inquire into the Vassall Case and Related Matters, Cmnd. 2009 (1963).
Lord Denning's Report, Cmnd. 2152 (1963).
Royal Commission on Tribunals of Inquiry, Cmnd. 3121 (1966).
Report of the Committee of Privy Councillors Appointed to Inquire into 'D' Notice Matters, Cmnd. 3309 (1967).
The 'D' Notice System, Cmnd. 3312 (1967).
Report of the Committee on Immigration Appeals, Cmnd. 3387 (1967).
Report of the Committee on Privacy, Cmnd. 5012 (1972).
Report of the Departmental Committee on the Reform of the Official Secrets Act 1911, Cmnd. 5014 (1972).
Government Views on the Recommendations of the Royal Commission on Tribunals of Inquiry and the Inter-Departmental Committee on the Law of Contempt as it Affects Tribunals of Inquiry, Cmnd. 5313 (1973).
Report of the Committee of Privy Councillors on Ministerial Memoirs, Cmnd. 6386 (1976).
Committee on the Political Activities of Civil Servants, Cmnd. 7057 (1978).
Report of the Committee on Data Protection, Cmnd. 7341 (1978).
The Interception of Communications in Great Britain, Cmnd. 7873 (1980).
Report of the Royal Commission on Criminal Procedure, Cmnd. 8092 (1981).
Modern Public Records: Selection and Access, Report of a Committee Appointed by the Lord Chancellor, Cmnd. 8204 (1981).
The Interception of Communications in the United Kingdom, Cmnd. 9438 (1985).
Review of the Operation of the Prevention of Terrorism (Temporary Provisions) Act 1984 by Viscount Colville of Culross, QC, Cm. 264 (1987).
Reform of Section 2 of the Official Secrets Act 1911, Cm. 408 (1988).
Government Reply to the Third Report from the Home Affairs Committee, Session 1989–90, Cm. 1163 (1990).

Review of Press Self Regulation, Cm. 2135 (1993).

Government Reply to the 1st Report from the Home Affairs Committee, Session 1992–93, Cm. 2197. (1993).

Report of the Royal Commission on Criminal Justice, Cm. 2263 (1993).

Open Government, Cm. 2290 (1993).

Disclosure of Criminal Records for Vetting Purposes, Cm. 2319 (1993).

Parliamentary Papers

Report of the Royal Commission on the Post Office (PP 1844).

Epitome of the Reports from the Committee of the Public Accounts, 1857 to 1937 (1938), HC 154.

Report to the Home Secretary From the Commissioner of Police of the Metropolis on the Actions of the Police Concerned With the Case of Kenneth Joseph Lennon (1973–74), HC 351.

Third Report of the Defence Committee 'The D Notice System' (1979–80), HC 773.

Ninth Report of the Public Accounts Committee, Ministry of Defence Chevaline Improvements to the Polaris Missile System (1981–82), HC 269.

First Report from the Defence Select Committee: The Handling of the Press and Public During the Falklands War (1982–83), HC 17.

Fourth Report of the Defence Committee, Previous Recommendations of the Committee (1982–83), HC 55.

First Report of the Liaison Committee (1982–83), HC 92.

First Report from the Select Committee on Defence, Positive Vetting Procedures in Her Majesty's Services and the Ministry of Defence (1982–83), HC 242.

Third Report from the Home Affairs Committee, British Nationality Fees (1982–83), HC 248.

Home Affairs Committee, Fourth Report, 'Special Branch' (1984–85), HC 71.

House of Commons Select Committee on Employment Third Report, The Implications for Industrial Relations and Employment of the Introduction of the Polygraph (1984–85), HC 98.

Defence Committee, Fourth Report, Westland plc: The Government's Decision-Making (1985–86), HC 519.

First Report From the Defence Committee, Expenditure on Major Defence Projects: Accountability to the House of Commons (1986–87), HC 340.

First Report from the Committee of Privileges, Speaker's Order of 22 January 1987 on a Matter Concerning National Security (1986–87), HC 365.

Third Report From the Home Affairs Committee, Criminal Records (1989–90), HC 285.

32nd Annual Report of the Keeper of the Public Records on the Work of the Public Records Office and 32nd Report of the Advisory Council on Public Records (1990–91), HC 561.

First Report from the Home Affairs Select Committee, Accountability of the Security Service (1992–93), HC 265.

Trade and Industry Committee, Second Report, Exports to Iraq: Project Babylon and Long Range Guns (1991–92), HC 86.

Return to an Address of the Honourable House of Commons Dated 22 October 1992 for the Inquiry Into the Supervision of the Bank of Credit and Commerce International (1992–93), HC 198.

Supply Estimates (1992–93), HC 273–xix.

Foreign Affairs Committee, 4th Report Expenditure Plans of the Foreign and Commonwealth Office and the Overseas Development Administration (1992–93), HC 562.

Series

Reports of the Security Commission
Bossard and Allen, Cmnd. 2722 (1965).
Reen, Cmnd. 3151 (1966).
Keenan, Cmnd. 3365 (1967).
Britten, Cmnd. 3856 (1968).
Bland, Cmnd. 3892 (1969).
Bingham and Hinchcliffe, Cmnd. 5362 (1973).
Lambton and Jellicoe, Cmnd. 5367 (1973).
Wagstaff, Cmnd. 8235 (1981).
Statement on the Recommendations of the Security Commission, Cmnd. 8540 (1982).
Prime, Cmnd. 8876 (1983).
Ritchie, (printed at *HC Debs.*, vol. 46, cols. 517–23w (July 28, 1983)).
Aldridge, Cmnd. 9212 (1984).
Bettaney, Cmnd. 9514 (1985).
9th Signals Regiment, Cmnd. 9923 (1986).

Annual Reports of the Interception of Communications Commissioner
Interception of Communications Act 1985 Chapter 56: Report of the Commissioner for 1986, Cm.
    108 (1987).
Report of the Commissioner for 1987, Cm. 351 (1988).
Report of the Commissioner for 1988, Cm. 652 (1989).
Report of the Commissioner for 1989, Cm. 1063 (1990).
Report of the Commissioner for 1990, Cm. 1489 (1991).
Report of the Commissioner for 1991, Cm. 1942 (1992).
Report of the Commissioner for 1992, Cm. 2173 (1993).

Annual Reports of the Security Service Commissioner
Security Service Act 1989: Report of the Commissioner for the Security Service for 1990, Cm. 1480
    (1991).
Report of the Commissioner for 1991, Cm. 1946 (1992).
Report of the Commissioner for 1992, Cm. 2174 (1993).

Others
Law Commission Report No. 83, *Criminal Law: Report on Defences of General Application*
    (1977).
Law Commission Working Paper No. 72, *Sedition, Treason and Allied Offences* (1977).
Foreign Office, T. Bingham, and S. Gray, *Report on the Supply of Petroleum and Petroleum
    Products to Rhodesia* (London, 1978).
MI5: The Security Service (London, 1993).
Central Intelligence Machinery (London, 1993).
Lord Chancellor's Department, *Infringement of Privacy* (London, 1993).
Ministry of Defence, *The Defence Advisory Notices: A Review of the D Notice System*, Ministry
    of Defence Open Government Document 93/06 (1993).

CANADA

Report of the Royal Commission on Security (Ottawa, 1969).

Law Reform Commission of Canada, *Commissions of Inquiry: A New Act* (Ottawa, 1977).

Commission of Inquiry into Certain RCMP Activities, Freedom and Security Under the Law (Ottawa, 1980), vol. 1.

Refugee Determination in Canada: A Report to the Hon. Flora McDonald, Minister of Employment and Immigration by W. Gunther Plaut (Ottawa, 1985).

Open and Shut: Report of the Standing Committee on Justice and the Solicitor General on the Review of the Access to Information Act and the Privacy Act (Ottawa, 1987).

SIRC, *Amending the CSIS Act: Proposals for the Special Committee of the House of Commons* (Ottawa, 1989).

Report of the Special Committee on the Review of the CSIS Act and the Security Offences Act, In Flux But Not in Crisis (Ottawa, 1990).

Solicitor General Canada, *On Course: National Security for the 1990s* (Ottawa, 1991).

SIRC, *Annual Reports*
1986– (Ottawa, 1987–).

Annual Reports of the Privacy Commissioner
1985– (Ottawa, 1986–).

Annual Reports of the Information Commissioner
1985– (Ottawa, 1986–).

AUSTRALIA

Royal Commission on Intelligence and Security, *Fourth Report* (Canberra, 1977).

Special Branch Security Records: Initial Report to the Honourable Donald Allen Dunstan Premier of South Australia (Adelaide, 1977).

Joint Select Committee on Telecommunications Interception (Parliamentary Paper No. 306/1986).

ASIO *Annual Reports to Parliament*, 1986– (Canberra, 1987–).

Annual Reports of the Inspector-General of Security and Intelligence, 1986– (Canberra, 1987–).

Freedom of Information, Report by the Senate Standing Committee on Constitutional and Legal Affairs on the Freedom of Information Bill 1978 and Aspects of the Archives Bill 1978 (Canberra, 1978).

Report of the Joint Parliamentary Committee on the Australian Security Intelligence Organization, ASIO and the Archives Act: The Effect on ASIO of the Operation of the Archives Act (Canberra, 1992).

UNITED STATES

Report of the Congressional Committees Investigating the Iran–Contra Affair, S. Rep., No. 216, H. Rep., No. 433 (1986).

Table of Treaties and Conventions

Table of Cases

Table of Statutes

Index